Working with Stories

in Your Community or Organization

PARTICIPATORY NARRATIVE INQUIRY

Third Edition

Cynthia F. Kurtz

I dedicate
this book
to my favorite storyteller.

Foreword

by Stephen Shimshock

On a rainy September Seattle day I ventured into the wild. There are many wild places in the Pacific Northwest, but on this day the wild was the Internet. My interest was piqued by an email. It was a friend request from a social networking site that focuses on story work.

The request came as a shock; I was hardly worthy of "member" status on the site. Story work just wasn't my thing. I joined the site to oblige an acquaintance who was a member of a social networking site I had started. My profile was less than forthcoming, which was why I felt a little leery of a friend request from someone I didn't know. In this new world of the Internet a friend request can be an invitation to loads of unwanted solicitations.

So, I did my usual routine of checking their profile, looking at their other friends, and examining the contents of their conversations with others. Clicking feverishly and doing a quick scan, I determined that things seemed innocuous enough; it was just a new guy to the site trying to make friends with everyone.

In the process of clicking around, I saw a picture of a member, a woman with camera in hand. As an avid photographer, I was intrigued. I clicked on her profile and found nothing about photography. However, I discovered that she self-published a book on-line entitled *Working with Stories*. I am always game for a new resource, especially ones that are made available for free.

What I found surprised me. Remember, story work isn't my thing. When people refer to story work they generally seem focused on the telling side of the story, with the intent to sell a product, a point of view, or something in between. *Working with Stories* is different. The focus of the book is on eliciting, listening to, and deriving meaning from stories.

The timing of this find was perfect. I quickly read through a few pages of the book on-line and instantly knew I had to print it—I was going to read it all. I was in the middle of my dissertation project, which was stalled at the time. I felt a sense of relief, like I had found a missing piece of a puzzle. It wasn't the final piece of the puzzle, but that piece that seemed to open up new ways for the other pieces to fall into place.

My project involved working with a group of community service providers who serve youth aging out of foster care. They are held together by their mutual passion and commitment to the youth in their city, yet like most coalition groups they lack any cohesive infrastructure. This informal structure opens up many possibilities for creative solutions to tough social problems, but can prove problematic when it comes to knowledge management, evaluation, or any other type of group assessment.

Inspired by what I was seeing on the Internet in terms of open source projects, I thought it would be interesting to apply open source principles to evaluation. Can a community group conduct and author their own evaluation? The more I explored the topic with the group, the more we realized that evaluation was not what they were looking for, at least in the traditional sense of the word. Evaluation of social services can be quite difficult because at any given time there are multiple variables that you simply cannot control.

We changed the paradigm from measuring effectiveness of the collaboration to gaining insight into how the group learns and takes action. The final report would not need to make any truth claim about effectiveness of the program, but rather explain how the group learns and how they take action based on what they learn. Things that are working (effective) and things in need of improvement would become self-evident in the narrative about their learning.

Intuitively I felt like things were on the right track. I was now faced with a simple question: "How do you go about doing this type of work?" *Working with Stories* quickly became my methodology guide.

I believe story work, specifically story listening, is a very effective tool for understanding how a community creates and acts on knowledge. It also provides ample opportunity for the group being studied to signify and make sense out of their own information. This can result in groups creating contextually specific summaries of what is happening in their community and/or group and what they plan to do as a result.

I use the phrase "contextually specific" to denote that the end result isn't necessarily meant to lend itself to being replicated in other contexts, as is expected with most evaluations seeking to find "best practices." It may turn out that other groups find the information useful, but the primary focus on this group was to improve local decision making regarding services to young adults.

As a long time member of a quality assurance team, I am no stranger to the buzz phrase "best practice." The phrase has infiltrated both the private and public sector. Personally, I dislike the term because it implies that the "best" is rooted in the practice and not in the practitioner. I feel like the phrase privileges codification of knowledge over the emergent and constantly-co-evolving aspects of knowledge. A good recipe is simply no substitute for a good cook. Both aspects of knowledge are very important, and I believe story work creates space for both. Taking on a story project will likely become an intervention in and of itself.

I could continue to use hundreds or even thousands of words to "codify" the experience of the emergent aspects of this work, but that's a little oxymoronic. This is where I will ask you to take a leap of faith. If you're reading this, it's likely because you are looking for something different. In your gut you know what it is, but you just haven't been able to put your finger on it. That's where I was. And, if you're a fairly logical thinker, like me, you want the step-by-step playbook for story work.

Well, I have some good news and some bad news. The good news is you found the playbook. The bad news is you will likely not realize it until you are halfway through your project. My copy of *Working with Stories* is tattered, dog-eared, highlighted and littered with hand-written notes. Do not expect to read it then go out and run a successful story project. My parting codified advice to you is simple: read a little, then do a little, then read again, and repeat as necessary. Good luck on your journey.

Stephen Shimshock

Contents

Chapter One

Introduction

Why are stories so important to human life? Because they are made of the same thing we are made of: time. Stories are tiny simulations of life itself. When I think of people and stories I always think of that line from the bible: "Mary treasured up all these things and pondered them in her heart."

That's what people do. We treasure up things that happen—and things that could and couldn't and should and shouldn't happen—and we ponder them in our hearts. We build them and play with them and give and receive them as we make sense of the overarching stories that are our lives. This is what I mean by *working* with stories.

You might think *you* do not work with stories, perhaps because you are not professionally connected with storytelling or oral history. But have you ever noticed yourself telling the same story to several people? Did the story change as you told it twice, three times, ten times? Did it get simpler? Did it get just a *bit* further away from the literal truth? Do you think you may have been incorporating it into the larger story you tell yourself about yourself? When you do these things, you are working with stories.

People do vary in the extent to which stories enter into their daily lives. Some people seem to live and breathe stories, while others rely more strongly on other ways of making sense of things, like working through options or making lists. But I've yet to meet anyone who *never* works with stories.

Just as individuals work with stories as they make sense of their individual lives, families,

communities, and organizations work with stories as they make sense of their collective endeavors. Groups plan, discuss, argue, gossip, and chat, and some of what they say takes the form of stories. All groups do this naturally, but conscious attention to working with stories can improve a group's collective ability to achieve its common goals.

Conscious attention to working with stories is what this book is about. I have been helping groups work with their stories since 1999, and I have learned much. This work is my attempt to pass on what I have learned and help other people and groups learn how to work with their own stories to further their own goals. Put simply, when they listen to each other's stories, people can learn and achieve things that they cannot achieve in any other way. That simple fact is the basis of every word in this book.

One thing I should say at the very start: this is a book of *practice*, not of theory or inspiration. My goal is to provide you with tools, not change your mind. You can find many books on why people tell stories and why stories are worth paying attention to. This book concentrates on helping you help people gather and work with their stories to achieve positive outcomes. If that is what you are looking for, read on.

WHY WORK WITH STORIES?

When I first talk to people about working with stories, the most common question they have is: "Why work with stories?" So it is this question I will assume you want to ask as well.

I have come to understand that the question "Why work with stories?" is really three different questions:

1. *Why* work with stories? What can I get out of story work? What is its purpose? What is its return on investment?

2. Why *work* with stories? Why not just tell them and listen to them? What do you mean by "working with" stories and what is the purpose of that?

3. Why work with *stories?* Why not ask questions or solicit opinions? What do stories offer that other modes of communication don't?

To each of these questions I have a different answer.

WHY work with stories?

The *why* part of the question "Why work with stories?" has to do with return on investment. People want to know what *results* they can get from working with stories.

Here are some results you can achieve when you work with stories.

Find things out

By asking people to tell you stories on particular topics, and then asking them some questions about the stories they have told, you can discover useful *patterns*, especially when many of these stories are considered together. An example of a project that finds things out might be one where you ask a group of nursing home patients to tell stories about interactions with their doctors.

Catch emerging trends

Catching trends is like finding things out, but it covers situations where you don't know what sorts of things people are concerned about, and you don't have any particular questions to ask, but simply want to know what problems or opportunities might be on the horizon. An example of a project that catches emerging trends might be one where you ask a group of teenagers to tell you about volunteer work they have enjoyed.

Make decisions

Looking at patterns in told stories can provide practical support when choosing between available options. This is especially true when people can look at patterns together. Working with stories to support decision making might involve moving into fictional space to consider alternative possibilities for the future. An example of a project that helps people make decisions might be one that presents stories representing three different possible futures of a town, and asks townspeople to answer questions about their reactions to the stories and respond with stories of their own.

Get new ideas

If you want to plan for the future or solve a problem, and you want to find as many possible options as you can, you can cast a wide net and invite a large group of people to brainstorm with you by asking them to tell you stories. An example of a project that gets new ideas might be one that asks people in an area plagued with gang violence to tell stories about times when they saw tense confrontations defused without violence.

Resolve conflicts

One way to help people in a group understand life from the eyes of people in another group is to collect anonymous stories from both groups and make them available in ways that make it easy to connect stories across traditional boundaries. An example of a project that resolves conflicts might be one that asks kids from all over the world to tell about their first friendship or their happiest day with their parents or their proudest accomplishment, and reveals their nationality only after the story has been read.

Connect people

Stories can connect people within as well as between groups. Providing a means for people to tell stories about their experiences in a group can help new members understand the unwritten rules of the community as well as provide a cultural language for resolving disputes. An example of a project that connects people might be one where university students are asked about their first day in their dormitory.

Help people learn

Telling stories to help people understand complex topics is both an ancient practice and an innate capacity. Providing a means to collect, provide context for, organize, and make available such learning stories can help a community become more collectively productive. An example of a project that helps people learn might be one where a piece of software incorporates "Eureka!" and "Help!" buttons which encourage users to tell the story of what they discovered or what went wrong. In the "Help!" instance, the story could also function as a search pattern to help the user find a solution to their problem. Such stories could also help other users articulate their needs and tell software designers about improvements they could make.

Enlighten people

Groups with a mandate to educate people about particular subjects will find that story work can be helpful to them in two ways. First, collecting stories of real experiences about a topic can help plan the best method of communicating a message. Second, one of the best ways to persuade people is to show them the experiences of real people like themselves, not more of the hype and prepared advertising they are already immersed in. An example of a project that changes minds might be one that collects stories about adoption and makes them available to people on the fence about becoming adoptive parents.

Story work can include any one or more of these purposes, and probably more I haven't thought of as well.

What you can't do with stories

So what *can't* you do when you work with stories? You can't find specific answers, test hypotheses, or conduct experiments as you would in a scientific endeavor. You can't *prove* anything by working with stories. If conducting a proper scientific experiment is like using a tiny scalpel, asking people to tell stories is like using a bludgeon: it's a blunt instrument. You can come up with hypotheses, but you can't control how people will interpret the questions you ask them, so you can never be sure if those hypotheses were proven or disproven. You can't create a control group, because you can't control how people will react.

Is this a problem? I don't think so. I have come to believe that when your subject is human beings and the things they feel and believe, proof isn't a very useful thing. What is useful is *help* coming to decisions. For that purpose, working with stories has an excellent record of accomplishment.

The other thing you can't do when you work with stories is *lie*. If you try to use the stories people tell you to create propaganda that distorts what they said (though not all propaganda does), chances are the truth will come out. And when it does, nobody will ever want to tell you stories again. So you can't really *use* stories; you can just *work with* them. And they sure do know how to defend themselves!

Why WORK with stories?

There are two sub-questions within this question: Why pay attention to stories? And why do *more* with stories than just exchange them?

Why pay attention to stories?

The first sub-question has to do with the *intentional* nature of working with stories. People ask: Why pay conscious attention to stories? Don't stories work well enough already, in the way people naturally share their experiences? Isn't this a natural process? Why attempt to shape it? Won't you just impose order on something that ought to take natural shape?

Yes, people telling each other stories in unstructured, everyday conversation is a constant human activity. It seems people cannot talk without telling stories, at least some of the time. We all do it every day. Some do it more and some do it less, but nobody *never* tells stories. However, having said that, we tell stories in daily life far less than we used to.

To spare you reading everything I could say about this state of affairs, let me just state my case quickly. I believe that the number of personal stories told in natural, everyday, casual conversation by any random person in any industrialized country today is likely to be smaller than at any time in the past, reaching back tens of thousands of years. If you doubt this, ask anyone over the age of eighty about their grandparents.

Many factors have come together to create this change in the narrative life of families and communities: the time-stealing mass media, the whirrs of our various labor-saving devices, the loss of leisure time, the two-earner household, and the rise of commercially super-sized stories that make our own tales of daily life seem unworthy of attention. We just don't tell stories the way we used to. So part of the answer to the question "Don't stories work well enough already?" is that they don't. They don't work well enough anymore, that is.

The fact is, we need to *reskill ourselves* in story exchange. At least some of the collective capacity we once had to share and work with stories in our communities has been lost, and for the most part we aren't even aware of what we have lost. Paying conscious attention to sharing and working with stories helps to restore the balance.

Why not just exchange stories?

The second sub-question is this: Why not just collect stories and distribute them? Isn't that enough? Why *do* anything with them other than support their exchange? What is all this about decision support? What is the point of "making sense" of stories?

My answer to this question can only be a practical one. Doing more with stories simply works better. I have seen the benefits of these techniques many dozens of times. I have seen people arrive at insights that had been eluding them for decades. I have seen people overturn assumptions harder than stones and bigger than boulders. I have seen people release unhoped-for fountains of energy to solve problems. All of these things happened because people did more with their stories than just telling them and hearing them. I hope the many brief stories about real projects scattered throughout this book, and the longer stories in the book's companion volume (*More Work with Stories*), will give you an idea of exactly what real people have achieved by working with real stories.

Based on the experiences I describe in this book, I believe that if you could run an experiment in which community A simply shares stories while community B both shares stories and conducts sessions in which people work with their stories to build something together, community B will arrive at better, more robust, more resilient, more *grounded* decisions. The decisions made by community B will be ones everyone who participated in the effort can understand and explain, but more importantly the decisions will be ones everyone who participated can live with, even if they don't agree with every last part of them.

But don't take my word for it! Try it yourself and see if it works for you. Or better, *make it work* for your community or organization. If you start small and work your way into greater understanding of the techniques I describe in this book, I am confident that you will gain something useful from them. These techniques were developed and refined over the course of many projects, and they share concepts and ideas in common with many other methods of participatory work. Pick up any book about participatory action research, community therapy, participatory theatre, or decision support, and you will find parallels to what you read here. In fact I strongly encourage you to draw widely from many techniques designed to help people think and make decisions together.

In the end, you and your community, and what happens in your community, are the ultimate authorities as to what works best. The ideas and techniques I describe in this book don't matter in the abstract. If they don't work in the particular context of your needs and hopes, they don't work. It is your task to make them work, or to build what *does* work for you. It is *my* task to help you do that.

Why work with STORIES?

What is the advantage of working with *stories* rather than with facts, opinions, or answers to direct questions? Why pay attention to stories in particular? Why do they matter? I can think of ten answers to those questions, in three categories.

Stories for negotiation

These aspects of narrative utility have to do with the position of stories and storytelling in social life, as a mechanism for the ritualized negotiation of truths.

Social function. People who are telling and listening to stories act differently and expect different things than when they are talking normally. This gives the sharing of stories both a unique function in society and a unique advantage when one wants to understand feelings and beliefs. When a person tells a story in a group, that person is given both the floor and the attention (and silence) of the group. Asking people to tell *you* stories sends them the message that you have given them the floor and your attention. It sends the message "I am listening" rather than the message "I am interrogating," and thus triggers a different social response.

Emotional safety. The separation between *narrative* events (storytellings) and *narrated* events (what takes place in stories) provides an emotional distance that creates the safety people need to disclose deeply held feelings and beliefs.

Compare these two mini-surveys.

1. Do you think your local government is doing a terrible, good enough, or excellent job meeting your needs?
2. What was the last interaction you had with your local government? Can you tell us what happened? (Then after the story is told…) How do you feel about that story? What do you think it says about your local government?

Which do you think would give you a better picture of what people feel and believe?

A story is a socially accepted package in which people have learned from a young age to wrap up their feelings, beliefs, and opinions. When they tell and listen to stories, people often reveal things about their feelings or opinions on a subject that they wouldn't have been willing or able to reveal when talking about the topic directly. People know that they can metaphorically place a story on a table and invite others to view and internalize it without exposing themselves to the same degree as they would if they stated those feelings, beliefs, and opinions directly.

Providing a voice. Most people are accustomed to being asked for their opinions in standard surveys, and they get out their well-practiced poker faces for that game. Asking people to tell stories puts away that game and starts another one. The storytelling game is inherently one in which greater respect is afforded to both players.

Asking people to tell stories shows respect by legitimizing their experiences as valuable communications. Respect is also communicated by giving people the freedom to choose what story they will tell and how the story will take form. The mere fact of saying "we really do want to know what has happened to you" is something many people have rarely experienced. In fact, I have come to expect that among the stories told in any project I will find some that express *gratitude* for the chance to tell the story. Can you imagine people expressing gratitude for the chance to fill out a survey?

Stories for thinking

These aspects of narrative utility have to do with stories as cognitive devices.

Engagement. I remember once sitting in my kitchen leafing through a magazine that had come in the mail. I was not paying much attention, but all of a sudden my hand jerked the magazine up to my eyes and demanded that I look at it more closely. The full-page advertisement I found myself examining started out with very small type, then had the word BECAUSE in large type, then descended into small type again. The reason I had thrust the page in front of myself with such force was that I absolutely had to know what was *because* of what.

We do that. People seem to compulsively think, over and over, every day, about the way things happen. We tell and listen to stories in part because it helps us refine our model of the way the world works so we can predict what might happen next. It's a survival skill.

To fulfill this cognitive function, every story has a natural shape, with a situation, a tension, and a resolution. People usually find it difficult to "exit" the story before the tension has been resolved, whether they are telling it or listening to it. The story pulls them in and engages them until it has completed its course. In the context of inquiry, this reduces the frequency of participants answering questions without giving them much thought. Even if people had *meant* to ignore the inquiry, they are sometimes captivated by the storytelling aspect and stay longer (and say more) than they would have otherwise.

Articulation. When people tell stories, they sometimes reveal feelings and beliefs of which they themselves are not aware. When the answer to a direct question is, "I don't know," asking for a story may provide the contextual triggers that bring out the tacit knowledge and relevant experience required. After the story has been told, the storyteller may *still* not know the answer to the direct question. But the answer is there in their story, and if you ask them *about* the story (and do so with many other stories and many other storytellers), the answers will form into meaningful patterns.

Interpretation. When you ask people to tell stories, and then ask them questions about their stories, you are asking them to *interpret* rather than opine. This displacement gives people both the freedom to say forbidden things—it's about the *story*, not about me—and the safety to admit fault or place blame. Also, people tend to have stronger reactions to hearing stories, in terms of the emotions they show, than they have to hearing factual information (see page 67 for more on reactions to stories). I've noticed that listeners tend to fidget less and lean in more when a story is being told than when someone is giving opinions or relaying information. This makes asking people to interpret their own stories a useful means of surfacing their feelings about important issues.

Imagination. When a topic is complex and many-layered, the best course is to increase diversity, generate many ideas, think out of the box, and prepare for surprise. Asking a diverse range of people to tell you what they have done and seen enlists their imagination along with your own. This both broadens the net of exploration (by opening the inquiry to the varieties of human experience) and increases its flexibility (by capturing multidimensional content which can be plumbed again and again as needs emerge). In contrast, direct questioning, though precise, is narrowly focused, and produces unidimensional content that can provide only one answer.

Stories for explaining

These aspects of narrative utility have to do with stories as knowledge transfer devices.

Authenticity. When the goal of a project is communicative, stories convey complex emotions with more *ground truth* than any other means of communication. Direct questioning may generate more precise measurements, but story elicitation ensures greater *depths* of insight and understanding into complex topics and complex people. The act of listening to a story told by another person creates a suspension of disbelief and displacement of perspective that helps people see through new eyes into a different world of truth.

Contextual richness. When you ask direct questions, it is easy to guess wrongly about what sorts of answers people might have and even about what sorts of questions might lead to useful answers. This is often a problem when exploring complex topics. Asking people to talk about their experiences can sometimes lead to useful answers *even if the wrong questions were asked,* because the contextual richness of stories provides information in excess of what was directly sought. In fact, being surprised by the questions posed (and answered) by collected stories is a standard outcome of narrative inquiry.

Redirection. A well-constructed story elicitation results in fewer non-response behaviors (answering without considering, manipulating the survey to promote an agenda, trying too hard to do what seems to be expected, and so on) than direct questioning. These behaviors don't go away when people tell stories, but they are both reduced and more obvious when they do occur. Because telling a story pulls in both teller and listener, the reluctant pay more attention, those with agendas reveal their true thoughts (even while promoting their agendas), and performers have a harder time guessing what they are supposed to say (and switch to telling the best story they can). Also, non-responses are easier to spot in narrative results, because the texts of the stories themselves provide clues to why people gave the answers they did.

WHY I WROTE THIS BOOK

I have been a researcher and consultant in the field of organizational and community narrative since 1999. (You can read about my work history in the Acknowledgements and Biography at the end of the book on page 631.) Over the years of this work, as story projects came and went, I kept thinking about the fact that the wonderful ideas and techniques I was developing were bottled up and available only to giant corporations, government agencies, and academic institutions with money and knowledge and power. While being grateful that those powerful bodies were willing to pay me to do this work, I could see that the people most in need of story techniques were Margaret Mead's small groups of thoughtful, committed citizens trying to change the world.

I began to imagine what would happen if *every* community around the world was uncovering such insights by sharing and working with their stories. I thought of people trying to negotiate better working conditions on migrant farms, or coping with refugee status, or recovering from floods, or working to bring back a struggling city block, or trying to get compensation for incidents like the Bhopal disaster, or trying to "green up" their community. If *they* could benefit from some of these understandings about stories; if *they* could use this power to discover insights and create positive change; it could change the world one small community at a time.

The urgency of this task increased when I encountered a wonderful book called *Where There Is No Doctor*, by David Werner with Carol Thuman and Jane Maxwell. I think I picked it up in a bookstore sometime around 2003. The following statement in the introduction of the book created a deep connection with the discomfort I had been feeling about my work with stories.

> *Where There Is No Doctor* was written for anyone who wants to do something about his or her own and other people's health. However, it has been widely used as a training and work manual for community health workers. For this reason, an introductory section has been added for the health worker, making clear that the health worker's first job is to share her knowledge and help educate people.
>
> Today in over-developed as well as under-developed countries, existing health care systems are in a state of crisis. Often, human needs are not being well met. There is too little fairness. Too much is in the hands of too few.
>
> Let us hope that through a more generous sharing of knowledge, and through learning to use what is best in both traditional and modern ways of healing, people everywhere will develop a kinder, more sensible approach to caring—for their own health, and for each other.

The Wikipedia page on *Where There Is No Doctor* quotes a review in the British Medical Journal that says:

> Chances are that if you visited a remote district hospital in a developing country you would find a well thumbed copy of *Where There Is No Doctor* in its library. The book is intended primarily for village health workers, but generations of doctors and medical missionaries who have worked in under-resourced communities globally will vouch for its value in providing concise reliable information.

Where There Is No Doctor spoke to me. It said: You are like a health worker in your work with stories, and like them your first job should be to share your knowledge and help educate people. It said: In the world of stories as in the world of medicine, too much knowledge is in the hands of too few. It said: Through a more generous sharing of knowledge, and through learning to use what is best in both traditional and modern ways of story work, people everywhere will develop a kinder, more sensible approach to caring for their stories—for their own narrative health, and for each other.

Why did I believe too much was in the hands of too few? Because I had seen it for myself. I noticed the displacement of ordinary people from ordinary stories in my very first story projects. Time after time I have watched people balk at being asked to tell stories—because they think "story" means "Hollywood" or "front page." They think any story they could tell would not be "good enough." They also balk when they are asked to work with stories—to build something out of them, for example—because they do not believe they are *qualified* to do so. Indeed, people sometimes respond with something akin to fear when I've asked them to tell or work with stories. It is as though I have asked them to cut out a tumor or build a skyscraper.

I can still remember the moment I first discovered this perception of not being qualified to tell stories. I was transcribing an audiotape from one of my very first group story sessions. One participant in the session told story after story, each of them fascinating and useful, and then—literally in the next breath—said, "But I can't think of any stories to tell." It's a good thing I was listening to a tape and not in the room with the person, because my jaw dropped to the floor.

Since then I have often pondered, at great length: *What made that person say that?* And I can't help wondering as well: Would someone have said it a thousand years ago? A hundred?

It is not so much that people have lost the *ability* to tell stories as much as they have lost the expectation that it is their *place* to tell stories. Their place, apparently, is in the audience. But when people are qualified only to *consume* stories, they give up the power that can arise from familiarity with using stories to make sense of their lives. And by extension, *groups* of people who have given up the power to work with stories lose the ability to use their combined stories to make sense together of the goals and trials of their organization or community.

I am of course not the only person who has noticed this trend. Robert Fulford put it well in his book *The Triumph of Narrative: Storytelling in the Age of Mass Culture:*

> This has been the century of mass storytelling. We live under a Niagara of stories: print, television, movies, radio and the Internet deliver to us far more stories than our ancestors could have imagined, and the number of stories available to us seems to grow larger every year. This phenomenon, the rise of industrialized narrative—storytelling that's engineered for mass reproduction and distribution—has emerged as the most striking cultural fact of the twentieth century and the most far-reaching development in the history of narrative.

Jack Maguire, in *The Power of Personal Storytelling*, put it this way:

> Once upon a time, when people made more of their own things, they created more stories about their life experiences. They told these tales to each other regularly, gracefully, and productively. They did it to give each other insights, to entertain each other, and to engage each other in times of celebration, trial, mourning, or reverence. But primarily they did it to connect with each other. Sharing real-life stories was an essential element in forging friendships, alliances, families, and communities. It brought individuals

a greater intimacy with each other and, simultaneously, a stronger sense of self.

Since that time, for all the wonderful progress made in communication technology, the world has grown alarmingly less personal. People have given over much of their individual power to the collective, and have let themselves be increasingly distracted from personal storytelling by flashier but ultimately less gratifying activities that compete for their attention. As a result, we citizens of today's world have lost some of our core vitality—our feeling of having direct contact with the lives we lead, of relating meaningfully with others, and of being individuals in our own right, with our own clear identities.

Thus I, and others, found the narrative situation today to be a perfect analogue of the situation *Where There Is No Doctor* was written to address.

With this realization I began to have an idea. What if next to every copy of *Where There Is No Doctor* there could sit *another book,* one that helps people take care of their own stories the way they take care of their own health? What if I could write such a book, or at least start it?

Ambitious, yes, and probably arrogant, but sincerely meant. That idea led me to this book, and to the revision you are looking at now. (And to splitting the book into two books, because it got too long—did I mention ambition?) My hope is that this book (and, um, the other) will get at least some people started along the road to taking control of the narrative health of their own organizations and communities.

THIS BOOK AND YOU

In writing and updating this book and its companion volume *More Work with Stories,* I have thought of you, my reader, in three ways.

1. You might know little or nothing about story work, simply aiming to explore what this approach can do for your community or organization. You will be looking for clarity in explanations and instructions, proof of effectiveness, and ideas to feed your own

ingenuity. Long treatises on fine points and advanced topics will stand in the way of your learning, at least at first.

2. You might be peering over at what I've written from expertise in a related field such as oral history, participatory action research, narrative inquiry, or qualitative research. In that case you will already have a perspective on stories, participation, or inquiry. You will not need much foundational explanation, though you might need me to fill in some gaps in areas you are less familiar with. Most of all, you will need me to explain the utility of the methods I propose you consider using.

3. You might already do professional work very similar to what I describe here. Perhaps you don't call it exactly what I call it, but you don't need me to define the work or explain its fundamentals. You will be interested in fine points of practice, because you have an interest in improving your skills.

So who are these books *for*? As they say, that's a long story. I began the book project thinking only of the first type of reader. I wrote the first edition of the book in a burst of energy over six weeks in early 2008. That first edition was about a hundred pages long. The second edition in 2009 mainly added some case studies and increased the book's length to about 120 pages.

After the second edition of the book had been out for a while, I found myself wanting to write down more of what I knew and make the book a stronger resource. I also hoped to sell printed copies of the book to support my work, and I felt I needed a stronger "product" to do so. So in late 2009 I started writing new sections. I posted these new sections onto my blog (at storycoloredglasses.com). (Why? To advertise my business and get consulting work! I have bills too!) Somewhere between a quarter and a third of the content of both books came from those blog posts.

Writing on a blog changed the way I thought about my writing, which changed my writing. Because people commented on my blog posts, my writing got chattier and more conversational. Because many of my blog readers were professional story workers already, my writing

started to take on more of a "your work in story" tone. Without my planning it, the two professional audiences above crept in and found a place in the book's readership.

Around 2011, I stopped keeping up the blog as often and turned my attention to finishing the book. The last portion of the book I wrote in the months and years that followed, sewing together the old and new, finding the gaps that remained, and filling them.

During this time I tried to keep all three portraits of you in mind, side by side, watching me work. I worried that the first type of reader might end up confused by the great volume of writing I ended up putting together, so I tried to work on ways to help everyone find what they needed. The main way in which I have done this is to segregate most of the professional-reader content into the companion book, *More Work with Stories*.

I still want very much to speak to my first and original reader, the interested newcomer. If you are that reader, I want you to know that helping you was the reason I started writing this book, and helping you was the reason I improved it. But you will also have to understand that the other readers are here with you. I suggest you put aside the companion volume until you have become comfortable with this book. You might also want to skim or jump over some of the sections of this book marked as optional (such as "Optional elaborations" in the exercise sections).

If you are in either of the two groups of professional readers, you also should be aware that the other two groups are here with you in your reading. I expect that you will be equally interested in this book and in its companion volume; but in *More Work with Stories* I speak more directly to you.

I am not at all sure that I have succeeded in my efforts to keep both of these books clear to all of my readers. Whatever your background, you are likely to find that my tone of voice jumps around from formal to chatty and abstract to concrete. I have tried to smooth out some of the worst peaks and valleys in tone, but I am sure the entire work remains a patchwork. Still,

I hope you will be able to make what you—all of you—need from it.

THE STRUCTURE OF THE BOOK

The first part of this book is about stories: what they are, how and why we tell them, what they are for, how they flow in communities and organizations. I think of Part One as a sort of primer of basic knowledge about stories that you'll need if you want to work with them. Part Two is all about participatory narrative inquiry, a method you can use to create positive change by working with stories in your community or organization.

NOTES ON THE BOOK

Here are a few miscellaneous notes on the book, which I should mention to you at the outset.

Our pigeonhole (if you want one)

This is a textbook for a course in participatory narrative inquiry (or maybe two courses, basic in this book and advanced in *More Work with Stories*). Both books could be used in a high school or community college or adult learning or university course, or they could be used in a self-study course, in a group or alone.

Each chapter concludes with a summary and some questions and activities I suggest would help you make sense of the information in the chapter and put it to good use. I never do activities in books myself, though I always think I will, for a little while. So I wrote them to be equally useful if you *do* them or if you just *think* about doing them.

Why this book is so awfully long

One day I was in a restaurant with some friends. I ordered some iced tea. It came without sugar, so I dumped a spoonful of sugar into the glass and started stirring it in. It made a noise, ching ching ching. I was engaged in conversation, so I kept stirring as I talked and listened. Evidently I forgot I was doing this and kept on ching-chinging for a very long time, because suddenly a waitress rushed up, grabbed my hand, and shouted, "Stop!"

That's just how I am, people. When I get started on something, it takes on a life of its own and goes on and on. This book project has been ching-chinging along for more than five years, taking up vast amounts of my time and entering into my conversations, thoughts, and dreams. I'm terribly sorry the whole thing turned out to be so long, but it's just who I am that I should write a monster of a thing like this. You will have to take it, and me, as you find us.

To reduce the ching-ching sound as much as I could, I have made a sincere attempt to reduce redundancy, which explains the many cross-references to similar topics covered in other places (the book's index should help you navigate those connections). I have tried to make a strong separation between what is important (the fundamentals) and what is nice to have (the advanced topics). I had originally meant this distinction to happen within one book, but the writing got *so* long that I had to move the advanced topics to their own volume. Finally, I have tried to lay out both books clearly so you can jump around in them to meet your needs. Hopefully that will make the books work for you despite their combined length.

Changes in this edition

In moving from the second to the third edition of this book I have increased its size nearly ten-fold (see previous backhanded apology) and divided it into two volumes, of which this is the first. While expanding the book, I addressed shortcomings that readers of previous editions told me about. I added more conceptual depth. I attempted to prove the value of the approach more than I had previously done. I told many more stories from my own experience (because readers asked me to). I evaluated my usage of specialized terms and removed or revamped those people had trouble understanding. I added more references and quotes. I added more than three hundred illustrations. I improved my recommended-books list to provide greater utility. Finally, I bound the books together with a new subtitle (Participatory Narrative Inquiry) that helps people better understand what the books are about. All of these changes are apparent in the new edition. Most of the writing from the first and second editions remains, but it is embedded in new writing and updated based on new understandings.

He, she, and they

My preferred solution to the pronoun problem (he, she, he or she, s/he) is to use what the style guides call "the singular they," such as for example "each storyteller has their own style." This form is often attacked as ungrammatical yet is growing in common usage. I have tried various methods but keep settling back on it as least distracting. Apparently the singular they is nothing new but was in common use in medieval times. Even Jane Austen used the singular they. As Austen's Emma Woodhouse says: "It is very unfair to judge of any body's conduct, without an intimate knowledge of their situation." Agreed.

Photo credits for the book cover

The woven image in the cover background is part of a photograph from the Wikipedia commons, where it is described as a "Dai woven textile" in the "weaving collection in the Yunnan Nationalities Museum, Kunming, Yunnan, China." The image is (according to Wikipedia) in the public domain.

The four photographs of people on the cover are all from the U.S. Library of Congress database from the Farm Security Administration (FSA) collection. All are described as having "no known restrictions" on publication. (I made sure none of the people in the pictures were famous, to avoid infringing on rights of publication, or probably still alive, to avoid infringing on rights of privacy.)

The photographs are described on the Library of Congress web site thus:

- Nine young women sitting on chairs talking: Meeting of NYA (National Youth Administration) girls with an instructor at the Good Shepherd Community Center. Chicago, Illinois. Photo released January 1942 by Russell Lee (1903–1986).
- Woman holding clipboard talking to women and boy: Farm laborer being interviewed by FSA home management supervisor for eligibility in the FSA labor program. Utuado, Puerto Rico (vicinity). Photo released April 1941 by Jack Delano (1914–1997).
- Two men talking, one with plow: Parish FSA supervisor talking and discussing farm problems with brother-in-law of rural rehabilitation borrower who had been cultivating his cotton. West Carroll Parish, Louisiana. Photo released June 1940 by Marion Post Wolcott (1910–1990).
- Six people at a table looking at a map: Meeting of the neighborhood or community land use planning committee in Locust Hill. Caswell County, North Carolina. Photo released October 1940 by Marion Post Wolcott (1910–1990).

Note that the people in these pictures are not necessarily working with stories. I chose these pictures for the cover because I wanted to show that the book is primarily about *people*. I wanted to show *real* people, not stock-photo people, who always look somehow robotic. The Farm Security Administration was created to help poor farmers improve their living conditions. As far as I can tell, that meant people were interviewed and meetings were held, but there was nothing explicitly narrative about the work. There was no oral history component to it, for example. So most of what is going on in these pictures is straightforward discussion, though I'm sure stories had to have been told, heard, and passed on. Still, the many photographs taken by FSA photographers brought the faces of rural poverty to the rest of the country, so that's a sort of narrative intervention in itself.

Part I

Fundamentals of Story Work

To help you get started in story work, I thought about my own discoveries in the field as well as conversations I have had with other people making the same journey.

By my best estimation, these are the questions you are most likely to have at this point:

1. What is a story?
2. What are stories for?
3. How do stories work?
4. How do stories work in my community?

Thus, this part of the book contemplates each of these questions in order to give you an essential grounding in narrative.

Chapter Two (What Is a Story? on page 15) explores varying definitions of stories and presents three story dimensions of form, function, and phenomenon.

Chapter Three (What Are Stories For? on page 25) describes stories as maps of experience, sounding devices, elements of play, and packages of meaning.

Chapter Four (How Do Stories Work? on page 35) explores aspects of how stories function in conversation, with purpose and without, inside and alongside other stories, and in society in general.

Chapter Five (Stories in Communities and Organizations, on page 63) looks specifically at how stories work in groups of people who live and work together. Because this book assumes that you are interested in actively working with stories in your own community or organization, Chapter Five serves as a bridge to the second part of the book—which moves beyond theory and into practice.

Chapter Two

What Is a Story?

This chapter explores definitions of the word "story" and sets up a working definition we will use for the remainder of the book.

Most definitions of story have two parts to them: stories are this, and stories are *not* that. I've read hundreds of such definitions, and maybe you have too. If you gather together all the definitions of story you can find and compare them, you will notice something curious. What makes a story a story to one person sometimes makes it *not* a story to another. So who is right and who is wrong?

I used to say what everyone else said: *I'm* right, of course, and the people who wrote these other definitions are wrong. But over time I've come to realize that *every* definition of story I have ever read—including my own—has been completely wrong. Or rather, wrongly complete. The reason good people disagree on the definition of story isn't that some are right and some are wrong; it is that they are looking at different parts of the same elephant.

So rather than tell you what is and is not a story, I will tell you about *three essential dimensions* of story that among them contain every conceivable definition of the word (see Figure 2.1 on the following page).

The *form* of a story is its communicative structure and meaning.

In the domain of form, a story works because it fits our cultural expectations of what a narrative communication ought to be like, and uses that fit to deliver a value-laden *message*. Within those expectations, many structural and stylis-

tic nuances of setting, character, plot, value, conflict, and theme can be used to produce particular effects for the story's intended audience and purpose.

The *function* of a story is its utility to thought, decision, and action.

In the domain of function, a story works when we encounter it in the right place at the right time, when it helps us to understand something useful, or when it reminds us of something we need to know and use. Function deals with *connections:* between story characters and their plans, goals, and actions; between cause and effect; between the story and other stories that explore related issues and teach complementary lessons; between situations in the story and analogous situations in our lives.

The *phenomenon* of a story is its life history as it moves through time and society.

In the domain of phenomenon, a story works when it survives and spreads through the conversation and memory of people. Phenomenon deals with *context:* when and where the story's events took place; when and where it first took form and was told; when and where it was retold; how it developed and changed over time; its current use, range, and variations. Phenomenon also involves interpretations of narrated events (in the story) and narrative events (storytellings) by storytellers, audiences, observers, subjects, and all other participants in the life of the story.

THE ANT AND THE DOVE

To illustrate what it means to consider a story from each of these dimensions, consider this fable from Aesop.

> An ant went to the bank of a river to quench its thirst, and being carried away by the rush of the stream, was on the point of drowning.

> A dove sitting on a tree overhanging the water plucked a leaf and let it fall into the stream close to her. The ant climbed onto it and floated in safety to the bank.

> Shortly afterwards a birdcatcher came and stood under the tree, and laid his

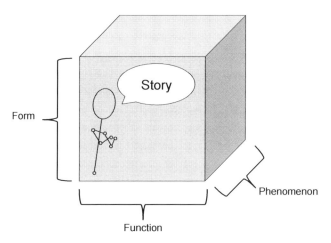

Figure 2.1. Stories can be seen in three ways: as form, function, and phenomenon.

lime-twigs [trap] for the dove, which sat in the branches. The ant, perceiving his design, stung him in the foot.

In pain the birdcatcher threw down the twigs, and the noise made the dove take wing.

That's *just* the sort of story Aesop would tell, isn't it? The old rascal. The story never comes right out and says *anything*, but we know what it means. That sort of understanding is what people do best. So, we apply the instrument, as follows.

Story form

We can describe story form in "The Ant and the Dove" as follows. (See Figure 2.2 on the next page.) The physical setting encompasses a river and a tree, in warm weather (no ice on the river), probably in the daytime. The story covers a time frame of perhaps an hour or two.

The social setting is remarkable: it includes unrealistically intelligent animals, though the bird-catcher does not seem aware of this, to his detriment. The protagonist of the story is the dove; the antagonist is the bird-catcher; the ant functions as a teacher or helper to the dove.

Contrasts between characters are important in the story. The ant is helpless against the current but can bite the man. The dove cannot attack its enemy but can fly from danger. The plot begins with an initiating event (the ant is carried away), continues with a protagonist action (the

dove saves the ant), encounters a complicating event (the man sets a trap for the dove), and ends with a helper action (the ant saves the dove) that is the story's resolution.

Change in this story appears when two characters who have no prior relationship form a bond of mutual salvation. The cause of this change is primarily the dove's (the protagonist's) choice to take on a risk to save the ant. The dove literally sticks out its neck to help the ant, and the ant reciprocates by taking another risk, as it could easily be stepped on by the man as it bites him.

The story contains internal conflict (should I help or stay where it's safe?), inter-character conflict (the bird-catcher's attempt to trap the dove), and external conflict (the river's dangerous current).

The symmetry of the two actions makes reciprocity a strong theme; thus the controlling idea of the story is the same as that expressed by the proverb "what goes around comes around." Also notice the story's style, with each sentence describing an apparently unconnected event. It never actually says either animal saved the other, or even that they meant to; only that they took certain actions that had certain outcomes. This gives the story a secondary theme about the undercurrents of connection that go on beneath actions and events that seem unconnected. Thus the story is a cleverly put together package meant to persuade its audience that the proverb is true.

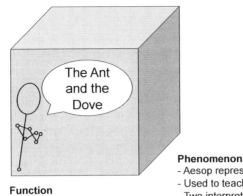

Form
- River, tree, hour
- Intelligent animals
- Dove saves ant
- Ant saves dove
- Risk, aid, reciprocation
- Mutual salvation
- Safety

Phenomenon
- Aesop represents oral traditions
- Used to teach children about social life
- Two interpretations compete for dominance:
1. One good turn deserves another
(ant and dove are friends beforehand)
2. What goes around comes around
(ant and dove are strangers beforehand)

Function
- Expectation: self-preservation
- Violation: risk taken to help other
- Result: gain to self
- Lesson: Helping is worthwhile

Figure 2.2. Story form is about communication; story function is about learning; story phenomenon is about sociality.

Story function

We can describe story function in "The Ant and the Dove" as follows. The expectation in such a situation is that people (for this is a story about people) are usually not willing to take risks to help each other, especially if they are strangers, as seems to be the case here. The violation of expectation explored by the story is that sometimes taking a risk for no apparent gain results in greater safety in the long run. The animals in this story share similar goals, to survive, and this similarity binds the two animals together in a reciprocal relationship. (Imagine if the ant had been the man's pet; would it have helped the dove?)

Also important to this story is the detection of plans: the ant is able to discern both the dove's plan (dropping the leaf) and the man's (setting the lime twigs). This is why the ant is a helper in the story and not a co-protagonist. The dove, unlike the ant, discerns no plans, not even the man's after the ant has bit him (only the noise made the bird take wing, not any dawning awareness of the man's plans).

It is in fact critical to the story's function that the protagonist, who risked her life to help another without promise of return, be unaware of any plans being made. Why? Because that is the lesson of the story: helping without expectation of return is worthwhile. Imagine if the dove had known the man was coming to lay a trap: would its help of the ant constitute help without expectation of return? No; it would be calculating, not taking a leap of faith in unseen reciprocity.

In terms of cognitive play and life-event simulation, the utility of this story lies in considering the relative merits of risk-taking in a world in which intentions and motivations vary and may be difficult to detect. Many folk tales explore related lessons, including some where the hero unselfishly helps others and is rewarded in return, as well as opposing stories where unselfish actions result not in aid but in vulnerability to attack by deceptive antagonists. Little Red Riding Hood and other cautionary tales stand in contrast to stories of reciprocity like this one in a multi-faceted exploration of help, hindrance, trust, and deceit.

Story phenomenon

We can describe story phenomenon in "The Ant and the Dove" as follows. Aesop may or may not have been an actual person. Some claim he lived in ancient Greece, though it is also possible that he is an amalgam of several or even many famed storytellers of the time. Thus it is not clear that anyone named Aesop, or any one person, created Aesop's hundreds of moralistic fables. It is much more likely that they were handed down in oral traditions for many hundreds of years before some number of persons began writing them down.

Over the past few thousand years, many compilations of "Aesop's" fables have been printed and reprinted many times in many languages, and they have developed variations through these printings. Today they are read to and by children, referred to in conversation, and performed in person, in writing, and in film. People use Aesop's fables to teach children about human social realities; to reference truisms in summarized proverbs; to entertain with witty performances; to pursue arguments in subtle, oblique ways; and for many other social purposes. The tales are generally considered part of the cultural heritage of Europeans and people whose ancestors came from those lands, though few people have read all of the fables in the collection or know what is an "Aesop's" fable and what is not.

In the many retellings of this particular fable, the reciprocal relationship between the two main characters remains stable, but details of what each did to save the other may vary, as may the identity and actions of the antagonist.

In the particular narrative event in which I read this story as I prepared this chapter of this book, I reflected on times when I have helped others, times when others have helped me, and times when neither of these things has happened. I reflected on times when, like the dove in the story, I helped a struggling ant—only to find the ant climbing a tree intent on biting me! I thought about how my writing this book is, in a way, a story of my dropping a leaf in a stream, having spent years in the endeavor of writing, unsure that the effort will benefit me or anyone else. I reflected that if the dove in this story is a fool, so am I a fool, but a fool proud of her folly. I wondered if pride in folly is itself folly (and that thought went round and round a few more times before it wound down).

Next I wondered about the people who have told this story over the past few thousand years. I wondered what they thought of it and how its meaning and reception has changed, as it has cast its ripples into the millions of lives into which it has entered. I started reading and listening to versions of the story on the internet.

I was surprised to discover a variety of interpretations of the story's essential meaning. Many versions gave its moral as "One good turn deserves another." This interpretation presents the ant as a protagonist who receives an obligation to help the dove. Other versions give the story's moral as "A kindness is never wasted," matching my interpretation.

These two interpretations seem to have been waging a war for dominance. One portrays a tit-for-tat world in which people rightly help only those who have helped them, and the other portrays a world of unselfish aid in which people do good for the sake of good and are rewarded through the natural balance of the cosmos.

Obviously I favor the natural-balance interpretation. Tellingly, I found myself wanting to copy every interpretation that matched my own and paste it here to show you. I will confine myself to just one: "The Dove did a good deed. And that good deed later saved her own life." Hooray for the right side of the story! Though at the same time I can see the value of the other moral, as I reflect on the naive idealism in my framing of the tale; if I were not of two minds I would not call the dove a fool.

One more thing (you may be able to discern at this point that I find the phenomenon dimension fascinating). Many contemporary tellings of this story do away with the surface-level disconnectedness of the older story, instead having the ant and dove form a close bond of friendship for "many days" before the ant is called upon to help the dove (or even making them friends from the start!). This is again a lesson—help your friends, never mind strangers—that favors the tit-for-tat worldview. Does the rise of the friendship-first interpretation say something about isolationism and xenophobia in the modern world? It's an interesting idea.

Three ways to look at a story

So, there you have three entirely different yet equally useful ways to look at a story. How do they come together? Well, I like to look at it this way: a story is like a cell in our bodies.

Internally, a cell has a complex *structure,* including other organisms-that-were such as mitochondria living their lives inside of ours, much like some stories live inside other stories. Story *form* is like cell structure: both are engaged in managing internal consistency in order to conduct operations that keep the organism alive.

Moving outward, the cell *membrane* is not simply the border of the cell; it is almost like a brain in its detailed control of transport and communication. Story *function* is like the cell membrane: both are engaged in negotiating the interface between what lies within (events, processes) and what lies without (connection, meaning).

If we zoom out our microscopes and look at the larger *tissues* of the organism, we see cells embedded in the contexts of their tiny destinies, some never moving and some traveling vast distances. We see them come together, form things, move apart, die. Story *phenomenon* is like cell tissues: both are engaged in exchanging materials, developing gradient and step-like patterns, pursuing complex large-scale movements that depend on their constituent parts yet add up to more than can be counted.

What is life? It is all of this. What is story? It is all of this.

STORIES OF DEFINITION

One thing I have noticed about the three dimensions of story is that nobody ever seems to make use of all of them at once. You are likely to have encountered some definitions of story already, if you have been reading in this area, and you are most likely to have encountered people saying that story is defined by one or two of these three dimensions.

Try it right now. Pick up any book about stories or storytelling, and you will find that the definition of "story" given in it describes, either only or primarily, one or two of these dimensions. I have read many such books and have yet to find *one* that covers all three dimensions. (See Figure 2.3 on the following page.)

Let me show you a few examples.

What definition of story does this author favor?

> Structure is a selection of events from the characters' life stories that is composed

into a strategic sequence to arouse specific emotions and to express a specific view of life.

Did you guess story form? The quote is from Robert McKee's *Story*, the bible of aspiring screenwriters, and it exclusively defines story in terms of form.

Here is another:

> We must recognize that the symbolic forms we call folklore have their primary existence in the action of people and their roots in social and cultural life. The texts we are accustomed to viewing as the raw materials of oral literature are merely the thin and partial record of deeply situated human behavior.

The quote is from Richard Bauman's *Story, Performance and Event*, a work concerned almost exclusively with story phenomenon.

A third quote:

> When a prior experience is indexed cleverly, we can call it to mind to help us understand a current situation. This process can lead to brand-new insights. All people reason from experience. The differences among reasoners depend upon how they have coded their prior experiences in the first place. We are not all reminded of the same things at the same time.

Which dimension did you pick? The quote is from Roger Schank's *Tell Me a Story*, a treatise on stories in their functional role.

A fourth example:

> We can say about stories what W. H. Auden said about books: some stories maybe unjustly forgotten, but no stories are unjustly remembered. They do not survive through the vagaries of whim. If a story has been swimming in the vast ocean of human consciousness for decades or centuries or even millennia, it has earned its place.

Which dimension of story does *that* description cover? It describes stories as societal phenomena. The quote is from Robert Fulford's book *The Triumph of Narrative*, which explores the

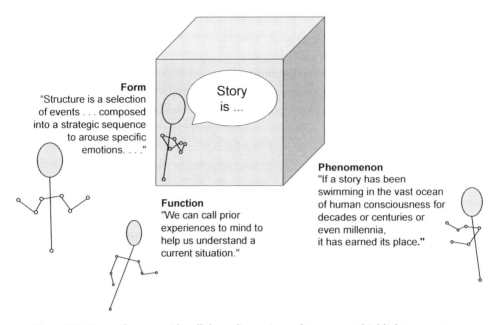

Form
"Structure is a selection of events . . . composed into a strategic sequence to arouse specific emotions. . . ."

Story is ...

Phenomenon
"If a story has been swimming in the vast ocean of human consciousness for decades or centuries or even millennia, it has earned its place."

Function
"We can call prior experiences to mind to help us understand a current situation."

Figure 2.3. Few authors consider all three dimensions of story; most highlight one or two.

roles of stories in society from gossip to urban legends to television.

Here is a quote from an author who covers two dimensions.

> The stories that people tell about their lives are of considerable importance to us, for there is an intimate connection between the ways in which people construe themselves and the ways in which they are likely to behave. ... It is because of this that we are often concerned enough to challenge the stories that people tell about themselves. ... There is an intricate political process at work here; what I should like to call the politics of narrative identity whereby we assert and maintain our own interests not just by advancing a particular view of ourselves, but by undermining the views that others advance of themselves. Stories and counter-stories are told; history is written, subverted, and rewritten. And in this game of strategy, those who have the last word also have considerable power over those who do not.

Can you guess which two dimensions it covers? It is by David Novitz in a chapter called "Art, Narrative, and Human Nature" in the book

Memory, Identity, Community. The quote has cognitive features of story function (connections, prediction, strategy) but also deals with stories as social phenomena (politics, representation, identity, power). But do you see much attention to story *form* there? Setting, character, plot, value, conflict, theme?

Do I believe these dimensions are a new, all-encompassing and fundamental truth about stories, which everyone should adjust their views to accommodate? No. It's more like: I found a way of thinking about stories that helps me think about stories in their entirety, and I think it might work for you too.

Am I saying a lack of lucid awareness of all dimensions of story at all times is a problem or failing? Do I believe it is *wrong* for these authors to speak of stories as one dimension and not others? Certainly not. Everyone naturally gravitates to one or two of these dimensions of story more strongly than the others, and that gravitation colors the way they think about stories and what they think makes a story a story. I began my career studying animal behavior, so I think about cognition and social signals a lot, and that explains why I gravitate to a definition that blends story function and phenomenon. Other people come at story from other backgrounds and personalities, so they experience different things, so story takes on different shapes to them. You yourself will most likely find one of these three dimensions most "true" when it comes to your own experiences with stories.

What I am saying is that *your definition of story is a story* about you and your life. This means that no definition of story can be truly complete without considering *all* of these dimensions, in the same way that no story of humanity can be truly complete without including the story of every single human being. I don't think we need a melting pot of story definition, just some respect for multiple perspectives and maybe some interfaith dialogue. If you live and breathe cognitive science, why not read Augusto Boal's *Theatre of the Oppressed?* If you dream in community therapy, why not pick up a book on screenwriting? If you design perfect characters, why not read up on expert systems or indigenous knowledge? Travel broadens the mind.

Does this mean I believe people must use *every* story dimension in story work all the time? No. Different dimensions of story have different *practical utility* in different contexts. That's a good thing. While it is good to practice moving outside the story dimension we know best, it is not always the best course of action to include every story dimension in the specific contexts in which we are working at any one time.

If you are reaching an audience or sending a message, you need stories to be memorable and motivating. They should have strong plots and characters in conflict. When you need to approach stories in that context, read Robert McKee's *Story* and Michael Toolan's *Narrative*.

If you are creating a narrative knowledge management system or learning from mistakes, you need stories to increase understanding. Your stories should present dilemmas, discoveries, surprises, and solutions. When you need to approach stories in that context, read Roger Schank's *Tell Me a Story* and Gary Klein's *Sources of Power*.

If you are bringing together a community or writing to your grandchildren, you need stories to achieve a lasting positive impact. They should resonate and connect in context. When you need to approach stories in that context,

read Richard Bauman's *Story, Performance and Event* and Augusto Boal's *Theatre of the Oppressed*.

The particular combination of goals in any story project will determine the particular combination of story dimensions it can most fruitfully use to the best effect. Thus, the more you develop your agility at handling various combinations of story dimensions, the stronger your ability will be to carry out effective story work.

Most of all, form, function, and phenomenon are *aspective*, not partitive, dimensions. They do not divide and exclude: they interpenetrate and augment. Not coincidentally, this is *exactly* what stories do, and it's why they have such a central place in human life. Stories are among our most aspective elements of thought and conversation. They deserve an aspective framework of understanding.

A WORKING DEFINITION

So my first answer to the question of what is a story, as you have seen, is that stories have aspects of form, function, and phenomenon. This is a *general* definition of story, suitable for any purpose. My second answer is that for my purposes in this book, that is, in helping you develop your ability to help people work with their stories to achieve goals, I would like to set up a *working definition* of story. A working definition (by definition) does not make any claims to "what is" in a *general* sense; rather, it establishes a set of agreed-upon assumptions we will use as we begin to work together with a specific purpose in mind.

Our working definition of story (which will form a part of the story of our work together) will be as follows.

A story is a recounting of events during which you wonder what is going to happen, and then you find out. In order for you to wonder what is going to happen there has to be a tension between two or more possibilities (it's why there needs to be a comma in that first sentence). Aristotle called this tension the contrast between *potentiality* (what could happen) and *actuality* (what does happen). The simplest recountings of events are not stories—for example, lists of things that happened on different

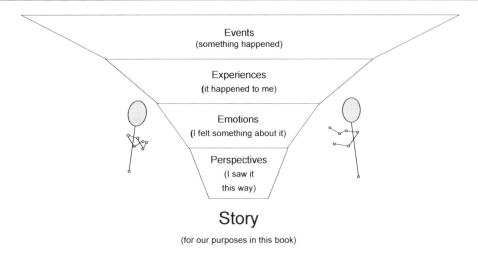

Figure 2.4. For the purposes of this book, we define a story as a recounting of events that conveys experiences, emotions, and perspectives.

dates, or places you stopped on your way to the coast—because if there is no *uncertainty* there is no story. Uncertainty is the reason stories draw us in and engage us, because they tap into problem-solving instincts that have evolved over millions of years.

The dominant metaphor I use throughout this book is that *stories are like seeds*. I like this metaphor because it captures how stories condense complex understandings and perspectives into packages that can be transmitted and stored, then retrieved from storage, planted, and germinated again in the fertile soil of receptive minds. And like seeds, stories are organisms of their own, worthy of respect and admiration.

THE BEST STORIES FOR STORY WORK

To narrow our focus even further, I will now explain what sorts of stories I believe have the greatest utility in helping people work together to make better decisions. The best story for our purposes is *a recounting of events based on emotional experience from a perspective*. Let's look at each part of that statement (see Figure 2.4).

Events

In story work, you need to collect stories about *things that happened*. Watch out for platitudes, opinions, suggestions, and complaints; they gather around questions like moths to a flame. People are very used to being asked for their opinions, but they are not used to being asked *what has happened* to them. It often takes time and effort (and practice) to get this point across.

Experiences

You need to collect true, raw experiences, not reports of fact. Stories can be second-hand, third-hand, or even rumored—even newspaper stories are fine—as long as the story contains *some* element of personal experience. In the case of second-hand stories there are really two stories being told: the original story, and the story of its *resonation* with the storyteller (which is worthy of notice in itself). But if a person says "our company motto is: we always overcome," that is not a story, because nobody *experienced* anything in it. If nobody is *in* the stories, working with them will produce little useful result.

Emotions

It's not hard to get people to tell you what happened during a period of time if you only ask for the facts. But in story work you need to know more than facts; you need to know how people *felt* when they had the experiences they did. Why? Because emotions are our pilots. Reason might keep the machine operating, but without emotions we have nowhere to go. If you map only rational explanations, you might end up with fine specifications for vehicular machinery, but you will have no idea where people want to go, long to go, and fear ending up.

Perspectives

The final thing you need when you work with stories is individual perspectives on events. You need people to tell *their own stories*. For example, people might tell you what happened in an incident, but may be afraid or unable to tell you how they *themselves* felt about it. That sort of story is less able to "work" in the way you need it to than a story told from the person's own perspective.

I suspect these boundary lines will seem arbitrary to you if you have not yet read the rest of this book. Rest assured, the abundant reasons that lie behind each of these qualifications will become obvious in time, if I have done my job well.

STORIES AND HALF-STORIES

You should now be able to guess at what I think stories are *not*—again, *for the purposes of this book.* If nothing *happened,* it is not a story. If nobody has told about their *experiences,* it is not a story. If no *emotions* are expressed, it is not a story. And if no particular *perspective* is apparent, it is not a story.

When you ask people to tell you stories, you will collect many responses I put in the category of *half-stories*, because they are somewhat useful but not the same as a recounting of events based on emotional experience from a perspective.

These are some common types of half-stories.

Situations

People might say something like, "I had a hard time my first day at work. Nobody thought I would be able to pick this stuff up fast enough." Quite often people will stop there, only having described a situation without resolving it. If this sort of thing happens in a group session or interview, you can of course say "And *then* what happened?" But if you have no such opportunity (the question is in a survey, or the people doing the interviewing are following a script or are otherwise untrained), the full story can be lost.

Scenarios

Sometimes people generalize their experiences into a sort of generic story, like this: "You click here, you click there, it doesn't do what you think it will, you give up, and then later you find out you just didn't wait long enough, but there was no way of knowing it was doing something." Obviously this must have happened a few times, but the generalized scenario is not as good as the particular story, because too much telling detail has been lost.

References

Sometimes people don't tell a story but simply refer to it, expecting that others will pick up on the reference. This is sometimes a problem in group sessions. People might say something like, "Remember that time in the elevator? It was like that." This is fine for the people who know what happened in the elevator, but not much use to anyone else.

SUMMARY

Stories can be seen as having three dimensions: form, function, and phenomenon. Story form is about communicative structure and meaning: setting, character, plot, value, conflict, theme, audience, purpose.

Story function is about utility to thought, decision, and action: connections, plans, goals, actions, lessons, analogies.

Story phenomenon is about a story's life history as it moves through time and society: telling, retelling, development, change, circumstances, variations, rights, norms.

Many definitions of story feature only one or two of these perspectives. This is not a flaw of such definitions; it is better seen as describing their context of application. For every application of story work one or two of the story dimensions will be most relevant, and a working definition of story should suit one's goals in practice.

The working definition of story we will use for the purposes of this book is that a story is *a recounting of events based on emotional experience from a perspective.*

QUESTIONS

Which of the three story dimensions best suits your background and personality? Why do you think that is?

Examine your experience with stories in relation to the three story dimensions. Is it evenly balanced? Are there gaps you want to fill?

What is *your* working definition of story? Why does it work for you? In what contexts does it work best, and in what contexts does it work less well?

Of the four parts of our working definition of story (events, experiences, emotions, perspectives), which are the most central to your own working definition of story? Why is that?

Can you think of some half-stories you have heard in conversation? What would it take to make them into full stories?

ACTIVITIES

Look up as many definitions of the word "story" as you can find. Search the internet for the phrase "What is a story?" For each definition you find, think about what dimensions of story are covered, and why, and what that says about the context in which the definition was made, and perhaps the background story of the definer. Now search again, but this time search for the phrase "For our purposes, a story is." Do the purpose-driven definitions as a whole have a different character than the open-ended ones? Do they have a tighter focus?

Choose a favorite folk tale and consider it from each of the three dimensions of story. If you can, compare different versions of the story through time. Did you discover anything you hadn't realized about it before?

Do the same thing as you did with the folk tale, but this time choose a story that has been passed down in your family.

Do the same thing again, but with a story you heard in conversation and jotted down or recorded.

Chapter Three

What Are Stories For?

Stories serve (at least) four functions in human life.

1. We use stories to *chart* maps of the world of our experiences. Sharing stories helps us validate and improve each other's maps.
2. We use stories to *sound* the terrain around us with evidential reasoning, enhancing our maps with additional dimensions.
3. We use stories to *tour* important locations on our maps, entering into serious play that transports us without danger and develops our understanding of difficult terrain.
4. We use stories to *package* the information on our maps, reducing cognitive overhead in well-known areas and freeing up resources to explore where exploration is needed most.

This chapter explores each of these functions.

STORIES ARE MAPS OF EXPERIENCE

In order to make the decisions required to survive, all organisms need to form some idea of what the world around them contains. For humans this is true in the physical sense and in many other senses as well: emotional, social, political, spiritual. From childhood on we build maps of the world we experience. The stories we tell to ourselves and others form part of those maps.

Recently the University of Minnesota's *Eurek-Alert!* online science news service described some ground-breaking research into storytelling, or the replay of lived experience, in the brain. Researchers placed electrode "hats" on rats as they ran around in mazes, essentially watching the rats map their worlds.

Says the news article:

> The hippocampus, a part of the brain essential for memory, has long been known to "replay" recently experienced events. Previously, replay was believed to be a simple process of reviewing recent experiences in order to help consolidate them into long-term memory.

The "replay of experienced events" is not that different from what we mean by storytelling, even if it is not communicated to another person (or rat). If you stand on your porch and remember the time you sat there eating Chinese food as a celebration after you finished a long-running project, you would not be all that different from a rat remembering the time it found some excellent cheese in a maze.

By watching firing patterns in the brains of these rats, the researchers were able to find out not only where the rat was located at any time but also what locations the rat was *thinking* of as it ran about (or didn't). The presence of "cognitive maps" in the brain, in which "place cells" describe the animal's current location, have been researched for a few decades already. But this combination of detecting "where I am" and "where I am remembering being" gave the researchers a way to compare lived experience with the replay of lived experience. Here is the exciting part of the article:

> [The researchers] found that it was not the more recent experiences that were played back in the hippocampus, but instead, the animals were most frequently playing back the experiences they had encountered the least. They also discovered that some of the sequences played out by the animal were ones they had never before experienced.

So the rats were not going over what they had experienced often, like eating breakfast, but what they had rarely experienced, like a frightening accident. And some of the stories they told themselves were fictional.

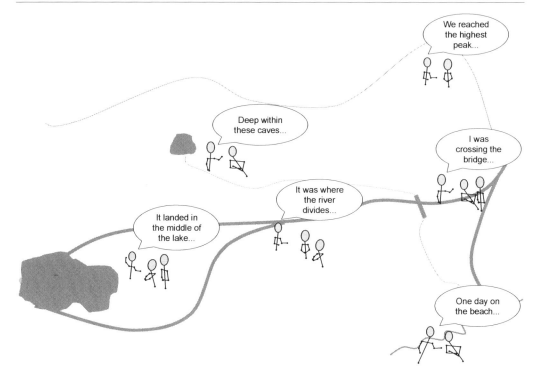

Figure 3.1. Stories map the extremes of experience, where memorable lessons will be most valuable to us. In familiar circumstances, stories are less often used.

When I read this, it reminded me strongly of Gary Klein's work (described in his book *Sources of Power*) on *naturalistic decision making*. This body of work describes how people make decisions in part by recalling cases from the past. Like the rats in the maze, Klein's firefighters did not recall their great masses of *mundane* experience; they compared what they were sensing mainly to the *extremes* of experience.

My strongest memory from Klein's book is of a firefighter entering a room, feeling a hot floor, remembering a time when a floor gave way because there was fire beneath it, and ordering everyone out—just before the floor collapsed.

What these and other similar bodies of research tell us is that as people tell stories (to themselves and others), they explore the areas of their worlds that hold the most opportunity and danger: the *edges* of experience.

Why pay so much attention to the edges? Because telling stories takes time and energy, and only at the edges is it worth the expense. Exploring the well-known simply does not pay off. (See Figure 3.1.)

Stories about rules are valuable, yes, but a modicum of those will suffice. Stories about *exceptions* to rules are more valuable, and the more the better because every exception is different. Remember Tolstoy's famous quote, that happy families are all alike, but every unhappy family is unhappy in its own way? This is why folk tale collections are made not of people sowing wheat and baking bread but of babies who drink oceans and tumble-down huts full of gold. If stories map our worlds, those at the outer edges are the ones we can least afford to lose.

I anticipate two nay-saying responses to this statement. First, when you read about stories in organizational settings, stories of unwritten rules, of "how we do things around here," are often brought up as foundational. Yes, such foundational stories *are* important to most organizations and communities. But they are not told on an everyday basis to those who already know them.

Instead, foundational stories tend to be told to newcomers and outsiders, for whom they *are* at the edge of experience. This is similar to the way in which people who pride themselves on the museums and monuments of their cities go near them only when visiting relatives require a tour. Foundational stories are also told when someone is in danger of breaking the unwritten rules, and in this case serve to reorient a person whose map is faulty (and for whom the edge may have been mistaken for the center).

The other nay-saying response that comes to mind about stories and edges has to do with *scripts*. Cognitive scientists often talk about how people learn how to live in the world by following scripts given to them by others in the form of stories.

Roger Schank says in *Tell Me a Story:*

> A script is a set of expectations about what will happen next in a well-under-stood situation. In a sense, many situations in life have the people who participate in them seemingly reading their roles in a kind of play. The waitress reads from the waitress part in the restaurant script, and the customer reads the line of the customer. Life experience means quite often knowing how to act and how others will act in given stereotypical situations. That knowledge is called a script.

By this view we need stories in the center, in "stereotypical situations," because they prepare us to act in ways that will keep us out of danger. But functioning adults do not exchange scripts of everyday life. Such script-stories are told to children or cultural outsiders, for whom they are at the *edges* of experience.

A child's map of experience starts very small and grows throughout childhood. Around the age of five or six, stories help children map the newly-acquired edge space of interacting with waiters and waitresses in a restaurant. But nobody would tell stories to a child of sixteen about how to behave in a restaurant, because by then the experience would be centrally located in their larger map.

STORIES ARE SOUNDING DEVICES

Stories help us make decisions about what to believe in what we see and hear. A favorite example here is Lance Bennett's "Storytelling in Criminal Trials" (in the book *Memory, Identity, Community*). Bennett makes the point that we judge the story a person tells about a situation by carrying out three "cognitive operations" on the story.

We judge a story's *consistency* by examining its internal *regularity*. We say a story "hangs together" or "ticks" or "runs like a fine machine." We also assess the story's consistency with cultural *standards* of story form: setting, character, plot, scene, action. Most adults can assess narrative consistency and know how to repair a story that is not functioning properly. In order to answer the question, "*Could* it have happened this way?" we ask the question, "Does the story hold together?"

We judge a story's *completeness* by looking for plot *holes* and unexplained gaps and omissions. We say a story "doesn't hold water" or "isn't the whole story" if we sense such inadequacies. In order to answer the question, "Is this the *whole* truth?" we ask the question, "Is there anything missing from this story?"

We judge a story's *veracity* by examining *connections* between it and the collection of stories in our memories, both those we have experienced directly and those we have learned about vicariously. We speak about whether a story "rings true" or "strikes a chord" in light of our experience. In order to answer the question, "*Did* it happen this way?" we ask the question, "What stories stand with or against this story?" (See Figure 3.2 on the next page.)

The fact that nearly everyone has the skills required to work with stories makes this an essential tool in a system of jury by one's peers.

Says Bennett:

> [I]n the [U.S.] courtroom jurors must understand that their judgments satisfy standards of "reasonable doubt." They must try to withhold final judgements until "all the evidence is in." They must try to be "fair." They must try to be "objective." These dimensions of interpretation are stipulated within the foreign context of a trial, yet the basis for this knowledge must be part of the juror's everyday equipment for living. A solution to this problem is suggested by the story model:

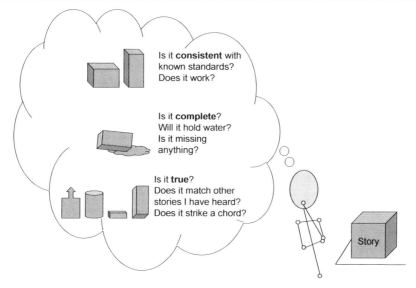

Figure 3.2. When we hear a story, we judge whether it is consistent, whole, and true in the light of our own experiences. This helps us judge the messages contained in the story.

The cognitive operations made possible by placing evidence into a story framework provide implicit measures of these justice criteria. … This, in a nutshell, is our everyday measure of "doubt."

In other words, we decide whether something is true by trying to put it into a story, then testing the story; and when information is given to us *as* a story, we test that story directly.

Bennett warns, however, that consistency and completeness criteria must not be allowed to overwhelm veracity (and he feels strongly enough about this to place the last two of the three sentences in italics):

> [I]ssues of truth or fact in our adjudication (and social judgment) processes are intimately tied to the symbolization of accounts and the ways in which the symbolizations fit into the story model. *This means that in some instances perfectly true accounts will be disbelieved due to improper symbolization or structurally inadequate presentations. Conversely, false accounts may be believed due to the skillful juxtaposition of internally consistent symbols.*

Those who tell wonderful stories can also tell wonderful lies. But Bennett sees evaluation based on story structure as a double-edged sword, noting that:

> In no case can "empirical" standards alone produce a completely adequate judgment, and there are cases for which structural characteristics alone are far and away the critical elements in determining the truth of a story.

What does this mean for everyday storytelling? If you watch people exchanging stories, you can see them judging elements of consistency, completeness, and veracity in stories. You can see them adapt and repair their stories as they detect deficiencies in any of these qualities, either in their own judgment or that of their audience. Sometimes you can see storyteller and audience negotiate over these qualities in conversation. (The upcoming section on conversational storytelling, starting on page 35, will explore this more fully.)

Other researchers and theorists have noticed the connection between stories and judgment as well. The function of stories in judgment forms a part of Walter Fisher's famous *narrative paradigm,* his description of how people use stories to make sense of the world.

This quote in particular (from Fisher's book *Human Communication as Narration*) relates to our discussion:

> Rationality is determined by the nature of persons as narrative beings—their inherent awareness of *narrative probability*, what constitutes a coherent story, and their constant habit of testing *narrative fidelity*, whether or not the stories they experience ring true with the stories they know to be true in their lives.

Fisher's narrative probability relates to Bennett's consistency and completeness, and his fidelity to Bennett's veracity. Fisher believes that we tell stories in order to develop "good reasons" with which to guide our decisions (such as whether to convict or acquit a peer).

Alasdair MacIntyre (in *After Virtue*) speaks of stories providing *accountability* among people:

> The other aspect of narrative selfhood is correlative: I am not only accountable, I am one who can always ask others for an account, who can put others to the question. I am part of their story, as they are part of mine. The narrative of any one life is part of an interlocking set of narratives. Moreover this asking for and giving of accounts itself plays an important part in constituting narratives. Asking you what you did and why, saying what I did and why, pondering the differences between your account of what I did and my account of what I did, and *vice versa*, these are essential constituents of all but the very simplest and barest of narratives.

I said earlier that we use stories to map experience. Evaluative aspects of story comprehension such as are explored by Bennett, Fisher, and MacIntyre add a third dimension to our maps, distinguishing peaks of truth from valleys of doubt.

Here there be dragons, say our stories; there sirens, there giants, and there lush fields of green. Without such detailed maps we would be ill equipped to survive.

STORIES ARE ELEMENTS OF PLAY

Another aspect of stories in thought and memory to which I want to bring your attention is their participation in play. Certainly the play of children is included in this, but I also refer to play in adults, individually and in groups.

If you think about it, you are already familiar with stories as objects of play. Think of phrases like "the suspension of disbelief" and "the play's the thing" (the thing we play with, that is), and think of role-playing games, which are essentially participatory stories.

Because stories are simulations, they provide the same benefits every other type of simulation provides. An article on medical simulation (by Carl Patow, in the journal *Simulation Learning*) explains:

> Medical simulation with computer-controlled simulation technology enables students and providers to learn, practice, and repeat procedures as often as necessary in order to correct mistakes, fine-tune their skills, and optimize clinical outcomes. They can develop and refine their skills without compromising the safety of real patients.

In a similar way, everyone uses stories to consider and correct their mistakes in order to increase their skills to cope with every aspect of life (see Figure 3.3 on the following page).

If you have ever watched a child tell stories in daily life, you have seen the play function of stories. The events of daily life—an encounter with a scary stranger, a challenging task, a visit to relatives, reports of a distant war, a mosquito bite, a parent's fears, a birthday party—all enter into fictional stories and are played and replayed from many angles until they have been thoroughly explored and can be put to rest.

For an explanation of stories as play I could not possibly say anything better than this quote from Brian Boyd's *On the Origin of Stories*.

> All participants must understand behaviors like chasing and rough-and-tumble as play and not real attack. To initiate play, canids have a ritualized play bow,

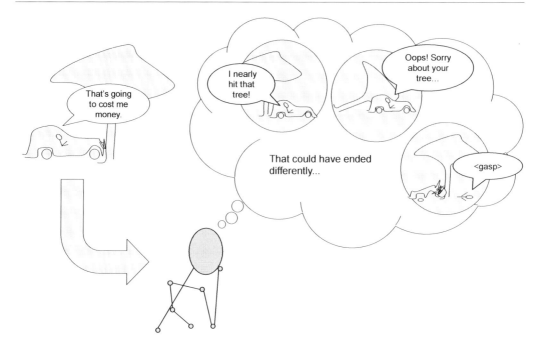

Figure 3.3. Stories help us play with events to make sense of things that have happened and to think about things that haven't.

particularly stereotyped in the young, like the "Once upon a time" that signals to a human child a partial suspension of the rules of the real. All movements and postures become loose in play. Baboons have a gamboling gait and a relaxed open-mouthed play-face—closely related to the human smile—to indicate "This is not in earnest." Play constitutes a first decoupling of the real, detaching aggression or any other "serious" behavior from its painful consequences so as to explore and master the possibilities of attack and defense. In play we act as if within quotation marks, as if these were hooks to lift the behavior from its context to let us turn it around for inspection. Within the frame of play, animals make a first step toward the representation or re-presentation of the real that thought and language provide and that allow us to rotate things freely in the mind, exploring them from new angles.

"A partial suspension of the rules of the real" is one of the many things stories bring to us, as children and as adults. Gary Klein calls this "mental simulation" and explains that when de-

cision makers in situations of rapid-fire action cannot recall cases that match current conditions well, they mix and match elements from previous experience to create new scenarios. The fact that stories take place in a sort of bubble where special rules apply makes this simulation possible with no damage to what surrounds it.

Says Boyd:

> Play permits detachment, yet does so by engaging players intensely. Inviting, engrossing, energetic, this self-rewarding concentrate of ordinary action makes it possible to develop rapidly skills that it would be dangerous to learn, and impossible to overlearn, within the urgencies of the real.

So stories create a relationship that seems paradoxical: they pull us in while simultaneously pushing away the "urgencies of the real." But this is not a paradox; it is a journey, a flight through possibility. A game.

One critical aspect of games in social life is their volunteer nature. As James P. Carse famously put it in *Finite and Infinite Games:*

> If you *must* play, you cannot *play.*

This is why told stories are wrapped in such elaborate rituals of social agreement. They are a means by which we help each other make sense of life. Play is serious business, even for children. Anyone who thinks play is for entertainment alone has never seen a young child frantically re-enact a frightening experience a dozen times in rapid succession, seeking the resolution of understanding.

STORIES ARE PACKAGES OF MEANING

When I tell you a story, I contract the total of my experience on that subject into a more condensed matter. Items particular to me are either excluded or explained, and items I can expect us to share ride along unstated, taking no space. When you read or hear the story, you re-expand it, making use of all the materials we share for the extraction of the story.

Try it. Here is a tiny story from storybytes.com.

> "Some things in life are so easy to do," the man thought, falling to his death.
>
> —G.S. Evans

You can almost *feel* that story expanding in your mind.

In terms of memory and thought, a story is a way of wrapping up experience into a robust, internally stable package suitable for travel through time and space. The structures of a story protect it from dissolution in the same way the bindings of a suitcase protect the clothing within it from scattering in the wind on the train platform. (See Figure 3.4 on the next page.)

Here is an appropriate quote from Vladimir Nabokov's *The Gift.*

> Now he read in three dimensions, as it were, carefully exploring each poem, lifted out like a cube from among the rest and bathed from all sides in that wonderful, fluffy country air after which one is always so tired in the evening. In other words, as he read, he again made use of all the materials already once gathered by his memory for the extraction of the present poems, and reconstructed everything, absolutely everything, as a returning traveler sees in an orphan's eyes not only the smile of its mother, whom he had known in his youth, but also an avenue ending in a burst of yellow light and that auburn leaf on the bench, and everything, everything.

Sometimes problems occur when we don't share enough experience to make the re-expansion of a story work. The degree to which re-expansion correctly reconstructs the original meaning depends on the emotional, cultural, temporal, and experiential distance between storyteller and listener. Let us put these together and call them *narrative distance.* The greater the narrative distance in a storytelling event, not only is the possible compression smaller, but re-expansion errors compound. It's like trying to send computer files to a nomad on a camel, or trying to send camel hair to a computer file. The mappings are all wrong.

To give an example: my hobby is reading old novels and folk tales, with rare twentieth century exceptions. When I choose book editions to read, I pay attention to whether the editions have notes of historical reference. Why? Because when they don't, it's just not as much fun. When I read Russian novels, for example, some of the narrative compressions come across very well—Dostoyevsky mentions putting straw under the table at Christmas, which I grew up doing, so no problem there. But other things, like the uses of bast and kvass, the moods of samovars, the types of carriages, and the nuances of the various grades of civil service, I cannot re-expand correctly without help.

Similarly, I can think of three well-known children's stories—Lewis Carroll's *Alice in Wonderland*, Jonathan Swift's *Gulliver's Travels*, and L. Frank Baum's *The Wizard of Oz*—in which cultural and political messages are compressed inside and inaccessible without help from notes and introductions.

In fact, *all* stories have such inaccessible parts in them, not just stories written hundreds of

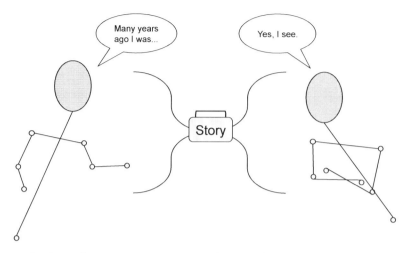

Figure 3.4. Stories package up our experiences and protect them so they can be opened and expanded again on the other side of the communicative link.

years ago. And this is not simply an element of communication between people; it can take place within one person's experience. Have you ever read an old diary entry and had no idea what you were talking about? You could not re-expand the compressed story you set down decades ago because you had forgotten too much of the surrounding context.

Extreme compression

There are two forms of story that take compression to an extreme: *proverbs* and *story references.*

Almost all proverbs are actually stories once you expand them. Here's an exercise: find some random proverbs and expand them into stories. I'll try a few.

1. The proverb: A chain is only as strong as its weakest link. The story: A bunch of people were trying to do something. They were all needed. One of them failed. The whole effort failed.

2. The proverb: A friend in need is a friend indeed. The story: I had a friend. I wasn't sure how good a friend he was. I had a crisis, and the friend came through for me. Now I know that he is really my friend.

3. The proverb: First things first. The story: I started on a project. I knew what I should do first, but I put it off. The project failed.

4. The proverb: Ignorance is bliss. The story: I used to love traipsing through the woods, listening to the birds in the trees. What a peaceful time I had! Now I have become a birdwatcher. All I can think about is whether I have the correct identification.

Proverbs are not just very short stories, however; they have a unique function that relies on their obliqueness. People use proverbs as a protective coating to tell stories they think may be unwelcome (including propaganda).

The second kind of ultra-compact story is the story reference. You know the old joke about the place where everybody knows all the jokes so well that they've reduced them to numbers? And one guy says "forty seven" and nobody laughs? And he says, "Ah, well, I never could tell a joke"? That's a perfect example of a story reference. Story references are like proverbs, except that they don't travel at all. They are *designed* not to travel.

SUMMARY

We use stories to build maps of the world we experience so we can make decisions about how to act. The edges of experience are particularly important to map, because it is at the edges that exceptional things happen for which we may not be prepared.

We use stories to make decisions about what to believe in what we see and hear. We judge a story's consistency, completeness, and veracity in order to hold accountable those who tell them and make them happen.

We use stories to playfully simulate possible outcomes before we commit to a course of action. Stories provide a "partial suspension of the rules of the real" that helps us safely explore the future.

We use stories to condense experience into packages that re-expand in the minds of listeners. Stories are like communicative suitcases: wrappings that protect experiences, feelings, and beliefs so that they can connect people through time and space.

QUESTIONS

Gary Klein's work on naturalistic decision making has been pursued to some extent in contraposition to the work of researchers such as Kahneman and Tversky on rational (or normative) decision making theory. In the language of the rational school, "anecdotal" reasoning involves flaws and biases, and only the careful analysis of outcomes leads to optimal decisions. Still others (such as Herbert Simon) have advanced the idea of "bounded" rationality, where different strategies work best in different situations. What do *you* think? In what situations is making decisions by recalling and comparing stories a superior method, and in what situations does it lead to bias?

Do you agree that stories about exceptions to rules are more valuable than stories about rules? In what ways does that statement connect, or not, with your own experiences?

Consistency, completeness, veracity: what do these words mean to you? How would *you* describe the ways in which people use told stories to make assessments about events? Are there words, or ways of explaining this, that you think work better than those used by Bennett?

Say you told me a story about a frightening experience you had. Then I told you about a scary movie I saw. In what ways were we both playing with the stories we told? How did our uses of narrative play differ, and how were they similar? What are some ways in which people can "play" with stories?

ACTIVITIES

Choose a story, either from your own experience or from something you have read. Consider how it works (or doesn't) as a map of experience. What sort of landscape picture is painted by the story? In the landscape of your life, where is the story located? Is it central or peripheral? How far into the extremes of your experience does it go? What does it reveal (or conceal, or distort)?

Now think of the same story as a sounding device. Consider its consistency, completeness, and veracity. What have you discovered about the story? Where is it strong or weak? How do you judge it? Where it is weak, what could you do to repair it? What would make the story sound?

Think of the same story as an element of play. What are the rules of the game it presents? What sort of game is it? What is its outcome? What roles are present in the game? What is the game's meaning? What are its boundaries? How do you feel about the game? Is it a game you want to play? Would you rather play a different game? If so, what would *that* game be?

Think of the same story as a package of meaning. What has been left out of the story, assuming its audience will be able to fill in what is missing? What has been kept in, as necessary explanation? How much is the story compressed? What does its audience do to re-expand it? How would a different audience re-expand it? What would work well, and what would create misunderstandings or misconceptions?

Think of a story someone told you that you found painful. Perhaps it was about yourself or about an issue you care about. Consider how difficult it is to confront the story directly. Now play with the story. Translate it to fiction; change the setting or characters; turn it into a folk tale. What does this exercise do for you?

Find some proverbs and expand them out into stories. Does what you found surprise you? Ask someone to tell you a story about something, then ask them to help you expand out the story to fill in all the details they didn't include. Did you learn anything you didn't know?

Chapter Four

How Do Stories Work?

In the first chapters of this book, I have been building up explanations based on typical questions people ask about stories. We have already covered what makes a story a story, and what stories are for. The next question people ask usually turns to practical utility. They ask: How do stories work? What makes them tick?

To answer this question, I would like to take you on a journey through stories as they work within our lives. We will start with a magnified view of stories as they are told in conversation, and end with a global view of stories as they move through society. Along the way, we will consider some intermediate-scope aspects of stories in use.

STORIES IN CONVERSATION

One summer evening, you and I are sitting together with a group of friends. We just came from a social event, say a sports event, and we are chatting about it. Our conversation has a tick-tock rhythm to it: you speak, I speak, she speaks, he speaks. We hand off the conversation to each other regularly and frequently by exchanging sentences, phrases, and paragraphs. When one person has been holding forth for a while on some subjects, the others in the group signal their willingness to listen by chiming in with "uh-huh" and "really" and "you don't say" from time to time. Though we don't know it, we are all watching the rhythm of the conversation and keeping it on course.

Have you ever met a person who didn't seem to understand this natural rhythm, who held the floor by force or volume and refused to hand over the conversational baton? Did you want to talk to them again? Not likely. Conversation is a negotiated ritual of give and take, and we know when it is working and when it isn't.

Now let's say you begin to tell a story. "I remember a time," you say. There is a brief pause as you glance around. The attentive looks and body language you see are welcoming, so you plunge in. During your story the ums and ahs continue, but in a subdued manner that signals you hold the floor and the permission to speak uninterrupted. If there was a talking stick you would have it. Soon you complete your story, transmitting another recognized signal that your turn has ended, and the conversation returns to its previous tick-tock pattern.

This dance, with its rhythms and signals and negotiations, is something all children learn to expect and participate in as they grow. It is probably tens of thousands of years old. It is only recently that people have begun to study conversational rhythms like these. What they have found out can tell us much about helping people work with their stories.

An iceberg model of conversational story

A story told in conversation has a structure somewhat like an iceberg. The story floating on the surface may appear to be unaccompanied, but it is in fact supported by a larger part of itself below the water's surface. This structure was first elucidated by William Labov and Joshua Waletzky in the 1960s. My iceberg diagram, Figure 4.1 on the following page, is a slight modification of their diamond-shaped diagram.

The story proper, what you see above the water, contains three parts.

1. In the *orientation* of the story, the story-teller *sets* the story into context and *settles* questions of *setting:* time, place, characters, location. Whether a story is told just after it happened or centuries later, the orientation serves to define the *ground rules* of how the story is to be understood and interpreted. If the story is fictional, it is so la-

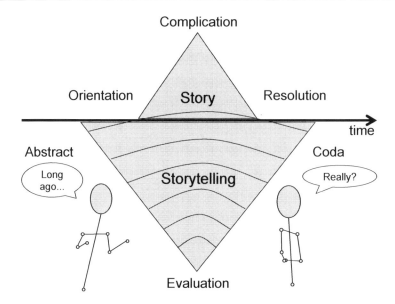

Figure 4.1. A model of conversational story (inspired by Labov and Waletzky's diagram).

beled here. If it originated in a rumor, or is true but not widely known, this is explained as well.

2. In the *complication* of the story, as they say, things get complicated. Some sort of dilemma or problem presents itself to the story's protagonist, and the protagonist responds. What will happen next? This is where the uncertainty comes in: we *cannot* know what will happen next, but we *want* to know. This is the hook that keeps us listening.

3. In the *resolution* of the story, we find out what *did* happen. The story comes to an end, for good or ill, and things stop happening.

That's a pretty simple structure, right? Now let's look at what lies beneath the waves.

Abstract: Negotiating permission

The *abstract* of a conversational story is a sort of prelude in which the potential storyteller asks their potential audience for permission to tell a potential story. Abstracts often contain *formulaic* phrases ("Here's one you might not have heard" or "That reminds me of a story") or *references* to elements of an offered story. For example, a person may reference a time frame ("One day I"), a memory ("I remember when"), an experience ("I survived an avalanche!"), an action

("I ate glass once"), an event ("The dam broke up"), a place ("That park wasn't always a park"), a person ("My dad was such a character"), or a rumor ("I heard about this guy who").

Note that these references share a past-tense frame, signifying entry into the recounting of a series of narrated events. Such formulas and references offer advance proof of the worth of what is to come and declare an intent to hold the floor. (I did the same thing at the start of this chapter, when I said, "One summer evening." I wanted you to know a story was coming.)

But an abstract is not simply a performance; it also involves elements that represent *negotiated accommodation* between storyteller and audience. These include *restarts* ("I—I saw this—this man"), *repetitions* ("Did you hear about—Did you hear"), and *reframings* ("I had this dog—One day I was walking my dog—This was years ago"). I like to think of these accommodations like the minute course adjustments made by pilots as they gain altitude and seek their planned flight path (there the "audience" is the features of the physical atmosphere). During such adjustments, the audience may actively attempt to channel the proposed story into a presentation they prefer over what has been offered at the start. Perhaps they want the story to be more exciting than has been presented, or more on topic, or less revealing.

Negotiations may encompass tone of voice, body language, and facial expression as well as words.

Not only must a storyteller establish their story's tellability during this period; they must also establish their *right* to tell the story. What constitutes both tellability and qualification to tell can vary widely depending on the social context of each possible storytelling event. Having participated in the events of the story may be important, or knowing the topic, or having a certain status within the group. Sometimes others in the group will insist on their participation (or even domination) in the telling of the story—"I was there too, you know" being a bid to share in the right to tell.

As the story abstract comes to an end, any one of a few possible outcomes may have taken place. The storyteller may have gained the group's full permission and attention to speak freely. Or a different form of the basic story may have been approved, in which case the storyteller quickly adapts the story to what can be told in context. Or the storyteller may have been given permission to tell the story only if they share its telling with another person also (or more) qualified to tell the story. Or the storyteller may have been given partial or grudging permission from the group, or permission from some members but not others, and they may decide to tell the story to a partial or half-listening audience, or give up and keep quiet. Or, finally, the group may roundly refuse to hear the story, in which case the storyteller may end their attempt, or (if they are particularly socially inept) forge ahead regardless, heedless of the failed negotiation.

Evaluation: Comment and annotation

The second element of a story told in conversation, shown here by the lowest point in the underwater triangle, and from which waves radiate out even above the water's surface, is a told story's statements of *evaluation*. These are direct lines of communication from storyteller to audience, and they all contain one message: this story is worth hearing. And it is still worth hearing, and it is still worth hearing.

Wait a second, you say: *Didn't the abstract prove the story's worth?* Yes, but statements of evalu-

ation tend to be scattered *throughout* told stories, as continual proof that the floor should remain in the storyteller's control. Any part of the story that does not explicitly contain a narrated event (thing that happens in the story) is usually an evaluation.

Say I am telling you a story about my dog being old and tired. When I get to the part where he was too old to walk up the driveway, I say, "I *never* saw a dog so *exhausted* in my *life*." Why did I say that when simply saying "he was very tired" would have sufficed to recount the event? The *real* meaning of that sentence was, "This story stands out from my entire experience as significant, thus it will be significant for you too—so I recommend you keep listening."

As with abstracts, evaluation statements are often *repetitive* ("I never—*never*—saw anything like it—*anything*") or *formulaic* ("isn't that *something*" or "doesn't that beat *all*"). They may reference a *comparison* to other experiences (my dog-story evaluation fits here) or an *authority* figure ("My dad said he'd never seen *anything* like it"). They may even ask the audience for *feedback,* the better to make any needed course corrections ("Can you believe *that?*"). Often evaluation statements stand out from other parts of the story as being spoken with an unusual volume, pitch, or tone; and the teller's body language may also indicate increased intensity.

There are also two forms of evaluation that are technically found within the story proper but which still count as evaluation. These are *reported speech* and *parallel events*.

Reported speech is what happens when a storyteller puts aside the usual narrative style of "this happened, then that happened" and temporarily does some play-acting, as though they were one of the people in the story. They might say something like "And then he comes in and, 'Yes sir, we *did* lose your luggage.'" Reported speech serves to draw attention to particular statements made in the story and to point out their importance to the overall point of the story. Especially when people report speech in ways that preserve the tone of the original speaker, perhaps with caricatured exaggeration, reported speech becomes a strong source of evaluation.

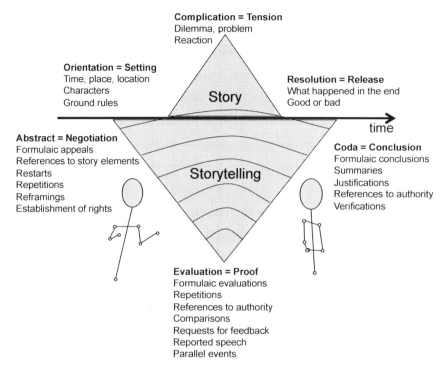

Figure 4.2. The iceberg model with the conversational elements expanded.

Parallel events are elements that take place at some distance from each other within the story, but which are reported in such similar fashion, for example with identical phrasing, that it is clear the storyteller is attempting to draw the audience's attention to a comparison between the events. A storyteller might say, near the start of the story, "I could *not* stop laughing!" and then repeat the exact same statement at its end, to emphasize that the story marks an occurrence of superlative comedy.

Coda: Back to conversation

The ending point of a conversational story, called its *coda,* is yet another piece of ritualistic negotiation. In a story's coda, the storyteller closes the circle of narrated events and ends the narrative event, returning the time frame to the present and the control of the floor to the group. For this purpose codas tend to include formulaic *conclusions* ("And that was that" or "And I lived to tell the tale") and *summaries* of what has been said ("And so you see he never went back").

When possible, the coda also serves to consolidate the worth of the story with additional evaluations such as *justifications* ("And that was

how I learned not to trust that man"), references to *authority* ("My boss said he was amazed"), and *verifications* ("Did you ever hear anything like that?"). (See Figure 4.2 for a summary of all of these elements.)

Why do we enclose our stories in these complex layers of ritualized negotiations? Why don't we just tell them as they are?

I like to explain negotiation during storytelling using the metaphor of wrapping paper. When we bring someone a present and wrap it with special paper, the paper is a physical representation of a ritualized message. It says, "This gift is an offering from me to you. Out of consideration for my feelings, please do not destroy or discard the gift in front of me. At least *pretend* you like it and appreciate the gesture."

People often surround gift-giving with gestures that communicate a wrapper-like appeal: tentative, do-you-like-it smiles; open, extended hands or arms; "ta-da!" performances in singsong voices; banners strung across doorways. All of these are social signals that set up a context of noncritical acceptance. We teach our children to recognize these signals and accept gifts graciously even (or especially) when they are unwanted.

Stories work in the same way, and at two levels. An outer layer of wrapping is made up of conversational rituals that surround storytelling and wrap stories in banner-like announcements of intent and preferred response. An inner layer is the story itself, which is a package we use to safely disclose feelings, beliefs, and opinions without making claims to truth that would be open to immediate dispute without it. Most well-brought-up people recognize the double-layered wrappings of a story and respond accordingly. Those who will not let others tell stories probably don't get many wrapped-up gifts either.

Examples of conversational stories

We can now use the iceberg model to examine three real conversational stories.

Example One: A well-told story

Here is an anonymized storytelling from a group story session that shows the parts of a told story. I will comment on each fragment as we go.

> I don't know what—I've got a good story. I don't know where it fits in here either.

Here the speaker puts forth the story's *abstract*. Note that the circumstance is contrived, since these people were asked to tell each other stories; but still the speaker started with a formulaic statement. Also notice the hesitation and reframing, and the negotiation of the "I don't know" statement, and a direct reference to fitting in to the conversation.

The group apparently responded positively to this start, so the storyteller went on.

> It just happened last week. My wife and I had our anniversary. And we went out to dinner.

This is the start of the story's *orientation*, with a time frame, a roster of characters, and a social setting.

> And I ate a small lunch and a small breakfast. I wanted to make sure I was good and hungry when I went out because we were going to have a nice meal.

This statement, though still in the orientation, contains both evaluation (this meal was to be important, thus what follows will be important) and foreshadowing (to heighten suspense).

> So we went to this rather new place, it's one of the oldest buildings in town, but they've converted it into a real nice restaurant. And we went there and looked at the menu, and I was hungry, and there was a sixteen-ounce Porterhouse on the menu.

> And I thought, well, I could do a sixteen-ounce Porterhouse here tonight. I feel like I'm in a steak mood.

> So I ordered the Porterhouse.

Here is the end of the orientation. Note the repetition of "sixteen-ounce Porterhouse"—this is evaluative, showing us that this particular Porterhouse is going to be important and that we should pay attention to it.

> And it took about an hour for the food to come—apparently there was a larger group that was in front of us—it was a small place—and the waitress comes out—and she was a pleasant enough person—

We begin the *complication* of the story with a tantalizing hint that things will soon be going downhill. Notice the reframings in this section, possibly indicating some mental adjustment of the story to the social context as the teller recalls the events and prepares his presentation.

> She comes out, and she sets this THING in front of me, this PLATE. And it's got these little three-inch diameter, less than a quarter of an inch thick slabs of meat.

> And I looked at her and I said, THAT'S a PORTERHOUSE?

> [laughter]

> And she says, yes, that's how we do our Porterhouse here.

> I said, THAT'S a PORTERHOUSE?

> YES, sir, that's how we do our Porterhouse here.

> I said, I've never SEEN anything like that.

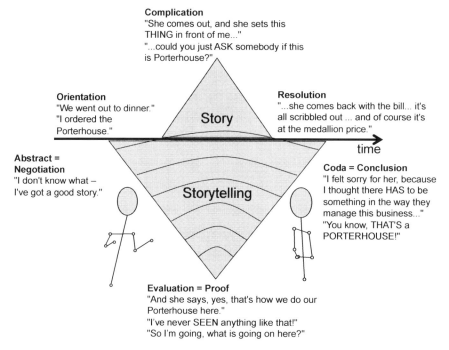

Figure 4.3. The iceberg model used to describe a story recorded from conversation (the "Porterhouse" story).

This part of the complication is dramatic and sounds almost rehearsed. Probably this part of the story varies little from telling to telling. It contains no hesitation at all and is chock full of evaluation. First there is the waitress whose "coming out" is repeated twice, then *this* thing, *this* plate, *these* slabs of meat. Then "THAT'S a PORTERHOUSE?" is repeated, and with such enthusiasm that this *might* be the central message of the story. However, it is quickly outranked by the waitress' response, which contains not only word-for-word repetition of an entire sentence, but reported speech as well. The lie framed by "That's how we do our Porterhouse here," we are meant to understand, is the point of the story.

So I just accepted that. So I sat down and I took a couple of bites, and I thought, this is, this is, I don't know WHAT this is. And I didn't even really like it, but I had just about finished the meal, and I couldn't eat any more, I just didn't LIKE it.

Here we have a bit of a quiet spot, but still there is repetition around "this is" and "I didn't like it." Something is brewing, we know.

And I said to her, I said, you know, could you—I'll bet you—I'll just bet you that this isn't Porterhouse. Could you just go and ASK somebody if this actually is Porterhouse—there was some of it left on my plate—could you just ASK somebody if this is Porterhouse?

Okay, okay, sir, I'll do that for you.

Reported speech again, and repetitions of "I'll bet you" and "could you ASK somebody" as the protagonist prepares to take action. This is a buildup of suspense, like watching the hero in achingly slow motion as he bounds toward the enemy to return the unjust blow.

So a little while later she comes back.

And meanwhile, I said to my wife, I said, I think this is pork medallions. It was the one below the Porterhouse on the menu. I think this is pork medallions, that's not Porterhouse steak, clearly. And I had a pretty good hint at this.

Here we have a common element of engagement in stories, and not just conversational ones. We the audience share with the storyteller some knowledge the antagonist of the story does not know. We audiences love that sort of thing, and this storyteller uses it well.

> She comes back and she says, well, the person that KNOWS is busy right now.

> So now I'm getting a real clue. So I said, The person that knows is busy? Could you ask somebody else?

> Well, no, that's really the only person that knows.

> So I'm going, what is going on here?

Notice the last sentence: this is not something that really *happened* in the story, but an evaluative comment. The teller wants us to know he was mystified; thus there is a mystery; thus we should keep listening to find out how the mystery will be resolved.

> So I said, Well, did you know that—I really think this is the pork medallions, and it's five dollars less, it's a meal that costs five dollars less than the Porterhouse. So when I get my bill, I really kind of expect to see at least the PRICE for the medallions, not the Porterhouse.

> Well, I don't know, sir.

Now the protagonist has made his full response to the complicating action. He has called out the waitress on her lie and stated his terms. We shall see what happens next.

> So a little while later she comes back with the bill, and it's got—it's all scribbled out where the order was, and it's got written "Porterhouse" there, and of course it's at the medallion price.

Here finally is the story's ironic and funny *resolution*. (I also think, having watched this story being told, that it was the crux of the story as well, though quietly spoken. The ironic twist carried all with it. As I recall, this sentence ended with the teller sitting abruptly back in his chair with a motion of "and there it is, folks" in his face and body language.)

> And even THEN she denied that—

> [laughter]

Note that this laughter is not, I think, indicative of the audience laughing *at* the sentence fragment "And even THEN she denied that." I think the resolution that came before it took a few seconds to sink in, during which time the storyteller began the story coda.

> —that it wasn't Porterhouse. To her it was still Porterhouse.

> And she was a pleasant enough waitress, and I kept—I felt sorry for her, because I thought there HAS to be something in the way they manage this business for her to take that stance, like if you make a mistake on the order, that you have to pay for it or something like that, because why else would she be so ridiculously—

> You know, THAT'S a PORTERHOUSE!

Now we have the story's *coda*, which contains quite an encyclopedia of evaluation. It begins with a summary of the story: the waitress denied the facts. Next there are two qualifying statements that attempt to control the reception and interpretation of the story. The teller prevents any possible interpretation of himself as unjust by making it clear he does not place blame on the put-upon waitress herself. And he explains what he thinks was the root cause of the problem, thus validating that the story is worthy of consideration when discussing the topic of organizational mismanagement (a topic on which several previous stories had been told). And finally, he caps off the story with a stunning piece of repetitive evaluation: *That's a Porterhouse!*

Figure 4.3 on the facing page shows some quotes from the Porterhouse story placed on the iceberg model.

Example Two: A story finds its footing

Here is another example, again from a group story session, that will give us a bit more practice understanding told stories.

> Well—it's funny because—like I said—we have Dilbertsville—all cubes.

This is an interesting story *abstract* for a few reasons. The phrase "like I said" refers to a similar statement the speaker made a few minutes back in the conversation, a statement that started with, "See now—our place is Dilbertsville—cubes everywhere." The full previous statement contained many more hesitations and restarts, and in fact sounds just like a story abstract.

It is likely that the earlier statement was *meant* to start a story but failed. The other speakers did not break their conversational rhythm until this line, with its "like I said," was spoken, after which they took the hint and gave the story their full attention. I wonder if the speaker's reference to a *setting*, though formulaic (Dilbertsville), rather than an event or memory, was too weak to sufficiently communicate a request to tell a story, and that only its repetition (as a sort of second application) succeeded in obtaining the group's permission to speak.

> And me and the person I sit next to—for years we were working on a lot of the same stuff—so we took out half of our partition between us, so—because otherwise we were constantly talking over the wall.

The speaker continues with what appears to be a complete, if brief, story. It has a complication (the wall divided workers) and a resolution (they took out the wall). But in fact this is just an introduction to a larger story, an *orientation* in the form of a story. Notice the three reframings, which show that the storyteller is working out how to tell the story in context.

> And for a long time I had to walk past HER cube to get to mine. So we just took out the wall and that was nice.

Here the storyteller repeats the same orientation story, but this time with no hesitations or reframings. His confidence, or his audience's attention, seems to be growing.

> We sat like that for like eight years.

The orientation ends with a sort of bridging statement, one that creates suspense (because surely *something* happened after those eight years). This is a signal that we are about to move into a new part of the story.

> And just last year they remodeled the whole building, and we managed to keep together, but they put us in cubes.

Now the storyteller has moved into the *complication* of his larger story: they put us in cubes *again*. Now we can see why the previous embedded stories were necessary: so we could understand the importance of the second erection of dividing cubes. Notice how the word "cubes" ties back to the previous embedded stories, signifying that *this* is the main story the smaller stories were meant to lead up to.

> And we said, eight, nine, ten, times to the people who were doing the planning, we said, we don't want that wall in there. Once they were putting up the partitions we said, get that partition out of there. Three months later we couldn't get ANYBODY to take that wall down.

Finally the storyteller has leave to emphasize the points he wants to bring forth, and he takes advantage of it by adding evaluations. The phrase "eight, nine, ten, times" is formulaic. The repetition of "we said" and "that wall" and "there" emphasizes the dilemma of the protagonist facing recalcitrance on the part of the planning people.

> So one night I stayed late, brought in my wrenches, and it's DOWN.

Here is the protagonist's response and the crux of the story. Note the complete lack of hesitation, dramatic word choices, and rehearsed quality of this sentence. (I also seem to recall the word "DOWN" being accompanied by a triumphant arm movement.)

> But we're the only two people in that whole area that have bucked the system, broke the rules, and got our open space back. So we've got a nice open space, we—our square footage had shrunk, and we both felt real cramped after having an open space, so—now we've got an open space.

This is a lovely bit of evaluation. It is not necessary to explain that pulling down a wall will increase the enclosed square footage, so this stands outside the story events as commentary on the protagonist's action. There is both formula *and* repetition in "bucked the system, broke the rules." The term "open space" is repeated no less than *four* times. This cements

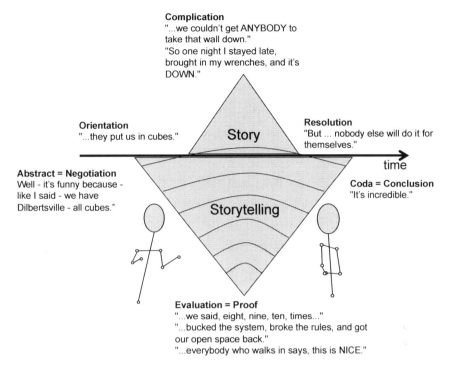

Complication
"...we couldn't get ANYBODY to take that wall down."
"So one night I stayed late, brought in my wrenches, and it's DOWN."

Orientation
"...they put us in cubes."

Story

Resolution
"But ... nobody else will do it for themselves."

time

Abstract = Negotiation
Well - it's funny because - like I said - we have Dilbertsville - all cubes."

Storytelling

Coda = Conclusion
"It's incredible."

Evaluation = Proof
"...we said, eight, nine, ten, times..."
"...bucked the system, broke the rules, and got our open space back."
"...everybody who walks in says, this is NICE."

Figure 4.4. The iceberg model used to describe another story recorded from conversation (the "Dilbertsville" story).

the importance of its contrast to the earlier repetitions of the word "cubes."

And everybody who walks in says, this is NICE. But the system doesn't want it and nobody else will do it for themselves.

Here is the *resolution* of the story: not that the wall is down, but that *other* people find this good but *will not do it for themselves*. If everyone in the office followed suit this would be a very different story, a story of a leader inspiring crowds. But this is not that story: it is the story of a lone voice crying in the wilderness.

It's incredible.

And here is the very short *coda*, with a superlative statement of evaluation. Enough said.

Figure 4.4 shows some quotes from the Dilbertsville story placed on the iceberg model.

Example Three: Collaborative story repair
Another fascinating element of conversational storytelling is the collaborative repair of stories that need some fine-tuning to fit the context of the conversation and meet the needs of speaker and audience. You saw how the tellers of the two previous stories recrafted their stories to fit the situation. Here is an example of a group making such a repair collaboratively.

The speaker Debbie begins to tell a story. (I've made up these names.)

Debbie: I'm in the middle of a development project, but the people putting it together are from the technical side, and they say [whispering] no, we're not ready to show customers, we're not ready to show customers.

[laughter]

Debbie: Meanwhile the market opportunity is slamming closed. And it takes time to get the sales and communications side of the—the mind share side of this thing going—so the pieces of this that we can actually start showing—

Debbie's complication ("we're not ready") goes on past the laughter into an excessive additional explanation of the dilemma. Both Debbie and her audience seem to have perceived this, and Debbie has communicated a need for feed-

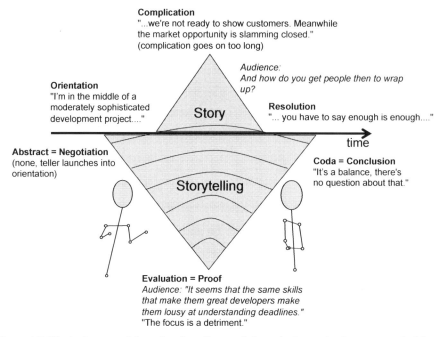

Figure 4.5. The iceberg model used to describe a collaboratively repaired story recorded from conversation (the "we're not ready" story).

back by pausing and restarting, perhaps unsure of how much detail to provide.

Karen: And how do you get the people then to wrap up?

Audience member Karen gives Debbie feedback in the form of a nudge in the direction of closure. (It's ironic that the repair of the story's excessive complication section parallels events in the story itself, with its perfectionism over software. It's almost as if Debbie is unconsciously demonstrating the events of her story in its delivery.)

Debbie: You basically—I mean, you can be polite about it—but you have to say enough is enough—or—you know—you have this version where—you're willing to go.

Debbie takes the hint and delivers the story's resolution, though with several pauses that show she is still open to negotiation over how the rest of the story should play out.

Debbie: It's a balance, there's no question about that.

After this (maybe in response to body language or looks from the others?) Debbie seems

to come to a decision that no more detail is needed. She adds her coda (no hesitations there) which signals the end of the story events, along with some evaluation. In effect she is saying, "Okay, I've finished the story as requested, how is that?"

John: It seems that the same skills that make them great developers make them lousy at understanding deadlines.

Debbie: Yeah. The focus is a detriment.

Finally John, a different member of the group (not Karen, the original hint-giver), signals to Debbie that the story has been accepted (as improved) by participating in the coda with his own evaluative comment. Debbie responds with an additional evaluation to signal her agreement to close the story and move on.

Figure 4.5 shows some quotes from the "we're not ready" story placed on the iceberg model.

By the way, I got these three stories from a transcript of a story session I conducted many years ago. I do not know who these people were, but I'm pretty sure they would not mind me using their stories, general as they were; otherwise I would not tell the stories here.

Variations in conversational storytelling

Now that I have laid out for you such a clear-cut key to how everyone tells stories to everyone, let me give you a warning. This is an idealized version of conversational storytelling. It *sometimes* works out this way, but not always, and variations on this form are enormous.

To quote Neal Norrick in *Conversational Narrative:*

> In genuine conversation, stories often surge up and recede again in topical talk. They may consist of fragments produced by separate speakers among extraneous talk and random interruptions, so that it is often difficult to say just where they begin or end. Indeed, it is sometimes impossible to determine the legitimate teller, or even the main teller. Listeners must piece together narrative structures and reconstruct chronologies to make sense of the storytelling they experience.

Here is Erving Goffman in *The Presentation of Self in Everyday Life:*

> I would like to conclude by mentioning two general strategies regarding tact with respect to tact. First, the performer must be sensitive to hints and ready to take them, for it is through hints that the audience can warn the performer that his show is unacceptable and that he had better modify it quickly if the situation is to be saved.

> Secondly, if the performer is to misrepresent the facts in any way, he must do so in accordance with the etiquette for misrepresentation; he must not leave himself in a position from which even the lamest excuse and the most cooperative audience cannot extricate him.... Thus balding men who affect a hat indoors and out are more or less excused, since it is possible that they have a cold, that they merely forgot to take their hat off, or that rain can fall in unexpected places; a toupee, however, offers the wearer no excuse and the audience no excuse for excuse.

In fact there is a sense in which the category of impostor ... can be defined as a person who makes it impossible for his audience to be tactful about observed misrepresentation.

STORIES AND PERSONALITIES

Storytelling is built into all human brains; it is part of how we think. But through upbringing, culture, personality, and habits, some people tell a *lot* more stories than other people do. If you think about the people of your acquaintance, odds are you can think of someone who seems to think and talk in nothing other than stories, and someone from whom a story seems strange. Or think about how many stories you tell per day, on average, then think about how many stories other people you know tell. There's probably a pretty big range.

Let's just assume for the sake of argument that you agree with me that people vary in how much they tell stories, and that some people think in stories more than others do. Here's what I have noticed. There is an astounding lack of correlation between whether people tell stories and whether they *think* they tell stories. If storytelling is innate, it is not always conscious. It seems to be one of those things people do without knowing how they do it, or that they do it at all. I myself am one of those people who tell story after story, but it was only *after* I discovered the field of organizational story that I had any inkling I did this.

Taking these two scales and pretending they are simple dichotomies (which they aren't) and combining them, you end up with four states, as follows:

1. The natural storyteller: I don't think I tell stories, but I do.
2. The confident non-story teller: I think I tell stories, but I don't.
3. The story performer: I think I tell stories, and I'm right.
4. The unaccustomed storyteller: I don't think I tell stories, and I'm right.

Now of course these are caricatures I have created to talk about extremes, and not real representations of real people. Nobody inhabits

Figure 4.6. Natural storytellers tell stories even when they think they aren't telling stories.

these extremes perfectly, but most people do *approach* them occasionally at different times and in different contexts. The categories are not fixed for life, or even for a day. Most people act differently with respect to narrative in their personal and professional lives and among different groups of people. Also, groups can develop a sort of storytelling culture (or a non-storytelling culture) over time.

Even whom you are talking to has an effect on whether you tell stories or not. Because telling a story requires holding the floor of conversation for longer than the usual turn-taking, it requires an understanding among everyone involved, an understanding which is not always present. You have probably met someone who seems to suck all the stories around them into a black hole because they won't let anyone have the floor long enough to tell one. So there are complex patterns that determine whether stories actually get told. But having said all that, people tend to be more at home in some of these areas than others.

Caveats in place, I've noticed some things about what happens when each of these behavioral/perceptual combinations is met with a request to tell stories.

The natural storyteller

The superheroes of story collection are the people who *think* they don't tell stories but do. These people come up with story after wonderful story, and the best part is that the stories are absolutely natural and authentic. Since these people don't see themselves as great storytellers, they don't try to perform or create a sensation. They just talk about what happened to them, in the way they usually talk, which is in stories. (See Figure 4.6.)

I love these people. When you have listened to a hundred people drone on and on, and then one of *these* people starts talking, it's like a light has been turned on. Once in a while I find one and just let them go to town. It's hard not to rush up and hug them, to be honest.

A conversation with a natural storyteller might go like this.

> You: What happened on your first day at the plant?

> Them: Let's see, I think I got there at five that morning. I was so determined to prove myself. When I went through the front gate my stomach was in knots. I remember I kept fixating on the company

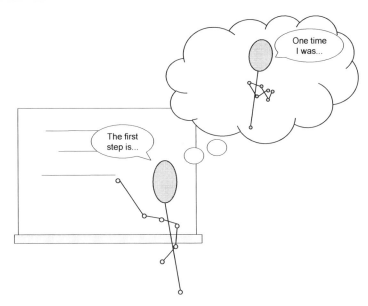

Figure 4.7. Confident non-story tellers think they are telling stories, but they aren't.

logo and trying to memorize it, in case they asked me any questions. Which is really funny, you know, because why would they do that? (laughter) I can still remember how worried I was that I'd drop something on somebody's foot. (etc., etc., etc.)

You: (secret grin)

Notice a few things about this fake interview. First, the storyteller narrates events unfolding over time: this happened, then that happened. (You'd be amazed how many people *don't* do that.) Second, they give details that provide context, emotion, motivation, and visual description—in realistic proportion. Third, they respond to their own story as they tell it, meaning that they add that-was-then-this-is-now metadata (which is immensely useful in story listening).

The confident non-story teller

The absolutely worst combination is when people *think* they tell stories, but they actually don't. Often these people don't understand what you mean by "story," and they think a story is a message or lesson or report or joke. (See Figure 4.7.)

I've found that confident non-story tellers often appear in positions of power. My guess is that it may have something to do with how power cre-ates a reality distortion field around itself. Confident non-story tellers can be difficult to work with because they are sometimes unwilling to reexamine their definitions and assumptions. A story is what they *say* it is, and nothing *you* say can turn them from that course. So no matter what you ask for, they give you what they want to say, and call it a story.

A conversation with a confident non-story teller might go like this.

You: What happened on your first day at the plant?

Them: Well, back then we knew how to work hard. I didn't give up at the first little problem like these kids do today.

You: Can you tell me about a *specific* problem that happened?

Them: Sure. I never let up, you know? I kept trying. I didn't let things get me down. Today all the new hires whine and complain and want us to hold their hands. It's *disgusting*.

You: So what *happened* on that first day?

Them: It was hard at first, but I kept going. I'm still here, aren't I?

You: (secret sigh)

Figure 4.8. Story performers know they are telling stories. The danger is that they may think they are telling even better stories than they really are.

Notice how the teller keeps drifting from narrating events back to giving opinions. They don't *mean* to frustrate the story listener; they think they *are* doing what they have been asked to do, and can't understand what else you could possibly want.

The story performer

The second-worst combination is when people tell great stories *and know it*. These people *mean* well, they really do. But they can't help getting out the big circus tent and climbing up to that trapeze, no matter what you ask them to do. (See Figure 4.8.)

A conversation with a story performer might go like this.

> You: What happened on your first day at the plant?
>
> Them: Oooooh, you should have *been* there. I was shaking in my boots. I had sweat dripping off my brow. I was there at three in the morning, and I drove around the plant *two hundred times!* Finally the guy at the gate let me in, and he said, I've never seen *anybody* in all my years here so scared. You really take the cake. And then I *fainted.*

> You: You really fainted?
>
> Them: Well, I *felt* faint! But anyway I was scared.
>
> You: What happened next?
>
> Them: What happened next I will never forget. I was ushered into a room and the CEO of the Worldwide Conglomerate *himself* walked in and slapped me full in the face.
>
> You: What?
>
> Them: Well, it was more like, the head of HR in our town bumped into me, but it *felt* like that.
>
> You: (secret sigh)

Story performers tend to exaggerate and claim to be the best or worst or first or last, not because they are braggarts but because it makes the story better. They drive things to extremes in the service of drama. I'll give a funny example. I once was in a conference and somebody proposed something I thought was unethical. I said so, and we talked about other solutions. A few years later, I heard that same person tell a group that a "roomful of draft dodgers" had berated them until they changed their policy.

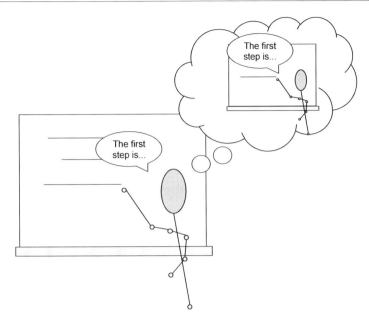

Figure 4.9. Unaccustomed storytellers don't tell stories, and they don't think they tell stories either.

Afterward I went up to them and said, "Hey, that roomful of draft dodgers was me, wasn't it?" They said, "Yeah, but it made a better story that way."

You know what? There is nothing in the world wrong with that sort of embellishment. The truth should never stand in the way of a good story, and all that. It makes life fun. It's play. But—unless it's well marked out so you can distinguish it—this sort of thing is not what you are looking for when you want to listen to stories for a reason. It obscures what you actually do need, which is what really happened and how people really felt about it.

By the way, in case I sound pompous and judgmental about performers, here is an admission: I used to be a "natural," but I've found that the more I identify with my career in organizational story the more I turn into a story performer. I've caught myself "hamming it up" with a story more times than I'd like to admit, because this little neon sign lights up in my head that says "Oooh, I can be *admired* for this!" And it's hard, hard, hard to turn that little sign off. That's why natural storytellers are so hard to find and so valuable. (It's the same reason sequels are never any good, and it's the reason "Yeah, but he knows it" is a negative comment.) Naturals

and performers have the same talents, but in performers the talent is hampered by awareness.

It's like playing an instrument: the more you think about how you play it, the less well you can play it. When I play the piano I just have to trust my hands and let them do what they know how to do. But I'm a duffer on the piano and I know it. I'm sure if I became a goat herder I'd be a great natural storyteller again, but in this career it takes an effort.

The unaccustomed storyteller

These are people who don't tell stories and don't think they do. They just don't think in stories. It's not their thing. (See Figure 4.9.)

If you work in stories and have not bounced off the sheer impenetrability of a personality like this yet, you are either inexperienced or in denial. They are out there, people.

You'd think this would be the worst group, but really they are not that bad. Unlike the two groups who *think* they tell stories, these people are usually willing to help you get what you need. You just have to help them get there.

A conversation with an unaccustomed storyteller might go like this.

You: What happened on your first day at the plant?

Them: It was a hard day.

(silence)

You: When did you arrive?

Them: Around six in the morning.

(silence)

You: What happened when you got there?

Them: I went in at the gate.

(silence)

You: How did you feel right then?

Them: Pretty scared. I was scared that whole day, come to think of it.

(silence)

You: What happened next?

Them: I got my ID card. The picture didn't come out at first and I had to wait. That was scary.

(silence)

You: That's interesting. What was scary about it?

(and so on)

Note how you have to keep drawing the story out, not because the storyteller is recalcitrant but because they are just not used to recounting chains of events.

Sometimes unaccustomed storytellers get the point after a while and start anticipating your "what happened next" and "how did that feel" questions, and you don't have to prompt them quite so much. But some people need help all the way through. That doesn't have to mean they can't or won't tell the stories you need. It just means they need help. They also need more time than other storytellers, so if you know you will be dealing with unaccustomed storytellers, give yourself extra time.

STORIES IN USE

When I ask people to tell me a story, I like to watch the forms taken by their responses, both in what they say and in their body language (when I can see it). I have noticed that people veer off into one or more of three predictable trajectories at the mention of the word "story." I've been amazed by the consistency in the responses I've seen. People even use the same words even though they have never heard other people use them. I have found this to be true whether I am talking with people face to face, on the phone, or over the web.

Shown in Figure 4.10 on the next page are categories of responses I've seen to the word "story" mapped in relation to three uses stories provide: they *engage* our attention, they *influence* our beliefs or actions, and they *transfer* knowledge and information.

Note that some perceptions of story involve more than one purpose. A lesson engages and informs; a performance influences and engages; an opinion influences and informs. Fables (folk tales) are the most powerful and adaptable stories because they include all three elements.

For each of these uses of story one dimension of story is most important: story form engages, story function transfers knowledge and information, and story phenomenon influences. However, it is easy to make the case that all dimensions of story play a part in all uses of story.

Figure 4.11 on page 52 shows the same divisions, but with synonyms of the word "story" from the online thesaurus at thesaurus.com.

I thought at first while doing this little thesaurus exercise that there was nothing in the "joke" spot. But soon I realized that stories as gossip and rumor fit well there, because they engage people in connecting with emotional resonance on issues that are difficult to talk about. In that sense jokes, gossip, and rumors are all methods of oblique emotional engagement through stories.

By the way, if you are looking for a place to locate "a sense of belonging," I place that in the engagement slot as well, because engagement means more than just excitement; it means drawing together, connecting, including.

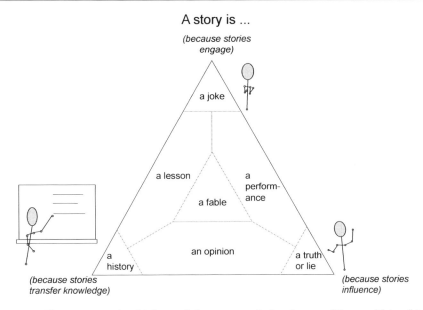

A story is ...

(because stories engage)

a joke

a lesson

a fable

a performance

a history

an opinion

a truth or lie

(because stories transfer knowledge)

(because stories influence)

Figure 4.10. These are ways in which people have responded to the use of the word "story" in my experience using the word.

Considering purposeful stories

You can envision two copies of this triangular model occupying two parallel planes (Figure 4.12 on page 53): the plane of naturally occurring stories and the plane of purposeful stories. And then you can envision another triangular plane beneath: the plane of life itself (which is of course why we tell stories in the first place). People, and groups of people, need to sustain their energy, interact with other people and groups, and learn from experience to better survive and thrive.

The natural state of wild stories is *people talking about things that have happened to them because the things have happened to them.* A naturally occurring story has no purpose in the same way that a crow has no purpose. Or if the purpose of a crow is to make more crows, the purpose of a naturally occurring story is to make more stories.

Purposeful stories, on the other hand, are like domesticated animals. The purpose of a domesticated chicken so dominates its existence that the chicken is unable to survive in the wild.

The function of a purposeful story, or its place on the triangle, is designed in advance. But the function of a naturally occurring story—if it has

one—becomes apparent only *after* it has been told.

When we shape a naturally occurring story to fit our needs, we are essentially domesticating it to suit a purpose. We do this naturally and without realizing it all the time. We encounter many wild stories every day, but we select some to tame based on needs we may only be vaguely aware of (or may deny). For example, the first time little Joey says "dog," one parent will tell the other simply because it happened. The second time Joey's parent tells the story to a neighbor, they might add some details that emphasize how precocious little Joey is. By the time little Joey is a dog trainer with a syndicated TV show, the story may have grown to an elaborate fantasy about how Joey had a precocious empathy with dogs never seen before or since—a full-blown purposeful fable.

I'm sure someone will be saying here that there are no completely purpose-less stories, that even the shyest of wild stories has some purpose whether we admit it or not. I agree, and that is why I drew a center *region* on the model instead of a center point, because the center point is theoretical and probably never seen in real human conversation.

Synonyms of "story"

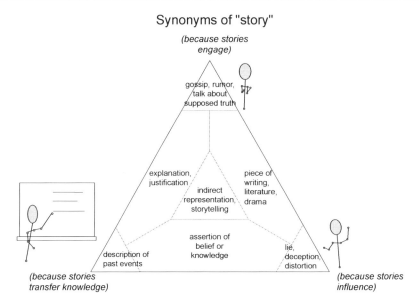

Figure 4.11. These are synonyms for the word "story" as retrieved from the online resource thesaurus.com.

STORIES IN STORIES

Like a ripple in a pond, every story has a story and is part of a story. As we explored in the section on stories in conversation (page 35), not all of the elements of a story are about things happening. A story's *narrated* events are usually interspersed with elements that are not narrated *events* but narrations *about* events. This distinction is crucial to understanding stories.

Mikhail Bakhtin, in *The Dialogic Imagination*, said it this way:

> ... before us are two events—the event that is narrated in the work and the event of the narration itself (we ourselves participate in the latter, as listeners or readers); these events take place in different times (which are marked by different durations as well) and in different places, but at the same time these two events are indissolubly united in a single but complex event that we might call the work in the totality of all its events....

So, "the work in the totality of all its events" includes at least two stories: that which is recounted, and that which constitutes the recounting (see Figure 4.13 on page 54). Consider retelling and remembering, and it's, as they say, turtles all the way down.

A simple exercise will prove my point. Choose a story about yourself as a child. Now follow that story as it moved through your life. I'll send you a dollar if you don't find several other stories wrapped around it.

All right, I'll go first. One of my favorite stories from childhood is from when I was exactly six years old. The neighbor kid started squashing a worm, out by the mailboxes (I can show you the spot) and I pulled her away, shouting, "That worm has just as much right to live as you do!"

I've thought about this story for a long time. Why do I remember it in so much detail—the location, the exact words, the fact that I was exactly six years old? For a long time I told myself the story that it was important because it said something about who I am, deep down, what sorts of moral sensitivities I (uniquely of course) was born with.

Now fast forward in time to a few years ago. On having a child I of course bought all the Dr. Seuss books I could find, including my two all-time favorites *Horton Hears a Who!* (about which movie I once threw a screaming fit because my horrid, horrid siblings wanted to watch something else), and *The Lorax*, a creature dear to my heart. So my son and I are sitting in the big chair and I'm reading *Horton*

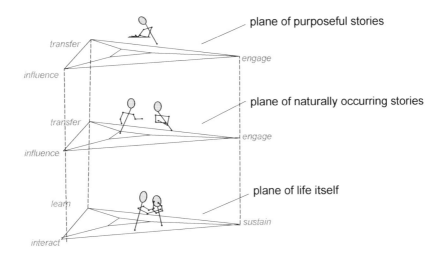

Figure 4.12. Naturally occurring stories follow the contours of life itself as people talk about what has happened to them. Purposeful stories follow the same contours, but with a goal.

Hears a Who! to him for the very first time, with great excitement, and I read these lines:

> Please don't harm all my little folks, who
>
> Have as much right to live as us bigger folks do!

I suddenly realize that it is irrefutably true that, in my memorable six-year-old outburst, I was parroting Dr. Seuss. Sensing a pattern, I reach for *The Lorax*. Sure enough, another one of my favorite sayings, which I thought only I in the whole world had ever said: "(Truffula) Trees are what everyone needs." I am a Dr. Seuss disciple, not an original thinker or a born moralist. (That doesn't make me any less wonderful, of course, but the point is that a new layer of story has formed.)

This new story makes me want to read more about Dr. Seuss (Theodore Geisel) and why he wrote those books, and what impact they have had on society, and how his books have become parts of the stories of other lives. When I go looking, I find out that many of Geisel's books are parts of larger stories about the country and the times he wrote them in.

For example, Geisel apparently wrote *Horton Hears a Who!* as an allegory for the American internment of Japanese-Americans and the Hiroshima bombing and subsequent occupation in Japan—and as an apology for supporting the internment during the war. He dedicated the book to a Japanese friend he met while touring Japan after the war. I didn't know any of that when I was six, but I did absorb the book's essential lesson of equality.

Apparently, so did many other children. As Charles Cohen recounts in his book *The Seuss, the Whole Seuss and Nothing But the Seuss:*

> The next time you're in a discussion about intolerance, see how many people cite a childhood encounter with *The Sneetches and Other Stories* or *Horton Hears a Who!* as the first time they learned about it. Ted's [Geisel's] long maturation process helped him surmount the attitudes of his day to become a pioneer in the fight for equality, so that children would grow up already knowing what it took him several decades to recognize.

And *The Lorax*? Geisel himself said, "It's one of the few things I ever set out to do that was straight propaganda." *The Lorax* was published just before the first anniversary of Earth Day, so it was a part of that larger story as well.

So the more I look, the more the stories keep on (if you will excuse me) biggering and biggering.

When I try to visualize these sets of interacting stories as ripples in a pond, the whole thing be-

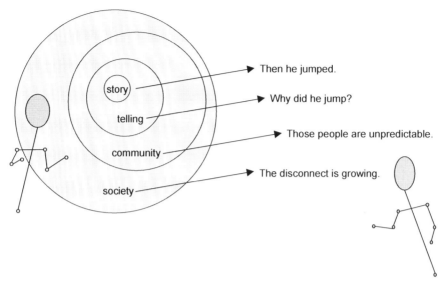

Figure 4.13. Every story has a story and is part of a story.

comes massively complex. Actually, I no longer believe that a story is like a ripple on a pond. Stories are like *rain* on a pond. A story may have its own stories, but stories also interact with other stories, which have their own stories, and it all gets sort of muddled together into an impressionistic wash, until a new story drops into the mix. We can sometimes see ripples and even circles, but it takes conscious effort to distinguish them from all the ... life ... going on.

STORIES IN SOCIETY

Now we have arrived at the last stop in our tour: a global view of stories as they live and breathe in human society.

The understanding I have developed of stories in society is not the same understanding another person might have developed. It has a story of its own, you could say. I was originally an ecologist and evolutionary biologist; so when I came to work with stories, I brought metaphors from those fields to work with me. The best way I know to explain stories in society is to use two ecological metaphors, and I think you will just have to excuse my not knowing how else to explain it. The metaphors relate stories to soil seed banks and species life cycles.

Story banks

To save you the trouble of finding it again, I'll repeat the relevant part of my story definition from the previous "What is a story" chapter (page 15).

> Stories are like seeds. They condense complex understandings and perspectives into packages that can be transmitted and stored, then retrieved from storage, planted, and germinated again in the fertile soil of receptive minds. And like seeds, stories are organisms of their own, worthy of respect and admiration.

Now let me expand on that by drawing a series of parallels between stories and seeds.

In a natural ecosystem, the *soil seed bank* is the community of living seeds present in the soil. In a human ecosystem, the *memory story bank* is the community of living stories present in the minds of people. You can separate and classify the stories in society, just as you can sort and label the seeds in the soil by family, genus, and species. Taken together, the bank of stories represents a collective capacity for growth.

The soil seed bank is constantly being *updated* by new seeds falling and being churned deep into the soil by water percolation, decomposition, and disturbances such as falling trees. As the soil churns, old seeds come to the sur-

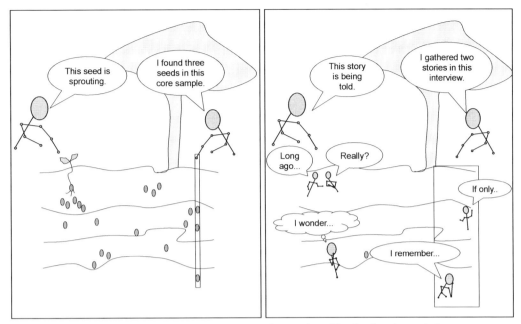

Figure 4.14. Stories in human society are like seeds in soil seed banks, forming a vital resource which can be studied and supported to help societies become more resilient in times of crisis.

face and germinate. Likewise the memory story bank is constantly being updated by new stories being told and churning deep into minds by the percolation of ideas, the decomposition of forgetting, and disturbances such as relocations and deaths. As minds reflect, old stories come to the surface and are told and heard again. Like messages hidden deep inside ancient structures, a story may sit unattended for thousands of years, only to reappear and take root in new minds.

Soil seed banks are like living *museums* of the plant community, places where dormant organisms are held in memory for future growth and in safety for use after a cataclysmic event. Memory story banks are like living museums of the human community, places where dormant stories are held in memory for future understanding and in safety for use when they are most needed. What will be needed, by whom, when, and for what purpose cannot be predicted. The only real preparation is to preserve the biodiversity—and narrative diversity—of the system.

A soil seed bank is a *reflection* of what is going on above the soil. Studying the soil seed bank can reveal patterns that give us important insights into the biological community and its

unique characteristics and needs, and it can give us a glimpse into the past and future of the ecosystem. A memory story bank is a reflection of what is going on in the world of human endeavor. Studying the memory story bank can reveal patterns that give us important insights into the human community and its unique characteristics and needs, and it can give us a glimpse into the past and future of the community. Ecologists, oral historians, and sociologists work on similar problems, though they may not know it. (See Figure 4.14.)

One of the problems with large-scale commercial agriculture is that though it produces short-term vigor, it reduces *diversity* in the soil seed bank. This *impoverishes* the system and reduces its ability to help the plant community survive and recover from catastrophe. Similarly, one of the problems with large-scale commercial storytelling is that though it produces short-term entertainment (and even the occasional insight), it reduces diversity in the memory story bank. This impoverishes the system and reduces its ability to help the human community survive and recover from catastrophe. The modern age has been marked by a decline in biological, agricultural, and narrative diversity in most parts of the world.

Some of the seeds in the soil seed bank are of *keystone species,* whose impact on the community's diversity and resilience is disproportional to their abundance. *Sacred stories* have a similarly disproportional impact on a human community's diversity and resilience. Neither keystone species nor sacred stories can be detected in advance or from afar; but if either is removed from the community the loss can have devastating effects.

In the soil seed bank *key species,* and in the memory seed bank *dominant stories,* sometimes *appear* to be the most important, because they dominate the community in number or visibility. Colossal trees and myths seem at times to define the community. But this is an illusion; the removal of key species or dominant stories does not damage community vigor as strongly as does the removal of keystone species or sacred stories. The discovery and preservation of keystone species and sacred stories is a goal of conservation efforts in nature and in human life.

A place where these metaphors come together is in exploring local indigenous knowledge to support ecological conservation. Species held sacred by local peoples often turn out to hold keystone roles in their ecosystems. Sacred stories point the way to their counterparts in nature.

Biodiversity and narrative diversity

What do ecologists do when faced with a dangerous loss of biodiversity? I can think of three complementary activities. Each has a corresponding activity also carried out by story workers.

Discovery

Ecologists map biodiversity, and its absence, in order to understand how best to strengthen it. Global maps of biodiversity, extinction risks, human impacts on the natural world, indicator species, and responses to climate change all help people decide where resources for study and action should be concentrated. Decision makers use such maps to coordinate cooperative efforts and arrive at mutually-acceptable plans for action.

In the same way, story workers help their communities or organizations build maps of meaning using collected stories that reveal hotspots of conflict, zones of complacency, opportunities for exploration, and other features. Maps of meaning differ from ecological maps in that they integrate many perspectives on sometimes contentious issues; but their utility is similar. The creation of such a map is often a turning point in story work because it creates a new language people in the community can use to discuss issues in a negotiated framework.

Sensemaking

Based on the maps they have constructed, ecologists make sense of what is going on in the natural world. They look for ways to find a sustainable balance between human activity and natural abundance in order to provide recommendations to policy-makers and help them make better long-term decisions. One of the pieces of work in this area I recall from my ecology days was research done on wildlife corridors, or passages between patches of viable habitat. Such corridors are critical to the preservation of biodiversity in the patchwork of wild places between human habitations. Natural corridors are both a requirement of biodiversity and an opportunity to support it, which is why their discovery was such a boon to the field of ecology.

In the same way, story workers use the stories they have gathered to make sense of what is going on in the community. They look for ways to find sustainable balances between forces at work in their community or organization. The process of making sense of the stories people in a community or organization are telling often reveals opportunities that, like wildlife corridors, moderate the damaging effects of problems, such as the stresses of corporate mergers or waves of immigration.

Support

Ecologists actively strengthen biodiversity by creating and maintaining *seed banks.* A seed bank is an artificially created collection of seeds maintained in order to preserve diversity in the face of depleted soil seed banks. One of the challenges in managing biological seed banks is the need to constantly replant seeds in order to maintain the viability of the stored seeds. In par-

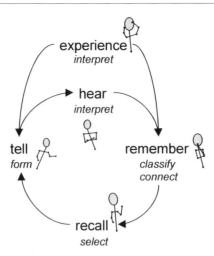

Figure 4.15. Stories cycle around in experience, memory, and retelling.

ticular, maintaining the endosperm layer that surrounds the seed embryo, which provides sustenance to keep the dormant seed alive and able to germinate, can be a challenge. Seeds whose endosperm is lost cannot survive.

In the same way, story workers actively boost narrative diversity by creating and maintaining *story banks*. A story bank is an artificially created collection of stories maintained in order to preserve diversity in the face of depleted memory story banks. One of the challenges in managing story banks is the need to constantly retell stories in order to maintain the viability of the stored stories. In particular, maintaining the layer of context that surrounds the story embryo, which provides memorability to keep the dormant story alive and able to be told, can be a challenge. Stories whose context is lost cannot survive.

Story cycles

As I said in the section above, when I started working with stories I naturally wanted to consider the ecology of stories, including their natural histories and life cycles. This is a much more difficult thing with stories than with tadpoles or mushrooms, because stories mingle and morph in ways that creatures can't. Still, we can learn something from the attempt.

Every time a person experiences something, a new story enters the narrative cycle of telling, hearing, remembering, and recalling (see Figure 4.15). Even if the person doesn't tell anyone

the story, the story still enters the cycle; only it stays in the person's own orbit. The narrative cycle has many orbits, or scales, from individual to family to community, society, and epoch.

In the narrative cycle, pockets of stillness and eddies of movement are constantly forming and dissolving. Sometimes a person has an experience but is unable to tell others about it or even think about it for years. This can happen because the experience is painful, or it can just happen benignly, because nothing calls the experience to mind. Conversely, sometimes a story takes on a life of its own and swirls about with great energy in a person or family or group or society for a time.

The little extra words in this diagram, by the way, are things that also happen at each stage that I think are interesting to think about. I originally had them as little recursive sub-cycles within each stage of the cycle, but the whole thing got too busy and I took them out (but you can picture them that way).

Some interesting points about these sub-cycles: Notice that interpretation takes place during direct experience *and* during story listening. When a story is remembered, it is usually also classified and connected to other stories; and this process can be continual as thoughts churn. (That's why I hate using the term "store" or "keep" for the process of remembering, because it implies no activity.) Recall of a story requires selection, usually for a purpose, though the purpose is not always known to the selector,

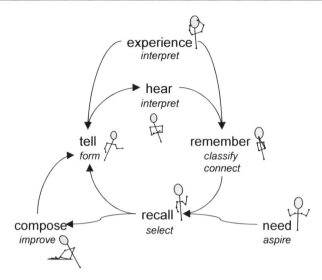

Figure 4.16. Purposeful storytelling adds "buds" of purpose and need to the natural cycle of story flow.

at least not at first. As stories are told over and over they usually solidify and take on a form, though that form can change later.

Note that I did not mention *events* in the narrative cycle. Not all events create experiences, and not all experiences require events. Perhaps something grows over time, imperceptibly at first but larger and larger until you can definitely say you have had an *experience* of something but you cannot point to any single *event* that defines or constrains it in time. A belief dies; a friendship grows; an awareness coalesces; an ability you once relied on slips away. Even if one day you suddenly realize it has been happening and will continue to happen, it's hard to say where the event is in the experience. What if it started before you started and will end after you end?

Now if you will permit me an aside, I will illustrate this independence of experiences and events by introducing you to an old friend from my days studying animal behavior. This is a conceptual model of information use in decision making which I've found useful for thinking about all kinds of decisions, be they made by lizards or birds or people.

We can classify the information used by organisms thus. *External* information is what we typically think of as information: what time it is, the temperature of the air, how many seeds are un-

der a tree. *Internal* information is about one's internal state: how hungry I am, how tired, how thirsty. *Relational* information is about how it all fits together: that if I'm hungry and tired, and it's cold outside and there is little food left, then I am in danger.

All of these types of information are required for decision making; if any is lacking the equations will be off. The reason I bring this up is that stories can come about from experiences involving *any or all* of these informational sources, and this is not obvious. We typically think of stories as arising from external experiences *caused by events,* such as when a tree falls on a house. But stories can also come from internal or relational experiences, and those stories are sometimes harder to spot in the wild. An internal-experience story might be one where I realize my memory is not what it was. A relational-experience story might be one where my family realizes *why* my memory is not what it was. Or where a scientist realizes why the memory of so many people is not what it was.

But I have not drawn the complete story life cycle, not yet. People don't only tell stories casually, in a simple line from recalling to telling. People have always told stories for a purpose, whether they had graphic presentation tools or not. In *The Walking People*, Paula Underwood describes how her people long ago created the first cave painting of a bear in order to warn

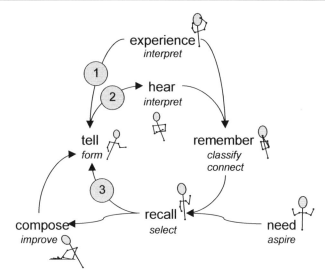

Figure 4.17. Narrative pulses are times when people experience an instinctual urge to pass on a story. Like steam in a boiler, these pulses of energy fuel the story cycle.

others about bears in caves. That is an early example of a purposeful story. (By the way, *The Walking People* is a recording of a millennia-old oral history by the last member of a Native American tribe, and well worth reading.)

So, adding purposeful storytelling to the picture, you get something like Figure 4.16 on the preceding page. Now the narrative cycle has another inflow: the need for a story to suit a purpose. And it has a sort of bud where a purposeful story is composed (out of the material of recalled stories) before being told and entering the inner portion of the narrative cycle.

Narrative pulses

I've saved my favorite part for last. This was an idea I came across around 2000, quite by accident. (I'm sure the idea is much, much older than my acquaintance with it!) What happened was, I was working in my little dark office at IBM Research when I made a discovery or solved some problem ... can't remember what. I rushed out of my office and looked for people in the hallways to tell my Eureka story to. I found a few people and *tried* to spill out the story to them, but nobody was interested in hearing how I had got a troublesome screen widget to work (or whatever it was). So the story died, and I soon forgot about it. But later I reflected on that experience, and began to call what I had ex-

perienced a "narrative pulse." Here is my theory of it.

When something happens to a person, they (sometimes, not always) have a little *narrative pulse*, or burst, or surge, of energy or motivation to pass it on. If you graphed a narrative pulse it would look like a little earthquake. But usually, because no one happens to be in the right state to *receive* the story, the narrative pulse dissipates, and the story is gone. But here's the thing: *every story is needed somewhere, by somebody, sometime*. In that sense a story is like a wisp of steam that, if put to good use, could provide power; but many of the best stories dissipate and are lost.

Over time I've come to realize that there are other, smaller pulses, something like echoes of the first and largest pulse. The second is when a person first hears a story: they may be inspired to pass it on right away. Again the steam may escape and be lost if no one is ready to receive it. The third pulse is when a person suddenly recalls a story, often as the result of something someone said. Again they experience a little pulse of motivation to pass on the story, and again it is often moot. (See Figure 4.17.)

A long time ago people spent so much time talking together (often as they collaborated on tasks that were difficult and tedious *but quiet*) that narrative pulses were caught and held simply because audiences were available. If the right person was not around to catch the pulse when it first arose, someone who knew such a person was around, and the story made its way to where it needed to go. Not today. In our modern, convenient, noisy, isolated world, we walk among great banks of dissipated story steam.

However, even today, when a person has a *way* to quickly and easily pass on a story, they will take advantage of it, especially if it becomes a habit. People who build ways to help people tell each other stories can think about narrative pulses and how to help them move through society. For example, one way to capture story steam as it rises would be to give people a "Eureka!" button or sheet of paper or phone number or … something, so that the energy can be captured and put to good use before it dissipates. There are of course all sorts of "hotlines" for this or that emergency, but I've never seen one for telling stories whose purpose is to help other people facing the same situation by catching story steam as it comes pulsing out of lived experience. My guess is that the *first* pulse is the most useful to support with a ready mechanism. But the others provide some energy as well and can be tapped. For example, when a person is reading a story in an online forum, it should be easy to do something right away in relation to the story, to put the pulse to use.

You could say that there are bursts of energy when people have a need for a story or when they are composing one for a purpose. But that's a different type of energy. It's the energy of purpose. The pulses I'm talking about are more like *instincts* than ideas. They arise spontaneously, without a conscious plan. That's exactly what makes them valuable.

In addition to narrative pulses, there are similar but larger-scale bursts of narrative energy. Call these *narrative waves*. These take place not in individuals but in groups, communities, and societies. I don't mean the "grand narratives" that societies construct about why things are the way they are. I'm talking more about why and when people become *motivated* to tell stories, and how those patterns of motivation move around in groups of people. Where is the narrative energy, and when does it happen, and why?

One example of a narrative wave is what is going on in the "tell all" world of television talk shows and reality shows. For some reason large numbers of ordinary people in the United States (less so in other places) have been driven recently to tell intimate stories about their own lives and troubles to audiences that would have been inconceivable only a few decades ago. Obviously some of this is done to make money; but that can't be the only place this tell-all energy is coming from. What is driving that particular narrative wave? Could it be a craving for celebrity, people wanting their "fifteen minutes" of fame? Or is it about people craving connection and reacting to increased societal isolation? Or is it just a transformation of the village gossip people no longer have to rely on? (And what does that transformation mean?)

Another wave of energy around stories concerns *fabulists*, the people who throughout history have packaged and repackaged the stories everyone has told since the beginning of time. Aesop didn't actually tell all of the hundreds of stories attached to his name. He was just a storyteller people knew about, so if they heard a clever story they said "that must be one of Aesop's." The same thing happened with the Brothers Grimm, Hans Christian Andersen, Andrew Lang, and many others. When reading Dostoyevsky I kept coming across somebody named Krylov, who was the Aesop of that place and time. It seems that there is a need for societies to have an Aesop, somebody whose name means "the keeper of the old tales" and serves as a quick reference to the collective wisdom contained in folklore. My guess is that whenever enough time goes by for the current fabulist-in-residence to fade, a narrative wave forms and a new fabulist (who is created not by any effort of their own but by popular need) is born. Who are today's fabulists? Maybe talk-show hosts?

SUMMARY

Trading stories in conversation is a dance, one we all learn during childhood. Learning to interpret and understand the dance of conversational storytelling can help people work with stories. A story has an orientation (things get set up), complication (things get complicated) and resolution (things come to an end). This is embedded in the larger conversational context of an abstract (permission to tell is negotiated), evaluation (proof of value is given), and coda (performance is concluded). The rituals that surround storytelling are like wrapping paper; we use them to communicate intent and negotiate interaction.

People vary in how much they tell stories, and they also vary in how much they *think* they tell stories. Those who wish to gather stories from people who experience narrative in these different ways should think about these dimensions of variation as they work.

Stories engage our attention, influence our beliefs or actions, and transfer knowledge and information. People tell naturally occurring stories simply to share experiences; people tell purposeful stories to create an impact.

Stories never exist independently but are embedded in layers of stories. Story workers need to pay attention to this.

Like seeds in a soil seed bank, stories represent the collective experience of a group of people. They reflect the lives of the people and can be studied to learn about problems. Reduced diversity in story banks impoverishes the natural system and renders it less resilient in the face of catastrophe. Story workers, like ecologists, support a community's bank of stories by mapping its features, making sense of what they find, and supporting the health of the system.

Stories move in cycles of telling, hearing, remembering, and recalling. Story work involves watching these cycles and helping them move as they should. Sometimes stories move in pulses and waves, and story workers can be aware of those dynamics as well.

QUESTIONS

I said that variations on the "normal" form of conversational storytelling are enormous. What variations have *you* seen? As you read the description of how conversational storytelling plays out, where have you noticed differences in groups or communities you belong to? What do you think those variations say about those groups or communities?

Do you tell stories? Do you *think* you tell stories? What about people you know? What does that mean about your conversations with them? What about the people in your community or organization? What is your storytelling culture like?

How do you habitually think of stories? Do you think of them more as engaging, influencing, or transferring? What about other people you know? Do any of those forms seem more safe or conforming in your community or organization? Why is that?

If your community or organization were an ecosystem, and you dug down into the soil and pulled up some stories, what would you find? Which stories are dominant in your ecosystem, and which are essential? How is your story ecosystem diverse? Where is it healthy and where is it faltering? Where does it need support?

Are stories like seeds? Does that metaphor work for you? If it does, why does it? If it doesn't, what metaphor does work for you? Can you develop your own metaphor and use it to consider some of the dynamics considered using the seed metaphor in this chapter?

What sorts of cycles do you see stories traveling in? If you developed your own theory of narrative cycles (and pulses and waves), what would it look like?

ACTIVITIES

Watch yourself tell stories. One day, follow yourself around and write down all of the stories you told on that day. How did you start each story? Did you include statements of evaluation? When and how did you do that? How did you end the stories? Why do you think you framed the stories in the ways you did?

In conversation with another person, fish for a story. See if you can get them to tell one without your using the word "story" or letting on that you are influencing them toward storytelling. Then insert a story into the conversation. Answer some question or observation of theirs with a story. See how they respond to it. Do they negotiate with you over what story you should tell? Do they modify the story as you tell it?

Ask two or three friends if you can record a conversation you all have. During the conversation, pay attention to the ebb and flow of stories. Jot down some notes. Count up how many stories you hear. Try to bring stories out if you can. Later, listen to the recorded conversation. Transcribe it if you like. (Use the advice in the section on transcribing storytelling, page 183, to help you get down the important points of the storytelling event.) How does your understanding of the storytelling change after you listen to the conversation? Can you hear things you didn't hear before? Do your story counts during and after listening to the conversation agree? Do this exercise a few more times. Do you find out more each time you try it?

Think of ten people you know well. Decide where each of them fits in reference to the sections of this chapter on stories in personalities (Do they tell stories? Do they think they tell stories?) and stories in use (What do they use stories for? What do they think stories are used for?). What does that exercise tell you about those people and about these models of story use? Can you improve on the models based on what you have observed?

Choose a story about yourself as a child. Now follow that story as it moved through your life. What other stories do you find wrapped around it? Do this for stories other people have told you.

As you look at the diagrams of the narrative cycle, think of moments that fit into each location. What makes them fit there? What does that mean about your community or organization? Can you think of any narrative pulses or waves that take place in your community or organization?

Chapter Five

Stories in Communities and Organizations

In the previous chapter, we covered how stories work at a range of scales from individual to society-wide. Now it is time to start thinking about communities and organizations, and about *your* community or organization in particular. This chapter begins by examining the flow of stories in communities and organizations, and ends with an assessment test you can use to think about story sharing in your own community or organization.

FUNCTIONS OF STORY SHARING IN COMMUNITIES AND ORGANIZATIONS

Why do people in communities and organizations share stories? What is their function in this context?

Narrative functionality began to be researched in earnest in the 1980s, and there are a number of studies describing it in the scientific literature. My reading of that literature, along with my own experiences collecting stories and helping people work with them, leads me to suggest a four-fold division of functionality, thus. Stories help people negotiate a social contract, create shared meaning, meet challenges, and play with possibility. Let's go over the categories in turn. Within each category, I'll bring to your attention some related research.

Negotiating a social contract

People share stories in communities and organizations to negotiate the unwritten rules of the contract that binds them. Stories help to settle such questions as what members can and cannot do, what is fair and just, who gets to decide what, and what happens when the social contract is broken. This process brings people together and generates commitment and solidarity, a process Mary Boyce, in a 1995 paper, called *collective centering*.

At the same time, the sharing of stories constantly *decenters* the community or organization, challenging it to find ways to accommodate disagreement and difference without dissolution. The forces of centering and decentering dance around each other as stories flow. It is the unique nature of stories, as negotiation devices that can contain conflict without resolving it, that makes them so useful to the process of creating and maintaining a social contract.

As people negotiate and renegotiate the social contract, they also *represent* its implications by telling stories. Because stories bring the abstract into the concrete, they translate values, beliefs, assumptions, and norms into memorable, flexible instantiations people can apply readily to everyday life. Stories communicate shared values and assumptions to new members, warn members who are in danger of violating the social contract, and mediate between views of "the way things are" in ambiguous areas. Such stories aid in the transmission of what Charles Perrow calls "third-order controls" (the first order being direct control and the second procedural control) and Edgar Schein calls "shared basic assumptions."

To cite a famous example of negotiation through story exchange, Yiannis Gabriel, in a seminal 1995 paper called "The unmanaged organization," gives an account of an accident in which a fire extinguisher exploded in a research laboratory. He collected four unsolicited, surprisingly different accounts of the same incident, as follows (and see Figure 5.1 on the next page).

Raymond, a manager, downplayed the incident, giving only a "detached description emphasizing the material damage." He "did not invest

Figure 5.1. In a 1995 paper, Yiannis Gabriel recounted how four employees who witnessed the explosion of a fire extinguisher told strikingly different stories about the incident, each casting themselves into a different role in the organization.

the events with any emotion or symbolic significance."

Maureen, the employee who had been closest to the fire extinguisher, half-seriously presented the incident as a "personal attack" on her by the management. "They failed on that attempt to kill me!" she said. Her joking account of the incident cast her supervisors in the role of the story's villain.

Chris wanted to make it clear that he was not frightened during the event: "I realized that everyone was trying to get out of the room, so I thought 'I better go then.'" His account "cast himself in contrast to the others, in the role of a person who is not easily rattled or panic-stricken."

Peter jokingly represented the event as a failed opportunity to inflict damage "upstairs" (on the management). In Peter's account, Maureen was cast as an "agent of retribution" who should "aim better" next time.

In each of these recountings, members of the organization used the story as a vehicle to negotiate elements of power and procedure. In all of the stories but the first, elements of fantasy came into play. Says Gabriel:

> Each [story] reveals a different way of constituting the subject, whether as hero, as heroic survivor or as victim. Each narrative highlights the plasticity of turning every-day experience into meaningful stories. In doing so, the storytellers neither accept nor reject 'reality'. Instead, they seek to mould it, shape it and infuse it with meaning, each in a distinct and individual way.

By telling stories, people don't just *convey* rules and assumptions; they rehearse, explore, perform, and refine them. There is an interplay between communication and negotiation in story sharing: neither happens without the other. Even the simplest "how we do things around here" story told to an outsider or newcomer contains a nugget of renegotiation as the story is told anew.

Creating shared meaning

People who live and work together need more than just a social contract; they need a *reason*

Figure 5.2. The "executive confronted by lowly employee" story is commonly told in organizations, where it is (paradoxically) used to demonstrate the uniqueness of the organization.

to live and work together. Of course, people have to live somewhere, and most people work for money. But few people live or work entirely by accident or misfortune. Most people have made at least some choices in where and how they live and make money. People use stories to make those choices, and to rehearse, explore, perform, and refine them. If stories about the social contract negotiate what we do and don't do, stories about meaning and purpose negotiate what we are and are not.

A useful example of creating shared meaning is the work of Joanne Martin and her colleagues, who (in a classic paper called "The Uniqueness Paradox in Organizational Stories") collected commonly shared stories from a variety of organizations. Based on this collection, they identified seven types of stories commonly found in organizations. While their seven story types negotiate behavioral norms, they also go further into negotiating the unique collective identity of each organization.

The seven types of stories Martin and her colleagues found in their collection explored the following questions.

What do I do when a higher status person breaks a rule? In these stories, a high-rank-ing executive attempts to do something that is against a company rule (usually of safety or security). An employee of low status confronts the executive, demanding that they follow the rule. The executive complies (or does not), and the rule is strengthened (or weakened) as a result.

At IBM, for example, a twenty-two-year-old employee confronted Thomas Watson, Jr., "the intimidating chairman of IBM's board," because he did not have the "green badge" required to enter a security area. Martin et al. tell the rest of the story thus.

"I was trembling in my uniform, which was far too big," she recalled. "It hid my shakes but not my voice. 'I'm sorry,' I said to him. I knew who he was all right. 'You cannot enter. Your admittance is not recognized.' That's what we were supposed to say."

"The men accompanying Watson were stricken; the moment held unpredictable possibilities. 'Don't you know who he is?' Someone hissed. Watson raised his hand for silence, while one of the party strode off and returned with the appropriate badge."

A similar story was collected from a plant supervisor at another company. Again an executive (again male) wanted to enter an area, and again he was forbidden to do so by a low-status employee (again female).

> "He leaned over one of the assembly line workers and asked her how things were going. She interrupted him abruptly and said firmly, 'I'm sorry, but you can't come in this area without your safety glasses.' He apologized, red with embarrassment, went back to get his safety glasses, and then came back and complimented her on her guts."

In each case, say Martin et al, "The inequality in power sets up a tension: Will the high status person pull rank and be angry at the attempt to enforce the rules?" In most stories the rule-breaker does not pull rank; but in some organizations the opposite story is told. (See Figure 5.2 on the preceding page for an illustration of both stories.)

Is the big boss human? Here a high-ranking executive is presented with an opportunity to perform a "status-equalization act," such as answering a telephone or fixing a broken machine. The executive does or does not "abrogate his/her high status temporarily by exhibiting 'human' qualities."

Here is a representative story from the collection:

> "Charles Brown was the chief executive officer at Illinois Bell during the late 1960's. A bad strike had crippled the organization, as craftspeople refused to work for several months. On the weekends, 'Charlie,' as he was known, would grab some tools, and start repairing telephones. One weekend, the country club where he belonged called with a complaint about a broken telephone. 'Without batting an eyelash,' or changing his clothes, Charlie went out and fixed the country club telephone."

The evaluative statement "without batting an eyelash" marks the story as a negotiating device for creating meaning about the type of organization employees at Illinois Bell saw it to be.

Can the little person rise to the top? This is the Horatio Alger story of an employee with low status who rises through the hierarchy through hard work and a positive attitude. On the flip side, other versions of the story tell about unfairness, as when a a deserving employee is not rewarded, or an undeserving one is. (I won't cite any more examples of the fascinating stories in Martin et al.'s paper, but you can find it and read it yourself.)

Will I get fired? These stories are about what happens when people have to be fired or laid off en masse. Those in power handle the decision with integrity (as with Alan Wilkins' famous "nine-day fortnight" story, see page 488) or with cruel indifference.

Will the organization help me when I have to move? These stories concern another traumatic event in organizational life: being asked to relocate (sometimes for good reasons, sometimes not). As with the firing stories, those in charge can be caring or cruel.

How will the boss react to mistakes? In these stories an employee makes a mistake and is either "graciously forgiven" or punished mercilessly.

How will the organization deal with obstacles? The most frequent of the seven types, these stories concern employees, or groups, encountering problems and solving them, or failing to solve them.

Martin and her colleagues saw three dimensions of negotiated meaning in these seven story types. The first three story types deal with *equality*, or questions of status, power, and rights. The next three types deal with *security*, or the safety of one's position in varying circumstances. The last (and most populous) story type deals with *control* over decision making. By telling stories that explore these common themes of organizational life, people build a larger shared story about what sort of organization they belong to (and whether they want to belong to it).

The paradox of the article's title is that even though these seven story types are common across many organizations, the stories themselves are often used as proof that a particular organization is unique. Whether the stories are positive or negative, they portray the organization as uniquely the best or worst of all possible organizations.

Say Martin et al.:

> ... these attributions endow the institution with uniqueness, enabling employees to identify with a benevolent organization or to distance themselves from a less desirable institution.

In other words, people share stories around common themes in order to create a negotiated portrait of the organization and its meaning in their lives.

Meeting challenges

Another function of stories in communities and organizations is as an aid to collective sensemaking, as people work to solve problems and achieve goals together. People share stories to transfer knowledge, discover useful insights, and make decisions.

In a 1991 study, David Boje studied organizational storytelling in over 100 hours of conversations taped at an office-supply distribution firm. He identified several functional patterns in the stories he heard.

For example:

- A *series* of stories might be told in which a common theme is repeated, "as a way to draw parallels between two patterns."
- A *composite* story might grow up around a central theme based on the experiences of multiple tellers; thus "an analysis of the story is embedded in the telling."
- A *predictive* story might feature an analogy from the past replayed as a possible future, which "allows people to predict what may happen if a similar incident should recur."
- A *word on the street* story might "leak" a rumor (possibly one everyone already knows) to explore forces in play. "Referencing how the story has been leaked," says Boje, "adds credibility to the performance."

From his observations, Boje concluded that:

> These stakeholders ... performed stories not only to make sense of their setting but to negotiate alternative interpreta-

tions and to accommodate new precedents for decision and action. They tell stories about the past, present, and future to make sense of and manage their struggles with their environment.

Much of the rest of this book will be about helping people in exactly this capacity: using stories to make sense of complex situations and build better decisions upon that sensemaking. (After you have read about working with stories in the rest of the book, I invite you to come back and compare each of Boje's functional story patterns to the group story exercises covered later in the book.)

Playing with possibility

Stories revitalize, challenge, and motivate people in communities and organizations by helping them explore. People share stories to conduct what-if experiments, create new visions of hoped-for futures, process painful events, and play with the uncertainties and potentials of collective life.

The paper I want to tell you about in this section is one that has been widely cited as proof that stories have power to persuade. In the paper, called "Truth or Corporate Propaganda: The Value of a Good War Story," Joanne Martin and Melanie Powers describe a two-part study they carried out on perceptions of stories in comparison to other information.

In their first experiment, Martin and Powers presented people (whom they call "quantitatively well-trained M.B.A. subjects") with an advertisement for a winery. The advertisement claimed that the winery "used many of the same excellent winemaking techniques as used in the famed Chablis region of France, thus producing California wine as fine as French chablis." They then asked the subjects to indicate to what extent they believed the advertisement's claim (see Figure 5.3 on the next page).

Accompanying each advertisement was supplementary information, of one of three types:

1. a personal story about the founder of the winery ("My father would have been proud of this wine.")

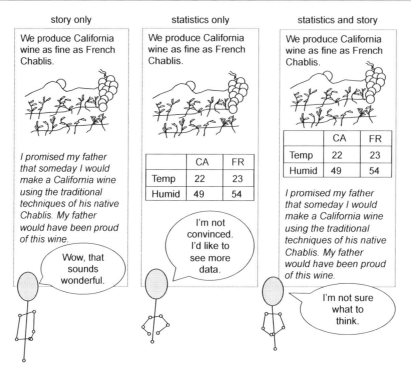

Figure 5.3. In an experiment, people were more willing to believe an advertised claim when it was accompanied by a personal story than they were if it was accompanied by a table of facts, or with facts and story combined. (These texts are paraphrased from the ones used in the experiment.)

2. a table of statistics comparing the winery's methods with those of the Chablis region of France

3. a combination of story and statistics

Subjects who read *only* the story "were significantly more likely to believe that the advertisement was truthful, to believe that the Beaumont winery actually had used the French wine-making procedures, and to distort their memory of the policy statement, in a direction favorable to the winery."

In their second experiment, Martin and Powers set up the same situation: a claim to truth followed by either a story, a table of statistics, or a combination of story and statistics. Their scenario this time was about Alan Wilkins' "nine-day fortnight" story (see page 488), in which managers avoided layoffs by asking everyone (including themselves) to take a cut in pay and work time. The claim this time was that the nine-day fortnight policy had been put into place.

However, for this second experiment the researchers set up a second dimension of variation. Some people got a table of statistics that confirmed the claim to truth (showing across-the-board pay cuts and no layoffs), and some got statistics that disconfirmed it (showing no pay cuts and mass layoffs). Some people got a story that reinforced the claim to truth, and some got a story that contradicted it.

As with the first experiment, people who read the confirming story more strongly believed the claim to truth than people who read the confirming statistics. However, when the story *contradicted* the claim to truth, it was dismissed "as the single exception to the general rule," and the statistical information held more persuasive power (see Figure 5.4 on the facing page). Said Martin and Powers, "The results of the second experiment suggest that if a story is to have strong impact, it must be congruent with previously available information."

The reason I find this paper fascinating is that it points to the contextual boundedness of story-based play. People share stories to play with

story confirming statement   story disconfirming statement

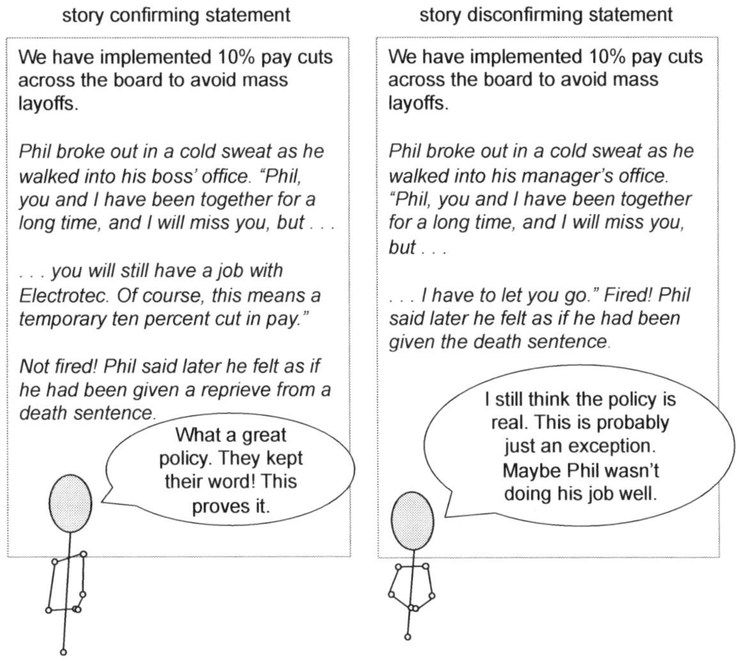

We have implemented 10% pay cuts across the board to avoid mass layoffs.

Phil broke out in a cold sweat as he walked into his boss' office. "Phil, you and I have been together for a long time, and I will miss you, but . . .

. . . you will still have a job with Electrotec. Of course, this means a temporary ten percent cut in pay."

Not fired! Phil said later he felt as if he had been given a reprieve from a death sentence.

What a great policy. They kept their word! This proves it.

We have implemented 10% pay cuts across the board to avoid mass layoffs.

Phil broke out in a cold sweat as he walked into his manager's office. "Phil, you and I have been together for a long time, and I will miss you, but . . .

. . . I have to let you go." Fired! Phil said later he felt as if he had been given the death sentence.

I still think the policy is real. This is probably just an exception. Maybe Phil wasn't doing his job well.

Figure 5.4. In a second experiment, people were more likely to believe an advertised claim when it was accompanied by a personal story, but they were *less* likely to disbelieve the claim when a story contradicted it. They considered the story a probable exception rather than proof that the claim was false. (These texts are paraphrased from the ones used in the experiment.)

possibility, but they know it is a game, and they follow the rules of the game within the game. Outside the game, the rules are different. You might say that such a game is too limited to be powerful; but in fact it is powerful precisely *because* it is limited. The power of bounded narrative exploration helps communities and organizations prepare for the future.

LOCAL STORY SHARING CULTURES

Do you remember, when I talked about stories in conversation in the previous chapter (page 35), how I mentioned that people vary in how they tell each other stories? At the level of a community or organization, such variations tend to gather together and form a local culture of storytelling. Members of any community or organization know how to tell stories and how to listen to them in a way that will be socially acceptable in context. People who belong to more than one community learn how to switch from one context to another as they move between worlds.

Shirley Brice Heath gives an excellent example of local story sharing cultures in her work observing how people in two neighboring towns tell stories. She gives the towns the anonymous names of Trackton and Roadville. "People in both Trackton and Roadville spend a lot of time telling stories," she says, but "the patterns of interaction surrounding the actual telling of a story vary considerably."

Stories in Roadville seem pretty cut and dried:

Roadville story-tellers use formulaic openings.... Their stories maintain a strict chronicity, with direct discourse reported, and no explicit exposition of meaning or direct expression of evaluation of the behavior of the main character allowed. Stories end with a summary statement of a moral or a proverb, or a Biblical quotation.

But in Trackton things are more complex:

Trackton story-tellers use few formulaic openings, except the story-teller's own introduction of himself. ... Stories maintain little chronicity; they move from event to event with numerous interspersions of evaluation of the behaviors of story characters and reiterations of the point of the story. Stories have no formulaic closing, but may have a reassertion of the strengths of the main character, which may be only the opening to yet another tale of adventure.

The two communities also differ in their opinions on what constitutes both a story and a true story:

The stories of Roadville are true to the facts of an event; they qualify exaggeration and hedge if they might seem to be veering from an accurate reporting of events. ... Roadville adults see their stories as didactic: the purpose of a story is to make a point—a point about the conventions of behavior.

But:

The content of Trackton's stories ... ranges widely, and there is "truth" only in the universals of human strength and persistence praised and illustrated in the tale. Fact is often hard to find, though it is usually the seed of the story. ... In Trackton, stories often have no point; they may go on as long as the audience enjoys the story-teller's entertainment. ... [Trackton] Stories do not teach lessons about proper behavior; they tell of individuals who excel by outwitting the rules of conventional behavior.

Brice Heath also found differences in telling rights:

In Roadville, a story must be invited or announced by someone other than the story-teller. Only certain community members are designated good story-tellers. .... Trackton story-tellers, from a young age, must be aggressive in inserting their stories into an on-going stream of discourse. Story-telling is highly competitive. Everyone in a conversation may want to tell a story, so only the most aggressive wins out.

Here is another example of local variations in story sharing cultures. Nigel Cross and Rhiannon Barker, in "The Sahel Oral History Project" (in *The Oral History Reader*), say of their work gathering stories:

Problems sometimes arose from men wanting to take over and disrupt interviews with women. Men would decide that they should act as mediators between their wives (or other female relatives) and the interviewer. In some cases it appeared that the woman was reassured by male encouragement; at other times the consequences were disastrous, with the woman feeling unable to talk about certain issues and the man asserting that he knew the woman's mind better than she.

And Hugo Slim (et al.) said (in "Ways of listening" in *The Oral History Reader*) of storytelling traditions:

Storytelling may also have a seasonal dimension. In Ladakh, for example, winter is the time for telling stories. It is considered an inappropriate activity during the busy summer months when the agricultural workload is at its peak, as a local saying makes clear: "As long as the earth is green, no tale should be told." It would be an ill-prepared and disappointed oral testimony project that set out to collect traditional stories in Ladakh during the summer!

These are all examples of local particularities in the way stories are told. The more you can learn about the way your community or organization shares stories, the better equipped you will be to help people within it share stories with each other.

WHY LOCAL STORY SHARING MATTERS

Why does it matter if people in communities or organizations share stories? More importantly, why should *you* care about supporting story sharing in your community or organization?

To put it simply, a community or organization with a strong tradition of story sharing is a better place to live and work. Now let me put forth some evidence to support that statement.

Alan Wilkins, in his seminal 1983 paper "Organizational Stories as Symbols that Control the Organization," spoke of two organizations he studied for his doctoral research. He called them Company A and Company Z. Wilkins chose these names based on William Ouchi's "Theory Z" of management. In Wilkins' phrasing, a Type A company features "highly specialized tasks, relatively high turnover, and contractual relations between employees." A Type Z company is characterized by "low task specialization, low turnover, and primary or wholistic relations between employees." In other words, you and I would prefer to work at a Type Z company. The work would be interesting; people wouldn't flee the first chance they got; and we'd be treated like real people.

As Wilkins reported on the stories he collected in companies A and Z:

> When I systematically interviewed participants at the middle management and operator levels at both companies, I found significantly more "shared stories" (stories told by several people) in company Z than in company A.

Thus Wilkins claims that organizations in which sharing stories is customary and familiar are more likely to be places in which people want to work.

I do find Wilkins' next finding problematical, however.

> I also found that a significantly greater proportion (33%) of the stories told by participants in company Z were used to illustrate or legitimate the management philosophy than was the case at company A (14%). These stories were concrete symbols of how management applied their philosophy. Apparently, company Z executives ... focus consistently on general themes which lower participants use as the theme for stories which they tell and pass on. The result at company Z is that stories are significant symbols of shared values and shared perspectives which participants must learn to function effectively.

That all sounds a little too wonderful to match with the reality I've seen in my own work. Yiannis Gabriel also disagrees with Wilkins. In his book *Storytelling in Organizations*, he claims to have collected only a "tiny minority" of positive stories about management in the five companies in which he collected stories (he says "the overwhelming majority are either neutral or oppositional"). While Gabriel agrees with Wilkins that story sharing organizations are better places to work, he believes that state is sometimes achieved *despite* the best efforts of those in charge.

Says Gabriel (again in *Storytelling in Organizations*):

> We shall not be surprised if some of the richest narratives and 'strongest' cultures are found not in 'excellent companies' but in oppressive, exploitative, no-nonsense organizations. In such organizations, jokes, stories, and gossip are indispensable mechanisms of psychological survival. Having a laugh at the expense of an arrogant manager or an awkward customer is a standard way of defeating boredom, generating solidarity, and restoring justice, albeit in a symbolic way. ... Culture (including that part of culture that is expressed through stories) does not stand in a mechanical relation to these conditions [of hegemonic or egalitarian infrastructures], but, in different ways, it expresses them, opposes them, justifies them, and seeks to offer consolations and compensations for them.

What I think Gabriel is saying to Wilkins is that a strong story sharing culture does not magically create fairness and universally shared values. Instead, a strong story sharing culture is *resilient* in the face of attempts to simplify its true nature, as a group of *people* with needs and ideas of their own, into something that can be easily controlled. Stories keep an organization or community *alive*—in all the messy, unpredictable, unmanageable, amazing ways *people* can be alive.

This all sounds very pat, however. The scientist in me hates it when people trot out thirty-year-old never-validated results to "prove" some truth "we all know." *Does* greater story sharing lead to greater satisfaction and resilience? I'm not sure. I can't find Wilkins' original research paper (his doctoral dissertation), which might tell me how many stories he collected and how. So if you think this is flimsy evidence for such a claim, you'll find me in agreement. Also, correlation is not causation; maybe it works the other way around. Maybe if you live or work in a community or organization that's a better place to be (for lots of reasons), you're more likely to share stories. It's hard to say.

Here's something I *do* know. In the scores of story projects I've worked on, it has become a standard experience to see ordinary people getting excited about the potential for sharing more stories in their communities and organizations. If people want something, it must be something they see as worth having; so it must be something they believe will make their community or organization a better place to live and work. That's the best evidence I can give you.

But don't believe what *I* say either. Find out what things are like in *your* community or organization. (In the next section I give you an assessment test so you can do just that.)

Right now you might be saying to yourself: *If all groups of people share stories, even when they are oppressed and controlled, maybe story sharing isn't something that needs fixing. Maybe it's fine the way it is. Why do I need to pay attention to this? Why should I learn about it?*

That's a valid question. My answer is to paraphrase George Orwell in *Animal Farm*. Now that I've said that all communities and organizations share stories, I'll change that to: *All communities and organizations share stories, but some share more than others.*

Gabriel starts out his book *Storytelling in Organizations* by saying:

> The argument that will emerge through the pages of this book is that storytelling is not dead in most organizations. Organizations do possess a living folklore, though this is not equally dense or equally vibrant in all of them.

Notice how Gabriel doesn't say that most organizations have dense and vibrant storytelling traditions. He says storytelling is "not dead." This means he must face or expect a perception among his readers that storytelling *is* dead in organizations (and maybe in communities too). My own experience in helping people share stories during projects has convinced me that in the majority of communities and organizations today people have an unmet hunger for greater story sharing. Your community or organization might be the exception. Maybe you already share stories as fully and vibrantly as you need to. But if you aren't sure about that, read on.

ASSESSING STORY SHARING

In this section I've written up a little test you can use to assess the strength and vitality of story sharing in your own community or organization.

Here's how to use the test. First, read over the test below, so you know what questions you are looking to answer.

Next, spend some time listening to people talk in regular conversations at various places in your community or organization. Sit in a café or lunchroom; walk around in the hallways of the town hall or lobby; hang around the edges of community events where people are coming and going. Also see if you can sit in on some gatherings where people are working together on things: meetings, conferences, volunteer sessions, and so on. Listen to the stories people tell. Collect as many contextual details as you can about each story: who told it, when, where, how; how the audience responded; any negotiations between storyteller and audience; any evaluative comments; laughter, silence, scorn; and so on.

When you reach the point of saturation, that is, when what you hear becomes familiar and predictable, answer the questions in the test. After you've done that, you can calculate your score.

If you are working in a team, do the same thing, only do it *separately*. Everyone should go out and listen to stories on their own. Don't talk about the stories you hear, and don't talk about your methods either. Keep all of your assessments independent, so that when you assemble them later their variety will mean something.

The twenty questions of this assessment test are in groups of five, under four headings: freedom, flow, knowledge, and unity.

Narrative freedom: Are people free to tell stories?

A lack of narrative freedom means that people want to tell stories but can't. That doesn't necessarily mean the iron hand of authority is pressing them down; it could just mean that the culture itself is repressive or tight-lipped and prevents people from recounting their experiences freely. In any case, a lack of freedom to tell stories puts a damper on all the things story sharing can do for a community or organization.

1. Counter-stories

As you listened to people talk, how often did you hear a person respond to a story with another story that countered it in some way?

 a. Never. I never saw that.

 b. I saw it happen a few times.

 c. It happened sometimes, but not often.

 d. Most of the stories I heard either *had* counter-stories or *were* counter-stories.

 e. I'm not sure.

2. Authority

When someone who was obviously in authority was telling stories, how much time and attention did they get?

 a. Everyone practically took notes.

 b. People sat silently and listened.

 c. People were respectful, but *nobody* could derail the conversation for very long.

 d. I can't tell the difference between those storytellings and the others.

 e. I'm not sure.

3. Mistakes

How many times did you hear people tell stories about mistakes?

 a. Not even once.

 b. I heard a few.

 c. They came up now and then, but not often.

 d. I heard *lots* of mistake stories.

 e. I'm not sure.

4. Silencing

When somebody started telling a story and another person stopped them, *how* did they stop them? What sort of thing did they say?

 a. A warning, like "You could get in trouble for telling a story like that."

 b. A caution, like "I think it would be better if you stopped talking now."

 c. A request, like "Can we please not talk about that right now?"

 d. A joke or mild insult, like "Oh, they don't want to hear about that old thing."

 e. I'm not sure.

5. Conflict

When somebody was telling a story and another person disagreed with the storyteller, *how* did they disagree? What sort of thing did they say? (See Figure 5.5 on the next page for an illustration.)

 a. A demand, like "Nobody listen. This didn't happen. Let's leave."

 b. A criticism, like "You should get your facts straight before you go around saying things like that."

 c. A comment, like "That's not what *I* heard."

 d. A joke or mild insult, like "Yeah, right, you're full of it."

 e. I'm not sure.

Narrative flow: Do people tell stories?

This assessment category is about whether people actually do tell stories when they are given the chance. It's about whether story sharing is a comfortable and familiar habit, a part of daily life people participate in without even noticing.

Figure 5.5. In a healthy story sharing culture, stories about conflicts are not avoided but are surrounded with other stories. (Note how, in the healthier example below, the original story is quickly linked to three additional stories.)

6. Remindings

When you listened to people telling stories, did you ever hear people say "that reminds me of the time" and then tell a story in response? If they did, how many stories did you see getting told in a row?

a. Nobody *ever* responded to a story by telling a story.

b. I saw it happen several times.

c. Quite often people swapped two or three stories before the exchange petered out.

d. In just about every conversation, people kept swapping stories until the conversation ended or the subject of discussion changed.

e. I'm not sure.

7. Retellings

How often did you hear people pass on stories they heard from other people? What proportion of stories were told second-hand or third-hand?

a. I never heard a story that was not first-hand.

b. I heard second-hand stories a few times, but it was pretty rare.

c. About a tenth of the stories were second-hand or third-hand.

d. A quarter to half of the stories I heard were second-hand or third-hand.

e. I'm not sure.

8. Folklore

In his book *Storytelling in Organizations*, Yiannis Gabriel says:

> We shall refer to organizational folklore as a range of cultural practices and texts that fulfill three conditions: first, they are

richly symbolic; secondly, they are not manufactured or legislated, but emerge spontaneously through informal interactions among participants; and, thirdly, they are not one-offs, but become part of traditions, emulated, reproduced, and re-enacted. Stories, proverbs, generalizations, nicknames, puns, jokes, rituals, slang, graffiti, cartoons, material objects of use or display, codes, gestures, uses of physical space, body language are among the many ingredients of organizational folklore.

Were the stories you heard richly symbolic? Were they informally spontaneous? Were they traditionally re-enacted? In other words, how much evidence did you find for narrative folklore in your community or organization?

a. None. Nothing.

b. Little and weak, but real.

c. I definitely saw some elements that could be described as folklore. I wouldn't call it strong, but it was there.

d. Based on this definition, I believe I can confidently describe what I saw as obvious, strong, and resilient narrative folklore.

e. I'm not sure.

9. Story types

Gabriel also lists five story types or "poetic modes" that describe stories he heard across five organizations: the comic story (about a fool), the tragic story (about an undeserving victim), the epic story (about a hero), the romantic story (about love or nostalgia), and the funny story (about a trickster or wizard). As you listened to people tell stories in your community or organization, do you recall hearing any stories that resembled these types?

a. I don't recall any stories that match those descriptions.

b. I think I could list a few stories for one or two of those types.

c. I'd say I could find one story for each type, if I look through my notes.

d. I can give you three examples of each of those right now.

e. I'm not sure.

10. Sensemaking

In your observations of people, you must have seen some people making *decisions* together, even if it was only about where to have lunch. Did you ever see people share stories as they prepared to make decisions?

a. No. I never saw that happen.

b. I saw one or two decisions in which stories were told.

c. I saw this happen occasionally, but not often.

d. When I saw people make a decision, they almost always told a few stories on the way to making it.

e. I'm not sure.

Narrative knowledge: Do people know how to tell stories?

This assessment category looks at your community or organization's collective knowledge about the way story sharing works in groups of people: how a story starts and ends, when stories can and can't be told, how to reframe a story to match an audience's expectations, and so on.

11. Real stories

In Chapter Two, I said that the best stories for story work are recountings of events based on emotional experiences from particular perspectives (see page 22). Think about how often the stories you heard met those criteria. Did people talk about things that happened, in their experiences, from their perspectives, and with emotion? Or did they tell half-stories, describing situations, scenarios, or references?

a. I don't think I heard a single story that was a recounting of events based on emotional experience from a perspective.

b. I'd say about a quarter of the stories I heard had all of those qualities.

c. Maybe about half the stories met the definition fully.

Figure 5.6. In a healthy story sharing culture, storytelling audiences participate in negotiating the telling and interpretation of stories. In an unhealthy story sharing culture, people might condemn the story or storyteller in their minds, but they do not actively negotiate.

d. Nearly every story I heard was a recounting of events based on emotional experience from a perspective.

e. I'm not sure.

12. Negotiation

Look over the "Stories in conversation" section again (page 35). Then think about the stories you heard people tell in your community or organization. How lively were the negotiations you heard going on between storytellers and audiences? Were there reframings and adjustments? Did audiences participate in making these adjustments? (See Figure 5.6 for an illustration.)

a. I never saw *any* kind of negotiation take place between storyteller and audience.

b. I saw a bit of negotiation a few times, but overall it was rare.

c. People did negotiate over how stories should be told, but it was mild enough that I would never have noticed it happening if I hadn't read that section of the book.

d. I heard no story told without ample and obvious negotiation by storyteller and audience.

e. I'm not sure.

13. Co-telling

Did you ever see two or more people tell a story together, that is, share in its telling by contributing different parts or aspects to the story?

a. No, I never saw that.

b. I saw it happen a few times, but that was all.

c. I'd say a tenth to a quarter of the stories were told in that way.

d. At least half of the stories I heard were told by more than one person.

e. I'm not sure.

14. Blunders

How many times did you hear story choice blunders, in which someone started to tell the wrong story to the wrong people at the wrong time, and things got all awkward?

a. Quite a few of the storytellings I observed turned out awkwardly because they were told in front of the wrong person or at the wrong time. People didn't seem to know when to tell about what and to whom.

b. I saw this happen often enough to amount to a pattern, if a weak one.

c. I saw it happen once or twice, but it was usually a person who was new or distracted or tired or something. It wasn't *systemic* or anything.

d. I never saw that happen, not even once.

e. I'm not sure.

15. Accounting

Go back to the section of Chapter Three called "Stories are Sounding Devices" (page 27) and find the quote from Alasdair MacIntyre about storytelling and accountability (it starts out, "The other aspect of narrative selfhood is correlative...").

Did *you* see people account for their actions and choices by telling each other stories? Did you ever, for example, see someone tell a story whose message was essentially that the storyteller was a reasonable person who could be trusted? Or that someone else could or couldn't be trusted?

a. No, I can't say that I *ever* saw anyone tell a story whose goal was to account for their actions or choices.

b. I did see this happen once or twice.

c. I'd say a quarter of the stories I heard had something to do with accounting for actions or choices.

d. At least half of the stories I heard could be described as the "giving of accounts" of actions or choices.

e. I'm not sure.

Narrative unity: Do people tell the same stories?

The last assessment category has to do with whether stories are shared within the community or organization.

16. Common stories

If you were to create a list of stories that any randomly chosen member of your community or organization could be expected to know, stories that are common knowledge, how easy would your task be? (See Figure 5.7 on the next page for an illustration.)

a. I couldn't possibly make such a list, because there isn't one.

b. Let me look through my notes. There might be a few stories like that.

c. I'd have to double-check, but I think I could come up with some common stories.

d. I can tell you the stories right now.

e. I'm not sure.

17. Sacred stories

Now let's pretend you are going to make another list, of stories any member would know and consider important to understanding the community or organization. Stephen Crites calls these *sacred* stories, and says of them (in his chapter "The Narrative Quality of Experience" in *Memory, Identity, Community*):

Such stories, and the symbolic worlds they project, are not like monuments that men behold, but like dwelling places. People live in them. ... People do not sit down on a cool afternoon and think themselves up a sacred story. They awaken to a sacred story, and their most significant mundane [everyday] stories are told in the effort, never fully successful, to articulate it. ... [A]ll a people's mundane stories are implicit in its sacred story, and every mundane story takes soundings in the sacred story.

Figure 5.7. In a healthy story sharing culture, most people can think of at least a few stories that are well known within the community or organization.

Based on what you've heard, how easy would it be to make a list of your community's or organization's sacred stories?

a. I don't think we have any sacred stories.

b. I could probably find one or two, if I look carefully through what I've written down.

c. Definitely there have been some stories I remember, but I'd have to skim through what I've written to be sure.

d. I can tell you those stories right now.

e. I'm not sure.

18. Condensed stories

One more time I'm going to ask you to (pretend to) make a list of commonly known stories. This time it's of compressed, condensed stories, in the form of proverbs and references, things people say that expand out to form detailed stories in the minds of their audience members. How easy would it be to make a list like that?

a. I've got nothing.

b. I may have heard a few of those. Let me check.

c. Yes, some spring to mind. I'll see if they were repeated often enough to be considered common.

d. Are you ready? Here they are.

e. I'm not sure.

19. Intermingled stories

Here's Alasdair MacIntyre again, this time talking about intermingling:

> . . . what the agent is able to do and say intelligibly as an actor is deeply affected by the fact that we are never more (and sometimes less) than the co-authors of our own narratives. Only in fantasy do we live what story we please. In life, as both Aristotle and Engles noted, we are always under certain constraints. We enter upon a stage which we did not design and we find ourselves part of an action that was not of our making. Each of us

being a main character in his own drama plays subordinate parts in the dramas of others, and each drama constrains the others. In my drama, perhaps, I am Hamlet or Iago or at least the swineherd who may yet become a prince, but to you I am only A Gentleman or at best Second Murderer, while you are my Polonius or my Gravedigger, but your own hero. Each of our dramas exerts constraints on each other's, making the whole different from the parts, but still dramatic. . . . I can only answer the question "What am I to do?" if I can answer the prior question "Of what story or stories do I find myself a part?"

Did *you* hear stories in which you saw evidence of people playing subordinate parts in the dramas of others? Did you see people's dramas constrain the dramas of others? Were the stories people told intermingled?

    a. I have no idea what MacIntyre was talking about. The stories I heard were not connected to each other in any way.

    b. I can see where MacIntyre is coming from, but I didn't see much intermingling. Maybe a few times.

    c. Fifty-fifty. Some of the stories I heard were connected, but a lot weren't.

    d. MacIntyre describes what I heard perfectly. I don't think I *ever* heard a story that was not intermingled with other stories around it.

    e. I'm not sure.

20. Storytelling culture

Go back and reread the section in this chapter about Shirley Brice Heath's groundbreaking study of local differences in story sharing (page 69).

Based on what you have heard in *your* community or organization, how easily could you write a description of its local storytelling culture like Brice Heath did for Trackton and Roadville?

    a. I couldn't begin to describe our "local storytelling culture" because there isn't one.

    b. I could write a paragraph or two about some things I've seen, but I haven't really seen anything coherent enough to describe in depth.

    c. Yes, I could write something. It would be only a few pages long, but I could describe the way we generally share stories.

    d. I could write a book on our local storytelling culture, *and* it would be a bestseller.

    e. I'm not sure.

Scoring your test results

After you've answered all of these questions, you can calculate your story-sharing score. But first, count how many "e" answers you entered. If you have more than five (out of twenty), go back and listen to some more stories, then reconsider the questions you answered "I'm not sure." Keep doing that until you have fewer than five questions with that answer. If you are working in a group, keep sending people out again until everyone has at least fifteen not-unsure answers.

But remember, you should be answering these questions based on your considered opinion. This is not a scientific measurement, and you can't prove anything by doing it. It's just an aid to thought. So before you go out and spend hours more listening to stories, look to see if you have an intuitive response to each question. That's all you need.

Once you have fewer than five "e" answers, start adding up numbers. All of the answer sets go from bad to good. For every "a" answer, give yourself a zero; for every "b" answer give yourself a one; for every "c" answer two; for every "d" answer three. (Any remaining "e" answers should also get a zero.) The highest possible score should be sixty. If your score comes in from zero to twenty, you have next to no story sharing culture in your community or organization. If your score is between twenty and forty, you have a story sharing culture, but it needs some work. If your score is between forty and sixty, you have a strong and vital story sharing culture (but it could always be stronger!).

If you are working as a team, you can either use your variety to choose the most popular answers to each question and create one composite score, or you can calculate each person's score separately and compare them. Or try it both ways and see what you find. It might be interesting to find out which questions show the most variation in opinion.

In addition to your total score, you can calculate scores for each of the four areas of the test (freedom, flow, knowledge, unity), then get out your markers and create some diagrams that lay out in which areas investment in story sharing might pay off best in your community or organization.

Going deeper

I've given you a quick test you can apply to your observations of story sharing in your community or organization. If you want to explore more deeply into the assessment of story sharing knowledge and skills, take a look at Terrence Garguilo's book *The Strategic Use of Stories in Organizational Communication and Learning*. The last eighty pages of the book present a comprehensive guide to improving story sharing skills at the individual level.

Terrence's "Competency Map" approach helps you assess and improve your skills in story eliciting, listening, observing, indexing, synthesizing, reflecting, selecting, telling, and modeling. You could use *The Strategic Use of Stories* to train yourself and others in how to share stories more effectively. That's not the same thing as making your community or organization a more story-sharing place; but spreading more awareness and skills about story sharing can only be a good thing.

Taking action

The last chapter of this book (Narrative Return) has a section, called "Ideas for supporting ongoing story sharing," that explains how you as a story worker can help your community or organization create and preserve a strong, vital culture of story sharing (see page 565). I put that section in the last chapter instead of here because supporting ongoing story sharing depends on more than just a little knowledge about how stories work in practice. I want you to learn more about how to work with stories, and even try out some techniques, before you take on such a complex task. But if you want to read about how you can improve the story sharing in your community or organization right now, jump ahead to page 565.

SUMMARY

People share stories in communities and organizations to negotiate a social contract, create shared meaning, meet challenges together, and play with possibility. All communities and organizations share stories, but some share more than others. Those in which people share more stories are more likely to be considered good places to live and work.

To consider whether people in your community or organization have a strong and vibrant story sharing tradition, ask yourself these questions: Are people *free* to share stories? Do they *habitually* share stories? Do they know *how* to share stories safely and with respect? Do they share a *common pool* of stories?

QUESTIONS

At the start of this chapter I listed four functions of story sharing in communities and organizations (negotiating a social contract, creating shared meaning, meeting challenges, playing with possibility). How do these functions apply to *your* community or organization? If you were to recall, say, three stories you heard in the past month, how would each of those stories negotiate a social contract? How would they create shared meaning? How would they meet challenges? How would they play with possibility? Are any of my functions missing from any of your stories? Do your stories suggest other functions I have not listed?

Would you rather live in Trackton or Roadville? Which story sharing culture is most similar to your own? Can you guess why? Do you know anyone who lives in a community similar to the one you *don't* belong to? What happens when people from the two communities come together?

Let's assume that you did this chapter's assessment test about story sharing in your community or organization. What in your test results surprised you? Which parts present challenges and which present opportunities? What can you do about the challenges? How can you build on the opportunities? What sorts of projects do your test results inspire you to carry out?

ACTIVITIES

In this chapter I listed four functions of story sharing in communities and organizations (negotiating a social contract, creating shared meaning, meeting challenges, playing with possibility). Think of one more. Write a paragraph or two describing the function. Include some example stories from your own experience that show how your addition to the list works.

Did you do the assessment test in this chapter for your community or organization? If not, do it now (or at least *think* about doing it). What did you find out?

Find another community or organization you belong to, and do the assessment test for it. What can you learn by comparing the responses to each question in the assessment test?

Get a copy of Terrence Garguilo's *The Strategic Use of Stories in Organizational Communication and Learning,* and use his competency map to assess your skills in story work (and the skills of others) more deeply.

Study story sharing in your community or organization like Shirley Brice Heath did for Trackton and Roadville. Write up a page or two describing how people share stories, complete with examples. Then do the same thing for another community or organization you belong to. Compare the two story sharing cultures. What have you learned?

Get a copy of Brice Heath's book *Ways with Words*—or her recent update to the original study, *Words at Work and Play*—and study your community or organization's story sharing culture (and some others) even more deeply based on what you read there.

Part II

A Guide to Participatory Narrative Inquiry

The second part of this book is a nuts-and-bolts guide to participatory narrative inquiry (PNI), an approach to working with stories for organizational and community change.

Chapter Six (Introducing Participatory Narrative Inquiry, on page 85) defines the PNI approach: its origins, connections, and principles.

Chapter Seven (Project Planning, on page 93) covers the process of making decisions before and as your PNI project gets started.

Chapter Eight (Story Collection, on page 109) helps you encourage people to tell stories, listen to the stories people tell, and ask people questions about their stories.

Chapter Nine (Group Exercises for Story Collection, on page 187) explains how to use three structured exercises to help groups tell stories together.

Chapter Ten (Narrative Catalysis, on page 215) shows you how, by using mixed-methods data analysis, you can create "food for thought" that helps people in your community or organization discover useful new insights.

Chapter Eleven (Narrative Sensemaking, on page 299) takes you through conducting a sensemaking session where members of your community or organization work with the stories you collected (and possibly the catalytic material you prepared) as they explore the project's topic together.

Chapter Twelve (Group Exercises for Narrative Sensemaking, on page 385) explains how to use five structured exercises to help groups make sense of collected stories together.

Chapter Thirteen (Narrative Intervention, on page 473) gives you ideas for intervening in the flow of stories in your community or organization.

Chapter Fourteen (Narrative Return, on page 543) guides you through the process of helping stories return to your community or organization as your project winds down.

Chapter Six

Introducing Participatory Narrative Inquiry

This chapter briefly defines participatory narrative inquiry (PNI) and summarizes its essential features and principles.

PNI Definitions

As you can tell from the primary title of this book, I like the phrase "working with stories." To me it connotes both shaping nouns like clay or wood and cooperating with verbs like people or animals or plants (which are not static objects but dynamic phenomena). Because stories are both nouns and verbs, the phrase works in both senses.

Still, over time I have found that many people become confused when they read the phrase "working with stories." Some think it has something to do with fiction or screenwriting; some think it means using stories to sell products; some think it means using stories to understand research subjects. To address these issues, I felt I needed a more precise name for the approach described in the book. I decided to call it participatory narrative inquiry, or PNI.

Here is a working definition of PNI we can use. Participatory narrative inquiry is an approach in which groups of people participate in gathering and working with raw stories of personal experience in order to make sense of complex situations for better decision making. PNI focuses on the profound consideration of values, beliefs, feelings, and perspectives through the recounting and interpretation of lived experience. Elements of fact, truth, evidence, opinion, argument, and proof may be used as material for sensemaking in PNI, but they are always used *from* a perspective and to *gain* perspective. This focus defines, shapes, and limits the approach.

Here is the recipe for building PNI:

1. Begin by mixing together large portions of narrative inquiry and participatory action research.
2. When this mixture stabilizes, add smaller yet substantial amounts of mixed-methods research and oral history.
3. Add, as desired and useful, flavorings drawn from cultural anthropology, folklore studies, narrative therapy, participatory theatre, complexity theory, and decision support.

Put this all together, stir well, bake, and taste. Repeat many times, and you will have the approach described in this book (see Figure 6.1 on the following page). So PNI is not so much a single idea as it is a way of putting together ideas into a package that works.

More than anything else, PNI is a *practical* method. It grew over the course of more than eighty real projects with real participants, real needs, real constraints, and real collaborators. What didn't work was dropped and what worked stayed in. I believe the ideas in PNI will also work for you.

I did not coin the term "participatory narrative inquiry," by the way. It has been in use for decades to denote the general addition of participation to narrative inquiry. For the most part, my use of the term agrees with prior usage. (The section of *More Work with Stories* called "PNI In Context" cites prior uses of the term. That section also explains in more detail how each of the fields in my PNI "recipe" contributes to and overlaps with PNI.)

PNI Elements

Figure 6.2 on page 87 illustrates the three basic elements of PNI.

Figure 6.1. These are the ingredients from which participatory narrative inquiry is made.

Narrative

The most essential part of PNI is narrative. PNI is founded on the use of *raw stories of personal experience*. In this respect it differs from other sensemaking and decision-support approaches that *sometimes* incorporate narrative but do not *require* it. Why are stories essential to PNI? Because without them its ability to address its core goals would be reduced.

PNI is not a superior method for all decision support projects, only those for which the profound consideration of *values, beliefs, feelings, and perspectives* is required. There are many situations in which facts, opinions, arguments, evidence, and proof are of superior utility. For example, if you want to know which of two treatment protocols has a greater effect on the reduction of chronic inflammation, PNI will not give you the result you need. However, if you want to understand the influences of societal taboos and stigmas when supporting patients with various treatment protocols, PNI is likely to give you a more deeply meaningful result than direct questioning.

Participation

Unlike its sibling narrative inquiry, *PNI invites its participants to work with their own stories.* Participation in PNI can vary in degree from simply answering questions about stories to participating in structured group sensemaking activities where groups of participants ponder issues and problems.

In general, a person who facilitates a PNI project does not tell or interpret or change or even select stories. All of these things are done only by *those in the group of interest.* What a PNI facilitator does is *help the stories get to where they need to go* to help the community achieve a goal. To do this a PNI facilitator might collect stories, ask questions about them, and help people look at, think about, and talk about the stories, the answers, and the patterns they form. But a PNI facilitator never decides for the community, by themselves, what stories *mean.*

Inquiry

In every PNI project *somebody finds out something about something*. They might better understand a conflict, or their own feelings, or the nuances of a topic, or how things got to be the way they are, or how things could improve,

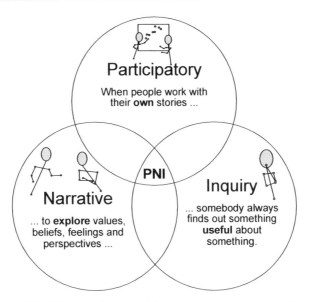

Figure 6.2. PNI depends on participation, stories, and exploration.

or any number of things. But the approach is never just about connecting or teaching or persuading people with stories. Even when a PNI project makes something happen, it happens because somebody found a new way to look at something. Including the inquiry word also makes it clear that the approach is not about telling stories (at least not all by itself). Nor is it about listening simply for the sake of listening. There is always somewhere new to get to, something to achieve.

PNI PHASES

A PNI project involves three *essential phases,* as follows (see Figure 6.3 on the following page).

Collection. Community members tell stories around a topic of concern, and those stories are collected in some way. The nature of collection can vary widely, from twenty stories gathered and used in an hour-long workshop to a thousand stories gathered over a year and used for many years afterward. But in one way or another, *all PNI projects start with stories.* Whenever possible, people interpret their own stories by answering questions like "Would you say this experience is common or rare?" and "Would you tell this story to your neighbor?" (Even better, people can interpret stories told by others, so that each story becomes surrounded by a cloud of interpretations from many perspec-

tives.) The questions used should pertain to the community and to the goals of the project.

Sensemaking. Some or all community members (and sometimes interested others) participate in group activities in which they negotiate meaning as they construct larger stories, possibly in the form of artifacts such as timelines, landscapes, and story elements. Sensemaking may take place on the same day as story collection or months later; it may involve few or many people; it may take place in person or through some form of mediated contact; and it may be strongly or weakly structured and facilitated. But in some way, *all PNI projects involve somebody making some use of gathered stories to better understand some situation or issue.*

Return. What has been gathered and produced in the first two phases is returned to the community and enters into collective discourse. Such a return may include formal reports and communications, and it may involve a wide or narrow distribution of collected stories. But it is also likely to include informal story exchanges about people's experiences surrounding the project. These informal storytellings may be more influential than the formal outputs, for better or worse, and they merit attention on their own terms. *All PNI projects involve someone telling stories they would not have told before the project took place.* Whether this is a

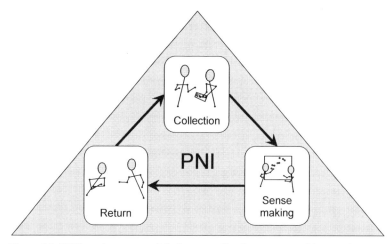

Figure 6.3. PNI has three essential phases: collection, sensemaking, and return.

stated goal of the project or not, it always happens, because the project is itself a story that takes place in the community. The return phase is one project planners might be unprepared for and might prefer to sweep under the rug; but it is futile to pretend storytellers and audiences are unaffected by storytelling. In fact, conscious attention to the return phase is a mark of projects that have lasting positive impacts.

The essential phases of PNI are egalitarian and multivocal in nature. They involve little top-down control, and in each phase the unique perspective of each participant is heard and included without coercion or artificial consensus. In the ideal PNI project all members of the community join in all essential phases, though in some projects some members may participate more in some phases than others. This is sometimes due to power differences, but not always or completely. Rarely is the entire community able, willing, and motivated to participate in every phase of the process. For example, often many people will participate in the collection and return of stories, but fewer will be able or willing to invest the time required to participate in sensemaking. Trust in representation is a critical element when everyone cannot participate—whatever the reason.

A PNI project can optionally include up to three *supporting phases*, as shown in Figure 6.4 on the next page.

Planning. Collection is sometimes preceded by a phase in which elements such as questions, group sessions, and exercises are chosen and/or designed. For example, a small pilot project might be used to test questions and methods before the larger project takes place. Planning serves to promote the success of the overall project, not to constrict or censor what is collected and said. Note that planning may be influenced by the return phases of previous projects.

Catalysis. Sensemaking can be preceded by a phase in which mixed-methods analysis is used to discover patterns in collected stories and interpretations.

I call this step catalysis (as opposed to analysis) because catalysis speeds up chemical reactions and catabolic processes break down molecules (while anabolic processes build them up). Thus catalysis serves to *enhance* sensemaking by asking questions, not avoid it by providing answers.

The catalytic material produced (for example, annotated images describing patterns across stories) is used as *food for thought* in the sensemaking process, but never as conclusive evidence or proof. To ensure that the material is catalytic rather than analytic, precautions are taken to *separate statements* (into observations, interpretations, and ideas) and *provide provoking perspectives* that generate questions rather than supply answers.

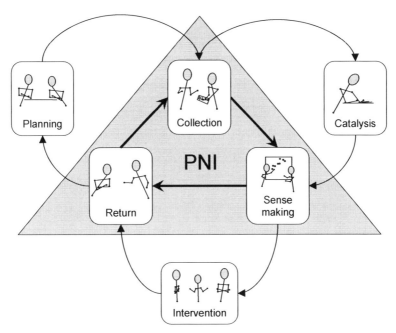

Figure 6.4. PNI has three optional phases: planning (before collection), catalysis (before sensemaking) and intervention (before return).

Intervention. The return phase is sometimes preceded by an intervention phase in which action is taken based on sensemaking. Some examples of narrative interventions are story-sharing spaces, narrative orientations, narrative mentoring networks, and participatory theatre events. (You can find out more about these and other interventions in the Intervention chapter on page 473.) Intervention serves to enhance the return of stories to the community, not to control or arrest it. Ideally, interventions grounded in effective narrative sensemaking produce positive change, sparking a spiral of storytelling that leads naturally into future projects.

The supporting phases of PNI *can* be carried out by all community members, but in practice—and much more so than in the essential phases—they are usually carried out by limited numbers of people with the time, patience, motivation, expertise, and/or authority to do the concentrated and sometimes difficult work required. However, the supporting phases are not levers that control the project, as anyone who seizes them for that purpose will find out. Since the essential phases are participatory and egalitarian in nature, any attempt to

constrict or control them through the supporting phases will cause the entire project to fail. Outsiders in particular cannot participate in or control the essential triangle of PNI (without causing some damage) but must maintain a purely supportive role in those areas.

PNI PRINCIPLES

These are some principles that help to define what PNI is and isn't. Where did they come from? They emerged. I kept finding myself saying them to people over and over, and I looked at that and thought, hmmm, those things must be important. There is much more to say about what defines PNI in the companion volume to this book (*More Work with Stories*), but this will get you started.

It's all about decisions. The primary goal of PNI is decision support augmented by sensemaking improved by narrative discourse. PNI does not focus on the goals of investigation, preservation, or communication, though those things do often happen in PNI projects. All of the ideas and methods in PNI focus on helping people make better decisions together, decisions everyone can live with in peace. Why?

Because it's what the world needs most. (That's what PNI thinks, anyway.)

The play's the thing. Play takes a central role in PNI, for the very serious reason that play creates the most effective decision support. The telling of stories is a form of play in human life, a partial suspension of the rules of the real which helps people resolve problems. PNI expands on this essential function of stories by incorporating play into every element of its activity, from planning projects to collecting stories to helping people make sense of them.

PNI practitioners take on a trickster role in the community or organization they aim to help, to avoid the taint of authority and to increase the benefit of participation. They shift their shapes; they lie; they break the rules; they say what cannot be said; they stand between worlds; but they do all of this play in earnest and with the most constructive purpose. One of the most important elements of learning how to "do PNI" well is learning how to play effectively. (The section of *More Work with Stories* called "PNI Skills" goes into some depth on the trickster role in PNI.)

PNI helps stories get to where they need to go. The most important thing a PNI project does is not to collect stories for safekeeping or tell stories for enlightenment or analyze stories for proof. The most important thing a PNI project does is to help stories get to where they need to go to have a positive impact on the community or organization. This distinguishes PNI from many other forms of narrative work whose goals are to preserve or persuade or study. All of the methods and ideas that make up PNI focus on discovering where stories need to go and helping them get there. Both of these tasks are rarely obvious or simple except in retrospect.

People know their stories. There is no better foundation on which to work with stories than stories combined with what their tellers say about them. No outsider to any community can be fully aware of this foundation. Context can upend content, rendering lies as truth and truth as lies, a fact that makes external interpretation not just futile but dangerously misleading. Therefore the more people work with their own stories the stronger any narrative project will be. PNI casts aside expert interpretation as in-

sufficiently beneficial to participatory decision support, and instead gives a central place to the interpretation of stories by people with the closest possible relationships to the stories told.

Don't mess with the stories. For the goals PNI addresses, true, raw, real stories of personal experience are more useful than stories of fiction. Any attempt to control or change or adapt raw stories will reduce the authenticity and therefore the effectiveness of a PNI project. There is no use helping stories get to where they need to go if they are not the stories that need to be going there. Therefore PNI never alters or "improves" the stories it considers but keeps them in as raw a form as possible, no matter where they are carried and no matter who encounters them.

Don't boil stories down, and don't boil them out; boil them up. This principle says that PNI should never be used to pretend to address an issue by collecting stories, then "boiling them down" to boil out emotion or pain or negativity or unwelcome views. PNI takes the stance that progress can be paradoxical: that the best way to create a positive future is to respect and work with all of the community's or organization's stories. Many of the methods of PNI help people respect and work equally with all the stories they collect, through ritual, juxtaposition, and play.

Stories nest. A common misconception about PNI is that its purpose is to build one common, merged, single-perspective story agreeable to all, as a kind of consensus building. This is not the focus of PNI. Consensus-building has its merits, and methods that build consensus are worthy of respect and attention and use. But PNI does something different: it works in situations where only partial trust is in place and consensus cannot be reached.

Why this focus? Unique among our forms of communication, stories do not force unity but *preserve conflict and contrast at all scales.* This is why many folk tales have other stories nested within them, sometimes several levels deep. The Arab story-of-stories *One Thousand and One Nights* is the most famous example of narrative nesting. Likewise, a story project can contain other story projects. It is because a community's story project can contain—without controlling—the projects of its sub-communities and families that the community may discover valuable insights about its conflicts *and* agreements.

If you do not make PNI your own, you are not doing PNI. PNI is not a dogmatic set of fixed prescriptions. It is a changing, idiosyncratic, connected, diverse, complex, of-its-time-and-place, living body of work. It is not a star; it is a constellation. It belongs to no one; it belongs to everyone. PNI challenges each of its practitioners and participants to add their unique talents and styles to PNI, to make it grow larger than it was before they got to it.

SUMMARY

Participatory narrative inquiry is an approach in which groups of people participate in gathering and working with raw stories of personal experience in order to make sense of complex situations for better decision making. PNI is primarily a marriage of narrative inquiry and participatory action research, though it also incorporates elements of mixed-methods research and oral history, along with some other smaller elements.

The most essential part of PNI is narrative; it is founded on the use of raw stories of personal experience. Unlike narrative inquiry, PNI invites its storytellers to participate in working with their own stories. PNI facilitators do not tell or interpret or change or even select stories; they limit their role to helping stories get to where they need to go to help the community achieve a goal. PNI is also about inquiry: in every PNI project somebody finds out something about something.

A PNI project has three essential phases: collection, when community members tell stories; sensemaking, when community members make sense of collected stories; and return, when stories return to the community. A PNI project can also optionally include three supporting phases: planning, when the project is designed; catalysis, when materials to improve sensemaking are prepared; and intervention, when some action is taken based on sensemaking. Support from outsiders is appropriate in

all phases, but outside *direction* is only appropriate in the optional phases of PNI.

PNI is about serious play for decision support. PNI believes that people are the best authorities on the meanings of their own stories, that outsiders or those in authority should not alter or control stories, and that stories should not be hidden or censored. Finally, PNI belongs to everyone. No one may control it; everyone who uses it should add to it.

QUESTIONS

In each of the components of PNI there is something that, for some people in some contexts, constitutes a barrier. For narrative, people sometimes find it hard to keep sensitive stories raw, preferring to curate them into something cleaner and safer. For participation, people sometimes find it hard to keep participants in the loop, believing they are unqualified to conduct serious research. For inquiry, people sometimes want to collect and use stories, perhaps to persuade, but don't want to address problems that might come up in the stories. Do you think any of these barriers exist in your community or organization? Might keeping stories raw, or keeping participants involved, or creating change, be a problem? If so, what can you do about that?

Conversely, in each of the components of PNI there is something that, for some people in some contexts, constitutes a source of energy. For narrative, sometimes the opportunity to be heard enlivens people who believed no one cared about their experiences. For participation, sometimes the opportunity to be included in sensemaking is empowering to those who feel their "data" has been often "extracted" from them and given to others considered more qualified to work with it. For inquiry, sometimes a new opportunity to address longstanding problems draws out energy people didn't know they had. Do you think any of these sources of energy exist in your community or organization? If so, how can you draw them out and build on them (without erecting barriers)?

What do you think about the last statement in this chapter, the one that says you have to make PNI your own? Does that seem like a positive or negative aspect of PNI to you? (Or both?) If you were to add your unique talent and style to PNI, how would it change? How could you do that?

ACTIVITIES

Take each ingredient listed in the recipe for building PNI (on the first page of this chapter) and (if you don't know about it already) look it up on the internet. Think about how each element influences PNI in general. Now think about your own goals and your own community or organization, and write your own recipe for your own PNI. What works for you?

Reread the section on PNI principles (starting on page 89) and make a list of all the *statements of fact,* like "context can upend content" and "progress can be paradoxical." For each statement in your list, think about how it interacts with your experience. Can you think of situations in which the statement was true and situations in which it was false? If you were to rewrite the section on principles from your unique perspective, how would *you* write it? What does that mean about your own version of PNI?

The three main PNI phases (collection, sensemaking, return) are not artificial contrivances but descriptions of what happens naturally in communities. If you sit watching any group of people who belong to a community or organization talk about something of mutual interest, you can see them going through the three PNI phases. So, when you can watch people discuss the community or organization and its goals, listen and take notes on elements of the conversation you can identify as: story collection (people are trading stories); sensemaking (people are juxtaposing elements of those stories); and return (people are telling different stories after the sensemaking has taken place).

After you have watched a group of people go through the three main PNI phases, think about how you might have added the optional helping phases to the process (planning, catalysis, intervention). What might you have done and said that might have enhanced the conversation? How could you have strengthened the story collection with planning? (Could you have prepared some questions to spur storytelling?) How could you have empowered the sensemak-

ing with catalysis? (Could you have taken notes on common story themes and shared them?) How could you have deepened the return with intervention? (Could you have told a story that related to a realization the group had?)

This one is challenging; but if you like, at another meeting, try a few small experiments in planning story collection, catalyzing sensemaking, and intervening in story return. The helping phases of PNI don't have to be huge projects; they can be simple suggestions or questions added to a discussion. Try a few and see what happens.

Chapter Seven

Project Planning

This chapter takes you through the process of planning a PNI project. It helps you make decisions about what you will do in your project, how and when, and with whom.

A PROJECT TO PLAN A PROJECT

The best planning process for a successful PNI project is a successful PNI project. What does this mean? PNI projects can range in size from something three people do in an hour to something ten thousand people do in ten years. So unless your project is very small, the best way to plan it is to *embed* a smaller project into its planning phase (see Figure 7.1 on the following page).

Such a planning project will most likely involve a small number of people meeting in a room or over the telephone for not more than an hour or two. But just like a larger PNI project, it should include story collection, sensemaking, and return, all focused on the larger project of which it is a part. If you are working alone you can do this alone, but it is best to find someone to help you think about the project even if they won't be able to participate in any other part of it.

Why do I recommend using PNI methods to plan PNI projects? Because I've compared projects planned with PNI methods and projects planned without PNI methods. Using PNI to plan PNI simply works better. Projects soaked in narrative and participation from start to finish result in longer lasting, more deeply rooted, stronger outcomes. Projects that attempt to keep participation and narrative out of the planning process tend to misfire more

often, producing results that fail to meet the hopes of the project planners (usually because they didn't sufficiently explore and understand those hopes from the start).

I often find that people are reluctant to use narrative techniques in the planning phases of narrative projects. They want a cut-and-dried plan without the touchy-feely aspects of emotion and hope. They want the *participants* in the projects they plan to emote, but they want to be saved from exploring their *own* emotions. Watch out for that distancing reaction in yourself. It can destroy well-meant investments in PNI projects. Soak yourself in stories from the start to the end.

PROJECT STORIES

For the collection phase of your project-within-a-project, tell each other stories about your project. Tell your stories as *future histories,* as if your project had already taken place.

Start with scenarios

Start each story with a scenario or situation, like these.

Ask me anything

If you could *ask* any person any question and would be guaranteed to get an honest answer (magically), whom would you ask, about what, and why? Tell a story about what might happen in that circumstance—play out the story. An example story might begin, "I asked my grandfather how he came to this country because I wanted to understand my heritage." Or, "I asked all the customers who have stopped coming here why they left, because I wanted to keep other customers from doing the same thing."

Magic ears

If you could *overhear* anyone talking to anyone at any time and in any place, whom would you want to listen to, where and when, and why? Tell a story of what might happen if you could do that. An example story might begin, "I overheard lots of people making the decision to commit a burglary, because I wanted to find out what motivated them." Or, "I overheard people talking honestly about whether they think I'd make a good mayor, because I wanted to know if I should run."

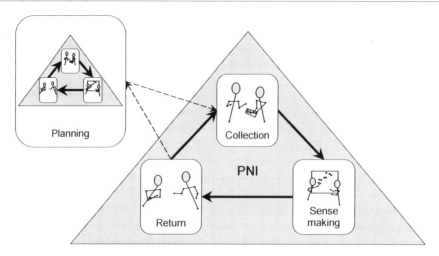

Figure 7.1. The best way to plan a PNI project is to embed a mini-project within the planning phase.

Fly on the wall

If you could *observe* any situation or event, what situation would you want to witness, and why? Tell a story of what might happen if you could do that (see Figure 7.2 on the next page). An example story might begin, "I was a fly on the wall the very first time a person sat behind the wheel of a car, because I wanted to understand their needs." Or, "I was a fly on the wall when people were finding courage they didn't know they had in terrible circumstances, because I wanted to help other people do that too."

Project aspects

Read over the next few sections on project settings: the people you will be asking to tell stories, the topic you will be exploring, and issues of privacy. When anything there reminds you of an aspect of your project—perhaps you recognize that your participants will be busy executives—tell a story about how that aspect shapes the project. An example story might begin, "We knew we wanted to hear stories from both native-born citizens and immigrants." Or, "We knew that asking people about their political history was going to be difficult, because we expected many people to have never thought much about it."

End with outcomes

Next, for each story of possibility, try ending it with each of these three *outcomes*.

Colossal success

Tell the story of your project succeeding far better than you had expected. What happened, and how did it feel? An example story might begin, "Because I asked my grandfather how he came to this country, I understand my own past in ways I had never imagined. This is so exciting!" Or, "I overheard lots of people making the decision to commit a burglary, and now I know how I can prevent other people making the same choice. I am eager to put these insights to good use."

Miserable failure

Tell the story of the project failing miserably. What went wrong, and how did you feel about it? An example story might begin, "I overheard people talking honestly about whether they think I'd make a good mayor. But they *weren't* honest. They were cruel. They judged me unfairly. I don't understand why they *said* those awful things. I can't go on." Or, "I asked all the customers who have stopped coming here why they left, but I didn't really find out anything I didn't know already. The whole project was a total waste of time I can't get back again."

Acceptable outcome

After you've mapped out the extremes of success and failure, tell a story about the project that falls somewhere in the middle, not perfect but not a waste of time either. What would constitute a minimally acceptable outcome for your project? Tell a story about that. An exam-

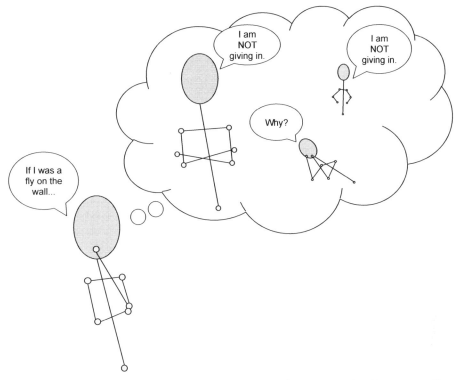

Figure 7.2. Imagine stories about the ways your project might turn out. What if you were a fly on the wall? What might you hear?

ple story might begin, "Our signage could definitely do with some improvement, and I have some ideas I'd like to try." Or, "I knew about all of these issues before we did the project, but this gives me a better idea of how people feel about them. I can use that."

You should be able to churn out a dozen or so of these stories in a group, just chatting for a half-hour or more. Each person should come up with at least two stories, with good, bad, and acceptable endings for each (that's six stories each). Don't stop to critique the stories; just spill them out as fast as you can. Bring out your hopes and fears.

Pilot projects

Now I don't want to confuse you, but you *might* want to extend your project-within-a-project planning one more level down by doing a pilot project. In a pilot project you plan and carry out a small test project that involves more people than your little planning group. You collect a number of stories, possibly in the dozens or even hundreds, and maybe do a small amount

of catalysis before sensemaking. The return of such a pilot project will influence the planning of your larger project.

There are two conditions under which you should do a pilot project: when you are not able to tell the planning stories you need without one, and when the project you are planning is very ambitious. (What's ambitious? Many people, many stories, many questions, many topics, or a great need to answer specific questions fully.) In the first case the project needs more definition to give it a foundation, and in the second case it is a simple matter of a small seed investment enabling a greater return on a larger investment.

A pilot project grounds your plan for the larger project in the community's reality in the same way that the larger project will ground decisions made after it is completed. I have seen pilot projects improve results in several large projects, and definitely recommend them when you intend to conduct large, ambitious, or sensitive story collections. However, if your project or skills are modest, put this aside for a later time.

THE SETTING OF YOUR PROJECT

Here are some elements of your project's setting that will impact its shape: consider them in your project planning.

Knowing your participants

It is possible to diminish or even destroy a project if you don't take the time to get to know your participants before you ask them to tell stories. Your most precious resource is not your time or your computer; it is the time and attention of the people you want to hear from. Take the time to think about your participants so that everyone can benefit from their participation.

Consider these questions about the group you will be asking to tell stories (or about any subgroups, if there are differences).

How much does authority matter to your participants?

Will you be collecting stories from people who expect to be obeyed or ignored? With people who are used to having authority, you may need to prove the worthiness of your project; you may need to approach them in a respectful or even subservient way; and you may need to guide them towards telling stories, which they may disdain as beneath them. For people unused to having authority, or afraid to say something that people in authority will hear, you may need to convince them that you really do want to hear their voices. (See Figure 7.3 on the facing page.)

If you are dealing with a community or organization that is highly stratified, you have to be careful bringing people of different ranks together. It is sometimes better to separate groups of people who will inhibit each other from storytelling.

If authority is not an issue in your group of participants, for example if they are just people who live on the same block, you can ignore these issues. But watch out—there may be authority lurking where you hadn't expected it.

Maybe the older people will expect more deference, or the people who have lived on the block longer, or the people who keep the park clean, and so on. One useful way to find out if there will be authority issues is to ask people who you think might have different levels of authority how they would feel about participating in a group session with people from another group. If they say something like, "What? With them?" then you have an issue to attend to.

What is your participants' level of confidence?

Are they timid or boastful? With people who tend to boast, you have to watch out for lectures and attempts to "set things straight," and you may need to focus their energy on telling real stories of their experiences. With people who are excessively timid, you may need to provide extra measures of privacy and ways to contribute without becoming exposed to possible ridicule.

How busy are your participants?

Some people literally cannot give you five minutes out of their day, and others can give you days and days. If people are very busy, you will probably need to avoid asynchronous methods such as email (they will not respond), and you probably will not be able to get them to commit to a planned group session. You may have to content yourself with a half-hour interview conducted over the phone during their lunch hour (but that still may be very fruitful). When people have plenty of time to give you, you can have the luxury of asking them to go through exercises, answer many questions, and so on (though see the section on cognitive budget, page 134).

What subgroups do you expect to hear from?

Think about how you would categorize the different groups of people being asked to tell stories, in terms of how they will respond to the request. What are the most important distinctions between them?

If you need to juxtapose the views of more than one group of people, you may have difficulty getting the same quantity of stories from all groups. For example, at most organizations it is easier to get stories from employees than it is to get stories from people who use their ser-

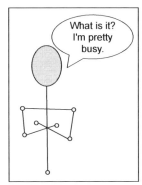

Figure 7.3. Will your participants be bold or timid?

vices (customers, visitors, etc). You may need to spend more time and energy on one group than another in order to make sure the focus and range of your project are supported.

Of the groups you expect to respond, which are the most important to hear from? If the project "worked" best for one group over the others, which of these would be most important to make it work for? Or if for some reason only one group was able to participate, which would be most important to the success of the project?

How much importance do your participants place on succeeding?

You would be amazed at the number of people who try to figure out how to "win" when you ask them to tell stories. They assume there is one right response and try their hardest to succeed. Depending on your participants, this issue can range from trivial to ruinous. For example, some participants refuse to tell a negative story, no matter how horrible their experiences with something have been, because they think they will succeed only by telling about something wonderful. Or they think you want to hear "useful" stories, so they try very hard to tell a story that is obviously elucidating, even if it is not something that happened to them or anyone else. These attempts to "win" can be illuminating (what do they think it means to win?), but when mixed in with real experiences, they can make it harder to find out what is actually happening in a situation.

When you have indications that your participants will be trying too hard to succeed (rather than just talking about their experiences), there are two ways to deal with it. First, you can ex-

plain carefully the point of what you are doing and how they can succeed in helping you—thereby using their drive to succeed in useful ways.

Alternatively, you can disrupt their drive to succeed by asking questions in ways that don't provide an obvious way to succeed. For example, instead of asking "What was the best day you ever had at work?" you might ask "What happened the first time you went out on a client project?" By directing them to a very specific recollection, you can avoid giving them the option of choosing an astoundingly wonderful story with which to win the game.

How concerned are your participants with privacy?

This one is obvious: if you think the group of people you will be asking to tell stories will be more aware of security and privacy issues than most people, you need to pay more attention to your privacy policy. Don't assume; ask, because people might be more wary than you think. Also, if you will be talking to two groups and one is more concerned than the other, you might want to use two different methods to talk to them.

How large of a bag of grievances are your participants carrying?

Is there a lot of pent-up emotion in this group of people? If you expect to release a lot of emotion, you need to pay attention to privacy and make it very clear what the goals of the project are. This will help to prevent people taking out their negative emotions on you instead of releasing them by telling you what they are upset about. Helping people feel that it is safe to talk

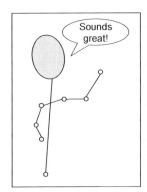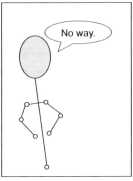

Figure 7.4. Will your participants be welcoming and friendly, or wary and distrusting?

about their negative feelings is important, because probably the goal of your project is to understand those feelings and find out what can be done to ameliorate the situation. If you can't help people surface their negative feelings in a safe and productive way, your efforts will have been in vain.

What are your participants' feelings about you and the project?

Will the people you will be asking to tell stories view you (and possibly the group you represent) as a friendly helper or as a hostile force? (See Figure 7.4.) If you will be viewed as hostile, you can either follow the procedures for the "bag of grievances" situation (strong anonymity, clear goals), or you can remove yourself from the center of the project by having someone *else* elicit stories. For example, asking people to interview each other, or asking outsiders to conduct interviews or run group sessions, can help people open up and talk about you when you are the problem they are upset about.

How seriously will your participants take the project?

I remember once answering a phone call and being asked if Coke or Pepsi was more in line with my lifestyle. I said, "It's sugar water!" (As I recall, the interviewer dryly commented, "Oh, a philosopher.") My point is that some people may not think your project is as important as you think it is. This often happens when the participants are young people. I don't know how many story collections I've seen where one of the dominant answers was "this thing is STUPID!!!" Sigh. (See Figure 7.5 on the facing page.)

When you think your participants will not take the project seriously, either because they think the subject matter is unimportant or because they think nothing anyone does can change anything (even if the subject matter is important), you will need to *sell* the project to people in order to draw them in. You can do this either by impressing people with a sense of purpose or by entertaining and engaging them (or both).

Does your project cover narrative distance?

Do you remember the section called "Stories are packages of meaning" in the "What are stories for" chapter (page 31)? Almost all story projects involve both narrative compression and narrative distance. There is almost always a gap to be bridged, whether it is between doctor and patient, company and customer, or neighbor and neighbor. This is one of the reasons for my caveats about "those in the group of interest" being the best interpreters of stories; others may insert erroneous elements during the necessary narrative expansion.

There are two ways to deal with narrative compression and distance in a story project. One is to *capture more of the context* of a story when it is told. This can be done, to some extent, by asking questions about the story and about the storyteller. Asking contextual questions can be particularly helpful when you are asking people from different groups to learn from each other's experiences.

The second option is to have people tell and work with stories *within the original group,* and make the necessary translations not on individual stories but on the *constructed artifacts* created during group sensemaking. Because of

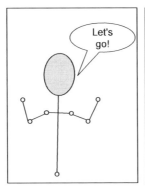

Figure 7.5. Will your participants be energized or disengaged?

the integrative act that produces them, such artifacts constitute a richer and more complex compression that communicates more of the essential meaning than the raw stories themselves.

What do your participants think of stories and storytelling?

People vary on whether they think stories are worth telling. I've found that whenever the group you want to tell stories is made up mostly of analytical, logical, careful thinkers, it can be difficult to convince them that the effort is not just "fluff." That mindset makes it difficult to get people to contribute, both because they aren't used to telling stories and because they don't think their experiences could possibly be helpful.

With this sort of group I've found a mini-course on the power of stories to create change is sometimes necessary. It can come in the form of a three minute talk at the start of an interview or group session or a two-sentence introduction in an email or on a web site. As with the situation of taking the project seriously, you need to sell the project to these people before they will be willing to tell you anything useful.

You also have to be careful if the group you want to tell stories is of the opposite type. If they are people who pride themselves on being great storytellers, they will be more likely to derail the project in another way. They may be more apt to perform or to tell a good story that is exciting but not actually useful.

Summary of participant reactions

We can summarize all of these questions by simply asking one question. Which of these things is most likely to happen when the people you expect to tell stories are asked to do so?

- Will people see the story elicitation as a *test* of their competence, and try to *zero in* on the "right" answer?
- Will people see the story elicitation as a *forum* to air their grievances, and try to *use* the forum to complain?
- Will people see the story elicitation as an *opportunity to help,* and try to *provide* useful information? (And will they try *too* hard to do that?)
- Will people see the story elicitation as an *opportunity to promote* themselves, and try to make *themselves* look good?
- Will people see the story elicitation as a *friendly ear,* and *reminisce* about their experiences and feelings?

You are likely to find a mixture of these tendencies; but you should be able to guess at the mix you will find beforehand. The mix of motivations you expect to find will guide how you approach the people who will be telling stories. If you *can't* guess, spend a little more time listening to people before you finish planning the project. Check within your planning group to see if you agree or disagree on what you expect to find.

Knowing your topic

The topic you want to ask about interacts with the people you will be asking to talk, so it is impossible to consider them separately. These questions pertain to that interaction rather than to the topic alone.

Is the topic sensitive?

Some topics are more private than others, no matter who is talking about them. If you know in advance that the topic is something the group you are talking to will be sensitive about, like things that touch on health, families, religious belief, and so on, you need to take special precautions to make sure privacy is dealt with carefully. You may also need to avoid methods of story collection that involve people talking in front of others.

Is the topic something people will know their own feelings about?

On some emotional issues that may be buried deep beneath the surface, people may need help expressing their feelings. Group sessions and exercises can be helpful with this, as can one-on-one interviews with a real person to provide a listening ear and help people probe deeper into things they hesitantly hint at. In this case a simple survey may not get much useful information because it will not stimulate people to dig deeper.

Is the topic vulnerable to self-promotion?

Some topics may invite people to promote themselves, which can reduce the usefulness of the resulting stories. For example, if you run an open-source programming forum and you ask people to tell stories about their greatest programming success, you are likely to end up with essentially a heap of résumés and advertisements instead of useful stories of real experience. If the topic you want people to talk about has this potential element, you can avoid self-promotion by making the project's goals clear and asking carefully worded questions that ask people to select experiences based on usefulness to the project rather than boast-worthiness (e.g., "Can you remember the worst day you ever spent as a programmer?").

Does the topic cover a long or short time period?

If you want people to talk about things that happened over a long period of time, you will need different techniques than if you are asking about shorter time scales. People remembering long spans of time, such as careers, tend to generalize and may need help selecting *particular* experiences to talk about. Best-worst questions can help with this, as can exercises.

Considering privacy

For some groups and some subjects privacy will not be an issue. But because story projects often delve into deeper and more emotional areas than surveys about favorite fast foods, chances are you will need to think about how you will reassure people that their privacy will be respected.

For most story projects it will be important to think carefully about the privacy policy you will create; to communicate the policy with the people you are asking to contribute; and importantly, not to change your policy after story collection has started. Usually you will be able to summarize your policy in a few sentences, and you should place these sentences in every communication with participants to head off questions and problems. By the way, I've found guidelines for oral history projects to be useful in understanding the issue of privacy in listening to people telling stories. Type "oral history privacy guidelines" into an internet search engine and you'll find lots of good information on this topic.

There are four essential aspects to privacy in a story project: collection, identification, distribution, and review.

What will be collected?

In a typical PNI project you collect stories and answers to questions about them. But it is possible to collect information about stories *without* collecting the stories themselves. This method is especially useful if the topic is so sensitive that you won't be able to get results in any other way. (See Figure 7.6 on the next page.)

There are two ways to collect answers without stories. First, you can ask people to tell stories to an interviewer or group and to answer some questions about them, but record only the answers and not the stories. The stories will exist only in the memory of the interviewer or group, but the answers to the questions will remain, and patterns in these may be helpful to your project.

Figure 7.6. Don't frighten people off by asking for more information than you need. Help them tell the stories you need to hear.

Secondly, you can ask people to think of a story but *not tell it*, then answer some questions about it. This method protects the storyteller completely, since nobody hears the story at all. It is slightly dangerous, however, in that the resulting answers may not be truthful. For example, your participants may not be enthused enough about participating to answer the questions carefully. If you are conducting interviews in person, it may be possible to discern whether people are answering truthfully or not.

Will participants be identified, and if so, how?

There are two ways for stories to be dangerous: dangerous to tell you, and dangerous to tell other people.

If telling the story you need to hear will get people in trouble with *you* (i.e., you are in the government or you are their employer), you have three choices:

1. retain all identifying information (and get much less than the truth);
2. ask a third party to retain identifying information and only allow you access under particular circumstances and with particular safeguards in place to protect privacy (and get some of the truth);
3. retain no identifying information (and get the most truth you can get).

By giving up the ability to collect information useful for one purpose (like finding people who did things) you can often gain the ability to collect information useful for another purpose (like understanding why people do things). For example, if you wanted to know why people stole things from store shelves, you might ask people to tell stories about times they'd stolen and gotten away with it. Obviously if you asked them to give you their name and address you wouldn't get much of value. So you might have to give up the ability to track down admissions of guilt in order to better understand motivations and prevent thefts in the future.

If telling the story you need to hear will get people in trouble with *other* people (i.e., the stories are about people who may not be happy to have the story told), you have more choices:

1. retain and publicize all identifying information (and get much less than the truth);
2. retain but don't publicize identifying information (and get some of the truth);
3. ask a third party to retain identifying information and only allow you access under particular circumstances and with particular safeguards in place to protect privacy (and get more of the truth);
4. retain no identifying information (and get the most truth you can get).

Which of these levels of protection you give people depends on the goals of your project, what you want people to talk about (your focus) and whom you will be asking to speak.

If you don't collect identifying information, how will you make *sure* people will not be able to be identified as individuals? If you invite specific people to group sessions or send emails to specific people, you can't very well forget who they are, but you *can* disassociate any stories they tell and questions they answer from identifying details. For example, if you hold a group session, you can record the session but destroy the tapes after anonymous transcripts have been created. If you elicit responding emails, you can copy the information from the emails, paste it into a text file or spreadsheet, remove any identifying details, and delete the original emails. In this way you can reassure your participants that nothing they say will be connected to their name.

Related to this issue is that of web security. If you are asking for information through email or on a web form, how will you assure people that the email or web communication will not be intercepted? Some online survey taking services offer secure connections, which can help (though people may still have misgivings). Email cannot easily be made secure, so I don't recommend using it if your topic is especially sensitive or your group of people is especially wary. Phone or in-person meetings and interviews avoid this problem.

How much non-identifying (but still personal) information will you need to gather about the people who tell stories? Typically age and gender is important, but you may need to know other things like ethnic background, nationality, and location. It's usually best to keep the list as short as possible. Try making the case for why you need each piece of information, and if you can't make a convincing case, don't collect it. Also, it is usually best to offer a "rather not say" option for all such information. The section of the book on asking questions about stories (page 133) has more advice on privacy and question asking.

To whom will solicited information be distributed?

For some projects you will only need to have a few people read contributed stories and answers to questions. For others you will be distributing collected stories very widely, perhaps to the whole internet. The more widely you will be distributing stories, the more carefully you should review each piece of information you gather and think about who should have access to it. There are many partial solutions; for example, you might know the ages and genders

and nationalities of participants, but you might post only the stories on a community site.

Will participants be able to review and change their information?

Another way to reassure participants, if you plan to incorporate their stories into a resource that is shown to other people, is to allow them to review and change their contributions after the initial storytelling session or interview. Giving people a chance to go back and review their statements, and possibly to remove things they feel, on later reflection, that they should not have revealed (no questions asked), will help them to open up in the first place. Of course, offering such an option may be technologically difficult, and it will require that you hold on to information about individuals (so that you can show them what they said again). But often people who will not be willing to participate under any other conditions will agree to contribute if they have the right to review, edit, and delete entries.

MAKING SENSE OF YOUR PROJECT PLANS

Now that we have considered some aspects of your project's setting, let us return to your project planning meeting.

After you have collected a dozen or more stories about possible project outcomes, and you feel that you have explored the possibilities of the project well, it is time to move into mini-sensemaking.

Look at the chapter called "Group Exercises for Narrative Sensemaking" (page 385) and choose one of the sensemaking exercises to do in miniature. Thinking of the stories you collected, build a timeline or landscape or set of story elements or composite story about the project. Choose whichever exercise appeals most to your sense of the project.

This need not take a long time; an hour and two will suffice, and even half an hour will do in a pinch. All of the exercises in PNI can shrink or grow in scope depending on context and purpose; scale down the exercise (or exercises) you choose to fit your time and needs. As few as five or ten story elements, events on a timeline, issues on a landscape, or plot points in a composite story can help you make sense of your stories about the project's past, present, and future.

Perhaps the idea of choosing a sensemaking exercise seems daunting, or the project you are planning is so small that you don't think it merits the time needed for an exercise. In that case (and *only* in that case, because otherwise I would prefer you choose an exercise that fits your needs) I will make a suggestion. I have found that constructing themes (and themes only) is useful in planning projects when there is little time or attention available in the planning group. You can do this in fifteen minutes, so there is no excuse to avoid doing at least a *little* sensemaking as you plan.

Here is a simple theming technique in a very tiny nutshell.

1. For each story, answer the question, "What is this story *about?*" Simply and quickly, describe what happened in the story. Write things like "everybody passed the buck" or "there was a miscommunication" or "we pulled together to help each other."

2. Once you have at least twenty answers to the question, cluster the answers into *groups*. Put answers closer together when they seem more connected, but don't worry about *why* they seem more connected. Just put like with like.

3. Give each group of answers a short *name* so you can remember it, like "unexpected assets" or "blame" or "missed opportunities."

4. Now *describe* the groups. Give each group a few positive and negative *attributes*, good and bad things about it, opportunities and dangers, like "this is hard but it makes us stronger" or "if we don't get a handle on this it may grow out of control" or "this is how we should treat each other."

5. Finally, take your attributes away from their groups and cluster them together, like with like. Give each cluster of attributes a short name: a *theme*.

The themes you have created in this exercise represent your collective assessment of your community or organization, with respect to the topic of your project, as you find it today; and they represent your hopes and fears for the future. These themes will help you move forward into making decisions about how you will carry out the project.

PNI Planning Questions

As you come out of the mini-sensemaking phase of your project planning, answer these six *PNI planning questions* using what you have built (Figure 7.7 on the following page). If you cannot answer these questions to your satisfaction, you are not done with the sensemaking part of your project planning. Go back and do some more. You will thank yourself later, I promise.

Goals: Why are you doing the project?

A project's goals seem like its most straightforward part, the part least in need of sensemaking. People who start a project know why they are doing it, right? But I've seen more projects fail because of misunderstandings and mismatches in goals than in any other area. Sometimes the people in a project group *think* they all understand the project's goals, when in fact each sees a different project. At other times, people go into projects without becoming fully aware of their *own* reasons for wanting to carry them out. You need to align your visions of the project's goals so that everyone is applying their energy to the same outcome.

Relations: Who are you in the community or organization?

A project's relations are things like: who provides the energy for the project; who tells the stories; who works with them; who hears them; who pays for any services that take part in the project; and who provides the services. Two projects run by different groups can have drastically different outcomes even if they explore the same issues in the same community. It is important to be clear on these relations before the project starts. As you make your plans, consider how the different groups involved will react to them. The sections earlier in this chapter on "Knowing your participants" (page 96) and "Considering privacy" (page 100) will be relevant in thinking about relations.

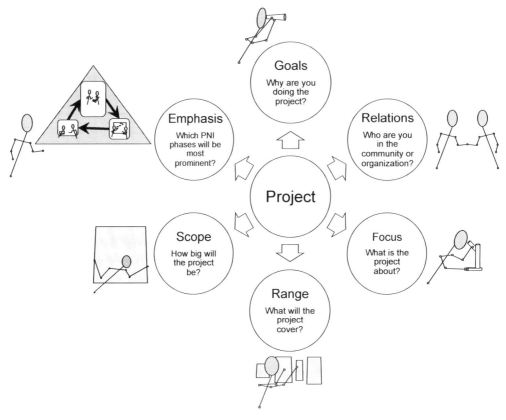

Figure 7.7. To plan your PNI project, think about its goals, relations, focus, range, scope, and emphasis.

Focus: What is the project about?

A project's focus, or center, has a lot to do with its goals; but focus is more like the "what" instead of the "why" of the project.

The focus of a project can include things like:

- a topic (our community's ten year vision)
- a question (what is the range of views about the planned bridge?)
- a decision (should we build a shopping center or a park?)
- a problem (what can we do about science illiteracy?)
- a goal (we would like to improve our services to patients)
- a group of people (our family's story)
- a perspective (how new immigrants see our town)
- a person (stories about our founder)

As you consider focus, consider any materials you have already gathered about the project, such as statements of purpose. Is anything *missing* from your consideration of focus that is in those materials? Why is that? Is it because the issue is not that important, or because it was avoided? If it was avoided, are you sure you want to avoid it? Conversely, is there anything in your materials that didn't come up in your consideration of focus? Why do you think that happened? Should any area of your focus be investigated in greater detail? Are there sub-areas you want to investigate? Or are you trying to cover too many topics? If you have come up with a series of topics, you can rank them and cut off some of the less important ones.

Range: What will the project cover?

All PNI projects cover a range of experience as well as focus on issues, but range is more often overlooked in project planning. The range of experience usually involves juxtaposition, or comparing things side by side.

For example, range might cover things like:

- possibilities (shopping center, park, and bridge)
- groups of people (immigrants and natives)
- perspectives (attract business, protect the environment, preserve the past)
- time frames (views today and views from the turn of the century)
- locations (views from around the county)
- goals (things we'd like to accomplish in the next ten years)

Range is not so much about why you are doing the project but what will make it succeed. For example, you aren't going to be able to find out what your community's ten year vision should be unless you include people from all parts of the community (all ages, all perspectives) and stories from the community's past.

Scope: How big will the project be?

The collection of stories and other information generated by a story project should be *rich in meaning*. That does not necessarily mean it needs to be *large*. There is a tension between the sheer number of stories you collect and how many questions you can ask about each of them (and get meaningful answers). I've seen story sets with fifty stories that were richer in meaning than story sets with five hundred stories in them (but in which either few questions were asked or few meaningful answers were given).

As far as a minimum, I wouldn't recommend collecting fewer than thirty stories. One hundred stories is a good number: enough to show some useful patterns and trends, but not enough to be hard to manage. When you get over three hundred stories, dealing with the volume starts to get limiting. (I write more about this issue in the section called "How many stories to collect" on page 132.)

But this decision depends on what you will be doing with the stories. If you will be looking for patterns in them yourself, volume is a more important consideration than if you will be making them available for people to look at and talk about. It also depends on how many projects you've done and what sorts of methods you've worked out for processing the stories. If you're just starting, a nice manageable project where you ask thirty people to tell two stories each is a good idea.

Emphasis: Which PNI phases will be most prominent?

Some PNI projects are arrayed like sunflowers, with equally sized petals, while others are like orchids, with some petals much more prominent than others. Which phases of PNI are most important to the project? Which are critical? Which are less important to success? What would happen if each phase were bigger or smaller? Which are you the most excited about, and which seem featureless?

After you have answered these six PNI planning questions, take some time to talk about them without any formal structure. In your discussion, evaluate whether you are happy with your answers to the questions. Are they complete? Are they accurate? Are they realistic? Do they miss anything important?

YOUR PROJECT SYNOPSIS

After you have answered the PNI planning questions, you can build a *project synopsis*. Combine your answers to the six questions into a nice clean sentence (or two), which you can use to describe the project to anyone involved.

Here are some fictional examples:

- In order to find out what people want for our community in the future (goal), our group of community council members (relations) will ask people from all demographic categories in our community (range) to tell at least two stories (scope) about the next ten years of our community (focus), and we will look for patterns in the stories told (emphasis).
- In order to rediscover forgotten ideas and get new ideas for extending the art of photography (goal), our group of students (relations) will ask twenty current photographers (scope) to meet and talk about (emphasis) stories about decisions and dilemmas (focus), which were originally collected from 150 photographers (scope) going back through fifteen decades (range).
- In order to improve our patient care (goal), our group of hospital support staff (relations)

will collect stories about office visits (focus) from fifty patients and doctors (scope) across a wide spectrum of disorders and complaints (range). Then a group of patients and doctors (relations) will meet (emphasis) to look at and think about the patterns they see in the stories. Our group (relations) will disseminate a report on the meeting (emphasis) to all doctors and waiting rooms in the network (relations).

- In order to help foreign students succeed at our university (goal), staff members at the university's international student center (relations) will ask thirty students (scope) from all countries attending the university (range) to tell stories about their first month at the university (focus). Those stories will be made available to other foreign students who need help settling in (emphasis).

Can you write a sentence or two like these that describes *your* project well? If you can't, go back to your sensemaking and see what you left out. It is better to go round a second time on a mini-project than to start the larger project without a firm foundation.

Your project synopsis will serve you as a touchstone throughout the project. To some extent your synopsis is an agreement, a constitution for collaboration, among all participants in the project. You should be able to return to it to settle disputes and answer questions as the project proceeds. Be sure it is ready to support the project before you move on to collecting stories.

SUMMARY

The best way to plan a PNI project is to embed a smaller PNI project within its planning phase. In your group or even by yourself, you can collect stories, make sense of them, and return them to the group (or simply your own thoughts) and thereby derive insights that will help you plan the larger project. To bring out useful stories, try thinking about situations in which the project goes well or badly, and reflect on what might happen to create that outcome.

If you cannot tell your own stories about how your project might play out, do some pilot story

collection to give you a better grounding in the context of the project.

Some questions about your project's setting you might want to consider are:

- How much do power and authority matter to your participants?
- What is their level of confidence?
- How busy are they?
- What subgroups are involved?
- How much importance do people place on succeeding?
- How concerned are people with privacy?
- Are people angry or sad about something?
- How do people feel about you and the project?
- Will people take the project seriously?
- Are there gaps between the experiences of different participants?
- What do people think about stories?
- Is your topic sensitive, difficult to understand, apt to lead to self-promotion, hard to remember?
- How will you handle privacy concerns?
- Do you need to identify people?
- Who will be able to read the stories?
- Will people have access to their stories later?

Consider all of these questions in your storytelling and sensemaking during project planning.

As you come out of your planning project-within-a-project, you should look to answer several framing questions that set out the project's goals, relations, focus, range, scope, and emphasis. You should be able to write your answers to these questions in the form of a short declaration that encapsulates the most important points about the project. When you have done this, and you feel that your declaration truly represents what your project is about, your planning process is complete.

QUESTIONS

How do you (or how does your team) usually plan projects? Do you usually write out statements and checklists and schedules, or do you come up with vague goals and see what comes next? As you read through the recommended activities for planning a PNI project in this chapter, what parts of it strike you as difficult or unnecessary? Does answering a set of questions seem too fixed? Does telling yourself stories seem too fuzzy? How can you combine what I've written here with your unique strengths to plan your PNI project in the best way you can?

How does your community or organization usually plan projects? What parts of this chapter seem difficult, not necessarily for *you*, but for your community? What can you do about that? What is the best planning process you can build for your community?

ACTIVITIES

Look at the scenarios I listed for stories you might tell in your mini-collection project as you plan a PNI project (ask me anything, magic ears, fly on the wall, project aspects). Come up with one more scenario that might help you plan PNI projects. Then try it out.

Look at the questions I asked about the participants and topics of projects in the "setting of your project" section of this chapter (page 96). Come up with a question about project settings that I didn't think of, one that applies to your project. (If you don't have a project in mind, think of one you might do someday.) What is it about your project's context and goals that I didn't anticipate for you? Now ask yourself that question about your project. Think about how you can incorporate it into your project planning process.

Come up with three projects you could conceivably (or inconceivably) do in your community or organization given the right opportunity. For each project, go through the phases outlined in this chapter: tell yourself some stories, do some sensemaking with those stories, then answer the PNI planning questions and write a project synopsis. Develop your skills at considering all the aspects required to plan PNI projects in a variety of situations.

Find a resource about another method of narrative work, say oral history or narrative analysis. Then find a resource related to participatory work, like a book on action research or participatory policy analysis. Compare how those re-sources recommend planning projects to what you read here. How do they differ? What do you like better and worse than what you find here? What might you want to incorporate from those approaches to complement this one?

Chapter Eight

Story Collection

This chapter covers how to go about collecting stories in a PNI project. It starts by describing the pros and cons of nine methods of collecting stories. The chapter then goes into particulars on how you can elicit stories and ask useful questions about them and about their tellers. Some sample question sets are given to help you understand what story elicitation looks like. Finally, the chapter ends with some advice on facilitating sessions in which people tell stories together.

METHODS OF STORY COLLECTION

This section describes nine methods of collecting stories: one-on-one interviews, group interviews, peer interviews, group story sessions, surveys, observation, journaling, narrative incident reports, and gleaned stories. Each method works better in some contexts and not as well in others.

One-on-one expert interviews

A one-on-one expert interview is an interview of one person conducted by one other person who knows a lot about stories or about the subject matter being explored in the interview (see Figure 8.1 on the next page).

I haven't found one-on-one expert interviews all that useful for collecting raw stories of personal experience as material for participatory sensemaking. I have worked on projects that relied on expert interviewing, and I found the stories collected in those projects, in comparison, to be somewhat less penetrating than stories

people told to other people who shared their situations and concerns.

This is partly because stories lead to stories, but it is also related to the high demands of narrative interviewing. Interviewing is an art few can practice well, and narrative interviewing is even more difficult.

Says Yiannis Gabriel in *Storytelling in Organizations:*

> In finding stories, researchers must be aware that they are furtive, fragile, and delicate creatures. They can easily be driven away, they can emerge without being noticed, they can rigidify into descriptions or reports, and they can be killed. The researcher's demeanour, attentiveness, and reactions play a decisive role in the generation of stories. ... The stand advocated here is that of a fellow-traveller on the narrative, someone keen to engage with it emotionally, displaying interest, empathy, and pleasure in the storytelling process. ... Like a traveller, the researcher is subject to the narrative's momentum, never seeking to control it or derail it, yet constantly and attentively engaged with it, encouraging it, sometimes nudging it forward, sometimes slowing it down.

This is a high level of expertise indeed, one few can reach without years of experience. Certainly few people who are trying to start working with stories in their own communities or organizations will be able to bring this level of interviewing skill to bear on their first project. For this reason, I don't recommend conducting interviews yourself unless you have a natural knack for interviewing (some do) or considerable experience in interviewing from another field.

Having said all that, there are some specific situations where an expert interview is either required or recommended to ensure the quality of the stories collected. A one-on-one interview may be best when the topic is so private or sensitive that a person can only speak in a private session with a person for whom they have already built up trust, such as a doctor, therapist, or minister. Also, a one-on-one interview may

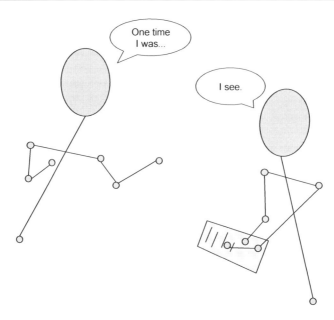

Figure 8.1. In a one-on-one interview, a professional interviewer asks questions and listens to the stories one interviewee tells in response.

be best when the interviewee is so busy or used to authority that they cannot (or will not) find the time to participate unless the interview has the status of being conducted by an expert. One would not, for example, be likely to ask the highest official in a country to attend group or peer interviews.

The process of conducting a one-on-one expert interview in PNI is no different than doing the same in any field of qualitative inquiry: find your interviewees, arrange times to speak to them, prepare your script, rehearse the interview, prepare your recording equipment, and start interviewing. If you need help preparing to interview people, I suggest you consult some of the plentiful sources of information on conducting interviews for oral history or qualitative research. Many experienced oral historians, for example, have written advice far better than I could give on interviewing skills and techniques.

Group interviews

A group interview is an expert interview in which more than one person is interviewed at once (see Figure 8.2 on the facing page). Typically a script of some kind is followed, though the best interviewers will be able to adapt the interview to the conditions they find. As with peer

interviews and group sessions, people in group interviews remind each other of experiences. But unlike those methods, group interviews are strongly controlled by the central interviewer, who is usually expert in the subject matter or in story work.

The best time to use group interviews is when you want the mutual prompting created as people listen to each other telling stories, but you need to remain engaged in the conversation to keep it moving and in the right direction. I have seen four situations in which the central control of group interviewing is most useful. They are when collecting stories from people with high or low status, or the very young or old.

The high and mighty

People of high status such as experts and executives do not always take kindly to being given tasks to complete. If you ask high-status people to tell each other stories and write down characters in them on sticky notes, they may simply refuse to do so, or they may give these apparently clerical tasks to underlings. I remember watching one lofty executive tell story after story without touching pen to paper, surrounded by several people busily carrying out the assigned task by marking things on sticky notes. When the others in the group spoke, the

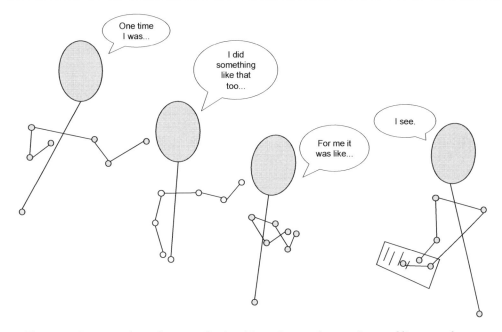

Figure 8.2. In a group interview, a professional interviewer asks questions and listens to the stories two or more interviewees tell in response.

executive radiated kind (though limited) permission to speak, but avoided taking any action that might place him in proximity to the vulgar sticky-note task.

I am exaggerating for effect, and not everyone in power is like this, but some people simply cannot be reached unless you place them in a position where their wisdom can be received in the form in which they prefer to provide it. A group interview clearly places them in this position.

The downtrodden

People of very *low* status also respond better to group interviews than to group sessions. This is not because they mind being given a task; it is because they do not believe they can complete it to your satisfaction. I have seen people in this position simply sit and stare at the ground when given storytelling tasks. Sometimes a group of fearful people will pass the task around like a hot potato, hoping *someone* will step up and take the risk. Or they may stall until they can get out of the task by asking questions or finding excuses in unimportant problems ("Our pen isn't working. We lost our sticky notes. What does this instruction mean?").

For this group, an interview can provide the constant encouragement and friendly reception they need to speak out. Hearing others tell about their experiences can also help to "clear the air" so the timid can speak.

Little kids

Younger children, say up to eight or ten, do better with group interviews than with one-on-one interviews or group sessions. Leaving them alone to do tasks will fail because they will spin off into unrelated activities. They aren't likely to fill out forms well either. But interviewing children one-on-one, especially when they don't know the interviewer, is likely to result more in performance than recall. Having other kids around helps to nudge things into the space between random play and scripted performance, which is where they should be to tell stories that explore their experiences related to the targeted issues.

Of course, if kids are recounting private or sensitive stories it is better to interview them singly; but for a typical project examining issues like, for example, educational methods or learning cultures, a group interview works well. Once kids can form groups and carry out tasks, a group session or peer interview is better, because it engages their imagination in working together.

Older folks

Group interviews also work well for elderly people in declining health. Old people know more about everything than anybody else can. They often hold the key to a community's collective experience on important issues. But older people often have a constellation of limitations that make collecting stories by other methods difficult. First, they don't have much physical energy, so asking them to walk around putting sticky notes on a wall is out of the question. Second, they are likely to feel they have earned the right to refuse to do tasks that don't interest them. Third, their attention and memory (and wakefulness) may wander, so they may need help keeping to any task set before them. Fourth, they may have had so many experiences in any given area that they may find it difficult to choose which to tell about, and may describe generic scenarios rather than specific experiences.

All of these things combine to mean that older people are not the best participants in group story sessions or peer interviews, even if they are willing to participate. Unlike children, who when given a task run off in random directions full of energy, older people usually go in the right direction, but quickly run out of steam. A one-on-one interview can provide energy, but it tends to crash into yet another limitation of the elderly, which is that the memories you need them to recall may be buried deep.

Many older people are so used to running through their small repertoire of oft-repeated stories that they need help reaching past them into other experiences they have explored less fully. Expert interviewers can provide that help, but they need to be exceptionally skilled and knowledgeable about the topics under consideration. When two or three older people are interviewed together, they can help each other draw up memories from sources of which their interviewer is only dimly aware.

For the people who are not in any of these four groups, I like group story sessions best. I think you get better stories when people talk to each other than when they talk to an interviewer. But

group sessions are like strenuous physical exercise, which makes healthy bodies stronger but frail bodies weaker. If your group can *handle* a group session it will produce better results. But if the strain of a group session is too much for the group, consider holding a group interview instead.

When you conduct a group interview, keep your task toolkit ready. The line between the conversation of a group interview and the tasks of a group story session is blurry. Come to your group interview familiar with the methods of a group session, so that if the group seems ready for a task you can give them one.

The details of conducting a group interview are much like those of conducting one-on-one interviews. They are also much like focus groups in that the facilitator guides the conversation, though people can talk with one another as well. All good advice on running interviews and focus groups can apply to group interviews where stories are elicited.

Peer interviews

Peer interviews are those in which the people who are being asked to tell stories interview each other (see Figure 8.3 on the next page).

Charles T. Morrissey explains what these are like (he calls them "volunteer" interviews) in "On Oral History Interviewing" (in *The Oral History Reader*):

> We had what we called volunteer interviews at the outset of the Kennedy project, about 135 of them, who did a total of about 300 interviews. When I say volunteers, I mean journalists, people in the administration, colleagues of people to be interviewed, friends, all sorts of arrangements, put on a kind of person-to-person, informal basis.

The person-to-person, informal basis of peer interviews is both their strength and weakness. Peer interviews are useful when poorly articulated or deeply held beliefs and feelings need to be brought out in the open. When people interview each other about an issue they know they share experiences about, different things come out than when a person speaks to you knowing you come to them from a different world. Peo-

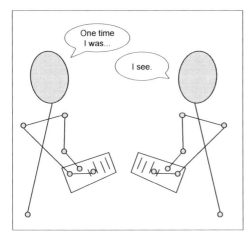

Figure 8.3. In a peer interview, two or more participants interview each other, following a script with story-eliciting questions.

ple remind each other of memories and draw out experiences buried deep.

This drawing out is especially useful when your project involves long experience, such as with people remembering their careers. It is also helpful when you are an outsider and people will self-censor when speaking to you. For example, say you want to gather stories from two ethnic groups who grudgingly share a city block. In this case your project is more likely to succeed if you start with peer interviews within each group than if you attempt a group story session or expert interviews.

However, peer interviews do have some limitations. Peer interviewers may avoid issues they know to be taboo, and they may leave unsaid things "everyone" knows. So while peer interviews improve the depth to which memory and articulation penetrate, they place limits on the range of experience covered. If experience is a landscape, peer interviews drill deep but stay close to home. For some projects this may be just what you need; but for others it may be best to complement peer interviews with another method that increases the range of experience, such as an anonymous survey submitted via telephone, computer, or paper.

I didn't want to clutter up this section with instructions, so I've written about facilitating peer interviews on page 164.

Group story sessions

While a group interviewer engages with the group in conversation, a group story session facilitator provides *tasks* for groups to complete. If you picture the meeting as a stream, a group interviewer swims *in* the stream with the interviewees, but a session facilitator stands on the bank, dipping into the stream only occasionally to test the waters. The momentum of the stream comes from the participants, not the facilitator (see Figure 8.4 on the following page). In fact, the facilitator of a group session may not even be present in the room; they might be represented only by a set of instructions on paper.

I have consistently found stories collected in group sessions to provide superior "food for thought" for sensemaking than stories collected in any other way. When you can get people into the flow of group story exchange, things happen that just don't happen in other settings. People open up and reveal feelings, beliefs, and perspectives that strike deep into the heart of the issues being explored.

However, group story sessions have fairly high requirements in practice. I guess you could say they are high input and high output. They can by physically difficult to set up, since people need to be able to come together into one room. Even the type of room has to be just right; an auditorium or classroom, for example, won't work because people need to be able to move

Figure 8.4. In a group story session, participants interact as they carry out tasks while a facilitator observes from the side.

around in small groups. Group sessions require a certain amount of motivation on the part of participants, since people are being asked to do more than respond to simple cues. They require a freedom to speak freely that excludes the most and least powerful in most societies. Group sessions also require more facilitation expertise than scripted peer interviews, though less than expert or group interviews. Specifically, they require the ability to guide participation without taking charge of it, and this is not something everyone can do.

You will find much information about conducting and facilitating group story sessions later in this chapter (see page 166). Because sessions are more unique to PNI, and because more of my experience is with them, that section is far longer than those on any other method of story collection.

Surveys

In a narrative survey, people tell their stories without direct human contact. This can be done through a telephone, a piece of paper, a web form, a software interface or an email. But no matter the medium, the interaction in a survey is a distant, one-way communication, more

like a message in a bottle than a conversation (see Figure 8.5 on the next page).

Surveys have their good points and bad points. On the good side, a survey is easy to administer. There is no need to gather people in a room and keep them interested in staying there; just send out a survey and hope some percentage of its recipients respond. You can reach far more people, and more diverse groups, with a survey than you can gather in a room. You don't need a travel budget, just an address. If your expected population of participants is large, diverse, widespread, or busy, or if your resources are very small, a survey may be the only realistic way you can collect stories at all.

On the bad side, a survey is as easy to ignore as it is to administer. Unless your community or organization is exceptionally cooperative, the minority of recipients who do respond will not be a random subset of the population. Even to get that small percentage you might have to pay people or force them to comply, and that would distort your story collection as well. Because there is no human face behind it, a survey is easy to laugh at, game, rush through thoughtlessly, half-complete, or even subvert. No matter how well prepared your earnest explanations of your goals, you have no control

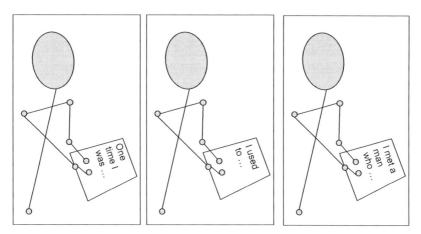

Figure 8.5. In a survey, people tell their stories without direct human contact.

over whether people will read them or pass over them. I have seen survey story collections where up to a quarter of those who filled out the survey in the first place (a small fraction of those asked) completed the survey without actually telling any stories. That's slim pickings.

When someone tells me they plan to conduct a narrative survey, the first thing I do is ask *why* they want to do this. Let us pretend you have just said, "I think we'll use a survey," and I'll respond.

Do you want to use a survey so you can collect a great number of stories? Do not be misled by the attraction of volume. It is *narrative richness* you need to support sensemaking, and volume does not always lead directly to richness. Sometimes people coming from quantitative analysis fields think you need to collect thousands of stories to consider an issue; but this is not true. (It may be true if proof is your object, but it is not true if decision support is your goal.) The necessary level of narrative richness can be achieved through depth or breadth, or any combination thereof. I usually find that a combination of depth and breadth works better than either in isolation. If you send a survey to a thousand people, why not also ask thirty or fifty to join you in a session? The difference in what people said through a survey and in person can provide useful sensemaking material in itself.

Do you want to use a survey because you cannot reach people in any other way, for example because people are too widely spread geographically? A survey may be the only way you can

reach *everyone*, but it is probably not the only way you can reach *anyone*. Perhaps you can reach *most* people with a survey but supplement your narrative richness with the depth provided by a small number of group sessions or peer interviews.

Do you want to use a survey because you don't have the resources to support anything but survey work? If so, could you gain more resources by narrowing your focus? For example, if you have the budget to survey four hundred people, perhaps you could use that same budget to survey two hundred and ask one hundred to participate in peer interviews, or ask fifty to participate in group sessions.

Do you want to use a survey because you don't think people will be willing to participate in anything more involved? Then what *would* make the project into something people would be willing to put more effort into? If there is such a difference between *your* motivation to complete the project and the motivation of the people who will be telling stories, is the project what it should be? Maybe you should do some pilot story collection to find out where you might discover more motivation to participate.

Do you want to use a survey because you are just getting started in story work and don't think you will be able to organize or facilitate anything more complicated? If so, remember that you can get started on facilitating groups with very small projects and very small numbers of people. What sort of story work do you want to do next year, and the year after that? If you want to facilitate group sessions someday, try to *supplement* your survey with a small face-to-face session, so you can round out your experience for future use.

Do you want to use a survey because you want to ask people about sensitive topics they might not be willing to discuss in front of others? That is in fact one of the best uses of surveys. But even so, you will need to prove to your survey-takers that they can trust you with their story.

I have a funny story about this one. In the days when I worked at IBM Research, I sat in my basement office like a grain of rice in the belly of the beast. One day I was surfing the company intranet (with good purpose, I assure you) and came upon some sort of personality survey. I can't remember its exact use; perhaps it had something to do with improving your time management skills. I had a strong sense of big-brother IBM looking over my shoulder, so I was wary of describing my frailties to those who oversaw my employment.

But the start of the survey surprised me in a way I have never forgotten. It said something to the effect of, "When you finish this survey you *must* print it, because after you click that button we will have no way of getting your information back for you. The information you provide in the survey is kept *only* in the aggregate. So don't come back to us the next day asking to print your results, because *we don't know who you are.*" What a concept: the administrators of this survey *proved* that my results were private by broadcasting their inability to connect my words with my identity. Whether this was actually true or not, I believed it at the time and filled out the survey with relish.

I use that experience when I design narrative surveys today. For example, say I am designing a form for participants in an online story collection to fill out. I will say something like this: "Do you see this number? It is your anonymous identifying number. Please *write that number down* and keep it somewhere. When your stories appear in the collection, along with all the other stories we are collecting, *you* will be the only one who knows what that number is. *We don't know who you are,* so you won't be able to find your stories again unless you keep that number." I find that people are universally

surprised to hear this, usually pleasantly so, and it provides them with the proof they need to speak. Yes, sometimes people do lose their identifying numbers and can't find their stories again; but that is a better problem than people refusing to speak in the first place.

You can do the same thing in your surveys, and of course it follows that you can do the same thing in every other mode of story collection. So while a survey can provide anonymity, it is not the only means by which you can provide it. Peer interviews are sometimes even better for anonymity, because you can ask people to choose someone they trust within the organization or community and interview each other. You don't need to know who interviewed whom, at least not in detail, and that means you can give people the freedom to choose what makes them the most comfortable.

It sounds like I hate surveys, but I don't. I find them useful and sometimes necessary, but rarely sufficient. They are like the dry bread of story collection, and they cry out for something to give them flavor.

One advantage of written surveys is that there is a wealth of excellent advice on how to write a good survey. Any well-regarded book on qualitative research is likely to yield helpful tips on such things as avoiding leading questions, choosing types of questions, making questions clear, and so on.

Observation

What if you don't want to *ask* people to tell stories? What about finding a place in which people are apt to tell stories, seeking out a nook where you can watch them unobserved, wedging yourself in place, and listening to conversations? (See Figure 8.6 on the facing page.)

Pure observation of unprompted story exchange sounds exciting in theory, but in practice it rarely happens. Laws and standards of privacy will usually prevent you from recording the conversations of others without making that recording known. Certainly I *have* sat in public places listening to stories as they flowed around me. I strongly recommend doing this to improve your own understanding of how stories circulate in conversation. But I can't think

Figure 8.6. Observing stories means surreptitiously listening to people who are telling stories to each other.

of any story project in which I have secretly observed story exchanges myself, and I don't think I have ever worked with stories collected in that way either.

I don't recommend including pure observation in a PNI project. Why? Because it is missing something critical to the success of PNI: *asking the people who told the stories what they mean.* You cannot walk up to somebody whose story you have just eavesdropped on and ask them to interpret it. You could theoretically ask an entire population to answer questions about surreptitiously collected stories, but you would run the risk of people recognizing themselves or others and your secret collections being found out. Secrecy and participation are like fire and water; you can have one or the other, but not both.

Besides, cloak-and-dagger story collection is not all that useful anyway. Says Neal Norrick in *Conversational Narrative:*

> After incurring the wrath of two friends I had recorded and increasingly experiencing pangs of conscience, I decided always to ask in advance of taping. Moreover, my comparison of openly recorded

versus clandestinely recorded conversation turned up only momentary taping effects. As often as not, my subjects registered surprise that the recorder was still running—proof positive that they had forgotten they were being recorded. My experience has been that conversationalists can only orient themselves to the tape recorder for a short period, and that their behavior returns to normal fairly rapidly. While we constantly react to the contextualization cues of our interlocutors, and we can adjust our speaking register to accommodate all sorts of changes in our visible audience, we seem hard put to key on hearers not directly present vis-a-vis. A tape recorder on a book shelf or a coffee table has little if any effect on a speaker directly engaged in conversation with a friend.

I have found the same thing, which is that most people don't mind all that much if you place a small audio recorder on the table. If they object to the recording, they will get up and leave at the start. But if they don't object, they will soon stop paying attention. They may speak haltingly for a minute or two, but they will soon forget the thing is there and speak as if you were not recording them.

I do find, by the way, that *videotaping* people is disruptive to storytelling. People remain acutely aware that a camera is focused on them, and can't stop performing for it or hiding from it. Maybe it is because the camera's staring eye has a stronger presence than the audio recorder's ear, and they can't put it out of mind. For this reason I don't recommend capturing videos of people telling stories unless you have some compelling reason to do so, such as for example that you need to pick up on body language.

The one exception to the no-video rule is that when you are capturing stories from *children*, video sometimes works better than audio. As long as children are not telling stories about sensitive topics (like abuse), and as long as they don't have any issues about the way they appear visually (some do), children are often more interested in participating if there is video involved, just because it makes the whole thing more interesting. This is even more true if you use peer interviewing; kids love to interview each other and pretend they are on television. For most adults in most situations, though, the no-video rule holds.

Journaling

Journal-based story collection is a lot like surveying, but instead of asking people to tell you stories once, you ask them to tell you stories every so often, for example daily for a month or weekly for a year. You can also ask people to fill out a journal entry whenever they think of it, usually when something significant has just happened (see Figure 8.7 on the next page).

Collecting stories via journaling is most useful when you want to get an in-depth look at what people are thinking and feeling as things happen to them in their daily lives. It's not the best method to use if you want people to look back over a long period of time, but it's an excellent focuser on things as they are right now. If you need people to bounce stories off each other, this is also not the best method to use, because it is an individual method of story collection. However, journaling is useful if you need people to look inside their emotions and practices,

because it's a private, reflective activity. It's also useful if your topic is so sensitive that people won't be able to reveal their true feelings in a group.

Asking people to fill out periodic diaries is a standard tool in the psychological and sociological toolboxes. Diary-based research has been practiced for several decades. However, most diary-based research projects use structured forms with check boxes and rating scales. This is mainly because collecting frequent diary entries tends to result in a *lot* of data. While a survey might gather ten data points about each participant, a month of daily journaling might collect hundreds. For that reason, diary-based research rarely asks people open-ended questions or asks them to tell stories.

An interesting exception can be found in Teresa Amabile's research on motivation at work, as described in her book *The Progress Principle*. You might find the appendix of her book, in which she describes her research methods in detail, interesting reading (I did). On each day of their participation in the study (on average, about a hundred days), Amabile asked her forty participants to "briefly describe one event from today that stands out in your mind." Then she asked people questions about the event they had just recounted.

Says Amabile:

> The idea behind the daily questionnaire was to track both inner work life and the stream of events occurring in the daily work lives of our participants in a way that was both detailed and relatively unobtrusive. In addition, the questionnaire would give us a way to examine specific reactions to the reported events— sensemaking about them, emotional reactions, and motivational responses.

That sounds a lot like story collection in PNI. But Amabile's research project was a mammoth undertaking. She and her team collected over eleven thousand diary entries in total, each of which they read multiple times. They also answered several qualitative questions about the stories (for example, whether the reported emotions were positive, neutral, or negative), then analyzed the patterns created by the answers.

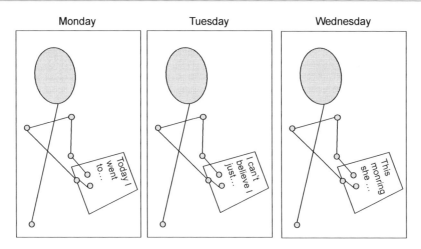

Figure 8.7. Journaling as a means of story collection means asking people to keep track of things that happen to them, on a periodic basis, on an episodic basis, or both.

You can imagine that this process must have taken a lot of time, and you can see why so few researchers collect stories in diary entries!

Of course, most PNI projects are far smaller than this. But if you decide to collect stories via journaling, be aware that the volume of stories you collect may quickly grow larger than you expected, especially if people can add stories to their journals whenever they like. You can deal with this issue in advance, by asking fewer people, by running the journaling period for a shorter time, or by asking people to journal less often. Even asking people to add to their journals every *other* day will collect half as many stories. Or you can deal with the issue after your collection is complete, by sampling fewer stories to use in later phases of your project.

If your topic is sensitive, you can avoid collecting journal stories at all. You can give your journal-keepers sole access to their stories, and collect only their answers to questions about the stories. When people reflect on private matters, the stories they are willing to tell *themselves* can reveal more useful patterns than the stories they are willing to tell *you*.

Another example of a journal-based story collection (this time a participatory one) is a web application called the 3-Minute Journal (3minutejournal.com). Site users are encouraged to spend three minutes at the end of each day describing one or more significant events of the day. People can also enter events as they happen.

After a user enters a story, they can answer some questions about it, like how they feel about what happened and how long they'll remember it. Over time, these answers build up into patterns people can use to make sense of what has been happening to them. You could say the 3-Minute Journal helps people do their own personal PNI.

Says John Caddell, the creator of the 3-Minute Journal, in an article on the web site 99u.com:

> Talk about Big Data is everywhere these days. But for managing your development, Little Data is much more useful. Little Data is data about you. ... Have you made progress this week, this month, or this year? How many days have you felt encouraged as opposed to frustrated? What mistakes have you made and do they fall into a pattern? ... [T]his insight forms the raw data needed in order to make your own judgments about your performance and development needs. Most importantly, when someone asks you about your accomplishments, say, at an annual performance review with a raise on the line, you'll be able to easily answer.

You can imagine how having lots of people tell themselves stories in this way could add up to

Figure 8.8. Incident reports are facts about events recorded by people who observed or participated in them. Narrative incident reports are stories about events, which can include emotional reactions to the events.

useful patterns when all of the private reflections are combined.

Narrative incident reports

In most methods of story collection, you ask people to recall stories about events that have happened to them or that they have heard about from others. In this method, you don't ask people to recall stories. You ask people to *watch stories happen.*

Let me give you an example. Say you are the director of education at a museum. Say you have asked twenty volunteers to follow people around the museum taking notes on what they do: where they stop and read, where they glance and move on, which hands-on activities they touch. Your observing volunteers will probably make their notes on forms with defined places for collected data, such as the length of time each visitor spent at each exhibit, with perhaps a check box for whether people touched any hands-on activities.

Incident reports like these are common tools in the world of anthropological and sociological research. When collecting incident reports, researchers aim to maximize objectivity so as to provide solid proof. If you were conducting a hypothesis-based research project, it would be inappropriate to ask your observers if they were *surprised* by the museum visit they watched, or how much they thought people learned by it, or whether they felt proud of the museum after the visit.

But let's say you are doing a PNI project for your museum. In that case, you can collect *narrative* incident reports. You can ask your volunteers to tell you what happened as they watched people—to the people, *and to them.* Of course each volunteer will be biased in their reactions. But if the project collects some anonymous information *about* each volunteer (say, age, gender, background, some opinions about the museum), and if volunteers are chosen to create a balance of views, their biases can add narrative richness to the story collection (see Figure 8.8). Not only that, but you can *combine* narrative incident reports with stories collected directly from museum visitors (from kiosk surveys or exit interviews, for example) to create an even richer body of stories.

Narrative incident reports can be collected by watching people in a variety of situations: eating at sidewalk cafés, making appointments at doctors' offices, browsing in supermarkets, waiting at airports, and so on. Anywhere people can be observed without compromising their privacy—that is, any public place—is a legitimate place to collect narrative incident reports.

You can collect narrative incident reports from observers, as in my museum example, or you can collect them from people who interact with people directly. For example, nurses, waiters, teachers, police officers, utility workers, and firefighters are all people who could collect narrative incident reports. Most of these people collect some kind of incident reports already, so all it would take to collect stories for a PNI project would be to add a few story-eliciting and story-interpreting questions to the factual data people already collect.

As in my example above, you can also ask the people on the other end of the interaction to recount their own versions of events. Especially in projects where interactions are important, say between staff and customers, such "we said, they said" story collections can provide valuable insights.

In terms of their structure, narrative incident reports are much like surveys and journal entries, so any guidelines you can find on writing surveys will apply to all three of these form-based methods of story collection.

Gleaned stories

There is one circumstance in which I believe it is legitimate to observe storytelling without the participation of the storytellers (and still call it PNI), and that is when the stories were told before you got there. Sometimes you may not be able to ask people to tell stories about a particular topic, but you do have access to records of their conversations made beforehand, possibly for some other reason. For example, say you have discovered in the archives division of your corporation a repository of thousands of discussions stretching back decades. Such a treasure trove of stories could provide valuable sensemaking material to a project bridging the past and future of the organization. I do consider it participatory to make use of such material when it is available, though it is better used as a *complement* to teller-interpreted stories than as a replacement for them.

I have done several projects in which the stories we worked with were gleaned from texts recorded as people spoke without knowing we would later make use of their stories. They were generally on-line chats and forums, as well as public records of conversations that took place in official settings such as court rooms and congressional debates. For example, I once assembled some stories about asymmetric conflicts in international relations. Some of the material I used was drawn from historical records and newspapers, but I also poked around on internet chat sites and discussion forums to find stories people told that pertained to the issues I was exploring. This material, intermixed with contemporary stories, was used in sensemaking sessions, and provided much useful food for thought.

How do you find stories when they are mixed in with other text? There are some fairly simple techniques. Look for past tense verbs, like "said" and "did" and "went." Look for personal pronouns like "he" and "she" and "we" and "they." Look for story-starting statements: a reference to a time ("one day"), memory ("I remember when"), experience ("I had" or "I did"), action ("I went"), event ("It rained"), place ("That house"), person ("He liked") or rumor ("I heard"). Look for story-continuation statements like "and then" or "soon" or "finally" or "the next thing that happened." In general, if something is *happening* it's a story. You will find that after you've carefully located the first dozen or so stories you will develop an intuition and not have to look for them; you'll just see them.

CHOOSING STORY COLLECTION METHODS

As you have seen, there are many ways to collect stories, perhaps a bewildering number of ways. But the decision of which methods to use really comes down to two simple questions.

With you or without you?

Do you want people to tell *you* stories, or would you rather listen as people tell stories to others?

This decision depends on your relationship to those who will be telling stories. Ask yourself which conversation will best produce the stories your project needs: one *with* you in it or one *without* you in it? The wider the narrative distance between you and your participants, the more likely your presence will disrupt the natural flow of stories.

Methods of direct engagement include one-on-one interviews, group interviews, surveys, journaling, and narrative incident reports. Methods of indirect listening include peer interviews, group story sessions, and gleaned stories.

Alone or together?

Do you want to hear people tell stories *singly* or in *groups?* This decision depends on relationships *among* the people who will be telling stories. Ask yourself which conversation will best produce the stories your project needs: one in which one person tells their stories alone, or one in which two or more people share stories together?

Speaking in groups has contradictory impacts on storytelling. On the one hand, people can sometimes open up more freely and explore experiences more deeply in a group of their peers; but on the other hand, groups can apply subtle pressure on individuals to tell only the stories the group finds acceptable. So this decision is a complex one, dependent on many factors about your topic, participants, situation, goals, and resources. I find that pairing individual and group story collection is often the best response to this dilemma.

Methods of individual story collection include one-on-one interviews, surveys, journaling, and narrative incident reports. Methods of group story collection include group interviews and group story sessions. Peer interviews lie halfway between single and group story collection. Gleaned stories can be collected from individual reflection, group discussion, or both.

One method or two?

Also remember that it is perfectly reasonable, and sometimes advantageous, to collect stories in two ways during the same project. Sometimes you need to do this because different groups of people cannot be reached in the same way. But even if you only have one group of people, using two methods of story collection

at once (say group sessions *and* a survey) can broaden the range of experiences you gather.

For example, you can imagine asking people to keep a private journal for a week or month (in which they are asked to reflect individually on the project's topic), then asking them to come to a group story session where they can explore the same topic with other people. Each element (private reflection, group story exchange) will add a complementary aspect to the story collection, and their combined effect will enhance your ability to support sensemaking.

Using multiple story collection methods is not an easy task, so you should not take it on during your first few projects. But remember that it is an option when you gain more experience.

ASKING PEOPLE TO TELL STORIES

No matter what method you use to collect stories, you need to find a way to ask people to tell them.

The best way to ask for stories

What is the best way to ask people to tell stories?

1. You could *ask directly* for a story. You could say, "Tell me a story about trust."

2. You could *tell a story* yourself. You could say, for example, "Trust saved my life one day. I was driving, and my wife suddenly grabbed the steering wheel. If I hadn't trusted her, I wouldn't have let her avoid the truck that was about to hit us." And then you could wait and see what people say in response.

3. You could *ask a question whose answer is a story*. You could say, "Have you ever trusted anyone with your life? What happened?"

I have seen all of these techniques used to gather stories, and in my considered professional opinion, only the third method is useful. Let me explain why I *don't* recommend the first two approaches.

Asking directly for stories

You can imagine saying something like "Can you give me a story about health care in your community?" or "Could you share a story with us about what courage means to you?" This does make it perfectly clear what you want. If the people you will be asking to tell stories are unlikely to understand an indirect request, it could be useful to mention that you actually want stories, to avoid people misunderstanding less obvious requests. But people may react negatively to such a question, because it seems to them that you are asking them to give you something that belongs to them.

Asking directly for stories designates them as nouns. Stories *are* nouns, but they are also verbs, in the sense that they are communicative events that unfold in conversation. Asking *for* stories places undue emphasis on stories as objects. People have a stronger "why do you need to know that" radar today than they used to (because every time they buy a thumbtack online they are asked for a ton of information) and may be wary. If you are asking questions in a survey, people may walk away in droves without your knowing why. I do find it adds spice to slip in a "tell me a story" element in a session *after* you have already got people telling stories. But *starting* with a command, or only using commands, will produce only compliance or refusal, not communication.

Another disadvantage of asking directly for stories is that people aren't always aware of whether they tell stories or not. As you read in the section on "Stories in personalities" (page 45), some people say "I never tell stories" and then proceed to do so, while other people present themselves as great storytellers, then proceed to deliver opinions and lectures, but tell no stories. If you ask *explicitly* for stories, you run the risk of people who think they don't tell stories (but actually do) turning away with an "I never tell stories" response.

A variant of asking directly for stories is to ask for *memories* (or recollections, reminiscences, experiences, history, reflections, remembrances). This implies looking back over the past, which hints at storytelling, but doesn't come right out and ask "for" a story. You might ask, for example, "Can you describe some of your memories from your years working here?" or "Can you share some of your experiences with your headache medicine?" This approach

avoids putting off people who won't want to "give" you a story, but it may end up collecting too many half-stories, fragments that don't come to completion. People might say "My experience was that the headache medicine was okay" or "My memory is that this has been a great place to work." When you get to the point of trying to make sense of the topic with these fragments, they will make for poor support.

Telling stories to get stories

This approach involves telling a story, then asking people to respond to it (or just waiting to see if they do). The advantage of this approach is that it is a strong focuser: it helps people understand exactly what you want. However, the disadvantage of this approach is *also* that it is a strong focuser. It helps people understand *exactly* what you want.

Telling a story gives people a *template* to copy. For most people in most situations, this tends to constrain their response to what they think best matches the template rather than what actually *happened* to them. That might be useful if you wanted to find out what people thought you *wanted* them to say, but it is not useful if you want to find out what people have experienced. It is true that if you were in a group you knew well, like in your own family, telling a story and noting responses would work. But rarely do people collect stories for purposeful story projects in such casual settings.

Asking questions whose answers are stories

Questions whose answers are stories do not command, objectify, or constrain (see Figure 8.9 on the next page). They start conversations, and conversations are the natural homes of stories. I was once open to using requests and examples to elicit stories, and I'm certainly not going to take offense if you try them! But I base this recommendation on my experiences watching people use these methods and watching how other people responded to them. Questions just work better.

Ways to ask people to tell stories

How do you come up with questions whose answers are stories? Practice and testing. One thing I recommend is to come up with a question, then try answering it *in every other way than by telling a story,* because people will try

Figure 8.9. Don't ask for stories, and don't tell stories. Ask questions whose answers are stories.

to find a way to do that. If you can't find any way to answer the question *except* by telling a story, it's a good story-eliciting question. And *test your questions.* It is almost impossible to guess whether questions will result in stories. People always surprise you. Testing questions is the best way to find out whether they result in storytelling.

Asking what happened

I put this up front because I've found that adding the question "What happened?" to nearly any story-eliciting question can cure most problems of perception. Compare these two questions:

1. Can you remember your first day at work?
2. Can you remember your first day at work? What happened on that day?

The first question breaks the cardinal rule of asking a question whose answer is a story, and the second doesn't. The "what happened" bandage can fix many an ailing question. Of course, it can be irritating to have "what happened" stuck onto the end of every question you ask. But sometimes it is not necessary, and when it is, it can be reworded in many ways, like asking what people did or said. You can also add

it into the question itself, as with "Can you tell me what happened on your first day at work?"

Asking directed and undirected questions

A directed question is one that directly asks someone to talk about an issue important to the project.

Examples of directed questions are:

- Was there ever a time when you were surprised by how *connected* or disconnected you were to the community?
- Have you ever felt *overwhelmed* with information?
- When you came into our office this morning, did anything happen that made you feel more or less *important* to us?
- Can you remember ever waking up and not wanting to go to work because you felt you couldn't face such a *hostile* environment again?

An *undirected* story-eliciting question is one that doesn't ask about a particular issue, but asks about the person's experiences in general.

Examples of undirected questions are:

- What happened on your *first day* at work?

- Tell me about your *wedding.*
- Can you tell me about your *visit* to the doctor's office today?
- Can you remember your *best moment* as a doctor?

When you ask undirected questions, you tend to get more raw emotions and honest reflections. People love to talk about things like the day they met their spouse or the moment they first skydived. The disadvantage of using undirected questions is that you cannot control *what* people will talk about, and only a fraction of the stories may be about topics important to the project. Directed questions focus on the issues you want to know about, but because you are asking people for something specific, people will be more likely to try to give you what they think you want rather than speaking freely from experience.

If your topics are very broad or if you care about several things, you might be able to ask an undirected question, then ask a question *about the story* that captures what topic it is about. For example, if you wanted to know about trust, you might ask a question about how important trust is to the story. If your topics are narrow or few, or you think people will be unlikely to talk about the topics unless you ask them to, you will need to ask directed questions. Another approach is to balance your questions between directed and undirected, seeking both goals (authenticity and specificity) at once.

Asking people to recall a point in time

This approach asks people to select a time reference of importance (a moment, time, point, minute, hour, day, week, month, year) and tell what happened during it.

The moment can be selected on the basis of general memorability, as with these questions:

- What was the most *memorable* hour of your career at this company?
- Can you recall what day of your tenure at the university *stands out* most in your memory?
- What moment of your visit to the zoo was most *interesting* to you?

Or the point in time can be selected on the basis of emotions, thus:

- Could you describe the week when your campaign *struggled* the most?
- Can you tell us about your *proudest* hour as a firefighter?
- You waited in a line in our department today. Was there a time during your wait when you felt *frustrated?*

Or the point in time can be selected in terms particular to an issue the project cares about, thus:

- Was there ever a moment when you felt that *trust* in your team was either strengthened or weakened?
- At what point during your stay at our hotel did you find yourself the most *relaxed?*
- Can you describe a time when you made a major *discovery* in your understanding of your research topic?

The advantage of the point-in-time approach is that it helps people with long experience to avoid generalizing or summarizing. Asking for a particular time reference helps people to understand that you want to know about something that happened *in time,* not outside of it. The disadvantage is that people might tell you what block of time was important without actually telling you what *happened* during it. They might say something like "The worst day was that day at the zoo." Adding "What happened?" at the end of the question can help with that problem.

Note, as in the "trust was strengthened or weakened" example above, that it is perfectly reasonable to give two options within one question. Often people who are not willing to tell one story will tell another. Asking two questions in one (without confusing people) is one way to maximize the number of stories you collect.

Asking people to recall an event

Another method similar to asking about a point in time is asking people to select an event (or episode, incident, occurrence, occasion, situation, circumstance) and tell about it (or describe, recount, depict, relate).

The episode can be selected on the basis of general memorability, thus:

- What event most *stands out* in your mind from your years as a mail carrier?
- Did anyone speak to you today in a way you will *remember* for a long time?
- Can you describe an occasion you remember as being *important* on your bus route in the past year?

Or the event can be selected on the basis of emotions, as with these questions:

- Is there a particular incident you feel the most *distressed* about that happened while you were in hospital?
- Tell me about a time when you felt too *worn out* to come to work.
- Can you recount for us an event that took place during your time here when you felt particularly *calm* and at ease?

Or the event can be selected in terms particular to an issue the project cares about, for example:

- Our museum's motto is "Everyone wants to *learn.*" Was there a moment during your visit today in which that motto was particularly well supported by someone you met?
- When you think of the phrase "*trust* takes years to build but can be broken in a second," what one event of the past seven years stands out most in your mind?
- Could you relate to us a situation when your *leadership* skills were challenged?

The advantage of asking about an event is that it makes it clear that you want people to recall things that happened to them. This may prod people who don't understand the recounting nature of the task to understand what is being asked of them. A disadvantage, however, is that people might feel that the events they remember are not sufficiently important to be counted as Events—with a capital E—and may not respond. People are *terrible* judges of whether something is important, especially when it comes to personal stories.

So if you have a particularly meek group of participants who think you couldn't possibly want to know what happened to *them*, an event question could be hazardous. On the other hand, if you have a group disposed to pontification, an

event question might keep them centered on the recounting of actual events.

Asking people to recall an extreme

This approach involves asking people to remember exceptional experiences.

An extreme can be selected in general, thus:

- Can you tell us about the *highlight* of your last project?
- What was the *worst* thing that ever happened in your years in the department?
- What was the *best* moment of your visit to the library today?

Or an extreme might stand out in emotional terms, as in these examples:

- As your car was being worked on today, when did you feel the most *frustrated* with the process?
- What was the *angriest* you ever felt in all the years you worked at this job?
- Can you remember the *happiest* you ever felt in this community?

Or an extreme might be selected in terms particular to an issue the project cares about, as in these questions:

- Can you remember feeling particularly *appreciated* in your work?
- Have you ever been exceptionally frustrated at a *communication* gap between yourself and your students?
- During your school day today, when did you feel you *learned* the most?

You might be asking right now: *Doesn't asking about extremes distort experience? Why not ask about common, everyday experiences?* I'm not saying you should *avoid* stories you expect to be common, just that a small number of common stories goes a long way.

For example, I don't find this question to be very useful in practice:

> What's a typical day like for you? What was yesterday like?

If people tell stories of actual events in response to that question, their stories are not likely to hold much useful information about the issues

Figure 8.10. Asking people about an extreme emotion or event helps them focus on one episode in a long history.

you want to explore. But often people do *not* tell stories of actual events when you ask them for "representative" stories. Instead, they tend to give you scenarios, like "I generally get up around nine, and I like oatmeal for breakfast" and so on.

I am not saying everyday stories are *never* useful. For example, if you are building an oral history as a record of a community's culture, you need to map the *entire* space. Why? Because your audience might be located in another place or time—say a hundred years in the future—and your center may be their edge. When two groups of people know nothing about each other, the mundane can be extreme. You have probably seen "Day in the Life" books that describe a typical day in the life of someone from another culture or lifestyle. If I was gathering stories from two groups with little knowledge of each other, with a goal to help them build mutual understanding, I would gather much more of the everyday than otherwise.

But in most projects that take place within one community and one time frame, I find questions like this one are best:

> If you look back on your career and think about trust and responsibility, what one day stands out for you as being a day you would tell children of the next generation about? What happened on that day?

When you ask a question like this (note how it focuses on themes important to the project) you direct people to recount the extremes of the experiential map they have built on that topic. When you put together dozens or hun-

dreds of these maps, you are more likely to discover useful insights about trust and responsibility than if you had asked the same people a question about trust in mundane stories (see Figure 8.10).

Watch out for a possible misfire here. If you ask people something like "Can you remember feeling frustrated?" you run the risk of them saying "Yes" and nothing else. Or even if you say, "What was the worst thing that ever happened?" they might respond with, "The bank closing." For this reason, I always recommend either adding the "what happened" addendum to any extreme question or combining it with another question type, like an event or point-in-time question.

You might have noticed in my examples above that some questions elicited negative experiences (such as, "What was the angriest you ever felt?"). When should you ask people about negative experiences? When negative experiences are less common. In most projects, where improvements are sought to a mostly-working system, stories of best practice are not as useful as stories of worst practice, because negative stories are "encountered the least"—that is, exceptional, or at the edges. However, in projects where the system is mostly broken, *positive* stories are encountered the least, so you should make a special effort to draw them out.

Asking people to recall surprise and change

This approach asks people to remember a time in which their expectations have been overturned or in which something important changed (other useful words are surprise, turning point, shift, change, climax, crux, transition, crisis, and critical moment).

For example, you might ask:

• Can you remember a time when you were *surprised* at how well a project was going?
• Was there ever a moment when things seemed to shift and *change,* and after that nothing was the same again?
• Can you tell me about a time during our training class today when you were *surprised* by something the teacher said?
• Tell us about a memorable *crisis* at the police station.
• What do you think was a *turning point* in your thinking about diplomacy?
• Can you tell us about a *critical moment* in your estate planning process?

The advantage of this approach is that it can help people who think they have nothing to say find something to say. It helps them select an event to tell about.

The disadvantage is that it opens the door for people who don't want to respond to say, "No, I've never been surprised," or, "No, nothing has ever changed." If you expect indifference or hostility to your questions, you might not want to give people this exit. But if people are going to be meek or find it difficult to choose things to talk about (perhaps because you are asking them to reminisce about a forty-year career), this approach can be helpful.

Asking people to recall specific decisions, people, places, or things

This approach asks people to recall a particular decision, location, person, or object and talk about their experiences with it.

Some example questions might be:

• What happened at the moment when you decided to join our *faculty?*
• When you drove into town today, did you notice the new *park?* Or did you drive right by it without seeing it? What happened as you drove by it?
• Do you remember the first time you walked into this *courtroom?* What happened on that day?

• Can you recount for us the day you first met your *spouse?*
• You've been driving this *car* for nearly twenty years now. When you look at it, do any special times come to mind?

The advantage of this approach is that it focuses people on something you want them to talk about. The disadvantage is that after you've focused them on the subject, they may forget to tell a story about it and simply start talking about it.

Asking questions using a fictional scenario

Another method involves asking a question that sets up a fictional situation.

For example, you might say:

> A parent you met at your school's open house calls you and says she is going to send her son to another school because "nobody here cares anymore." What story might you tell, either from your own experience or that you heard about, to help her decide what to do?

This approach can be useful when the people you are asking to tell stories will not be willing to tell you their real opinion about a sensitive topic. Asking them about a fictional situation navigates them past their automatic reaction and may get them to talk about a touchy subject when a more direct question would not.

However, results of this approach can be hit-or-miss, mainly because the reasoning required to understand the request is convoluted. People sometimes reply to fictional-scenario questions with one of two misfires: they *refer* to the story they would tell without actually telling it ("I'd tell them about when I first moved here"), or they forget all about telling a story and just say what they would tell the person ("I'd tell them to give my school another try").

If if you expect people to be very reluctant or closed-mouthed or unwilling to admit things, this approach *might* prod them to reveal things they wouldn't have otherwise, though they may need some help getting there. Otherwise I would use it only when there are other options available for those who can't or won't follow you down the path of fictional exploration.

Mixing approaches within one question

It is a good idea to mix different approaches to story-eliciting questions within one question.

Some examples of mixed questions are:

- What do you think you might tell your grandchildren about the best moment of your career at the company? (fictional scenario, extreme, time reference)

- At what time during your visit to the church today did you feel the most connected to everyone else? (time reference, issue of interest, extreme)

- Can you remember a moment in which you were surprised about the trust in your team? What happened in that moment? (time reference, surprise, issue of interest, what happened)

- Can you recall a memory about a time you've had volunteering in which you felt the most fulfilled? (memory, time reference, extreme, issue of interest)

Why is it useful to create mixed questions like these? Because it gives people multiple subtle cues that you are looking for stories, and the cues work in complementary ways to get your message across.

Finding words that work

In one of my first projects collecting stories, my colleagues and I had a lot of trouble getting across the point of what we were trying to do. People came to our group story sessions with a wide variety of misunderstandings about what we were doing. Since our first sessions were about software, a lot of the people thought we wanted lists of bugs. Some other people thought we were giving a training course, and they were upset because they thought we were going to tell them how to use the software. Other people just didn't know what the session was for. When they found out that we wanted to hear about their experiences, some people said, "I don't have time for this!" and walked out.

Finally we came upon a phrase that worked like magic. We would say: "We already know how to use this software, but we want to know what it's *really* like to use it every day." As soon as we said that, it was *easy* to get people to tell stories. They would say, "Oh, *that's* what you want."

I don't even know exactly what it *is* in those words that worked so well. My guess is that it has something to do with the difference between information and experience. If you are talking about information, you want to know what does what or what leads to what. But if you are talking about what something is *really* like, you want to know *what has happened to you.* (See Figure 8.11 on the next page.)

Those words worked in *that* context, but I cannot say to you, "use the phrase 'what is it really like,'" because *your* phrase will be different. I have noticed that in each project words keep coming up, throughout the planning and collection phases, and those words have *power* in the context of the project. Stories seem to cluster around those words. You are bound to notice words like that yourself. For the particular projects I started with, "what it's *really* like" were the right words. Look for the right words for your project, because they are there, somewhere. When you say something and people respond by recounting events based on emotional experiences from a perspective, you've found the right words to use.

Diverse questions for diverse motivations

When I first started asking people questions whose answers were stories, I asked everyone the same questions. I would work long and hard to find a few questions everyone could answer, and I would ask the questions one after the other. What I found was that people varied in whether each question spoke to them. Some people would respond strongly to question one but weakly to question two, and others would do the reverse. At some point I stopped asking everyone the same questions and started giving people a *menu* of questions to choose from. This improved story collection tremendously. (See Figure 8.12 on page 131.)

So what I now recommend is that if you want to ask people to tell you three stories, you don't have to find the three perfect questions that will lead each of those people to describe their experiences. You will have better luck if you present the people with all three questions at once, or even five questions, and say: choose the question you like best and answer it. Then tell me

Figure 8.11. Find the right words that help people understand what you are hoping to hear from them.

which question you chose and why you chose it. Now choose another.

Why build a menu of diverse questions? To match the diversity of your participants. Say for example you know that some of your participants are more motivated to talk about a taboo issue than others. You can build in some questions that give reluctant speakers a safe way to reveal only a little about the topic, and balance those with questions that give other people an excuse to "spill the beans" as fits their enthusiasm.

A question for the reluctant might be something like this:

> Think of a time when you saw somebody doing something in a way that made you think, "If everybody acted that way, things would go a lot more smoothly around here." Or think of a time when you said to yourself, "If everybody acted that way, things would be a lot more difficult." What happened that made you think that?

This question is intermediate:

> When you compare the way things are now to the way they used to be, does any particular incident come to mind that illustrates the change?

And for the rabble-rousers, questions like these will signal freedom to speak:

> How do you think things got to be the way they are now? Have you heard any rumors about what happened?

Matching diversity with diversity requires understanding your participants and topic well. It takes more effort than asking everyone the same questions. And it requires your participants to process more information as they consider the questions. So the menu approach is not appropriate for the simplest of projects. Still, I find that this method collects more and better stories because it gives everyone a question they can answer.

How should you offer your menu of eliciting questions? A menu fits in more easily to some venues than others. In a group session, you can

Figure 8.12. If you give people a menu of questions, they can all choose the questions they want to answer.

write your menu on a white board or hand out paper menus. On a survey form, you can ask people to choose a question to answer before telling their story.

In any kind of *interview,* however, presenting a menu of questions is more difficult.

If you are interviewing someone face to face, whether you should read the questions to them or simply *hand* them the sheet of paper depends on the person being interviewed. For some people, like me, who read quickly and don't process audio all that well, giving me the paper is better. (When I do interviews, I always try to peek at the page the interviewer is reading from, because I can take in the information better that way.) But for some people who process audio well and read more slowly, it would be better to read the questions out loud. If you are interviewing someone face to face and have the luxury of being able to show them your page of questions, you can simply ask them: "Would you like me to ask you these questions? Or would you rather read them yourself?" You are likely to get a range of responses.

Over the phone, it is impossible to hand anybody anything. When a menu can't be presented visually, you can keep your menu small, keep your questions short, and give your questions memorable *names.*

For example, in a phone interview you might say:

> I am going to read you three questions and ask you to choose one you want to answer. Here is the first. Did you ever see somebody do something and think that if *everybody* acted that way we'd all be better off, or worse off? We'll call that the *if everybody did that* question.

Then you would explain the second question with its name, then the third and its name. At the end you would restate all three question names, then ask which the person would like to answer. This takes a bit of rehearsal, but it's worth it when you can do it.

But as useful as the menu-of-questions approach is, it is not for all projects. If your participants are *very* reluctant, or you can get only a little of their time and attention, a menu of questions might put up too much of a barrier to

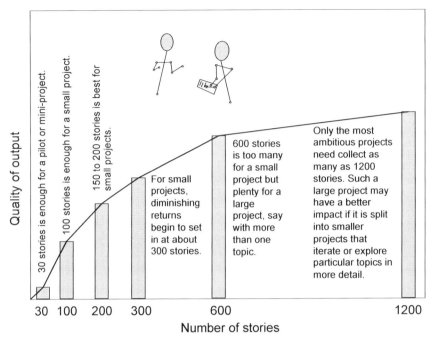

Figure 8.13. There are diminishing returns on the number of stories you collect in a project.
When you plan how many stories you will collect, consider narrative *richness* as well as volume.

participation. If you are facing such a situation, put this idea away for another time when you can better afford it.

How many stories to collect

One of the most common questions I get when people start looking at doing a real story project is: *How many stories should we collect?*

My suggestion is to maximize *narrative richness,* or the degree to which the collected stories address the goals of the project. Narrative richness relies on both the *volume* of stories collected and the *utility* of each story. A story's utility depends on whether it taps into a rich vein of experience (this can be improved by facilitation in story gathering) and on the number and utility of answers to interpretive questions about it. So maximizing narrative richness might mean collecting a lot of stories in some projects, but in others it may mean asking more questions about fewer stories, or collecting fewer stories in a more effective way. In still other projects, narrative richness may mean *connecting* the collected stories in ways that add richness to the collection (perhaps through sensemaking) so that it becomes something richer than the sum of its stories. The best

combination of volume, depth, and connection depends on a project's defining characteristics.

Having said that, for particular elements of a PNI project, specifically catalysis of sensemaking using patterns in interpretation, there are some quantity requirements to keep in mind. When you have fewer than 100 stories, the sample sizes of subsets with particular characteristics (told by men, about dogs, etc.) become too small to support strong statements about trends. I usually recommend gathering at least 100 or 150 stories if people want to look at patterns in interpretation.

Collecting between 200 and 300 stories tends to sort the very important trends from the less important, so you get better definition in your patterns. I'm happy when I see 200 stories, especially if more than one issue is being explored. But at the same time, as soon as you get over 300 stories you start hitting difficulties in processing and distributing stories. The range between 200 and 300 is a sort of sweet spot for getting enough to work with without becoming overwhelmed.

When you get over 300 stories, you get into diminishing returns for most projects (see Figure 8.13 on the preceding page). I see a second level of utility up to about 600 stories, but after that the returns drop off dramatically.

If your goal is quantification or strong proof, or you have a mandate to preserve a wide range of stories (perhaps for historical reasons), or your topic is very broad or ambitious, gaining very strong resolution on issues may be important. But for most projects in support of *sensemaking*, the effort required to collect so many stories is just not worth it.

Also, huge volumes of stories close off other possibilities, such as keeping within a scale that works for distribution. Collecting something everybody in the community can read in a half hour may be more important than developing strong patterns, in some cases.

If you have the resources to collect many thousands of stories, stop and think before you plan to collect all the stories you can. Would it be better to split your resources up and conduct a series of projects, each of which informs the planning of the next? Or might you want to pursue several projects that focus on particular topics or geographical areas or populations in detail? Or would you be better off collecting fewer stories, but asking twice as many interpretive questions about each, or asking a wider variety of people to interpret each story? Or perhaps you should use your resources to help people make more *use* of the stories you collect in facilitated sensemaking sessions? There are many ways to apportion resources in support of a PNI project. I find it is usually better to keep your options open by remaining light and agile in your movements.

Projects with multiple sub-projects

Now that I've warned you not to collect too many stories, I'll add a complication to that warning. When I say that diminishing returns set in at around 300 stories, this does *not* hold if your project aims to explore more than one topic in depth, or to represent more than one group of people in detail. For projects that hold significant sub-projects inside them, it is the *sub-projects* that should determine how many stories you collect.

I worked on a project once where I failed to understand the implications of this fact. My client wanted to learn more about the experiences of people with six medical conditions. For each of those conditions, they wanted to consider the perspectives of doctors, patients, and family members. As we designed the project, I thought we should collect 600 stories, with 100 stories per medical condition. I thought those were the topics my client wanted to explore in depth. However, I didn't understand that my client wanted to explore in depth *each* combination of medical condition and perspective. I thought we were doing a six-part project, but they thought we were doing an *eighteen*-part project. Splitting our 600 stories into eighteen groups created samples of only thirty-three stories each. As a result, my client was dissatisfied with the depth of the exploration we achieved. Now I'm more careful during project planning to make sure I understand all of the sub-projects people have in mind.

As you plan your story collection, think of how many sub-projects your project has within it. Are there multiple distinct topics of inquiry, or areas of exploration, or groups of people, that will determine the success of your project? If you plan to explore only one topic or area, you can collect 100 to 300 stories, as I said above. But if your project's success will depend on the significant exploration of multiple topics or areas, your project contains sub-projects. For each of those sub-projects you will need to collect 100 to 300 stories. If you don't have the resources to explore all of the sub-projects within your project, you might need to narrow your focus and explore fewer areas.

ASKING QUESTIONS ABOUT STORIES

Asking questions about stories means asking people to consider and interpret their stories, and perhaps those of others as well.

My thinking on asking questions about stories has evolved over time. At this point in the previous editions of this book I had this sentence:

> You don't have to ask people to answer any questions about the stories they have told. If you have a very small project (and you are in the group of interest so you can interpret stories directly) you

may want to just collect stories and leave it at that.

I have since changed my mind about this. It was in 2010, around the time I decided on the name of participatory narrative inquiry, that I realized I had reached a tipping point on this issue. Why did I change my mind? Because I had finally seen enough differences between projects with and without reflection on the part of the story-tellers. Asking people what their stories mean, and then comparing what different people say, just works too well to write it up as optional. (If you want more details on why I made this decision, see the section called "PNI Justified" in this book's companion volume, *More Work with Stories*.)

So this aspect of PNI, asking questions about stories, is not optional; it's *critical*. I said in the earlier editions of the book, just after the "you don't have to" section above:

> However, asking people to interpret stories can be a powerful way of finding out more about their feelings and beliefs, especially if you can juxtapose many such interpretations and look for patterns in them. Stories and answers to questions about them reinforce each other and provide a richer base of meaning than either can alone.

Take out the "however," and I would say the same thing now.

Asking questions about stories is not anything new or unnatural; it's only what people have always done. If you listen to anyone tell a story in person, they will almost always surround it with some metadata about why they are telling the story, where they heard it, who it happened to, why you should listen to it, who you can feel permitted to pass it on to, and so on. And the people who listen to the story often ask questions and add their own metadata while the narrative event is going on. When we put questions on a story-elicitation form, we are just trying to mimic some of these natural processes.

In the sections that follow, we will explore topics related to asking questions about stories: how many questions to ask, types of questions you can ask, and finally, putting your questions together into sets that start conversations about stories.

How many questions to ask

When thinking about how many questions you can ask about stories, you need to consider your *cognitive budget*. This is how much mental energy people can put into responding. The number and complexity of the questions you can ask (as well as how many stories you can ask people to tell) will depend on the cognitive budget you have to work with.

Cognitive budget is an amalgam of time, attention, interest, and ability to concentrate. Time is the obvious standout, but all of these factors can come into play. Be careful not to think that if you have a lot of people's time you have a large cognitive budget. Any of the non-time factors can reduce your cognitive budget.

For example:

- You might have an hour of somebody's time, but their attention might be divided between answering your questions and watching their toddler.
- You might have only three minutes of somebody's time, but you may have their complete attention and concentration as well as enthusiasm to help.
- You might have a captive audience required to sit at a desk and fill out a form until it is complete, even if it has a hundred questions in it, but that doesn't mean they will pay attention to the ninety-ninth question (or even the twenty-first, or even the first).
- You may have a group with lots of time, attention, and ability to concentrate, but little interest in the project.

How many questions can you ask about a story? I categorize conditions of questioning into three situations: kiosk, volunteer, and commitment.

Kiosk situations

In a *kiosk* situation, you have not more than a few minutes of someone's time. They have chanced to walk by a kiosk, or picked up a brochure, or clicked a button on a web site (see Figure 8.14 on the facing page). They feel no obligation whatsoever to help, only a momen-

Figure 8.14. In a kiosk or momentary-interest situation, only ask for one story, and never ask more than three to five questions about it.

tary speck of interest so insubstantial that a breath of wind will waft it away. In this situation, collect no more than *one* story per person, and ask no more than *three to five* questions about the story (with as many about the participant). That's not much information, but it's better than pushing too hard and getting nothing at all.

Volunteer situations

In a *volunteer* situation, a participant is moderately interested in your project. The only real difference between kiosk and volunteer situations is that the volunteer has already stated in public that they support the project or its goals or mission, so they feel a social *obligation* to follow through on that pledge (see Figure 8.15 on the next page). They might donate to your non-profit or buy your product or come to your coffee shop or vote in your community, so they feel a *bit* connected.

Volunteers are held by their social obligation *for a while,* but they can also toss off the obligation if they feel any kind of boundary has been crossed in what has been asked of them. For this level I usually suggest collecting *two* stories and asking *six to nine* questions about each story (with as many about the participant).

Commitment situations

In a *commitment* situation, a participant has more than a social obligation to assist the project: they consider themselves *part* of it. The project represents some part of their *identity,* not just an obligation. They may be an employee with a mandate to work on the issue, or they may consider it part of their professional

work, or they may consider themselves committed to the issues being explored (see Figure 8.16 on page 137). If you collected stories about story collection, I'd be a committed participant.

It is only in situations of true commitment that you can push people to answer a relatively high number of questions. Here I would go up to *three* stories per person and *ten to fifteen* questions per story (with as many about the participant). Note the larger range here, due to a larger range of variation in how much commitment people can feel.

A common error in those starting story work is to mistake volunteers for committed participants. The great majority of projects involve volunteers, while the great majority of project *planners* hope to have committed participants. Be honest with yourself. Just because somebody works where you work or lives where you live does not mean they will commit to your project. Perhaps you have not hit on the essential element of their identity that will ensure their commitment. Perhaps they think the project could be run better. Maybe they just don't like you.

People are *never* as prolific with their answers as well-meaning project planners want them to be. You can be justifiably angry and disappointed about people not rising to the occasion and participating as much as you feel the project needs; but if you don't meet people where they are, you will waste what they *do* have to give you. It's like that joke about fight-

Figure 8.15. In a volunteer situation, participants feel a social obligation to respond, so you can ask for two stories and collect six to nine answers to questions about stories.

ing with your spouse: do you want to be *right* or do you want to be *married?*

In the story collection chapter of *More Work with Stories*, the section called "How not to ask too many questions about stories" goes into more depth on issues of the number of questions you can ask, including ways to reduce your question wish-list to fit the conditions you find.

Questions to ask

These next few sections will cover the *topics* of questions to ask about stories and storytellers. Later sections will examine the best ways to go about asking those questions.

Questions about project goals

Goal-directed questions are those that specifically ask about the issues you defined as being important to your project, *as they apply to each story.*

Some examples of goal-directed questions are:

- Would you say that the people in this story *trusted* each other?
- Would you say that the people in this story showed *compassion* for each other?
- When you read this story, what did it say to you about *democracy?*
- Did this story make you feel more or less confident about *technology* as an enabler?

A good way to write goal-directed questions is to go back to the themes you defined in your project planning phase, rank them in terms of importance, and write a few questions for each of the most important themes. Try to maximize the breadth of ways you ask the questions within each theme. Then you can choose between all of the questions you created based on either how you *think* people will respond or how people *do* respond in a test run.

Questions based on story elements. A specific type of goal-directed question with great utility in *some* situations is the *story element* question. As is explained in the chapter on sensemaking exercises (page 419), story elements are abstract packages of meaning about behaviors, beliefs, values, situations, themes, or other areas of interest to the project. They are derived during an exercise in which stories are considered and meaning emerges from interactions among people. If you conducted an exercise like this as part of a story project, you may have already collected some of these elements, and you can use them as a way to ask people questions about stories.

Some examples of story elements might be:

- Self-serving fear-mongers (character)
- On the ropes (situation)
- Can't get no respect (theme)
- We're all in the same boat (value)

When story elements are used as questions, the general question is, "How *present* is this element in the story?" So for example when a person has just told a story about people helping each other after a tornado, they might rate the "We're all in the same boat" element as having a strong presence.

Figure 8.16. In a commitment situation, participation is part of each person's identity, not just an obligation. In this situation you can collect more stories and ask more questions about them.

Story element questions tend to require more preparation than non-element questions, because people may not know at a glance what the brief name of each element means, especially if the group is varied. For example, some elements may include cultural references that not all of your participants understand. Say you run an exercise during a group session and the element "Only the Shadow Knows" emerges. Younger participants will not know that "The Shadow" was a popular comic-book and radio character from the 1930s, so you may get blank or nonsensical answers from that group. It can help to translate narrowly-understood terms to more general terms ("Only the Shadow Knows" could be changed to "mysterious powers" or something). Also, for people who think more literally, story element questions may leave them confused or uninterested.

However, with that warning in mind, if the group you are asking to tell stories is fairly coherent, that is, will understand internal references, story elements can provide powerful ways for people to safely disclose sensitive information. For example, if you ask someone whether bureaucracy stifled their options in the story they just told, you might not get a truthful response; but if you offer them a chance to link the story to an element that makes sense to everyone in the organization, you may get more of a telling response.

Questions about story fundamentals

Many of the best questions about stories derive from considering one or more of the three essential dimensions of stories: form, function, and phenomenon. These are some questions I have used and recommend for each of the dimensions of story (see Figure 8.17 on the next page).

Story form. These questions pertain to the internal structure of a story.

1. Who was the main character in this story?
2. Who or what worked *against* the main character in this story?
3. From the perspective of its main character, would you say this story ended well or badly?
4. What did the main character in this story want or need?
5. Who or what helped the main character in this story get what they wanted or needed?
6. How strongly did the main character want or need something?
7. Did the main character get what they wanted or needed in the story?
8. How much help did the main character get towards getting what they wanted or needed?
9. Which of these things, if they had been available to the main character of the story, would have helped them?
10. What changed in this story?
11. Describe any [values, conflicts, risks, challenges, strengths, ...] you see in this story.
12. How long ago did the events in this story happen?

Form
- Who was the main character?
- How did the story end for them?
- Who or what helped or hindered them?
- What did they want or need?
- Did they get it?
- Why or why not?
- What changed?

Function
- Was this a happy or sad story?
- Why was it told?
- How long will you remember it?
- Did it surprise you?
- What does it remind you of?
- How does it connect with other stories?
- How did people behave in it?

Phenomenon
- Where did this story came from?
- Are stories like this common?
- What would people say about it?
- Is it consistent? Complete? True?
- Who can tell it? Who can't?
- Where and when can it be told?
- Why should it be told? Why shouldn't it?

Figure 8.17. You can ask questions that invite people to interpret stories as form, function, and phenomenon.

13. At what point in the history of your interaction with [the topic] did the events in this story happen?

14. Where did the events of this story take place?

Story function. These questions relate to a story's role in thinking about the topics raised.

1. How do you feel about this story?
2. What is the emotional tone of this story?
3. Why was this story told?
4. How surprised were you by the events of this story?
5. What surprised you about the events of this story?
6. What did you learn from the events of this story?
7. To which of the questions we asked you is this story an answer?
8. How long do you think you will remember this story?
9. Does this story remind you of any proverbs or sayings?
10. Does this story affirm or contradict any other stories you have heard or experienced?
11. Who was most responsible for the events that took place in this story?

12. Who *should* have been responsible for the events that took place in this story?

13. Who showed [respect, trust, cooperation, honor, . . .] in this story?

14. How predictable would you say the events in this story were?

Story phenomenon. These questions pertain to a story's life in society.

1. Where did this story come from?
2. Based on what you know of [the community or organization], do you consider the events described in this story to be common or rare?
3. What scope of [the organization or community] is involved in this story?
4. Which of these [roles, events, groups] are present in this story?
5. What do you think [other people, or another group, in the organization or community] would say about the events in this story? [Would they say the events were common? Would they say the story turned out well? Where would they say the story came from? How long would they remember it?]
6. What would you like [other people, or another group, in the organization or community] to say about the events in this story?

[Would you like them to say the events were common? Would you like them to say the story turned out well? Where would you like them to say the story came from? How long would you like them to remember it?]

7. If this story was more widely heard, what would be its impact on [the organization or community]?

8. Are there any people or groups whom you think particularly need to hear this story?

9. What does this story say to you about [rules, cooperation, trust, power, hope, conflict, …] in this community?

10. Would you say this story holds together well or poorly? (ask this only about stories told by others or official stories)

11. Is there anything missing from this story? (ask this only about stories told by others or official stories)

12. Does this story ring true? (ask this only about stories told by others or official stories)

Each of these questions is listed simply here, but expanded into several paragraphs of explanation in the chapter on story collection in *More Work with Stories.*

Questions about participants

It is always useful to juxtapose questions about the storyteller and question-answerer (who may or may not be the same person) with questions about the stories they told (or answered questions about). For basic demographic questions, such as age, gender, income level, education, housing, marital status, children, profession, location, position, background, memberships, and so on, there is no need for me to go into details.

There are four non-demographic categories of participant questions I have found useful: questions about personality, role, views on topics, and views on the community.

Personality questions. Sometimes a project needs to distinguish between participants by the way they habitually think about things. Well-known distinctions such as those posed by the Myers-Briggs Type Indicator and other similar systems can be useful in some projects, especially those that deal with personality issues like

learning, cooperation, and dealing with challenge. For example, you may discover that introverts saw a problem as less tractable than extraverts, or that big-picture thinkers found a challenge refreshing while detail thinkers found it overwhelming.

The questions about personality I have used mostly have to do with interaction (introvert, extravert), cognitive styles (detail-oriented thinkers, big-picture thinkers), reactions to ambiguity and chaos (avoid, embrace), and attitudes about such things as hard work, luck, and justice. I have not used but can imagine a question on learning styles (visual, auditory, kinesthetic, etc) as well.

Questions about personality differences can be tricky, because they produce hit-or-miss results. Sometimes you think a question will highlight a fault line between styles, but it turns out to show nothing. Other times you will ask simply because there is room to do so, and a difference will jump out and overwhelm everything else.

Role questions. Questions about roles ask people about their positions in the organization or community and what those positions involve. What is their position's scope of responsibility? What sort of thinking does it require? Do they work with people, or with numbers, or with words, or with tools? Does their work vary? Do they like their work? Are they looking around for something better? And so on. The reason to ask these questions is to look for differences in the stories people tell that link to their positions and responsibilities, which is often a source of insight.

For example, perhaps people with a large purview in the organization tell a different story about trust than people responsible for only their own work. Or perhaps people whose work never varies from day to day speak differently about innovation than people whose work skews wildly around depending on needs of the moment.

In organizations, questions about roles are easier to answer (and are usually more often answered) than questions about personality, since most people know their job descriptions well. In communities, things tend to be more nebulous, and these questions are less sure of producing benefits.

Issue view questions. Asking direct questions about views essentially embeds a non-narrative survey within a story collection.

For example, you might ask:

- Would you say the government is doing a good job?
- Do you think our company puts customers first?
- Do you feel like you have enough support to do the work you are asked to do?
- How would you say that living in our town ranks among places you have lived?
- What is your position on the corporation's policy towards diversity?

You might wonder: *If I already asked people about their views through their stories, why should I ask all over again?* Because asking directly about views causes people to think in a different way about the topic of your project. The combination of these two complementary approaches (direct and indirect questioning) produces a more detailed, complex picture than either approach can alone.

Usually answers to questions like these are given on a range from supporting an initiative or viewpoint to being firmly against it. Sometimes differences between what people say about an issue directly and the stories they tell related to the issue (and what they say about those stories) provide some of the best insights in a project.

In one project I can remember, those who supported the organization's official policy most strongly also told the *worst* stories about it, and felt the most work stress related to the topic. These people, mostly in positions of oversight, were in a double bind: they *had* to support the policy in public, but they also experienced some of its most difficult repercussions. In other projects, people contradicted themselves not because of official roles but because the issue presented them with mixed feelings, some on the surface (thus easy to state) and some more deeply held and only accessible through recounting their experiences.

Community view questions. Finally, you can ask direct questions about views on the community or organization.

For example:

- You might ask people how they view the organization, say as a graceful dancer or a plodding mule.
- You might ask people whether they see the community as united or in conflict, moving forward or heaping mistake upon mistake.
- You might ask people whether they see the project itself as reaching deep to improve conditions or going through the motions and putting on a show.

When you combine stated views of the community or organization with the stories people tell about it (as with views on topics), it is in the contradictions that the insights lay. If I say people in our community hate outsiders, but tell story after story about people welcoming immigrants, I have revealed to you a knot of tension that begs to be explored. It may contain an explanation, a solution, a culprit, or an opportunity.

Ways to ask questions

For each question you want to ask, there are a few different ways you can ask it. Which is best depends on the question, the project, the participants, and the venue.

Free-entry text versus answer list

Free-entry questions are those where you don't predefine any answers, but just write down exactly what people say, or ask them to write or type whatever they like. Other questions have predefined lists of answers.

Free-entry questions have the benefit of allowing unexpected trends to emerge, but they come with the burden of reading and checking over and making sense of a lot of text (see Figure 8.18 on the facing page). If you are collecting few stories, using mostly free-entry questions can be illuminating. But if you want to look at patterns across stories, free-entry questions are less useful because you can't count them up. You can categorize them and count how many are in each category, but that takes time.

Figure 8.18. Free entry texts offer flexibility, but take time to process. Fixed lists are quick but leave gaps.

The advantage of using a fixed list of choices is that you will get quick responses. Choice questions don't use up as much of your participants' time and attention, because recognition is easier than recall. The disadvantage is that if you have not correctly anticipated all possible answers you may miss some. For questions where you know all possible answers, like age ranges or locations, this sort of question is best. You can add an "other" choice when you are not sure you have a complete list.

Ordinal versus nominal list

An *ordinal* list of choices is one where the *order* matters (age ranges, for example). A *nominal* list of choices is one where only the *name* of each item matters (gender, for example). For many questions this will be a simple characteristic of the list of choices, but for some you could present the same question either way.

For example, you could ask:

How do you feel about this story?

[ ] It doesn't bother me

[ ] I'm quite upset about it

[ ] It makes me feel warm and fuzzy

[ ] I'm boiling over with anger

[ ] I'm amused

[ ] I think I learned something from it

Or you could ask:

How do you feel about this story?

[ ] very bad [ ] bad

[ ] neither good nor bad

[ ] good [ ] very good

In the first case, the list incorporates items that represent many dimensions of meaning instead of just one; but people have to read through the whole list, and it may not include the feeling they have. In the second case, the list covers the whole ground and is very quick to scan; but it gives only unidimensional information.

Unipolar versus bipolar list

A *unipolar* list of ordinal choices is one that goes from nothing to something, such as in these questions:

- How much do you think trust matters in this story? (not at all, very little, somewhat, to a great extent)

Figure 8.19. Unipolar (one sided) scales are sometimes a problem because people choose the answer they think is most reasonable or socially acceptable.

- How skeptical do you think the people in this story are?
- How completely would you say that this story illustrates the proverb "Too many cooks spoil the broth?"

A *bipolar* list of ordinal choices is one that goes from one thing to another thing, such as in these questions:

- How would you say the people in this story respond to danger? (extreme fear, some fear, neither fear nor excitement, some excitement, extreme excitement)
- How would you characterize management support for employee satisfaction in this story? (no support, some support, adequate support, more support than is comfortable, suffocating support)
- How do the people in this story interact? (extreme cooperation, some cooperation, neither cooperation nor competition, some competition, extreme competition)

The advantage of unipolar lists is that they are easy to understand quickly. The disadvantage is that it is easy to see what the "correct" or socially acceptable answer is (see Figure 8.19). You can break that pattern by switching the direction of the lists (i.e., putting the "best" answer on one side, then the other), but people may still hunt for the "right" side.

Bipolar lists thwart people who are trying to find the right answer, because there isn't one. They also give you a richer answer than unipolar lists, because a wider range of possibilities can be included. However, bipolar lists have a serious disadvantage: they can be hard to understand, so they use up time and attention. Thus they increase the possibility of getting "rush past" answers instead of real answers.

There is also the problem that people can't pick *both* sides of the list at once when issues are complex, for example when the people in the story show both fear *and* excitement. You can try to anticipate these issues, but sometimes they will surprise you. (See Figure 8.20 on the facing page.)

If you think people will try to conform to "correct" answers, bipolar lists are better—but only if you will have enough of your participants' time and attention to work with. If you know you will have limited time and attention to work with (say a participant will be standing momentarily in front of a kiosk), it is better to stick with the faster unipolar list.

The middle option

If you use a bipolar list, you will need to decide whether to include a middle "neither" option. Some researchers say that having a middle option gives people a way to avoid answering the question and so distorts your results.

For example, say you ask the question, "How do you feel about this story?" You could provide answers like this:

[ ] very bad

[ ] bad

[ ] neither good nor bad

[ ] good

[ ] very good

Figure 8.20. Bipolar (two sided) scales can help people avoid knee-jerk answers, but they can also confuse or offend.

Or you could provide answers like this:

[ ] very bad

[ ] more bad than good

[ ] more good than bad

[ ] very good

A person choosing from the second set of answers will not be able to find a noncommittal option, and will have to make a real choice. If you have a reason to expect strong conformity in your participants, you may want to take away the "whatever everybody always says" option.

However, if you *do* take out the middle option, be sure to provide a "not sure" option to avoid the situation of people choosing "more good than bad" only because there is no noncommittal choice available. That way people can choose to either mark a meaningful answer or decline to answer.

List versus scale

When you want to ask a person a question to which the answer is some point along a scale, you can ask using words (e.g., tiny, small, medium, large, huge) or scales. Scales can be numerical (e.g., "please choose a number between zero and ten") or graphical (e.g., "please make a mark on this line").

The advantage of using words is that people can respond to them quickly by recognizing which word best matches their feeling. However, it is sometimes hard to come up with lists of words that work, and different people may interpret the same words differently; linguists call this "semantic ambiguity." (See Figure 8.21 on the next page for a comparison of these options.)

A numerical scale is free of the interpretation of terms, but quantification is sometimes a hard thing for people to do, especially if the question is about an emotional issue. Sometimes making a mark on a line is easier to do than choosing a number, but then again people can become confused when they see a simple line with nothing written on it, and there can be a higher up-front cost to explaining what they are about to do.

To give an example of some of the options here: there is a lot of debate in the medical community about the best way to assess how much pain a patient is in. These are some of the pain scales that have been developed.

• The *Verbal Rating Scale* uses names for pain categories, like "none," "mild," "discomforting," "distressing," "horrible," and "excruciating."

• The *Wong-Baker Pain Faces Scale* shows the patient six faces with expressions ranging from very happy to crying, and with labels showing both a number and a text, ranging from zero ("no hurt") to five ("hurts worst"). There has been some criticism of this scale because the worst face is shown crying, and some people (especially children) think they cannot choose that option unless they are *actually* crying. Hence, interpretation matters even if pictures are used instead of words.

• The *Numerical Pain Scale* asks the person to describe their pain by choosing a number between zero and ten, with zero representing "no pain" and ten representing the "worst possible pain."

• The *Visual Analogue Scale* uses a line with numbers from zero to ten, with the left side

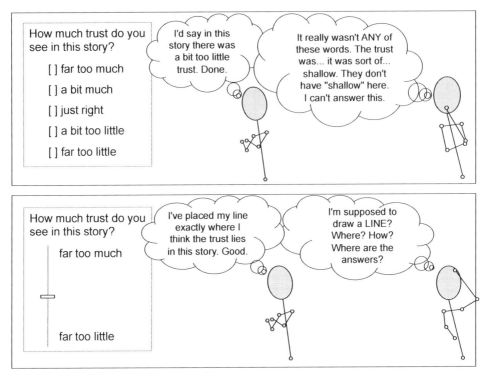

Figure 8.21. Scales designated by words are quick to comprehend but may not adequately represent people's feelings. Graphical scales provide more flexibility but sometimes create more confusion.

labeled "no pain" and the right side labeled "worst possible pain," on which the patient is instructed to either circle a number or make a mark.

There are all sorts of studies showing that each of these is better than the others in one situation or another, but as far as I can tell there is no overall consensus as to which is best; each has its strengths and weaknesses. Often people use all three methods (words, numbers, lines) at the same time and don't specify which method the patient should use. That approach avoids difficulties in understanding, but it increases the amount of time and attention needed to answer the question.

I myself am a big fan of graphical line scales where each extreme is marked with a label but there are no intermediate labels. With this method there is some up-front explaining to be done, but most people pick up the format quickly, and they can mark a spot on the line easily with their pencil (or mouse, on a computer). Problems with intermediate labels go

away; you don't need to find a perfect way to say "sometimes but not all that often." It is just a spot on the line. Coming up with good names for the two ends of the line is still a difficulty, but you would have that task in either case. However, there are times when named lists are superior to scales, especially when many dimensions are needed or when labels are well established.

As you design your questions, remember that most questions can be asked in multiple ways. Don't allow yourself to fall into the trap of believing that there is only one way to ask a particular question. I have been friends with some particular questions, like "when did this story take place," for a long time, and some have surprised me by working even better with new clothes on. Why not try a few different ways to ask the same question and see what works best for you?

Advice on writing questions about stories

Here is some general advice on asking questions about stories. Each of the sections below represents a lesson I learned in practical experience (usually the hard way) from which you can benefit.

Ask questions that matter and resonate

Find questions that want to be asked. Don't just pull out a standard list: think more deeply, more emotionally, more aspirationally. Think about what you want to achieve with your project. Think about its fondest hopes and dreams. Find questions those dreams want to ask. Pretend you are sitting with the stories and answers you intend to collect. In a perfect world, what do they tell you? Then come at it from the other side: what do your participants have to say, want to say, need to say? If you can't guess, collect some unadorned stories before you design any questions about them. Find the place where what you need to hear and what needs to be said come together.

Transmit your excitement and energy

You are doing your project because you hope to achieve some goal that is important to you and to the participants. What is it about that goal that moves you the most? Does that excitement come through in your questions? Do your questions, as a whole, feel like a contribution to something positive and helpful, or do they feel like a tax form? If you can't tell, try your questions out on anyone you can find who will be in your group of participants. Watch them as they look over the questions. Are your questions communicating your energy to them? Does their interest leap up to meet it? Or do your questions serve as a poor conduit for your enthusiasm?

Gather interpretations, not opinions

When you ask questions about stories, you want people to direct their attention to the story and away from themselves. This creates the *narrative displacement* you need to get past defensive walls and gather authentic ground truths about the topic you are exploring together. So make sure your questions keep people engaged in *interpretation* and don't allow them to wander over into *opinion*. For example, even if you

are one hundred percent sure that each of your participants will be the protagonist of their own stories, don't ask a question like, "In this story, what did you need to solve a problem?" Doing that will remove them from the context of story interpretation and place their attention back on themselves. Instead, ask "In this story, what did the main person need to solve a problem?" *Keep them in the story*.

It's a bit tricky figuring out how to refer to whoever is in the story without saying "you" and "your story" to people. Rarely can you use the word *protagonist*, because most non-screenwriters will not understand what you mean. Instead, it's better to talk about the *main or central person or character*. *Character* is more broadly understood than *protagonist*, but it can be a dangerous word to use with suspicious participants or sensitive topics, because it can be taken to imply that the story is a fiction or lie. *Person*, though not very exciting, is the least risky.

When you ask questions about the story's main character, make sure to ask *who* that is. I've seen a few question sets that asked about behaviors, beliefs, and characteristics of the central person, but then forgot to ask who that person was. When this happens the answers get mixed together and lose their utility—was it the teacher or the student who showed compassion? Was it the sales agent or the customer who needed information? I hate it when this happens, because people often reveal things about themselves as a story character that they are less willing or able to reveal directly. A simple question like "Who is the central person of this story?" or "Who is this story about?" (and then some choices based on the important societal/topical roles of people who might be in the story) can avoid this problem.

You might think that the question "How do you feel about this story?" presents an exception to the keep-their-eyes-on-the-story rule. But it doesn't, because it asks for an interpretation of the *story*, not an opinion of the storyteller's. If you asked the question, "What does your story mean?" or, "What is your story about?" you would open the gates to the world of platitudes and close down the path to ground truth.

Figure 8.22. Watch out for directing messages that tell people what you want them to say.

Don't ask people why they *told* their story. If you do that, you might as well skip the story and go straight to "what do you think about this issue." Instead, ask people *what the story says to them*. That's still interpretation, and that's still magic.

Mind your messages

It is so very easy to slip subtle messages into questions about stories. We all betray ourselves when we ask questions; it's human. Some messages, like "I am excited about this project" and "I hope you will find yourself heard here" and "I'm here to listen" and "I respect your viewpoint" are messages you *want* to communicate. But other messages can creep in, ones that damage the potential of the project. Those are worth finding and removing.

I can think of three types of message you might send in your questions about stories: directing messages (what to do), characterizing messages (who you are, who we are), and shared-value messages (what we all believe).

Directing messages. A directing message tells people which responses are acceptable and which are not (see Figure 8.22). This is close to a "leading question" in direct questioning surveys (but since we are telling stories, I call it directing since it is like you being the director of their story). The most extreme directing message is what I call the "do you want to keep your job" question, in which the correct answer to the question is painfully obvious. Projects with questions like these are foregone conclusions and aren't worth finishing. But many lesser grades of directing questions can slip under your radar.

Say you are asking patients for stories about their relationships with their doctors. Say you ask what the story shows about the doctor's commitment to quality medical care. If all of the available answers are positive, ranging from "satisfactory" to "excellent," for example, you have communicated to your participants that you do not want them dishing any dirt on their doctors. "Quack" is not a possibility, nor is incompetent, dishonest, burned out, or confused. The message is: you will say this, and you will *not* say that. The worst part about a message like this is that it will affect not only the answers to that question, but *every answer* and *every story* people tell after they see it. It will infect the whole interaction.

Or say you are looking at innovation among the employees of your organization. One of your questions has to do with what the main characters in stories do with their work time. It would be a project-killer to include "play" or "chatting" or "messing around" as possible answers, even though this is the sort of thing you are looking for, because nobody in their right mind would choose that. But if you put in an answer like "unconstructed exploration" or "collaborative brainstorming" you are likely to find the play you are looking for.

This is not to say you should not direct people when you ask questions about stories. Certainly you want to nudge people! You want them to reflect on their story, to consider the questions carefully, to recall the information you need, to explore their feelings. Keep those directions and lose the others. My suggestion is to have a range of people read the questions and report on their feelings about where they feel nudged.

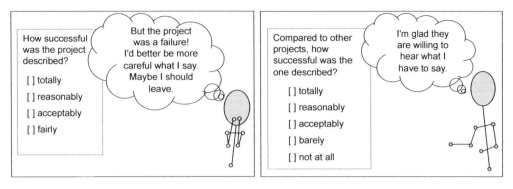

Figure 8.23. Watch out for characterizing messages that limit the responses people can give.

Are they nudged in the way you'd like them to be?

Characterizing messages. When you make a statement that describes your participants in some way, for some of them, your statement might not be correct. To those people your statement constitutes a message, intended or not. The message is: this is not for you. (See Figure 8.23.)

The classic example of this sort of characterization is in the riddle that goes like this.

> A man and his son are rushed to the hospital, both badly hurt. The surgeon on duty in the emergency room cries out, "I cannot operate on this boy! He is my son!"

At this point so many people know this story that it's just a funny little test to see if there's anyone left who can't guess the answer. But think how the surgeon would respond to questions that assume she is a man. What would she do? She might try very hard to prove she can still be considered worthy of speaking; she might lose enthusiasm and plod through the rest of the required task without giving due consideration to anything; she might answer the questions vindictively; or she might simply walk away and exclude herself from the project. *All* of these responses are misfires for a PNI project.

A few more examples. The available list of possible answers to the question "How do you feel about this story?" shows people what sorts of emotions you expect them to have. Say the list includes "hysterical" but not "calm," or "motivated" but not "desperate," or "happy" but not "sad." That communicates a message. I like to check for counter-balancing answers. If there is a "desperate" there should be a "reassured" or "content." If there is "to create" there should be "to destroy." Or if there is a long list of possible problems, one answer should be "there *wasn't* a problem." Why? Because if you *don't* have that answer the message is "you are a person who has problems."

Shared-valued messages. Also watch out for "of course everybody thinks this" shared-value messages. These make a statement about the worldview of your participants by describing *your* worldview and making it clear that you assume they share it. Again these can be so subtle that you don't notice them. Even the names you use for places and people can communicate presumably shared values. Listen to this sentence from Wikipedia on the name of one of the airports in Washington, D.C.:

> The airport is commonly known as "National," "Washington National," "Reagan," and "Reagan National."

Which of these names you call that airport has something to do with your feelings about Ronald Reagan and his politics, and your age and history in the area. Every city has a few of these tellingly-named landmarks. Even the names of some whole cities, and countries, are indicative (Mumbai or Bombay? Burma or Myanmar?). Most people in official roles can also be referred to in several ways. Is a teacher different from an instructor? How about an educator? A trainer? What is the difference between a cop, a policeman, a police officer, a law enforcement agent, and an officer of the law? A page on Wikipedia lists nearly three hundred slang terms for police officer. (Wow. Important?)

It is so easy not to notice characterizing messages that I suggest always having someone *else* look for them. Of course you can't write questions that encompass the worldview of every sentient being on the planet, but you can aim to get to the point where most of your participants believe the project is about them and not someone else.

Build a two-way conversation

The answers you make available for people to choose are the participants' part of the conversation. If you give people a voice that consistently matches what they would say if they were speaking to you, they will be more likely to find answers they can choose. This will both motivate them and save precious time.

For example, the issue of whether your participants are "educated" is important in asking them questions about stories. By "educated" I don't mean smart or well-informed. I mean something closer to cultural homogeneity, more like "educated about the way people usually ask questions in surveys." Social scientists are used to throwing around precise terms, graphs, scales, ratings, and other social constructs, and sometimes they forget that not everybody is equally used to these things.

For example, if your participants are not academic or professional people, the question "How do you feel about this story?" is far superior to "Please rate the emotional intensity of this story." And if they *are* academics or professionals, the latter version will probably work better than the more conversational, candid, personal form.

Think about the mindset of your participants and meet them where they are. Put on their shoes. Picture yourself as one of the people you will be asking questions. Imagine yourself where your participants will be: in an interview, in a room you have reserved for a session, at their home computer using your web site. If a question seems intrusive or rude, fix it. If a question is confusing, fix it. Put your questions aside for a few days, then surprise yourself by

"finding" them next to your bed in the morning. See how they appear then.

Also, be consistent: don't mix casual statements like "I like my work" with more formal statements like "I am satisfied with my current situation." Give the storyteller a coherent voice, a solid character. The more the character you present matches their real character, the better their responses can be. Yes, you will not be able to do this perfectly, not being them. But it is better to build the most coherent voice you can than to ignore consistency and present a confused cacophony of voices.

Do not judge; do not appear to judge

Make sure none of your questions can possibly be taken as *critical* examinations of the person's story (see Figure 8.24 on the facing page). Don't ask if the story shows a change in value, because people might think you are saying the story *should* have showed a change in value and is deficient otherwise. Don't ask if the main character meets a challenge, because people will worry that they *should* have met a challenge. For some reason I have never completely understood, people tend to be nervous about the quality of their told stories and are quick to jump to the conclusion that you are judging their storytelling skills. A common response is panic (as in: Oh no, did I get it wrong?) followed by either thrashing about trying to get things right or withdrawal into non-response.

To avoid the appearance of judgment, I try to adorn my questions with signs indicating an invitation to *reflect* rather than *judge*. Some useful reflection-pointing signs include: in your experience; based on what you have seen; when you consider; as you contemplate; when you think about; what would you say about; how do you find; what appears to you; how would you characterize; what do you see; what do you think.

Avoid the words "opinion" and "judgment" and all synonyms, because they bring criticism back in. Asking people to judge their own stories implies that you *also* will be judging them, which will trigger a defense reaction. Reflection, consideration, contemplation, meditation: these are the cognitive functions you want to activate. Criticizing, analyzing, inspecting, scrutinizing, evaluating, dissecting, finding fault or praise,

Figure 8.24. Be careful to avoid the appearance of judging stories for narrative quality.

rating, categorizing, nitpicking, defending, attacking: these are *not* what you want people to be doing with their stories.

Why pamper people like this? Why does this matter? For a simple reason. Judgment does not produce high-quality catalytic material for participatory sensemaking, which is why you are asking people questions in the first place. Remember, you are not asking people questions in order to *prove* anything. You are asking people questions so that the patterns their answers form will stimulate thought and discussion. Reflection opens; judgment closes.

Write questions that stand on their own

When I watch people look at a form full of questions about stories, this is what I see. First, people flick their eyes over the introductory part of the form, the part that tells them the *context* in which the questions are being asked. Next, they look at how many questions are on the form, to assess the *scope* of the task. Then their eyes hop down the form from one question to the next (jumping over answers) to understand the *intent* of the form at a high level. Finally they come back and read the *details* in the answers they see as they begin the task.

In other words, when they see your questions, people will ask these questions, in this order:

1. Why should I do this?
2. How long is it?
3. What is it about?
4. What do I have to do?

Now a quiz. Based on that understanding, should you or should you not include a question like this one?

In your experience, which of these statements is true?

No, you should not. Why? Because the question skimmer will have no idea what the question is until they have read the *answers*, on their fourth pass over the form. Which of *what* statements? About *what*? Memorize this fact: *people don't look at the available answers* while they are skimming through the questions. I can't tell you how many people I have seen make this mistake.

Why does this matter? Because you want people to understand the totality of the task placed before them *as they assess the task* in order to decide whether to put their energy into it. You want them to understand how the questions relate to the story they just told. You want your questions to *tell them the story* of their answering the questions, a story that highlights the opportunities the task will provide for reflection and insight. You want people to see *what's in it for them*. If the questions mean nothing at first glance, people will not be motivated to complete the task. At least they will not be *intrinsically* motivated; extrinsic motivation results in a different outcome, a less meaningful one, usually.

So: make sure your questions are skim-ready. Each question must stand on its own and communicate its intent with or without its answers. To check this, drop out your answers and show *only the questions* to a willing friend. Then ask the friend what they think each question is about. Next, show them the version with the answers and ask if any of the questions seem different now. If their idea of what the questions are about differs before and after they see the answers, reword the questions until the story of the task comes out from the questions alone.

Believe it or not, the same rule holds for answers: *they* must stand alone as well. Yes, I am actually saying that people will forget what question they are answering while reading the answers to that question. (All who have done this and marked the wrong answer in consequence raise their hands.... Now I have to go back to typing....) Answers as well as questions must communicate intent.

So the above question should say:

> In your experience, which of these statements about trust at work is true?

And *then* the answers should say "trust at work is strong" and so on. The rule is: *don't make people grope* for any of the essential information the question form provides: context, scope, intent, or details. It wastes motivation and cognitive budget.

Ask why (when you can)

If you have the opportunity to collect some stories in a pilot project before you start your larger project (a method I recommend), ask people *why* they answered the way they did. For example, say you plan to ask the question, "Are there any people or groups whom you think particularly need to hear this story?" Say you are doing some pilot work to refine your questions. Since your pilot story collection should be more open, do not only ask *which* people or groups should hear the story, but *why* they should hear it. You may be surprised by what people say, and it may help you plan the project better.

Asking why in a larger story collection may lead to difficulties dealing with the volume of material produced. But you can still give people the *opportunity* to say why, even if it is not something you plan to rely on. You can do this by having lots of empty space on your question form and telling people they can make any elucidating comments they like about why they answered any question the way they did. Some people will probably take you up on the offer.

Do not conflate

One of the worst destroyers of answers to questions about stories is *conflation:* answers that mean "I feel this way" mixed indistinguishably together with answers that mean "I couldn't find the answer I wanted, so I picked this one instead." Conflation happens when people cannot find an answer in your list that matches the answer in their minds. Badly conflated answers usually have to be thrown out because they cannot reveal useful patterns, and they usually result from inadequate preparation.

The best antidote to conflation is pilot testing of questions. When that is not possible, I use and suggest a simple exercise to detect possible conflation. It goes like this. First, make a list of people with widely varying backgrounds and personalities. It's best if they are in the group of people you will be asking to tell stories, but if that's not possible, just consider people you know or remember. They can even be fictional or historical. The important thing is that they be *diverse* in their perceptions. Consider a priest of your acquaintance, a thief, a politician, a gardener—you get the picture.

Now that you have some people in mind, take your question list and mentally picture each person answering the questions. On each question that has predefined answers, picture the person with their pencil hovering over the possible answers to the question. Is there an answer for that person? Do they find something that works for them? If they can't find an answer, what can you do to help them answer the question? You can also multiply the people by situations, and picture them telling stories that come out well and poorly, and so on. When you get to the point where everyone can find an answer in every situation, you have a set of answers that will not ooze together into a meaningless mass.

Do not ask for more information than you need

Within each question (never mind how many questions you ask), don't ask for anything you don't need, for two reasons. First, people don't like being pried open. That much is obvious. Second, asking for more detail takes up more of your cognitive budget. It takes longer to consider more possible choices.

For choice questions, the number of possible answers you should provide follows the same rule as the number of questions. For a kiosk situation, provide only three to five possible answers; for volunteers, six to nine; for committed participants, ten to fifteen. Why? When a question has too many answers for the prevailing participation level, people either ignore the last answers or ignore the whole question. I've seen questions with too many answers where the first three answers are disproportionately chosen. This usually does not mean those answers are best. It means people looked at the long list, said "ugh" to themselves, and truncated it for you (but each in their own way!). The result is muddied patterns and thrown-out questions.

I find that question designers often design overly fine-grained answers out of zeal to meet their project's goals. But over-reaching on answer detail can reduce, not improve, your ability to discover insights. For example, if you are asking "when did this story happen," how much resolution do you need? Do you need to distinguish between events that happened six months and a year ago? When I'm looking over answers, I often find random assignments when the meanings of answers are too close together. People rarely have the time or energy to make precise distinctions between feelings. It may seem useful to differentiate between whether people told a story "to explain" or "to inform" or "to clarify," but storytellers often will not want to slice things so finely. Remember, the point of the whole thing is not to prove or measure anything. The point is to provide food for thought, and this can only happen if you don't bog things down with too much detail.

An exercise that works here is to explain the differences between answers to yourself (or in a group). If the explanation is long or confusing, maybe you don't need two separate answers. Justify each small difference. For example, say you have "frustrated" and "irritated" in your answers to your "how do you feel" question. Why do you need *both* of those? What situations are you trying to separate? Do they *need* to be separated? Do you want to use some of your cognitive budget on having people assign their feelings to those small categories? (Sometimes such a fine division is necessary; if so, be sure to free up some budget from somewhere else to make room for it.)

Note that above (in "Do not conflate") I said that having too *few* answers to a question can be a problem, because people can't find the answers they need in the list. This seems like contradictory advice, and it is! You need both accuracy *and* brevity in your answers, and you need to find the best balance between them.

Do not give non-responders nothing to say

That's a pile of negatives, isn't it? I'll wait while you work it out.

Getting no response is a fact of asking questions, and not just with four-year-olds. For every question there will be some people who cannot or don't want to answer it. This hard fact sometimes hits up against walls of pride in project planners. Sometimes the people designing questions do not want to admit (even to themselves) that those responding may not want to choose an answer. Admit to yourself that some people will not have an answer, or will not want to think hard about it, or will not want to tell you what they really think.

Once your little pity party is over, look to your creativity to gain information even when people do not respond. How? By giving people multiple ways to not respond (see Figure 8.25 on the next page). Turning a lack of response into response can create insights, for example by distinguishing when someone didn't understand, didn't remember, didn't care, didn't want to spend the time, didn't know, or knew and didn't want to tell you. Within reason, the more information you can help people give you about *why* they aren't answering, the better you can support sensemaking.

My favorite example of this was on a project where we were doing a pilot story collection to test some questions. On the "how do you feel about this story" question, most of the participants chose the answer "good." They did this for all sorts of stories, from the mundane to the catastrophic. What happened was, not seeing a noncommittal option, they decided that "good" *was* the noncommittal option. The clear message was that for this particular set of people, telling stories about this particular topic, some of them needed a way to say "I'd rather not tell you that." When we took out "good" and added "I'd rather not say," the utility of the story collec-

Figure 8.25. Be sure to give people who don't have an answer a way to explain why they don't have an answer.

tion improved. Some of the worst misfires I've seen have been ones where participants could not find a place to put non-responses and muddied up the real responses with them.

In particular, I find the phrase "I would rather not say" worth including in every question where it makes sense. I remember on one project we noticed that the more probing the question, the lower the ratio of "I would rather not say" to simply leaving the question unanswered. On those questions the response reached past "I would rather not say" to "I would rather not say 'I would rather not say.'" That's a useful piece of responding non-response, isn't it? We could then compare stories on either side of those answers.

All of these non-response responses are legitimate in one context or other:

- I don't know
- I'm not sure
- I'd rather not say
- That's too private
- I'd like to skip this question

- I don't understand the question
- The question doesn't apply
- I don't like the question
- I don't think the question makes sense
- None of these answers work for me
- None of these
- My answer is (blank)
- (nothing marked on the question at all)

Several of these answers are subtly different from each other in ways that match some contexts better than others. Of course you would never use more than probably two of these per question, but don't leave them out. They might save the project.

Advice on writing questions about participants

A few simple rules apply to all direct questions about people and their views.

Do not ask for any more detail than you need

If you are used to conducting standard surveys, you may think it natural to ask people for their exact ages, incomes, and other information.

But this is not a standard survey. You don't need to know whether people are forty-five, forty-six, or forty-seven years old; you just need to know if they are young, middle aged, or elderly. You don't need to know their income down to the penny; you just need to know if they live in an apartment, a detached house, or a mansion. For any demographic question, push it down to the minimal amount of detail you need. Make yourself justify each bit of information you collect, and if you can't justify it, drop it.

People often think I'm some kind of privacy zealot when I say not to ask for more information than you need. Nobody cares about privacy anymore, they say. I remember a conversation with a person who was asking people for their telephone number in an online form. I said, "What do you need their phone number for?" And he said, "Oh, I don't really, it's just the usual thing." That kind of might-as-well thinking might make sense in bureaucratic contexts, but for story work it can be risky. Why? It has to do with the volunteer nature of storytelling: if you *must* play, you cannot *play*.

Whether people are willing to answer questions about themselves is just the tip of the iceberg of assent. In story work there are many ways to refuse, and a lot of them look exactly like compliance. When you cross the invisible line (different for each person) between reasonable inquiry and unreasonable intrusion, people don't necessarily stop telling stories. They just tell *different* stories. And those different stories produce a different outcome for your project, perhaps not the one you were after. So this justify-asking-it rule is not (only) a moral stance; it is a tactical plan.

Find the right words

When you write questions about people, you may be asking for personal information, so watch out for anything that will spook people. For example, in some communities the marital-status answer "living together" may raise no eyebrows, but in others it may turn people away. In other communities, leaving that option *off* the list will irritate people. Be careful to avoid any answer (or omission) that will offend. Test your questions to find out.

Even subtle wordings can be offensive. How about, "Are you a homeowner or do you rent?" Do you see the difference? One is a solid citizen noun; the other is denied the status of solid reality. How about, "Do you rent or own your home?" That's another way I've seen that question asked, but it always galled me in the days when I rented: it felt like they were rubbing my nose in the fact that it wasn't *my* home I lived in. How about, "Do you rent or own your place of residence?" That's better, though it sounds stilted. (I didn't say it was *easy;* I just said it mattered.)

Close no doors

I don't suggest ever *requiring* answers to questions about participants, unless one of the answers is "not sure" or "rather not say." Story listening is not interrogation; it's a game. If you give people a way out, they will tell you more in the questions they do choose to answer. Also, those who do answer the question will be comforted by the fact that they had a way out even if they didn't take it.

Ask after

Ask people about themselves *after* you ask them about their stories. If you are going to scare anybody off, do it after you have heard their views. Is that manipulative? A bit. But there is far more value in stories without demographic information than in demographics without stories.

There's a nice reason to do this too, though. After a participant has told a story, their answers to questions about their opinions will have been placed into a richer context, and this will help them justify their views (in their own minds) better than if they had been asked point-blank about their views. That's part of what storytelling is for: to communicate views with more nuance and depth than with simple statements. Let people tell their stories before you ask them direct questions, and they'll be more comfortable telling you what they think. (See Figure 8.26 on the following page.)

Building question sets

A set of questions about a story is half of a conversation you hope to have with people about the story. To make sure the question set grows into a full conversation (of the kind that leads

Figure 8.26. Never ask people questions about themselves or their views *before* you collect their stories. Get the stories out first.

to excellent catalyzing material for sensemaking), here are some guidelines you can follow in how you put questions together.

Create an interesting, varied experience

I recommend creating a *mixture* of question types (free entry, named choices, scales) within any set of questions about stories. I recommend this for two reasons. First, mixtures keep the question-answering activity interesting by reducing monotony. Even though people may be able to read and understand questions more quickly if they are all the same type, people may get one question confused with another or get bored. There is a natural tension between people's need to understand (hence the need for clarity and consistency) and their tendency to get bored or lose interest when things repeat (hence the need for variety). You can create clarity without sacrificing variety.

Secondly, varied questions produce more interesting patterns to catalyze sensemaking. If you asked every single question with a fixed choice list, for example, all of your catalytic images would be bar graphs of counts (this many people told about dogs, this many about cats, etc.). But if you asked some fixed-choice questions, some scalar questions, and some free-entry questions, you will end up with several types of images: scatterplots, bubble correlation diagrams, annotated lists, even 3D landscapes. The point of catalysis is to stimulate thought and discussion, and for this diversity of images is a boon. So build diversity into your questions, the better to work with the answers later.

As I said in the section about ways to ask questions (page 140), I love questions with continuous scales between extremes. This is partly because people tend to understand them quickly, but it is also because the answers to these questions come together to produce scatterplots. Looking at a scatterplot is like looking at a starry sky or a mountain stream or a fireplace. I have noticed that people seem to enjoy contemplating scatterplots more than bar graphs, which look too much like conclusions to permit freedom to imagine and discover. So I recommend using at least some continuous-variation scales when you can. But having said that, I would never design a question set with *only* scales, because it would produce *only* scatterplots, not an array of diverse images for the sensemaking parade.

Design a conversational flow

Order your questions like a conversation. Make them flow naturally. If you were asking someone questions in person, which would you start with? Having to switch gears or answer questions in an order that doesn't seem natural wastes cognitive budget. It is more important that a question seem related to the ones around it *by what it asks about* than by what type it is. Try asking your questions out loud. Listen to whether the order jars or flows freely. Does it make sense to ask about this after that? Does the story of the conversation flow naturally?

One thing I've found, for example, is that the "how do you feel" question likes to be asked right after the story is told. Doing this sets the stage for the questions that come after it. It communicates to the participants that you will be asking them to think about their personal feelings about the story, not asking them for facts and figures. In general, the further away you get from the story, the less vivid the storyteller's emotions about it will be, so it is often best to ask the more factual questions later. Asking factual questions first can put people into classification mode and reduce their emotional response when you need it most.

Create a question form that supports the flow of stories

At some point you will make a transition from a *list* of questions to a *form* with questions on it, some kind of presentation you will make to the people you want to speak with. In an interview, the form will be spoken, but in a group session or survey, the form will be on paper or on a screen. The following advice pertains to paper or screen forms. (For interview guidance, I suggest consulting oral history guidelines; they give much better advice than I can. Still, some of what follows may be useful in an interview setting as well.)

Your question form should *answer all expected questions* about the purpose of the session. For example, if you anticipate concerns about anonymity or the distribution of collected stories, address them on the form.

Your form should be *concise*. You cannot expect people to spend more than about thirty seconds reviewing the form, so you need to use that tiny budget wisely. Keep your statements to a few short sentences. For example, "Today we are sharing experiences about our town's wildlife. Your input is anonymous. The stories we tell today will support future discussions."

Your form should be abundantly *clear*. To test this, take a draft of your form and place it in front of anyone you can find—neighbors, relatives, children—and ask them to skim it, then explain what they think it says. If what they say it says is not what you meant it to say, make another draft. The last thing you need is to have your group story session snagged on ten minutes of people asking what you mean by "new urbanism" or some other bit of jargon out of place.

Your form should *not* include a lecture about stories or storytelling. This is a common mistake of inexperienced story collectors. It does not matter if participants know what a story is. It only matters if they tell stories. Whether they tell stories is more likely to be damaged than improved by information that will only make them self-conscious.

Your form should be *grammatically perfect*. I know that sounds pedantic, but believe me, there *will* be pedants in any group of participants, and you will irritate them. The non-pedants will not be irritated, but they will still be distracted. Trivial things like subjects and verbs that don't agree, such as "How long ago does the events in this story take place" can stop people up. *Never disrupt the flow of stories.*

This might be a good place to list some of the things I have seen well-meaning people do in writing questions about stories, each of which causes me to grind my teeth in annoyance. (It had to go *somewhere*.)

- Do not end a statement with a question mark, like this: "Choose which of these roles are present in your story?" Conversely, do not end a question with a period, like this: "What roles are represented in this story." Grrrrr.

- Do not misspell. Do you think this story shows resposibilie behavior? Do you? Or are you distracted by that monstrous word? Misspelling means: *We don't care*. We want *you* to put forth your best, but *we* didn't bother. Not very motivating.

Figure 8.27. Mistakes on question forms slow people down, irritate them, and reduce their confidence in you. Don't waste your precious opportunity to gather their input. (How many mistakes can you find in the bad version of this form? I count at least twenty.)

- Do not include nonsensical commands. A statement like "select the no more than three questions for this answer" will drain energy into a useless pool of confusion.

- Do not get basic facts about the community or organization wrong. I confess to having done this a few times due to outsider ignorance. I cringe in horror when this happens, because it communicates a message: we know nothing about you or your world. Not good for storytelling.

- Do not give answers that are of different categories, like "cat" and "dog" followed by "it's raining" and "why not try Stilton cheese?" You are looking to create *an experience that flows without hitches or bumps.* Things in lists should be of the same type so they don't bump.

- Do not give answer ranges that overlap, like for age: up to twenty-five years, twenty-five to fifty years, fifty-plus years. What is a twenty-five-year-old to do? Scream?

- Do not overuse capital letters. It takes longer to read capital letters, and they are rude out of place. Don't use them for things that are *not* alarming, like "PLEASE ANSWER THESE QUESTIONS" or "GIVE YOUR STORY A TITLE." Use them sparingly, for things you really do *need* people to notice, like "circle only ONE answer" or "please GIVE US your completed form."

- Do not switch back and forth between "I" and "you." I have seen this one a lot. One question says, "The title I would give this story is ... " and the next says, "How do you feel about this story?" Choose to refer to the participant as "I" or "you" and then stick with it. (Actually I hate the "I" form, because it implies the participant is talking to themselves. I think it is better to engage people in conversation, even if it is an imaginary one. Why not speak to them as "you?" Seems more natural to me.)

- Do not highlight parts of some questions but not others. I like to write my questions so that one or two words are highlighted (usually in bold) in each, like "Which of these best matches the **theme** of this story?" I find high-lighting helps people skim the form quickly to get an idea of the conversation before they start it in earnest. If you choose to use high-lighting, make sure it is evenly applied, not haphazard.

- Do not use jargon if you can help it. Read your questions out loud. This is a *conversation* you are trying to imagine, not a treatise. Even with professionals you can write conversationally.

The more smoothly your questions flow, the better the results you will see. Keep people focused on their own reflective processes, not on your presentation and its flaws. And be careful: once you've been working on a question set for a while, it all begins to seem perfectly logical even if it isn't. Try your questions out on somebody you can watch, and see where they pause and ponder. Where does their pencil hover? Is it because they are thinking about the story, or because they are trying to figure out what you meant by your poorly presented question? Increase the former and reduce the latter (see Figure 8.27 on the preceding page).

Your form should be *attractive,* even appealing. People respond to beautiful design. Handing your participants something printed badly in an unreadable mélange of fonts sends a message that you don't value their contribution, because you didn't bother preparing something nice for them to work with. It's like inviting someone to visit your home, then asking them to sit on a dirty floor. Give people something beautiful that will feel like an honor to use. This may sound silly, but I've seen it make a difference. When you want to get people telling stories, use every opportunity at your disposal to send a message of appreciation and respect. Pick up a book on "design for dummies" and take its advice.

Lastly, your form should be a thought *landscape,* not a thought jail. Drop a casual hint at the start of the session that people can use their forms to take notes or make comments on the questions or the session or anything they like. Mention that if they don't like a question they can write that, or if they can't decide between two answers they can circle both (and say *why* they circled both, if they like). If they have a random thought about the project, they can feel free to jot down some notes on it. Leave room on the pages for all of this, or even mark out a section that says "your notes." If you can have a small photocopier in the room so people can keep a copy of their pages if they like, that will help make the point as well.

This mindset may be alien to both you and your participants, and the physical form of a sheet of questions may constrain your thought about the interaction. Allowing changes to the expected form will help shift expectations toward participation. You want people to see the form as an opportunity to reflect, not a trial to endure. You want them to create, not simply dump out, their interpretations, because in that way they will participate in sensemaking as they reflect.

Why go to all this trouble? Why shift expectations toward participation? Because it will improve the catalytic material that results, which will improve the sensemaking that comes later. It will also have an impact on the return of stories to your community or organization.

I remember once doing a group story session as part of pilot planning for a larger project. When I got back the paper forms from the session I saw right away that our questions needed some work. Quite a few of the participants had drawn long, raking lines—gashes, really—across several of the questions. It was fortunate that they felt encouraged to take such measures. On looking at which questions were defaced, I realized that they were a cluster of questions the participants felt were insulting to their professional status. We reworded the questions in the next session, and responses improved.

In another project, one of our questions contained a factual error about the organization. The participants let us know this by surrounding the mistake with question marks and exclamation points. In both cases, if we had ignored the annotating marks, or had given explicit instructions to use the forms exactly as they were written, we would have missed an important understanding that improved the project.

Sample question sets

In this section I have pretended to be starting three separate projects with different goals, and

I have put together question sets for each to give you an idea of how questions can come together.

Sample one: museum renovation

This sample imagines an organizational environment (a museum) with a kiosk situation and one-on-one interviews.

Goals: Why are you doing the project? In preparation for our historical museum's renovation project in the spring, we want to find out if there are any problems the museum should be addressing in its educational displays. Our hope is to provide input to the renovation process that will help the museum staff refine its exhibits to better serve the community.

Relations: Who are you in the community or organization? We are the Friends of the Museum. Our project is supported in spirit by the museum, but we are providing all the volunteer time to make it happen. We have shown our plan to the museum staff, and we plan to meet with them for a final sensemaking meeting, but what comes in between will be our work.

Focus: What is the project about? We will mainly focus on *gaps*—places where the museum isn't helping its visitors learn as much as they could about our area's past. When people leave the museum puzzled about the past, we want to know why.

Range: What will the project cover? We want to cover three ranges of visitor characteristics: from first-time guest to dedicated member; from local resident to regional or foreign traveler; and from all levels of educational background. We will assess our range at a few different times during the project and try to balance out our collections by seeking out visitors in areas where we have few stories.

Scope: How big will the project be? Our plan is to sit in the museum lobby and ask departing visitors for a few moments of their time. We have ten volunteer interviewers who will do the interviewing. Our interviews will be no more than a few minutes long. We will ask each visitor to tell one story. We will ask four questions about each story, and four about each participant. Each volunteer will collect ten stories, for a total of one hundred stories. We will record the stories on audiotape and fill out paper forms as we do the interviews.

Emphasis: Which PNI phases will be most prominent? After the interviews are collected, we will transcribe the recordings. Then we (the Friends) will have a catalytic meeting to work together on patterns. We will print each story and its answers to questions on a card; then we will sort the cards together and take pictures of the results. Together we will choose which patterns we find strongest and prepare some notes in multiple interpretations. Next we will hold a sensemaking meeting of the Friends and the museum staff, where we will work with the stories and with our observations and interpretations. We will invite interested members of the public, including those who told stories, to come to the sensemaking session. Together we hope to finish the sensemaking meeting with some suggestions and ideas for the renovation.

Our interview script is as follows.

Hi. My name is [say name]. I'm a volunteer with the *Friends of the Museum.* [Show volunteer badge.] I'm helping with a project to improve our museum's educational displays. May I ask you a few questions about your visit to the museum today?

Thank you! This will just take a *few minutes.* I'd like to *record* our interview so I can be sure to catch what you say. After we transcribe the interview, we will destroy the recording. This is *completely anonymous.* I won't be asking for your name. Is the recording all right with you?

- It is? Great. [turn on tape recorder]
- No? Then I won't turn on the recorder. I'll just take notes while you talk. [be prepared with notepad to write notes]

Now let's begin. Looking back over your visit to the museum today, can you remember a *time* when you felt *confused* or *puzzled* by anything? Maybe you said to yourself "What's that?" What happened when you felt that way?

[Extra questions, if this one doesn't get a response (use only when necessary):]

- (if they say they never felt confused) Okay, then can you recall a time when you had *questions* that you didn't feel were answered? What happened then?

- (if they say all their questions were answered) Okay, then did you encounter any signs or educational displays that weren't as *complete* as you wanted them to be? What happened then?

- (if they still say this was not true) Okay, then can you just tell me *what happened* during your visit?

[after the story is told]

May I ask you a few questions about the experience you just told me about? Thanks.

1. How do you *feel* about that story? Can you show me a spot on this line that describes how you feel about it? [they hold up a large card with a line on it, with "wonderful" on one side and "horrible" on the other]

2. Thanks. Where were you in the museum when this happened? [only ask this if they didn't say it in the story][open ended answers, classify later]

3. Great. How *common* do you think this experience is among visitors to the museum? Do you think it is something *everybody* would have a problem with, or just a *few* people? Can you show me where you would mark your answer on this line? [from few people to everybody]

4. What do you think would have made that story *turn out differently?* [they listen to the answer or note it down]

Now I'd like to ask you a few questions about *yourself.*

1. Do you live in the *local* area, in the *state, outside* the state, or outside the *country?*

2. *How long* have you been coming to the museum? [choose answer from fixed list based on what they say]

3. Can you tell me roughly what your *educational experience* has been? High school, community college, university, and so on? [write down level mentioned]

4. Finally, is there anything you would like to say to the people who will be doing the renovation next spring?

Thank you very much for your time. Would you like a flower or a chocolate as a token of thanks for participating? Great.

If you are interested, you can *participate* in the meeting where we will be using our stories to help the museum plan its renovation. Here is some information on that meeting. [hand them the prepared paper] If you have any *questions* about the project, call this number *here.*

We will be posting a report on the project in next month's *Friends of the Museum newsletter,* like this one. You can pick these up at the museum or find them online at our web site. I've written that information *here.*

Thanks again for your help!

Also: each interviewer notes, without asking, age category, gender, apparent level of interest, whether the participant allowed the recording, and any other significant comments the participant made before or after the recording.

Sample two: neighborhood park

This sample imagines a community environment (people who live near a park) with a volunteer situation and one-on-one interviews.

Goals: Why are you doing the project? I got dragged into it, that's why. We picked this house ten years ago partly because it had such a great park across the street, and we've been going there ever since our oldest was in a stroller. Well. A few weeks ago the kids found a … I don't know the *technical* term for it, but it has something to do with drugs, in the park. I was pretty freaked out, I'll tell you. I told the kids the park is off-limits for the time being while we figure out what is going on. Joyce next door said she was walking her dog last week and saw the remains of a campfire and some beer cans, and that isn't supposed to be happening in our park either. It's a *playground* for goodness' sake!

Anyway, so Joyce and I, and Martin who has three kids too got together and we are going to talk to everybody along both sides of the street to see if we can figure out what's going on and what we can do about it. I went down to the town hall and told them what we are doing and they said that's fine, they will support us. So here we go, we're doing a project, as Joyce says.

Relations: Who are you in the community or organization? We are just concerned parents who worry about our kids and our park which is supposed to be a fun place for them to play, not a dangerous drug hang-out. What is this world coming to? Anyway like I said Joe at the town office said he wanted to hear what we find out, and Karen at the desk said she'd help us too.

Focus: What is the project about? We just want to hear from everybody who lives around the park and find out what they've seen and heard in the park over the last year or two. Things have been changing and we want to know what is going on. Who is using the park and what are they using it for? We aren't vigilantes or anything, don't get me wrong. Martin says it is a listening tour. That sounds about right.

Range: What will the project cover? Well like I said we plan to walk up and down all around the park talking to people. Martin said, and I guess I agree, that we should make sure to get over to the university dormitories too because he thinks some of the college kids are coming over to the park at night and maybe not cleaning up after themselves. He says what's the point of hearing what's going on only from one perspective? Which is kind of a point. He works at the university so I guess he can ask around there to find kids to talk to. He already asked the housing person there and they said they will support him if anybody gives him a hard time about it.

Scope: How big will the project be? Well, there's about twenty houses near the park, and then if you put in say ten kids from the dorms that'd be about thirty conversations with people. Also Martin says he'll hang out in the park for a few hours in the morning and evening to catch hold of anybody else who might not live nearby, so that might be another five or ten. If we ask each person about one or two things that happened to them, then just ask them a few questions about that, I think we should be able to get some kind of picture of things. I've never done this kind of thing before and I'd rather do something small to start with. Joyce did a project like this last year in her school so she is the expert here, I've been just peppering her with questions.

Emphasis: Which PNI phases will be most prominent? Collection I think, mostly. I have no idea what to do with the stories once we get them. Joyce says she can make some graphs using her computer. Me, I'm focused on just getting the stories to the town and I guess the university so people can be more *aware* of things. I do have this kind of thought in my head that if those college kids, who maybe are the ones hanging out at night, hear about us folks wanting our little kids to be safe running around in the park, maybe they'll think twice about leaving stuff around. I mean I went to college a hundred years ago and I remember those times, but they could be more considerate, you know? Maybe they just aren't *aware*. I was pretty clueless at that age.

So hearing from people, looking for patterns a little, and maybe getting some stories to some people who need to hear them? That's as far as I'm thinking. Karen says she'll be happy to give out copies of the stories to anybody who wants them and comes to the town hall.

Here's what we're thinking about asking people when we walk around. We don't have anything written down but this is what we've been practicing saying. Well I guess it's *my* version of it anyway. Let's pretend to have the interview right now. You be the interviewee.

———————

Hi neighbor! (That part's important, *neighbor*, because it means I'm part of the same community as them.) I'm Mary Smith and I live down on Orchard Street right across from the park? Yeah, and so me and Joyce and Martin, do you know them? are just walking around talking to people about the park. The Orchard Street park, you know it, right? Yeah?

Anyway so we're just walking around talking to people about the park and what has been going on there lately. We're calling what we're doing *Eyes and Ears for the Park* (that part's important so they have a name to remember the project). We just want to keep an eye on the park for our kids, and maybe help people remember that it's everybody's park, you know what I mean?

So our plan is to write down what people tell us, then give our notes to the town so they can be aware of what's going on. That's the whole thing, it's just, it's a *listening tour* about the park (that's another good name people can remember). Anybody can look at all the notes in the town hall, just ask Karen at the desk for a copy. Now, we aren't writing down any names even if we *know* your name so don't worry about that, it's all anonymous. But anybody will be able to hear what you say about the park. So, are you okay with telling me about the park? Yeah?

Great. Okay then, here's my question. *Has anything ever happened at the park that you especially remember,* like especially good or bad on any day? Can you tell me what happened?

(And here I'll wait while they tell me what happened. I'll take notes on whatever they say. If they don't tell a story, I'll gently guide them to giving an example of *something that actually happened.* I've practiced doing that, I think I've got it down.)

(So now this *next* part is the part that comes *after* they finish telling the story. But by the way I'm not going to *say* the word "story" ever. I think it would just confuse people.)

How do you feel about what happened? Like, does that make you feel happy? Or sad or what?

And that was when?

You know lots of people go to the park, along these streets and even from the university. What you just told me about, how do you think *other* people would react to it? I mean, would they feel the same way you did about it, or would they feel different? (That's to ask people how they think everybody else wants to use the park.)

Can I ask you one more question? If the park was perfect, how would it be different from what you just told me about? Or was it perfect then already? (That's to ask what people want the park to be.)

Do you think that would be perfect for *everybody* or just for *you?* (More on what they think other people want.)

Wow thanks a *lot.* I'm really glad to hear from you. Like I said no names here. Is there anything *else* that happened at the park you think the town should know about? (If they want to tell another story I'll write that down, then I'll ask the same five questions again.)

Now can I just ask you a few questions about using the park? How often do you go to the park? What time of day do you usually go there? What do you do there?

That's great. Like I said, we will be giving our notes to the town to look at. Karen should have all our notes by probably about a week from now, so you can go look at them there. Thanks for helping make our park better!

And then we'll all write down, not *who* they are but how old they are and how far away from the park they live and whether it's a house or apartment or dorm or whatever. All that's roundabout and not exact so they are still anonymous.

That's the plan. Wish us luck!

Sample three: coffee shop

This sample imagines a combined organizational and community environment (a coffee shop and people in the community who visit it) with a volunteer situation and a survey.

Goals: Why are you doing the project? Joe Schmo's is an institution in this town. My grandfather started it sixty years ago next fall. I'm the up-and-coming generation, and I guess I want to put my mark on things. I want to know more about what people in the town think of Joe Schmo's, where we have been, where we are now, and where we are going in the future. I want some new ideas.

Relations: Who are you in the community or organization? This year I'm taking over running Joe Schmo's from my dad and mom who are retiring. I also have three cousins and my brother who come by sometimes and pitch in when we have something big going on. So there's kind of a generational change thing going on. The customers who come here are different than they used to be, too. There used to be more regular regulars, you know? Old guys who would come in every morning before work. But now the demographics are changing. There's soccer moms coming in with little kids in strollers, and there's couples on the weekends getting an egg bagel. There's more of an occasional regular pattern. Also some of the university kids are showing up looking for a new place now that they shut down that student-run cafeteria over there in the business school. So who are we? We are part of this town, but what that means exactly has been changing, and I guess I want to know about that.

Focus: What is the project about? What is it about? What happens at Joe's. I want to know what used to happen here, what happens now, and what people want to happen. I know enough about what *seems* to happen here, or what happens on the surface. We have our sandwiches and our different kinds of coffee. We have our reading groups and our private rooms and our lectures and live music and all that. I know about all of that. What I want to know is what all that looks like, not to me and my family, but to all the people of the town. People who have come here for sixty years, or ten years, or a year. What happens at Joe Schmo's for *them?* What's good and bad about that? What do they want to happen, and when does that happen or not happen? That's the focus.

Range: What will the project cover? I want to make sure we hear from all ages, that's first. Then, weekdays and weekends is big. Time of day, some people come in at six in the morning and some stay until we close at midnight. And then I want to hear from people who come here for lots of different reasons: to meet friends, to find other single people, just to hang out in public, to go to meetings and lectures, to hear great music, to drink great coffee, everything, everything. What else in terms of range? Let me think. I guess people from all walks of life and income levels, yeah, and people who speak different languages, and ... whatever. Just everyone who comes here for any reason.

Scope: How big will the project be? My cousin Joey will be graduating next spring and he's just a computer whiz. He is doing a student project of some kind and I said why not build me a kiosk? So he's doing a whole thing where he's putting up a little soundproof booth in the corner for people to go in, either by themselves or together, and talk about what happens at Joe Schmo's. We will be recording the stories for something like a month. Joey's got a whole survey thing up on the kiosk computer to ask peo-

ple about their stories. We know people won't want to spend much time, so we're keeping it short and sweet, like a five minute thing. Of course free coffee for doing it, but I don't think anybody will do it for the coffee! Joey's idea of asking people to interview each other, if they come to Joe's together, is a great one. I can imagine some of the old folks doing that. I'm also going to get mom and dad and grandpa and every cousin I can round up to spend some time in there too.

Emphasis: Which PNI phases will be most prominent? Collection obviously, but after a month or we have enough stories, I'm planning to hold a "It's Happening at Joe's" night. Great title, huh? It'll be a sort of party, with free food and great music, and we'll ask people to listen to stories and talk about Joe's and what happens here, and kind of help us figure out what we should do to stay the institution we are going forward. My brother, that's Joseph right over there at the coffee machine, see him? He's been reading about this story stuff, and he wants to get people to build a time line of happenings at Joe's over the years and into the future. He says if I *don't* get any new ideas from it he will buy me a coffee every day for a week. I said Joseph, how can you buy *me* coffee? I *sell* coffee! But anyway, he says he knows what he's doing and I trust him. Just don't tell him I said that, all right? But that's the plan.

Want to take a look at the kiosk? Joey is still working on it, but you can see what he has so far.

It's Happening at Joe's

Thank you for being a part of Joe Schmo's and our town. We would be so glad if you could help us keep Joe's going strong by telling us *what has happened to you* at Joe Schmo's.

Will you do it? Will you talk to us?

(This is a completely anonymous story collection. The audio recordings and answers you give in this booth will not be identified *in any way*. If you want to change *anything* you said here later, ask a Joe's employee and they'll help you find your contribution and remove or change anything you like about it.)

[Count me in!] [No thanks.]

——————

Thanks neighbor!

First question. *Your biggest surprise ever* at Joe's: What was it? When did you say to yourself, "I cannot *believe* this just happened!" What was it that happened, good or bad?

[Press this button to
start recording your answer]

——————

Was it a good or a bad thing that happened? (Mark a dot on this line.)

[super great] ————- [just awful]

Do you think what you just told us about could *only* have happened at Joe Schmo's? Or could it have happened anywhere?

[only at Joe's] ————- [anywhere]

Now think ten years into the future. Say the thing you just told us about happens *every day*. What would Joe's be like if that happened every day?

[Press this button to
start recording your answer]

——————

Second question. *Best or worst time ever* at Joe's. Be honest! We want to hear it either way, you choose. What happened? What stands out? When did you say to yourself, "I'm so *glad* I came here today!" or "I wish I had *never* come here today!"

[Press this button to
start recording your answer]

——————

Was that a good or a bad thing?

[super great] ———— [just awful]

Could *that* have happened only at Joe's? Or could it have happened anywhere?

[only at Joe's] ————- [anywhere]

If that sort of thing happened at Joe's every day, what would Joe's be like?

[Press this button to
start recording your answer]

——————

Thanks so much for telling us about those things!

Can you tell us what decade you were born in?

[20s] [30s] [40s] [50s]

[60s] [70s] [80s] [90s] [00s]

[rather not say]

How long have you been coming to Joe's?

[decades] [years] [months]

[weeks] [days] [don't know]

How often do you come here, on average?

[daily] [weekly] [monthly]

[occasionally] [rarely] [don't know]

What do you do here? (check as many as you like)

[get coffee and run out again]

[drink coffee]

[get lunch to go] [eat lunch here]

[hang out] [listen to music]

[people-watch] [meet people]

[go out with family] [go out with friends]

[go to events] [go to meetings]

——————

Anything else you want to say? Anything at all?

[Press this button to
start recording your answer]

Thanks so much for being part of "It's Happening at Joe's" !!

[Press this button to
print your coupon for
free coffee or ice cream!]

Save the date: June 20th is "It's Happening at Joe's" night! We'll have free coffee and food, great live music, and a chance to influence what Joe Schmo's will be like ten years from now! We will be listening to audio recordings, looking at patterns, and building crazy castles in the air. It'll be fun! Come and have a say in what Joe's becomes! We need you!

——————

Like it? I love it. I can't wait to see what happens.

FACILITATING PEER INTERVIEWS

This section provides some instructions on setting up and running peer interviews (where people interview each other; see page 112).

Most peer interviews are done in pairs where each person interviews the other, but trios can also work. Once the number gets up to four it becomes less an interview than a group story session, and I would recommend different methods for that situation.

The peer interview script

Peer interviews rely on a *script* people will use to interview each other. The script should include *eliciting questions* that lead to stories interspersed with *interpretation questions* to be considered after each story is told. Keep the script as short as you can, and speak plainly. Read the script aloud, because your interviewers will. Take out anything that seems awkward or confusing. Then listen as other people read it aloud. Find some people who know nothing about the project or about stories—your neighbors, your grandchildren—and ask them to read it aloud. Listen to how it comes out of *their* mouths. It may come out more confusing and less obvious than it seemed when *you* said it. If it isn't perfectly clear, improve it and try again.

Be careful not to make any assumptions about what your interviewers will know about stories. Remember that many people don't realize they tell stories and that many people don't know what is a story and what isn't a story. *You* may know how to respond when you ask for a story and get an opinion, but your interviewers won't. They will just move on to the next question, oblivious to the problem. Write the script so that it communicates what you need *through* the interviewer to the interviewee.

But don't use the script to *teach* the interviewer or interviewee about stories. If you are lucky enough to have found some people to work with who are very motivated to learn, that's great: give them a fifteen-minute lecture on what makes a story a story, then send them off on peer interviews. But don't try to *embed* a lecture in the script. People will skip over it to get to the good stuff. (Wouldn't you?)

Finally, make sure the script includes motivational elements in it for both interviewer and interviewee. In other words, if you expect both people to care about the project's goals, mention those goals in the script itself. Get people involved through what you ask them to *say* to each other.

Setting up peer interviews

How do you go about getting people to interview each other? I know of three ways.

Unplanned matching

You can ask your participants to create their own pairs or trios by giving them a matching criterion and asking them to apply it. This is similar to saying in a group session "find someone with the same color shirt as you have on." You might ask people to find another person to work with who knows something they don't about the organization or community; or works in a different department; or comes from a different educational background; or was born in a different decade. When people are motivated to participate in the project this method is best, because it gives people more ownership over their part of the project. They can feel that through their choice they have improved the quality of stories collected.

When people are *not* motivated to participate in the project, however, you may find that few pairs or trios form after such an announcement. If that happens, stop and rethink whether your project is truly participatory. What project *would* people jump to find a partner to work on? Why is your project *not* that project? If you think your project is truly participatory, is there *another* reason people haven't paired up? Perhaps they don't have enough time, or they don't know people? Maybe you need to help them? If so, consider another of these matching methods.

Half-planned matching

In this method you select *one* set of participants and ask them to find a person in the other group to interview. This is similar to the "ask your grandparents about their grandparents" method of oral history. Typically the person asked to find someone to interview is younger, has more time, or is more motivated to participate in the project. In this case the interview may or may not be mutual; the grandparent may or may not interview the grandchild. It depends on how much you can expect the found interviewees to participate. Answering some questions when approached by a respectful volunteer might be as far as they are willing or able to go.

This method can produce useful results because it uses the energy of participation where it finds it and doesn't go looking for participation where it can't be found. If you know your participants will fall into two classes of motivation, this method might help you gain the support you need.

Planned matching

Peer groups can be created by pairing up people, either randomly or using a criterion such as age or position. This is similar to saying in a group session, "meet up with the person whose number matches the number you were given when you came into the room" (a number you set up in advance). In this case you will simply give each person instructions that specify whom they should work with, along with what questions they should ask and how they should submit their results. This method is best if you expect little participation from anyone, but still want to gain the benefits peer interviewing can provide in terms of mutual reminding of stories.

Recording peer interviews

How do you record peer interviews? There are many options, some more and some less dependent on technology, some more or less dependent on trust and volunteerism. These are just a few ideas.

Recorders

You can hand out small audio recorders and ask people to bring them back to your office, or send and receive small audio recorders by mail. This is relatively inexpensive if you get the recorders back, but expensive if you don't. If you can trust the people to send back the recorders, this can be a nice way to get people to do peer interviews. Seeing the little recorder you sent tends to motivate people to "fill it up"

with their interviews. It also shows them that the task you are asking them to do is important to the project, important enough to send them a real tool to carry it out with. People do have to meet in person in order to record the conversation, so this may be difficult if people are not close together geographically. (You can also use a smartphone application to send this same message, if you can expect everyone to have a phone.)

A recording service

You can ask people to use a telephone or online voice service you have set up that records their call and gives you access to the recording. This is relatively inexpensive and easy to manage. Many such services exist, and some even provide transcription services. On the phone, people won't have to figure out which buttons to push or deal with dead batteries in an audio recorder. However, using a telephone service does mean the people interviewing each other have to be on separate phones, which might not create the immediacy a face-to-face interview can have. A speaker phone might get around that problem, but still, the necessary mediation might put off the conversation in ways that turning on and then forgetting an audio recorder would not. Also, some people might not be comfortable with their conversation being recorded over the phone; it might seem more controlling on your part than if they can make the recording themselves (even if they send it to you).

A recording location

If all of the people are close together geographically, perhaps in your town, you can give each pair or trio a scheduled time slot during which they will come to a particular room where you will record their mutual interviews and stand by to provide help if they need it. This option is useful when you worry that people will have technical difficulties recording their conversation or understanding the tasks, but will not mind being recorded. This method also helps you make sure the peer interviews do take place, because you can remind people of their appointments and make sure they meet.

No recording, just notes

You can ask people not to *record* their mutual interview but to take notes on it and send the notes via mail or email. This method is easy to carry out and easy to transmit, but will yield a variety of interpretations of what such notes should contain. Some people might write notes that are close to transcripts of their interviews, while others might write next to nothing.

Still, this is a low-cost, low-trouble, flexible method that people may prefer if they are unfamiliar with technology or unwilling to be recorded. Peer interviewers can talk to each other in any way that works for them—in person, over the phone, through chat or email or even old-fashioned letters. They can tell you as much or as little as they want to about the stories they shared with each other. Asking for notes on stories allows each pair to choose how much they will tell you. This gives people more control over what is distributed than any method of recording interviews. Even if you do plan to record interviews, it may be useful to give the unwilling this option so you can hear their voices as well.

FACILITATING GROUP STORY SESSIONS

This section goes through the basics of facilitating a session in which you ask people to tell each other stories.

Planning your group story session

Planning a group story session is all about making decisions. Here are some that are likely to come up.

Whom to invite

Whom will you ask to come to your group story sessions? You should have already considered participation in your project in general; but not everyone has to tell stories in the same way. Perhaps you will ask some people to come to a story session and ask others for phone interviews. Or you may give people the option of coming to a group session or filling out an online survey. Which options to offer people depends on your goals and their characteristics.

One consideration in thinking about who will come to story sessions has to do with power distribution. Never mix people in different power roles in any community or organization. It will

severely hamper the natural flow of stories. If you have, say, patients and doctors, or council members and police officers, or farmers and soldiers, keep them in separate sessions if you can, or in different ends of a large room if you can't.

Group story sessions can range in size from five or six people all the way up to forty or fifty. How many people you invite to each session will depend on your expertise at facilitation, how much facilitation help you will have, how willing the participants will be to help out, and what sort of physical facilities you can use. Ten or twelve people is a nice number for a group story session: enough to get the busy hubbub of three or four small groups going, but not enough to overwhelm your powers of facilitation or require a giant room.

How to invite people

How will you invite people to participate in group story sessions? I know of five ways to do this, and I have arranged them from the greatest to the least reliance on prior planning.

Commands. You can *order* people to come to the sessions. In this method you map out the hierarchy of control, get the cooperation of those *above* the people you need to tell stories, and push the buttons of command. This method only makes sense where there *is* a hierarchy of control, usually in an organization. When there is a strong hierarchy this may be the only way you can get people to participate, since their time may not be their own but may be controlled from above. When you order a session, it is important to remember that the hierarchy may force people's *bodies* to show up in the room, but it cannot force their *minds* to be present. There are no conscripts in story work, only volunteers.

Networks. You can use networks to issue invitations to the sessions. In this method you map out the network of connections, then start a telephone tree (or its equivalent in some other medium of communication). Each person should reach out to some number of others with an invitation to participate and a session schedule. This method is best when there is no hierarchy of control but there is a strong network of connection among the people you want to reach. Unlike hierarchical control, which by definition reaches everyone in the organization, a network may skip newcomers or the socially isolated. For this reason I suggest you not rely entirely on networking to invite people but supplement this method with one of the others below to reach the unconnected. If you think people will garble the message as they send it along, make it too beautiful to garble: send out a fancy invitation card or "official" text or something people will pass on unaltered.

Broadcasting. You can broadcast invitations to the sessions. In this method you gather a list of potential participants, usually from those with a supervisory or census-like function, then send people on the list repeated notices of the upcoming session schedule. This is a common method when people are trying to reach customers who buy a product or other scattered but listed groups. Broadcasting does not always result in high participation, since many people get so much unwanted solicitation already. This method works best if it can be combined with another such as networking or advertising.

Advertising. You can advertise the sessions. In this method you put up a sign somewhere you know people congregate or pass by, giving information about the project's goals and the session schedule. This method is useful if you know who you want to come, but you don't want to (or can't) force or pester the reluctant into showing up. Getting only the people who respond to an advertisement will create a biased sample, but I don't know of any method that doesn't, actually. Like I said about hierarchical control, getting people into a room isn't the same as getting them to tell stories, or getting them to tell the stories that matter. Participatory work requires participation, and interest in participation is always unequally distributed, no matter how well you have listened at the start. Still, it does help to balance things out by combining advertisement with another method, perhaps by asking the people who respond to the advertisement to bring a friend along (network) and pass on the advertisement to other places people meet (broadcast).

Spontaneous sessions. You can *spark* sessions. In this method you go to a place where people congregate and simply hold a session on the spot, asking people as they walk by to come in and participate. This is like advertisement except that it involves no scheduling, just walk-in serendipity. It is a disorganized, spur-of-the-moment, near-chaotic method of holding a session, but sometimes it can be magical.

I once worked with a guy who could go out into any parking lot in the world, given a nice suit and ten minutes, and find ten people willing to do just about anything. He was just *that* interesting; whatever he said people would be doing, they wanted to do it. And he didn't lie to people; he just had an amazing ability to appear upbeat and exciting. Few of us are *that* persuasive. I know I'm not; I don't think I could get people to follow me out of a burning building. It's a gift I can only view from afar with wonder. If you can find one of these naturally motivating people (and keep them from lying, which is a common downside to the gift), you can ask them to help you draw people in to spur-of-the-moment story sessions.

Because this method is scatter-shot it should never be used in isolation. But as a spice, it can add flavor to one of the more plodding methods of invitation. For example, if people have been ordered to attend sessions, you can have a great motivator stand outside the room addressing people as they trudge wearily up to carry out their assigned task, converting them to enthusiastic participants. (Don't laugh; some people really can do this.)

The invitations you use in each of these situations should be identical: they should be clear, transparent, positive, and encouraging. They should give people a reason to want to come to the session, not because you are a master at getting people to do things they don't want to do, but because you understand what people want to do and have designed the session and the project to match it. As with all other materials you intend to put before people, test your invitations by putting them in front of a variety of people and watching how they respond.

Of course you should always recruit more people than you actually need, because some people will change their minds or get too busy at the last moment. This ratio is somewhat higher in story work than in when people get together for other reasons. Better to have a larger session than a very small one.

How to help participants find time to participate

There are two ways I know of to help people who want to participate but need a little extra help finding the time: paying them outright, and giving them unexpected gifts.

Paying participants. That sounds like an oxymoron, doesn't it? Does a project in which people are *paid* to participate qualify as a project of participatory narrative inquiry? It depends. Actually I have worked on several projects in which people were paid to participate, either as a one-time fee or as part of their daily work. When payment is given as a means to help busy or resource-poor people who want to participate find the time to do so, when otherwise they could not, payment can be helpful. It can be a sign of respect and recognition rather than a crass exchange of money for stories. Say you wanted me to tell stories about gathering stories. As much as I would like to help you with your laudable project, I have many things to do (like write this book) and really can't afford the time. If you could pay me to help out I might be able to find more time, not because I am uninterested, but because I really do have to choose carefully what I do with my scant resources.

To give an example, I can remember a few projects in which doctors were paid to tell stories about various aspects of medical care. In those cases the payment was less a motivation, as the doctors were undoubtedly interested in the beneficial outcome of the projects, than a recognition that they simply could not find the time otherwise.

Did the doctors participate in the projects? Looking across projects, I'd say about ten percent of the doctors typically didn't participate even though they were paid. They told ridiculously brief stories and obviously didn't consider the questions with their full attention. About sixty percent of the doctors did what they were asked but no more. Their participation was agreeable and ungrudging, but not eager. The remaining thirty percent responded with an enthusiasm that obviously relied little on payment and would have been given regard-

less. Did payment taint the contributions of either the agreeable or eager participants? I don't think so. It just helped them find the time to do what they wanted to do, some more and some less.

So here's a test on payment. If you pay participants in your project because they *want* to help but can't spare the time without some help from you, payment is appropriate in a PNI project. However, if you pay participants in your project in order to *convince* them to help, that is not participatory, and it has no place in a PNI project. Sometimes it is hard to tell which of these you are doing. To check, imagine the project taking place in a world in which everyone has infinite time and money at their disposal. Would the people you intend to pay participate? If most of them would participate in a perfect world, it is reasonable to pay them. If most of them would not participate in a perfect world, a payment scheme is *not* appropriate, and you should rethink your project to make it truly participatory.

Giving gifts to participants. Giving people an unexpected gift at the start of a group story session, an interaction I have found useful in creating a climate of mild and enjoyable social obligation, is nothing like payment. When people come to a group story session without expecting any kind of reward, handing a small gift to each participant is an excellent way to send a sign of respect and appreciation for their participation in the project (see Figure 8.28 on the facing page).

If you search the internet for "thank-you gifts for volunteers" you will find many ideas along these lines: seed packets, candles, greeting cards, note pads, flashlights, magnets, mugs, bookmarks, pens, cookies, gift cards, coupons for local stores or restaurants, photo frames, books; the list goes on and on.

My favorite thing to do is to *give a gift that tells a story* about the project and participation in it. If your project is about environmental conservation, you might give out tree seedlings. If your project is about a fund-raising campaign to erect a monument, you might give out signed copies of early monument designs. If your project is about improving the lives of senior citizens in your town, you might give out

Figure 8.28. Giving an unexpected gift at the start of a group story session can create a climate of mild and enjoyable social obligation. It's also fun. (The story depicted here actually happened in a session I facilitated once.)

copies of a hard-to-find oral history book about everyday life in the 1930s. Even the location of the session can be a gift, if going there confers an honor on participants, or if it's seen as a special place.

The very best thing is to give out a gift that cannot be gotten in any other way than by participating in the project, a gift that tells a *unique* story of participation. From gifts like these, the stories you collect can gain an "I was there when it happened" boost, as people understand just how important their contributions are to the success of the project. (And you are not lying to them about this; their participation really *is* what will make the project succeed or fail.) I still have a few of these little I-was-there mementos tucked away in my desk drawers from projects I was part of. I'll bet a lot of people have such things. Well chosen gifts do more than please; they spread motivation around the community through storytelling about participation in the project. This can impact not only your own project but those that come after it.

Where to hold the sessions

Not every location is a good place to hold a group story session. Some of the more involved exercises require physical spaces such as walls or tables on which people can affix sticky notes. Small groups must have enough space to spread out so that recorded conversations don't mingle. The rule of thumb I usually follow is to find a room built to handle about twice as many people as you expect to participate. Also, chairs and tables should be easily moved around to accommodate different tasks, so an auditorium-style room with fixed chairs is a bad spot. A room with circular tables surrounded by chairs, like the ones found in many hotel conference centers, is good. If you know from the start that your location will not be large, either reduce the number of people in each session or choose (or adapt) an exercise that fits the room well.

Can you hold a group story session outside? Certainly! Fresh air stimulates the imagination. Just check to make sure there isn't too much background noise (so you can hear the storytellings on recordings). If you plan to do any exercises that require the physical manipulation of objects, bring some tables or boards or blankets or planks, which people can place their work on. Also, watch out for things that could derail the conversation, like passing traffic or proximity to distractions that will draw people away from the activity.

Please note that I have decided *not* to cover virtual (online) story sessions. I do cover online *sensemaking* sessions briefly in the chapter on sensemaking; see the section called "Facilitating sensemaking in virtual space" on page 371.

Session length and timing

Deciding how much of your participants' time you can take is an important choice. The more time you can get people to give you, the more and better stories you will get; but the more time you ask for, the fewer people will be able to give it. For some groups (especially busy people) you will get more stories from a shorter time period, because more people will be able to contribute, and when they do contribute they will be able to attend fully for that short time. For other groups you will get more stories from a longer time period, because though fewer people may contribute, those that do will be able to plumb deep into their feelings, perhaps using exercises.

I would say that the absolute minimum time frame in which you can hold a group story session is one hour. There is always time required at the start for explanations and stragglers, and a corresponding wrap-up time at the end. As to an upper limit, I have seen sessions that lasted whole days (from breakfast to the evening meal) with highly motivated groups. Usually when a session is that long, some sensemaking is mixed in with the story collection. A *typical* session with moderately motivated participants and a reasonably ambitious project will be two to four hours long.

The time of day can have an impact as well on the success of a story session. In most contexts the time of day has cultural meaning, so that a session scheduled at nine o'clock in the morning sends a different message than one scheduled at seven o'clock in the evening. Even within a busy workday there are particular days and times that stand out. I read somewhere that Tuesday afternoon is a good time for meetings about decision making, because the week is well on its way but people don't yet feel they have fallen behind in their tasks. Similarly, meetings held on Friday afternoons tend to be taken in a more relaxed way: the pressure of work is off and it is time to reflect in peace.

Think about the people you want to reach and how their daily activities change depending on the time of day. Think about what they do with their time and how you can fit the session around that. Maybe you need to schedule sessions for different groups at different times, one for working moms and another for stay-at-home moms, for example. Meet people where they live.

Small groups for quiet story exchange

Whether you intend to use storytelling exercises or not, any group story session with six or more people in it should be split up into small groups. Why? Because storytelling works best in small groups, and because you will be able to collect more stories if you split large groups up. Here are a few guidelines on creating small groups.

To begin with, never ask two people to tell each other stories. I know putting people in pairs is a common practice in other kinds of participatory work, but it does not work with storytelling. I'm not sure why, but people in pairs in story sessions stare at the floor (see Figure 8.29 on the next page). Maybe it has to do with the "three's a crowd" nature of conversational narrative. Three people is enough for two to form an audience, so it seems natural to tell a story. With two people there is no audience, no stage. But I'm just making that up, really; all I know is, when I have put participants in pairs it has not turned out well. The stories have been stilted and unnatural compared to those told in groups of three or more.

The largest small group is, I think, five people. Above that and the audience starts to have a back row, a disengaged element from which people begin to look around the room and see what everyone else is doing (see Figure 8.30 on the facing page). Wandering audience members distract other groups, and the whole thing starts to unravel. Keep people engaged by keeping each group small.

One more thing about small groups: avoid making only two groups in a group session. Again I don't know why this happens, but when there are exactly two small groups, people in each group can't help checking constantly on what the other group is doing (see Figure 8.31 on the next page). With at least three small groups, people find it too difficult to keep tabs and give up checking, returning their attention to their small group where it belongs. As with the two-person group, there is something about a dyad that seems to necessitate continual checking. Three of anything and it goes away.

So if you have ten people in your session, say, form two groups of three and one of four. Don't form two groups of five, and don't form five groups of two. If you have seven people, I'd form one group of four and one of three. That breaks the two-groups rule but keeps each group larger than two. The two-person stare is worse than the two-group check.

Figure 8.29. Don't let people form small groups of only two for storytelling. They will just stare at the floor.

Figure 8.30. Don't let people form groups with larger than five people for storytelling. The people in the "back row" will drift off and lose interest.

Figure 8.31. Don't create only two groups in a room. People will waste time comparing what they are doing with what the other group is doing.

What is the upper limit on the number of small groups? The size of your room. Even if you are not recording the conversations, it is imperative to have enough physical room between groups so they cannot hear each other. People who hear other groups, especially if their group is large, tend to wander off either physically or mentally from the task at hand.

What are the best small groups? My suggestion is to create a balance between *comfort,* where people speak to people who think the same way as they do, and *diversity,* where people speak to people who think differently than they do. Too much to either side and things will go badly. If there is too much comfort and too little diversity, people will relax, but their stories might come out dull and internally focused (*we* all know how things are, don't we?). If there is too much diversity and too little comfort, people will feel the frisson of contrast, but their stories might come out either hysterically protective (I can't say the truth in front of *them*) or combative (I'll show *them* what's what). Find a balance

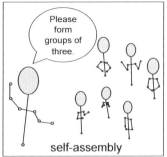

Figure 8.32. You can form small groups through direct assignment, through a group-forming rule, or simply by asking people to break into groups.

where people are neither asleep with contentment nor hyperactive with tension.

Now, how should you go about forming small groups? You can form groups by *assignment*, using matchings you set up in advance. This is best when you know the participants well and think they might not comply with requests or summon the energy to create groups on their own. Imagine asking the people you expect in the session to form groups. If they sit still in their seats and glare at you like snarling bulldogs, or curl up like abandoned fawns, take over the group-forming task yourself.

You can also form groups using a group formation *rule* that highlights diversity (find someone who lives in another part of the town), comfort (find someone you know), or both (find someone you know who is at least ten years younger or older than you are).

Or you can leave the whole thing up to the participants and just *ask* them to form groups without any other explanation; call this approach *self-assembly*. (See Figure 8.32 for an illustration of these three methods of group formation.)

If your participants will be strangers to each other, you can use a short ice-breaking activity to help them find people to connect with. If you look around at participatory group methods you can find in books or on the internet, you will find that people have come up with hundreds of interesting ways to get people to form small groups.

Asking people to share stories in groups

In a group story session you give people tasks to complete, tasks that involve telling stories, which are collected as they flow. These tasks can be as complex as several-part multi-layered exercises, or they can be very simple. The simplest task you can give people is the task of listening to and accepting your expectation that stories will flow as they speak, putting in motion the self-fulfilling prophecy that fuels the session.

If you don't want to use organized storytelling exercises, how should you get stories going? As I mentioned in the section on asking people to tell stories (page 122), asking questions whose answers are stories is (in my experience) the best way to get people started telling stories. Therefore I will presume here that you have prepared a set of questions you mean to use to elicit stories.

Once you have asked the people in your session to split up into small groups, you can give people questions to spur their storytelling in a few different ways.

You can simply *read* your questions out loud. I don't like this option much; I've tried it and have seen other people try it. People only remember the first or last thing you tell them. Every time I have seen a facilitator give people two or three tasks to complete, the people do the first task, then flounder. Every time I have seen a facilitator give people three questions to choose from, they choose the first or last one they heard. If you must read your questions out loud, use another method as well. If you have no means to write anything down (say you are holding an impromptu story session in a moving bus), give your questions short memorable names and keep repeating them. Be like the

Figure 8.33. Create a self-fulfilling prophecy about storytelling. Tell people it usually happens, and they will believe you, so it will happen.

oral storytellers and memorize a rhythmic pattern.

You can *write* the questions on a white board or large sheet of paper. This works well. Just make sure people can read the questions from anywhere in the room. People might need to move around to find acoustical isolation from other groups, so don't chain them down by writing the questions too small to read from far away.

You can *hand out* prepared sheets with your questions on them. This is the method I like best. Hand out only one sheet per small group, because it gives people something to share as they negotiate their common tasks. If you give each person their own sheet, it sends a message that even though they are in a group the task is for them to complete individually. That's not the message you want to send. Handing out one sheet per group also keeps each group's attention focused inwardly and reduces their need to look around the room, reducing distractions.

There are of course many other ways to get people telling stories in groups. If you look through some of what is available for work in participatory theatre, you will find a wide variety of ice-breaking and conversation-starting techniques. Asking questions isn't the only way; it's just the way I know and can write about. Why not find out what is possible? If something speaks to you, try it.

Supporting story exchange

These are some things you can do to help stories flow in group sessions.

Create a self-fulfilling prophecy

I recommend using a very simple technique to get people to tell stories in groups. Tell them that when people talk in groups like the one they are in right now, stories naturally arise: *and they will* (see Figure 8.33). This may sound too simple to be true, but it works better than some more complicated methods. It isn't a lie or a trick; people *do* naturally tell stories in groups. Telling people it is likely to happen just makes it that much more likely to happen. This positive feedback mechanism requires fuel to prime the pump, however, and that fuel is confidence. Your confidence in the method will spread out into the group, *if you have it*.

How do you get the confidence to create a self-fulfilling prophecy? Don't go into your very first story session without having done one already. That sounds impossible, but what I mean is that you can always find a way to collect stories

Figure 8.34. Don't explain what makes a story a story, and don't answer questions about it either. Just get people telling stories.

more casually, with family and friends, before you try to collect stories from strangers. Prove to yourself that people naturally tell stories in groups; and then you will be able to say that they do; and then they will. Before each step, place a smaller step, and in that way the journey will provide its own power.

Whatever you do, do *not* tell people what is a story and what is not a story (see Figure 8.34). That will break the cycle of positive feedback by injecting negative feedback. The moment you define a story, people will stop telling stories and start *trying* to tell stories. Nobody needs to know how their lungs work to breathe, and nobody needs to know what a story is to tell one. You may need to tell people why you want to *hear* stories, but you do not need to tell them what a story is. If people press you for an explanation, say "talk about what happened" or some other short answer. Don't get drawn into definition.

Project patience and calm confidence

Even though people naturally tell each other stories in groups, it can take time to get started. I've seen both interviews and group sessions where most of the good stories came in the last quarter of the time. That's fine, as long as it hap-

pens. Don't let silence bother you. Sometimes it means people are about to come out with something important. Wait it out, at least for a while, and don't jump to fill up every lull. A jumpy, under-confident story elicitor doesn't elicit very many stories. The self-fulfilling prophecy applies to you, too: the more you believe you will elicit stories, the more you will.

But at the same time, don't allow yourself to get over-confident either. Don't expect to be welcomed with flowers. At least at the start, expect to find some people irritated at what seems to be a waste of their time. In every group session or batch of interviews there is always going to be one nay-sayer who doesn't get the point, who thinks what you are doing is stupid, and who attacks your methods and skills. Develop a thick skin about it and move on. Sometimes people will even walk out of the interview or group session. But most of the people will participate, and that is all that matters.

Know yourself

One of the most important things in doing this sort of work is to know the resources you have to work with, including yourself. If you are going to have a hard time asking people to do things they don't want to do (answer personal questions, come to a group session, do an exercise), find someone who can help you do that. If reading dozens of long email interviews will bore you to tears, find someone else who likes to do that sort of thing. You may have to experiment to find what works, and you may find abilities and interests you didn't know you had, but be prepared to adapt what you do to what you feel comfortable with and can do well.

If you have the good fortune to have a team of people doing the project, talk about how you can complement each other in carrying out the project. Perhaps one person can handle the technological side of things; one can process the data; one can write the persuasive messages that encourage people to contribute; one can conduct interviews; and so on.

The reason I mention the probably obvious fact that people can work together in PNI is that I've met a lot of people who think story work is monolithic, or that only some people can do it. They say, "I can't do this, I'm not good with people." Or they say, "I can't do this, I can't use a spreadsheet." Those things don't matter. Everyone can work with stories as long as they work together.

Use what you know about conversational stories to keep stories flowing

If you read the section of the book on stories in conversation (page 35), you should know something about how stories flow. But don't just read that. Go out and listen to stories being told. Practice noticing the different parts of told stories. Ask people to let you record their conversations, then mark out parts of transcripts, like I did in my explanation. Get used to noticing the elements of told stories (abstract, evaluation, coda). Then get used to helping people tell stories in conversation.

Support story abstracts. A story's negotiation, compromise, retrenching, and eventual agreement (or not) happens in seconds, often with no particular words spoken by anyone beyond a simple "one time I . . . " put forth by a member of the group. It might seem impossible to notice this rapid series of interactions, let alone influence them. Still, your ability to spot such negotiations will grow with practice, as will your ability to manage your responses to them.

Have you ever heard someone start to tell a story, and then heard someone else interrupt them—and saw the look of disappointment on the face of the storyteller? Or have you heard someone tell a story, and then heard a pause that made it obvious the other person was not really listening, but was waiting for the storyteller to finish so they could speak? Telling a story is taking a risk in terms of conversational give and take. For this reason people can be reluctant to do it *even if you say you want them to.* This is one of the most common mistakes people make in asking people to tell them stories: they *ask,* but they do not *give permission.*

I remember one project where people were asked to interview each other about a factory that was closing down. As I listened to the interview tapes, I heard the same conversation over and over, thus.

> Interviewer: Do you remember your first day at the factory?
>
> Interviewee: Yes, I do.
>
> (very long silence)
>
> Interviewer: I guess we should do the next question.

I could tell that many of the interviewees *wanted* to tell those stories of their first day at the factory, but they did not feel they had *permission* to do so.

After you have watched people tell stories long enough, you will know what it looks like when people want permission to tell a story, and you will be able to respond naturally. Often people will start telling a story, then *pause* to see if people are going to listen to their performance (in effect, to find out whether they have the floor). If other people respond, they go ahead; otherwise they stop. If you happen to be one of the people responding, you can recognize the start of a story and nudge the storytelling to happen, by just looking at the storyteller in a listening sort of way, or by saying "Uh-huh?" or "What happened?" or "I'd like to hear about it" or some such thing. (See Figure 8.35 on the next page.)

In the case of a survey, you can help people get over the obstacle of starting to tell the story by being very encouraging in the questions you ask and in the statements you make about how

Figure 8.35. Give people positive feedback when they are offering evaluations during their storytelling. Give them a reason to keep talking.

useful the stories will be to your project goals. Making it clear to people that you need *the insights only they can provide* will help them to open up.

Support story evaluations. As you listen to stories, practice teasing out evaluation statements. One way to do this is to record people talking in conversation, in video or audio, then make your own transcripts, marking as you go not only elements of intensity and vocal tone but also evaluation statements. It can be hard to recognize evaluations on the spur of the moment, but when you can pore over conversations, perhaps repeating certain points over and over, you can improve your ability to quickly pick up on evaluative speech.

In many told stories you can make out a point where the evaluative statements rise to a sort of climax. This is usually the part of the story that holds the greatest importance to its teller. If you can cue in on this crux of the story you can often gain insight into why the teller told the story, or if they told it in answer to a question, why they chose that particular story to tell.

When you see the crux of a story taking place in conversation, you can know two things: first, that this is why the storyteller is telling the story, and second, that they need your support. At this moment the storyteller needs their audience to pay attention if the storytelling event is to reach a successful completion. If you are conducting an individual interview, you can just lean in and look at the storyteller so that they know you are listening. If they are telling the story in a group of which you are a part, you can't make anybody

else listen, but you can make sure the storyteller knows that you at least are attending.

Support story codas. When you are supporting storytelling and recognize a coda taking place, it's a good idea to say something that reinforces the story's validity so as to encourage the teller, and others in the group, to consider it safe to tell another story later. Some types of useful reinforcing statements are *appreciative* ("Wow" or "That's interesting" or "I never heard that before" or "That's worth remembering"), *summarizing* ("So they caught the guy, huh?" or "So you left the zoo?"), *questioning* ("Does it seem different years later?") or *grateful* ("I'm glad you shared that").

Note that it is *not* a good idea to thank people *for* a story ("Thanks for that story"), because the "a story is a possession" mindset creeps in and people can close down (see Figure 8.36 on the facing page). But you do need to give people *something* to go on, some kind of positive response, because otherwise they may not venture forth out of the safety of silence again. I have seen people's faces fall after they have told a story and got no response.

Often it's the second or third story people tell that is the most useful, partly because they start to understand what you want to know, and partly because they feel safe enough to tell about deeper things. So it's important to help people get over the point of vulnerability found at the end of the first story they tell.

If you are asking for stories through writing, as silly as it seems, it's fine to put a line that says "That's interesting" or some such thing at the bottom of web form or email. You can also put

Figure 8.36. When people finish a story, recognize the story's ending by saying something appreciative or asking questions. But don't *thank* people for their stories; it makes the story seem like a commodity.

something less silly but still to the point like "We appreciate your help very much" at the end of the form. It serves the same purpose.

Restarting stalled storytelling

Often storytelling in a group session starts out well enough, but the group stalls when it seems like all the stories have been told. Usually at this point there are more (and possibly more useful) truths the session can reveal, but the participants need some help expanding the dialogue. These are some techniques I've seen work to get storytelling going again.

Encourage reminding

Stories told in casual settings often flow from one to the next on threads of reminding: my dog was like your horse; my day at the zoo was like your trip to the carnival; my car breaking down was like your pipe bursting. The ways in which one story leads to another are rich and varied in groups that know and trust each other. When people come together to tell stories but don't know everyone in the room, the flow from story to story doesn't take place as easily. People may be hesitant to claim a link for fear that it

won't meet the needs of the group or project. As the group's facilitator, you can reassure people that you do want them to link story to story, and you can help guide the links in ways that work for the project.

If someone has told a story and a long silence follows it, you might ask people to think about whether the told story reminds them of anything—anything at all—and see where it leads. The reminding can proceed from any of the elements of the story—characters, behaviors, feelings, events, settings, conclusions, challenges, and so on.

For example, you might say things like:

- Does that plant manager remind anybody of anyone else they know?
- Trust was broken in that story. Can anyone else recall a story where trust was broken?
- Does that old building bring any other memories up?
- Those people were talking past each other, weren't they? Can you remember any other times like that?

• What a surprise that the man didn't know he was already in the place he needed to be! Anybody else have a surprise like that?

If you practice linking stories together in your own conversations, you can prepare yourself to support it when other people are exchanging stories.

Encourage alternatives

Another reminding tactic is to ask about *alternatives* that could have happened in the story just told. For example, if the story ended with a project succeeding, you could ask what could have made the project fail. This can remind people of other similar stories (e.g., when other projects failed, when the thing that could have made that project fail happened, and so on). Think of something you can change about a story, like whom it happened to, or where or when it happened, or who told it, or how it came out. Ask people to think about what might have happened if the story was retold that way.

It can even be helpful to talk about things that couldn't possibly happen, just to get people to expand their thinking into new areas. For example, if someone just told a story about storming out of a town meeting after feeling that nobody was listening to their input, you might say "I wonder what would have happened if you had been in charge of the meeting" or "I wonder how that would have played out if the meeting had been on a desert island."

Encourage expansion

If people are telling only the safest stories and you don't feel that they are reaching their true feelings, you can gently push things to the extremes by asking people for more of whatever they are talking about, in whatever direction the storytelling is timidly heading. For example, if someone has just told a story that hints at not being trusted—perhaps they were irked at not being allowed to fill the water cooler themselves—you can say something like "Has anybody experienced anything worse than that?"

What this does is two things: first, it communicates to people that it's okay to move to the extremes, and second, it taps into the universal urge to compare ourselves to others and try to do as well as they have done or better. This may

urge people to go further than they would have in opening up an area they were reluctant to talk about. However, be careful with this one: it can bring out performances instead of honest reflections as people try to "win the game" by "going one better." Use it for the timid, not the bold.

Finding facilitation balance

The degree to which you facilitate a group story session could vary all the way from the hovering presence of multiple facilitators, each dedicated to making sure every little group of three or four people completes the stated tasks perfectly, to the complete *absence* of facilitators, with nothing but a printed set of instructions in the hands of session participants. Which is best depends on the skills, resources, and motivation you and your participants bring to the session. What your participants bring is likely to be the more important part of the equation, since you would probably not attempt to run a session without *any* preparation.

I have facilitated sessions in which I could have left the room for hours and things would have moved on just the same, just as long as I left my notes behind, because the participants were manning the oars as well as I could. I have facilitated other sessions where the participants, metaphorically speaking, bleated like sheep on the raft I was propelling and steering alone, sure to tumble off and drown if I took my hand off the rudder for a moment.

To guess what sort of crowd you will face, talk to some of the participants before the day of the session. Do they show a strong interest in the goals of the day? Do they quiz you about methods and plans? Or do they say something like, "My boss told me to show up, but he didn't say I had to *do* anything." Let them tell you what they need. If you can't talk to people before the session, prepare a few different agendas, then get to the session early and watch people as they settle into being in the room with you. Usually within a few minutes you can make a decision about which course to take. You can also make small adjustments to the amount of facilitation you give as the session goes on.

I find that the best storytelling takes place when facilitators stay out of the way of storytelling as much as they possibly can, but no more. A facilitator is not a director or participant, but a resource and guide. In the "PNI Skills" section of *More Work with Stories*, I describe how facilitating group story sessions is one of the best examples of the half-in, half-out nature of story work.

Listening for balance

How can you tell if you are facilitating the right amount, and not too much or too little? Listen to what people say. Here is a bit of a transcript from a story session that illustrates this balance.

In this excerpt of conversation, just after (the person I'm calling) Steve told a story in which asking "dumb" questions was put forth as a smart thing to do (on account of dumb questions being those you weren't supposed to ask), the conversation went like this.

> Jennifer: Let me ask a dumb question. [The topic] is an interesting issue. Are we doing the assignment? Because I missed the beginning part.
>
> Steve: I don't know.
>
> [laughter]
>
> Larry: I think we're doing pretty good. I think that the idea is to try and think of stories around [the topic], but I think the stories themselves are very relevant.
>
> Jennifer: Have you come up with what you think is the best story?
>
> Steve: We haven't voted yet, we haven't voted, but I think that we're—I think the hardest thing is being sure which ones are really relevant to [the topic]. I think there's a general lack of familiarity with [the topic] to know which ones to go with. But I think we've had some great stories, I'd say here, so...
>
> [laughter]
>
> Jennifer: Well, the theme is definitely *silence*. And the use of silence.
>
> Steve: Yes, and asking dumb questions. [then he tells a long story]

First Jennifer takes advantage of the "dumb question" joke to label her question as "dumb." I take this as her signal that she is not judging the others in the group on how well *they* are doing in the exercise (a typical offer of face saving) while also signaling her need to make sure the group is "on task." Steve replies "I don't know"—even though he just finished telling a story, thus fulfilling the task—and everyone laughs, thus admitting that they are half following instructions and half doing their own thing. As an observer I am happy to see this, because it means stories are flowing naturally despite the contrived task people were given.

Next Larry says he thinks the group is doing well on the task, which means they don't need any corrective measures. Jennifer, who didn't hear the instructions, asks if they have come up with the "best" story. Coming up with the best story was not in fact *in* the instructions. They were asked to choose the story most *relevant* to the topic they were discussing. Steve uses the word "relevant" in the next sentence, but he also says "we haven't voted yet." They were not asked to vote either.

Steve explains that the topic is difficult to address but that "we've had some great stories" which is apparently his understanding of the gist of what they were asked to do. There is laughter again, which I take to mean "we all agree that we're fine." However, Jennifer is *still* not satisfied, so she makes another attempt to guess at the instructions she didn't hear and proposes a *theme* to their stories, possibly believing they were to create one. She then repeats her theme before allowing Steve to plunge back into storytelling.

You should see many examples of this sort of "what are we doing" negotiation going on in groups you have asked to tell stories. These are good signs. If you hear only people doing *exactly* what you told them to do, without ever discussing it, you need to loosen up your instructions a little to let people interpret the task in a way that allows the natural flow of storytelling to come through. Conversely, if you often find that groups veer completely off the topic and task without even *mentioning* what it was you asked them to do, your task mandate needs to be stronger.

Intermediate facilitation techniques

Here are a few ideas for achieving intermediate facilitation in story sessions.

Intermittent facilitation. This is when you keep jumping into and out of the stream of activity. You might for example give people a task, then leave the room and come back five minutes later to check if things are going as expected. Intermittent facilitation sends the message that you are willing to share control of events with the participants, to make it not your session but theirs.

Only practice intermittent facilitation if your instincts tell you the people in your session are ready for it. Don't leave even for a minute if you think people will abandon the task or sit waiting (with the excuse of a question) for prodding from you. A good sign is when people become so wrapped in their task that they stop paying attention to you. When you see this, and when their task is on target, this is a good time to send the "you can do it without me" signal. As you leave, be sure to indicate your faith in the participants, and get their agreement to take the reins of the session. Say something like, "Right, I think you know what you are doing, so I'll get that cup of coffee I've been wanting. Back in five minutes, okay?" They will probably think you just need your coffee, but you are *really* doing this to give them ownership of their participation. This might seem a silly stunt, but it can change the stories that come out of the session.

Available facilitation. This is similar to the intermittent option, except that instead of leaving the room entirely, you withdraw to a part of the room where you can't hear conversations but can still be seen and beckoned over when your help is needed. You can pretend to be busy with something, or make no excuse at all. From your distant perch you can still sense the tenor of what is going on, so you can tell if you need to plunge back into the stream of participation; but you can stay out of the storytelling itself. Usually you can tell from afar whether people are telling stories or just talking, because during storytelling one person is talking and others are listening for a longer period of time than usual.

My colleague Dave Snowden likes to use this technique, and he says that some of his best facilitations have taken place where he didn't understand the language in which the stories were being told. In those settings he could still be asked questions (as the people also understood English) but he didn't form a part of the audience for the storytelling that took place. That is a fine half-in, half-out position for a facilitator to maintain.

Voices and music

How loud is your normal speaking voice? Do people always tell you to speak up or tone it down? If your voice carries, practice your whispering. If you speak quietly, learn to speak up, or work with someone who can be heard. (I speak *very* quietly, so I like to find people I can use as microphones when I need to address a large group.) You may think this is a trivial matter, but in a room with ten people in it, a facilitator's voice is like a lighthouse on the shore. If it is too strong it can strand people on the rocks of distraction, mesmerized, their task forgotten. If it is too quiet, people can crash from confusion about what has been asked of them, wandering, their task lost in fog.

People in group sessions are usually nearly but not *quite* sure that they know what they are supposed to do. This is actually just where you want them: on board enough to do *something* related to the goal, but with enough freedom to apply their own ingenuity to the tasks at hand. But it can be hard to put off those who can't help seeking more and more explanation when they should be relying on their own power. This is a bigger problem, in my experience, than reining in those who hear half the explanation and start off at a sprint. The sprinters will get *somewhere*, and it will probably not be all that far off the target. The foot-draggers will not get *anywhere* unless you bring them to understand that they need to do the walking for themselves. At some point you need to just stop explaining and give them a push off into the sea of participation.

Here's another favorite trick in finding facilitation balance: use music as a cue. The reason restaurants play music is that it covers the sounds of conversation so people can talk. The same thing works in story sessions. Music works perfectly as a signal that guidance has been withdrawn for a purpose.

When you are giving instructions, the music should be off. But when the instructions cease, the music should go on and any clarifications should be given quietly, to individuals or small groups, not to the whole room. If you need to tell *everyone* in the room something—well, first, maybe you don't. If three small groups are engaged in a task it may be better to repeat the clarification three times quietly than to disrupt everything. Stepping in when a task is "in session" can disrupt the flow of stories. It reminds people that they are being watched. Don't do it if you don't have to. But if you do have to make a room-wide announcement, turn off the music to make it, then turn the music back on again. It's a nice simple aid to understanding. Only make sure the music you choose has no words, is unobjectionable to everyone in the room (no death metal), and doesn't make people think about anything in particular (no movie music). It is there as a signal and an aid; it should draw no attention to itself.

Fitting in question asking

Asking questions about stories fits more naturally into some story collection venues than others. In a survey, questions about stories naturally intermingle with questions whose answers are stories. In a one-on-one interview, you can intersperse the two types of questions, though you may need to do some extra reminding about what each question pertains to.

When people are telling stories in groups, asking questions about stories is more difficult, since you don't want to disrupt the flow of storytelling to ask questions as each story is told.

One method that always seems to work well in a group setting is to greet everyone when they come in with a short stack of paper forms, one for each of the stories you expect them to tell in the session. People will probably look over them briefly as the session starts. This produces three useful outcomes.

1. They will read the beautifully crafted statement at the top of each form about why they are meeting today. This will bring them on board even before you start the session.

2. They will see what they are expected to do in relation to each story (since the form says things like "please give the story you told a name" and so on). They will begin to visualize what will happen and gear themselves up to complete the required task.

3. Possibly most important of all, they will see that *everyone else in the room got the same stack of forms.* This is positive peer pressure you can use. It says, "We are all going to do this together." If you think this doesn't matter, watch people as they look at their forms. They always look around to see if everyone got one.

When should people fill out their forms? Right after they tell a story? Not then. There are two problems with asking people to answer questions about their story in a group right after they have told it. First, rarely will anybody remember the form as they finish their story. This means you will have to swoop in and give them a poke to get them to do it. This will confuse people and possibly embarrass them, and it will disrupt the conversation and possibly hinder the connection between one story and another that might come after. Second, nobody likes to do anything when they are the only ones who have to do it. They will feel singled out: everybody else gets to have fun talking but I have to fill out this boring form.

Instead, what I find works best is to build short breaks into your session plans, say five minutes out of every half hour. During those breaks ask everyone to fill in the forms in reference to whatever stories they have told since the last break. Because everyone is doing the same task at the same time, there is peer pressure to do it all around. If you watch people at these times you can see that they glance around (just like at the start of the session) to make sure everyone is doing the task along with them.

How can you match the stories on forms to the stories people told on the audio recording? This does take a bit of thought and advance planning, but it is not difficult. The general idea is to give each story some kind of *identifier* that is the same in the audio recording and on paper.

You can have someone give the story an explicit *name*. The name can be supplied by the storyteller, others in their group, or a facilitating helper. Or you can have someone list a few identifying *details* about the story, perhaps a visual image in it like a green door or a blue car, and make that the link. Which you choose depends on the relative amounts of energy you expect to have in facilitation and participation.

For example, any of these situations might take place.

- Our session has one small group. I am facilitating. Every time a person finishes a story I say, "So, what do you think would be a good name for that story?" When they say the name I say, "Could you write that on one of your forms?" Then in the break I ask them to fill out each form with a story name on it.

- Our session has five small groups. As the facilitator, I give each of the groups a task to tell each other stories. I ask the people who are *not* telling the story to remind the storyteller to name their story and write down the name. This is a group of scientists, so I expect they will follow directions well. I watch them and see that they are carrying out the instructions perfectly.

- Our session has three small groups. As facilitator, I have predicted that the participants will not be particularly motivated and are not likely to carry out any tasks I give them. For this reason I have arranged to have one facilitating helper for each small group. The helpers do not ask anyone to do anything, but they listen and write down a few identifying details of each story on a sticky note, along with a number that identifies its teller. During the break, each helper hands each storyteller's sticky notes to them. They ask the participants to name their stories based on the identifying details, and write the names on their forms as they complete them.

- Our session has ten small groups. I figured out in advance that the participants will be highly motivated to contribute. At the start of the session I write on the board where everyone can see: "1. Give each story a name. 2. Write the name on one of your forms. 3. Make sure everybody else is doing the same thing." While the storytelling is going on, I

hover around all the tables making sure everyone is following the instructions. When I see people forgetting to write down story names, I chide them in a joking way and ask their group members to help them remember.

- Our session has three small groups. One other facilitator and I sit next to two of the groups and listen to the conversations. As each story ends we write down the number of the speaker (they have placards in front of them) and a name we have made up for their story. During the break, we hand each participant a list of story names to copy to their forms. We are careful to name the stories by some visual detail, like "the long hallway" or "the garden path" because we do not want to insert any interpretation into the name. Because we know we cannot cover the third group, we ask for a volunteer at the start of the session. One participant offers to help, and we give them one minute of instructions. They do as well as we do ourselves.

Think about how much facilitation and participation you will have in your session and plan based on that. If you know in advance that you will get little participation from the people you have invited to the session, ask your friends or colleagues to help you facilitate so you can balance the shortage of help in that way. Another way to gain more help is to seed the session with some participants you know will be exceptionally helpful. For example, say you are asking people on your city street to come to a session. If you don't know some of the people and can't guess how much they will participate, ask some neighbors you do know (and know to be helpful) so you can increase the odds of getting the help you need.

That covers asking questions about stories in a group story session, but what about in a group interview? A group interview is mid-way between a single interview and a group session. The degree of participation in a group interview will be lower than a group session but higher than a one-on-one interview. So you *might* be able to ask each storyteller questions about their story just after it is told, as if the teller were in a one-on-one interview, as the other people listen. Gauge the level of accommodation you find in the group as you start. If you have few questions, say three or four, your group might not mind waiting the short time required while the storyteller answers the questions. They might even enjoy hearing the responses. In some particularly friendly groups you might even be able to ask *everyone* the questions about each story. When you can find such an opportunity, seize it, because it gives you a multi-perspective view on each story.

On transcribing storytelling

Because storytelling is a performance and a negotiation, transcribing conversational storytelling is not the same as transcribing other kinds of conversation. Some differences between transcribing conversational storytelling and transcribing non-narrative conversation are as follows.

Evaluations. Words said with particular emphasis or emotion, like "I couldn't *believe* that happened", often represent evaluation statements by the storyteller that communicate the point or meaning of their story. A transcript of conversational storytelling should preserve the strength of emphasis in these words. For example, if your transcript doesn't distinguish between "*we* knew what to do," "we *knew* what to do", "we knew *what* to do," and "we knew what to *do*," you might not know which of these stories is being told (and these are quite different stories). A simple notation such as asterisks around emphasized words will make such emphases clear.

Disfluencies. Most transcriptions of conversations remove the ums and ahs of informal speech. Transcriptions of conversational storytelling should not, because such breaks, irregularities, hesitations, repetitions, and confusions can be important indicators of negotiation and reframing of stories as they are being told in context.

Socially significant sounds. Most conversational transcripts ignore background noises like laughter, muttering, the sound of shuffling feet, and silence. But when someone is telling a story, those sorts of social cues can be useful indications of what is going on in the storyteller's and audience's minds. Simple notations such as [laughter] and [long silence] can be helpful.

One colleague of mine developed a method of denoting laughter in transcripts by putting one [HA] for each unit of laughter (as he defined it), so a long bout of laughter registered as [HAHA-HAHA]. It's also useful to note who is laughing, or umming, or coughing, if you can tell that.

Pauses are also important. A common practice is to use dashes for short pauses and ellipses for long pauses. All of these things are evidence of the formation of the story in the event of its telling.

Non-text cues. As we know from written communications, a lot of the verbal and visual cues we give each other in person are lost when our words are translated into unadorned text. Transcribers of storytelling should be aware of things that might not come across the same in text and make notations that preserve the spoken meaning. For example, you might add notes like "said with a sarcastic tone" or "said in a Darth Vader voice" or "waving hand around" or "pointing out window" and so on. Especially reported speech, when someone takes on the words of another person, even sometimes taking on their vocal tones, has an evaluative meaning that should be kept in the transcription.

SUMMARY

The first decision to be made about collecting stories is whether you want people to tell you stories or whether you want to listen to people tell each other stories. Methods of direct engagement (people telling you stories) include one-on-one interviews, group interviews, journaling, narrative incident reports, and surveys. Methods of indirect listening (people telling each other stories) include peer interviews, group story sessions, and gleaned stories. Each of these methods is more useful in some circumstances than others.

The best way to ask people to tell stories is to ask them questions whose answers are stories. Within this guideline a variety of question types is possible. You might ask people, for example, about a point in time; about an event; about an extreme; about surprise or change; about specific decisions, people, places, or things; or using a fictional scenario. For each of these types of story-eliciting question, a directed question asks people to think about their experiences with regard to a specific topic, while an undirected question asks people to simply recall memorable experiences.

For each project there will be some words that convey what it is you are looking for in the stories you collect. Find those words and use them.

When asking questions to collect stories, it is best to use a "menu" approach, where participants can choose to respond to the questions that appeal to them most. The menu approach helps people find questions that match their varying experiences and motivations to participate in the project.

The sweet spot in story collection for PNI is between one and three hundred stories. With fewer than one hundred stories, patterns are weak. With more than three hundred stories, you start to encounter diminishing returns for your efforts. If you have the resources to collect many stories, you might better use your resources to conduct multiple smaller projects rather than fewer larger ones. However, if you project contains significant sub-projects within it (areas you want to explore in depth), collect 100–300 stories per sub-project.

Asking questions about stories is a mainstay of PNI practice. Asking questions about project goals is relatively straightforward; for example, you might ask people to say how strongly the people in a story trusted each other. You can also ask questions about the fundamental features of story form, function, and phenomenon. Asking questions about people complements the practice of asking people about stories; it creates juxtaposition that reveal useful trends. You can ask people about their personalities, their roles in the community, and their views about the community.

There are many ways to ask people questions about stories. You can ask them to fill in a blank, to pick one or more choices in a list, or to mark a line on a scale. It is best to mix styles of question asking to keep people interested.

The number of questions you can ask people about stories depends on the cognitive budget you have available: their time, attention, interest, and ability to concentrate. In a kiosk situation, where you have only moments of someone's time, you can ask three to five questions about a story. In a volunteer situation, in which the person feels a social obligation to answer the questions, you can ask six to nine questions. In a commitment situation you can ask ten to fifteen questions.

Some advice on writing questions about stories is as follows. Ask questions that matter and resonate. Transmit your excitement and energy. Gather interpretations, not opinions. Mind your messages. Build a two-way conversation. Do not judge. Write questions that stand on their own. Ask why. Do not conflate. Do not ask for more information than you need. Find ways to make a lack of response useful.

Sets of questions given to participants should flow naturally and easily. They represent a conversation between your project and its participants. The conversation should be polite, respectful, and easy to understand.

When you plan a group story session, you need to decide whom to invite, how to invite them, whether to compensate or reward them for coming, where to hold the sessions, and when and how long the sessions will be. These decisions pivot on your project's goals and context.

When forming small groups in a story session, avoid having groups of two, and avoid having two groups.

To help stories flow, create a self-fulfilling prophecy (that people will tell stories). Project patience and calm confidence. Know your strengths and weaknesses. Use what you know about conversational stories to keep stories flowing. Support story beginnings, evaluations, and endings. To restart stalled storytelling, encourage reminding, alternatives, and expansions.

Find the right balance of facilitation for storytelling between control and freedom. Listen for balance, and respond if things have moved too far into control or anarchy. Practice intermediate facilitation. Pay attention to the volume of voices. Use music to signal times of quiet group work.

When asking questions about stories in a group session, schedule short breaks for reflection, and make sure everyone knows they are all completing the same tasks so that no one feels singled out.

Questions

Which of the methods of collecting stories described in this chapter seem most natural to you? Which seem easiest, which hardest? Which seem fun and which onerous? If you were going to choose one method to start with, which would best suit you? Why is that? Is there something about your background or interests that makes one method of story collection more appealing than others?

As you read through the sections in this chapter on methods of collecting stories, did any connections jump out at you regarding your own community or organization? Do you recognize anything that tells you one or more methods will be particularly useful (or difficult, or damaging) in your situation? Can you rank the methods in terms of how appropriate you think they will be in your context?

Methods of collecting stories come up in several fields you may already be familiar with: oral history, participatory theatre, narrative analysis, journalism, memoir writing, and so on. Based on what you have seen in these fields, how do the descriptions here compare? In what ways are they similar and different? If you were to add together what you think best from what you have read here and what you have read elsewhere about story collection, what sort of methods and recommendations might you compile?

Activities

Try collecting a few stories using every method mentioned in this chapter. Interview one person. Interview three or four people together. Give two people a script and a tape recorder, then (later) listen as they interview each other. Facilitate a group story session. Hand out a survey form. Watch some people chatting. Ask someone to keep a journal. Ask someone to report on events. Find some stories on the internet. Even if you do each of these things with only a few people, you will get a sense for the ways in which each of these methods holds unique benefits and difficulties. Learn for your-self how each method feels. What was easy and hard about each method? Which method did you enjoy most? How did the stories that came out of each method differ?

For one full day, carry a notepad around with you. Every time you hear somebody tell a story, jot down some notes on how the story got started. Did someone ask a question that led to it? Did it flow from another story? Did it come up as part of a task people were doing? Did you elicit the story or did you overhear it? At the end of the day, think about each storytelling event. If you had *purposefully* collected each of the stories you heard, which of the methods described in this chapter would have been best used to gather it? In which situation would each story have arisen most naturally? Are there any methods by which that particular story would *not* have been told, or would have been told differently?

Think of a project you'd like to do in your community or organization. Describe its goals, relations, focus, range, scope, and emphasis. Write a sample question set for the project like the ones in this chapter, as a practice. Show your project description—but not your questions—to a friend or colleague. Ask them to come up with questions they might ask in such a project. How do their questions compare with yours? How do both sets compare with the question sets shown here? What can you learn from that?

Chapter Nine

Group Exercises for Story Collection

This chapter covers three group exercises you can use to help people tell each other stories: twice-told stories, timelines, and landscapes.

WHY USE GROUP EXERCISES TO COLLECT STORIES?

Group exercises dig deeper than unstructured conversation. They help people bring out feelings that are difficult to articulate or deep below the surface, and they generate diversity in situations where it is lacking. If you think it will be difficult for your participants to articulate their feelings about your topic, or they will tell only official or safe stories, or they will be more likely to give lectures or opinions than tell stories, or you have very little of their time and want to make the most of it, choosing some group exercises might be useful to your project.

However, using exercises requires motivation on both your part and the part of your participants. If a group story session is a high-input, high-output option for collecting stories, a story collection exercise is even more so. You need to facilitate without exerting too much control; and your participants need to meet you halfway in completing the task. Group exercises ask more of people than just sitting in a circle talking. If you have very little time to run your project, or you aren't very experienced collecting stories, or you can't get people together physically, or you think your participants will resist doing anything that seems artificial or re-quires effort, you are better off asking people to tell each other stories without an exercise.

I cover five narrative exercises in this book: twice-told stories, timelines, landscapes, story elements, and composite stories. The first three of these appear in both collection and sensemaking chapters, since they work well for both. The last two are more useful for sensemaking than for story collection, so I cover them only in the sensemaking chapter. All of the exercises can be used for both purposes, but I have placed them where I think they work best.

A note on finding your style. I've seen quite a few people do these exercises in group sessions. One thing I've noticed is that everyone does them differently and, for the most part, everyone does them right. You can bring your own experience and knowledge to bear to make these exercises work for you and your needs. You don't need to adhere to a strict recipe. Please take these descriptions as food for your own thought processes. (The "Your own style" sections in the exercise descriptions give you some ideas on variations to consider.)

TWICE-TOLD STORIES

In a twice-told stories exercise, when it is used for story collection, people in small groups tell stories to each other while choosing one or more stories from among those told to retell more widely.

When to use it

The point of this exercise is to give small groups of people a concrete yet very simple task that encourages people to tell stories and shapes the stories they tell. It is meant as story work for a beginning story worker and beginning participants. When people are capable of more complex exploration it is *not* the best exercise because it is too simple and more can be done.

What it requires

Six to fifteen people; at least an hour; a room with enough space to distinguish as many small group conversations as you will have small groups; some way to record stories; some way to record answers to questions about stories.

How to do it

Step One: Introduce the exercise and form groups

Five minutes. Explain the exercise and its purpose briefly. Ask people to form groups of three to four people (not two; not five or more unless necessary). Turn on any audio recorders.

Step Two: Select criteria

Five minutes. Each small group should choose a criterion by which they will choose a story they will tell to the larger group afterward. It must be a criterion of *utility* rather than quality, and it must be related to the purpose of the session. (If you think people will not be able or willing to choose criteria, you can do this for them, and just *tell* them about the criterion you have chosen.)

Step Three: Exchange stories

Twenty-five minutes. Small groups exchange stories. As they do this they name the stories, say the names on the recording, and note them down on their forms.

Step Four: Answer questions about stories

Five minutes. Each person fills out a question form for each story they told.

Step Five: Retell stories

Fifteen minutes. Each small group chooses a member to retell their chosen story to the whole session. Divide up the time and watch the clock so every group gets a chance to tell their story.

Step Six: Wrap-up

Five minutes. Wrap-up and general discussion of all stories told and the topic.

If you have less time

You can trim this exercise down to forty-five minutes by hurrying the first two steps into five minutes (introduce the exercise and form groups, plus select criteria), exchanging stories for only twenty minutes, and either cutting the retelling short or dropping the wrap-up period. I don't think the exercise can get any shorter than that.

As far as converting this exercise into a simple fifteen-minute task, I don't think it can be done. The exercise is very simple already. You *could*

have people tell each other stories and choose which they would retell *if they had time* to do so. But that isn't much different from trading stories without any selection going on. If I didn't have time for this exercise, I'd use some other method of getting people telling each other stories (like just asking them to trade experiences).

If you have more time

If you have two hours, double the time in the sections longer than five minutes (and the last discussion period). If you have three hours, don't triple the time; choose a second criterion, choose another exercise, or open up the storytelling outside of an exercise.

Before you start

The great thing about the twice-told stories exercise is that it requires no preparation whatsoever. You can start one of these things at any time in any setting, as long as you have enough people to form two groups of at least three people each. You could start one of these in a restaurant or while waiting for a bus or after church. In fact, starting quick on-the-spot exercises of this type (and not recording any stories) is a good way to improve your skills at facilitating story collection.

Optional elaborations

If there is time and people are interested, each person in each small group can answer questions sheets about the stories they *heard* as well as told. People can also do this at the end of the session about stories they heard repeated from other groups.

How you will know it's working

The time this exercise needs to work is in the small group story exchanges, since that is the heart of the storytelling. If people in the small groups are telling stories, they will be intent on each other, and they will be taking long turns in the conversation. Watch the small groups, and if you see a group wandering around or looking at what other groups are doing, go and offer them some help.

What can go wrong

People choose quality criteria

If people choose a criterion for selecting a story that has to do with quality ("we decided to pick the best story" and so on), just let them go. It is better not to say anything to the group, because they may take the criticism badly and stop telling stories entirely. Just think about how you can improve your instructions the next time so this becomes less frequent.

People abandon the topic

Don't step in to fix things if people wander off the topic. Think about how to improve things next time. Any hint of censorship will reduce storytelling.

You get behind time

The period for retelling stories is the part of the exercise that can shrink. Do not shrink the exchange, question answering, or wrap-up. You need the exchange to record the stories; you need the questions answered; and if you don't allow time for wrap-up people will feel a lack of closure. If the retelling time does shrink, divide the time by the number of groups and ask people to summarize their stories.

Here's a tip: halfway through the small group story exchange period, go around and say "how's it going" just to be available for quiet questions. Then, about five minutes before the period ends, throw out a "your story should be ready for retelling in five minutes" to the whole group. If people are behind schedule or off the task, you will see them suddenly huddle to complete the task. If you see an awful lot of huddling, you can give people a few extra minutes.

You are disappointed at how few stories you got

This is a low facilitation expertise method, but it is also a low output method. With minimal instruction people are not likely to tell epic tales. That's all right. For a small project it may be just what you need. Don't over-reach. Start small and you will be more likely to be pleasantly surprised.

Try it yourself first

This exercise doesn't require any materials, so it is an easy one to try out without anyone knowing you are doing it. Just insert two questions into any casual conversation with at least two other people in it. First, ask about the topic: "Did you ever get soaked in the rain?" or something. Then, after people have traded a few stories about the topic, slip in the second question, as if you just thought of it: "I wonder which of those stories says more about umbrellas." Or use a third party reference, like "Which of those stories do you think Josh would be most likely to tell?" The point is not to trick people into revealing anything; it's just to observe what happens when people trade stories and choose among them. If you do this several times, you will probably pick up some observations about the process, even though you didn't do it in a formal way. You can of course also ask friends or family to do the whole exercise with you, with your prepared statements, as a rehearsal. But I think messing about with some barely-nudged conversations is an even better preparation for the real thing.

Your own style

Because this exercise is built on so basic a frame, you can imagine bolting all sorts of elaborations onto it. Perhaps people could tell other groups their stories in a round-robin fashion. Maybe people could move around the room to different "memory jogging" stations as they tell each other stories. You might ask people to choose one story from those retold and stage it as a final play before the session wrap-up. If you like, fill up the empty spaces in this exercise with ideas of your own design.

Where it came from

I developed this exercise with my colleague Neal Keller at IBM Research in 2000. We specifically aimed our research at developing something people could use with no preparation or knowledge of narrative. We called the method a "small pill" people could take to get started collecting stories, perhaps on their way to more elaborate exercises, perhaps not. I think it is valuable to people who are just getting started collecting stories and don't want to think about any of the more complicated methods available. Usually people won't stick with this method alone, but will keep it in their repertoire for

Figure 9.1. Each group should draw a line on the space and mark the starting and ending dates.

times when they are rushed for time or working in a new, unfamiliar area.

How to find more on these ideas

This exercise is described only in this book, but it has so much in common with many hundreds of simple participatory exercises that I'm sure you can add some interesting wrinkles to it from looking over those. Many ice-breaker exercises are like this one: break into groups, then do a simple task with one moving part. If you read about participatory exercises you are sure to find variations on the same idea you can use.

TIMELINES

In a timelines exercise, when it is used for story collection, people build linear progressions of events, factual and/or fictional, from the stories they tell each other.

When to use it

Building timelines is particularly useful when people are considering a topic that has a strong time component to it. It might be something that happened to all of the people in the session together (a flood, an election), something that happened to them individually but is similar enough to be considered together (going to university, having a baby), or something that happened in the entire society (the rise of the internet, the sad decline of the "pet rock" fad). If you ask people about their experiences and they say, "I don't know, it all blends together," having them build a timeline is a useful way to get them to find experiences to talk about.

If your topic does *not* have an inherent time component, like a project on trust or leadership or cookies, asking people to build a timeline may lead to confusion. To test if this exercise will be useful to your project, try to picture (or build) a simple timeline of experience. If the exercise seems nonsensical to you, it will to others as well.

What it requires

At least three people and up to as many as the room will comfortably hold; at least ninety minutes; large sticky notes of a few different colors; large markers; places to put sticky notes (walls, large tables, clean floor); some way to record stories; some way to record answers to questions about stories.

How to do it

Step One: Introduce the exercise and form groups

Five minutes. Explain the exercise and its purpose. If you have enough people, split into small groups of three or four people each. Show people the walls, markers and sticky notes you have prepared for their use. Turn on any audio recorders.

Step Two: Choose topics and dates

Five minutes. Ask each group to agree on a *topic* their timeline will explore. The topic should be related to the goals of the project, like "how our town grew" or "beekeeping through the years" or "a journey through our medical system." Also ask each group to choose *starting and ending dates* for their timeline (Figure 9.1). Have them mark these dates with sticky notes (usually with the starting date on the left and the ending date

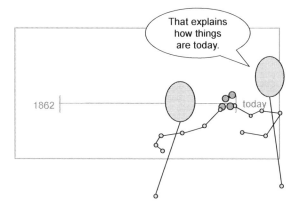

Figure 9.2. Groups should place a cluster of sticky notes with names of stories that describe the situation at the ending date.

on the right). In most contexts the ending date will be the present moment, but not in all cases.

Step Three: Describe the situation at the ending date

Ten minutes. Ask each group to tell some stories that capture an essential description of the end of the timeline. They should write a brief title for each story and build a cluster of these notes at the end (usually the right hand side) of the timeline space (see Figure 9.2). They should also write the story titles on their question answering sheets. Each group should aim to place at least three descriptive stories at the ending date.

Step Four: Work backwards to the starting date

Forty minutes. Now have each group work backwards through time, telling stories along the way (see Figure 9.3 on the next page). What happened before that? What happened before that? And so on.

Also ask people to mark *turning points,* or times when things changed in significant ways, on their timeline.

Step Five: Answer questions about stories

Ten minutes. Ask everyone to fill out question forms for every story they told (whose titles they should copy to their question forms).

Step Six: Visit timelines

Ten minutes. Ask everyone to walk around the room looking over all of the timelines created and talking about the experiences described there. Have one person from each group stay at

their own timeline to answer any questions or tell any stories people want to hear. (If you only have one group, leave this step out.)

Step Seven: Whole-room discussion

Ten minutes. Bring everyone together into a discussion of all the timelines. See if any additional stories come to mind.

If you have less time

You can trim this exercise down to forty-five minutes by including only these steps.

1. Introduce the exercise and form groups. Five minutes.
2. Choose topics and dates. Five minutes.
3. Describe the situation at the ending date. Five minutes.
4. Work backwards to the starting date. Twenty minutes. (No mention of turning points.)
5. Answer questions about stories. Five minutes. (Fewer stories.)
6. Visit timelines. Five minutes. (Or schedule a break after and tell people they can visit timelines during the break.)

This will be very fast-paced, and you'll have to keep people on their toes, and the timelines will be simpler and more sparse, but it will still work.

To convert the exercise into a simple fifteen-minute task, don't worry about start and end dates; don't worry about a topic; and don't worry about turning points. Just ask people, as

Figure 9.3. Groups should work backwards, filling in the timeline with stories about events. Use a different color of sticky note to denote turning points along the timeline.

they tell stories together, to place the names of the stories on a timeline that grows as it gets more stories in it. It won't matter if each timeline has three or ten or twenty stories in it; that isn't the point. The point is just to give people a little help telling stories by placing them in juxtaposition through time.

If you have more time

To add more time to this exercise, include one or more elaborations, or add time to the steps in this order:

1. Work backwards to the starting date
2. Visit timelines
3. Whole-room discussion
4. Answer questions about stories
5. Describe the situation at the ending date
6. Choose topics and dates
7. Introduce the exercise and form groups.

The maximum time I would suggest for this exercise would be about three hours.

Before you start

If you want to ask people to consider more than one type of turning point in their timelines, you will need to come up with a list of these things, and test it, before the exercise starts. Not half an hour before the exercise starts! Ideally you should have your list a week before the session, so you can try it out with various people before you put it to serious use.

Optional elaborations

Use multiple types of turning point

Depending on the goals of your project, you may want to ask people to think about particular *types* of turning points, like problems, decisions, dilemmas, learning moments, times of joy or despair, times of solidarity or conflict, breakthroughs, accidents, surprises, and so on.

I suggest giving people no more than three types of turning point. You'll confuse them with too many. Use different colored sticky notes to denote the different types of turning point. The more people seem willing to do complicated things, the more elaborate you can ask them to get about turning points. If you like, you can ask people to make up their own types of turning point.

Add utopian and dystopian timelines

If you want to get into speculative fiction, you can add this optional step just before participants answer questions about their stories. Give it thirty to sixty minutes.

First, ask each group to talk together about an inconceivably utopian, perfect, heavenly state of affairs. Ask people to tell some fictional stories around what that state might be like. Ask them to give each of those stories a name, then place the cluster of sticky notes in relation to the ending-date cluster (see Figure 9.4 on the facing page).

Next you have a choice: you can ask people to describe the *future* (and place the utopian cluster to the right of the ending date) or an *alternative ending date* (and place the utopian cluster directly above the actual ending date).

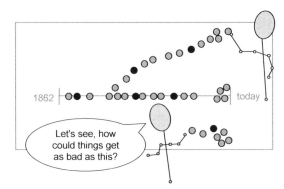

Figure 9.4. Groups can add fictional utopian and dystopian timelines to consider what-if scenarios.

Exploring the future is best when the goal of the project includes planning of some kind. Exploring alternatives to the past is better when the goal of the project has more to do with making sense of what has happened in the past. For example, if you are helping people think about the immigrant experience in the 1950s, it would not make much sense to ask them to think of a future state. On the other hand, if you are asking people to think about immigration in past, present, and future, asking them to come up with alternative futures is likely to be useful.

After the utopian cluster is placed, ask each group to work the utopian timeline backwards and finish it by connecting it at some point already located on the factual timeline (but *not* to the ending date). It is important to anchor the fictional timeline to the factual one, so that events diverge more and more from the possible. Along the way, ask people to tell fictional stories that show how the state of affairs transforms into the state of perfection. As with the main timeline, you can ask people to describe turning points, such as decisions, dilemmas, accidents, and so on.

When the utopian timeline is done, ask people to think about its opposite: an inconceivably *dystopian*, horrible, ruined state of affairs. Ask them to do the same storytelling around that state, placing the cluster near the bottom of the wall. Then have them work that fictional line back to the factual line in the same way as with the utopian line.

You don't have to start with utopia; either timeline can be done first. Some groups of people will prefer to think about utopia first, and others will prefer it the other way. You can let people choose which timeline they do first.

If you have a very motivated group and a big wall to work on, you can have people create multiple utopias and dystopias, the better to explore many possibilities. When people answer questions about their stories, they should consider the fictional stories as well; only make sure they label them as such (and utopian or dystopian too).

Add descriptors to timelines

Another optional elaboration is to have people add *descriptors* to each item in their timelines (factual and fictional). Place this step just after all the timelines are built and before the review period, and give it anywhere from ten to sixty minutes.

Ask people to go back over their events and place one or two additional items next to each story. (See Figure 9.5 on page 195.) Some example descriptors might be beliefs, feelings, motivations, forces, goals, fears, hopes, capabilities, deficiencies, resources, connections: things that matter for making sense of how things played out.

I like to ask people to place descriptors above and below the main line of events, creating up and down cityscapes along the main line. You can use the vertical value dimension to add meaning: hopes and fears, capabilities and deficiencies, beliefs and disbeliefs (or misbeliefs), cooperation and conflict. I always picture this as balloons rising up and plumb bobs falling down. Using lines, or even actual strings, to connect event items to descriptors might make the connections more explicit. This might help people think of more stories to add to the timeline, which is wonderful; squeeze them in and keep going.

Add multiple perspectives

Yet another optional elaboration is to include multiple perspectives on one timeline (see Figure 9.6 on the facing page). This is easy to do (with two perspectives) for the main timeline: simply displace each event from the line slightly to the top or bottom (balloons and plumb bobs again). Use separate colors as well, in case placements are not perfect or notes fall off the wall.

Be a bit careful here, because whatever perspective gains the top spot will seem more dominant. It might be best to put the underdogs on top to counter knee-jerk reactions. For fictional timelines this gets more difficult to fit into the space. Rarely will two competing views have the same utopian and dystopian situations, so create four fiction lines. Just make sure there is room for each set and label them clearly.

Exploring multiple perspectives is an elaborate activity that will take time and concentration, so you should only do it if you have people dedicated to a longer time frame, say a half-day or day-long session. But when your goal focuses on drawing out stories from multiple perspectives, say from two sides of a conflict over rights, I've seen this method work very well. The stories from one side of the line tend to spark stories on the other side, and in interesting ways: one group's surprise is another group's plan, one group's crisis is another group's opportunity. Interesting stuff.

Compare timelines to published models

After the timelines have been filled in, you can ask groups to compare their timelines to one or more published models that incorporate phases or stages. See the chapter on sensemaking exercises for instructions (page 397), and see Appendix A for a list of models useful in the timeline exercise.

Create follow-on timelines

Often when people are constructing a timeline they think of another timeline they could have (or should have) explored. People say things like, "What if we had considered not just *this* oil crisis but the two before it?" Or, "What if we had done this from the immigrant point of view?" Or, "What if we had gone through the telegraph as well as the telephone?" So another way to plan your session is to leave time for a second timeline after the first, then give people the option not to fictionalize or elaborate on their first timeline, but to start all over again with another time span and topic. Sometimes you will get better stories with a second run through the exercise with a new time frame or a new topic. Or you can ask people to expand their original timeline further into the past or future.

If people need you to hold their hand the whole way through this exercise, you will need to make these decisions for them ("Now you should create a second timeline this one makes you think of"). If they are ready to run on their own power, simply present all the elaboration options you can adequately describe and support, then let them pick what works for them.

How you will know it's working

Keep an eye on the timelines as they form. If the storytelling is going well, each will have a number of items scattered around it. If you see "blotchy" timelines, with some parts well populated and others bare, people may be going into too much detail. You might find that people vary a lot in how detailed their timelines are: one group may have fifty items while another has ten. There is not much you can do about this (and besides, the narrative richness in the sparse-item group might be greater anyway).

What can go wrong

People fuss too much over their timelines

Be careful not to give people the impression that the timeline they are building is to be an authoritative and coherent history. When used for story collection, timelines are like scaffolding. They provide support as people search through their experiences for moments to tell stories about, but they have no other purpose. Don't let people get the idea that the scaffolding is the building, because they might spend too much time on it and too little on the stories.

I like to use the words "rough timeline" to help people understand that precision isn't the point.

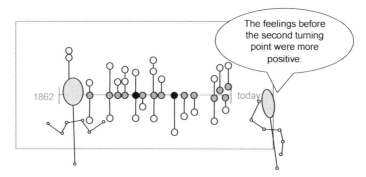

Figure 9.5. Groups can include descriptors that add detail to each event, such as beliefs, motivations, and capabilities.

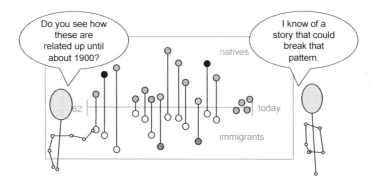

Figure 9.6. Groups can describe the same events from multiple perspectives, with one perspective on the top (displaced by some meaningful distance) and the other on the bottom.

If people do spend all their time fussing around getting things perfect on their timelines, explain that they don't need to precisely place each event, that the sequences don't have to be perfect, and that they can place multiple stories on the same spot. The idea is to help draw out experiences by thinking about the sequence of what happened, not to create a history lesson.

People can't fill up their timelines

Sometimes people look at a blank timeline and can't think of anything to place on it. Turning points are useful for this. If they aren't helping, see if you can come up with better ones, or ask people what sorts of turning points they would like to consider. Simple things like surprises and high or low points can help people find events to talk about.

I like to use a sort of "change between" method: go to two points with nothing between them and say, "What happened between these two events that changed things?" Then that empty space can get filled in. If you keep doing this for every empty spot, you will fill in the timeline.

Another method is to ask people about seasons or holidays as markers. For example, you could say, "Thinking about the spring of this year, do you remember what the situation was like? Did anything memorable happen during that spring?" And so on. Yet another tack is to ask people to place nouns on the timeline (places, people, objects) that surged up in importance during an event. Perhaps during protest marches an orange flower became significant. Bringing in nouns can add reminders that don't come up when only verbs are in front.

People describe events as dry facts

Sometimes people mistake the timeline exercise as a list-making exercise and place only events on it. The stories they tell are not actually recountings of personal experience, but simple lists of dates and incident reports, like "On November the third we lost our house. On

November the ninth we filled out the insurance claim." This is an unavoidable vulnerability of timelines: that they seem like, well, timelines. People may be used to timelines from history lessons, and may not be able to break out of dull recitations of information.

Here's a trick: spice up your turning points. Suggest more emotional turning points, like seizures of fear, sinking feelings in the stomach, leaps of elation, flights of fancy, and so on. If people ignore your recommendations and plod on marking out the mundane, set up some rules for what the timeline must contain. Say each timeline must contain at least three entirely unsuspected surprises, or at least four events about which there are conflicting reports, or at least five arguments. It is better if you see this coming and give out the rule at the start or soon after, but the old "I forgot to mention" gambit can help if things are going wrong.

People go forward through time

Actually I don't consider the part about going backwards in time to be absolutely essential to this method. It's more of a "nice to have." Working backwards prevents people from plodding through what always happens next, so the timelines people create going backwards tend to be more creative and diverse than those they create going forwards. But you won't get *no* creation or diversity if people work forward; you will just get less. I would not give people a lecture or castigate them if they don't work backwards. Just think about how you can improve your explanation the next time. Sometimes it doesn't matter how well you present the ideas. Sometimes the backwards thing just doesn't float. It's not the end of the world.

People can't or won't go to utopia or dystopia

If you plan on a fictional part to your exercise, you may or may not succeed in getting people to go along with it. You may find yourself in a position where some groups are willing and some are not. I wouldn't force people into fiction if they don't want to go there. Instead, ask just-the-facts folks to add more detail to their factual timeline or build a second timeline of a related but different history. If they already talked about the history of the town, ask them to build the history of the town market. Or ask them to add another type of turning point

they haven't explored yet, or consider multiple perspectives on what has happened. Both the factual and fictional parts of this exercise can shrink or grow in time without ruining the outcome.

People run out of space

The longer the physical timeline people have to work with, the more they will put on it. I'd say people should be able to place at least twenty items comfortably side by side on any timeline space you have. If you can give people a twenty foot wall (and the time to fill it), go for it. Don't make the mistake of having people run out of space before they run out of stories, because stories are far more precious than space!

People forget the questions about stories

This exercise is so in-drawing that people might forget (and *you* might forget) to use the forms you prepared with questions about the stories. When you are using a timeline method to collect stories, the pause-and-reflect-on-paper step is critical, so pinch yourself (or have someone else pinch you) when it's time.

Try it yourself first

This is an easy method to try alone. Just choose your own topic, find your own space, and set to work. I have done this myself on real walls and on the computer (using a presentation program) when I needed to sort through an experience. If you can get a few friends to try it with you, all the better; but doing the exercise alone still has merit. In fact, I like to use a similar timeline exercise when I need to update my résumé. It helps me remember little stories I want to include to show the world how amazing I am. You might want to try it for the same thing.

Your own style

I was once embarrassed by a timeline. I was taking an art class, and the instructor asked us all to create timelines of our lives in art, noting when important things had happened to us. I took this instruction very seriously, and drew out a line with lovely little markers on specific dates on which specific events had taken place. Imagine my surprise when everybody else in the class wrote nothing but vague, gauzy statements like "for a while I thought I might like painting but now I like sewing together little

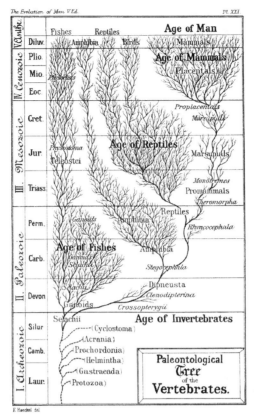

Figure 9.7. Ernst Haeckels' 1879 Paleontological Tree of Vertebrates showed time as a vertical chart, with relatedness as the second dimension. (Public domain image from Wikipedia.)

bottle caps." I was smugly reflecting on my exemplary display when the instructor looked at it and said, "Oh Cynthia, you're such a scientist." My memory of this event oscillates between my portrayal as the only intelligent person in the room and as the idiot who misunderstood the point of the whole thing. I do think the instructor succeeded, though, because I and the bottle-cap people were free to create what worked for us.

My point here is that "timeline" means many things to many people. It's not a word without prior meanings. It may not mean the same thing to you as it means to the people in your session. The best preparation is to accept that, figure out what you think timelines should look like, do what you can to steer things your way, and then let go and let people build what they think are timelines. And do the same thing with respect to what *I* think is a timeline, or anybody else who describes one. The general idea of building timelines is broad enough for fifty

people to walk abreast. Use it the way it works best for you. Maybe it should involve stones on the floor. Maybe it should involve play-acting. Maybe it should involve challenge and competition, or holding hands around a fire. Find your way.

Where it came from

The earliest timelines were chronological lists of events: coronations, harvests, floods, Olympic contests. The oldest preserved sequence of this type, the Parian Chronicle, was carved on a stone tablet in 264 BCE. It describes the history of the Greek world as a series of dated events.

Sometime in the first few centuries CE, time tables arose, with one column holding dates and the other events. This allowed the creators of time tables to expand the event column into two or more parallel categories, such as geographical regions. Many such time tables can be found in medieval books, looking much like the tables and spreadsheets we use today.

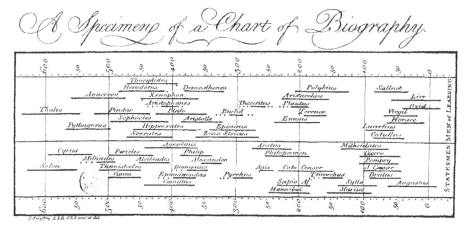

Figure 9.8. Joseph Priestley's 1765 timeline of the lives of important men shows the transition of chronological displays from time tables to time lines. (Public domain image from Wikipedia.)

Around the sixteenth and seventeenth centuries, two changes took place in the representation of time. One change was that ideas from the expanding field of cartography started leaking in to time representation. As a result, time tables began to experiment with new graphical representations of time in space. One example was the circular time table, which arranged its columns of events not in vertical lines but in concentric circles. The reader of a circular time table would turn a linear pointer, connected to the circle at its center, to view all the events that took place at that point in time. Many other representations of time were created, such as events displayed on a tree (see Figure 9.7 on the previous page), in a branching path, on a fanciful map, or on parts of a human or animal body.

The other change that took place in the creation of time tables was that the line between the year column and the event columns got thicker, and the lines between event columns got thinner. (See Figure 9.8.)

This was probably just an improvement in usability, because it was necessary to remember where the time periods were marked out. This trend continued until the line marking dates became a dominant feature of the representation (see Figure 9.9 on the next page). Thus time *tables* became time *lines*. (By the way, you can read about all of this in the fascinating book *Cartographies of Time: A History of the Timeline* by Daniel Rosenberg and Anthony Grafton.)

The long history of timelines means that this is one of the easiest representations of connected stories for people to understand. Timelines are particularly well suited to use with people who have had less experience with mathematical or graphical ways of representing information.

The *backwards* element of the fictional elaborations on this timeline exercise is somewhat new, and it is based on my own experiences. I'll tell you how it got added to the basic timeline. During some workshops Dave Snowden and I were conducting for the U.S. government with analysts and historians in 2001, we had people making fictional timelines to explore possible alternate histories related to asymmetric conflict. One of the groups drew their timeline backwards, from now to then instead of from then to now. We looked at that and thought "strange" but left them alone.

Just after that, we noticed that people seemed to add elements to their timelines that seemed appropriate based on what had happened before. In other words, they were plodding along in their thinking, running on *expectations* instead of exploring the fictional space. All of the groups did this, even the one that drew their line backwards. It was just the line, not the time frame they were considering, that was backwards.

But this "backwards" idea got us thinking. In the next exercise, we tried an experiment: we asked people to build one of their fictional timelines by working backwards through time,

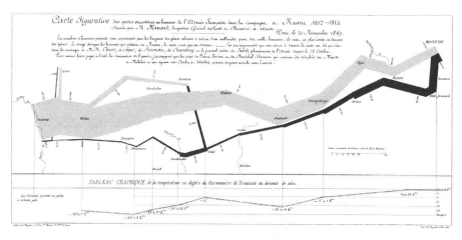

Figure 9.9. Charles Joseph Minard's 1869 chart of Napoleon's disastrous Russian campaign of 1812 shows time as a line arrayed in geographical space (and without dividing timetable marks). (Public domain image from Wikipedia.)

in effect telling the story from end to beginning. What we found was that the backwards timelines had more imaginative and multi-perspective elements, and seemed to allow people to range further in their consideration of possibilities. Going backwards stopped people from plodding along and forced them to think more creatively. After that workshop we changed the timeline method to use that discovery.

How to find more on these ideas

Dave Snowden calls this exercise "The Future, Backward." You can find descriptions of the method if you search the internet using that term. Searching the internet or books for any kind of "timeline" will also help you find ideas. You can also read about the history of timelines as representations of events in sequence to get ideas on other ways to show the flow of time. For example, some exercises use visualizations such as time as a flowing river. The idea of working backwards from the future is also widespread; I even came across a YouTube video with part of the movie *Back to the Future* run backward! (Untangle that!)

Time is something we all swim in, forward in experience and backward in memory, which is why methods like this are both useful and common. Search around and you are likely to find ideas that can augment your skills in helping people navigate in time for better storytelling.

LANDSCAPES

In a landscapes exercise, when it is used for story collection, people define a space with meaningful dimensions, then populate the space with stories called to mind by the combinations of conditions at each point. As the stories build up, a landscape of features comes into view. People describe these features and tell stories about them.

When to use it

Landscapes perform a complementary role in story elicitation to timelines, in that they work best for domains in which there is no dominant sequence of events through time. For example, while the timeline exercise is a natural choice for considering a community's development, the landscape exercise might be better for considering how the community uses its library. The landscape exercise takes what appear to be scattered experiences and finds ways in which they come together to create areas that invite deeper exploration.

What it requires

At least three people and up to as many as the room will comfortably hold; at least ninety minutes; large sticky notes of a few different colors; large markers; places to put sticky notes (walls, large tables, clean floor); some way to record stories; some way to record answers to questions about stories.

Figure 9.10. Give each group some dimensions to fill with stories.

How to do it

Step One: Introduce the exercise and form groups

Five minutes. Explain the exercise and its purpose. If you have enough people, split into small groups of three or four people each. Show people the walls, markers and sticky notes you have prepared for their use. Turn on any audio recorders.

Step Two: Present dimensions and corner points

Five to fifteen minutes. Ask each group to mark each axis of the space using dimensions you have chosen. Then ask people to label each corner point with descriptions of how the two dimensions come together at that corner: low trust, strong leadership, and so on (see Figure 9.10).

Step Three: Populate landscapes with stories

Forty minutes. Having defined their space, each group will now fill it up with stories (see Figure 9.11 on the next page).

Ask people to *put aside* their defined space at first and simply tell stories about the topic. As they tell each story, they should name the story, then write the name in two places: on a question sheet and on a sticky note. They should then place the story's sticky note on the space, discussing where it belongs as they do so. If they can't agree on one spot to place the note,

they can split it into two or three sticky notes, as long as they mark the aspect of the story each note refers to.

After each note is placed, more stories located in that area may jump out and beg to be told. If more stories don't jump out begging, the group should return to telling stories using *remindings* you have prepared: eliciting questions, categories of events (surprises, misconceptions, etc), or people, places, and things. You can give these out on paper or write them on a large white board, but have them ready to support the process.

You might ask: why not have people consider the *space* first rather than tell stories first? Because given an empty space, people tend to start drawing lines through it. They create quadrants and segments. That is not what you want. You want people to go on *journeys of discovery* through the space, wayfinding, exploring. You don't want them to chart the land's contours from a distant satellite. Why? Because you are looking for *ground truth*, of course! When people start telling stories *first*, they come down from the bird's eye view, land with a thump in the landscape, and start walking around in it. *That's* what you want.

Step Four: Discover (and tell stories about) features

Ten minutes. As people tell stories, patterns will naturally appear in the space they are filling

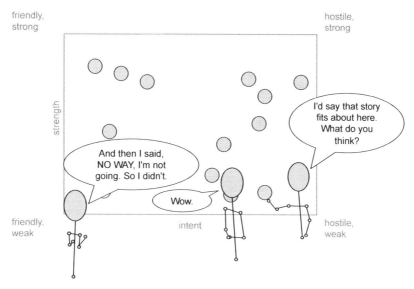

friendly, strong

hostile, strong

strength

I'd say that story fits about here. What do you think?

And then I said, NO WAY, I'm not going. So I didn't.

Wow.

friendly, weak

intent

hostile, weak

Figure 9.11. Groups should exchange stories normally, but as they do, they should place sticky notes with story titles into the space.

(see Figure 9.12 on the following page). Perhaps there are many stories in one spot but few in another, or the stories in one area form a line that divides one condition from another, or all the stories in one area mention dogs. After groups have populated their spaces, ask them to mark out features of the landscape. They can use marker, tape, string, sticky notes stuck to each other and arranged into chains: whatever works to make their meaning known.

Step Five: Answer questions about stories

Ten minutes. Now ask people to pause in their building and answer questions about each story they told. (If they are very tolerant or energetic, ask them if they will answer questions about the stories the *other* people in their group told as well.)

Step Six: Visit landscapes

Ten minutes. Ask everyone to walk around the room looking over all of the landscapes created and talking about the experiences described there. Have one person from each group stay at their own landscape to answer any questions or tell any stories people want to hear. (If you only have one group, leave this step out.)

Step Seven: Whole-room discussion

Ten minutes. Bring everyone together into a discussion of all the landscapes. See if any additional stories come to mind.

If you have less time

You can trim this exercise down to fit into forty-five minutes if you do only these parts.

1. Introduce the exercise and form groups. Five minutes.
2. Present dimensions and corner points. Five minutes.
3. Populate landscapes with stories. Twenty minutes.
4. Discover features. Five minutes.
5. Answer questions about stories. Five minutes.
6. Visit landscapes. Five minutes.

You can convert the exercise into a fifteen-minute task by presenting people with a pre-defined space and asking them to simply place stories in it as they tell them. Don't give people a special time period to discover features; just assume that they will notice some features as they tell stories. This will give people just a *bit* of help covering the topic of discussion.

If you have more time

To add more time to this exercise, include one or more elaborations, or add time to the steps in this order:

1. Populate landscapes with stories

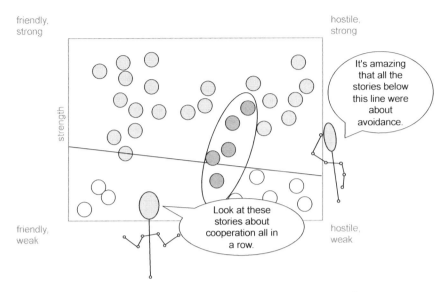

Figure 9.12. Groups should discover patterns among the stories in their spaces.

2. Discover (and tell stories about) features

3. Visit landscapes

4. Whole-room discussion

5. Answer questions about stories

6. Present dimensions and corner points

7. Introduce the exercise and form groups

The maximum time I would suggest for this exercise would be about three hours.

Before you start

Preparing to facilitate the landscape exercise requires you to think about dimensions of meaning that people can use to create landscapes. Where can you find dimensions of meaning? Look through the documents you have written (or remember discussions you have had) as you planned your project. Can you find two aspects you can expect to vary in meaningful ways among the stories you collect? If your project is about trust, would that dimension vary enough among stories to be useful if considered?

The two dimensions you choose should be *orthogonal*, or independent of each other. Non-orthogonal (dependent) dimensions are things that are usually related in general. Seeing them line up together in any *particular* case will not add useful meaning to the project.

Some examples of non-orthogonal dimensions might be:

• age with experience

• strength with capability

• fairness with equality

• trust with respect

• occupation with income

• fear with anxiety

In contrast, orthogonal dimensions might or might not be related in any particular case. So whether they turn out to be related in the case of your project *will* mean something useful to the project.

Some examples of orthogonal dimensions might be:

• trust with success

• innovation with fairness

• effectiveness with efficiency

• strength with generosity

• cooperation with innovation

• diversity with conflict

The one exception to the orthogonal-dimensions rule is that you *can* use dependent dimensions when they are *generally* connected but probably aren't in the case of your project. For example, usually respect and trust increase together. But you may know (say from a pilot story collection) that in the case of your project, trust and respect have become uncoupled in the community. In this case you might *deliberately* choose these dimensions as a means to get people to explore the trust-respect issue as they tell stories. Deliberately choosing dependent dimensions can be risky, because it can lead people to limit their storytelling to cases that fit the expected relationship. On the other hand, if the lack of an expected relationship is important to the project, asking people to address it head-on can help them probe a sensitive topic.

When you have found a dimension set you think works, test it by placing stories on it and showing it to people to see if they appear to understand it. Better yet, test a few different dimension sets and pick the best one. If you plan to use more than one dimension set, you will need to go through this process more than once.

Using dimensions from published models

You can draw your landscape dimensions from published models or frameworks that relate to the topic of your project. Any model that includes two or even three named dimensions will work as a landscape dimension set. You can find landscape-ready models in textbooks on any subject; there are even a few in this book. Just make sure the model's dimensions cover *continuous* ranges (low to high), not *discrete* categories (A or B). As an example, say your project is about learning, and you know of a model that places the degree of knowledge abstraction (from concrete to abstract) against the degree of cognitive complexity (from simple remembering to complex creation). Asking your participants to fill an abstraction-complexity space with stories might create useful diversity in a story collection on the topic of learning.

However, when you use published models in a landscape exercise, watch out for two things: familiarity and jargon. First, familiarity. If the model whose dimensions you use is very well known to your participants, it might restrict rather than enhance the stories they tell. For example, if you asked a group of educational consultants to tell stories in the space defined by a learning model they all knew, you would not necessarily get stories about their *experi-*

ences as much as you would get stories they believe fit the expectations set up by the model. In that case it would be better to break their expectations, perhaps by mixing dimensions from two familiar models, turning the model's dimensions around, renaming dimensions, or simply putting aside the well-known model entirely.

On the other hand, when people are very unfamiliar with a published model, the jargon issue comes into play. Fancy "ten dollar" words can intimidate participants, making the stories they tell more about performance to expectation than about lived experience. Yes, I am saying that published models can have the *same* impact on people who know them well *and* people who know them so little that every word in them is strange. Both extreme familiarity *and* extreme unfamiliarity lead towards performance and away from the recounting of lived experience. This is actually not all that surprising. People perform when they think they can't just talk. The problem is, you *need* people to "just talk." Participatory narrative inquiry only works well when ordinary people tell ordinary stories about their ordinary lives. Anything that stands in the way of authenticity will damage your project.

So using published models in story collection exercises is a double-edged sword: useful and dangerous as the same time. On the one hand, well-known models usually *become* well known because they are useful. Most such models come from long experience and serious research, and they have been improved over many uses by people dealing with the topic in practice. There is no doubt in my mind that using published models as scaffolding *can* improve a story collection's coverage of a topic. But on the other hand, I have seen fixed models stifle the authentic recounting of lived experiences in some circumstances. In particular, I've seen people who are used to following directions or are very literal-minded stick to published models like glue, unwilling to consider anything that even slightly "colors outside of the lines" of the model.

So if you find a model that seems like it will improve your story collection, check it for familiarity to your participants and for off-putting jargon. Try it out with some of the people you expect to tell stories. If you find people performing to an expectation they perceive in what you have presented, think of another way forward. There are many ways you can use a published model to *inform* the dimensions you use in a landscape exercise without using the model exactly as it was published. Think of published models as tools in your toolbox, not as blueprints you must follow.

Appendix A (page 589) lists examples of published models I think might be useful in story collection and sensemaking exercises.

Optional elaborations

Rename dimensions and corners

The simplest form of this exercise is to give people one fixed set of landscape dimensions and ask them to use the dimensions *exactly* as given. The benefit of the use-only-this option is that you can choose dimensions that you know match your project's context and goals well. The detriment is that by specifying dimensions up front you will miss any *better* ideas your participants might have. If you want to add just a *bit* more depth to the exercise, but don't want to overwhelm people with a complex task, you can ask people to *translate* the names you provide into names that seem more meaningful to them. Place this renaming activity after step two and add an extra five to ten minutes for it. There are many ways to describe the dimensions and areas that define a landscape. For example, "friendly" can be nice, kind, amiable, warm, sociable, neighborly, benign, agreeable, and so on. Encouraging people to find words that mean something *to them* can help them make better use of the dimensions.

Choose from multiple dimension sets

Instead of presenting people with *one* set of dimensions, you can prepare and present two or three such sets. Ask each group to choose one set they will work with. This gives people a way to customize the exercise somewhat to their needs, but still keeps some quality control in place. Add this activity after step two, and add an extra five to ten minutes for it, or more if you ask people to translate names into their own versions. You can allow multiple groups to use the same set, or you can have groups "claim" a

dimension set so that all of the sets get used by somebody.

Build dimension sets from a list of dimensions

You can provide people with a list of dimensions, then ask each group to choose which two will form the set that defines their landscape. For example, you might list six dimensions (which you chose before the session started) on a white board and ask each group to choose two. Place this activity after step two and add an extra five to ten minutes for it.

If you use this option, I suggest adding a dimensions-review period afterward (another five to ten minutes) in which each group *presents* their dimension set to the whole room. Explain the difference between orthogonal and non-orthogonal dimensions (as above) and ask people to consider that aspect of the choice. Each group should justify their dimensions as *relevant* to the project and likely to be *useful* when considered together.

A reader has pointed out that Robert Keidel's book *Seeing Organizational Patterns* lists many sets of dimensions which could be useful for considering dynamics in communities and organizations. I agree.

Create new dimensions and sets

As you might expect, you can expand participation further by asking people not only to build their own dimension sets, but to nominate their own dimensions as well. You should only use this option if you are sure your participants will be willing and able to go this far into participation with you. If you are not sure, you can drop back to one of the lesser forms of choice.

Or you can combine all three choice options by simultaneously presenting:

- some preselected dimension sets;
- some preselected dimensions, with instructions on how to pair them up into new sets (or permission to "pull apart" the preselected dimension sets and pair them up differently); and
- an invitation to come up with entirely new dimensions and pair them up (with or without preselected dimensions) into new sets.

This flexible method is more complicated for you to facilitate, but it handles the case of groups whose willingness and ability to participate vary. In any case, if you include any element of choice beyond the choice of sets, include a review period to ensure that sets are orthogonal, relevant, and potentially useful.

No matter how much freedom you want to give participants in naming and choosing dimensions, never attempt to do a landscape exercise without *some* prepared dimensions on hand. This is simply because you can never know when people will have difficulty coming up with dimensions they want to use. Choosing dimensions to define a space is fairly complex, abstract thinking. Not everyone is comfortable doing it. (As to competency, I think anybody can do anything given enough time. It's more a question of what works right now than what people are capable of doing.) If people can't do this task in the time you have, hand them something they can use and move on quickly. You could drain out most of your time in this stage if you let things drag on.

Add a third dimension

You can improve the landscapes you create by incorporating a third height dimension, which shows not just areas of space but mountains and valleys. A third dimension takes longer to incorporate, which is why I put it down here in the optional part. But more importantly, a third dimension requires a more complicated thought process on the part of your participants. If you think people can handle height, by all means bring it in; it will increase the utility of your output.

Here's how to up the dimensionality of your landscape. When you are setting up the space at the beginning of the session, suggest a third dimension. I do not recommend you give this one to people to control, because it is too easy to get wrong. I know of only two height dimensions that work well in landscape exercises: *value*, from desirable to undesirable; and *constancy*, from changeless to volatile. Each of these describes a critical evaluation people make about situations they face: Is it safe? Is it changing? A satiated, sleeping lion is unsafe but unlikely to move; rain after drought is welcome but liable to stop suddenly. Which is more useful, value

or constancy? Constancy has to do with future planning and prediction, so it is a good dimension to use when the goals of your project reach toward the future. Value is more useful in examining the past and present.

To add a height dimension, make a small amendment to your instructions when people begin to populate their spaces with stories. When they write each story's name on a sticky note, ask them to choose from a few *different colors* of notes that represent different states of value or constancy. I would not push this distinction beyond three colors (good, neutral, bad; or changeless, intermediate, volatile) because people will get confused. Yes, a limited number of sticky note colors creates pigeonholes in the third dimension, but not much can be done about that.

Now when people discover landscape features in their spaces, they will find more meaning. Perhaps all the blue volatile stories are clustered around the strong/friendly corner. Or maybe there is a line of green "very good" stories separating two pools of red "just awful" stories. The mapping gets more meaningful with a third dimension.

Consider multiple perspectives

You can ask people to represent every story, when possible, with two or more sticky notes that represent different points of view. If a story called "The dog came home" involves a dog, a neighbor, a town official, and a businessman, write out the title on four cards (three if you don't care about the dog) and place them in a position that matches the story from the perspective of that story character (also written on the note). Maybe the town official saw the story as an example of weak friendliness, while the neighbor saw the story as showing strong hostility. This is a good way to populate a space more quickly, by the way, if you think people will worry they didn't "do it right" unless they get lots of things into the space.

Add descriptors

Descriptors can also be added to the space, in the same way they were with timelines (see page 193). The only difficulty here is that you have to repeat the story title on each, so this is only feasible in practice if people are very mo-

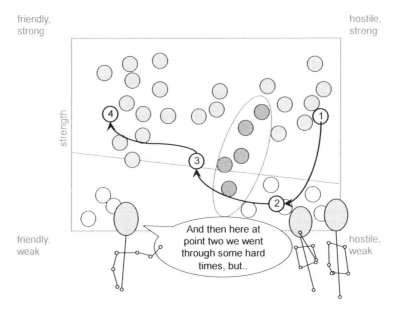

Figure 9.13. A landscape space filled with stories can help people think of more stories to tell, real or imagined.

tivated, or you have a lot of time, or you have some helpers who can help copy things down for people to use. Still, if you want even more depth you can get it in this way.

Build stories on landscapes

You can add an elaboration after step seven (discuss the landscapes) in which you ask people to use their landscapes to either build fanciful stories or tell real stories by describing a journey through the space (see Figure 9.13). Give people markers or string or tape and ask them to show the stages of their story as it unfolds. As always, encourage people to tell more stories this reminds them of.

How you will know it's working

In the first part of this exercise, when people are defining their space, check in with each group to make sure things are going as they should. Don't just watch during that time; ask. Why? Because if people don't have a solid foundation for their storytelling and story placement, things will founder soon after.

In the part of the exercise where people are supposed to be telling each other stories and placing them on the map, which is the heart of the exercise, they should be looking at *each other*, not the map. Look for storytelling during

that period, because that is where things will go wrong if they are paying too much attention to the map. During the later periods, the bulk of the storytelling will have taken place and the pressure on you to make sure stories are flowing will be reduced.

What can go wrong

People don't get the whole dimensions thing

There are two metaphors you can use to present the landscape exercise: *mapping* and *graphing*. Each works best with different people.

Most scientists and professionals are familiar with the practice of plotting data in spaces defined by dimensions. For these people it works best to speak of creating *graphs* that show patterns. Say things like "on the X axis, write your X dimension."

But a graph-based explanation will leave those who have little familiarity with graphs and charts confused, and a mapping explanation will work better. For these people, use *map* language. Avoid words like *dimension, axis, x, y, z, plot, figure,* and *diagram.* Instead use words like *direction, location, place, spot, site, land,* and *area.* When you ask people to define their dimensions, say "Consider what changes as you move from North to South, then from East to

West." When you ask people to define corners of the space, say "Write what it means to be located in the extreme North-West corner of the land."

Decide which metaphor you will use to speak to the people you will be working with, and stick to it.

People misunderstand the dimensions

It is important that everyone within each group understands and agrees on the group's dimensions. If one person is placing stories from strong to weak trust, and a second person is placing stories from present to absent trust, and another person is placing stories from my trust to your trust, the picture they create together will be meaningless. The best way to monitor this is to visit each group about five minutes into their storytelling, and ask them a few questions about their dimensions. See if they all tell you the same thing. If they don't, ask them to work out a better common definition of the terms.

People choose inadequate dimensions

Sometimes when you ask people to come up with their own dimensions (or give them the option to do so) they will come up with dimensions that don't work. One or both of the dimensions might work only with a fixed-choice list, which makes the space into a list of boxes. The two dimensions might be too close to each other, like the degree of trust and the degree of loyalty. Too-similar axes usually produce strong lines of association that hide differences. Also, watch out for story-quality dimensions creeping in, like memorability or noteworthiness.

If you catch a problem with dimensions early on, before any stories are told, you can help people improve it; but catch it quick or let it go. You should be very active in the period where people are defining or customizing their dimensions, then fade back after they start telling stories.

People draw boxes on the space

Remember to communicate that dimensions should go from something to something else, or from little to much of something, like number lines. Dimensions are not boxes; they are open spaces. If you catch people building boxed areas, stop them. Often I say "let it go" but this is

a case where you had better nip categorization in the bud. It will constrain the storytelling and damage the result.

People don't fill up the whole space

Sometimes, during the part of the exercise when people are telling stories to fill their maps, one part of the landscape becomes a "no man's land" where no stories can be found. People might avoid the strong-unfriendly area, or the place where trust breaks down and hope fails. When you are using this exercise for sensemaking, this is useful information; but when you are using it for story collection it is a problem.

What works is to set up a *coffee mug rule:* leave no space bigger than a coffee mug empty (see Figure 9.14 on the following page). If your map space is larger or smaller, or you hate coffee, adapt the rule: a coin, a notebook page, a plate, a book. Anything roughly one-fifth of the length or width of the space will work. Even one or two stories in a dead spot will improve the story collection. It is better to set up this rule in advance, as the groups begin to tell stories, rather than try to add it after people have become engaged in their activity.

The great thing about a coffee-mug rule is that if someone has a dead spot on their map you can just carry around a real coffee mug (or other object) and place it on their map without saying a word. This way there is less disruption, less offense, and more story flow.

People try too hard to map the space perfectly

This is the inverse of the previous problem: people try to create a perfect distribution of stories. While I said above that each part of the map should have some stories in it, the stories don't have be spread evenly with a butter knife. There should be natural variation in story distribution. If, say, there are ten stories clustered around one spot but only the minimum required by the coffee-mug rule in another spot, this is not a problem that needs to be fixed.

A landscape of stories is a mechanism to aid recall, not a creation to be perfected. Putting too much attention into the map takes away from attention to storytelling. For example, you might find people dividing the map into sections or quadrants (even though you said not

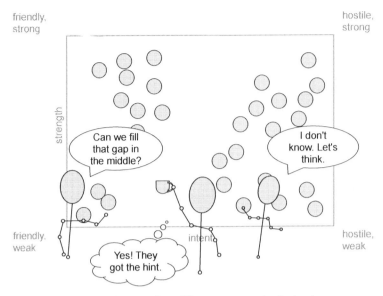

Figure 9.14. Nudge people to fill empty spaces in the landscape.

to) and counting the numbers of stories there. It is for this reason that you shouldn't mention feature-finding until *after* the story-filling period has passed, because people might stop telling stories and start obsessing over finding, or creating, features before it is the right time to do that.

Watch for groups not telling stories but pointing at their maps and arguing; if you see it, listen in and find out if you need to gently remind them what the map is for.

People can't find any features in their space

This does sometimes happen: people tell lots of stories and fill up the space, but they can't see any differences among the stories. They have mapped out a featureless plain, a desert of meaning.

When this happens, my suggestion is to be ready with a quick three-dimensional add-on exercise. If people complain that they have no features, ask them to take their markers and make one, two or three noticeable dots on each item, denoting a third dimension. Make it a simple question: Did the story end well? Or, did the story involve much change? If necessary, expand the feature-finding segment of the session by a few minutes to accommodate the extra activity. It is likely that *some* features will appear as a result, even if only a mild declivity is discov-

ered. (People can even do this more than once, if they are willing: red dots and blue dots.)

If a group completes such an annotation, and there are *still* no discernible features in their landscape, then *that* is the story of their landscape: that it has no features. Later they can talk about why the landscape came out the way it did and what that might mean. Sometimes a desert is all there is to find.

Try it yourself first

This is an easy exercise to try on your own or with a colleague or friend. You can use a wall or a computer. Try it with some topic you know well, so it will be easy to populate your landscape with stories.

By the way, you can also use this exercise while collecting stories in an interview, by populating a space yourself while you ask one or more people questions. You can use it as a way to check whether you have covered the range of topics you hoped to cover. Maps are flexible tools for recall and can be used in many ways.

Your own style

Remember what I said above about graphs versus maps? Of course the way you present the exercise should depend partly on your participants, but it should depend on you as well. If you are more comfortable with maps than

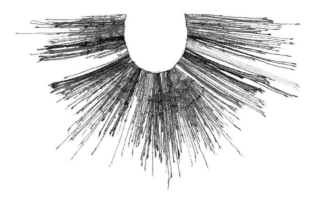

Figure 9.15. Incan quipus were used as maps of memory, much like today's graphs and diagrams. (Photograph from the Larco Museum in Lima, Peru; permission given under the Creative Commons Attribution-Share Alike 3.0 Unported license. Retrieved from Wikipedia.)

graphs, by all means present the idea that way. Whatever you can speak about with the most confidence and comfort is the way you should present it, as long as the participants can understand you.

Another element of style is whether you *talk* about the landscape or *show* it to people. By showing the landscape, I mean drawing one or building one with real objects, like books or mugs or coins you place into a space in front of people. Try a few different methods of presentation and see which comes off most naturally. Your own experiments using a map on your own will give you some insights into what metaphors (or lack thereof) work best for you.

Where it came from

The idea of mapping ideas in space is thousands of years old. Every ancient civilization seems to have developed maps as aids to memory, communication, and understanding. The Native American medicine wheel is one example that goes back perhaps five to ten thousand years. Physical recording systems such as Inca quipus (Figure 9.15) and North American wampum belts were maps of memory. Mandalas symbolically represent the universe, seen and unseen. Even the great Taj Mahal is considered by some to represent a map of the metaphysical world. You will find many such idea-maps spread throughout history. If time is the current of the river of life, space is the water we swim in.

My own experience with mapping stories came about in two ways: through my involvement in developing the Cynefin sensemaking framework (and later the Confluence sensemaking framework, see page 596), and through a project on discovering features of complex situations.

Here is an excerpt of what I wrote (in a paper, *The Wisdom of Clouds*) about the discovery of narrative landscapes:

> Dave Snowden, Alicia Juarrero and I were working together on a project for a government agency about helping people detect weak signals of upcoming problems by looking at public information such as newspaper articles. What challenges could government analysts find that could be addressed before they got too big to handle?
>
> During one phone call in particular, Alicia and I talked about the difficulties people had in finding features in a landscape of meaning. We wondered what it was about the features they could not see.
>
> In what I must say was a great feat of lateral thinking, Alicia mentioned how Einstein's revelation had been in discovering that a planet has gravity because space-time is curved around the planet, not because the planet has a "thing" called gravity. (Said physicist John Wheeler, "Matter tells space how to curve, and curved space tells matter how to move.")

This was a critical insight and turning point: we began to think about what would happen if you asked people to describe *the space itself*, not its features. Would useful features emerge from the space if you did this?

A quick look at the literature on topology showed us that interpolation among point measurements was a standard way of creating topological maps of geographic features. We already had much experience gathering and working with stories, which are essentially point measurements on geographies of meaning. What would be the result of interpolating among stories?

We then tested this idea. I collected some newspaper articles about aspects of large political situations, selecting stories that seemed to represent diverse perspectives and foci. I asked myself questions about each story, questions that would place each item on dimensions that seemed important to mapping such situations: change (stable to unstable), connectivity (tight to loose), reach (local to global), capability (weak to strong), intention (accidental to intentional), diversity (homogeneous to heterogeneous), conflict (cooperating to competing), morality (good to evil) and sophistication (civilized to barbaric).

The exercise generated some unexpected features of the spaces (pairing up dimensions in all possible ways, with change as the height dimension in all cases). To give one example, in the morality and sophistication landscape, the expected basin when all parties are good and civilized was not countered with a peak of instability where all parties are evil and barbaric—that area contained a stable basin as well, because evil is predictable. But there was a strong central peak where intentions are difficult to predict. In retrospect, such a pattern makes perfect sense, but if you asked people to generate such features from considering the whole situation, they might not have seen it.

This is the utility of all mapping techniques: they move from specific to general in order to reveal insights that were hidden in plain sight.

How to find more on these ideas

I'd like to point you at three avenues for further exploration of space and negotiated meaning. The first is the field of *information cartography*, or the spatial visualization of information. Many books and papers have been written about ways in which the visual display and examination of information can help people (usually analysts and decision makers) explore meaning and discover useful patterns in complex masses of data. Information cartography offers abundant ideas for creative visualization, but is rarely participatory.

A second avenue of exploration is the relatively new field of *knowledge cartography*. Work in this area uses methods such as mind mapping and concept mapping to array elements and linkages in space. Knowledge cartography, unlike information cartography, places much emphasis on sensemaking and participatory work, so it is closer to narrative landscape work. (A comprehensive resource here is the 2008 book *Knowledge Cartography: Software Tools and Mapping Techniques*, edited by Alexandra Okada, Simon Buckingham Shum, and Tony Sherborne.)

However, both information cartography and knowledge cartography, while they use space, do not use *meaningful* space. Even though both names include the word "cartographic," this is meant in a metaphorical sense only. Strictly speaking, what is produced in both information and knowledge cartography is not a true map but a *diagram*. In a diagram, relative *proximity* between elements matters, but absolute *location* does not. That doesn't mean these methods are flawed; it just means they are not the same as this exercise.

The third avenue you might want to explore is the field of *participatory mapping*, which uses continuous, meaningful dimensions. However, participatory mapping rarely makes use of *conceptual* space, which is the primary concern of both information and knowledge cartography.

So these three avenues go off in different directions. Information cartography is conceptual, but neither dimensioned nor participatory; knowledge cartography is conceptual and participatory, but not dimensioned; participatory mapping is dimensioned and participatory, but not conceptual. Learning more about each of these partial connections to narrative landscapes can help you improve your techniques in this area.

BUILD YOUR OWN STORY COLLECTION EXERCISE

I hate books that say "do these three things and call me in the morning." What I hope you will get from this part of the book isn't that these are The Exercises You Should Do (and Just As I Say). I hope you will learn that using exercises to help people draw out stories can be worthwhile and that you can develop them yourself, just as I did. These are some exercises I helped grow, and have come to know and love; but many more such exercises exist, and even more are possible. Some exercises may be waiting for *you* to develop them. (For an example of a story collection exercise I *didn't* develop but like a lot, look at Stéphane Dangel's "I forgive" exercise in the "PNI Stories" section of *More Work with Stories*.)

What are the essential features of a story collection exercise? I would say there are three.

A scaffold

A story collection exercise should create a *scaffold for recall:* a structure that reminds people of things they have forgotten. The scaffold should not require talents or expertise not available to all, unless it has been designed specifically for the use of one group alone. It should have something to do with memories and meanings. Timelines use time; landscapes use space; twice-told stories use simple themes; but there are other structures out of which you can build scaffolds.

A vehicle

A story collection exercise should create a *vehicle for exploration:* there should be something in it that draws on some kind of energy to pro-

pel people forward in their search for stories. The vehicle might specialize in broad or deep exploration, but *something should move* as the exercise unfolds. Such a vehicle makes the process a journey, not simply a task.

A tapestry

A story collection exercise should create a *tapestry for sensemaking:* something should be juxtaposed with something else for comparison. Similarities, differences and larger patterns should be considered. The resulting insights should enrich the stories collected so that the collection is not just populous but meaningful.

A story collection exercise usually starts as an idea or image: perhaps *this* will be useful. How to move it from a simple idea to a useful exercise? Just keep doing it. Start by playing with the idea yourself, then ask a friend to try it with you. At the end of each trial of your method, apply the above criteria to it. In what way does it create a scaffold, a vehicle, and a tapestry? If any of these are weak, how can you make them stronger? If the three features are unbalanced, how can you balance them?

As you keep trying your method, use it with larger groups. Listen very carefully to what people say during your experiments. If you can, record the whole session and transcribe it, then pore over everything everyone said. Sometimes people will give you transformative insights through off-hand comments or jokes that reveal dangers or opportunities you hadn't seen. Don't let those gems slip through your fingers. *Let the method teach you* how it should develop. That's the best way to move from a tantalizing idea to a solid technique.

ABOUT THOSE STICKY NOTES

In these sections about narrative exercises, I have made many references to "sticky notes." What I mean is those little pieces of paper with weakly adhesive backings which have become ubiquitous in contemporary office life. They started out as "Post-it Notes" from the 3M company, but they now come from everywhere. You can buy sticky notes at just about any store that sells general merchandise (even my grocery store has them).

You *can* use square or rectangular sticky notes, but if you can find hexagonal or round sticky notes, I recommend them. They are *much* better for use in exercises. Why? Because hexagonal or round notes fit together in a beehive pattern that makes it easy to cluster them together. Square notes define square spaces and are more likely to lead to categorization. It sounds strange to say that the shape of a note could influence thinking, but I've seen it happen. Believe me, it matters.

Several suppliers of hexagonal and round sticky notes are available, though such notes are often more expensive than the square kind. A colleague of mine has had success with buying square sticky notes, then cutting off the corners with a strong paper cutter. This is a great cost-cutter if you have a strong paper-cutter, not so much if you don't. But if you have some helpers, you can do the same with scissors and time.

Another idea is to use square notes but simply ask people to *rotate* them to create a diamond. That's not as good as using a different shape, but it's still better than the dead-on square.

It's usually a good idea to get several *colors* of sticky notes, because you can use the colors to annotate stories with additional meaning.

No matter what shape of sticky note you use, *use big ones*. When you have a wall filled with sticky notes, you need people to be able to see both the detail and the larger picture at the same time. Give people large markers, and ask them to write big. If you are doing the exercise on a computer, this can be daunting (it's the worst disadvantage really), but you can get around it partially by either having a large screen or zooming in and panning around a lot.

By the way, you can also buy *giant* sticky notes, two or three feet tall and wide. These are excellent for use when you need a place to stick your smaller sticky notes. When you finish your session, you can pull each giant sticky note off the wall (no damaging tape) and roll the whole thing up, ready to look at again when you get home.

SUMMARY

Three exercises are described whose purpose is to help people examine their experiences and share stories.

In a twice-told stories exercise, people in small groups choose selection criteria, then tell stories and choose one to retell to the larger group. As people consider the stories they are telling, they think of more stories they want to tell. This is a simple exercise suitable when participants and facilitators are inexperienced in story work.

In a timelines storytelling exercise, people build a timeline of events about which they tell each other stories. Timelines are especially useful when people are recounting a shared history (such as a town's history) or similar experiences (such as long careers). Optionally, people can explore fictional timelines and consider the same events from multiple perspectives.

In a landscapes exercise, people fill a two-dimensional space with stories that represent qualities of the different areas mapped out. Landscapes are useful when there is not a strong time component to what is being recalled, but exploring issues (represented by dimensions in the landscape) is important to the project. Optionally, people can add a third dimension, consider multiple perspectives, and use the landscape to build or recall stories.

To build your own story collection exercise, create a scaffold that helps people recall stories, a vehicle that helps people explore issues, and a tapestry that helps people make sense of the stories they tell.

QUESTIONS

Are you familiar with any group exercises from work in other areas? Have you ever used an ice-breaker exercise, for example, or started a group game, or ran a debate, or got people to brainstorm about something? How do the exercises in this chapter differ from what you have done before?

Do any parts of the exercises in this chapter seem particularly challenging to facilitate? Do any parts seem like they will be interesting or motivating to you? Do any parts seem trivial or dull? If you were to customize these exercises so that they perfectly fit your style of doing things, what changes would you make?

Think about people who might be involved in a group story session you might facilitate in your community or organization. How would these exercises go over with them? What parts might they find exciting, empowering, boring, worthless? If you were to customize these exercises so that they perfectly fit your community or organization, what changes would you make?

ACTIVITIES

Go back to each "try it yourself" section in this chapter and do what it says there. Select a story to retell in conversation; build a timeline; create a landscape. Then go back and reread the sections on each exercise. How does facilitating each exercise seem different now? What would you like to try next?

After you have tried each exercise yourself, try helping a small group of friends or colleagues carry out each exercise. What happens differently in a group than by yourself? What do you need to do before you will be ready to facilitate these exercises in a story session that is part of a project?

In the questions above, I asked what you might do if you were to customize these exercises for your own style and for your community or organization. Choose one of the exercises, make some changes to it, and try it out with some people in your community or organization. Take notes on what you learn from doing this.

Develop your own story collection exercise. Create a scaffold for recall, a vehicle for exploration, and a tapestry for sensemaking. Try it out in practice. Then write up the method so others can use it.

Chapter Ten

Narrative Catalysis

This chapter describes the process of preparing catalytic material, or observations and interpretations of stories and answers to questions about them, for use in sensemaking.

NARRATIVE CATALYSIS IN A NUTSHELL

Narrative catalysis creates food for thought that enhances group sensemaking about collected stories. This "food," or *catalytic material,* takes the form of interpreted observations about patterns formed by stories and answers to questions about them. Catalysis begins with a number of stories and answers to questions about them, and it ends with a report or presentation of some kind.

Why include catalysis in a PNI project? For two reasons. First, catalysis *concentrates and solidifies* the patterns spread across many stories and answers into a smaller number of coherent patterns. Second, catalysis *expands and multiplies* those patterns into a web of representations, interpretations, and ideas that spur thought and discussion around each pattern.

More than anything else, catalysis is an *amplification* process. It is not about simplification, nor it is about finding answers, solving problems, conveying messages, or supporting agendas. Catalysis results are like *false-color images* in which data, like temperature changes or lava flows or wind patterns or traffic jams, are highlighted and made more understandable and accessible by transforming them into visual information. Catalysis does the same thing with the stories people tell and the things they say

about those stories. It highlights trends and patterns not easily visible to the naked eye.

Catalysis is a supplementary, optional part of participatory narrative inquiry. It can be used to help improve the productivity of sensemaking, but it is an advanced, complicated activity. If you are a newcomer to PNI, you might want to set catalysis aside until you have mastered some of the more essential parts of the approach.

A simple example should help to explain what narrative catalysis looks like, and hopefully it will show what catalysis is good for as well.

Data to patterns

To begin with, consider Table 10.1 on the following page. It shows how many stories were annotated with each of several emotions by their tellers (in a real project).

Then consider Figure 10.1 on the next page, which represents the same data visually. Just rendering the pattern visually makes it more useful.

Patterns to observations

Now consider these observations about the counts of answers in Table 10.1. In narrative catalysis, observations are *statements about patterns that anyone can see.*

1. "Frustrated" was marked twice as often as "angry."
2. "Hopeful" was marked more than three times as often as "indifferent."
3. "Confused" was marked only once out of seventy-five total markings.

Observations to interpretations

Now consider the same observations, each expanded with the addition of three linked interpretations. In narrative catalysis, interpretations are *statements about the meanings of observations.* One of the principles of catalysis is that interpretations of any observation must be *multiple and varied.*

1. "Frustrated" was marked twice as often as "angry."
   a) This could mean that people feel the problems they face are systemic, not

Happy	Hopeful	Enthused	Relieved	Confused
13	13	10	6	1
Frustrated	Disappointed	Angry	Indifferent	
12	10	6	4	

Table 10.1. Raw data describing how some people answered questions about stories.

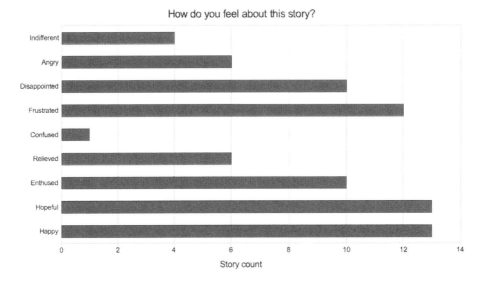

Figure 10.1. Converting raw data into a visual pattern makes it easier to comprehend.

anyone's fault, and perhaps unavoidable.

b) Or it could mean that the questions asked did not lead to stories being told about problems that involved direct action.

c) Or it could mean that people do not feel they are in a position to speak directly about anger, but can only express diffuse frustration.

2. "Hopeful" was marked more than three times as often as "indifferent."

a) This could mean that people are deeply optimistic and have faith in the community.

b) Or it could mean that people see it as part of their identity to appear anything but indifferent to what happens, and avoided marking that choice out of self-image.

c) Or it could mean that only people who have an immense reservoir of

hope choose this community, so they are naturally disposed to optimism through self-selection.

3. "Confused" was marked only once (out of seventy-five total markings).

a) Perhaps people see confusion, like indifference, as an image they are better off not projecting, being professionals (as we know they are).

b) Or maybe the stories that naturally sprung up in response to the questions were not stories about confusion.

c) Or this could mean that confusion is considered so "par for the course" of the events related in these stories that it did not seem worth commenting on.

Interpretations to ideas

Now consider the additional expansion of observations with *ideas* that follow from each interpretation. In narrative catalysis, ideas are *statements about possible actions* based on interpretations of observations. Generally there is one idea per interpretation, though there can be more.

1. "Frustrated" was marked twice as often as "angry."

   a) This could mean that people feel the problems they face are systemic, not anyone's fault, and perhaps unavoidable. *If this is true,* perhaps people feel unable to find solutions and are moving into a sense of learned helplessness, where they don't take action to help even though they could. Maybe we could find systemic problems we could relieve so that people feel they have the tools they need to change things.

   b) Or it could mean that the questions asked did not lead to stories being told about problems that involved direct action. *But we did ask* directly about behaviors of individuals. We did not ask about systemic issues. Still, if people did think we meant to ask about systemic issues, perhaps we could collect some more stories with a more direct focus and see if we get different answers.

   c) Or it could mean that people do not feel they are in a position to speak directly about anger, but can only express diffuse frustration. *If this is true,* perhaps the way in which we asked people to tell stories caused them to shy away from pointing fingers. It might be useful to follow up this story collection with one in which anonymity is more assured and people feel more free to talk about praise and blame.

2. "Hopeful" was marked more than three times as often as "indifferent."

   a) This could mean that people are deeply optimistic and have faith in the community. *If this is true,* perhaps it represents a resource we have not strongly considered in our work on solving community problems. If we think about hope and optimism in the community, maybe we can come up with new solutions that draw on that hope.

   b) Or it could mean that people see it as part of their identity to appear anything but indifferent to what happens, and avoided marking that choice out of self-image. *If this is true,* it would mean two things. First, it may be possible to gather help to solve problems by appealing to the self-image of community members as people who deeply care about the community. Second, it is important never to insult that self-image by implying that only we (the people supporting this project) care about the community and that everyone else is indifferent. Perhaps we have been doing that even now, in the way we ran this project.

   c) Or it could mean that only people who have an immense reservoir of hope choose this community, so they are naturally disposed to optimism through self-selection. *If this is true,* this might represent a useful way to draw more people into the community, and to ask people to commit to involvement or drop out. If we are "about" optimism, perhaps we can define ourselves better as a community using this feature.

3. "Confused" was marked only once (out of seventy-five total markings).

   a) Perhaps people see confusion, like indifference, as an image they are better off not projecting, being professionals. *If this is true,* could this mean that an unwillingness to appear "over one's head" is a weakness of this group? Perhaps finding a way to help people admit and work past confusion, without losing face, could help people find the help they need. Strengthening attention to private mentorship, for example, might help people reach out for help in quiet ways.

   b) Or maybe the stories that naturally sprung up in response to the questions were not stories about confusion. *If this is true,* it might be useful to gather some additional stories specifically centered around moments of confusion. Helping people deal with confusion is important to our goals, so we may need to take special steps to explore the topic more fully.

c) Or this could mean that confusion is considered so "par for the course" in the situations related in these stories that it did not seem worth commenting on. *If this is true,* it could mean either of two things (or both). First, it could mean that confusion really is a pervasive condition, in which case we should pay more attention to ways we can help people alleviate its impact. Second, it could indicate that a fatalistic attitude exists about confusion, in which people are giving up to confusion when solutions might be available. In either case, this interpretation leads one to the idea that we should examine the role of confusion in this work: how it varies by circumstance and role, how different people deal with it, how people cooperate or conflict over it, where they get help dealing with it, and where opportunities exist to help people cope with it.

Hopefully you can see in this small example how these observations, interpretations, and ideas add "false color" to the picture seen in the original data, and how this color can help enrich the depth and breadth of sensemaking about the data collected. If you picture a group of people encountering this pattern and its observations, interpretations, and ideas, in juxtaposition with the original stories, as part of a catalytic report, you can see how their sensemaking process would be enriched it. This is the purpose of narrative catalysis.

THE CATALYSIS PROCESS

The process of moving from raw stories and data to a finished catalysis report is illustrated in Figure 10.2 on the facing page.

Step One: Preparing your data

In this initial step you transfer the data you collected to a standardized form in which you can work with it more easily.

Step Two: Verifying data integrity

In this step you look for data that cannot form patterns because it came out muddled: people didn't respond, didn't understand, or didn't respond clearly. This sometimes reduces the amount of data to be considered, because some has to be put aside as incapable of supporting consideration.

Step Three: Scoping your exploration

Here you align your aspirations with your resources. You decide which types of graphs and tests you will create and which types you will leave out. You consider the goals of your project, the data you have collected, and your own resources and skills. Generally during this time some data is put aside as of insufficient variation to be considered given the time you have to work with it.

Step Four: Producing results

In this step you churn through the process of creating images you decided to create and running statistical tests you selected. This process winnows the data further by leaving aside some results as insignificant, weak, or inconclusive. But because one of the rules of catalysis to *explore exhaustively,* reduction of volume in this step is not large.

Step Five: Accumulating observations

Now you look through your results finding *remarkable* patterns. Results that tell you things anyone would already know, like that older people have been alive for longer, or that people who live in the tropics experience warmer weather, can be put aside. The computer doesn't know which results are obvious and which are useful, but you do. What is not obvious becomes a pattern. About each pattern you write a brief observation, like "Participants over sixty were more likely to say they felt happy about their story than any other group." Each observation should be something anyone can see and everyone can agree is true.

Step Six: Interpreting and exploring observations

This is the only stage in the catalysis process in which the material under consideration expands. This is also where catalysis departs from

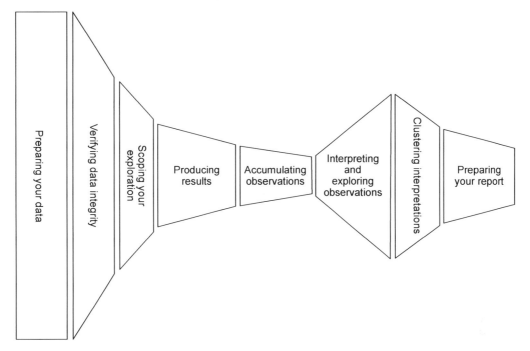

Figure 10.2. Stages in narrative catalysis. The height of each stage represents the volume of material worked with. Some stages increase the volume and some diminish it.

analysis. In this stage, each observation is annotated with multiple interpretations, and optionally multiple ideas as well. In this stage you follow "paths" through the data looking more deeply into observations, often reading stories and discovering new observations, which are themselves annotated with interpretations. Thus the increase in volume here represents both the expansion of each observation and the accumulation of additional observations that result from deeper exploration.

Step Seven: Clustering interpretations

In this stage, you cluster your interpretations to draw together the main points of what people said in what was collected.

Step Eight: Preparing your report

In the final stage you take your observations, interpretations, and possibly ideas, and you create a report or presentation that people can use in sensemaking.

The remaining sections in this chapter describe each of these stages in turn. Before we get into them, however, I will briefly mention the principles that guide catalytic work in PNI.

PRINCIPLES OF CATALYSIS

The principles of narrative catalysis, like those of PNI itself, were not received on tablets of stone but assembled from trial and error over the course of years spent supporting sensemaking. Taken together, they can help you maximize the extent to which you can help people make use of collected stories and data. At the same time, these principles can help you minimize the extent to which you can damage the sensemaking process by inserting your own bias or exerting your own control (see Figure 10.3 on the next page).

Separate Statements

Always separate any statements you make about stories and data into *observations* anyone can see, *interpretations* of what the observations mean, and *ideas* on actions that could be taken as a result. Make no statement that is not thus identified (see Figure 10.4 on page 221).

Provide Provoking Perspectives

Coming up with competing interpretations is one of the hardest parts of catalysis work, but it's also one of the best parts. It's hard because

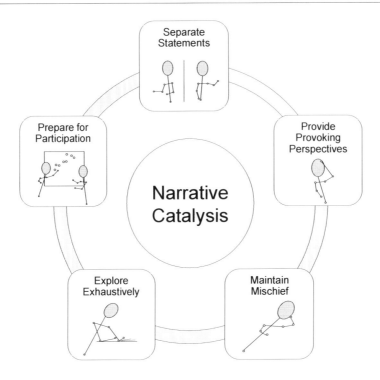

Figure 10.3. Narrative catalysis depends on five basic principles.

sometimes you have to kick yourself to find another interpretation, especially when the obvious one is so overwhelmingly obvious that anyone could see it. But it's also one of the best parts, because interpretation is the good stuff, the meat of catalysis, what leads most directly to useful sensemaking and decision support (see Figure 10.5 on page 222).

Maintain Mischief

Like a gingerbread man shouting "catch me if you can," make it clear in catalytic work that you have followed a *deliberately* obfuscatory procedure. When the burden of proof comes near, push it back to where it belongs, in the minds of those using the report to support their sensemaking and decision making. Encourage participation; entice with possibility. Get people fired up to figure things out on their own (see Figure 10.6 on page 223).

Explore Exhaustively

When doing catalytic work, present *all* the patterns you find, not only those that seem most surprising to you. The best way to remove the possibility of cherry-picking is to examine the

whole tree: every fruit, flower, leaf, twig, and root. This ensures that the observations you offer are *everything* anyone can see, and not a biased subset (see Figure 10.7 on page 224). The methods I recommend to follow this principle (and still get your catalysis work done on time) are detailed in the "Scoping your exploration" part of this chapter on page 226.

Prepare for Participation

When you are the creator of catalytic material, your responsibility is to create thought-provoking materials for group discussion and sensemaking. However, when you are the creator of anything that will be seen and judged by others, your tendency will be to want to create things that will make other people think you are smart and wonderful. These tendencies will sometimes be at odds. Keep the participation of the report's readers foremost in your mind (see Figure 10.8 on page 225).

Taken together, these principles create catalytic material for sensemaking that is useful and relatively free of bias.

Figure 10.4. Separate statements. When preparing catalytic material for sensemaking, always keep statements of fact separated from interpretations.

OUR EXAMPLE PROJECT

I wanted to show you what catalysis is like in practice, so throughout this chapter I will be describing a real catalysis project.

This is a project I carried out for a client who has graciously allowed me to write about the project here. I was not involved in setting up the project, but I looked at the data and prepared a catalysis report, selected portions of which you will see in this chapter. The project collected eighty-three stories from twenty-three people in order to explore the topic of leadership in firefighting.

To ensure confidentiality to my client, I have changed the names of all the stories (while attempting to retain their essential meanings). Also, no actual words from the collected stories are included here. However, *patterns* are what matter most to catalysis, and those are exactly as I found them.

In the project, each firefighter was asked these four questions, in this order.

1. Imagine you are sitting around with a group of your peers having coffee, and they start talking about some of the biggest mistakes they have ever seen made by someone in a leader's role in the workplace, both those which could have been avoided as well as those where there is no blame. Can you recall a recent event or a moment when you felt a mistake was made, perhaps unintentionally, by someone in a leadership role? Please describe it.

2. Thinking back over the past few years, what moment or situation have you observed or experienced that for you represented behavior that should be adopted by all leaders? What happened?

3. Imagine that you are helping to train a new employee. This new employee asks you a question about how leaders and managers interact between themselves or others and the difference in their roles. Share one experience that you or someone else observed of leaders and/or managers working really well together or where they noticeably did not work well together.

4. Thinking back through history, what leaders inspire you, and what one story from their lives typifies those qualities?

Each participant was asked these questions about each story they told.

1. The leader in your story typically reacts to challenges by ... (a scale from) relying on their own knowledge, skills and abilities, and not listening to anyone else (to) taking no responsibility themselves and relying completely on input and knowledge from others.

2. The leader's self-confidence in this story was ... (a scale from) completely lacking to the point that no one trusted their abilities or decisions (to) so over the top that they caused safety and other risks by taking on challenges beyond their abilities.

3. In your story the leader's demonstrated level of self-control was ... (a scale from) unpredictable and emotional; responded

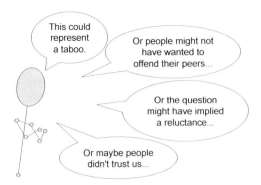

Figure 10.5. Provide provoking perspectives. Don't provide only one interpretation; look at patterns from multiple points of view.

and acted before thinking (to) overly calculated and mechanical; time to respond and act was way too slow.

4. In your story, the leaders developed the abilities of others by ... (a scale from) satisfying job description requirements or didn't give feedback or know what staff wanted (to) putting too much focus on future and not enough on present, didn't leave enough time to apply learning.

5. In your story, the leaders held other people accountable by ... (a scale from) never setting performance standards, just letting them do what they want (to) setting unrealistic expectations of performance or applying disciplinary action as a corrective measure.

6. The leaders in your story demonstrated leadership by ... (a scale from) being passive or providing no direction or team cohesiveness (to) blindly following corporate vision or being too narrowly focused on team.

7. How do you feel about this story? (choices of) happy, hopeful, enthused, relieved, confused, frustrated, disappointed, angry, indifferent.

8. How common do you think this story is? (choices of) not at all common, somewhat common, common, just the way things are around here.

9. What do you think this story is about? (choices including) managing resources, change management, leadership, teamwork and cooperation, planning, strategic thinking, etc.

10. What type of work is represented in this story? (choices including) fire line operations, aviation operations, field operations support, etc.

11. From what perspective is the story told? (choices including) fire crew member, management, etc.

In addition, each participant was asked their age, years of experience, and time in their current position.

DESCRIBING CATALYSIS

I am a programmer, and I develop the software I use to do my work as I use it. Probably few of my readers will do catalysis work in this way. But *anybody* can prepare catalytic materials. The process doesn't require any special training or computer skills. If you can compare and contrast, you can catalyze.

Because I was wary of writing something nobody but myself could use, I decided to work through the process of conducting an actual catalysis project (the firefighting project, mentioned previously) in three ways:

1. using hand-written paper cards;

2. using a spreadsheet (OpenOffice Calc, which is free); and

3. using NarraCat, my own free and open source software package dedicated to narrative catalysis.

Why include hand-written paper cards? Isn't that going too far? I don't think so. This book would not be about working with stories in *your*

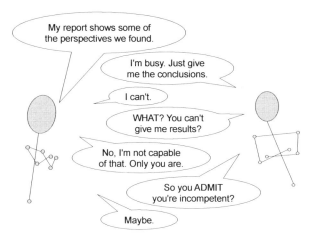

Figure 10.6. Maintain mischief. Help people think for themselves by refusing to give them easy answers.

community or organization if by "you" I only meant "people with access to and comfort with using computers." I can think of *lots* of people I know who are intensely curious and intelligent but just don't happen to use computers. Or they can use the computer to type a letter or check their email, but a spreadsheet is more than they are ready to use right now. Billions of such people exist, and they need to make sense of stories, and they can do catalysis as well as any computer maven can. Maybe *you* are one of those people. Or perhaps, like me, you simply refuse to become incapable of thought without a computer.

In my on-paper version of catalysis I have described the optional use of a photocopier, hand-held calculator, and camera, since I know many people today have access to these things and can use them. Of course, since I already carried out the project I am using as an example a few years ago, I did not do the *entire* project all over again on paper and with a spreadsheet. Instead I *replicated* some selected *aspects* of the project that show what it would be like if I *had* carried it out in those other ways.

You might think this coverage of three methods of producing results would cause this chapter to expand into three chapters. But in fact covering three methods only impacts four of the eight catalysis steps I have outlined (preparing your data, verifying data integrity, scoping your exploration, and producing results). In the other four steps (accumulating observations,

interpreting and exploring observations, clustering interpretations, and preparing your report), operations are the same regardless of the underlying technology used.

A final note about adapting methods to your purposes. In the chapters that describe other PNI phases, what I have written has been based on observation of both my own work and that of at least a dozen colleagues and friends. In the area of narrative catalysis, however, I can offer you observations about the practices of exactly three people: me, myself, and I. At the time I am writing this, nobody I know does mixed-methods data analysis for the purpose of preparing catalytic materials to support narrative sensemaking. Why? I have no idea. Probably there *are* other people who do this, perhaps with a different name for it, but I don't know any of them, or at least I don't know any of them well enough to know any details about what they do and how they do it.

Therefore what I have to tell you about in this part of the book is going to have to be idiosyncratic. You are almost *certainly* going to have to adapt what I say here to fit your specific needs. Still, I hope the description will be of value to you.

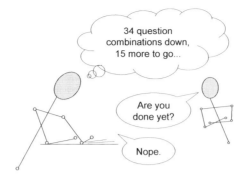

Figure 10.7. Explore exhaustively. Plan your catalysis work well, and you won't have to leave anything out.

THE FIRST FOUR STEPS IN GENERAL

In the sections that follow, I will first talk about the first four steps of catalysis in general, then with reference to my three chosen methods of carrying out the work (paper, spreadsheet, dedicated analysis package).

Preparing your data

The first step in building catalytic material is to prepare your data in a way that makes it easy to work with. You collected stories and answers to questions about them somehow; now you need to *convert* the original form in which you collected the information into something you can use to quickly build many comparisons of stories and answers.

No matter what tools you will use to work with your data, this means *standardizing* the data, or making all the records the same, so you can place them in *parallel* juxtaposition. Means of standardization vary, but in each case it is important to be careful, consistent, and patient in preparing your data for use. An hour of preparation can avoid dozens of hours spent fixing problems later on. So even if your time is limited, do not stint on data preparation.

Once you have prepared your data for comparison, it is critical to make sure that the data accurately reflects what people actually said about their stories. Many little mistakes can creep into the data, no matter how it has been pulled together. Information can be typed or written in the wrong places; stories can be assigned to the wrong participants; you might write or type

a yes when you meant to write or type a no; a computer program you used to collect your data might have a bug that garbles your information; and so on. The last thing you want is to discover trends only to find out later that you were mistaken and the trends were illusory.

In any of the three ways of working with data, the method of verifying accuracy is the same: check what you have prepared from the data against the original data itself. I do this by spot-checking: pulling a story out in whatever form it was *originally* collected, and comparing the original record to the data I have prepared. I usually do this with about two to three percent of the stories (thus answer sets) collected. If you have transferred your data more than once, for example from paper to spreadsheet to statistical package, I suggest sampling more stories, up to five percent. Checking accuracy doesn't take very long, but it is essential.

Verifying data integrity

Verifying data integrity means checking to see where your data holds together as a coherent and meaningful body of intentional communication, and where it doesn't. If you are used to doing data analysis, you will be familiar with this work already, though there are some special issues related to asking people questions about stories.

Every data set has places in it where it's obvious what people meant by what they said. And every data set has *muddles* in it. These are places where it's hard to guess what people meant by what they said. Muddles might be questions people didn't understand, answers

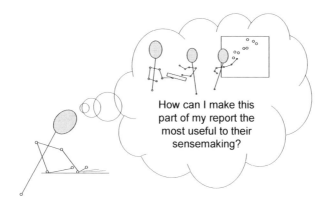

Figure 10.8. Prepare for participation. As you produce catalytic material, remember how it will be used.

that didn't fit what people wanted to say, participants who didn't respond, or answers that don't mean what they seem to mean.

It is important to manage muddles at the start of your catalysis effort and deal with them *before* you begin churning out any results. Why? Because if you don't deal with muddles up front, you might waste your time churning out results you didn't need to churn out (because they show nothing). Worse, you might churn out results and mistakenly think they are meaningful until you realize some of the data they *ought* to cover is missing. You might even go so far as to annotate your observations with interpretations and begin to build them up into clusters before you realize that some of the observations don't hold up.

Some types of muddles I have often come across in my catalysis work are as follows.

Muddles in scale data

For scale data (from this to that) these are muddles you are likely to encounter.

Midpoint clusters. This is where people answer the question by placing their marker at the exact midpoint of the range. Sometimes this means they think the answer is at the midpoint, and sometimes it means they didn't understand or didn't want to answer the question. If you find mid-point clusters, look to see if you can find a reason why people could have meaningfully answered the questions in that way.

End-point clusters. Sometimes you will find that people rush to one side or other of a scale as a way to avoid thinking about a question. Sometimes this is meaningful, but sometimes it simply represents a belief that one side is the "correct" side. If you are surprised by a rush to one side of a scale, look for patterns that explain why people favored one side over the other.

Too many "does not apply" or "not sure" answers. It is usually impossible to tell whether this means "the scale does not apply to this story" or "I don't understand the question" or "I am not paying attention to this task."

Muddles in choice data

Here are some muddles commonly found in choice data.

Lopsided answers. This situation happens when the responses to choices favor one or two choices to the near exclusion of others. Sometimes the answer that receives the lion's share of responses is the safe or noncommittal answer; this is especially true if there is no obvious noncommittal answer like "not sure" or "rather not say." But it may also represent the true nature of the community or organization. Reading stories can help to determine whether the answers represent true interpretations.

Too-heavy emphasis on the first few choices. Sometimes when a question has many possible answers, say ten or fifteen, people check the first answers disproportionately often. This sometimes means people were rushing through the question and didn't carefully read all possible answers, though it doesn't have to mean that.

Answers spread too thin. If there are too many possible answers to a question, and not that many stories were collected, you may end up in a situation where you have too few stories in any category to compare. You can sometimes fix this problem by lumping answers together.

Confused distinctions. Another pattern I often see in data is an apparent confusion between two similar choices. This is usually due to poor question design. For example, for the question "how common is this story" I used to use several choices, among them "common" and "everyday." I found that people couldn't distinguish between these choices, so they seemed to flip a mental coin. When I see confusion of answers like this, I usually go back and try out how the patterns look if the answers are lumped together: because really there is little to distinguish them.

Internally divided answers. Sometimes people perceive and respond to distinctions you didn't anticipate within one answer. For example, say you asked people what the main character of their story needed to succeed, and lots of people chose "help." But as you read the stories you come to realize that some people took "help" to mean tactical support, while others took it to mean the availability of information, and still others meant emotional support. If you can get at those multiple interpretations in some way—if you can link them to something that distinguishes them—multiple interpretations can be helpful, but sometimes they can simply waste everyone's time.

Muddle management methods

I use three methods to handle muddles in collected data, all at once.

Explore the contours of non-response. When people don't answer questions, you can sometimes find patterns in the way they didn't answer. Say there was much less variation in one particular scale than you expected. Does that mean everyone agreed on that answer? Or does it mean everyone perceived some subtle social signal in the question that meant only one answer was acceptable? When you attempt to gather responses and fail, look again at the empty spaces where people appeared to say nothing.

Add more information. It is almost never possible to go back and ask the original storytellers what they meant by their answers. But you can add more information yourself. The point is not to "correct" the assessments of the storytellers, but to add another dimension of interpretation. Every bit of contextual information you can add helps you make sense of what a pattern means.

Prune the dead wood. Sometimes you can't do anything at all with a muddle. In those times it is better to trim away what doesn't add value and move on to considering what does. Some losses of data can be happy events, because they free up more time to ponder the patterns you have more deeply. Sometimes it can be freeing to let things go and move on. Sometimes you have no choice, so you might as well see it as positive!

Note: What I wrote on this topic got so long that I moved it to the companion volume (*More Work with Stories*) for fear that it would bog you down when you wanted to get started working with your data. This section gives you only a summary of the topic. For the expanded version of this section, see "Details on verifying data integrity" in the catalysis chapter of *More Work with Stories*.

Scoping your exploration

There is never enough time to do narrative catalysis. Catalysis seems to expand to fill, and spill over, *any* amount of time allocated to it. Every estimate is wrong; every project runs over; every inquiry is a surprise. This has to do with our natural misperceptions of increase. As you add questions to a project you create a linear progression: 2, 4, 6, 8, 10 questions. But catalysis is not linear; it is geometrical, exponential: 4, 16, 36, 64, 100 question combinations. In catalysis we find patterns by putting things together. The more questions you ask, the more ways there are to put them together.

When (not if) you find yourself in the position where you are unable to generate or consider all the images and tests you could possibly generate or consider during catalysis on your project, try these options for reducing your task to fit into the time you have available.

Prune dead branches

Sometimes scoping problems just go away. In some projects you can put aside as many as a quarter of your questions because they show little variation across the stories collected. You can't *plan* on some questions falling flat, so don't ask extra questions expecting to use fewer; but things are not always as difficult as they seem at first.

Lump together weak spots

Sometimes you will see two or more answers to the same question whose counts are too small to include in your considerations, but if combined become stronger. When the meanings of the answers are close enough together, doing some careful lumping can strengthen a data set while reducing the time you need to work with it.

Trim twigs

If you think of your data like a tree, each level of the tree's structure you explore gets larger: one trunk, ten limbs, a hundred branches, a thousand twigs. If you drop off looking at the twigs, you can cut your work in half, without necessarily losing much of the strong meaning in the data. One easy way to trim the twigs is to use story counts as thresholds for consideration (only consider comparisons when there are at least some number of stories in each set). I call these methods *letting the patterns select themselves,* because by using these methods I *don't make any decisions* beyond what sorting criteria to use. If you explain your criteria well, people will be able to see how you fit the work into the time you had without distorting the results.

A second tree, one that interacts with the tree of your data, is the tree of methods you use to consider it. If you drop out an entire *category* of calculation, you haven't cherry-picked results, just limited the depth of exploration.

Triage trend strength

You can calculate a measure of pattern strength (a correlation coefficient, a t-test difference between means, a skew coefficient, a simple range or count) and sort your possible graphs by these measures, then generate images only for the strongest patterns. As with the method of twig-trimming, this does not allow bias to enter, be-cause the data themselves determine which patterns will be considered.

Improve efficiency

The faster you work, the more you can do in the same amount of time. If you do catalysis more than once and do not change the way you do it, you are not doing effective catalysis. You should learn and improve on each report.

Don't try anything fancy

This bit of advice goes against the one just above it. Always aim to improve the efficiency of your methods, but *not while you are doing them.* Improve your methods *between* projects, not during them.

Get help

You can expand the time you have available by getting some help from people or computers or both. Make sure every tool you add to your toolbox, and every member you add to your team, is added with a full understanding of the principles that keep catalysis useful to sensemaking. If you add capacity but turn explorations into fixed answers, you will not have solved a problem but created a new one.

Plan backward

If you plan to use catalysis in a project, think about it from the start. Calculate how many combinations of questions your design will create. If you cannot possibly cover all the combinations, think about what you should do about that. You can ask fewer questions; you can provide fewer answer choices; you can change the types of questions.

The less time you have to do your catalysis, the more likely you are to miss useful patterns, no matter how many time-saving techniques you use. But these techniques can help you minimize the risk that you will scope your effort in ways that introduce bias into the process.

Note: As with the section on verifying data integrity (page 224), this section ran far over its intended length, so I moved it to *More Work with Stories.* This is an abridged summary of what I wrote. You can find the rest of what I had to say about scoping catalytic work in the section called "Details on scoping catalytic exploration" in the catalysis chapter of *More Work with Stories.*

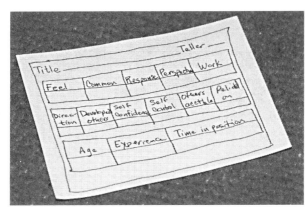

Figure 10.9. Create a blank card to hold the data for each story. It doesn't have to be perfect.

Producing graphical results

Once you have prepared your data, verified it, and decided on the scope of your explorations, it is time to put your nose to the grindstone and start churning out images and test results.

In this phase of the work I generally think very little. Once I have settled on a plan for image generation I plod through it methodically, never stopping to look up. I do this because I don't want to introduce any subtle biases into the images I generate. I do not consider the results as they come out, in case it leads me to abandon my plans to explore exhaustively. I wait until all images and tests are complete before I allow myself to consider any single result.

For each of the three methods I have selected (paper, spreadsheet, NarraCat) I will describe how to produce each of these types of graph.

1. A bar graph shows counts of stories about which people answered questions in various ways.

2. A contingency table shows counts of stories with particular combinations of answers to choice questions.

3. A histogram shows a distribution of scale values.

4. A scatterplot shows the relationship between two distributions of scale values.

After describing the creation of these graphs, the chapter will come back together to consider how to use them in catalysis.

THE FIRST FOUR STEPS ON PAPER

The following four sections will describe how you can carry out the first four steps of catalysis using nothing but such useful things as paper, pencil, your hands, your brilliant mind, your wonderful friends, and your precious time.

Preparing your data

Begin by copying each story's title and answers to questions onto a small card, like an index card. It is important that the cards be small, because otherwise it will be impossible to arrange them in any realistic space. Use a standard format so you can see the important information at a glance. If you can use a photocopier, it is a good idea to create a standard form and make lots of copies of it, so you only have to fill in the rest of the information. (If you don't have access to a photocopier, time can substitute; just write everything down lots of times.)

Whether you use a copied form or simply write the same thing on each card, be sure to choose a *standard* way to write each question's answer. Stick to it carefully so as not to introduce any errors. Write the information about the storyteller on the card as well. You don't have to write the whole story on the card; use the story's title to link between the story text (which you probably have written or typed elsewhere) and the information on the card. Check to see if you have multiple stories with the same name, and if you do, add numbers to them so you can distinguish them. If you have a computer but don't know how to use a spreadsheet, you can

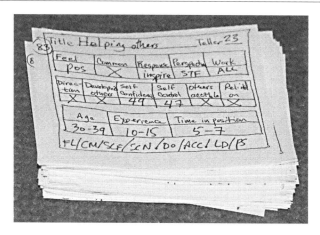

Figure 10.10. Here are eighty-three story cards with information about each story in my data set.

print the information onto card-sized sheets of paper and use them instead of writing the information down.

What if you asked people to mark a spot on a line for scale questions? Should you draw the same lines on your cards? You could, but it takes up a lot of space. What I do is use a ruler to measure how far from one end of the line each person marked each answer, then write that number down. Just make sure that your lines are all of equal length and encompass a nice round range (like ten centimeters) that makes the numbers more meaningful.

To make the cards for the on-paper version of this project, I first drew one nice clean entry form (which took three or four tries to get right; see Figure 10.9 on the preceding page). On the form I designated a place to write the story title and its teller, then boxes for each question answer: choices first, then scales, then questions about the participants.

I photocopied my "good enough" version of this form. Then I put the original and copy together and copied them again. I kept doing that until I had five little forms jammed into one sheet of paper. I copied about sixteen of those five-card sheets, then cut them apart with a paper cutter.

Shown in Figure 10.10 are the eighty-three cards after I filled them with information about each story. It took me hours and hours to do this, but don't let that bother you. If I had had helpers, or hands less crippled by decades of computer use, the task would have been done in much less time.

As you can see, I forgot to leave places for a few things on the card form: the number of the story (so I wrote it in the upper left hand corner and circled it to make it stand out), and the "story is about" question (whose answer I wrote in any remaining space at the bottom). Not clean and not pretty, but perfectly workable.

On paper: Verifying data integrity

How should you consider data integrity on paper? As you are going through your data, *highlight* anomalies so they stand out to you. When you find aberrant patterns, like a person who answered every single scale with a fifty out of 100, or an answer to a question that seemed to have been avoided, mark the data that stand out. Listen to your instincts and make marks. Draw circles around things; highlight things in yellow or blue; stick sticky notes on things; make extra cards about things; and so on. Make note of things you see that stand out as different.

Then, when you have lots of cards spread out in a space, those highlights you made will jump out, possibly in meaningful patterns. Maybe they will cluster in stories told by older participants, or in stories collected in one particular neighborhood or on one particular day. If a pattern concerns you, pursue it before you start churning out results in earnest. You may find that you need to put aside a question or some stories because of uncertainties you can't resolve or missing data you can't make up for.

When I wrote onto paper cards the data for the project I reconsidered for this chapter, I found

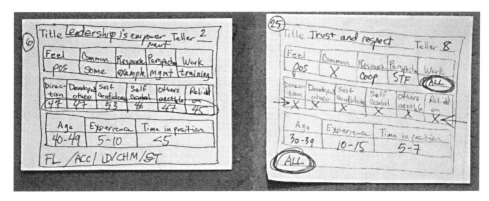

Figure 10.11. Circles and arrows show "muddles" or anomalous patterns in the collected data.

that data integrity issues (which I already knew about from the previous work) became more apparent, more palpable, you might say. I think if I had written out the data in this way the first time I had gone through the project, I would have paid more serious attention to the anomalies I found than I did when they were just blips on a screen. Even though there are undeniable advantages to fast computation using computers, there is definitely something to be said for literally holding your data in your hands.

As I wrote out the cards, I noticed three distinct problems with data integrity. First, some stories had values for all five scales very close to the center point, which might (or might not) be a lack of response masquerading as response. Second, on some stories, no scale marks were made at all, though the choice questions were answered. Third, on one question ("What is the story about?") people had not been asked to limit their responses, so some people checked all or nearly all the available answers. These three muddles were quickly apparent as I wrote out the cards, and I marked them as I went.

In Figure 10.11, on the card on the left, you can see that I've drawn a circle around the scale values: this means the variation among them is less than ten (out of one hundred) in all the scales. On the card on the right, the arrows point out the fact that *no* scale values were marked, and additional circles show that the participant checked every single possible answer for the "what is the story about" and "type of work represented" questions. Should the story on the right be dropped from the data set? Maybe, but it still has some markings: it

is a positive story about cooperation, about a leader with a short-term focus, and it was told by a person with particular demographics. That's not *no* information, just partial information.

These markings work out in practice in two ways. First, you can address them directly, before you begin producing any results. You can sort out all the cards with little scale variation or too many answers to a choice question, and look to see if there are any patterns in those particular cards. Secondly, as you build each result graph, the marked cards may (or may not) fall into patterns that tell you things about how the data muddles impact the observations you can draw.

Scoping your exploration

Making sure you don't have more work to do than you can handle is more important when you are working on paper than when you have the help of a computer, because that's what computers are for: slogging through lots of boring things that take forever. When you work on paper, you do the slogging yourself. That is not necessarily a bad thing! You will stay closer to your data and will get to know it better when you are in closer contact with it. But you do need to plan more carefully.

If you cannot get any help with catalysis, use all possible ways to reduce the amount of data you will be working with. To begin with, don't ask very many questions if you know you will be working on paper. Calculate how many graphs you will need to produce before you even begin asking questions. After you get your data, look for things you can remove from consideration, or put off until later. It sounds strange to look for ways to get rid of what you were so eager to collect, but it is better to work with less than to become overwhelmed and end up with nothing.

Where you have fixed answer sets, look for answers that gathered few responses and can be lumped together. One way to lump answers together when working on paper is to use color to add extra annotations to your cards. Let's say you had seven possible answers to the "how do you feel about the story" question. After counting up how many cards you have with each possible answer, you can see that some of the answers were rarely chosen, and that you would not lose much meaning by lumping the seven answers into three. But you've already written out your cards. Writing them all out again with new answers to the question would take forever. So instead you can add color to your answers, in one of two ways. You could *highlight* the answers on each card with one of three colored highlighters (say yellow, red, or blue). Or you could *affix* onto each card one of three colored stickers. Here I'm thinking of those small labeling dots you can find in office supply stores. The annotation on top of the original answer becomes the lumped answer, and you use that, rather than the original answer, when you build your graphs.

Because the number of graphs you need to produce is a combination of the answers you have, some careful and creative lumping can reduce your catalysis time by half.

If you are doing your project as part of a group, this is the time to get some help. When you first get your data, you might do some of the early work with it yourself, but once you are ready to build graphs, it's time to call in help. Think of it like a barn-raising. Choose an acceptable time and place; have some refreshments on hand; make the gathering fun. Ask people to participate in an exciting discovery, then get ready to help them work.

When people arrive to help, connect skills to tasks by explaining what needs to be done and asking people to do what they think they could do best. Usually in any random group you will find some people who are good at meticulous organization, some who arrange things beautifully, some who can find and fix problems quickly, some math wizards, and so on. The better you break up the tasks into discrete chunks, and are ready to explain each chunk, the more likely people will be to pitch in. For example, say you need to write out all the information you gathered on cards, then produce four kinds of graph. You might create an instruction sheet on how to create each type of graph, then place the sheets on a table. Then you can ask people to choose a type of graph they find easiest or most interesting to build. If people show up and you aren't ready to tell them anything other than "we need to make something useful," you are not likely to get much help. The better you prepare to get help, the better help you will get.

Producing graphical results

Each of the sections below describes how to produce one type of graph on paper: bar graphs, contingency tables, histograms, and scatterplots.

Bar graphs

A bar graph shows counts of stories about which people answered questions in various ways. To create a bar graph on paper, take your story cards and sort them into piles, looking only at the one question you want to consider.

In Figure 10.12 on the following page you can see that I have laid out my story cards in three columns (positive, negative, no answer) for the question "How do you feel about this story?" I have signified piles of ten stories by spreading them out from side to side; thus the column of positive answers on the left shows four spread-out piles of ten, plus two single stories on top. That's forty-two stories with positive answers to the question. The column of negative answers shows thirty-three stories, and the "no answer" column on the right shows eight single stories. (Those little diagonal lines like the one near the "neg" label are not meaningful; they are marks my zealot of a vacuum cleaner makes on the carpet.)

One way of producing graphs using paper cards is to lay out your cards like this and take photographs of them with a camera, letting the photographs *be* your graphs. As long as you write your graph title and row and column labels

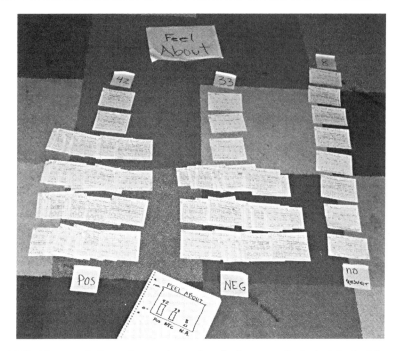

Figure 10.12. A bar graph shows the numbers of stories in categories by height. In this example, some stories have been combined into wider piles of ten to fit into the available space.

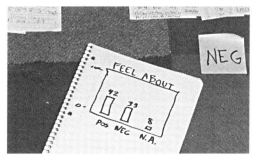

Figure 10.13. Here the bar graph has been copied onto a notebook.

very large, such photographs have the advantage of showing the cards as they were placed, not something derived from them. For the distrustful this is useful evidence. However, just because you can *take* photographs (for example, on a mobile phone) it doesn't mean you can print or rearrange or annotate the photographs easily to create your report. For that you need a printer or some way to annotate and move around your photographs in the camera itself. So whether the photos-as-graphs solution works for you depends only partly on whether you have and can use a camera.

Another option is to lay out your cards in the same way, but use that arrangement to draw your own graph of the results. In Figure 10.13 you can see how I have drawn, on a notebook page, a bar graph of the pattern produced by laying out the cards. I used a notebook because it has lines on it that help me easily make the bars the right heights.

When you can produce *both* drawings and photographs of the card layouts you create, you can keep the photographs as evidence and backup references for your drawings. You do have to reuse the same cards to make the next graph, so a photograph of where you put them for each graph helps you remember what you found out.

Figure 10.14. A contingency table shows stories placed into two categories at once.

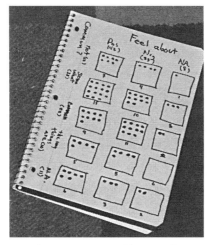

Figure 10.15. The contingency table copied to a notebook.

Contingency tables

Contingency tables are used to show counts of stories with particular combinations of answers to choice questions. To create a contingency table, take your story cards and sort them, just as with bar graphs, but this time sort them into categories formed by all possible conjunctions of answers to *two* choice questions. Figure 10.14 shows my story cards spread out into a contingency table, showing answers to the "how common" and "feel about" questions.

I marked out the graph space with some don't-fall-into-the-ditch poles, which form the horizontal and vertical lines of the graph. This time I made bundles of five cards, fanning them out

vertically. For example, the upper-left-hand corner cell of the graph (positive stories considered not common) has five story cards in a bundle followed by two single cards, or seven stories.

As with the bar graph, this photograph could be a graph in itself. There is certainly no *meaningful* difference between it and the most sophisticated, beautiful graph created by a professional information cartographer.

Before I picked up the story cards, I made a diagram of the result, which you can see in Figure 10.15. I made boxes on the diagram to represent each cell, and wrote dots in each to represent the number of items in it. Why not just write the numbers in the cells, you ask?

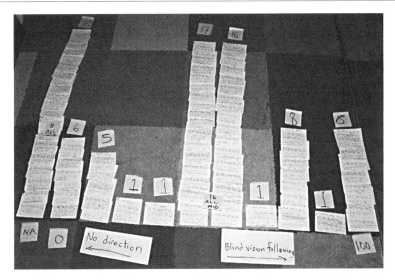

Figure 10.16. A histogram shows how many stories fit into each segment of the line between two labeled extremes.

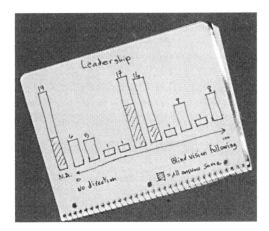

Figure 10.17. The histogram copied to a notebook.

Well, you could, but I find that for spurring exploratory thought, pictures say more than words. You can see the answers welling up in the "somewhat common" and "common" answers, and you can see that the pattern is nearly identical for positive and negative stories.

Histograms

Say you asked this question:

> How long do you think you will remember this story? Mark a spot on this line between zero (I've already forgotten it) and one hundred (I will remember it all my life).

Say you collected a hundred answers to this question, and you would like to see how the an-

swers would array themselves if you laid them all out. That is what a histogram is for.

If you are not familiar with what a histogram (or frequency distribution) looks like, here's an easy way to visualize it. Think about people. Say you have gathered a large group of people in a large room. As the organizer of the event, you write out height ranges on large signs, place them at intervals on a wall, then ask people to stand in front of the height range they fall into. "Everyone whose height is between five foot six and five foot eight, please stand in front of this sign," you say. After the people are grouped by height, you ask each group to form themselves into a line perpendicular to the wall. Some lines extend longer into the room than others.

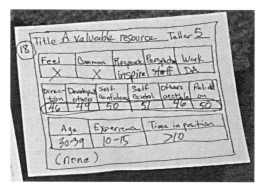

Figure 10.18. The circle around the numbers in the middle of this data card shows low variation among answers for this story.

When you climb up onto a tall ladder and look at the assembled crowd, what you see is a histogram. For histograms with answers to questions about stories, each scale value given by a participant is like a person in the histogram gymnasium.

To create a histogram, take your story cards and sort them into some number of "bins" along one scale, say ten bins for a scale of zero to one hundred. Then simply decide on a way in which you will fit the bins into the space you have available. Figure 10.16 on the facing page shows how I laid out my cards on the floor for the "Leadership direction" scale question. Note that I overlaid the cards by about half on each card; keeping to a standard card placement gave the height of the columns meaning, while still fitting the whole graph into the floor space I had available. The photograph has meaning just as it is.

Figure 10.17 on the preceding page shows the drawn version of the photograph, simply transferred by eye to my notebook.

You might notice the extra annotations shown in the shaded areas of the notebook graph. They represent a data integrity problem with the firefighting data set. The stories in those shaded areas are ones for which people either didn't mark an answer or chose the midpoint of the range for *all* the scale questions, not just this one (see Figure 10.18 for an example of such a story card). In other words, the reason those three columns are so high is not because people marked them often and meaningfully; it's because they contain many non-answers to the questions. If we mentally drop those answers out of consideration, the histogram has no strong peak in the center, but is closer to a uniform distribution across the range.

You might also find it useful to create histograms using *subsets* of your data, as marked out in choice questions. For example, what might graphs of scale values look like when only older or younger participants are considered? Or considering only common or uncommon stories? This is easy to do. Just sort your cards by the answers to a choice question *before* you prepare each histogram. Of course, you could end up multiplying the number of histograms you must create by many times, so choose carefully which answers are most important to distinguish.

Scatterplots

Scatterplots show relationships between distributions of scale values. To create a scatterplot, lay out a grid in space and fill each cell with the story cards that fit into it. Figure 10.19 on the next page shows a histogram comparing self-reliance with control in leadership.

In the scatterplot cells, I wrote sticky notes on top of piles with more than one story in them. I had a hard time keeping track of the cells where there were no story cards, so I hunted around and found some nails I could use to mark each empty spot. Those are the little dark lines in the places that have no story cards in them. Note that I marked a "no answer" line for each axis, culminating in a no-answer-for-either-question pile (eleven stories) in the upper right-hand corner.

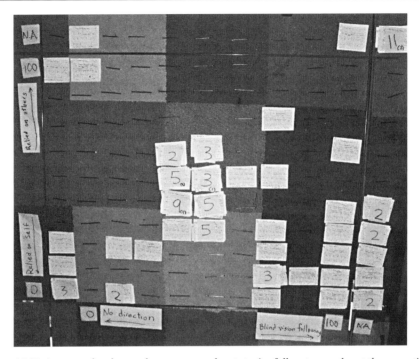

Figure 10.19. A scatterplot shows where answers about stories fall on two scales at the same time.

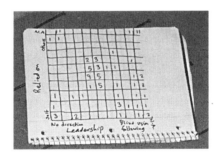

Figure 10.20. The scatterplot copied to a notebook page.

Figure 10.20 shows the notebook page drawn based on the card arrangement.

From this simple graph I can make a few possibly useful observations. For example, leaders who relied on themselves were more likely to be guilty of "blind vision following" than leaders who relied on others were to give no direction.

THE FIRST FOUR STEPS WITH A SPREADSHEET

The next four sections will describe how you can carry out the first four steps of catalysis using a computer spreadsheet program. I will describe the use of OpenOffice Calc (because it's free), but other spreadsheet programs will have comparable methods you can use.

If you need help with things like selecting spreadsheet cells, or finding out what a spreadsheet cell *is*, look on the internet or ask around. There is so much information available on these spreadsheet basics that it would be redundant for me to cover them here. I will assume that you know the basic terms used in spreadsheets (rows, columns, cells, formulas) and that you know how to select single and multiple spreadsheet cells and create simple formulas.

Story title	Participant	Relied on self to others	Self-confidence lacking to over the top	Feel about happy	Feel about hopeful
In front of others	1	7	61	0	0
Full support	1	46	49	0	0
We had to defend our tactics	1	16		1	0
He took a chance	1	67		0	1
Didnt see the value	2	4		0	0
Leadership is empowerment	2	45	53	0	0
Immature sarcasm	2	12		0	0
Doing the right thing	2	38	67	0	0
Off track meeting	3	11	85	0	0
Honest and fair	3	48	49	0	0
Out of touch	4	0	99	0	0
Respect and confidence	4			0	0
Paperwork versus results	4	5	88	0	0
Standing by his team	4			0	1
Inexperience	5	42	51	0	0

Figure 10.21. Place each story on a separate row, with answers to questions in each column.

Preparing your data

At the top of your spreadsheet file, use column headings to mark a short name for each question. Then enter each story as a row in your spreadsheet, with the story's title followed by answers to questions (about story and storyteller). You can enter the story's text in the file or keep it separately, linked by the title. If you find two identical story titles, add numbers to them to distinguish them. Choose a format for each column and *stick to it carefully* so as not to introduce any errors. For questions to which people could choose more than one answer, I suggest making one column per possible answer, because that makes it easier to count and graph the data.

The *most* important thing to do when entering data into a spreadsheet is to *be ridiculously consistent*. You can't count things if they don't match *exactly*, letter for letter. *You* might be able to understand at a glance that "happy" and "happey" are the same thing, but a computer cannot do this. This is the most common error I see when people are working with a spreadsheet for the first time: they don't realize how insanely consistent they have to be.

I remember working on a project once where people entered information into a spreadsheet for me to use. I spent a long time figuring out subtle inconsistencies, like a participant whose name was sometimes entered as "Charles" and sometimes as "Charlie," and ages sometimes entered as "25–30" and sometimes "25 to 30." To the people who entered the data, those near equivalences were trivial, but to the computer they were not only different but *meaninglessly different*.

Little details like this can throw a wrench into your attempts to find patterns. If you can't remember the exact words to use for each answer, copy and paste elements from a standard list you keep to the side. That way when you count how many instances of "happy" there are, you won't miss one that was mistyped as "happey."

In Figure 10.21 I have entered the same project data as I did on the paper cards; here the story from each card is a row in the spreadsheet. The title of each story is shown, as is its link to the (anonymous) participant who told it. In the figure you can see, after the story title and participant number, two scale questions (with numbers from zero to 100), followed by the first two answers for the "Feel about" choice question: happy and hopeful. (There are many more columns, but I could not show them all.)

For the scale questions I have written in numbers (or blanks if they didn't answer the question). The choice question shown here (feel about) uses one column per possible answer. I like to use the numbers zero and one to mean that an answer was checked, because it is much easier to add ones than it is to add instances of the word "yes." I *don't* recommend using a blank cell to mean "no" or anything like that, because it could also mean you forgot to put anything in the cell. I use a blank spreadsheet cell to mean only "there is no data in this cell." It reduces mistakes.

To be sure I have been ridiculously consistent in entering this data, I always check my spread-

Participant	MEAN FOR ALL SCALES	STANDARD DEV FOR ALL SCALES	NUMBER OF ANSWERS
4	34	26	19
4	0	0	12
4	56	46	21
4	0	0	8
5	47	18	19
5	50	4	18
5	49	3	17
5	49	2	7
6	32	15	11
6	47	20	14
6	21	18	17
7	65	35	27
8	51	40	9
8	0	0	25
8	0	0	31
8	0	0	35
9	61	44	12
9	49	27	20
9	57	11	21
9	47	15	24
10	29	25	18
10	47	21	23
10	53	4	21
10	51	3	24
11	23	18	17
11	35	18	14
11	50	35	21
11	50	25	8
12	36	17	22
12	48	17	20
12	50	8	30
12	47	3	8

Figure 10.22. Comparing patterns of where people filled in scale values with normal variation (white boxes), low variation (dark boxes) or no values at all (light gray boxes) can help you find problems in your data.

sheet for extra labels that don't match others. You can do this by using any available summarization method of your spreadsheet that shows you all the values you entered into a column. In OpenOffice Calc, I can go to any cell in any column, right-click, and choose "Selection List" from the pop-up menu. I then get a list of everything the spreadsheet has found in that column. If the list shows any entries other than what I had meant to include, I go and find those entries and change them.

You must find all near-matches and remove them if you want to use the computer to count occurrences of answers. I've learned to take all necessary time to resolve issues like this at the *start* of catalysis projects. It's much harder to fix such errors later, after I have started building graphs.

Verifying data integrity

When you have finished inputting your data into a spreadsheet, get out all the summarization tools you have available and start "walking around in the data" to see what it is like. For every column of data you have entered (that is, every question or answer), summarize and review the patterns you see.

For scale values, calculate the mean (average) and standard deviation (a measure of variation), and look at how much they differ from question to question. Once you set up a summarization cell for a column, you can copy it to other columns to make across-the-board comparisons.

For choice questions, you can use counting summarizations to look at how the various answers played out. How many zeroes and ones do you find? Are there any answers people had available to them yet never chose?

Also, bring together the data collected from each participant. What is the mean and standard deviation of each person's collected scale data? Did any participants consistently decline to answer questions?

One feature of spreadsheets you can use to aid in making sense of data is formatting: bold, italics, colors, etc. For example, I use the background colors of spreadsheet cells to mark out patterns I want to remember. I set up thresholds and color, for example, answers rarely given, stories with few answers, and stories with little or much variation in scale values. I use these colored areas to build a sort of landscape of coherence in the data. Doing this makes patterns of repetition jump out, and I can use the colors to ask questions.

When I finished creating the spreadsheet of data for the firefighting project, I set up formulas to calculate the mean and standard deviation for each scale question, and the "yes" (one) count for each answer to each choice question. I also summarized each story's row in the file: what was the mean and standard deviation of all scales for that story, and how many "yes" (one) answers were present in the row.

On doing this, I wondered if the relative lack of variety in the scale values was due to *particular* people responding poorly, or whether it was an overall lack of variation. So I looked for a correspondence between the participant number field and the (colored) fields showing low scale variation. In Figure 10.22 on the facing page you can see that for almost all of the stories told by participant five, the distribution of scale values was thin because the standard deviations were small.

This would support the idea that the low variation was driven by particular non-varying participants. However, participant five was the *only* participant who consistently answered with low variation in this way. (On one story, participant five also chose only seven of thirty-five possible "yes" answers.) All of the other participants marked low variation on only *some* of their stories. So that cleared up one muddle: this was a widespread issue, not one created only by the behavior of a few people.

I then looked to see if the low variation took place only in response to some of the story elicitation questions. I had noticed while reading the stories that the "inspiring leader" stories seemed weaker. Could the low variation be only on those stories? Again I lined up the answers, and again there was no clear correspondence. This pointed to a greater possibility that people actually *meant* to place their scale values all in the middle. If that was the case, it represented their intent to *answer*, not to avoid answering. They really did mean their answers to be there.

Spreadsheets are excellent devices for aiding memory recall. When you use the formatting properties of spreadsheet files to make notes to yourself about data integrity, you can leave all your notes in place as you build your graphs. Your spreadsheet file can become a record of your project, a repository of reminders, and the beginning of your report, all at once. Keeping a "trail of thought" is easier with a spreadsheet than with paper or an analytical package.

However, I *strongly* suggest you keep multiple versions of your spreadsheet. When you make changes such as marking up colors or adding summary columns and rows, don't just save the file; save a new file with a new name that reminds you of what is different from the last version. It is very easy to inadvertently destroy valuable information such as the original order of the rows and columns.

Scoping your exploration

The main thing I want to show you about scoping your exploration with a spreadsheet is how to lump together answers. Sometimes lumping is necessary because counts for some answers are too small to consider. Sometimes lumping is just more of a time-saver. Either way, reducing the number of columns you need to deal with will reduce the time you need to do catalysis.

Earlier I said I recommend using zero and one to mark answers in columns instead of texts like "yes" and "no." This is why. When the cells hold numbers, you can just *add them up* to lump them together.

In the example shown in Figure 10.23 on the next page, I noticed that the answers to the

=SUM(I3:L3)

I	J	P	Q	R	S
Feel about happy	Feel about hopeful	Feel: Angry	Feel: Indifferent	Feel about positive	Feel about negative
0	0	1	0	0	1
0	0	0	0	1	0
1	0	0	0	1	0
0	1	0	0	1	0
0	0	0	0	0	1
0	0	0	0	1	0
0	0	0	0	0	1
0	0	0	0	0	0
0	0	1	0	0	1
0	0	0	0	1	0
0	0	1	0	0	1

Figure 10.23. You can lump together values to create fewer categories by using the SUM function.

"Feel about" question were too sparsely distributed across the nine possible answers to be usefully compared. I decided to lump them into only two answer sets: positive and negative. It just so happened that the positive-answer columns were all in front (happy, hopeful, relieved), so all I had to do to create the "positive" lumped column was to add the first three column entries using the **SUM** formula. If the columns had not been next to each other, I would have used control-click to select them for the formula, or simply typed the cell names in to the formula.

Because these were *mutually exclusive* choices (the participant could choose only one), I could use the **SUM** formula all by itself, because the total could never be anything but zero or one. If they were not mutually exclusive choices, I would have added an **IF** statement to the formula that placed a one in the lumped column if the sum was *at least* one, and a zero if the sum was zero. That formula is **IF(SUM(I3:L3)>=1;1;0)**. Spelled out, this means that if the sum of the values in the cells from I3 to L3 is one or more, the spreadsheet should place the number one in cell R3; otherwise it should place the number zero in cell R3.

Sometimes lumping is difficult not because of *technical* issues but because of issues of *meaning*. Take the answer counts in the "how common" question for the firefighting project: not at all common (thirteen stories); somewhat common (twenty-eight stories); common (twenty-one stories); and just the way things are (ten stories). What I would *like* to do is lump together the answers in some way that would increase either of the two extremes above the small numbers of stories there. But the two middle answers could not possibly be meaningfully lumped with either extreme. In fact they seem to want to lump together; but that would produce a huge block of forty-nine somewhat/common answers. *Did* people consider "somewhat common" and "common" to be different answers? It's hard to say. In the end I decided not to do any lumping on that question, even though it would have saved time. Saving time is great, but saving meaning is more important.

Once you have made the decision on which questions should be lumped, be sure to make a new version of your spreadsheet, then *remove* the non-lumped answers from it. That way you won't work with the non-lumped data by accident. (Never mind how I know that.)

Producing graphical results

The sections below explain how to create graphs using a spreadsheet: bar graphs, contingency tables, histograms, and scatterplots.

Bar graphs

A bar graph shows counts of stories about which people answered questions in various ways. To create a bar graph, use a spreadsheet formula to sum up how many "yes" answers there are for each possible answer. In this example (see Figure 10.24 on the facing page), using OpenOffice Calc I first copied my column headings below the rows of story entries, then used the **COUNTIF** function to count how many times the word "yes" appeared in each column. (This was before I realized I should show you using ones and zeros; but I decided not to replace this example, because it works either way.)

| SUM | ▼ | f_x ✗ ✓ | =COUNTIF(O3:O85;"yes") | | | | | |

	O	P	Q	R	S	T	U	V	W
1	Feel about	Feel about	Feel about	Feel about	Feel about	Feel about	Feel about	Feel about	Feel about
2	Happy	Hopeful	Enthused	Relieved	Confused	Frustrated	Disappointed	Angry	Indifferent
73	yes	no	no	no	no	no	no	no	no
74	no	no	no	yes	no	no	no	no	no
75	no	no	no	no	no	no	yes	no	no
76	yes	yes	no	no	no	no	no	no	no
77	no	yes	no	no	no	no	no	no	no
78	no	no	no	no	no	no	no	no	no
79	no	no	no	no	no	no	yes	no	no
80	yes	no	no	no	no	no	no	no	no
81	no	no	no	no	no	no	no	no	yes
82	no	no	no	no	no	yes	no	no	no
83	no	no	yes	no	no	no	no	no	no
84	no	no	no	no	no	no	yes	no	no
85	no	yes	no	no	no	no	no	no	no
86									
87									
88									
89	Feel about	Feel about	Feel about	Feel about	Feel about	Feel about	Feel about	Feel about	Feel about
90	Happy	Hopeful	Enthused	Relieved	Confused	Frustrated	Disappointed	Angry	Indifferent
91	=COUNTIF(O3:O85;"yes")		10	6	1	12	10	6	4

Figure 10.24. Use the COUNTIF function to count how many occurrences of one particular answer occur in any column.

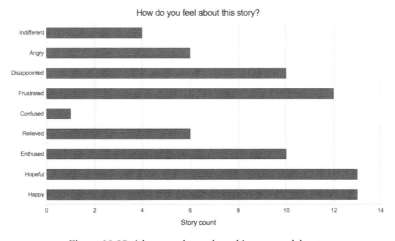

Figure 10.25. A bar graph produced in a spreadsheet.

If you have multiple answers in one column, just count the number of times each possible answer appeared; so the formula in this example might be **COUNTIF(L3:L85;"happy")** or **COUNTIF(L3:L85;"hopeful")**.

The next step is to select the cells with calculated totals, with the cells above them for labels, and choose **Insert-Chart** from the menu. You will get something like Figure 10.25.

I prefer to use horizontal bar graphs because the names on answers to questions are often too long to fit nicely into small spaces. Remember that clarity is more important to catalysis than beauty. You don't need lots of colors or 3D pop-outs: just make sure it is easy to see the patterns in the data.

Contingency tables

Contingency tables show counts of stories with particular combinations of answers to choice questions, like dog owners who told stories about cats. The way to produce these in a spreadsheet is to use a formula very similar to that you use for lumping. Just add up the values in the columns you want to combine. You can see now why lumping is so useful. If I had combined the seven original answers for the "feel about" question with the four answers for the "how common" question, that would mean I would have to calculate and graph twenty-eight columns of values, just to combine those two questions! With lumping, the number of comparisons goes down to eight.

In column Y of the spreadsheet in Figure 10.26 on the following page you can see that I used the summing operation (**SUM**) to produce

SUM				=IF(SUM(R3+T3)>=2;1;0)			
	R	S	T	U	Y	Z	AA	AB

	R	S	T	U	Y	Z	AA	AB
1	Feel about	Feel about	How common	How common	Pos+uncommon	Neg+uncommon	Pos+some	Neg+some
2	positive	negative	not at all	somewhat				
3	0	1	0	1	=IF(SUM(R3+T3)>=2;1;0)		0	1
4	1	0	0	1	0	0	1	0
5	1	0	0	1	0	0	1	0
6	1	0	0	1	0	0	1	0
7	0	1	0	0	0	0	0	0
8	1	0	0	1	0	0	1	0
9	0	1	0	0	0	0	0	0
10	0	0	1	0	0	0	0	0
11	0	1	1	0	0	1	0	0
12	1	0	0	0	0	0	0	0
13	0	1	0	0	0	0	0	0
14	1	0	1	0	1	0	0	0
15	0	1	0	0	0	0	0	0
88	42	33	13	28	7	4	15	10

Figure 10.26. Using the SUM function, you can produce counts of contingency or co-occurrence between answers.

		Feel about	
		Positive	Negative
How common	Not at all	7	4
	Somewhat	15	10
	Common	9	11
	The way things are	5	5

Figure 10.27. After summing up how many stories fit into each pair of categories, you can place them into a table in preparation for graphing.

counts of stories marked as positive *and* uncommon. However, because I wanted to know when people marked the story as *both* positive and uncommon, I needed to test for the condition where the sum was not one but two. So I used the **IF** function to place a one in the cell *only* if the total of the two cells was at least two.

You can see that I repeated this for the "Negative and uncommon" column, and you can also see the totals of each column in the area below the black line, showing that seven stories were marked positive and uncommon, while four were marked negative and uncommon.

With some careful editing, you can copy and paste these formulas to produce all possible combinations of answers between two questions and count the number of stories that match each.

When I'm placing lots of similar formulas and could easily slip up, I use the colored highlighting features of spreadsheets to double-check my work. For example, say I have laid out all eight combinations of answers for the "feel about" and "how common" questions. I have all my formulas in place; but to double-check, I run across each formula and double-click it. When I do that, OpenOffice Calc shows me a blue box on the first cell in my formula and a red box on the second cell. I use these colors to make sure my formulas are making use of the correct spreadsheet cells.

Now that I've done all of my conditional totaling, I can take the sums of each column and place them into a new table on another page of my spreadsheet, as in Figure 10.27.

How did I get those numbers into that table? I copied them there by hand. Shocking, isn't it? I am sure there are lots of great formula-laden ways to do this in an automated fashion. I know that people use things called "pivot tables" and "data pilots" to do this sort of combinatory operation. But I'll be honest with you: I'm not much of a spreadsheet user. I'm a programmer. Whenever I see rows and columns of data, my first thought is always, "Gee, if I wrote a little program I could get *it* to churn through all that without *my* having to keep track of it." When you have a hammer, everything looks like a nail, right?

So if you want to know everything there is to know about how to make spreadsheet software do what you want, you'll have to look elsewhere. The good news is that *you can*. There is an abundance of useful information available in books and on the internet. I'm sure if you start with the very basic techniques I describe here, then look for more information elsewhere, what I've

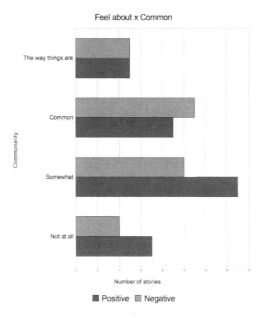

Figure 10.28. A contingency table produced in a spreadsheet.

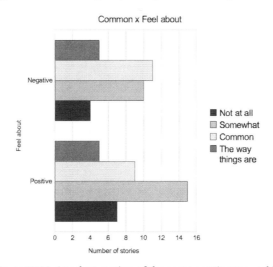

Figure 10.29. Another version of the same contingency table.

written will start to seem elementary after a while.

Still, always remember this: there is nothing on this earth wrong with copying things by yourself. Not everything has to be marvelous just because it's on a computer. Go ahead and copy things by hand. You are still allowed to, you know. Just go back and double check your work, like we did before we had computers.

Okay, so we've nearly made a contingency table. The last part is to select that new little table of answer combination counts, then choose

Insert-Chart. You will get a result like Figure 10.28.

I like to keep things simple and use plain bar graphs rather than anything fancier to show contingencies. In a simple graph it's easy to see exactly how many stories were told with every combination of answers without getting out a ruler and compass. One thing you may want to play with is how the rows and columns of your contingency table combine to produce your graph. Figure 10.29 shows the same graph, but with the **Data series in rows** option chosen (instead of columns). It is just as reasonable to show the relationship one way as the other, so you can experiment with which way of showing the numbers gives you the best feeling of insight into what the data show. In this case I can see a bit of a trend in positive stories being slightly less common (though it's so weak as to be probably meaningless). The trend is more obvious in the "feel about x common" graph, so I'd use that one. You can also choose one based on which is simplest to understand.

So that's how you put two choice questions together. If you asked, say, five choice questions, you will need to do this twenty-five times. That may seem daunting, but if you get started on it you will find that two things happen: you will fall naturally into a system where it goes faster, and you will learn how to explain how to do it to others who can help you. Who knows, you may travel far beyond me into the world of spreadsheet macros, and someday gaze fondly back on these insipid instructions as the scraps you started with, long ago.

Histograms

To create a histogram in OpenOffice Calc, I recommend you start by copying your scale values into a new sheet, maybe called "Histograms". (The "sheets" in your spreadsheet are like pages; you can see tabs for each at the bottom of your window. Give them memorable names so you can move back and forth easily.) You don't *have* to create a new sheet for your histograms, but you will have to create some new columns to build them, and it might get confusing with all the choice-question data in your way.

On your new sheet, add a column right next to each column of data where its matching histogram counts will be placed. That way you won't forget what goes with what. Title each matching column the same as its brother, but add "histogram" so you remember what the numbers are.

Now add one column of "bins" (or ranges or classes or groups) into which scale values will be sorted. I like using ten bins; not too few or too many. OpenOffice Calc's **FREQUENCY** function, which we will use to create the histograms, requires bin definitions at the *top* of

each range. Thus to sort all values within the range 0–9 into a bin, use the bin value 9. Make sure the top bin number is the highest possible number in your range, so no data is left out.

In Figure 10.30 on the facing page you can see how I have added histogram columns for the first two scales (Relied on, Self-confidence). They are empty for now. On the left is the list of bin definition values.

Next, select the cells in the results column in which you want the answers to appear. *Be sure to select the entire range,* with as many rows as you have bins defined. It should look something like Figure 10.31 on the next page.

Now choose **Insert-Function** from the menu. The Function Wizard window will appear. Being a programmer I usually eschew "wizards" and opt for typing out things "in code," but in this case the Function Wizard is *much* easier to use. All available functions are listed here; choose the one called **FREQUENCY**. (A quick way to get to the **FREQUENCY** function is to choose the category "Array" from the drop-down list of categories.)

After you select the **FREQUENCY** function, you will see two empty boxes on the right side of the window, marked "data" and "classes." Click in the box marked "data." Then move the wizard window aside and use your spreadsheet to select all of the data for the scale you want to consider. OpenOffice Calc will show you a blue box around the data, and it will show the data range in the "data" box, as in Figure 10.32 on page 246. (Your results selection will still be in force, as you can see by the lightly shaded area here.)

Next we need to do the same thing for the "classes" box. These are our bins. Click in the classes box on the wizard window, then again move your mouse to the spreadsheet itself and select your bin values (Figure 10.33 on page 246). Make sure you include all of them.

Now you have fully specified your data, the bins you want them sorted into, and the place where you want the results to appear. Click the **OK** button. The result cells you selected will fill in with counts of how many answers are in each bin (see Figure 10.34 on page 246).

A	B	C	D	E
Histogram bins (upper limits)	Relied on	Relied on histogram	Self-confidence	Self-confidence histogram
9	7		61	
19	46		49	
29	16			
39	67			
49	4			
59	45		53	
69	12			
79	38		67	
89	11		85	
100	48		49	

Figure 10.30. To define bins for histogram values to fill, specify their upper bounds.

A	B	C
Histogram bins (upper limits)	Relied on	Relied on histogram
9	7	
19	46	
29	16	
39	67	
49	4	
59	45	
69	12	
79	38	
89	11	
100	48	

Figure 10.31. Select the empty cells in which you want your histogram results to appear, with as many cells as bins.

Do this for each scale, moving across your columns.

To graph the histograms, start by adding one more column of graph labels. You could label your graph with just the upper-limit definitions of your bins (nine, nineteen, etc) but that would not be clear. Instead, add a corresponding column of labels with nicely readable ranges marked out. (Remember to format these cells as text, so the program doesn't interpret the hyphenated ranges as dates.) Figure 10.35 on page 247 shows my bin labels for graphing.

Now to make the graph, select the cells of bin labels, then hold down the Control (or on the Mac, Command) key and select the corresponding histogram counts for the scale you want to graph (Figure 10.36 on page 247). Once those are selected, choose **Insert-Chart** from the menu.

Choose a vertical bar chart. When you get to the stage of setting the data range(s) for the graph, tell the program that you mean the first column of what you have selected to be a range of labels ("**First column as label**"). If you don't do this,

the program may try to graph your labels as a set of bars.

Finally, set up the titles on the graph to show the question's name; see Figure 10.37 on page 248.

By the way, I *could* have selected the question name above my data and clicked the "First row as label" check box to make the name appear (in the legend) without my having to type it in. This would ensure I didn't type in the wrong question name by mistake. I tend to avoid using this, however, because it means I can't have two or more lines of labeling. I like lots of explanation in my spreadsheets so I can remember what things are, and I'm willing to do a little extra work to keep it. If you do projects like I do, where months sometimes elapse between glimpses of your "working copies" of data, you will want to maintain your ability to surround your work with documentation that will help you remember what it all means.

This is in fact one of the great strengths of spreadsheets, that their formulas work even though they are embedded in any quantity of notes and explanations about why you chose

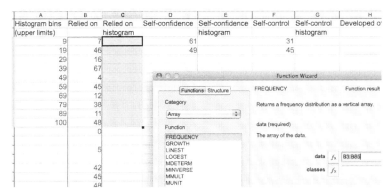

Figure 10.32. In the function wizard, first choose your data.

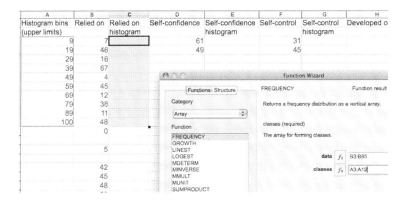

Figure 10.33. Still in the function wizard, select your bins, or classes.

A	B	C
Histogram bins (upper limits)	Relied on	Relied on histogram
9	7	11
19	46	7
29	16	6
39	67	10
49	4	17
59	45	10
69	12	6
79	38	1
89	11	0
100	48	2

Figure 10.34. Here are the resulting histogram counts. Eleven stories, for example, had values from zero to nine on the "Relied on" scale.

to use those formulas. This is not so true for the results of hand-work or the output of computer programs, where results are often stored separately from information on the way they were created and why they were chosen. My advice is to make full use of this embedded-documentation facility in spreadsheets by including everything you think you might forget, right in the place where you used it this time.

When you come back to the project next month or next year, you will be glad you did.

Finally, Figure 10.38 on page 248 shows our lovely histogram. Notice how I asked the program to write the number for each column above it. I find that sort of thing very helpful, especially if the graphs are to be used in discussion, because it avoids people arguing about how many items are in a column.

	A	B	
	Histogram bins (upper limits)	bin labels for graphing	
	9	0-9	
	19	10-19	
	29	20-29	
	39	30-39	
	49	40-49	
	59	50-59	
	69	60-69	
	79	70-79	
	89	80-89	
	100	90-100	

Figure 10.35. To create a nicer display for your graph, create labels that make the bin limits more clear.

A	B	C	D	
Histogram bins (upper limits)	bin labels for graphing	Relied on	Relied on histogram	
9	0-9	7	11	
19	10-19	46	7	
29	20-29	16	6	
39	30-39	67	10	
49	40-49	4	17	
59	50-59	45	10	
69	60-69	12	6	
79	70-79	38	1	
89	80-89	11	0	
100	90-100	48	2	

Figure 10.36. Select your bin limit labels and your histogram counts so you can graph them.

I can already see some interesting things in this graph. Nobody chose values between eighty and eighty-nine; in fact, the count of markings between fifty and one hundred is only nineteen, compared with fifty-one in the lower half of the range. So people thought these stories showed people relying on themselves quite a bit. Also notice the relatively large number of markings in the 0–9 bin. Those represent stories with extremely self-reliant main characters. If I was going to follow up this project with another, I might want to explore that very-self-reliant area in more detail. For example, I might want to ask what qualities people relied on: Endurance? Skill? Strength?

As you can see, building one histogram for each of your scale questions should not take very long, given a clean, neat spreadsheet and a little practice.

You may also want to create histograms for *subsets* of your data based on answers to choice questions. For example, you may want to compare histograms for memorability as marked by older versus younger participants, or with respect to stories considered "happy" versus "sad." This is perfectly doable in a spreadsheet, but it does require somewhat more organization than the other graphing operations I describe here. If you are just getting started using a spreadsheet, I recommend you put this elaboration aside until you have had more practice. Looking at subsets of data is often useful, but it is rarely the linchpin of a successful project. Don't worry if you are not ready for it yet; it will wait.

The safest way to work with subsets of scale data is to copy selected scale data to a new sheet for each subset you want to explore. Thus instead of having one sheet marked "Histograms" you might have a sheet marked "Histograms for positive feeling" and another marked "Histograms for negative feeling." This may create a lot of sheets, but it is safer and more clear than adding many columns to one large sheet.

There are two ways to create your subset sheets for histograms: sorting and the **IF** function. Sorting is simplest. Just select your entire spreadsheet (on a sheet where all the data is

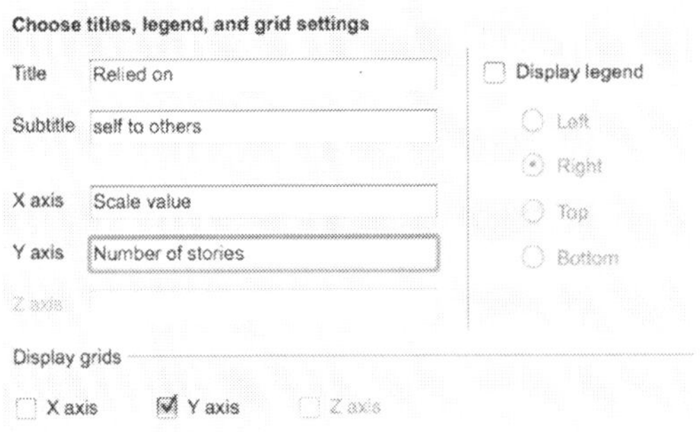

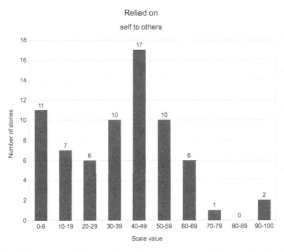

Figure 10.37. Here you are setting up the labels on the histogram graph.

Relied on

self to others

Figure 10.38. Here is a histogram of the scale values set by participants in the firefighter study, for the "Relied on" question.

together), then sort by whatever column(s) you want to create subsets from. Figure 10.39 on the next page shows an example of sorting scale data by whether the participant marked a positive emotion (zero, or no positive emotion, is sorted first).

Notice that the "feel: negative" column is not the reverse of the "feel: positive" column. The negative column does not have ones everywhere the positive column has zeroes. This is because sometimes the person marked neither a positive nor a negative answer to the "how do you feel" question (producing a line with zeroes in both places). Be careful not to make erroneous assumptions about subsets of your data, and be careful to mark your graphs so that the people who will be using your catalytic material don't make them either.

As you can see here, when you sort by answers to a choice question, *all* of your scale values get sorted at the same time. This makes it easy to create new sheets with subsets: just copy across all the scales with the value you want for the choice (in this case, ones in the "feel: positive" column), then paste the values into a new sheet (in this case it would be named "Histograms for positive feeling"). After you have created all the histogram sheets you want, it is simply a matter of working your way through them building each set of (well labeled) histograms.

The other way to copy out data for subset histograms is to use the **IF** function. Use this instead of sorting when you want to look at subsets of subsets: people over sixty who own cats, or stories people said were "scary" and also "the way things are around here." The **IF** function is harder to use than simple sorting, but you can

G Held others accountable	H Demonstrated leadership	R Feel about +	S Feel about -
97	1	0	1
	13	0	1
59	86	0	1
90	50	0	0
95		0	1
	3	0	1
89	90	0	1
45	50	0	0
46	46	0	0
46		0	1
		0	1
		0	1
92	91	0	1
96	11	0	1
87	94	0	1
49	47	1	0
65	75	1	0
39	54	1	0
47	47	1	0
47	47	1	0
		1	0
		1	0
51	56	1	0
50	46	1	0

Figure 10.39. To create histograms of subsets of data based on answers to choice questions, sort the data, then copy the values for one choice answer to a new sheet. Then carry out the steps described above to create a histogram.

FREQUENCY f_x =IF(AND(R4=1;SUM(T4:U4)=1);C4;" ")

C Relied on self to others	R Feel about positive	S Feel about negative	T How common not at all	U How common somewhat	V How common common	W How common the way things are	X Relied on Pos+less common
7	0	1	0	1	0	0	
46	1	0	0	1	0	0	=IF(AND(R4=1;SUM(T4:U4)=1);C4;" ")
16	1	0	0	1	0	0	IF(Test; Then_value; Otherwise_value)
67	1	0	0	1	0	0	67

Figure 10.40. You can also create histograms of value subsets by using the IF function to consider only some values.

use it to make sophisticated queries with many factors.

In Figure 10.40 you can see I've used an **IF** function to copy out values for the "Relied on" scale, but only in the condition that the participant reported positive emotions about the story (R4=1) and said the story was either "not at all" common or "somewhat" common (the sum of T4 and U4). I could have done this with an equality test, checking whether the sum of columns R, T and U was at least two; but I didn't think of that at the time and used an **AND** test instead. In any case, I used the **IF** function to place the "Relied on" scale value in X4 only if the result of the **AND** function was true. Otherwise I placed nothing there. So what was copied to the X column by the function was a subset of the scale values for the "Relied on" question.

I could now copy that formula and use it to subset all the other scale questions as well (updating the C4 reference in each); and then I could copy all of those filtered results to a new sheet named "Histograms for positive and less common" or something. In this way, with care, you can produce histograms for every interesting or useful subset of your data.

A side note about copying values that resulted from formulas into new sheets: when you go to paste the values you copied, don't use the standard Control-V paste operation. Choose **Edit-Paste Special**, then tell the program you want to paste only the *values,* not the calculations (uncheck "Formulas" and check "Numbers"). If you don't do that, the copied functions will try to operate in their new locations and will become confused. You want to paste only the raw numbers, not the formulas that created them.

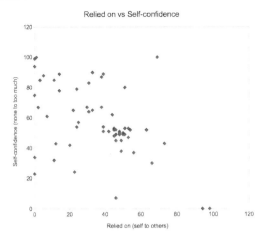

Figure 10.41. Building a scatterplot in a spreadsheet is easy: just use an XY graph.

Scatterplots

A scatterplot shows the relationship between two distributions of scale values. This is perhaps the easiest graph to create in a spreadsheet. You don't have to sum or sort anything; just select two columns full of scale data, choose **Insert-Chart**, then select **XY (Scatter)** as the graph type. You will get a graph that looks like Figure 10.41.

Each dot in the scatterplot indicates one story, with its two marked values placing it in the two-dimensional space. Be sure to label your axes, including with the meaning of each end of each range.

As you did with histograms, you may want to graph scatterplots for subsets of data by choice answer. I won't repeat the instructions here because they are the same: either sort your values or use the **IF** function to copy some values selectively. If you have already created some sheets in your spreadsheet for subset histograms, you can simply use those for scatterplots as well. The information you need is already there.

THE FIRST FOUR STEPS WITH ANALYTICAL SOFTWARE

The next four sections will describe how you can carry out the first four steps of catalysis using a dedicated computer analysis package, one that largely automates the creation of graphs (and possibly statistical tests) for your

use. Specifically, I describe how I use Narra-Cat, a package I developed for my own catalysis work (see Figure 10.42 on the facing page).

NarraCat is a set of Python scripts I built on top of the excellent open-source Python libraries matplotlib (graphics) and scipy (statistics). NarraCat is free and open source, so you can use it, though I will not pretend it is simple or easy to use for the uninitiated. This description is specific to NarraCat, but its general advice should apply to any sophisticated graphics and statistical package, such as R, SPSS, SAS, and others (some of which are far easier to use than Narra-Cat).

As of this writing, you can find my description of NarraCat at my blog, storycoloredglasses.com. If you don't find NarraCat there in the future, just try searching on the name and you will be likely to find it. In addition, there are dozens of free and commercial software programs available with which you can produce graphs and statistical results from tabulated data. Wikipedia's comprehensive list, which includes comparisons, is a good place to start any search for such tools (search for "information graphics software" or "analysis software").

Preparing your data

Most graphics and statistical packages can import data from a spreadsheet, so it is a good idea to get your data into spreadsheet format first. Doing this also gives you the flexibility to use multiple options as the need arises. I think a lot of people who use sophisticated analysis pack-

Figure 10.42. NarraCat is open source software for producing graphical and statistical results during narrative catalysis.

ages fall back onto using spreadsheets when they need to explore a question they have not programmed their system to automate. I tend to jump back and forth between NarraCat and a spreadsheet myself, so if I didn't have my data in both formats I would not be as able to converse as freely with the data as I do. It is unlikely that you would attempt to use a graphics package to work with your data if you did not already know how to use a spreadsheet, so this should not be a problem for you.

Any system that automates the creation of graphs or statistical tests will need you to tell it not just what data you have but what you want it to *do* with the data. To do this you need to *describe* your data to the tool in some way. You need to tell it things like what sort of data is in each column (numbers, words, choices), what images to build with it (bar charts, scatterplots, etc), what to call it, and so on. *You* use all this information when you work with a spreadsheet yourself, but it's so simple that you may not even realize you know it. Of course a column marked "name" has letters in it and a column marked "times repeated" has numbers in it. To give tasks to the computer, which knows nothing, you have to make the implicit explicit.

To import the data from our firefighting project into NarraCat, I first followed the directions in the spreadsheet section (especially the ridiculously consistent part) to make sure my data were entered cleanly. Then, since I would be asking NarraCat to step through the creation of many graphs and statistical tests on its own, I needed to build a *format description file*. This file describes to NarraCat the fields (columns) in my data file: which are scales, which choices; what to call them; how to display them; whether they are about stories or participants; what order to consider them in; whether to lump any of the answers together; and so on. Finally I specified, in a *configuration file,* the data and

format files I wanted to work with, as well as some options specific to my data and goals for the catalysis.

Figure 10.43 on the next page shows one (simplified) part of the format description file I used to ask NarraCat to read my data. For each column of the data file, a corresponding row tells NarraCat how to interpret what it reads: what to call each column (Field ID), whether it is about a story or its teller (About), what type of question it is (Response Type), what responses to the question can be expected (Responses), and what to do with the responses (Lumped).

The "Lumped" column shows off the advantages of using an automated results-creating system like NarraCat. I use response lumping to pull together data for answers that few people chose. In this project, too few people chose some of the individual "How do you feel" choices (happy, hopeful, enthused, etc) for useful comparison, so I lumped the answers into two general categories: positive and negative. I use this technique often when the numbers of received answers are very small. I sometimes iterate several times until I find a lumping configuration that works best to represent what the data show.

With NarraCat, unlike using a spreadsheet or working on paper, lumping takes place only during processing. The data file itself stays untouched, and I can change how the data is lumped with a few keystrokes. This sort of on-the-fly data manipulation is one of the strengths of using a programmed system. It is relatively easy to clean up data when you have such tools at your disposal. Of course, *getting* those tools to the point of being "at your disposal" requires a large up-front investment before you can get any results at all.

Field ID	About	Response Type	Responses	Lumped
Story title	story	Other Text Box		
Participant number	participant	Other Text Box		
Leader relied on	story	Numerical range		
Leader had self-confidence	story	Numerical range		
Leader had self-control	story	Numerical range		
Leader developed others	story	Numerical range		
Leader held others accountable	story	Numerical range		
Leader demonstrated leadership	story	Numerical range		
How feel about story	story	Single choice	happy	positive
How feel about story	story	Single choice	hopeful	positive
How feel about story	story	Single choice	enthused	positive
How feel about story	story	Single choice	relieved	positive
How feel about story	story	Single choice	confused	negative
How feel about story	story	Single choice	frustrated	negative
How feel about story	story	Single choice	disappointed	negative
How feel about story	story	Single choice	angry	negative
How feel about story	story	Single choice	indifferent	negative
How common	story	Single choice	not common	not common
How common	story	Single choice	somewhat common	somewhat common
How common	story	Single choice	common	common
How common	story	Single choice	the way things are	the way things are

Figure 10.43. NarraCat lumps answers on reading the data, when this operation is specified in the format description file.

Verifying data integrity

When you use analytical software, you can verify data integrity using a spreadsheet before you input the data into automation, or you can include data integrity checks in the automated results you run. In my own catalysis work I do a combination of both. I use my spreadsheet program to calculate summaries of the data, just as I described in the spreadsheet section. In addition, I use NarraCat to run through a series of standardized data checks before I even consider churning out results. Walking around in the data in a spreadsheet helps me find anomalies I hadn't anticipated in my standard checks, and running standard checks puts the data through its paces quickly and can sometimes pick out issues I miss by eye. Most graphical and statistical packages have some integrity-checking features you can use for these purposes.

One of the benefits of automated results creation is that because it's so easy to generate results, you have the luxury of producing and discarding waves of potential results as you try out ideas and methods for resolving problems. It's like building when you have heaps of scrap wood to try out ideas on: you can test crazy ideas without wasting good wood. I've noticed that I tend to do some "pilot" graph generation while I'm concentrating on data integrity. I run though some of the results-churning processes I will rely on later, but I don't *keep* the results. I simply generate them and throw them

away (again and again) as I find and fix anomalies in the data. Sometimes churning out results without treating them as definitive helps me find anomalies such as answers nobody chose and clusters of too-similar ratings. I am careful when I do this to label the results, so I don't get mixed up and take tentative results created before decisions have been made (such as whether to lump available answers) as definitive.

To look at data integrity with NarraCat, I typically run through a suite of summary graphs. This suite has grown over the years as I have encountered different muddles in my data. Essentially, every time I find a new problem I put in place a way to check for it so I am never surprised by it again. As I write this, my testing suite consists of the following procedures.

Giant graph of all values

The first thing I usually do is to graph *all* of the scale values in the entire project, taken together as one body of numbers. I look at the mean, median, and mode of the distribution. I look at its skewness and kurtosis. If the overall distribution is not as expected, it may signal an overall bias towards excessive conformity or avoidance of reflection.

Figure 10.44 on the facing page shows the graph of all scale values for the firefighting project. It shows a very strong peak at the midpoint of the scale. This could indicate a lack of interest or understanding. Usually when I see a strong

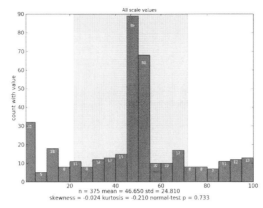

Figure 10.44. Looking at a histogram of all collected data helps you find anomalies in the data, such as a taboo on saying anything negative (or positive).

midpoint peak (and I see this often) I pull out those stories to see if there is anything different between them and the rest of the body of data. This particular peak, though strong, is not overwhelmingly so; I've seen much worse. It might indicate a lack of interest or a conformity to the accepted view, and I'll remember it later as I look at other trends.

Per-participant comparisons

Next I look at how people behaved as they told stories and answered questions about them. I calculate the mean value of each participant's scale values, then graph all the participant means (see Figure 10.45 on the next page). I do the same for the standard deviation of each person's scale values (see Figure 10.46 on the following page). The standard deviation graph is usually the more telling of the two: if it has a very low mean, each individual person chose very similar scale values for different questions, so they probably didn't pay all that much attention. This is the same thing you can see when you look at filled-in forms and see marks that line up, only you are using graphs to see the same patterns.

For the firefighting project the distributed mean values are central, meaning that people did not uniformly favor one side or the other of the scales given. Favoring one side does sometimes happen when people get the idea that one side or the other is inherently better or more acceptable, but it didn't happen here.

The distribution of standard deviations is more important, as I said, and in this case caused

me some concern. Quite of few of these participants varied little in the markings they made on scales. I would have liked to have seen that peak higher, perhaps at thirty.

Next I make mini-histograms that show each participant's scale values taken separately, as if each person were the only one in the project. I look over all of these single-participant results side-by-side (see Figure 10.47 on the next page). The comparison helps me see if some people answered in a very different way than others. Sometimes I find differences in styles of answering questions based on background or position. For one thing, people with bureaucratic jobs—secretaries, accountants—tend to answer questions more diligently than some others. You can often see patterns like that in by-participant histograms.

In Figure 10.47 on the following page you can see how participant one marked their scales with something closer to a normal distribution than participant four, who answered for the most part on the extremes of the scale. What concerned me more in the case of the firefighting project was that some participants (like five, ten, and fifteen) showed very little variation in their scale answers.

Wondering what this might mean, I looked at the data file (Figure 10.48 on page 255). It does not appear that very many *participants* marked all their answers the same, but it does appear that quite a few *stories* showed little variation. Which stories were marked like this might hold some meaning, so I added a column to my data set called "scale data quality" and marked it as

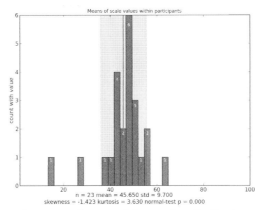

Figure 10.45. Looking at the means of per-participant value distributions can help you spot trends like people uniformly favoring one answer.

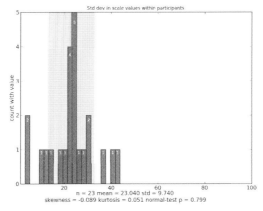

Figure 10.46. The standard deviation of each participant's scale values is a clue to how varied their answers were. Usually people who are telling a diverse set of stories (and who are thinking deeply about each one) will give you a wider range of scale values.

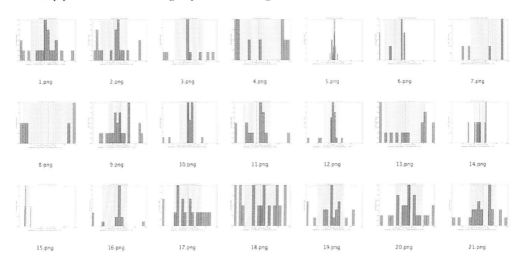

Figure 10.47. Looking at all the histograms of scale values by participant can help you spot problems such as people who didn't pay much attention to the questions.

Story title	Participant	Lea⋅	Lea⋅	Lea⋅	Lea⋅	Lea⋅	Lea⋅	Scale data quality	Number of scales marked
In front of others	1	7	61	31	0	97	1	normal	4 to 6
Full support	1	46	49	45	49	49	47	low	4 to 6
We had to defend our tac	1	16			37	65	75	normal	4 to 6
He took a chance	1	67			48	39	54	normal	4 to 6
Didn't see the value	2	4		10	12		13	low	4 to 6
Leadership is empowerm	2	45	53	46	47	47	47	low	4 to 6
Immature sarcasm	2	12		19		59	86	normal	4 to 6
Doing the right thing	2	38	67	46		90	50	normal	4 to 6
Off track meeting	3	11	85	2	70	95		normal	4 to 6
Honest and fair	3	48	49	45	45	47	47	low	4 to 6
Out of touch	4	0	99	25	45		3	normal	4 to 6
Respect and confidence	4							low	0 to 3
Paperwork versus results	4	5	88		6	89	90	normal	4 to 6
Standing by his team	4							low	0 to 3

Figure 10.48. The "Scale data quality" and "Number of scales marked" columns here were added to see if there were useful patterns between stories for which people marked a range of scale values and stories (like "Full support") in which the range was limited.

"low" when all the scale values for a story were within ten percentage points of each other. I also noticed a difference in how many scales the participant marked per story, so I added a "number of scales marked" column to see if that showed any patterns. I've found that I increasingly add data to my projects that describes not what people said but the *way* in which they said it.

Exploration of extremes

Next I write out the choice answer combinations with the highest and lowest frequencies. Sometimes these are as expected (no responses with feel about: positive and theme: mistake). But sometimes they are surprising and merit investigation (no responses with feel about: positive and theme: cooperation). I won't show this for the firefighting project, since nothing stuck out as being particularly noteworthy.

I also graph patterns of extreme response: very high and very low scale answers. This helps me pick out scale questions for which the patterns of response are abnormal and possibly reflect an unwillingness to answer the question.

Figure 10.49 on the following page shows the number of stories with the lowest markings for the firefighting project. The scale with the most low-end markings is "relied on self," so people often marked the main characters of stories as self-reliant.

Tied for most high-end markings (though I have not shown this graph) are self-confidence (too much) and holding others accountable (too much). Self-reliant, self-confident, with high

standards. All reasonable and meaningful, and probably not indicative of any data integrity problems.

Exploration of volubility

If people were given the option to tell any number of stories, there is sometimes useful information in how many stories each person chose to tell. In that case, I write out a spreadsheet that shows how the questions were answered by people who told each number of stories. If, say, people who told only one story were also likely to choose every possible noncommittal answer, it might mean they weren't motivated to finish the exercise. This would change how I would look at their answers, because they would also have been less likely to reflect deeply on their answers.

Figure 10.50 on the next page shows a spreadsheet that counts how many stories were told by each participant in the firefighting project. The usual way I would make sense of this confusing mix of patterns is to write a list of statements about it, thus:

1. The older the participant, the more stories they told.

2. The most *and* least experienced participants told the most stories.

3. People who had been in their current positions the shortest time told the most stories.

So, a person who told more stories might be older, very experienced, but in a new position; or older, new to firefighting, and in a new po-

Number of stories with value 20 or below

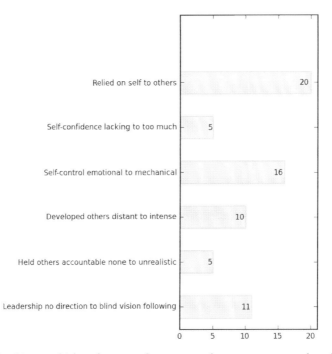

Figure 10.49. Looking at which scales were often answered at one extreme or the other can tell you things up front about the nature of the whole data set.

	A	B	C
	Question	Answer	Mean num stories
	Age	20-29 years	3.44
	Age	30-39 years	3.64
	Age	40-49 years	4
	Experience	Less than 5 years	4
	Experience	5 to 10 years	3.5
	Experience	10 to 15 years	3.43
	Experience	15 to 20 years	4
	Time in current position	Less than 5 years	3.71
	Time in current position	5 to 7 years	3.8
	Time in current position	7 to 10 years	3
	Time in current position	Over 10 years	3

Figure 10.50. When people can tell as many stories as they like, counting how many stories they told can sometimes show you useful things about the story collection as a whole.

sition. Not much to go on, and it's hard to say whether a difference of half a story, on average, is enough to matter. The strongest difference of the three is in the "time in current position" question; so maybe people whose positions are newest to them have the most stories to tell, or want to tell stories more eagerly. Worth thinking about, but too weak to support any observations.

Exploration of reluctance

Next I print out all write-in answers to choice questions, if they were elicited (as in "if none of these choices apply, please write in your answer"). Sometimes these "other" answers clear up muddles in choice answer patterns. Sometimes they enlighten me as to misfires where the available answers did not match what people had to say. The firefighting project didn't have any such write-in choices, so I can't show you anything there.

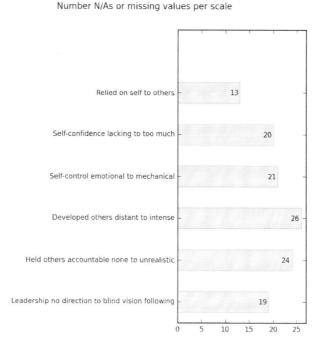

Number N/As or missing values per scale

Figure 10.51. Looking at which scales were most often put aside can provide insights into which questions were more or less appealing to participants.

Then I graph patterns of non-response: how many times each choice and scale question was *not* answered. Doing this can help point out questions people often avoided. Sometimes there is a pattern related to the order of questions, where the number of non-responses increases as the survey goes on: survey fatigue, I call it. Finding a pattern like that can help make sense of what might or might not be meaningful patterns in answers.

Figure 10.51 shows the patterns of non-response for scales in the firefighting project. Nothing jumps out as being wildly different, but the "developed others" scale might have been seen as difficult to answer, thus often skipped. When I see a scale often left blank, I always check to see where it fell in the list of questions. If it is near the end, the lack of response may be survey fatigue. The last question is usually answered more, out of people checking to see where the end of the list lies; but the next-to-last question often gets by on table scraps. I do notice that the "relied on self" scale was most often filled in, and this lines up with it also being often extreme. Could asking about

self-reliance have hit a vein with these participants? Possibly.

All of these integrity checks help me quickly scan the data for problems before I begin producing any real output. They increase the likelihood that patterns will be useful, and they reduce time requirements by trimming out nonproductive work. You can try these, and you are likely to come up with some of your own ideas for becoming familiar with the entire body of what the stories and answers you collected have to say.

Scoping your exploration

You might think there is no need to pay attention to scope when you have the magical assistance of a computer to churn out as many hundreds or thousands of graphs as you like. Not true. In fact, attention to scope is just as important when you can effortlessly churn out hundreds of graphs by clicking a button. Why? Because it is deceptively easy to create more graphs than you or anyone can usefully work with. When I see NarraCat piling up hundreds of images I always think of the old folk tale where the young person forgets how to tell the magic pot to stop, and it fills the whole village with soup.

A computer might be able to *create* graphs quickly, but it has no idea what they *mean*. You have to make sense of what things mean, and you have limits. The point of catalysis is not to dump masses of meaningless generated nonsense on people; it is to help them make sense of an issue with meaningful, well-chosen images that inspire thought and discussion.

What I often do when I use NarraCat for a project is triage the types of graph and statistical test I could do.

In the first category are *must-haves:* results I plan to generate and consider. These are usually things like summary graphs, simple comparisons, and tests of difference like t-tests and correlations.

In the second category are *stand-bys:* results I will *generate,* but not automatically *consider.* I'll run the operations to create them, but then I'll only glance over them, and decide later whether I need to consider them seriously. Maybe I'll dip into them if I'm exploring an issue and need to dig deeper into something. Differences in distribution shapes, like skew and kurtosis, sometimes fit here. These are things that provide extra detail but will probably not form major trends in the project.

In the third category are *drop-outs:* results I will forego even generating, either because they don't fit the project's goals or data, or because I know I won't have enough time to get into that depth of analysis. Cluster analysis is an example of an optional technique I can't usually use, because it requires perfectly matched numbers of scale values. 3D scatter graphs are another category of deeper-in work that sometimes has to be jettisoned due to lack of time or lack of usefully juxtaposed data.

Using a package like NarraCat makes it possible to have stand-bys, and even to bring back drop-outs if the need arises; doing the work just means clicking a button, after all. Using a spreadsheet or doing the work by hand cuts off the triage at one category, because there will rarely be enough time to generate results you don't have time to consider. You could argue for never having a drop-out category. But "glancing over" results still takes time, and those bits of time add up.

Producing graphical results

I'm not sure what to tell you about "how to" generate any of these types of graphs using NarraCat. The way you do it is, you choose the type of graphs you want to generate, then you click the button, and the graphs appear. In any package like NarraCat, the work lies in setting up the system so it knows what you want it to do and in checking to make sure it knows what you are giving it. Actually *creating* the graphs is done for you. I guess what I should do is just show you some graphs produced by NarraCat and see if there is anything worth telling you about what they are like.

Bar graphs

Figure 10.52 on the next page shows a graph of responses to the question "From whose perspective was this story told?" for the firefighting project. There is a fairly even spread across all possible answers, including "other" (for which there was no fill-in option). Nothing special to say about it.

Contingency tables

Figure 10.53 on the facing page shows an interesting contingency table for the firefighting project, with the results of a chi-squared statistical test overlaid on it. The darker circles show how many stories fit into each combination, and the lighter circles show how many would be expected in that combination if there was no relationship between the two questions. The question "what is this story about" had many possible answers, too many; and people could choose as many as they liked. Since I saw variation in this, I set up a data field that distinguished people who marked lots of answers from those who marked few.

People who marked either very few *or* very many answers to the story-is-about question also tended to mark their scales with low variation. I interpret this to mean that some participants paid much less attention to the entire process—across the board—than others. Again, why? Perhaps I might find clues to that question later. I might follow this path into reading the stories told by those who answered in more and less complete ways.

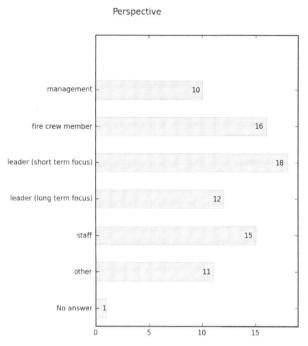

Figure 10.52. This is a bar graph produced by NarraCat showing answers to the question about from whose perspective stories were told.

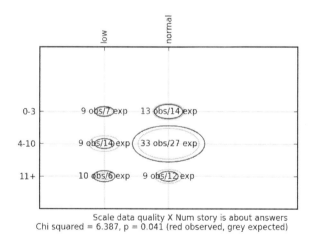

Figure 10.53. In this chi-squared diagram, you can see that people whose scale answers varied little also gave fewer answers to the question about the topic of their story.

Histograms

Figure 10.54 on the next page shows one of the histograms produced for the firefighting project, for the self-reliance question. The mean of the distribution is shown as a thin vertical line, and one standard deviation as a pale gray overlay. Beneath the graph are more detailed numerical results.

Interesting, right? Do you see how the right side of the scale (reliance on others) was avoided almost completely? Often (but not always) this kind of rush away from one side of a scale represents a taboo, something that must not be said. This is a pattern that would make me immediately perk up my ears and begin rooting around for something deeper.

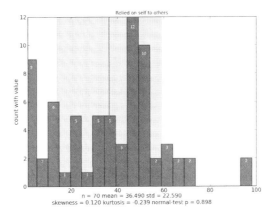

Figure 10.54. The histogram for reliance on self shows a lack of responses on the "relied on others" side of the scale.

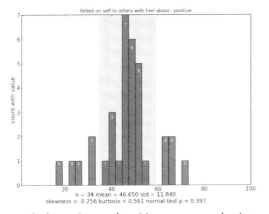

Figure 10.55. Looking at only the stories rated positive, we can see that intermediate self-reliance is most positively viewed.

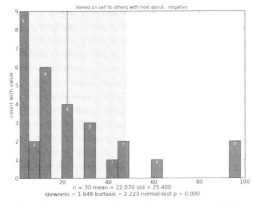

Figure 10.56. Looking only at the stories rated negative, we can see that excessive self-reliance was often associated with negative outcomes.

Figure 10.55 is a subset of the same histogram, but showing only stories marked as positive. Figure 10.56 shows only the stories marked as negative by their tellers. These add complexity to the picture, don't they? They don't show a rush away from a taboo on the right-hand side. They show the middle range as preferable. I am going to guess that the negative self-reliance stories are about mistakes. I won't show it here, but that guess holds up. The stories on the left

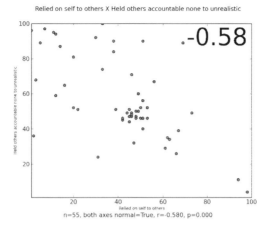

Figure 10.57. This scatterplot shows an inverse correlation between self-reliance and holding others accountable.

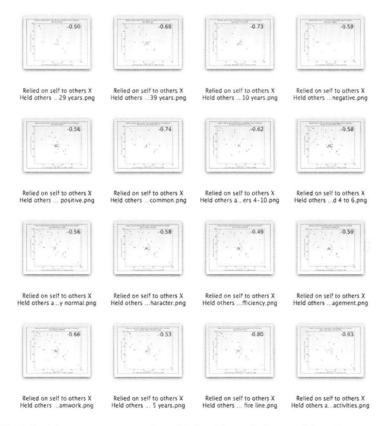

Figure 10.58. Looking at many scatterplots side by side can help you pick out larger patterns in the data.

are mostly stories about mistakes, which, as you will recall, people were asked to tell.

Scatterplots

Figure 10.57 shows a scatterplot from the firefighting project. Each dot represents one story marked with both scales (stories not marked on both scales cannot be shown and do not enter into the statistical result, which is why n=55). The giant number is the correlation coefficient (*r*) between the two sets of numbers. The reason it's giant is so I can compare lots of them side by side.

Clearly self-reliance was strongly associated by these participants with high standards of accountability towards others. You could say the motto here is "I work hard; you should too." This sort of strong result can feed lots of interesting explorations of the data, like in what contexts this correlation holds and who was more likely to display it. What I often do, after I see a nice strong pattern like this, is look for differences in the patterns among subsets of the data. Figure 10.58 on the previous page shows the same scatterplot for all subsets with at least twenty stories in them. What I would be looking for here is the correlation dropping off to nothing in some subsets. I don't see that here (if it did drop off, some giant correlation numbers would be absent). The correlation does get stronger in a few instances (I see -0.73 and -0.80), but that is not likely to be a strong distinction.

I do produce other images with NarraCat, such as three-dimensional scatterplots. But these four types of graph (which I have kept constant throughout the three ways to create them) are the bulk of what matters in most projects. You could get much more complicated and create all sorts of graphical finesse; but such things are beyond the scope of this book.

PRODUCING STATISTICAL RESULTS

I had a hard time deciding what to do about statistics for this book. On the one hand, statistics support decision making, especially in a collective setting, because they form a system of truth negotiation among people with varying perspectives; so they fit naturally into group sensemaking.

On the other hand, statistical methods are so deeply complicated that they continue to challenge fearless explorers decades into their explorations. If telling you how to prepare catalytic materials is difficult (and it is), telling you how to incorporate statistics into that practice is even more so; and it's fraught with difficult decisions. Should I describe how to do statistics on paper? With a calculator? With a spread-

sheet? Should I write a whole chapter about the basic unavoidable concepts on which statistical analysis stands? How long would *that* take?

In the end I decided to avoid the problem and ask you to look elsewhere for information on statistics. Why? For two reasons. First, though I may use statistical techniques in catalysis, I use only the bare minimum, and my knowledge of the field is pitiful compared to that of a bona fide statistician. So writing a chapter about the basics of statistics would not come as easily to me as, say, writing a chapter about how to prepare a catalysis report (which I have done dozens of times).

Second, you are not likely to be in any need of information from *me* about how to understand and use statistics. The amount of information freely available about statistics is overwhelming. Most of the basic techniques in use today were developed several decades ago, and it should be easy to find what you need in any library or used book store, or on the internet. What I will do is offer those of you who are unfamiliar with statistics a few pointers on what to look for if you want to incorporate statistical techniques into your work on catalysis.

The most important thing I could tell you about statistics is this: don't be daunted by it. At the most basic level, statistics are not really all that complicated. They are just means of comparing things in a careful way so we can speak together about what we see. And you don't have to learn *all* of statistics to use a little bit of it. You can gain benefit incrementally, without having to spend years learning each detail. Start modestly and work your way into more comfort and familiarity with statistical techniques as you go.

The first thing I suggest you read about statistics is how to create *graphs*, specifically histograms, bar charts, and scatterplots. This information will be similar to what I have described here, but it will help you produce your own graphs even more accurately and reliably.

Second, read about *descriptive statistics* of *frequency distributions: mean, median, mode, variance,* and *standard deviation*. Read about the *normal distribution* and *deviations* from it: tests for *normality, skew,* and *kurtosis*.

I will allow myself to say a brief word about why the normal distribution matters in story work. The normal distribution (or bell curve, or Gaussian distribution) came about because people (like Carl Friedrich Gauss) noticed something consistent in measurements of natural phenomena. If you measure the heights of a hundred people, or the lengths of a thousand blades of grass, or the size of ten thousand rocks on a hill, the numbers will often be distributed in a bell-like shape: very few very small, few small, lots medium, few large, very few very large. This bell-like shape tends to occur any time many small, unrelated factors interact to influence one measurement of something. When a distribution is *not* bell-shaped, it usually means that only one or a few strong factors have dominated the situation; and we can think about what those factors might be.

Applying this to story work: if you asked a hundred people how memorable they found their own stories to be, you would expect them to have been influenced by many small, unrelated factors, ranging from personality to context to what they had for breakfast. This should produce a normal distribution, and in fact many distributions of scalar answer sets do produce this pattern. When a distribution of answers to a question *deviates* from the normal expectation, it could be because all or most of the people misunderstood the question (in the same way), or felt they should stick to the "standard" or "accepted" version of things, or had similar experiences. These are exactly the kinds of patterns we want to explore as we prepare catalytic material. We read the stories on either end, looking for similarities and differences. We look at subsets of the stories: those told by men or women or teenagers or tourists. And so on. If a distribution of values is bimodal, meaning it has two peaks, it might mean that two different strong influences are overlaid. Looking at subsets of the stories and reading them might clarify what is creating such a two-peaked picture.

The third thing you should look up in whatever statistical reference you find is how to use and calculate three types of statistical test that can help you juxtapose answers to different types of question.

To compare choice questions with choice questions, look at *contingency table* methods used with *ordinal* (in a defined order) and *nominal* (just with names) data, specifically the *chi-squared test*. This method helps you detect combinations of answers that are more prevalent than others, such as that dog owners were more likely to tell stories about walking to work, or that stories about cats were less likely to involve conflict than stories about dogs.

To compare scales with scales, look at calculations of *correlation coefficients*. This will show you relationships of co-occurrence between values, such as that stories rated as memorable were also likely to be rated as rare. Be careful, however, not to equate correlation with causation. Memorability and rarity being correlated does not necessarily mean stories are memorable because they are rare, or rare because they are memorable. It just means they held together for some reason. Often reading the stories that make up the pattern helps to make sense of it. For example, you might compare very rare, very memorable stories with very common, forgettable stories. What the correlation points you to is not proof of any influence, but a good place to look to find differences of note.

To compare choice questions with scalar questions, look at the *t-test* for differences between means. This tells you whether a particular rating differed between subsets of stories connected to different choice answers, such as memorability in stories told by cat owners and dog owners.

Which statistical tests you need to use depends on which question types you used. If you used only choice questions, you need only contingency table methods. If you used only scale questions, you need only correlation methods.

You might wonder: *Why complicate things by having multiple types of question? Why not zoom in on answers more clearly?* Because the point of catalysis is to produce interesting, thought-provoking observations and interpretations. The more varied types of graph and result you can provide, the more intricate the contemplations you can promote. If analysis is like a speed train that gets people from point A to point B as quickly and predictably as possible, catalysis is more like a scenic, meandering ride through the countryside. The point is not to get anywhere in particular but to contemplate the view.

I'm sure you could use many more, and more elaborate, statistical tests than the few I have listed here. For the purposes of catalysis I have found these to be adequate for the majority of projects. Let's say your project has a large budget and you would like to delve deeply into complicated statistical analysis. In that case I would urge you to think about whether such depth is the best use of your funds. The point of PNI is participatory dialogue, not exhaustive proof. Why not use your budget to support a series of staged participatory projects? Why not reach more people, or provide more help with sensemaking, or create a longer-term narrative resource for the community? Once you have decided to use statistical techniques, be careful not to give them more power than they deserve.

Since I am not including a section on how to do statistics in the book, it follows that I don't have much to say about different means of doing them. But I do want to help you get started looking up information depending on how you are doing your analytical work.

Statistics on paper

Can you produce statistical results on paper? Of course you can. Statistics was invented long before computers! Details on how to carry out the most common statistical tests by hand are readily available to the interested beginner. One bit of advice: if you want to do statistics on paper, look for an older textbook, one at least twenty or thirty years old. A lot of the new textbooks limit their instructions to which menu items to choose in statistical software packages! The older books lay things out in more detail so you can do the work yourself.

As with all other paper methods, a systematic approach, lots of paper, room to work, time, any kind of computing power you might have (calculator, camera), and help from your friends goes a long way. You can for example buy handheld calculators that incorporate means of conducting the most common statistical tests without a computer. I remember relying heavily on a "scientific" calculator when I was in college

and couldn't afford a full-fledged personal computer.

Statistics using a spreadsheet

You may be surprised to discover that nearly every commonly used statistical test is available in nearly every commonly used spreadsheet program. So you don't need to use a dedicated statistical system to add some statistical elements to your catalysis. Just read about the correct formulas in your spreadsheet's help system or on the internet. All of the tests I mentioned above (normality, skew, kurtosis, chi-squared, t-test, correlation coefficient) are available in OpenOffice Calc and in Excel (and many more tests as well).

Statistics using analytical software

Most analytical software packages can be used to automate statistical analysis to some extent. NarraCat calculates statistics for ordinal, nominal, and scalar data based on the way data fields are defined. For example, chi-squared tests are automatically run on all combinations of choice questions. You don't have to pick out tests to apply: NarraCat just churns through them all. The difficulty in this case is not in carrying out the individual tests but in setting up the system correctly and making sense of the output it generates.

ACCUMULATING OBSERVATIONS

At this point in our journey through catalysis, in step five of eight, the difference between doing the work on paper, using a spreadsheet, and using a dedicated analytical package goes away. At this point human minds begin to do all the work. So the rest of this chapter will merge those methods and no longer distinguish between them. (And we can return to the stick-people figures, which is more fun than graphs and screenshots. At least it is for me!)

Before we continue, I want to remind you of something I said at the start of the chapter. This chapter describes a method I have developed to support sensemaking in my own work. But this is not the only way to support sensemaking by working with stories and answers to questions. I don't expect you to do catalysis in the same way as I do it! But I do hope that by explaining how I do catalysis, I can help you as

Figure 10.59. Divide your results into those that are remarkable (worthy of remark) and those that are unremarkable (not worth spending time on). Pretend you are reading the results in a newspaper.

you develop your own catalysis practice. Now let's move on.

After you have generated all of the images and test results included in the scope of exploration you decided on (no matter what methods you used to do that), the next stage is to work your way through those results choosing which to place into your report.

The central activity in this stage of catalysis is to make a binary distinction between *remarkable* and *unremarkable* results. Remarkable results are simply those you consider worthy of remark, attention, or observation.

Some made-up *unremarkable* results:

- Older people were more likely to say they had more seniority in the organization.
- When we asked people to tell stories about failures, people were more likely to say they felt negative emotions about those stories.
- When we asked people to tell stories about everyday events, people were more likely to say those stories represented common occurrences.
- Factory workers told more stories about assembly line incidents than managers, who told more stories about meetings.

Those are bona fide results, but marking them out for attention during sensemaking will probably not produce any great insights. They are *what you would expect to find* given the questions asked.

By contrast, here are some made-up *remarkable* results:

- Older people were more likely to tell stories they felt were common than younger people, who told more stories about less common events.
- When we asked people to tell stories about failures, people whose first language is not English were more likely to tell stories about misunderstandings.
- When we asked people to tell stories about everyday events, those stories were rated as significantly more negative than stories told in response to the question about extraordinary events.
- Factory workers told more stories about trust than managers.

How do you decide which patterns merit inclusion? Formulate them into statements of fact. Take each graph or result you are facing (in the list you are plodding through) and write it, or say it aloud, as a sentence. Think of your results like newspaper headlines. Which surprise you, and which seem not worth printing in the newspaper?

When you write or say this sentence and the next thing that comes out of your mind is "well of *course*," simply mark that result as considered, then move on to the next result (see Figure 10.59). If you do *not* immediately think "well of course," *don't stop and think about it* any more than that. Just pop the result into your remarkable list and move on to the next result. The decision should be binary, and it should be quick. Do this for all of the graphs and tests you have, and you have completed your accumulation of observations.

Here is an example of my practice accumulating observations. What *you* do is sure to vary, but this should help you get an idea of what is involved.

1. When I am sure I am done creating new results, I begin looking at my folders full of graphs and test results. I look at one graph or test, or at several in a row. I notice something, a pattern. There are more of these than those; a correlation is significant; a test is positive; a shape is apparent.

2. I concoct a statement, an *observation*, about that pattern. By the rules of catalysis, the observation has to be something *anyone* can see in the data and agree is there. I quickly classify the observation as remarkable or unremarkable.

3. If the classification is *unremarkable*, I leave the graph(s) or test(s) alone, but I *remember* that I have considered those files and thereby place them in the "considered and put aside" category. I generally plod through my generated results in the same order on each project (bar graphs, histograms, t-tests, and so on), so I know what is left to be done by what I am now doing.

4. If the classification is *remarkable*, I copy the graph or test result into a list. I like to use a slide presentation program like PowerPoint or OpenOffice Impress to accumulate observations, because I can quickly drag images into place and leave them there to be dealt with later. But *any* way of listing observations will work. You could type things into spreadsheet rows, or write them on index cards, or sort papers into stacks, or put sticky notes on things. What matters is that you preserve your decisions so you can find them again when you need them.

5. Using my slide presentation program, I type my observation onto one page, without elaboration or interpretation. If I type anything else on the page, it must be very, very short. No paragraphs and no complete sentences are allowed. Often I write one word: DETAIL. That means "I would like to come back and explore this later; it looks interesting." Or I might write "hmmm" or "wow" or "really!" This gives my feelings of enthusiasm somewhere to go without derailing the activity I need to be engaged in.

6. When I have reached the end of all the files I have generated, I stop accumulating observations, take a long walk, and get ready for the next stage of catalytic work. (A walk may not be what *you* need, but it is likely to be something similar: a simple yet absorbing activity you can use to stop yourself from paying too much attention while your mind works in the background. Find what works for you.)

If you are doing this stage of catalysis right, it should be about as exciting as watching paint dry. If you find yourself getting *interested* in what you are reading, you are not doing this stage right. *Do not think.* Just heap up results. To state it metaphorically: when I find myself reaching into the cookie jar and creating grand theories to explain what I see at this stage of catalysis, I slap my hand and say, "Not until dinner, young lady, you'll spoil your appetite."

Why plod along like this? Why not ponder each result deeply as you encounter it? I used to do that, years ago. I used to wade through the results I found on first contact, peering intently at each outcome, instead of dancing around on top of them as I do now. It didn't work as well as this does.

Let me see if I can explain why. A group of stories and answers to questions has something to say to you, but it never speaks with one voice. The first time you go through the mass of your accumulated results, what you see will be fragmented, in shards and slivers and wisps of meaning. If you try to think too hard about each shard as you encounter it, you will find yourself tossed this way and that. You will be sure of something, then of its opposite, then of something entirely new, until you get bogged down in confusion.

What I've found works better is to start by skimming lightly across all the results, getting a general sense of what is being said, but without

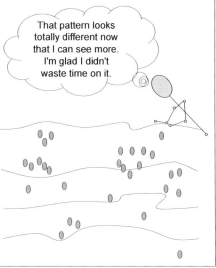

Figure 10.60. When you are accumulating observations, don't let yourself delve into detail. Let the big-picture view emerge before you follow promising trails. They may not be as promising later as they seem now.

allowing myself to delve deeper until I have skimmed *all* of the results. At some point, and I'm not sure how this happens, it all begins to cohere. The cacophony resolves itself into one voice and I can hear what the stories have to say. But this *never* happens right away, and it cannot be forced to happen ahead of time. It emerges, but it *won't* emerge if you try to *make* it emerge. You have to wait for it to happen.

I can easily see this in practice, because most of the notes I can't help making as I go through this stage seem perfectly idiotic on the next pass through (see Figure 10.60). My post-emergence response to "related to age issue?" might be "well of course it would *appear* that way, if you haven't seen the *other* parts of the puzzle yet." The data have a story to tell you, and the little bits of the story you see as you pass through it the first time may *seem* to lead in definite directions, but that all changes after you have seen *everything* the stories and data have to say.

I like to say, "Having finished, I'm ready to start." That rule applies *perfectly* to catalysis.

Avoiding bias in choosing what to interpret

I anticipate a reaction from the astute and careful. Is this binary choice of which results are remarkable a place where bias can be inserted? It certainly is. I consider the accumulating-observations stage to be the weakest part of the catalysis process. If you were to insert a bias it would be inserted here. Coming up with multiple interpretations insulates you from making claims to truth, but *choosing what to interpret* is shakier ground.

How can you reduce bias when accumulating catalytic observations? I use and suggest several methods, as follows.

Set thresholds, but don't obey them entirely

When I have a lot of decisions to make about what "stands out," I often use statistical tests and numerical calculations to create a decision-support scaffolding. Whenever you can say, "These ten graphs represent the ten strongest deviations from normality," or, "These are the ten most statistically significant differences between means," that's ten decisions you didn't have to make. You did make a decision about where to *place* the threshold, and bias could creep in there, but it's a smaller entry point.

However, be careful about putting *too* much reliance on strict thresholds. Sometimes I will encounter a situation where several patterns line up, each too small to reach over the threshold on its own, but taken together they say some-

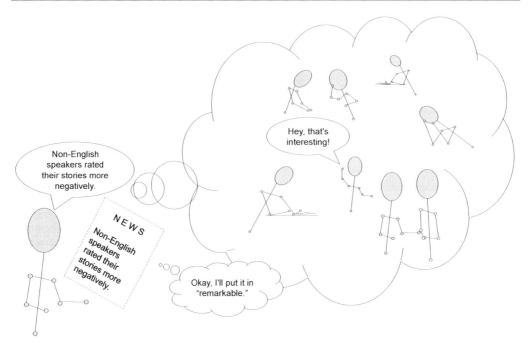

Figure 10.61. Imagine the reactions of people connected to the project when you're deciding whether patterns should be considered remarkable or unremarkable.

thing important that needs to be heard and considered. It's like the tiny people in *Horton Hears a Who!* Sometimes you can hear them saying "We are here!" only if every last one is calling out, and only if you are listening very quietly and respectfully with your very large ears.

So I have learned to set thresholds, then look *at* them and *beyond* them as well. When there is very little time, you sometimes have to let this fine point go, but when you can cast a quick glance for concurrent weak patterns it is better to include it. One method I like to use is to create visual displays for myself that juxtapose many patterns next to each other, like a hundred tiny graphs laid out in tidy rows. When you do that, sometimes repetitions of weak patterns jump out, and you find something worth investigating.

Speak to an imaginary audience

Yes, here I go again with one of my "imagine the nay-sayers" methods. What I like to do in this stage of catalysis is, I imagine that I am standing in front of a group of people that includes those funding the project, those carrying it out, and those who told the stories. I state each observation to the assembled group. If they all say "of course" and go back to doing what they had been doing before I interrupted them to speak, I move on past the result. If they look at me and say "really?" (or "*WHAT?!*") I include the result (see Figure 10.61). I try to be more inclusive than exclusive in this: if *anyone* in the audience looks up at what I have presented, I keep the result. This is one reason speaking the statements out loud helps: I can better imagine the response if I actually *say* the words than if I write them.

Preserve undigested results

At this stage of catalysis you need to decide what to pay attention to and what to put aside. This is in the nature of reducing the volume of material to cover, which is one reason to do catalysis (not the *only* one, but one). However, just because information is not considered in detail does not mean it has to be discarded completely. In most projects on which I do catalysis (for clients) I find that while some people just want to read the executive summary, there are some who want to pore over every page of the report, and there are still others who want to see the thousands of results I *chose* from in order to accumulate the observations that make up the report (see Figure 10.62 on the next page).

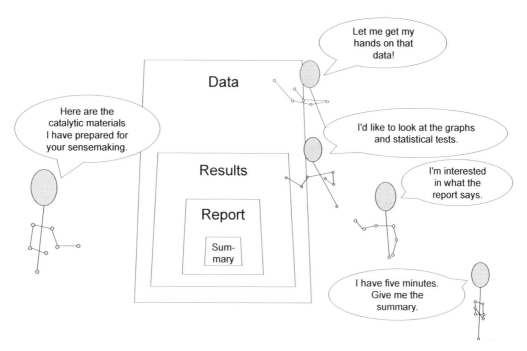

Figure 10.62. Different people want to explore different levels of detail in catalytic material. Preserving detail for those who want to delve into it reduces bias.

For this reason I make sure that even though I am choosing what will end up in the catalysis report, *the rest is still there* for those who want to dive in. This reduces the chance that I will damage the project by inserting my bias.

You can do this as well. Say you have generated 200 graphs and written up fifty observations you consider remarkable results. You can still present the other 150 graphs: just shrink them into a form where people can look over them very quickly. That way they can dive into the details *you* chose not to consider if *they* see something they want to pursue.

Iterate

Sometimes, when I feel simultaneously anxious about leaving things out and running out of time to consider everything, I iterate on this part of catalysis. I start with a very low threshold of inclusion, and mark more observations than I know I can use. Then, having seen how many observations I can accumulate, I go back and mark the *strength* of each observation: is this result knock-you-over-the-head strong, I-can-see-it medium, or you-have-to-squint-to-see-it weak? After I have marked these strengths, I

can then go back and mercilessly cull all observations that didn't make the cut. These are excellent candidates for the "undigested detail" stack, which only motivated participants will consider. To make decisions about selection and iteration, I pay attention to my feelings about the data, my anxieties and confidences. Worry can be a useful tool if you know how to listen to it. The important thing is to build your sense of confidence that *this is what the stories say,* that you have not misheard it, misunderstood it, or distorted it. When you feel more anxiety than confidence, try iterating over the process.

Delegate

I usually work alone when I do catalysis work, just because, well, it's what people hire me to do. But if *you* are doing projects in your own community or organization, there is no need for you to work alone. If you split up the process of accumulating observations, you can confuse bias by combining it with diversity. You can also cross-accumulate observations: have two or more people go through the same process independently, then use the union of their accumulations. This is somewhat similar to my "speak to an imaginary audience" method above, only the audience is you and it is real. In a perfect world, all catalysis would be done by everyone in the community, so diversity of interpretation would be preserved throughout. This is rarely possible in practice, but any step you can take toward increasing the diversity of catalysis will improve the outcome.

Re-scope

If you can't find an unbiased way of getting this stage of catalysis done in the time you have, even using all the methods above, my suggestion is to take a step back and return to the "scoping your exploration" step of catalysis (see page 226). Instead of forcing yourself to make decisions you will regret, choose one method of comparison to drop out of the process. Maybe you don't need to create three-dimensional landscape graphs, or you can put aside the t-tests you had planned (and pick them up again if things go faster than you expected).

Choosing to put aside one avenue of exploration might cause you to miss some trends, but it will not cause you to insert bias into your selections without knowing it. It is better to say "we put aside calculations of correlation coefficients" or "we drew bar graphs of single questions but not combinations of questions" than it is to say "we decided that what people said about their feelings didn't matter" or "we decided to put aside thinking about trust."

Why no story reading?

You may have noticed that I have not once mentioned reading stories in the stage of catalysis when you accumulate observations. That's because I don't recommend it.

I repeat: *do not read any stories* while you are accumulating observations. Reading the stories too early can damage catalysis. Yes, the stories *are* results and they need to be considered; but stories are full of compelling emotion and imagery. In general this is a strength of storytelling, but at this point in your catalysis work it can be a hindrance. The last thing you want at this point is for the powerful, well-told, amazing stories to dominate the weak, poor, not-very-well-told stories. Why? Because *every story matters*, not just those that speak well.

At this point you need to treat *all* of the reflections people gave you about their stories with equal respect and attention. If you read the stories at the start, you won't be able to stop yourself from placing more emphasis on the stories that stand out more to you, and on the interpretations of their tellers as a result. Nobody can be unmoved by stories, so don't try to be or pretend you can. Keep your susceptible self away from the stories until you have mapped out what your participants had to say about them.

INTERPRETING AND EXPLORING OBSERVATIONS

Now we come to the stage of catalysis in which you dive in deep. Here you enter into hearty and prolonged discussions with all of the data you have collected, both stories and their interpretations.

When you begin interpreting your observations, you should have in front of you a list of remarkable observations you collected in the previous stage. When I do this, I usually have my observations in the form of several files of slide presentations, each page containing two things: one graph or test result and one observation. You could have this list in the form of a spreadsheet, a document, or a bundle of papers with typed or handwritten notes on them.

When you enter this stage, put aside the results you produced earlier. Refer *only* to the observations you accumulated in the previous step. You may need to refer to your results again, as you need to answer new questions that come up. But keep the results from distracting you from your observations (see Figure 10.63 on the facing page).

So let's say you have put aside your heaps of results and are looking now only at your accumulated observations. What do you do next? I can divide the work, for each observation, into four steps: evaluate, interpret, explore, and explain.

Step One: Evaluate for relevance

When you first look at an observation, think about how important it is to the project. You need to do this, because you will never have

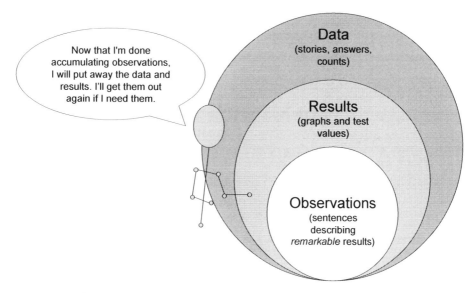

Figure 10.63. After you have finished accumulating observations, put away the results that led to them, so they won't distract you.

enough time to consider every observation as fully as you would like to. You need to budget your time.

Think about how each observation falls on each of four dimensions of importance:

1. Is this a strong observation on an *objective* scale? How high is the significance value? How far apart are the means of the distributions? Are the sample sizes huge or tiny? How strongly does the pattern assert itself in the data?

2. How important is this observation to the *goals* of the project? Is it directly about the topics being considered, or is it tangential?

3. How *surprising* is this observation? It has to be at least a little surprising, or at least noteworthy, to have been selected at all, because you removed the unremarkable patterns in the previous step. But just how big is the "wow" factor in this observation?

4. How strongly does this observation *interact* with other observations? Does it form part of a picture, or does it stand alone? (This is hard to gauge early on when you have a dim sense of the whole picture, but you will be able to evaluate this dimension better as you go.)

After you have looked at your observation in light of these four dimensions, you should get a feeling for how *relevant* it is to the project. This will help you decide how much of your time you should put into it. You could think of this as a process of triage, with three outcomes: drop it, explore it minimally, or explore it fully.

Dropping an observation is as simple as writing a note on the page that says "drop" and moving on. (You can delete the page later, but it's better to keep it in, just in case you find a need for it later.) Whether you should minimally or fully explore an observation is not really a binary choice, but a gradient. When I interpret observations, I find that the time I spend on each can vary all the way from five minutes to two or three hours. It depends on what avenues appear fruitful and what I find when I venture down them.

Should you *mark* your observations at this point as to their strengths? Yes, do, but consider these *preliminary* markings. You may change your mind about what matters most after you have worked your way through all of your observations.

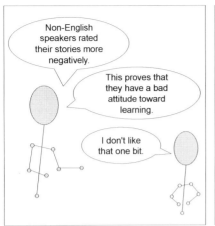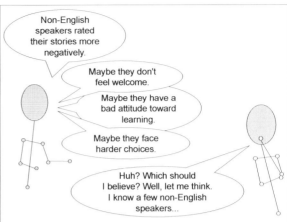

Figure 10.64. Multiple interpretations move people away from defense or attack and into exploration.

Step Two: Generate interpretations

Assuming you didn't drop the observation in the previous step, next you should interpret the observation from multiple points of view.

The first thing I ought to explain about writing multiple interpretations is *why you should bother*. Why not just tell people what the data have to say? Isn't that what research is about? Not participatory action research, and not participatory narrative inquiry. Both PAR and PNI are about much more than just *what the data have to say*. They are about *what the people have to say about what the data have to say*, which is not at all the same thing. PNI, like PAR, is not about proof, but about participation and perspective.

My placement of the generation of multiple interpretations at the center of catalysis is based on my observations of how people react to single interpretations of patterns. When people encounter one interpretation, you can see them taking sides: do I agree or don't I? Their attention is on the interpretation, not on their own feelings or beliefs or experiences. They put on their armor and prepare to do battle. It's clear to them that the one interpretation they see is the interpretation held by the author of the report: why else would they write it? And as the interpretations build throughout the report, people build explanations about the whole report: it's biased, or the author doesn't know what they are talking about, or the reasoning is flawed. All

of this stops sensemaking short and destroys any hope of productive thought or discussion.

In contrast, when you give people two or more *competing* interpretations of the same pattern, they turn their attention away from attacking or defending the interpretations and toward *exploring their own experiences*. This is what you *want* people to do. You *want* people to dwell on messy ambiguities, and to *use* them, until they resolve themselves naturally (or don't). If the author of the report has written two interpretations, the reader *can't tell* which is the author's own, so there is nothing to attack or defend, and there are no larger explanations about bias or ineptitude to build. The report author essentially walks out of the picture and lets the reader think. The reader can put away their armor and get out their maps and spyglasses. They can explore. (See Figure 10.64.)

You could visualize a single interpretation as a point in space, like a pinpoint of light: it's on (right) or it's off (wrong). There is no room inside that point for anyone but the author of the report to stand. And they can't be anywhere but there, can they? But two interpretations define a *line* in space, and three interpretations define a plane. Since the author of the report has not identified their position in the space but has merely laid it out and stepped away, the space is empty, thus inviting. The reader can enter the space, find their way around in it, and perhaps expand it as well. This is what sensemaking is about: finding our way around the world in order to make decisions about it.

Let me give you a more concrete example of how this works. Say I am looking at stories people told about their telephone service. Say I've seen a pattern that the younger the participant, the more likely they were to say they felt disappointed by the events in their story. If I give people one interpretation—that younger people are not happy with their telephone service—people start turning their binary switches off and on. Yes that's right, no that's wrong. But what happens if I say that younger people might not be happy with their telephone service, *or* older people might not understand the question, *or* younger people might be more willing to admit to disappointment (whereas older people might feel more pressure to say everything's fine), *or* younger people might be more disappointed about *other* things and it drifts over, and so on? I've marked out a space for exploration and invited people on a journey, instead of setting up a straw man to be knocked down.

Of course, not everybody is comfortable with competing interpretations. Sometimes people want *The Answers,* even when nobody can give them the answers. Stories don't provide answers, and patterns in stories don't provide answers, because none of this work is scientifically verifiable in reliable, valid, repeatable experiments. It's not meant to be. *It's all food for thought.*

Stories, and patterns in stories, are like seeds: seeds of potential conclusions, resolutions, explanations, plans. They can't grow into those things without the fertile soil of open, exploring minds and the light of discussion. Answers aren't seeds, and they can't grow, no matter what soil they fall into. They are not food for thought; they are food for use, for consumption. For some goals, like building bridges and designing telephone cables, answers are exactly what is needed, and growing conclusions would be ridiculous, even dangerous. But for complex issues of human interaction, food for thought is the only type of food worth having.

In what follows I'm going to assume that you have been convinced by the preceding arguments that including multiple interpretations

in your catalytic material is worth doing (or that you already agreed before I tried to convince you). I should next tell you *how* to generate multiple interpretations of an observation.

To generate multiple interpretations, simply describe to yourself what each observation *means* about the situation the project is meant to explore. Avoid clean prose for now, and just jot down notes to yourself. You will clean them up later. Start with the obvious interpretation, then come up with *at least one alternative explanation* for the same pattern. Do not move on to the next observation until you have come up with at least one competing explanation for what you see. Start a friendly argument with yourself.

How can I argue with myself? You might ask. *The data speak and I listen!* Don't just listen to the data. *Listen to yourself listening to the data.* What is your reaction to what you hear? There is always conflict even in the calmest of minds, if we let it surface. Use the conflict you find.

When I do this part of catalysis I play out little stories of conflict around observations. Usually while pacing around in my office, I tell myself my own interpretation about the observation, usually out loud. Then I cross my arms, put on my nay-saying scowl, and say "*ha!*" or "that's not what *I* see" or "that's what *you* think!" or some other stubborn-mule retort. Then a conflicting interpretation comes out (sometimes surprisingly), and I write it down. (See Figure 10.65 on the following page.)

Go ahead and try it right now. Pick a fact you can see around you, something anyone can see, like "the window is closed." Say, out loud, what you *actually* think that means, like, say, "it's a hot day outside." Then find something to say that *disagrees* with that interpretation, like "the air outside is polluted" or "people might hear me talking" or "it might rain today" or "the barking dog is distracting." Find other ways to explain the same fact. That's all there is to it.

A warning: the more highly trained you are in any scientific field, the more difficult this part of catalysis will be for you. People trained as scientists are so used to zeroing in on single truths that they find branching out into multiple perceptions difficult. Having said that, I

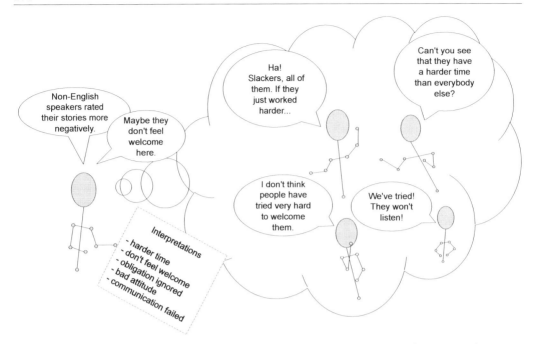

Figure 10.65. The process of generating multiple interpretations is a process of imaginatively arguing with yourself.

am absolutely sure that *anyone* can develop the capacity to argue with themselves fruitfully. It just takes practice. Call upon the diversity in yourself and in your life. Sometimes I pretend that I have temporarily become a person who I know would have a strong reaction to my first interpretation, and I say what *they* would say. Imagine arguing with your parents or grandparents or siblings or spouse or neighbors or colleagues. Such role playings can work wonders for your interpretive ability.

Here's a little fictional example of generating multiple interpretations. Say I have observed in my PNI project that people over sixty were more likely to say they kept their dogs outside. *Of course,* I might think, it's a generational thing. People used to treat dogs more like livestock, and younger people treat dogs more like members of the family. People are becoming more knowledgeable about dogs, thus more humane. *I* would never abandon a dog on a chain outside. Dogs are social animals, meant to be with people; and people are only beginning to understand that now.

That's my *first* interpretation, and it's my *own* interpretation. Now I cross my arms and scowl, and here's what comes out.

1. These young people have their priorities all wrong. These are *dogs,* for goodness' sake! Stop treating them like babies. Older people know how to survive in the world. What will you young people do when the hard times come and there is no food for *you,* let alone your precious pets? It's only because young people today are all spoiled brats who have never known hardship that they keep their pets inside. Take care of *yourself* first, not some dumb animal.

2. Young people today are isolated. They don't know their neighbors, they don't go to community events, they don't have real friends, and they don't have big families either. Because they are lonely, they bring their pets inside and fawn over them like they are children. Pets aren't children; they are animals! Older people know how to find other ways to connect, and they don't need to use pets for things they are not meant for. Young folks should make more *real* friends.

I would describe these three interpretations as:

1. Older people are more likely to keep dogs outside because they don't understand the true nature of dogs as social animals.

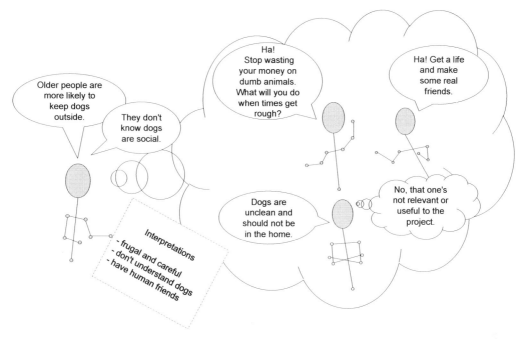

Figure 10.66. Keep only the interpretations that are reasonable, relevant, and useful to the project.

2. Older people are more likely to keep dogs outside because they know how to be frugal and careful in economic uncertainty.

3. Older people are more likely to keep dogs outside because they don't need surrogate family and friends.

Note how all of these statements begin with the observation (older people are more likely to keep dogs outside), then append a "because" and the interpretation of the cause of the pattern.

Now here's the tricky bit: even in your own notes to yourself, put your own personal interpretation first only randomly. *Even to yourself,* do not give your own views precedence. It is only natural to want to find evidence for your own views. Work against that.

How many interpretations are enough? As many as are reasonable, relevant, and useful to the project. Use your instincts. If you try *too* hard to come up with a plentiful variety of interpretations, two things will happen. First, the interpretations will start to become too similar to each other to be useful, and your report will become tedious. Second, you will start reaching too far beyond your actual experience into

things you know less about, and you will write things that either offend the readers of your report or give them little of substance to work with.

My general rule is to list two interpretations as a minimum, then let other interpretations "bubble up" as they will, until they stop bubbling. Then I remove those that are not reasonable, relevant, and useful to the project. In the outside-dogs example above, I actually thought of one more interpretation, from the perspective of a devout Muslim who believes dogs to be unclean animals not permitted near holy areas. I thought of this by remembering how some devout Muslims I've known have reacted to my own dogs being in the house. However, I later removed that interpretation from my list as insufficiently connected with the project's goals. I also realized that I was sliding into attempting to show off my knowledge of other cultures.

Beware: you are likely to find yourself proud of your broad experience as you write interpretations of patterns. It is easy to slip into including interpretations whose main purpose is not to expand thought but to show how very amazing *you* are: open-minded, widely read, a world traveler, a historian, a scholar, a philosopher, knowledgeable about the subject matter, whatever. I probably delete ten or twenty such I'm-so-great interpretations on every project. Watch for them, because you are sure to find them. They are *not* usually the most reasonable, relevant, and useful interpretations. (See Figure 10.66 on the previous page.)

Can a *group* of people generate multiple interpretations? Yes of course, and in fact that is likely to create a better outcome than if one person does all the interpreting. I do this work by myself because I'm hired to do it. But a group of people could do a better job than any one person working alone.

There is a trick to generating multiple interpretations in a group, though, that may not be obvious. You might think that all you'd need to do to have a group work on generating multiple interpretations is to simply have them all look at a pattern and write down what they think it means. That would be a disaster. First, the people working on the catalysis will be likely to agree on many things, because they are not likely to be a random subset of the population. Second, people asked to provide one interpretation usually cannot help defending it. They will begin arguing with each other instead of with themselves.

If you want to share this task in a group, ask each person to generate *at least two competing interpretations*. Ask them to conceal which is their *actual* interpretation (by keeping the tone consistent and the order random), then merge all of the interpretations together without keeping track of which came from whom. Then people can explore the interpretations together without feeling territorial about them.

Step Three: Explore interpretations

For each observation you have decided to keep, after you have generated at least two competing interpretations, explore your data set in search of answers to questions they bring up.

This part of catalysis is like working your way through a maze (see Figure 10.67 on the facing page). You might follow what seems to be a promising path, only to find yourself facing a blank wall; or you might enter a path you are sure will lead nowhere, only to find it branching out into several new and encouraging avenues. Be sure to explore each of your interpretations as you do this. Walk through the maze not as yourself but as a crowd. Bring along each of the nay-saying personalities that disagree with your interpretation.

In my dog example, from the knowledge-about-dogs interpretation I might want to ask questions like these.

- In stories about dogs told by older people, how do they characterize the nature of dogs as social animals? Do they seem to believe dogs have no social needs? What about in stories told by younger people?
- Do older people with outside dogs play with them a lot? Do they interact with them socially? Do people whose dogs live indoors report playing with them more?
- Do older people know less than younger people about the biology and evolutionary history of dogs as a species?

From the spoiled-brats interpretation I might want to ask questions like these.

- Do older people mention the high cost of taking care of dogs more than younger people? Do they speak of ways to reduce those costs more?
- Do younger people mention spending more on their dogs than older people? Do they mention more instances of impulse buying related to dog ownership?
- How does the "income group" question line up with the "dog inside or outside" question and the "age group" question? Are older people of all incomes more likely to keep their dogs outside, or is it only older people with lower incomes? Is this true among younger people?

From the surrogate-friends interpretation I might want to ask questions like these.

- How do older and younger people differ in their answers to the questions about social activities? Do older people with outside dogs report more weekly social activity than younger people with indoor dogs?
- In the stories told about dogs by older and younger people, and by people with inside

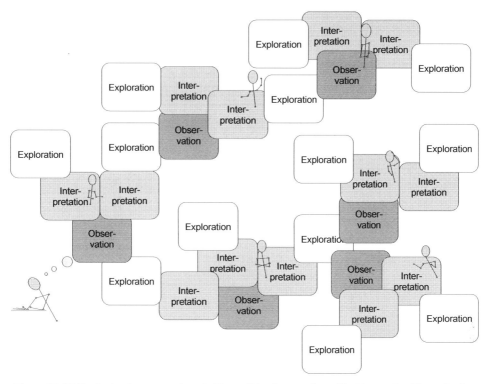

Figure 10.67. Exploring interpretations is like walking in a garden of forking paths. The point is not to arrive but to explore.

or outside dogs, what instances can we see where dogs are explicitly connected with social activity, or the lack thereof? Can we line up stories where people say things like, "I don't have many friends, but I have my dog," or, "Going out with my dog helps me meet people," side by side? Taken together, what picture do those stories present?

You might think that these explorations, this act of asking questions of the data in the service of these perceptions of the pattern, is a means of gathering *evidence* for one perception or another. You might think that the end goal is to *prove* one argument over another. It is not. You are unlikely to have collected so much data that you can prove conclusively, to all people in all places, that people keep dogs indoors as substitutes for social life, or anything else. Even if you *could,* that is not the point of catalysis. The reason you want to explore the manifestation of each of your interpretations is to help the people looking at the pattern think about it. If lower-income seniors were just as impulsive about their indoor-dog-related purchases

as higher-income young people, it doesn't disprove the spoiled-brat interpretation; it just provides more depth to the understanding of that perception.

Ways to explore interpretations

What are the ways in which you can explore your interpretations? I can think of several.

Look again

Sometimes a question that comes up as the result of an interpretation will cause you to look again at a graph you already considered, and perhaps discarded as being unremarkable. What was unimportant *in general* may be very important in the context of a focused question. When this happens, you can pull those images into your report.

Create new views

Quite often I will be in the middle of a project, with all of my graphs already generated and considered, and I'll be in the middle of exploring interpretations of a pattern, and I'll suddenly discover that I need an entirely new type of graph to answer a question. Maybe I want

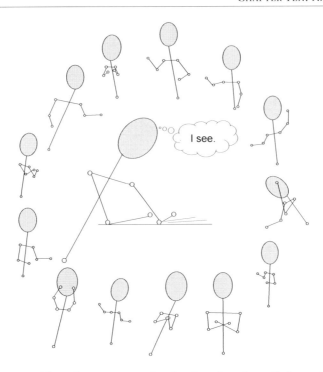

Figure 10.68. Sitting with stories means experiencing them in order to find out what they are saying collectively.

to know whether older people were more likely to say they "struggled to pay their bills" and "loved dogs" and "missed the old days," or whatever. When this happens, I refer to the decision I made in the first stage of this section: evaluation. Did I mark this pattern as being strong, medium, or weak in importance to the project? If I marked it as important, I may consider generating a new graph, or even a new category of graphs, to answer the question. If not, I may simply make a note on the page that "this issue would reward future exploration" and move on.

Sit with stories

Sometimes when a question is vague and can't be systematized easily, I will select two sets of stories about which people answered questions differently and just *sit with them* for a while (see Figure 10.68). I read the stories in each set and go back and forth between them, as though I was comparing two books of folk tales. Usually, after a while, an interesting difference will emerge from the two sets of stories. Say I notice that in one set of stories people keep saying "my dog" while in the other set people refer to a specific breed of dog—"my border collie" or "my shih tzu" or something. Or I notice that the

stories in one set often seem to mention taking dogs out to dog-related events like agility trials, while the ones in the other set rarely do.

These differences can sometimes be striking, but you can't predict them in advance. You just have to be with the stories long enough to notice them. Sitting with stories is like people-watching on a city street; you are guaranteed to notice patterns in what you see, but exactly what patterns you will notice is unpredictable in advance (and they depend on *you* as much as on the people and the street).

When I sit with stories and find useful differences between sets of them, I record the differences in my report by including particularly telling excerpts from the stories involved. I will note that I see a pattern here, and that the report readers can see the same pattern if they select stories with these criteria. By excerpting and instructing I don't set myself up as arbiter on these differences. Instead I use them to entice people to follow the trail I have laid out. Does this insert bias into the report? Possibly, but if you can illustrate the difference with excerpts, readers can decide for themselves the strength of what you see, because they can see it too.

Theme stories

Annotating stories with themes is a reasonable way to add depth to the catalytic method without inserting bias, if it is done correctly. By "theme" I mean what a story is about, its subject or essence or gist or plot; a shorthand for *what happens in the story*.

Some themes might be:

- I did my part but somebody else didn't
- The rules of the game are constantly changing
- I faced a difficult challenge and succeeded
- People have their limits

The method I have developed to draw out story themes is based loosely on grounded theory. It generally takes the form of three passes through the stories, thus.

1. First, write up one or more themes for each story. Summarize the story briefly, as if it was a newspaper headline (but not a sensationalist one!). Pay attention to the events of the story and describe what happened. Some stories will be well represented by one theme, but others will require more to fully describe them. I generally place a limit of three themes per story, to avoid diluting the meaning of the themes too much. As you write each theme, add it to a growing list. Don't pay attention to reuse on this pass through. If a particular story cries out for a theme you already have on your list, you can reuse it; but don't force conformity.

2. When you have read all the stories once, go back and read them again. This time, compare the themes you have for each story to your overall list. Whittle the theme list down so that each theme is uniquely meaningful (none are redundant), each is populated sufficiently (none have few stories), and the total number is manageable (typically eight to twelve themes). If your theme list is very large (say over twenty themes), you can use a clustering technique to merge some of them.

3. Finally, go back and read your stories a third time. This time, do not create any new

themes, or do any lumping or splitting of themes, *unless* you feel a story presents a serious challenge to the organization you have in place. When you finally feel that each story has been well described by its themes, you are finished.

Does this process of theme production insert bias? Yes, of course it does. But it limits the bias to describing the *events* of the story. Try to keep your themes *defensible*. Picture yourself making a case for each theme assignment in front of an assembled body of participants who nay-say it. If you *can't* defend the assignment, remove it. Also, two heads are always better than one; so if you can have two or more people come up with their own lists of themes, you can merge them to create a more complex description of the stories.

You can theme stories either as-needed, when a question pushes you to explore similarities and differences between juxtaposed groups of stories, or you can theme all of the stories in your collection. When I work on a project with few collected stories, say a hundred or fewer, I usually theme all the stories as a matter of course. On large projects, say over several hundred stories, it is usually impractical to read all the stories three times to derive themes; so I pull out subsets as explorations require them and do mini-theming runs.

No matter how and when they are derived, I often set up my generated themes as answers to a "story topic" or "story is about" question. When formatted this way, themes can then enter into all the generated graphs and provide useful insights. Because themes come not from what people said about their stories but from the stories themselves, they provide a different view on what was said.

Add questions

In addition to theming stories in general, you can answer new questions about stories to explore interpretations of patterns. Quite often in projects I work on, new questions arise that were not anticipated before the stories were collected. For example, in my outside-dogs project above, I might be led to ask to what extent each story incorporated anthropomorphism in speaking about dog behavior. Giving each story (either in the whole collection or ones in pertinent subsets) an anthropomorphism rating might provide more food for thought when pondering how people think about dogs as pets. These unanticipated questions can feed in to your graph generating system and deepen the catalytic materials you provide.

Yes, this may mean that you have to pause in your exploration of interpretations to go back and generate more graphs, and you might accumulate even more observations as a result. Sometimes this is impossible. Sometimes an enticing question cannot be answered given time constraints. But sometimes you encounter a question that shows such huge potential to add meaning to catalysis that you decide it's *worth* spending the time, possibly even at the expense of dropping something optional you had meant to do, or asking for more time, or bringing in more help. When your data surprise you, sometimes you have to be ready to rise to the occasion.

Study story texts

You can add to the mix of ways you explore interpretations a variety of textual analyses on the contents of the stories themselves. I'm personally not a big fan of generalized textual analyses like concordances (where you map out all the words that appear) in story work. I've tried it and been underwhelmed with its utility for supporting sensemaking.

There is one type of attention to story texts that I do find helpful and have used on occasion, especially when participant response has been thin. Usually when I read through a collection of stories, some *pivotal words* start rising up out of the collection. Not only do these words come up often, but when they do come up, they always resonate with emotion and meaning. Also, importantly, participants *vary* in the emotions that resonate around these words. That's why I call them pivotal; because the project pivots around them. For example, in a project on dogs the word "animal" might be used with fondness ("what a beautiful animal") or contempt ("it's just a dumb animal"). Pivotal words highlight a relevant conflict or tension in the community.

You can't decide what your pivotal words will be before you collect your stories; you can only dis-

cover them as you read what has been collected. In one medical project I worked on some years ago, I remember the words *better, worse,* and *normal* (as in back to normal, or living a normal life) being pivotal. The tension around those words had to do with the different perspectives with which patients and doctors saw the words in context. What was better for the patient was not always better for the doctor, and vice versa.

When I find pivotal words, I sometimes add a question to my list that marks whether each story contains them. This is a *kind* of textual analysis, but its energy is targeted where it can be most relevant. I find it much more useful than dumping the entire texts of stories into the meat grinder of blind textual analysis.

Step Four: Write the preliminary report text

In this step you write what your report is going to say about the interpretations you explored for each observation. The reason I call this a "preliminary" report text is that you are bound to revise some of these as you get into the stage of clustering interpretations.

Always *separate your statements* as you write. Make clear distinctions between observations (statements about patterns), interpretations (what patterns could mean) and ideas (suggestions for action). I've tried lots of different ways of denoting the separation in my catalysis reports over the years. I started out writing a label in front of each statement (observation, interpretation, idea), but after a while I found the repetition annoying. So I tried using formatting to denote the difference. I would write the observations in bold, say, then the interpretations in plain text and the ideas in italics. However, this approach also has problems because it supposes that people will read the "how to read this report" section, which few people do. So I am more or less explicit about the separation depending on the characteristics of the people who I think will be reading the report. If you are writing for meticulous readers, spare them the repetition. If you are writing for glancers, repeat.

Writing observations

When you write observations, go ahead and use the language of science. Here it is reasonable to

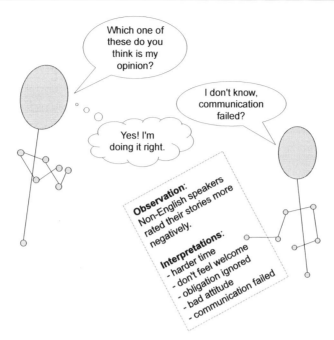

Figure 10.69. If you aren't sure you are hiding your own interpretations well enough, ask someone else to guess at which opinions are your own.

say that trends are clear and strong and valid, and all the authoritative words you find in analytical reports. This *one* part of your catalytic material should be strongly analytical. But it should the *only* part written thus.

Writing interpretations

The number one iron-clad rule of presenting multiple interpretations is: it should be *impossible to guess* which interpretation is your own. Nobody should ever be able to find *you* in the interpretations you provide. This is a form of *steganography,* of hiding a signal (your interpretation) in noise (interpretations you do not agree with). And believe me, there will always be a signal. You cannot be human and have no opinions at all, especially about the emotion-laden topics story projects probe.

I myself often have strong emotional reactions to the patterns I see in story project data. The patterns I see may, from my perspective, reveal injustices or prove the truth of disputed claims or promise help to the helpless. I can't *help* seeing things as I see things, and neither can you. It is not only futile to pretend you have no feelings about the patterns you see, it is a dangerous lie that can destroy the utility of your work.

So rather than try to suppress your reactions (or convince yourself that you have suppressed them when you haven't), it is better to *embed* your interpretations along with other interpretations you do not hold. Anyone who wants to do effective catalysis work has to learn to do this. You must protect the people you are helping from your own interpretations so that they can form their *own* interpretations, not simply adopt or attack yours.

To be sure you are following the steganography rule, occasionally test your catalysis writing. If you can get someone else to help you, ask them to read your report and make highlighting marks where they think you are speaking your mind (see Figure 10.69). If they are often correct in their assessment, you are not hiding your signal well enough. Spouses tend to be good at finding you in what you write since they know you so well.

If you can't get someone else to help (or if the report you are preparing is too private to show to anyone), read it yourself, but from a different perspective. How can you put yourself into a different perspective? Put yourself into a situation you rarely find yourself in, or do something strange to put yourself out of your normal habits. Read what you have written on a train, in the bathtub, without your morning coffee, in the middle of the night, in the garage, on a rock in a stream, while listening to the most grating music you can find. Find a way to be a different one of your own selves, and see if you can find yourself in what you have written. I often ask my husband to skim over bits of reports I am writing, but sometimes I also print out pages and take them off to some strange place to read.

I do catch myself breaking the steganography rule sometimes. It's hard not to. The more the project hits me in my soul the greater the danger is. I tend to love underdogs and the downtrodden, so when projects touch on such triggers I have to be especially careful. When I find myself slipping up, I go back and change how I phrase each interpretation to make sure that I am not favoring my own beliefs by stating them more often in a stronger way. Like coming up with multiple interpretations, this is another challenging yet rewarding part of catalysis work.

What sort of writing is best when explaining multiple interpretations? I like to use simple conversational forms to present multiple views, much as if two or three people were having a conversation in which differing opinions were offered—but everyone was courteous and respectful. To begin with, these respectful interpreters never speak in terms of absolute proof or certainty. They say that a result *supports, strengthens, encourages, promotes, advocates, corroborates, endorses*, or *favors* an interpretation; or that a result "could be seen as" doing any of these things. They *never* state unequivocally that a result *verifies, validates, authenticates, confirms*, or *proves* an interpretation.

To chain multiple interpretations together, a variety of methods are available. I tend to mix all of these together to make the report text more interesting.

- The simplest connections are straightforward *conjunctions*: but, or, instead, alternatively, however, maybe, perhaps, could be, might be.
- For spice, terms describing *viewpoints* can be added: one way to look at it, one way to see it, one view, another view, one perspective, one

interpretation, on the one hand, on the other hand, at the same time, a contrasting view.

- Terms describing fictional *speakers* are also useful: one might say, someone who disagrees might say, the nay-sayer response to this might be, one might think, explanations could range.
- Some terms related to *speculation* itself can be used: you could imagine, it is possible to see it as, the question arises, we can imagine.
- You can use terms of *appearance*: seems, appears, at first glance, on encountering, on consideration, seems to point to, one might expect, matches with, is surprising, could denote, could mean, may have to do with, seems to say. (Always follow these terms up with a "but" or "on the other hand" to avoid people jumping to the conclusion that you are making statements of proof.)

These are all methods of saying not "here are the results" or "here is a clear trend" but "here are some thoughts to get you going."

What if there is a clear trend? Doesn't that ever happen? Of course it does. But even clear trends rarely produce single interpretations. Just because the pattern is obvious doesn't mean its *meaning* is obvious, or obvious in the same way, to everyone. If you don't believe that, ask two people from opposite ends of the political spectrum what any economic graph *means* (not what it *says:* what it *means*) about what government policy should be.

One more tip on writing multiple interpretations: *let the stories speak*. When possible I like to place short excerpts from stories to illustrate each interpretation as I explore it. I make sure these are set off from my own writing with a special font or color or quotes, so people know this is not *me* speaking. This makes the report more relevant, understandable, and interesting to its readers. It brings the stories to people, you could say. I've watched people use my reports, and I've noticed that they sometimes jump across the stories in the report like stones on a stream, getting the gist of the thing, before they come back and dive into the detailed patterns.

Including excerpts from the stories also serves as a check on your interpretations as you write them. If you are writing up an interpretation and you *can't* find anything anybody actually said to illustrate it, maybe you strayed from what the stories were saying and inadvertently brought some of your own emotion to the interpretation. If it's real and useful, it should be there in the stories.

Writing ideas

After you write about each interpretation for your observation, there is an extra step you can take if your goals and context warrant it: you can add *ideas*. The essential form of an idea is: from the viewpoint of *this* interpretation of *this* observation, taking *this* action might create positive change. The action might be finding out more about something, making a change to policy, setting up a training program, or even doing nothing and letting things take their course. Usually when you are writing interpretations, ideas will "jump out" at you naturally. If older people don't know as much as they should about dogs, there might be ways to help them learn. If younger people waste money, maybe they need help managing financial risk. If younger people lack human community, maybe better meeting places would help. And so on.

While observations and interpretations are always useful, ideas are sometimes useful and sometimes not. It depends on the goals and context of your project. Ideas are most useful in projects where problems have been known about for some time and nobody has any new ideas about them. In such situations your ideas can spur people on to come up with their own good ideas. But in other situations, ideas can dampen rather than catalyze sensemaking. Usually these are situations in which the project touches on sensitive nerves. The topic might be personal and private, or there might be power differentials reflected in the participants and researchers, or you might unwittingly press on sore spots. The stronger and more dangerous the emotional undercurrents in your project, the less likely ideas will be helpful to it. If you aren't sure, try writing a few ideas, then test them out with a real or imaginary audience and gauge reactions.

If you choose to use ideas in your project, always remember that they are not advice. Their purpose is not to provide recommendations you expect people to actually carry out, but to help people come up with their *own* ideas. If you've done your catalysis right, some of your ideas will be perceived as completely off-base, even nonsensical. That's okay, because if you've done your catalysis right, your ideas will get people thinking of their *own*, probably much better, ideas in response. If people read your ideas and say, "No, *that's* no good, but how about *this?*" you're doing catalysis right.

CLUSTERING INTERPRETATIONS

When you have finished exploring all of your observations, and you have written up multiple interpretations (and maybe ideas) for each, the next step is to go back and tie your interpretations together.

Start on the first interpretation you wrote. Pass back through all the material you wrote in the order you wrote it. As you read what you have written for each observation, follow these four steps: revise, rate, cluster, compile.

Step one: Reconsider and revise

Read what you have written for each observation and reconsider it in the light of everything you have learned since you wrote it. Since you wrote about that observation, you might have written about many *other* observations. You learned many other things about the stories and answers you collected. You have a much deeper understanding of the observation than you did when you wrote it. From your more enlightened perspective, see if you need to clean up what you wrote before. Perhaps what you said then was tentative and now it can be solid. Maybe you thought the pattern would repeat elsewhere but it did not.

You might even decide, on this pass through, that an observation and its interpretations are too weak to include. You can drop an observation even at this late point in the process. Clean up your writing and make it make sense in the light of what you have found out.

Step two: Rate the observation

Now make your final *rating* of the strength of the observation. By now, since you have considered every one of your original observations, you should have a much better feeling for what is a strong, medium, or weak observation in relation to the totality of what you have learned. Mark the observation's page or pages with a rating that will stand in your final report. I usually do this with a color-coded visual key, but any method is fine as long as you stick with it.

Remember that you are rating the *observation*, not the interpretations that flow from it. You can't rate interpretations, because they are perceptions, not facts. To rate your observations, go back to the part marked "Step One: Evaluate for relevance" in the section on interpreting observations (page 270). It's the same process, except this time you know more about what matters most, and this is your *final* rating, the one your report readers will see and use.

Step three: Name and cluster

Give each interpretation a short *name*. This should not be difficult. You are likely to find, as I do, that memorable names for interpretations "jump out" as you work with patterns in the data. Often these names come from things people said in their stories, like "spoiled brats" or "dumb animals," that stand out as connecting well with patterns you see in the answers they gave to questions. In the firefighting project, some of the names that came up often were "perfectionism," "cowboy mentality," and "critical decisions."

At this point in the process, do not worry if your names will offend anybody who reads the report. They are only for *you* to use right now. You won't necessarily keep them later. What matters right now is that the names are *memorable* enough that you can use them to connect interpretations with each other. You should be able to look at the names in a list out of context and remember what they mean.

As you think of names for interpretations, try to *reuse* names you already thought of on other pages. (That's why the names have to be memorable, so you can remember to reuse them.) The rule is: never add a new name if an existing name can adequately express the interpretation. This will tie together interpretations into larger clusters by name. The clusters of interpretations you create by reusing names will become the pages of the summary section of your report. By drawing interpretations together into clusters, you make it easier for people to approach the complexity of the report.

For a small project exploring only one or a few simple topics, aim for three to seven clusters. For a more involved project, aim for five to ten clusters. It is better to have too many clusters than too few. With too many clusters you can lump some in your report (but preserve the detail so people can traverse it). With too few clusters you will need to split some, which means you will have to go back to your interpretations and reassign some. So if you are in doubt, generate more clusters rather than fewer.

Write each cluster name somewhere on the pages on which it appears. Write it in a way that you and your report readers can see it easily (even though you might change it later). I like to make my cluster names prominent on each page, either with colored "sticky note" boxes separate from the text or with special formatting (bold, colored) in the text itself. You want people to be able to see the cluster names as they skim the pages.

Step four: Compile a list

For each interpretation, after you have assigned it to a cluster, copy the interpretation name, the cluster name, the name of the observation the interpretation came from, the strength of the observation, and the page number on which the interpretation can be found, into a list (see Figure 10.70 on the next page). I usually do this in a spreadsheet so I can sort it by name as I go. There are two reasons to build this list: to keep track of your cluster names, and to build an index into your report that readers can use to drill down to the detail on each cluster of interpretations as they like.

For a long time after I started building catalysis reports, I refused to put any kind of summaries in them. I was afraid that summarization would present biased views of what mattered most in the report. Besides, I felt that if people weren't ready to make the commitment to read the whole thing I wasn't going to "boil it down" for them. I now think this was unrealistic, and I now build a summary section into each report.

CLUSTER	STRENGTH	SECTION	PAGE
it's not my problem	weak	F	18
it's not my problem	weak	F	26
it's not my problem	medium	F	4
it's not my problem	medium	F	19
it's not my problem	medium	F	67
why are we still here?	medium	C	3
why are we still here?	weak	F	7
why are we still here?	medium	F	9
why are we still here?	medium	F	64
why are we still here?	medium	D	6
why are we still here?	strong	F	5
why are we still here?	strong	E	13
why are we still here?	strong	E	14
why are we still here?	strong	E	10
why are we still here?	strong	E	21
why are we still here?	strong	E	37
why are we still here?	strong	F	48
we are the adults in the room	medium	F	9
we are the adults in the room	medium	F	67
we are the adults in the room	medium	F	13

Figure 10.70. Building a list of clusters and linking your interpretations and observations to it can help you build a summary of your report more quickly.

My position now is that it is acceptable to present multiple levels of detail in catalysis materials, as long as those levels *accurately* show what is in the rest of the report. What I do now is tie each summary statement to supporting details below it (using an index such as you see here) so that the reader can drill down to explore any issue more fully. This sort of *supported summarization* minimizes bias, though nothing can completely eliminate it. It is also strongly supportive of reader participation.

However, my advice is to *watch yourself closely* as you summarize. If you find yourself writing summaries that float above your details unsupported, in which it is impossible to follow statements downward into detail, you risk biasing your result more than you have to.

A side note about something I call *leakage* in catalysis. Every stage of catalysis leaks into the stage before it (see Figure 10.71 on the following page).

Thus:

- When you are producing *results*, you are not supposed to be choosing some to become *observations*, but you can't help noticing that some results stand out as remarkable.

- When you are accumulating *observations*, you are not supposed to be generating *interpretations*, but you can't help noticing what some observations might mean.

- When you are generating *interpretations*, you are not supposed to be building *connections* between them, but you can't help noticing that some things seem to fall together.

- When you are *clustering* interpretations, you are not supposed to be finishing your *report*, but you can't help doing a little clean-up as you cluster.

Leakage is a normal part of catalysis. It is not something you can stop entirely, but you *should* attempt to keep it to a minimum. Why bother reducing leakage? Because foresight is always foggy and often misleading. What seems solid turns out to be misty, and what seems irrelevant later becomes pivotal. Don't trust early glimpses; have patience and let the process work. Jumping the gun can lead you to erroneous statements and waste valuable time.

PREPARING YOUR REPORT

This is the stage of catalysis in which you will prepare to hand over your report to those who will be using it in sensemaking. There are a few last tasks to take care of at this point.

Clean house

This is the time to look over your cluster names and make sure they will be memorable and useful to your report readers. If something sounds catchy to you but may be offensive to your readers, find a way to reword it. I usually go through my cluster names at this point and make sure

Figure 10.71. Leakage, or jumping the gun to the next stage, is a normal part of catalysis; but try to keep it in check.

every single one of them can be found in a story somewhere. That way if anybody complains that I distorted things by making up strange names, I can point out that people really said these things in the stories.

This is the time to get your report ship-shape and ready to be read by people other than yourself. If you are like me you will have littered your report files with layers of notes to yourself. Find all of those notes and convert them into report prose or remove them.

Prepare for participation

This is the time to build the introductory section of your report. The introduction is where report readers will land first. It is where they will develop their assumptions for reading and using the report. This is where you need to make sure people understand the point of catalysis, and the use of catalytic materials, before they move on to use them.

The first part of your report should anticipate and deflect what I call "the duffer misconception." This is when people miss the point of catalysis and jump to the conclusion that you have offered multiple interpretations not because you invite people to think *with* you, but because you need them to think *for* you. They mistake effective catalysis for ineffective analysis. This is not an unreasonable expectation, just an erroneous one, often based on prior experience with analytical reports. But you are not *stupid:* you are *dancing.* You need people to

understand that from the start (see Figure 10.72 on the next page).

The best way I have found to avoid the duffer misconception is to explain the intentions, goals, and methods of catalysis initially, frequently, clearly, and in multiple ways. I tend to have a "how to read this report" page in each section, in case people didn't read the one at the beginning. I complement this by talking to the people who will use the report and explaining its methods. If the report is to be used in a sensemaking session, I ask the presenters to communicate to the participants the same messages.

These steps transform the perception of catalytic material from disputation to resource. This is necessary, because without an understanding of the meaning of mischief by all parties involved, catalysis has no power to support sensemaking. It is up to you to make sure that meaning is understood.

Prepare a bird's eye view

This is the time to build the summary section of your report. Give each of your clusters a page or two, not more. The summary is for people who don't have time or don't care to read the details of the report; so keep things brief. Copy onto each page a representative observation and interpretation for that cluster, one that you think shows the meaning of the cluster well.

Then—and do not forget this—*visit the stories* and find a few excerpts or stories that illustrate the meaning of each cluster well. Bring some

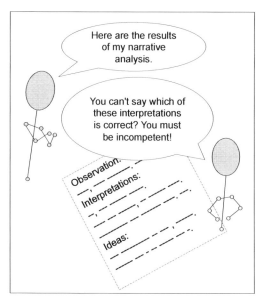 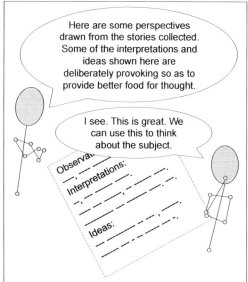

Figure 10.72. Avoid the "duffer misconception" by making it clear that you have provided multiple interpretations for helpful reasons rather than for reasons of ineptitude.

stories to the surface. This is the same process as I described for the individual interpretations (on page 282), but this time each story excerpt illustrates a whole cluster of interpretations. I usually include two or three such excerpts for each cluster. Place these story excerpts prominently on the page, and make it clear that these were the actual words spoken by participants. I usually set excerpts off with a special background color and quotes.

I've noticed that having these real quotes in the report summary helps people understand the clusters much better than they can by simply looking at graphs and reading things like, "the means of these two distributions were significantly different." (See Figure 10.73 on the following page.)

If you can't find any stories that illustrate a particular cluster well, stop right where you are. This is the equivalent of dropping a nail while walking around in your bare feet. Something is wrong. Stop and fix it. The stories *can't* be wrong, so it can only mean your cluster of interpretations is wrong. Go back and look over the interpretations in the cluster. Maybe they don't hold together in one cluster? Maybe small errors have compounded into a larger one?

This has never actually *happened* to me, by the way. Finding stories to illustrate clusters of in-

terpretations is usually as easy as falling off a log. In fact, I usually go straight to the best story for each cluster without having to read any, because of course I've read all the stories already, or most of them, and I'm very familiar with them. I've laughed and cried and lived with the stories by the time I get to writing my report summary, and I know just which ones ought to speak on the summary pages. If you know which stories ought to speak at this point in your work, you are doing catalysis right.

After you have illustrated each cluster with a pattern (graph or test result), an observation (statement of fact), an interpretation (statement of meaning from a perspective) and a story excerpt or two, copy the relevant part of your indexing list that shows where the detailed pages can be found for that cluster. This will help your report readers drill down into detail when they want to explore the clusters. When I'm running out of time I do this literally, with a simple grid (pasted directly from my spreadsheet) showing pages and sections and strengths. When I have more time I make the display a little more visually appealing, maybe with little bubbles of different sizes and so on.

In the drill-down section, provide some kind of count of how many observations are related to each interpretation cluster: this many strong,

Figure 10.73. Remember to include story excerpts in your report, especially in the report summary. Bring the stories to the people who need to see them.

this many medium, this many weak observations. But make sure you explain that these counts are not any kind of evidence or proof of the validity of the interpretations. After all, the same observation will appear on pages describing competing interpretations. The counts are indicators of how strongly each cluster of interpretations flows throughout the stories.

By the way, I am calling these things *clusters of interpretations* when I speak to you, because you understand the process they came from. But you might not want to call them that in your report.

I've struggled with what to call these conglomerations of interpretations for years. I've done some reports where I called the clusters clusters; I've done some where I called them patterns or trends; I've done some where I didn't label what the "things" were at all. Here's what I've noticed. Calling them trends or patterns seems to draw people towards analytical thinking. Calling them clusters leaves people confused and asking questions about the process. Calling them nothing at all leaves people searching for words they can use to discuss the things (they start talking about page numbers instead, and that becomes *really* confusing).

Recently I've settled on calling the clusters *perspectives,* that is, views on the topic under consideration. I like that solution because it gives people a word they can use, doesn't require an understanding of the process, and keeps the report from sounding analytical. Works for me.

EXCERPTS FROM A CATALYSIS REPORT

What follows are three examples of observations paired with interpretations and ideas taken from the report on firefighting we have been following in this chapter. These should illustrate what sorts of observations, interpretations, and ideas you might see in your own catalytic work.

Perfectionism? Or resourcefulness?

Observation

Excessive self-reliance in leaders tended to coincide with over-confidence, lack of self-control, and unrealistic expectations of others.

In Figure 10.74 on the next page you can see that when a story was marked as showing strong self-reliance (towards the left side of the X axis) it was also more likely to be marked as showing excessive confidence (toward the top of the Y axis).

In Figure 10.75 on page 290 you can see that when a story was marked as showing strong

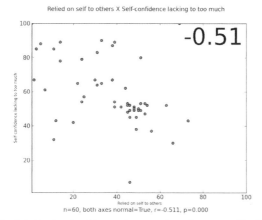

Figure 10.74. In the firefighting leadership project, stories of strong self-reliance tended also to be stories of excessive self-confidence.

self-reliance (towards the left side of the X axis) it was also more likely to be marked as showing "emotional" self control (towards the bottom of the Y axis). Recall that the "emotional" side of the self-control scale read, in full: "In the story the leader's demonstrated level of self-control was unpredictable and emotional: they responded and acted before thinking." So this result means that when a leader was portrayed as self-reliant, they were also portrayed as working from an emotional, not a rational, basis (whether that would be described as gut-feel or impulse would depend on perspective).

In Figure 10.76 on the next page you can see that when a story was marked as showing strong self-reliance (towards the left side of the X axis) it was also more likely to be marked as showing unrealistically high expectations for the accountability of others (towards the top of the Y axis).

Interpretations

The link between self-reliance and unrealistic standards of accountability is the most surprising of these three. It seems to say that some leaders have such high standards that no one can measure up to them, so they feel they have to do everything themselves. Perhaps perfectionists do not make good leaders? Perhaps being a good leader involves developing a nuanced understanding of the strengths and weaknesses of your team so that you can balance expectations and delegations?

The fact that the most emotional people are the most self-reliant is also surprising. You could imagine it going the other way, where the most rule-bound people are the most self-reliant. Another interpretation of these patterns might be that rules tend to distribute responsibility, so people who rely more heavily on mechanical rules are less likely to either choose to rely on themselves, or to have to rely on themselves. This would imply that when rules are lacking, leaders are pushed into positions that *appear* perfectionist, but stem not from personal tendencies but from lack of required support.

Ideas

Attention to perfectionism and its affects on team working might be useful. Another possible avenue for exploration would be exploring the varying official and unofficial rule structures teams put into place and how their use affects interdependence.

Empowerment? Or obstinacy?

Observation

For the scale describing how leaders in stories held others accountable, stories marked with positive emotions or told in response to a positive question tended to be clustered around the mid-range, with a smaller number on the right-hand side of the range (Figure 10.77 on the following page).

Negative-emotion stories covered the range with a fairly equal distribution (Figure 10.78 on page 291). Note that negative stories did not

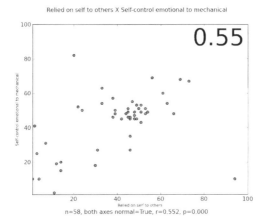

Figure 10.75. In the firefighting leadership project, stories of strong self-reliance tended also to be stories of emotional self-control.

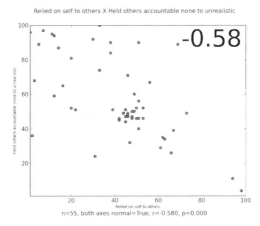

Figure 10.76. In the firefighting leadership project, stories of strong self-reliance tended also to be stories of unrealistic expectations of others.

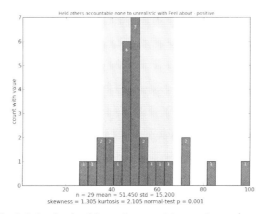

Figure 10.77. In the firefighting leadership project, positive stories took up mainly the middle of the accountability scale.

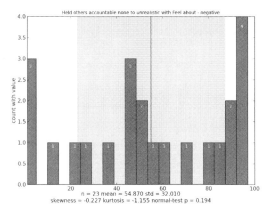

Figure 10.78. In the firefighting leadership project, negative stories took up the entire range of the accountability scale.

show a gap in the center, but covered it as well, with even a small peak there.

The fact that positive stories tended toward the middle and right says that the most positively viewed behaviors showed an intermediate or intense set of expectations about performance standards. The question arises as to whether high expectations for behavior are viewed positively when they refer to the storytellers themselves or to others.

Themes in the seven stories marked as showing high accountability and positive emotions were as follows:

- Leader gives subordinates difficult challenges and they respond with great performances (3 stories)
- Subordinates speak out to leader, don't back down, and win the case by having a superior approach (2 stories)
- Leaders work to help each other and both benefit (1 story)
- Leader works for benefit to all without taking credit for it (1 story)

Themes in the nine stories marked as showing high accountability and *negative* emotions were as follows:

- Leader demands absolute control, "my way or the highway," even when it results in danger and failure (3 stories)
- Leader berates subordinate(s) in front of others, or is rude and condescending (3 stories)

- Two leaders compete in "immature" power struggles (3 stories)

In summary, positive stories of high accountability had mainly to do with power sharing, and negative stories had to do with power hoarding. Positive stories also included successful confrontations of power hoarding. In negative stories the lack-of-respect theme appears as well.

Interpretations

Sharing responsibilities for group goals and succeeding at difficult challenges together is something these participants view with pride and almost a sense of entitlement. One might say that they see themselves as capable independent actors, almost to the point of not *needing* supervision. The best leaders, in their view, are people who don't lead at all, but serve.

An alternative interpretation of this pattern might be that the participants are cantankerous malcontents unable to work with authority figures, "cowboys" who need to learn how to get along and "take direction" in order for the fire service to be effective.

Ideas

Interpretations of this pattern could vary so widely that reactions could range from giving firefighting groups far greater autonomy to requiring all employees to take manners classes. A follow-up question might be: is the current system fine-grained enough to allow employees to move up in responsibility without relying on a great leader to recognize their skills? If becoming empowered to succeed is critical to effective firefighting, perhaps it should be made more systemic and less personality-driven?

High standards? Or critical decisions?

Observation

Unrealistic expectations (by leaders) were associated with over-intense skill development, blind vision following, and excessive self-reliance and self-confidence on the part of leaders.

In Figure 10.79 on the facing page you can see that when a story was marked as showing unrealistic expectations of accountability (towards the right side of the X axis) it was also more likely to be marked as showing "intense" development of others (towards the top of the Y axis). Recall that the full description of the "intense" side of the "Developed others" scale was this: "In the story the leader developed the abilities of others by putting too much focus on future and not enough on present; didn't leave enough time to apply learning." So, when a leader held people highly accountable, they also tended to push them to develop quickly, perhaps too quickly.

In Figure 10.80 on the next page you can see that when a story was marked as showing unrealistic expectations of accountability (towards the right side of the X axis) it was also more likely to be marked as showing "blind" vision following (towards the top of the Y axis). Recall that the full description of the "blind" side of the "Demonstrated leadership" scale was this: "In the story the leader demonstrated leadership by blindingly following corporate vision or being too narrowly focused on the team." So, when a leader held people highly accountable they also tended to follow handed-down visions blindly.

In Figure 10.81 on the facing page you can see that when a story was marked as showing unrealistic expectations of accountability (towards the right side of the X axis) it was also more likely to be marked as showing strong self-reliance (towards the bottom of the Y axis).

In Figure 10.82 on page 294 you can see that when a story was marked as showing unrealistic expectations of accountability (towards the right side of the X axis) it was also more

likely to be marked as showing excessive self-confidence (towards the top of the Y axis).

Interpretations

The portrait of an ineffective leader described here is of someone who has high standards for their team, but prefers not to, or cannot, share the pursuit of those high standards with others. The more likely leaders are to have high standards, the more likely they are to take most of the responsibility on themselves. This leads back to the "perfectionism" pattern seen earlier, the "nobody can do it right, so I have to do it myself" belief.

However, the nay-sayer response to this "ineffective perfectionism" interpretation is that because the decisions made by leaders in this field are so critical, leaders cannot *afford* to have subordinates make mistakes, and so in a sense perfectionism is *thrust* upon them. Perhaps the culture also demands accountability, such that saying "I gave them a challenge and they blew it" is not an adequate response. Perhaps leaders in this field have such a heavy responsibility that they simply *dare not* share power as much as they would like to. The situations in which people are learning may be so intense and difficult that allowing "necessary mistakes" may not be possible. If so, those working beneath leaders should respect their dedication and accept their difficult choices.

Ideas

If the first interpretation is more correct, the problem is of training leaders to recognize skills, share power and get along. If what keeps people from making necessary mistakes is cultural and personality-driven, the issue can be addressed by leader training or other means of cultural change management.

If the second interpretation is more correct, the problem is of training people to be good *followers*. Certainly "followship" skills are as necessary to the efficient operation of a high-expectations team as are good leadership skills. Both of these competing interpretations link to the promise of "safe mistake" capability, in which responsibilities can be earned through proof of competence in a way that does not threaten high standards of performance.

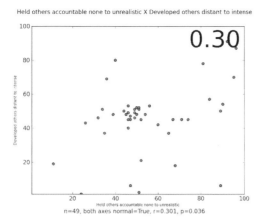

Figure 10.79. In the firefighting leadership project, stories in which leaders held others unrealistically accountable were also stories in which leaders developed the skills of others intensely.

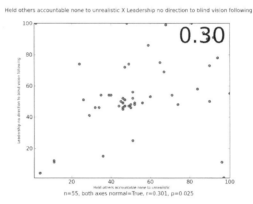

Figure 10.80. In the firefighting leadership project, stories in which leaders held others unrealistically accountable were also stories in which leaders followed handed-down visions blindly.

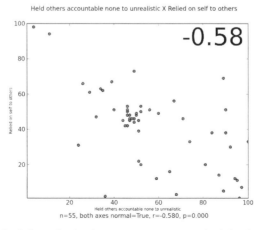

Figure 10.81. In the firefighting leadership project, stories in which leaders held others unrealistically accountable were also stories in which leaders relied only on themselves.

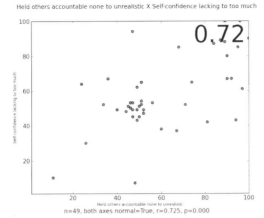

Figure 10.82. In the firefighting leadership project, stories in which leaders held others unrealistically accountable were also stories in which leaders were excessively self-confident.

USING CATALYSIS IN SENSEMAKING

The final thing to explain about catalytic materials is when and how to use them for sensemaking.

When to use catalytic material in sensemaking

When is it most useful to include catalytic material in sensemaking? Here are some situations in which you will find catalytic material especially useful.

When your goals are ambitious

Catalytic material is most useful in sensemaking when the project is ambitious and there are many stories and questions (thus possible patterns) to consider. If you have sixty stories about which people answered three questions, you have a lot less to make sense of than if you have a thousand stories about which people answered sixteen questions. The bigger the collection, the more catalysis helps participants in sensemaking work their way through what has been collected.

When your project is complex

Catalytic material is most useful in sensemaking when the topic is internally complex. Some projects address one very specific and narrow question, like, "How can we redesign our coffee maker to better meet the needs of our customers?" Others address broad questions with other layers of questions hidden inside them,

like, "Why do kids drop out of school?" The more intricately detailed a project's goals, the more it will benefit from catalytic material.

When your participants need help

Catalytic material is most useful in sensemaking when the participants need help counting and comparing stories and data. If your participants are analytical scientists, they can probably build their own graphs and charts. But it's rare to have a sensemaking session made up of only analytical scientists! The great majority of people are not used to detailed analytical work. For example, say your sensemaking session will be patients at your hospital or people who live on your street. Asking people to do things they don't know how to do will only confuse and alienate them. Generally the less scientifically educated your participants the more useful catalytic material will be.

When other methods have failed

Catalytic material is most useful in sensemaking when the topic is so well known that it's difficult to come up with any new ideas about it without some new energy. My experience has been that the narrative approach to topics is often brought in after other attempts to address the problem more directly (usually with surveys and focus groups) have failed to produce change. When there is a "been there done that" feeling about the topic of your project, when you expect people to come to your sensemaking session saying, "Why are we even here?"—

that's the time when catalytic material can be helpful.

When your topic is sensitive

Catalytic material is most useful in sensemaking when the topic is sensitive or the taboos against talking about (or even thinking about) certain things are strong enough that people need someone else to say what can't be said. However, this connection is not simple. Catalytic material is more useful in the middle range of sensitivity than at either end. When the topic will be considered trivial or safe (say it's about coffee makers), graphs and charts might be useful for other reasons, but they won't open up any issues waiting to be opened up. When the topic will be considered deeply sensitive or personal, to the point that people may refuse to speak about it at all (maybe it's about homelessness, with homeless people), opening things up with the playfully diverse interpretations of catalytic material may be too risky to work. It could turn people away instead of engaging them. It is in the middle ground, where there is some reluctance to talk about a topic, but people can get there with help, that this benefit appears.

When people need new ideas

Catalytic material is most useful in sensemaking when the project's goals are focused on new ideas. Some projects look more towards the past than the future, for example in organizing oral-history type exhibits. For a situation like that you might not need catalysis to spur thought, because you aren't looking to solve any problems. However, the majority of PNI projects address problems for which new ideas will be useful. The more welcome fresh ideas would be to your project, the more likely catalytic material will be helpful to sensemaking.

When you are ready to handle catalytic material in sensemaking

Catalytic material is most useful in sensemaking when the facilitator is ready to handle the complexity of adding catalytic material to sensemaking. Working with catalytic material does make facilitating sensemaking more complicated. People might have more questions; they might be confused about what they are supposed to do with the material; they might get into arguments about whether what the material says is correct. The more confident you

are that you can work catalytic material into your facilitated session, the more useful it will be in practice.

Does this mean that when your project doesn't meet these criteria, you should not include catalysis in your project? Not really. Using catalytic material in sensemaking is not a binary choice, it's a gradient. You can use any amount of what has been created, from one graph to hundreds of graphs, from no interpretations to a hundred-page report full of them. So the choice of whether to do catalysis is separate from the choice of how much catalytic material to include in sensemaking. Catalytic material can also help you plan the sensemaking, intervention, and return phases of a project. That's useful even if you use only a little of the material in your actual sensemaking sessions.

How to use catalytic material in sensemaking

Consider these scenarios of people using catalytic material.

- The catalytic report was sent to the people who sponsored the project. They read it. They did not discuss it.

- The catalytic report's summary was sent to the executive in charge, who glanced at it. The whole report was sent to the executive's staff, who pored over and discussed every detail. Later, the executive met with his staff, who provided input before the final decisions were made.

- In a meeting, the catalytic report's summary was presented to the executive in charge, who half-listened to the presentation but managed to draw out the most important points anyway. After the meeting, the full report was given to the executive's staff, who pored over and discussed every detail. Later, the executive met with her staff, who provided input before the final decisions were made.

- In a meeting, the catalytic report's summary was presented to the members of a group, who discussed it and its implications for future decisions. All group members received copies of the report. Most skimmed it or ignored it. One member who was particularly interested pored over every detail, then told other members about particular parts of the report, not in a formal meeting but here and there, when they would listen.

- In a meeting, the members of the group that sponsored the project looked at the catalytic report together. They discussed each page of the report's summary. On some pages they drilled down into detail, but after a while they ran out of time and had to rush through the rest. The group members took home copies of the full report. Afterward, some looked at it and some didn't.

- The full catalytic report was posted on the web site of the organization. Members of the organization, and of the public at large, were encouraged to read the report and enter into discussion about it in the web site's forums and chat areas. Some read only the summary, some the full report. The discussion went on for weeks. Later, summaries of the discussions were appended to the report, and the entire project was described in a paper published in an academic journal.

- In a half-day brainstorming session, members of the group were led through a sensemaking exercise by one member who was particularly interested in narrative work. The catalytic report's summary was used as background material for the exercise. The group members took home copies of the full report. Afterward, some looked at it and some didn't.

- In a full-day decision support workshop, members of the group were led through a series of sensemaking exercises by an external consultant. The entire catalytic report was printed and arrayed on the walls of the room, as were all of the collected stories. Some of the sensemaking exercises depended critically on the use of the report, so time was allocated to having groups "cruise" the walls on which the report was arrayed, discussing and debating points as they went.

Do you think I'm going to say that I have arranged these little vignettes in order from worst to best uses of catalytic materials? I'm not going to say that. People in *each* of these situations could use catalytic material well or badly. I've seen one person sit with a catalysis report, understand what it is for, and derive great benefit from simply reading it and reflecting on what they have read. I've also seen a room full of people miss the point of catalysis, attack a catalysis report for its lack of clear answers, and gain nothing from the effort.

The optimal use of catalytic material doesn't depend on fancy exercises or group processes or egalitarian decision making. It depends on the way the material is approached. You can drown in an inch of water, and you can misuse excellent catalytic material in any situation.

Using catalytic material in a group sensemaking session is not a guarantee of anything (positive or negative) happening. The way any group of participants in any sensemaking session will react to the inclusion of catalytic material depends on the unique mix of people in the room. Two groups considering the same issue using the same catalytic material will react differently. For some people, in some contexts, catalysis is a boon; for others it's an annoying distraction; for some it can even be seen as an attempt at control.

My favorite way to use catalytic material is to have it *on display but in the background* (as in Figure 10.83 on the facing page). I like to use it like wallpaper: on view but safe to ignore. You can use catalytic material just like real wallpaper, by "papering" a wall with the pages of a report. Or you can place a printed report on each table, or have a laptop with the report on it available for people to look at, or a printed copy on a side table.

Above all, never use catalytic material as you would an analytical report. Never present it as mandatory, definitive, authoritative, or even part of your session plan. Just make it *available*. Even when you are sure catalytic material will be useful (and welcomed) in sensemaking, you should *still* present it on the side. Participants should feel free to choose or set aside the materials, as they wish and as the need arises.

The best use of catalytic material depends on three things.

1. When catalytic material is used to reduce or resolve inquiry, it will fail. When it is used to multiply and energize inquiry, it will succeed.

2. When catalytic material is used to achieve conformity and end debate, it will fail.

Figure 10.83. Catalytic material can be a great help in a sensemaking session if it is presented as an optional resource, but not if it is presented as an authoritative analysis.

When it is used to achieve diversity and stimulate debate, it will succeed.

3. When catalytic material is used to reduce exposure to detailed content, it will fail. When it is used to facilitate and guide exposure to detailed content, it will succeed.

Certainly there are times and places to resolve, agree, and summarize. There are times to come to decisions, make plans, and firm up goals. Those times are *not* the times in which catalytic material is useful. It is useful *before* those times begin, in the times of expansion and exploration.

SUMMARY

Narrative catalysis begins with tasks standard to any data analysis project: *preparing data* and *verifying data integrity*. In those steps it is necessary to make sure you are working with what people actually said, not some misunderstood or mangled version of reality. The step of *scoping your exploration* is where you fit your plans to your time frame and goals. *Producing results* means generating graphs and statistical results that analyze the numerical data you have collected: counts, values, ratios. *Accumulation of observations* is a simple process of filtering remarkable from unremarkable results and describing the patterns seen.

It is in the next stage that catalysis departs from its sister process of analysis. Each observation is not given one interpretation but described from at least two *competing views*. These interpretations drive *exploration* of the stories and other data from multiple perspectives.

Finally, the explored interpretations are *clustered* into groups, and the entire exploration is used to create a summarized, accessible report ready to be used to support thought and discussion. Such catalytic material can be used fruitfully in many different settings, as long as it is used to energize inquiry, stimulate debate, and guide exposure to detailed content.

QUESTIONS

Consider the eight stages of narrative catalysis. In which of these stages do you think the tasks required are the best fit for your particular skills? Are you good at carefully entering and verifying data? Do you excel at creating clear diagrams? Does sorting through patterns seem easy to you? How about considering things from multiple points of view? What are your strong and weak points in relation to the tasks of catalysis? Might you want to seek help on some tasks from people who complement your skills?

Many elements of catalysis vary depending on the context and purposes of each particular project. When you think of yourself, and your community or organization, and the project or projects you hope to carry out, what shape do you think *your* catalysis will take on? Where will it be constrained by custom or expectation or practical issues, and where will it be free to expand? Are there some things you can't guess at in advance, like how a catalysis report might be received? How should you shape your work to deal with those uncertainties?

What do you think of the concept of narrative catalysis? Do you think the process is superior to the kind of analysis that produces conclusive answers? Can you advocate for and against catalysis as part of narrative project support? What are its strong and weak points? Now think about your answers to the first two questions above. How do those answers work together? Where does the nature of catalysis itself, as opposed to analysis, intersect with the particular characteristics of yourself and your community or organization? Do you see dangers and opportunities there?

ACTIVITIES

The best activity you can do to prepare yourself to do narrative catalysis is … to do narrative catalysis. All you need is some stories and some answers to questions to work with. Folk tale collections are excellent sources of stories with which you can practice narrative catalysis. Aesop's Fables, for example, are brief yet deep in meaning (and they are easily available on the internet). Pick out twenty or thirty stories, then answer three or four questions about each of them yourself. Use simple questions like "What emotion is strongest in this story?" or "To what extent does the main character of this story show exemplary behavior?"

If you want to practice doing all the comparisons described in this chapter, include at least one scale question and at least one choice question. Two of each would be best, because that way you would produce two bar graphs (choices), two histograms (scales), one contingency graph (choice x choice), four groups of subset histograms (scale x choice), one scatterplot (scale x scale), and two groups of subset scatterplots (scale x scale x choice). If you had (or created by lumping) three possible answers for each choice question, that would make twenty-four graphs in total (respectively, $2 + 2 + 1 + (2 * 2 * 3) + 1 + (1 * 2 * 3) = 24$). After you have your results, go through each of the steps outlined in this chapter and produce a simple report. But do this whole thing quickly; don't allow yourself to fuss over details. Catalysis doesn't have to be perfect the first time you do it; there just has to *be* a first time so you can come back and improve on it the *second* time you do it. A "dry run" through the catalysis process will prepare you to work with the stories you collect in your own community or organization.

Another mind-stretching activity is to go through the same catalysis process described above, but use *all three methods* of producing results in the same project. Make the same graphs by hand, using a spreadsheet, and using a dedicated data graphing and analysis package. If that's too much work, reduce the number of graphs you produce by not going down some of the more detailed paths. If you toss out the subset histograms and scatterplots, you will only be producing six graphs $(2 + 2 + 1 + 1)$. After you have produced your results in three ways, proceed to do the rest of the steps of catalysis. You are guaranteed to learn more about the process of narrative catalysis by doing it in three ways at once than you can learn by doing it in only one way. Each method of producing results has unique benefits and provides unique insights. Pay special attention to the methods you have little experience using, because they are likely to hold the greatest surprises.

Making sense of names somebody else gave to concepts can be a stumbling block in making a process work for you. With that in mind, reread the section of this chapter called "Principles of catalysis" (page 219). For each of those principles, think about what is written there and come up with your own explanation for why catalysis should be that way. If you don't think it should, think about that too. Maybe some of your own principles will be a bit more loose or tight than the ones I have written up here. Write your own principles of catalysis (then prepare to revise them as you gain more experience!). It is better to do this activity *after* you have gone through at least one catalysis process, whether you use folk tales or your own collected stories. You will probably not be ready to rewrite the principles until you've gone through the process yourself.

Chapter Eleven

Narrative Sensemaking

This chapter helps you help people in your community or organization work with collected stories together. The chapter begins with a definition of the term "sensemaking," describing its application to story work. The chapter then outlines four essential elements of effective narrative sensemaking (contact, churning, convergence, and change) and explains how to enable and support each element in practice. Finally, the chapter ends with advice on planning, setting up, and ending sensemaking sessions.

AN INTRODUCTION TO SENSEMAKING

Sensemaking is what people do when they think about situations as they face challenges and dilemmas. Group sensemaking is the same thing, only in a group. Narrative sensemaking is the same thing, only paying particular attention to the roles of storytelling and listening in the process. Narrative sensemaking in PNI can be natural and unaided, with simple discussion and sharing; and it can be organized and facilitated, with exercises and outcomes. Narrative sensemaking plays a big part in PNI because it helps communities and organizations create bridges between the stories they collect and the decisions they need to make. It's that simple.

What does narrative sensemaking in PNI look like? It usually looks like some people in a room together for a few hours, doing things with collected stories. Reading them, listening to them, talking about them, telling more stories in re-

sponse to them, and sometimes building larger stories with them in simple or complicated exercises. This activity can result in any or all of three things, which impact the project as a whole: an *experience* the people remember; a *record* of what went on in the sensemaking session; and some kind of *outcome* of the session, such as lists of stories, recommendations, ideas, concerns, and so on.

How can you as a PNI practitioner incorporate narrative sensemaking into your PNI projects? First of all, you don't need to *do* anything to incorporate narrative sensemaking into your projects. Every PNI project *already* contains a sensemaking phase, whether you plan one or not.

Any time you collect stories, whether it is an organized campaign or involves simply sitting down and listening to people, *somebody* is going to think about the stories, and somebody is going to return the stories to the community in some way. You could say that the PNI wheel is set in motion by the act of collecting stories, and that sensemaking and return follow as a natural result. Even an action as simple as asking an elder at a family gathering about their childhood starts a simple PNI wheel going. Indeed, this is a perfectly valid PNI project, as valid as one with a huge budget and printed reports.

At its simplest, PNI simply describes how people work with stories naturally. Even at its most complex, PNI builds upon that essential foundation.

Okay, you say, *let me rephrase the question. What can I do to improve the narrative sensemaking that goes on in my PNI projects?* You can learn what sensemaking is and how it works. You can learn how to support group narrative sensemaking. You can learn how to help people go through some organized exercises that make narrative sensemaking more productive. You can learn enough about sensemaking to grow your own sensemaking sessions made up of some sensemaking without exercises, some planned exercises (perhaps fitted together in a unique way), and some new exercises of your own creation, suited to your own situation like no packaged exercise can be. That's a lot, but

I believe you *can* do all that, with practice and patience.

Deeper into sensemaking

Are you ready to step deeper in to sensemaking? Let's start by working out a more detailed definition of the term we can use in practice.

The term "sensemaking" (and its hyphenated cousin "sense-making") originated in the research work of at least three groups. The organizational theorist Karl Weick is considered by many to be the originator of the term, which he first used in the 1970s (though his work drew on related prior scholarship by a number of social scientists and psychologists). At some point before or after that (it's murky) the term was also used by a group of researchers at Xerox PARC (led by Daniel Russell) to talk about the design of computer interfaces, and by the communication researcher Brenda Dervin to talk about the design of information systems. Each person or group put their own particular spin on the word, and people who talk about sensemaking today generally have read *something* written by one or more of these people or groups.

Why is sensemaking such a useful word? On the face of it, the word means what it says: making sense of things. But if that was all it meant, we might as well just define it as *being alive,* because making sense of things is what we all do every day. It can't mean *everything.*

I would love to put right here a simple quote (from somebody else's book) that clearly and brilliantly sums up sensemaking in one sentence or paragraph, so I don't have to explain it myself. I *could* send you off to read all of what has been written by Weick, Dervin, and others on the subject, but the fact is, I don't think *anybody* has yet done a great job of explaining what exactly is meant by this useful term. As far as I can tell, people seem to just struggle through tolerating it until it starts making sense to them. It's hard to point you at *any* definition of the term that doesn't seem designed to confuse you.

Here, for example, is an explanation from a 2005 paper by Karl Weick, Kathleen Sutcliffe, and David Obstfeld:

Sensemaking involves the ongoing retrospective development of plausible images that rationalize what people are doing. Viewed as a significant process of organizing, sensemaking unfolds as a sequence in which people concerned with identity in the social context of other actors engage ongoing circumstances from which they extract cues and make plausible sense retrospectively, while enacting more or less order into those ongoing circumstances.

Still awake?

How about a quote from Brenda Dervin (from the book *Sense-Making Methodology Reader*)? Will that clear things up?

Perhaps most fundamental of Sense-Making's metatheoretical assumptions is the idea of the human, a body-mind-heart-spirit living in a time-space, moving from a past, in a present, to a future, anchored in material conditions; yet at the same time with an assumed capacity to sense-make abstractions, dreams, memories, plans, ambitions, fantasies, stories, pretenses that can both transcend time-space and last beyond specific moments in time-space.

With all due respect to both Weick and Dervin, this is hard going.

To help clear things up for you, I spent some time looking through some of the most influential works on sensemaking (some easy to read, some not-so-much) and thinking through my own experiences with supporting sensemaking in practice. I whittled things down to the most essential aspects of sensemaking you need to know about in order to make good use of the term yourself. To make it easier to remember, I created a memory device out of three alliterative words: pertinent, practical, and playful.

Sensemaking is pertinent

Sensemaking happens for reasons that matter in situations that matter. Sensemaking centers on and surrounds the making of decisions. It comes between the information you perceive and the decision you make, and it comes between the decision you made and the explanation you give of it. Sensemaking is not random, meandering, abstract thought; it has a goal in a context, even when you don't realize or understand it. When you stand in front of your cupboard pondering whether you like your peanut butter best on a spoon or on toast, that's not sensemaking. It's just pondering. When you stand in front of your cupboard deciding what you want to make for your dinner party guests, then later reflect on what you made for your dinner party guests (and how that worked out), that *is* sensemaking, because *it happened for a reason and in a situation that mattered to you.*

When I say that sensemaking centers on the making of decisions, I don't mean to imply that it is merely secondary to or dependent on decision making. It is far more powerful than that. Sensemaking can change the nature of decision making itself. As people make sense of things, they sometimes discover new possibilities that lead them in directions and to decisions they would have never thought possible. Sensemaking and decision making are more like binary stars than they are like star and planet.

Weick calls this applied aspect of sensemaking *enactment;* he says that the activity of sensemaking is *effortful,* not passive; and he says it has to do with *priorities* and the extraction of relevant *cues* from the totality of experience. Dervin speaks about sensemaking as the act of building a *bridge* across a *gap* between the current *situation* and desired *outcomes.* Russell et al. speak of *task-specific* sensemaking activities.

Sensemaking is practical

Sensemaking happens in real life. Sensemaking is grounded in concrete reality, whether it involves one person or a family, organization or society. Abstract analysis and scientific proof are not included in sensemaking, because they are not grounded in the reality of people making unique decisions about their unique lives.

Weick speaks of the importance of *identity* and *social context* to sensemaking, how they both influence and are influenced by it. Central to the sensemaking process as described by Russell et al. are *frames* or *schemas,* ways of looking at the world particular to individuals or groups based on their unique histories and characteristics.

Dervin speaks of sensemaking as including the entire gamut of ways in which real people meet real challenges: not just rational thought but also emotion, intuition, and imagination. She also includes in her definition of sensemaking aspects of thought often excluded from what is considered correct or reasonable, such as power-brokering, the suppression of uncomfortable facts, and the creation of fantasies and illusions. These too are sensemaking activities, because they are human activities whose purpose is to thrive in the world.

Sensemaking is playful

Sensemaking happens improvisationally. It is less about organization, sorting and ranking than it is about construction, connection, and juxtaposition. Ordered methods of thinking, such as making lists and comparing options, may be *incorporated* into sensemaking; but they do not limit or define it. Sensemaking is about *preparing* for the future, not *predicting* it. It is about *processing* the past, not *proving* anything about it.

Weick says that sensemaking favors *plausibility over accuracy,* by which he means that it is more about what *works* than what *is.* Weick also talks about the importance to sensemaking of *ontological oscillation,* or rapid shuttling among different ways of looking at the world. This is also a feature of play.

Dervin speaks of the *verbings* of sensemaking; of simultaneous views from many perspectives; of the importance of gaps and muddles; and of the play between fluid and rigid, individual and group, order and chaos.

Russell et al. speak of a *learning loop complex* in which people (a) search for frames they can use to represent the situation at hand, (b) build representations of the situation using those chosen frames, (c) *shift* those frames where they don't fit with what has been observed, and (d) use the framed information to make decisions. I find their representation of this process to be somewhat limited by its machine-like frame; but if you look closely, it has elements of play in it. Repeatedly choosing from, building and adapting plausible representations with which to explore pertinent topics is something children do all day (and adults do when they forget to pretend they can't).

Finally, all of these authors speak of the importance of *time* in sensemaking: that it radiates out into the past and future. This is another playful element, because play is often about making sense of things that have happened and that could or couldn't or should or shouldn't happen in the future.

To sum up: Sensemaking is thinking about things in ways that are *pertinent* to decisions we will make or have made, of *practical* application to our real lives, and experimentally, improvisationally *playful*.

Sensemaking illustrated

Let me illustrate these three aspects of sensemaking with an example. Let's pretend you need to buy a car. Maybe your old car is dying, or you've never had a car before but need one now. What sort of car do you want to buy? How much will you pay? Will it be new or used? What brand? What style? With what features? What will it run on? Are you *sure* you need a car? All of these questions will need to be answered before you can make a final decision (see Figure 11.1 on the next page).

How will you go about preparing to make this decision? You might look at reviews of cars on the internet or in magazines. You might look through tables comparing safety ratings, maintenance costs, reported fuel consumption, customer satisfaction. You might visit a few car dealerships and drive some cars. You might read about the experiences of people who bought particular brands of car. You might talk to family and friends and neighbors about their cars. You might even ask people you see in parking lots how they like their cars. You might remember cars you or others had in the past. You might also think about your needs for a car and how they have changed over time. Is safety more important now than it was then? How about cargo capacity? Fuel efficiency?

After you have made the decision of what car to buy, and you have bought the car, what do you do afterward? How do you begin using the car? How do your perceptions of it change as you drive it? How do you tell the story to your-

self, and to your family and friends, about your choice? Do you experience buyer's remorse? Do you discover unexpected benefits? If someone comes to you for advice about their own decision-making process, what do you say to them? Figure 11.2 on the facing page shows how sensemaking plays a part after your decision.

We use the term sensemaking to describe all of the thoughts and actions that surround and pertain to your car-purchase decision. These thoughts and actions are *pertinent*, because you would not be doing them at all if you did not plan to make a decision about a car. They are *practical*, because you are not thinking about cars in the abstract; you are thinking about *your* car, *your* life, and *your* needs. Finally, your thoughts and actions are *playful*, because you play out possible scenarios that might result from different choices, both before and after the decision has been made.

Now for a contrast, let's say that I am the director of an organization that tests cars for safety. My team maintains a comprehensive web site listing our test results for each make and model of car being sold in the country. What sorts of things does my team do? We obtain representative cars of each make and model; we carefully test them under conditions of consistency and transparency; we publish the results; we provide clear and useful tools to consumers so they can make informed decisions.

Is our data collection and preparation process sensemaking? No, it is not. It is not *pertinent* in the sense of being related to any decision we *ourselves* are making. The information we produce *does* pertain to the decisions of those who seek it, but our activity is not pertinent to any decisions *we* are making about cars *we* are thinking about buying. Our work is not *practical*—to us—because it is not related to our *own* car purchases. And it is not at all *playful;* it follows exact procedures we have created outside the activity itself. (See Figure 11.3 on page 304.)

If you want to find sensemaking in my activity as the director of the safety-testing organization, you can certainly find it; but you must look in the spaces that surround our testing procedures (Figure 11.4 on page 304). For example, we must decide such things as: From what groups will we accept funding? How will

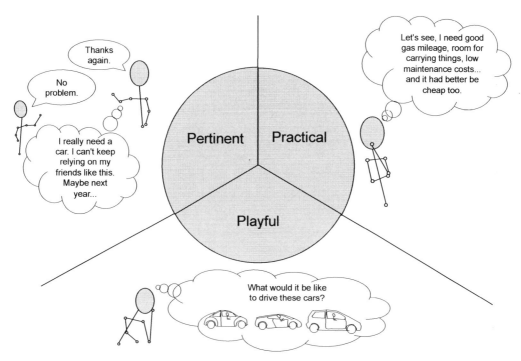

Figure 11.1. A person thinking about buying a car does sensemaking as they consider their needs and options.

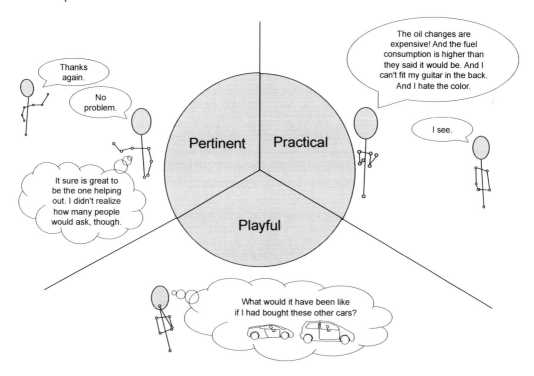

Figure 11.2. After the person has bought their car, they are still doing sensemaking, only now it's about how the decision played out.

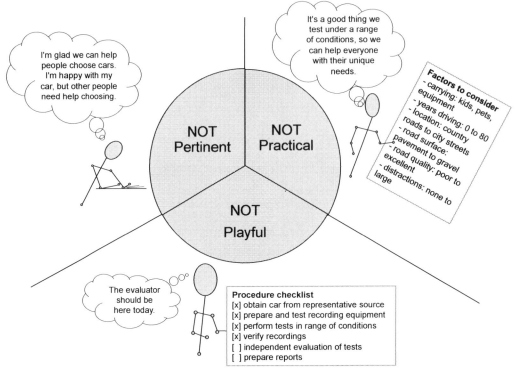

Figure 11.3. People who test cars for safety are not doing sensemaking when they follow procedures to help a large number of people (not just themselves) choose cars.

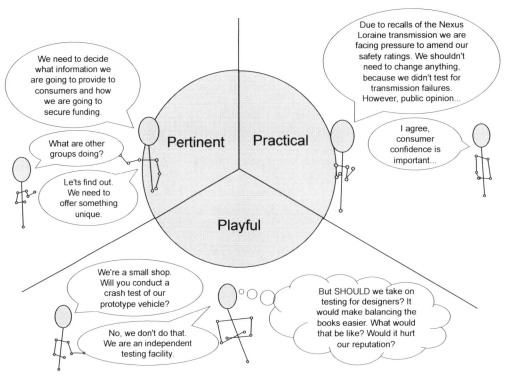

Figure 11.4. People who test cars for safety are doing sensemaking when they make decisions about how their organization will operate.

that choice impact views of the independence and trustworthiness of our reported results? How will we make sure we obtain representative cars similar to those any consumer might purchase? Which safety features will we prioritize? How will we speak to consumers, manufacturers, lawmakers? Will we attempt to lobby politically for safer vehicular design? Or will we choose to prioritize influencing consumer behavior? Making these decisions requires pertinent, practical, and playful work. That's sensemaking.

If you find this whole section confusing, put this book down. Don't read the rest of this chapter yet. As I write the rest of this chapter I will simply *have* to assume you understand what I'm trying to get at when I say "sensemaking." Maybe you *don't* understand.

If what I have written above did not adequately convey to you what the word "sensemaking" means, I suggest you look elsewhere for a better definition. Just because *I* couldn't find one doesn't mean *you* can't. A lot of people have written about this topic. I find reading the writings of Weick and Dervin on sensemaking to be equally frustrating and enlightening, but maybe that's just me. I've always thought that for every reader there is a writer (and vice versa), so maybe you will find someone who can help you understand this idea better than I can. Don't worry; I'm not jealous. I'll be here when you come back.

ADDING NARRATIVE TO SENSEMAKING

I've said above that sensemaking describes what people do as they make decisions that is pertinent, practical, and playful. Can you think of something *else* people do as they make decisions that is pertinent, practical, and playful? Hint: it has something to do with this book. Yes, it's telling and listening to stories. Stories *pertain* to things we make decisions about; they connect to our *practical* needs; and they bring *play* into our thinking.

Storytelling and sensemaking are not synonymous, nor does either contain the other. There is storytelling outside of sensemaking, because there are reasons to tell and hear stories that

don't connect directly to decision making. Stories can bind a community together, for example, or explain complex concepts, or entertain with humor, or communicate rules.

There is sensemaking outside of storytelling too: the comparison of options, the presentation of arguments, the discovery of connections between facts. Still, the two activities do connect and influence each other, like intersecting sets in a Venn diagram. When I speak of narrative sensemaking, I mean the place where the two sets intersect.

Some people might say the whole sensemaking circle is saturated with stories, but that isn't what I've seen. It's like what I said earlier in the book about how some people think in stories more than others. In the sensemaking of some people and some groups in some contexts, narrative is very strongly involved; and for some people and groups and contexts it is far less strongly involved.

To explain more explicitly why PNI and sensemaking go together so well, in Table 11.1 on the next page I link the PNI principles set out in the Introduction to PNI chapter (page 89) with the three aspects of sensemaking (pertinent, practical, playful) described in this chapter.

FOUR ESSENTIAL ELEMENTS OF EFFECTIVE NARRATIVE SENSEMAKING

At this point in the chapter we've talked about what sensemaking means, and we've talked about where it connects with stories and with PNI. Now here's what I think you need next. Knowing that sensemaking is pertinent, practical, and playful is not enough. You want to know what you can *do* to make sensemaking happen.

To figure out how to explain this to you, I have thought about what every successful sensemaking session I've ever seen has had in it that made it work, no matter how varied it might be in its specific context. Here's what I have come up with. In my experience, a successful PNI sensemaking session features elements of *contact, churning, convergence* and *change*. Let's examine the four elements one by one.

Sensemaking is	And PNI says	And these are related because
Pertinent	It's all about decisions.	Both PNI and sensemaking share an emphasis on decisions as the central point of what is being defined or made use of.
	PNI helps stories get to where they need to go.	PNI is not about simply recording history or connecting people. It is about making stories more pertinent to decision making by getting the right stories to the right people at the right time (and in the right way) to make the best decisions they can make.
	Don't boil stories down, and don't boil them out; boil them up.	The reason not to boil stories down is that effective sensemaking requires full contact with the detailed emotions and perspectives found in true stories.
Practical	People know their stories.	Both PNI and sensemaking are grounded in the reality of the people involved. Keeping things grounded means keeping the stories within reach of their tellers.
	Don't mess with the stories.	Changing stories, perhaps to make them more articulate or easier to read, may seem like a good way to improve their transmission for sensemaking. But it is impossible to "improve" a story in a way that does not compromise its authenticity. This fits with the idea in sensemaking of "frames," or ways of looking at events that may not survive a translation of the story to a more universal form.
Playful	The play's the thing.	It would not be wrong to say that PNI is a form of serious, adult, coordinated, purposeful play. Sensemaking too incorporates improvisational elements of play.
	Stories nest.	The fact that stories can contain (without altering) nested stories makes them a useful tool for participatory work. This is also a playful aspect of sensemaking, a way to prepare for the future and process the past. Weick's ontological oscillation is a form of nesting, in which one overall frame supports within it two opposing views.
	If you do not make PNI your own, you are not doing PNI.	You *could* call this a practical aspect of PNI, but the more important aspect here is improvisation, or the fitting of the general to the specific. There is no such thing as generic, context-free sensemaking, and there is no such thing as generic, context-free PNI.

Table 11.1. A comparison of PNI and sensemaking principles.

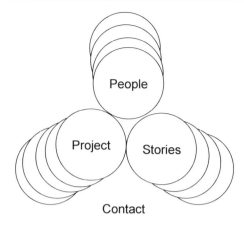

Figure 11.5. The first element of effective narrative sensemaking is that people, project, and stories should come into contact.

Contact

In order for people in a PNI project to make sense of its collected stories, interactions must take place between the *people,* the *stories,* and the *project.* Call it exposure, interface, proximity, communication: stories need to rub up against people and against the reason the stories were collected (see Figure 11.5).

I'd like to introduce three types of contact important in narrative sensemaking.

Contact between people and project

Contact between people and project means people understanding, accepting, and supporting the goals of the project. It also means people making the project their own through adapting its goals to their needs. If there is substantial conflict between the project's goals and the people's needs in a sensemaking session, it usually means the planning group didn't understand the needs of the people involved as they planned the project. Even when this does happen, there can be a negotiated compromise between the needs of the project and the needs of the people, at least to the extent that nobody has to leave the project (or the session) entirely.

Contact among people

Interpersonal contact means discussion, story exchange, and participation in group exercises. When it goes right, this means respectful attention and listening to the perspectives of others. It *doesn't* have to mean people agree! Some degree of constructive conflict can be useful in sensemaking, as long as people disagree on

ideas without attacking each other *personally.* You can also expect to see face-saving, avoidance, coalition building, rebellion, censoring, and all other normal aspects of group dynamics.

Contact between people and stories

People participating in sensemaking need to read or hear or otherwise experience some portion of the stories the project has collected. They need to get a sense not just of individual stories but of the body of collected stories as a whole.

Churning

After contact has been established, the next essential element is *repeated, varied* contact, or churning (Figure 11.6 on the next page). By this I mean not simply putting things together *once,* but putting them together and taking them apart many times in succession. Other synonyms for this element might be agitation, stirring, mixing, rearrangement, iterated juxtaposition, reshuffling, and recombination. It's as though somebody had a really big spoon (and a really big arm) to mash everything together with, over and over.

Why do you need churning for sensemaking to be effective? The magic of sensemaking, that thing-you-do that produces new ideas and discoveries, doesn't happen when you combine things *once.* It only happens when you combine them *many times in varied ways.* Churning in sensemaking is like plot development in stories: it is the journey that was begun by con-

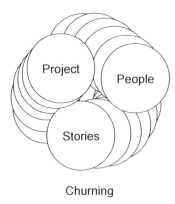

Churning

Figure 11.6. The second element of effective narrative sensemaking is churning: repeated, varied contact between people, project, and stories.

tact. No story is complete without the twists and turns of plot, and no sensemaking session is complete without some churning.

Churning between people and project

As session participants speak, listen, and negotiate, the reasons they have for doing what they are doing should shift and change. A session can start out being about one thing and end up being about another, without anyone becoming dissatisfied.

Churning among people

During sensemaking, people should move with and around each other physically, intellectually, and emotionally. Groups should form, interact, and dissolve as people explore meaning together.

Churning between people and stories

As stories are categorized and connected over and over in changing ways, new categories, new connections, and new meanings should emerge.

Convergence

After people, project, and stories have come into contact, and after things have been mixed and remixed many times, the third element of narrative sensemaking comes into play. Things begin to coalesce, clump, connect, cohere. What things? Discoveries, ideas, stories, goals, messages, values, learnings. (See Figure 11.7 on the facing page.)

Why is convergence essential for effective narrative sensemaking? Because without convergence, sensemaking doesn't follow through to effective decision support. Contact and churning produce small, isolated ideas and discoveries, but unless they join up to form something larger, they will dissipate after the session and become dissolved in the everyday.

I have seen narrative sensemaking sessions end without convergence. Churning follows contact, but nothing draws together. The time just runs out. People pack up their things and leave, still a bit confused and scattered, and go back to what they had been doing before the session started. There may be a recording of the session, but there is not much to *show* for what happened, in the sense of having arrived at any gathered conclusions that will support collective decisions. When convergence *does* happen, the session draws together in ways that prove useful later on.

Convergence between people and project

During sensemaking, the many projects in the minds of participants should negotiate compromises and linkages, until they are not as far apart as they were. They may never merge to become one grand project everyone can agree on, but they are likely to find common ground.

Convergence among people

The people participating in any sensemaking session should come to know each other better, either individually or in their roles in the community or organization. Gaps in understanding the perspectives of others should shrink during effective narrative sensemaking.

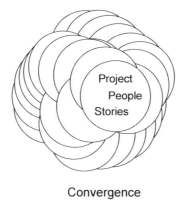

Convergence

Figure 11.7. The third element of effective narrative sensemaking is convergence: the creation of coherent, resonant meaning.

Convergence between people and stories

People who participate in sensemaking need to *connect* to the collected stories of the project. They might remember a story they read; they might discuss it; they might tell one or several stories related to it. The story, and the stories that surround it, might enter into the story of their own participation in the community or organization. If the people and stories don't draw together during sensemaking, it's unlikely anything useful will come out of it.

Change

If during your sensemaking session there has been contact, churning, and convergence of stories, people, and project, there should also be change (Figure 11.8 on the next page). Something should be different between the time before the session and the time after it. The change may take place during the session itself, or it may take place days or weeks later as people reflect on the experiences they had at the session. But *something* should change.

Why is change essential for effective narrative sensemaking? The goal of participatory narrative inquiry is to make better decisions together, and you can't use narrative sensemaking to meet that goal unless the sensemaking ends with change. Change in sensemaking completes the follow-through movement that goes from story collection into decision support and into the return of stories to the community.

You might say that change needs to take place during the intervention and return phases of PNI as well, and you'd be right to say that. The change that takes place during sensemaking tends to be intense, localized, and idiosyncratic, while change later on is diffuse, far-reaching, and cultural.

Change between people and project

The project you have *after* a sensemaking session should not be the same as the project you had *before* it. This should be true for everyone who attends the session. This type of change depends on who was at the session and what they did and said and experienced together.

Change among people

People who participate in sensemaking sessions should have different feelings of relationship to each other than they did before the session. They may never see those *particular* people again, but they should reason differently about people with those *characteristics* afterward. For example, a customer-facing staff member who has attended a sensemaking session *with* (not just about) customers should come out of it with a different understanding of customers than they went in with, and the same should be true for the customers.

Change between people and stories

People who have participated in sensemaking should come away from the experience with a new understanding of the topic because of the stories they encountered there. The body of collected stories used in the sensemaking should also grow in some way (in the number of stories, in interpretations, annotations, combinations, patterns, highlightings, mappings), and

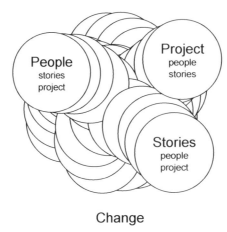

Change

Figure 11.8. The final element of effective narrative sensemaking is change: people, project, and stories are all different than they were before the session started.

this will be due to the unique identities of the people who worked with them in the session. The stories told in the community or organization will also change, even if what is written down does not reflect that.

FACILITATING THE FOUR ELEMENTS

Now that we've gone over the four elements in theory, it's time to start talking about what you can do to make sure they happen.

A note about sensemaking exercises. In this section I'll talk about sensemaking *without* exercises, because you don't need structured exercises to do sensemaking. Exercises are useful packages of procedure you can follow if you like, games to play together, and they have many uses. But they aren't the only way to do sensemaking, and they aren't even the best way in some situations. Even when you use exercises, you'll still need to know enough about supporting what happens *around* them (and under and over and between them) to make sensemaking work.

FACILITATING CONTACT

First let's talk about bringing people, project, and stories into contact in sensemaking. Because contact starts sensemaking going, it deserves more time than the other elements.

(What I mean by that is: brace yourself, because this is going to be a long section.)

Here I have tried to describe not what could happen in a perfect world, but what I have actually done and seen other people do, in real rooms with real people and real stories. You won't be doing exactly what I did or what I've seen other people do in your sensemaking sessions. You are bound to discover your own strengths and ideas as you support sensemaking in your own way.

Facilitating contact between people and project

How can you bring people and project into initial contact? I know of three ways: with a preparatory letter, with an orienting handout, and with an opening explanation. The more complicated the project, the more of these methods you need to use. Some projects will need all three, some will barely need the last.

Preparatory letters

You can start bringing people and project into contact days or weeks before your sensemaking session by sending a letter that explains why the session is being held and what people can expect to happen there.

The general rule about preparatory letters is: send them in situations in which people expect to receive them (see Figure 11.9 on the facing page). Pay attention to the *identities* the project calls to the front in the people you expect to participate. We are all bundles of identities, dif-

Figure 11.9. If you think people will expect to receive a preparatory letter, send them one. If you think it will alarm people, don't.

ferent people in different situations. With respect to the context of your project, who are your participants? What do they expect?

Some identities that might expect to receive a preparatory letter are professionals, managers, people embedded deep in bureaucracies, people used to being spoken to formally, respected elders, or just people who like to see things written down so they seem real, serious, worth spending time on. Anyone for whom any of these identities is foremost, in the context of the project, will contribute more in a sensemaking session if they are given the preparatory letter they expect to receive before an occasion that merits their attention. If they *don't* get such a letter, the occasion doesn't merit their attention, so even if they *come* to the meeting they might not *participate*.

Some identities that might be turned away by a preparatory letter are non-professionals, non-managers, working people, people not in an official or important or responsible position, people who see themselves as too "creative" to do formal things, people who don't like to plan ahead, people wary of official-sounding letters. Anyone for whom any of these identities is foremost, in the context of the project, will contribute *less* in a sensemaking session if they are given a preparatory letter. For example, say you're planning a sensemaking session among people on your street about upcoming town development. Sending out a formal prepara-

tory letter may seem out of place or even suspicious in that context. People might wonder why you're making it seem like you are some kind of authority, and what your motives might be for making things so formal. In that situation, for those people, in the identities the situation calls up in them, it would be better to just invite people to the meeting in person.

What does a preparatory letter look like? It should be brief (because no one will read it carefully), yet get across why the meeting is being held and what is expected out of those who participate. It might look something like this.

> Thank you for agreeing to participate in the New Roads project!
>
> Please come to **Room 212B** of the Community Center from **7–9 pm** on **Friday, October 21** for an idea session with other town residents.
>
> Together we will read and listen to stories we previously collected about town development, talk about our own experiences, and work together on ideas about what our town needs most.
>
> We hope to see you there! Your experiences and insights will help us make our town even better.
>
> If you have any questions, please call Sarah at 123–4567.

Figure 11.10. Don't use jargon if you don't have to. It puts people off, though they won't always tell you that.

Note that I didn't use the term "narrative sensemaking," using instead the less jargon-y (and totally made up) "idea session." In this book I am using jargon with *you*, but I use it for a very good reason: to have some way to say "a session in which people work with stories in order to support decision making by bringing things together lots of times" without having to write (and you read) that whole thing every time. But just because I use jargon to speak to *you*, that doesn't mean you should burden every participant in your project with it (see Figure 11.10).

Jargon is a device we use to contract words into smaller spaces. The jargon device saves time in the long run, but it relies on the investment of shared understandings, which take time to build up at first. In most of your interactions with participants in PNI projects, you won't have enough time to support the use of jargon, nor will you need to repeat yourself enough to make it worth investing in. The more times you need to say the same thing to the same person, the more reason there is to make the investment in jargon. If you expect to speak to a particular person exactly twice during your project, don't use the term "narrative sensemaking," because you and they won't benefit from it enough to make it worth all the explaining you have to do. However, if you expect to speak to a person fifty times during your project—perhaps they are especially interested, or they have volunteered to help—by all means use jar-

gon with *them*. There the investment will pay off.

One more thing about jargon: sometimes people use it not to save space but to make themselves seem more knowledgeable or authoritative, to themselves and others. You are likely to want to do that too. *Everyone* is susceptible to the draw of jargon as a creator of authority, myself included. I have put myself on jargon watch throughout this book project, trying to use it only when I think it will be *useful to you* rather than knowledgeable-sounding for me. I have eradicated as much jargon as I possibly could without writing a book twice as long. My advice in speaking to your PNI participants is to put yourself on jargon watch too. Don't spew fancy words when you feel under-confident; gain experience and build your confidence in other ways.

Why does this matter? Because explaining what jargon means takes time you need for other things. Because people don't always *tell* you when they don't understand what you are saying. Sometimes they just walk away and stop participating.

If you aren't sure whether something is jargon, show the things you are preparing to say or write to anyone who knows *nothing* about what you are doing. Ask your grandparent or grandchild or neighbor to look quickly over your preparatory letter. Ask them to read it back to you. Where do they get stuck? Why did they get stuck there? Don't *tell* them what the words mean; ask them what *they* think the words mean. If it's far off what you meant to say, rewrite the letter so it is more clear.

Finding the right words. Here's a question you might have right now. You might say: *If I don't want to call my session a "narrative sensemaking" session, what should I call it?* There are many names you can choose from, some more helpful than others. I suggest choosing a name that has these features.

Keep it positive. The name you use should have a *hopeful* slant. Mention ideas, issues, topics, and solutions. Don't mention problems or crises or dilemmas.

Keep it collaborative. The name should convey *participation*. People should *not* show up expecting to work on their own or listen to somebody else give a lecture. Use terms like workshop, session, working group, conversation, discussion, or dialogue. Don't call the session a presentation or seminar or conference or class. I also suggest avoiding the word "meeting" when possible. A meeting can be many things, but for most people it signals a structured gathering in which only some people speak and some people listen. You don't want people getting that idea.

Keep it open. The name should connote *discovery* rather than analysis. Talk about exploration, search, brainstorming, invention, innovation, solution gathering. Don't talk about calculation, investigation, review, explanation, measurement, or assessment. You might need to call a session an "evaluation" session, if that is its purpose, but prefix the word with "participatory" to make it clear that this is evaluation of a different sort. Another tricky word is "inquiry." I know it's the name of the method, but some people understand it to mean something to do with the police. Better to avoid it unless you are sure people understand you mean it as collaborative exploration, not the assignment of blame.

Once you have chosen a name for your session, stick with it. Use the same name on all your written and spoken statements, even to people who don't attend the session. That way nobody will be confused.

Orienting handouts

Another way you can create contact between people and project is by giving people an orienting handout as they enter the sensemaking session. I like doing this, myself. I find that people respond well to it. It is a demonstration of effort, a good faith offering, showing them that you will do your part in the work that lies ahead.

An orienting handout should be brief and simple, with just a few sentences on it. It should also be nice to look at: clear, clean, handsome. I like to use a Q&A format for the orienting handout, like this.

What's this meeting about? We are here to think together about revitalizing the downtown area.

How will we think together? We will start by considering some stories our townspeople have told us about their uses of town spaces.

Why stories? Because we want to think about different perspectives on development, and hearing about the experiences of our townspeople is a great way to do that. We will listen to stories and tell our own stories too.

What's our goal? To come up with some new ideas for downtown development.

What will be done with what we do here today? The session will *not* be recorded. We do plan to create some group constructions such as a timeline of stories, and those will be placed on the town's web site for everyone to see and discuss. Participation will be anonymous. (Questions? Concerns? Contact the town clerk at 123–4567.)

Note again the absence of jargon and the presence of clarity about what will be done with what is created.

You can also use orienting handouts to jump start collaboration. If your session is large enough to have multiple small groups, you can give out *only one* orienting handout per small group. This will give the people in each group something to share from the start of the session (see Figure 11.11 on the following page). If you

Figure 11.11. Giving each group only one copy of an orienting handout gives them something to negotiate over from the start, and it gives you information you need about the groups.

give each person a separate handout, that creates a relationship between you (the facilitator), the project, and the person *individually*. But if you want to have small groups work together, you want to create relationships *within* each group as well.

Handing out one orienting handout per group also gives you an opportunity to *observe* your small groups as they begin to negotiate how they will work together. For example, you might see one person grab their group's handout and place it "front and center"—centered in front of themselves, that is; and you might see others in the group react to that action, by moving the paper or themselves or both. In one way or another, people will use the document as an artifact of negotiation. Watching people do this can help you gain information up front on how you can help small groups work together in your session.

Opening explanations

No matter what you write down, the most important contact between people and project comes when you, the session facilitator, take a few minutes at the start of the session to explain what the project is about, what you hope to achieve, and what will be done with what is produced. You can't control whether people read *anything* you write, but you can usually get the attention of participants as you speak, at least if you keep things short and to the point.

They have already put in the effort to come to the session, so they are motivated to find out how they can make it a success.

The most important thing people need at the start of a sensemaking session is not *information*. It's *expectation*. People need to know what sort of gathering they are at so they know how to behave (see Figure 11.12 on the next page). Working together with collected stories is not something most people are used to doing. The first few minutes of the session is your time to set up the expectations that will make sensemaking work.

So what should you say? If you had the ideal audience, willing to sit quietly while you explained in perfect detail everything you wanted them to understand before you started your sensemaking session, you might say something like this.

> Today we will be reading [and possibly, listening to] and talking about stories previously collected in this project. We will give those stories our full and respectful attention.

> We may not *like* all of the stories we encounter. However, we agree to consider the collected stories as *legitimate recountings of lived experience*. To some extent we are putting aside considerations of fact and truth as we consider the

Figure 11.12. The most important thing people need at the start of a sensemaking session is not information. It's expectation.

experiences of those who told the stories. When we say that we consider a *story* legitimate, that does not have to mean that we accept as legitimate any *opinions* or version of *facts* expressed in it. Nor does it mean that we believe events really happened the way they were recounted.

As we consider these stories, we will tell some stories from our *own* experiences. The same rules for considering the previously collected stories will apply to stories told here. We will listen respectfully to the experiences recounted without either challenging or uncritically accepting facts or opinions. Everyone has a chance to tell their version of events *from their own experience* without censorship. However, we also agree that while telling stories we will avoid direct statements of opinion or fact. We will stick to describing *what has happened to us* and how we feel about it.

When I say "we will be working with stories today" you may think I mean we will be turning out big, complicated, polished, multi-media, Hollywood-style stories. That's *not* what we will be doing. We will be working with a different kind of stories today.

Every time you say "The bus was late today" or "That was the best sleep I've had in weeks" or "I forgot to buy apples at the store" you've told a story. *That's* the kind of story we will be working with to-

day: the stories of our community, our everyday, simple, raw, personal stories.

We can learn a lot just by thinking about *what has happened* to us and how we feel about it. This is true for the stories our project has already collected from people in our community, and it's true for the stories we will tell each other today. Why do we care about everyday stories? Because thinking and talking together about these experiences can help us make better decisions together. That's our final goal.

We are not here today to deal with facts or opinions. We are not here to debate, argue, or prove anything. We don't even need to reach agreement today. That is not our purpose. We are here today *to listen and to be listened to*.

We are here to see events through the eyes of others, and we are here to help others see events through our eyes. We are here to discover things we have never understood before, not about facts but about ourselves and about the people in our community, and about the experiences we and they have had. We are here to explore the topic of [what the project is about] through the eyes of everyone in our community, so we can find new ideas that will help everyone.

Some of the things we do today may be a bit outside your comfort zone. We will be asking you to do things you've never done before with people you may not know. You may have strong feelings about some of the topics we will consider. We don't want you to do *anything* you don't feel comfortable with. But we do ask you to keep an open mind and give the methods we will be using a try. Working with stories may seem strange or even silly to you, but we beg your indulgence in trying this approach. We know it works, and we have seen it work before. Let us show you how useful these methods can be for our community.

Please don't worry about doing anything wrong! Everything we will do today is entirely *natural* and as ancient as society. People tell stories every day, and they think about stories every day. We are just going to do this in a more concentrated way, with a more sustained purpose, and with greater attention to cooperation, than people usually do. But if you think you don't know how to work with stories, don't worry: you do. Everyone does.

Now I'll explain the process we will be going through. [And then a description of the session, broken into fifteen or thirty minute chunks of activity, ending with a description of the expected result to be created at the end of the session.]

Here are the records we will be keeping of the session. [And then a description of exactly how the session will be recorded and how anonymity, if any, will be preserved.]

Of course you couldn't actually *say* all of that in front of any group of real human beings. People would drift off and stop listening before you finished, if they didn't leave the room entirely. Let's see if we can trim it down to something you *can* say in front of a group.

> We are here today to work with *raw stories of personal experience* told by people in our community and by ourselves. Some stories have been recorded already, and we will tell some more. Please speak and listen with *respect* for the experiences of others.

> We are not here to debate or prove anything. We don't have to reach agreement. We are here *to listen and to be listened to*.

> We are also here to *discover new ideas* about [what the project is about] so that we can make better decisions together.

> Working with stories may seem strange, but in fact it is *ancient* and *natural*. Don't worry about doing this right. You already know how.

> Here's what we will do. [And then a very brief description of the process, product, and recording.]

That's quick, and you can write the important words (the ones I've placed in italics, plus a summary of the planned time slots) on a white board everyone can see.

Now let me ask you a question. After you explain the goals and basic plan for the session, should you stop and ask people if they need clarification? Should you ask them what *they* hope to achieve in the session? Should you ask people to participate in setting up plans and goals for the session with you?

Did you say yes? Well, the fact is, that all sounds great in theory, but in practice it's a bad idea (see Figure 11.13 on the facing page). I've seen people try to do this quite a few times. (Okay, one of them has been me.) It does not work. If you have already decided within your project planning group how the session will work out best, *don't* ask for input before you start. The session will just get derailed, and your results will be diminished. If you pause after your opening explanation, even for a minute, the session will go off its tracks. People will ask a million questions, attack the approach, drift off, propose doing something entirely different, and basically use up all the time and momentum you had. Don't let that happen. Just deliver your opening explanation, which you should have rehearsed so many times you can say it in your sleep (no, you *do* say it in your sleep). During the explanation, don't allow anyone to interrupt, and don't ask for input. Just say what you have to say, then plunge into the session itself.

I can imagine that some readers might find these instructions insufficiently participatory.

Figure 11.13. Don't ask for feedback or questions at the start of the session; things will get derailed. Just plunge in.

Don't get "buy-in" at the start of the session? Railroad people into doing what you say? Yes, but there's a good reason for it. Two reasons, actually. The first reason has to do with the nature of story work. Memorize this fact: *nobody understands story work until they do it*. It's just not something that is easily explained. People new to story work *always* misunderstand it, and they go on misunderstanding it right up until the moment when they understand it. So don't let people talk you out of what you plan to do: just ask them to leap into it with you. Sometimes I even ask people to "take a leap" into the session with me, because "all will become clear" in time. (And it *does* become clear, and I *know* it does, so when I *say* it does people *believe* me, so it *does*.)

The second reason not to stop and gather input is that in the situations in which narrative sensemaking is *most* useful to address a topic, people are *least* likely to understand their own goals about the topic. They may discover their goals for the session only as the session unfolds. This may also be true for you. *Don't worry about it.* You don't need to know exactly what you want or need before the session starts. It's not that kind of session. *Let the stories tell you* about your goals as you go. Share the session with your participants, not only in its *content* but in its *intent*.

The great thing about story work, unlike simple discussion or debate, is that it works *even better* when goals are unclear or unarticulated.

This is because it depends less on the rational surface level and more on the oblique, intuitive, allegorical, emotional, underlying, moving, shifting depths; and for *those* things, mixing in more goals (without articulating them) only increases the richness of the exploration.

Facilitating contact among people

Now that we've covered initial contact between people and project, let's turn our attention to people coming into contact with other people.

Interpersonal contact in sensemaking is all about small groups. The advice I gave you on small groups in story collection sessions applies here as well, so you might want to go back and look over that section again (see "Small groups for quiet story exchange" on page 170).

In forming groups, balance comfort with diversity, as before, though the balance should be a bit further on the scale towards diversity than comfort for sensemaking. That's because the goal of the session is less revelation and more working with previous revelation.

As before, you can form groups through *assignment* (assigning people to groups yourself), *rule* (you give people an assembly rule, leaving them to apply it) or *self-assembly* (you ask people to form groups but don't tell them how). That's the same.

Again, don't have only two groups if you can help it, because they will compete in sensemaking just as they do in storytelling. The only difference I can point to is that in sensemaking a group as small as two people *will* work. Pairs don't tell stories easily, but they are usually able to carry out a task together. That's probably because it doesn't feel like a performance, so they don't need an audience; they just need a team.

I don't have more to say about facilitating interpersonal contact, but that's because *lots* of *other* people do, so you don't need me to cover it. There is a wide literature on facilitating small groups. Search for "small groups" and "group dynamics" on the internet and you'll find much to explore. The dynamics of small-group facilitation are not very different in story work than they are in any other kind of collaborative group work. Read as much as you can, and talk to experienced people, about facilitating small groups of people doing things together. And practice.

Facilitating contact between people and stories

Facilitating people-story contact means understanding what people need as they begin to work with stories. Of the three combinations covered in this chapter (people-project, people-people, people-stories), I think this one has the highest possibility of success *and* the highest risk of failure in practice. Why? Because there are *so* many different ways you can bring people and stories together.

Come and walk with me, if you will, into three different sensemaking sessions taking place in three different rooms.

In Session A, twenty people are working with two hundred stories. Each person is huddled over their own laptop computer, peering at stories embedded in a spreadsheet along with masses of other data and graphs. In *theory* the people are talking together about the stories and making sense of them. But in practice it's hard to focus on any particular story in the masses of data, and it's hard for two people to look at a laptop screen together. Sometimes a person finds a story interesting, but it's such a hassle to explain to anyone else *which* story it is that they eventually give up and exchange less and less information as the session wears on. One person is writing down ideas and recommendations as they come up, and some do

come up, but the conversation keeps drifting off the subject. Some people are surreptitiously checking their email and only half listening to the conversation.

Down the hall in Session B, another twenty people are working with another two hundred stories. In this room one person is presenting the stories and graphs, one after another, to the group. The room is dark because the stories and graphs are displayed on a projection screen. Some people in the audience are listening, watching, and taking notes; some are arguing with the presenter; some are checking their email; some are asleep. The presenter wants to be able to claim that they have shown the group all the stories they selected as being most important in the time they have. It is important to them that they can claim that people have seen the stories, because they promised to include group sensemaking in the project. Once all of the stories have been shown, the presenter hands each participant a survey sheet with questions about what policy changes they recommend.

Now let's walk over to Session C. Here another twenty people are working with another two hundred stories. But these people are not peering into computer screens or sitting in the dark; they are walking around the room reading and talking together. Three of the four walls of the room are covered from floor to ceiling with stories. Each story is printed large enough to be read by several people at once from several feet away, with titles (given by the storytellers) prominently shown. Answers given by the storytellers to questions about their stories are shown beneath each story in smaller print. Scattered among the printed stories are graphs that show patterns among the answers, with provoking, competing catalytic interpretations beneath each one. The people point at, touch, and read aloud from the stories and patterns on the walls as they stand together looking at them.

On a large table in Session C, next to the coffee and cookies, are heaps of sensemaking supplies: sticky notes, colored markers, strings, tape, thumbtacks, glue sticks. The session participants frequently visit the table to get more food and supplies. What are they doing with the

These people are working with stories. | These people are working with stories. | These people are working with stories.

Figure 11.14. People can work with stories in a wide variety of ways, but some ways are more participatory (and productive) than others.

supplies? They are annotating the stories and graphs in the room as they speak about them. Some are linked together with strings and tape; some have large colored circles drawn on them; some are marked with symbols that reappear in other locations; some have sticky notes on them. On the fourth wall, the participants are building a landscape. On it are labels and drawings marking the meanings of certain areas, as well as sticky notes with names of stories and graphs, symbols drawn on multiple stories, colors, strings, and tape. As the session winds down, the participants begin listing outcomes of the session, under these headings: discoveries, ideas, suggestions, conflicts. The session runs a half-hour over, but nobody leaves the room: they know they are getting somewhere worth going.

In all of these sensemaking sessions people are coming into contact with stories, but the results could not be more different (see Figure 11.14). Of course these are caricatures, of two unimaginably bad sessions and one impossibly perfect one, but you get the point, I hope: that the way in which people come into contact with stories during sensemaking can have a huge impact on the value of sensemaking. Because of this huge impact, we will be spending more time on this aspect of facilitation than on any of the other combinations of element (contact, churning, convergence, change) and interaction (people-project, people-people, people-story) in this series.

To think about how a facilitator can support effective contact between people and stories, we can turn to supporting work, mainly in the fields of information design and data visualization, by people who have thought (a lot more than I have) about what people need as they contact information.

In his classic 1996 paper called "The Eyes Have It," Ben Shneiderman compiled a list of seven tasks people need help with when they work with collected bodies of information. I've found Shneiderman's tasks useful in thinking about helping people work with stories in sensemaking sessions. So let's use them to organize our thinking in this section.

In Shneiderman's words, the tasks are:

Overview: Gain an overview of the entire collection.

Zoom: Zoom in on items of interest.

Filter: Filter out uninteresting items.

Details-on-demand: Select an item or group and get details when needed.

Relate: View relationships among items.

History: Keep a history of actions to support undo, replay, and progressive refinement.

Extract: Allow extraction of sub-collections and of the query parameters.

For each of these tasks, I'll talk about what people need to use it in narrative sensemaking and how you can help them get it.

Let's make up an example context to explore. Say you are in a room with ten other people who are considering a hundred previously col-

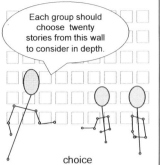

Figure 11.15. These are all valid ways of drawing samples from your collected stories in sensemaking.

lected stories, some told by themselves but most told by others in your community or organization. What do the people need you to help them do, and how should you help them?

Overview

You need to help *all* of the people in your sensemaking session become aware of *all* of the collected stories. Ideally you could just have everyone read or listen to every collected story, but in practice that is usually impossible due to time constraints. Generally it is necessary to *sample* the collected stories as sensemaking begins.

Ways to sample stories. I know of three ways to sample stories, each with its own merits (see Figure 11.15 for an illustration).

Pre-assigning stories. You can hand out *packets* of story cards in pre-sampled groups based on how many stories you think people will be willing and able to read in the time you have. The benefit of using prepared story packets is that you can control how the stories are sampled; you can design the session so it best meets the goals of the project. The detriment is that prepared packets may reduce participatory enthusiasm, because people may feel that your act in selecting what stories they will read (even if it's random) prevents them from starting the session in a participatory way.

(What are *story cards?* Just index-card-sized pieces of paper with the text, title, and answers to questions for each collected story written or printed on them. Using thick paper makes the cards easy to pick up and move around.)

To assemble story packets, you can choose stories *randomly,* either *with replacement* (the same story can be in two packets) or *without replacement* (a story can be in only one packet). Or you can *range* the stories within any one packet so that they cover an axis of variation important to the project, like the age or the stated political affiliation of the storyteller. You can also do this with or without replacement. The ranged approach makes sure that every participant starts the session with a view from multiple perspectives (and is most useful when a project goal is mutual understanding).

Asking people to choose stories. If you don't want to hand out prepared packets of stories, you can instead present all the stories you have collected and ask people to choose some stories to read. You can ask people to choose *without replacement* by having only one set of story cards for the whole room, or you can ask people to choose *with replacement* by having multiple copies of each story card (perhaps with a "pack" or "deck" of story cards for each table).

How can people choose stories to read without reading them? They can skim them. They can read each story's title and some scattered words on it, then choose to read it in full or move along. In fact, one benefit of this method is that it accommodates varying reading speeds. Some people read faster than others, and some people skim faster than others too. If you give people control over how many stories they will skim (in order to choose how many stories they will read in detail) you don't have the problem of fast readers reading half of the stories they could have read in the time. You don't have to

Figure 11.16. These are all valid ways of having people experience the stories they have sampled from your story collection.

specify the number of stories, either. You can just ask people to choose some stories and give them ten minutes to do it in. Some people will choose three, some will choose seven, some will choose twenty. That's fine, as long as people have become collectively exposed to the overview of the stories.

Asking people to play a game in which they choose stories. You also have the option of making story sampling into a participatory game, with rules like "You must have at least one story from each age group" or "Choose stories in pairs with opposing views on the topic we are exploring" or "You can't have more than two stories out of ten from any one part of town."

Ways to experience stories. After people have been given or have chosen some stories to consider, how should they *experience* those stories? (Not skim: fully consider.) To decide, think about these questions (see Figure 11.16).

Should people read or hear the stories? Reading is usually faster, but it's not when people can't read well or have difficulty seeing. If some can and some can't read well, all should listen, so the contact is even.

Should people experience the stories separately or in groups? If your stories are about a sensitive or taboo topic, separate experiences are better during initial contact. Later, people can experience additional stories in groups, but that first contact should be private.

If your stories are not sensitive, the answer to this question hinges on whether people are motivated to participate. People who are highly motivated to participate will do a quiet task

alone. In fact, quiet reflection by motivated participants is a good thing, because people will generate a wider variety of ideas by it. However, if people are *not* motivated to participate, it is better not to ask them to experience the stories separately, because some will pretend to read or listen instead of actually participating. In that case, giving groups tasks to complete will create a better contact situation.

Should every participant be asked to experience the same number of stories? Evenly distributed experience is useful if your participants have relatively uniform backgrounds. It is not useful if some people can work faster than others due to background or skills, because for some the same task would be unfairly onerous. It is also not useful if people are particularly unwilling to participate and will see your "everyone has to do it" instructions as inappropriately controlling.

Should participants have a task to do while experiencing the stories? A task is useful if people are not motivated, because it will give them a goal to work towards. A task is not useful if the stories are so sensitive that the task seems inappropriate in context. Only the most tactless person on earth would ask a group of women which rape stories rank as "most memorable." What if the stories are not sensitive and the people are motivated? In that case, a task is not needed, but it might be enjoyable, and it might help get people energized to participate even more in the exercises yet to come.

Should people evaluate stories? An evaluative task involves choosing or ranking stories based on some criterion of utility. For example, people might rank stories based on how well they answer the question, "Where do we want our organization to be in ten years?"

A non-evaluative task involves doing something with stories without evaluating them. For example, each person in a group might summarize to other group members the stories in their hands; or the group might make up two titles for each story written from opposing points of view.

Which type of task is best depends on the mindset of your participants coming in to the session. The more open they will be to new experiences, the more you can include elements of evaluation in the task. When people are ready to explore and learn, selection won't turn into blame or censorship. Conversely, the more you think people will start the session with closed minds (and will be unwilling to question their assumptions), the less evaluative the task should be.

Should the experience of encountering the stories be energetic or calm? If the stories you have collected are particularly sensitive or upsetting, making initial exposure into a game might seem disrespectful to the original storytellers. Also, if you think your participants will be initially reluctant or slow to warm up to participation, you might want to put off more active ways of engaging stories until people have gotten more into the spirit of the session. The last thing you want is a room full of wallflowers waiting for someone else to engage with a story.

On the other hand, if you expect strong participation and your topic is not sensitive, making initial contact with stories into a lively game might help the room build energy for shared work. Also, if you think people might be suspicious of your own actions in the session, such as believing you chose stories specifically to mislead or persuade them, asking people to experience the stories in a game with rules they can control might help them to understand that you intend to share the session with them.

Another game-like idea that can help people get started with the overview task is to place a short ice-breaker task in front of it. This is particularly useful if you expect people to be nervous or awkward with each other as the session starts. You can find descriptions of many ice-breaker exercises in books and on the internet, so I won't suggest any here. Any activity that gets people more at ease with each other will ease the way into encountering stories together.

Should people experience the stories before the session? Why not give people some stories to read *before* they come to the session? Why not assign the overview task as homework people do before they show up? I'll tell you why not, and I know why not because I've tried it. The problem is that only some people do the homework.

If you give stories out ahead of time, the people who did the homework will inevitably start working with the stories in their own minds *before* they come to the session, whether they intend to or not. Those people will show up already having categorized and combined and observed and interpreted stories (in an individual way), while others will arrive without having done any of those things. Thus sessions with assigned homework tend to split into two groups, the we-read-ours-first group and the we're-just-seeing-this-now group. These two groups end up doing two different versions of sensemaking, because they started the session at different points in the process.

I'm not saying people shouldn't be *allowed* to see your collected stories before a sensemaking session starts. But if *anyone* sees them *everyone* should, so the sensemaking stays balanced. I suppose you *could* assign homework, then split your participants up into groups depending on whether people did the homework or not, but it's a risky move. The groups might not be split evenly, and even within the homework group, people may vary from having read two stories to two hundred.

I find it works better to manage first contact with the stories so that *everyone has it together*. Not only do the participants have equal time for first exposure, they can see that everyone around them is experiencing the same thing. Reading stories alone is not the same as reading them in the context of a whole room of people preparing to work together.

Supporting overview later in the session. We have covered overview at the *start* of narrative

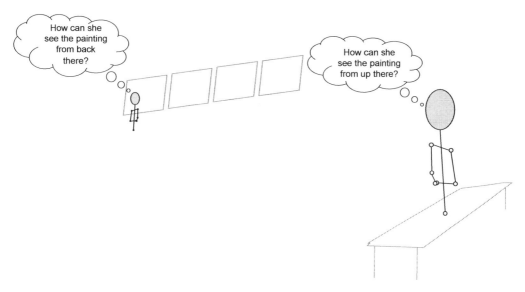

Figure 11.17. Zooming means switching between big-picture and detail views of something quickly and easily.

sensemaking, in first contact. But what about later in the session? How can you make sure that people *stay* aware of the entire body of stories collected? One way is to *repopulate* the body of stories (in whatever they were taken out of, pack or table or wall) after people have chosen some to read. In other words, even if people have chosen some stories to keep on hand, you and your helpers can make sure that *no story is ever removed from view*. You could imagine, for example, holding an initial contact game where people choose stories from a wall-o-stories; but after small groups are doing some intense thing where they don't look around much, you quietly repopulate the wall. Or you might quietly place a second story-card pack on each table and say something like, "Just in case you need more." In that way, if people want to go *back* to an overview of the whole story collection, it's easy for them to do that.

Zoom

Once I was visiting the Museum of Modern Art in New York City with my sister. At some point the two of us entered a large room in which was displayed one of Monet's famous paintings of water lilies. This one was forty feet long and took up an entire wall. At the time I aspired to become a something-creative, so I was hyper-aware of correct museum behavior. I quickly observed the distant benches on which people

were *obviously* supposed to go to properly appreciate the painting, so I made a beeline for them and sat primly down, smoothing my cherished identity. My sister the medical student, clueless to such nuances, strode up to within a few feet of the painting, then walked the length of it while I shrunk down on my distant bench, trying as hard as I could to look unrelated.

Sometimes when I tell that story to myself I come out smarter, and sometimes she does; but my *point* is that when I read about zooming in information retrieval, this is the image that always springs to mind (see Figure 11.17). Zooming is going back and forth between what I did and what my sister did. In an ideal presentation of information, zooming should be intuitive, obvious, and effortless. In other words, my sister and I were both hampered in our zooming, I because I couldn't bear to commit the faux pas of walking near the painting, and my sister because she thought the benches were just for sitting on when you got tired of standing up.

What does zooming mean when you are working with stories? It means switching back and forth between looking at *one* story and looking at *many* stories, quickly and easily. How can you support that? I'll give you two magic words. The first is *font,* and the second is *size.* Put those two words together and you can do much to support zooming.

Title:
Working its way down

Text:
It's not a pretty story. The people who made the mistake
would not own up to the mistake. It worked its way down.
The person who ultimately got stuck with it had nothing to
do with it. They were just the most defenseless. It's just the
way we do things here. Nobody talks about it. It's
impossible.

Questions about story:
Where did this story come from? first-hand
How do feel about the story? angry
How did it end? sad to happy: 9
How long will you remember it? trivial to memorable: 48
How much trust do you see in it? absent to abundant: 12

Questions about participant:
What is your position? manager
What is your age group? 41-60

Working its way down

It's not a pretty story. The people who made the **mistake**
would not own up to the mistake. It worked its way down.
The person who ultimately got **stuck** with it had nothing
to do with it. They were just the most **defenseless**. It's
just the way we do things here. Nobody talks about it. It's
impossible.

Remember	trivial _____	_____	memorable
Ending	sad _		happy
Trust	absent __		abundant

Source: **first-hand** second-hand rumor unsure
Feel: happy sad **angry** relieved enthused indifferent n.a.
Position: worker **manager** executive other
Age: <21 21-40 **41-60** 61+ declined

Figure 11.18. Well-designed story cards make it easy to zoom in and out between the detail of
one story and the big picture of many juxtaposed cards.

To show you zooming in story cards, I'm going to ask you to do something. Prop this book (or laptop or tablet or psycho-kinetic interface medium or whatever) up on something, then take about ten steps back, then compare the two versions of the same story in Figure 11.18. Please? Pretty please? It'll just take a minute.

The version of the story on the right is more amenable to zooming than the version on the left. I limited myself in this example to only changing font size and bolding. If you used color and visual details such as table borders, you could do more to make things stand out.

These are some features of the story card on the right that help zooming work better.

Large title. The name of the story is written in the largest font possible. Story names are handles we use to remember what's in the story. Making the name very large makes it possible to stand across the room from an array of stories on a wall and consider them together. Just this one thing can make a big difference all by itself.

Highlighted words. Three words of the story (mistake, stuck, defenseless) are highlighted with an enlarged font. This is to help people remember what the story is about while glancing at it from far away. If there is a visual word in the story, like "door" or "teapot," those words can also be good choices for highlighting. The point is not to emphasize the words that *matter*

most, but to use highlighting to help people *remember* stories quickly as they work with them.

However, be careful with this one. Choosing words to highlight can be seen as biasing, since *somebody* gets to say which words to highlight. If your stories are particularly controversial, or you expect your participants to be particularly suspicious of your intentions, it would be better *not* to highlight any words in your stories. But if those things aren't issues in your project, highlighting can help people recall stories to mind more quickly. If you are worried you won't be able to pick the right words to highlight, have two or three people choose words separately (with the rule "choose words that will best help recall the story to mind"), then look for coincidences.

Clarity. All extraneous labels have been removed. Remember, every extra word takes up the time and attention of your participants. You can rely on common knowledge to help you slim things down. If you put some words at the top of something and make them bigger, people will know it's a name or title without your having to waste their time reading the word "title." There might be fine distinctions in your data that you care about (like whether the question is about the story or about the storyteller) that are not useful to the session participants. Remove anything people don't need so as to clarify what is left. (If you would like to point out that I should have taken that advice while writing this book, you may do so now.)

Graphics. I've placed all three scale questions together and converted their numbers to graphical displays. You want people to be able to compare lots of these from far away, so set them up in groups of no more than three, and work on creating an order that makes sense in practice.

What you want to do is create what Edward Tufte calls "small multiples," which are displays similar enough to be compared (multiple) and shrunken so that many can be seen at once (small). In this case I put the "remember" question first, because the "ending "and "trust" answers were likely to appear together in most stories. The reason to have three scales per group is because that's the largest number of unlabeled things people can usually keep in mind without checking. After people have seen a few cards, they should be able to remember what is on top, in the middle, and on the bottom of each triad.

Patterns. I've placed all four choice questions together. Instead of showing only the answer given for each question, I have shown all possible answers, with the answer given highlighted in a larger font. You might complain that I've added more words, but this actually improves clarity, because I've converted something you have to *read* to understand into something you can just *glance* at to grasp.

Since the same answers always appear in the same locations, participants can compare *spatial* patterns without having to read the answers. If you picture one of those early computers with their rows of tiny lights you can get an idea of why this method is useful. People are very good at making sense of repeated patterns, which is good because it's also conducive to rapid zooming. Texts might become unreadable several paces back, but arrays of dots just become smaller arrays of dots. Even with this one-story example you can see how, if you were looking at a dozen or hundred of these, the patterns created by the larger words (first-hand, angry, manager, 41–60) would line up.

I didn't let myself use a table in this situation, but with a table you can make all the answer spaces the same size. That makes the spaces even more indicative of choices. Also, if you can use color, you can make the spaces "light up" to show the pattern of answers.

References. In the left-hand version of the story, questions are shown as they were asked. That looks fine, and it's transparent, but it repeats a lot of identical information. It's better to represent questions with brief (yet still understandable) names, and have a question look-up sheet somewhere that people can check if they forget what "feel" means. Saving space on the page saves time, and it leaves more space to create small multiples whose patterns will build up across stories.

Yes, learning what a system of lighting-up patterns means does require more effort. But when your goal is to make sense of more than, say, one hundred stories, a system to make patterns stand out will be pretty much required. You may need to ask people to put a few minutes into getting the system into their minds as they first encounter the patterns. If they are motivated to participate, and you have met them halfway by testing your representation and making it the best you can, you should be able to help them find patterns.

My makeover of the story I've shown here (which I made up) is a simple one. You could take a file of stories and clean it up in this way quickly, especially if you copied and pasted a story-card template many times, then changed formatting on existing answers rather than typing them in. Splitting up the task among three or four people can also help it move along quickly. If you can use macros or simple scripts, you can generate formatted text using a markup language like HTML. You can also write out cards like this by hand. Time, help, and knowledge can substitute for each other in producing output.

Filter

To understand what Shneiderman means by filtering, picture this scene. On a crisp fall day you are lying on the (dry, soft, not at all smelly) forest floor, gazing up at the branches of trees that wave softly above your head. Some of the leaves you see are still green, but most are red, orange, yellow, or brown. Some are lobed, some pointed, some serrated; some are worm-eaten, some whole. Once in a while a leaf drifts slowly down. The branches that hold the leaves are also variously sized and colored: birch white, beech gray, pine brown. Some of the branches are low to the ground, some much higher up, in layer upon layer of branches. Through the branches you can see the blue sky and the white clouds above the trees. As you lie there thinking, your eyes naturally filter in some elements of the complex scene and filter out others. You notice the sharp red leaves; you notice the bright blue sky; you notice the white branches of the birch gleaming in the sun.

In any sufficiently detailed visual landscape people tend to filter continuously, looking at one category of thing, then another. We can't help doing it, because it's one of the things that helps us survive. Filtering is an immensely useful activity when you're looking for food and prey (and predators) in a complex environment. People who design complex visual information displays know this and design their presentations to make use of it.

Have you ever seen one of those exploded diagrams of parts in a complicated mechanical system like a car engine? Can you recall how information like the names of parts and part numbers are often written in ways that make it easy to filter them in or out as your need requires? Usually different categories of information are denoted using different colors and fonts, and sometimes with different sorts of connecting lines. You can do the same thing in the story cards you prepare for people to use in sensemaking. The careful use of color, position, font, font size, font style, and diagrammatic components (lines, boxes, dots, highlighting, etc) can help people stand in front of a wall of stories and have patterns "jump out" at them as they filter the set, first by one element then by another.

How can you tell if the story cards you have made adequately support filtering? Test them. Start by building a draft story card format that you think represents your information well. Write up a small number of stories in your draft format, say eight or ten. Print or write the story cards so they are index-card sized. Next, tape your story cards on a wall or strew them around

on a table. Then stand several feet back from them and see what you can see.

Better yet, invite a few friends or colleagues to look at your story cards, and ask them what *they* can see. People should start saying things like, "Look, these ones all have values in the middle of the ranges" or "These ones all ended badly but the people said they were happy."

Ask people to move the cards around into patterns they see. If you find yourself (or see others) stepping forward to *read* the cards, or if nobody can come up with any reason to move any of the cards towards or away from each other, you might not yet have adequate support for filtering. Keep working until you feel that people will be able to filter by different aspects of the information on the cards *without* stepping back and forth.

Details on demand

This is an easy one: every bit of information you have on every story should be available to participants in your sensemaking session. Do this for two reasons: first because people might want to delve into the details, and second because nobody wants to think some information has been hidden from them.

Place the information you think people will be unlikely to need in very small print or on the backs of your story cards. Examples might be things like which participant told each story (anonymized with pseudonyms like "P1"), how the story was collected (survey, interview, session), the date of collection, how many stories the teller of the story told, and so on. If you know it, include it. But don't give every bit of data the same emphasis, to save time and attention.

It's also useful to make sure your participants know that *this is all the data you have*. Slipping in a mention that "here is all the data we collected" avoids people thinking you pre-selected what they would be using.

Relate: compare: count

I've expanded Shneiderman's "relate" task into two sub-tasks (comparing and constructing), because supporting sensemaking requires taking into account things people need to do with information beyond simply retrieving it. Relat-

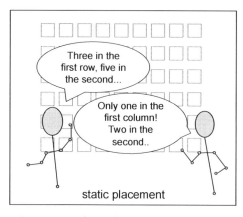

Figure 11.19. If you place story cards statically on a wall, people can point to count them. If you place them dynamically in packs, people can move them to count them.

ing by comparing includes within it the activities of *counting* and *ranking*.

Counting stories means adding up how many stories fall into categories suggested by the questions asked or by attributes of the stories themselves. Some examples might be: stories about which people said they felt happy; stories longer than sixty words; stories told by women; stories considered particularly memorable; stories with multiple protagonists; stories about cats.

Static versus dynamic placement. Counting is one place in which the tension between static and dynamic placement of stories comes into play (see Figure 11.19).

Let's say you have designed and printed a set of one hundred story cards representing the stories and other data you have collected prior to your sensemaking session. Should you array all of the cards on a wall, so that people can find them in the same places over and over? That would be a *static* placement. Or should you hand each table a pack of cards so they can manipulate the stories and rearrange them? That would be a *dynamic* placement.

On the one hand, having all of the collected stories statically arrayed makes it easy to count instances of stories by simply pointing and adding. If you have rows and columns of story cards, people can segment their counting: three in this row, five in this, that makes eight, and so on. When the array never changes, people can memorize it, so each count goes more quickly

than the last. It's like looking at a table in a book. Seeing how everything is laid out makes patterns that range across the space more clear. Static arrangements of story cards create a story landscape people can learn and use as they make sense of the stories collected. If your rows and columns are meaningful, like say arrayed from low to high memorability in the rows and from worst to best outcome in the columns, people can use the space to support their counting (and thinking). There's a lot to say for the reliability of a static arrangement.

On the other hand, people given a pack of cards can sort them into piles, then count the piles. In fact, card or pile sorting (it goes by both names) is a well recognized method used in cultural anthropology (where "informants" sort cards while researchers watch) and in information systems design (where users of information systems sort cards while designers watch). The beauty of dynamic placement is that people can quickly sort cards into many configurations, then count the piles of cards afterward. It's also more familiar than the wall-o-cards approach. Most adults have had some experience with playing cards, so they know what it means to sort and shuffle and rank and count cards.

I've seen people in sensemaking sessions make and sort cards when they were not even *given* cards; they take printed sheets with stories on them and move them around as if they were cards, even if the facilitators didn't set things up that way. Also, people don't always need to actually count cards when the differences are large. If people make two stacks of cards and one is obviously twice the height of the other, there is no need to count them.

One drawback of card sorting is that you have to keep reusing the same cards, so the pattern you saw in one comparison disappears in the next one. This doesn't happen when the arrangement is static. An inexpensive digital camera at each table can help people record their arrangements for later reference, but then you have the problem of seeing what's in the tiny pictures on the camera, or finding a way to get them off it easily.

Yet another way to support counting in sensemaking is to use both methods at the same time. If you can print multiple copies of your story cards, you can array them in rows and columns on a wall *and* give a "card deck" with the same stories in it to each table. Then you can tell people to sort the cards at their table *or* count the statically arrayed cards on the wall, as they choose. If you have thousands of stories, this may be hard to pull off, but if you have one or two hundred it should be doable.

Relate: compare: rank

Ranking stories is closely related to counting stories, but it's also different and requires different support. Counting is comparing stories by *kind;* ranking is comparing stories by *degree.*

People can count stories by pointing at story cards on a wall or by stacking story cards. But ranking stories means *spreading them out* in some form of meaningful space. People might rank stories in a line from most positive to most negative, or they might arrange them in two dimensions. This means that dynamic placement, at least of story *titles,* is necessary for ranking. If you don't have multiple copies of your story cards, you can ask people to copy story titles to sticky notes and arrange them.

Dimensions of comparison need not be on the story cards already; they might combine elements of data and reaction. For example, people might rank stories on an axis denoting how likely they would be to retell the story in their *own* family, or how much they think the story "speaks for the community," or how likely the story would be "to change things around here" if it were widely known. Both looking at rank-

ings already on the story cards and coming up with new rankings can create new insights in the sensemaking process.

Why support counting and ranking? At this point I'd like to pause and answer two questions I think you might have. The first is: *Why does it matter if people count and rank stories? Why do I need to support this?*

My answer to that question would have to be experiential, not theoretical. In every project I have worked on in which people have been asked questions about their stories, counting and ranking subsets of stories has revealed useful insights about the topic being explored. In fact, counting and ranking answers is most of the reason to ask questions in the first place.

This is probably something you are just going to have to see for yourself. The first time you see something surprisingly insightful—like that the older the participant the more likely they were to say their story was a rumor; or that when people said they felt "frustrated" about their story they were more likely to say they were "not sure" what caused the problem; or that men were more likely than women to tell stories in which they couldn't find help—the first time you see a thing like this, you will understand why counting matters. People who are making sense of stories together in order to arrive at new insights need to be able to find those patterns, so they need to be able to count and rank.

An analogy might help to explain my point. Have you ever played with Legos, those bits and pieces of plastic that come together to form anything you can imagine? People who build with Legos spend a lot of time sorting, counting, and comparing them.

In the sorting of Legos, many different criteria are used: size, color, function, type, material. In the sorting of stories the same is true: voice, length, speaker, theme, emotion, impact. Some sortings are large and permanent, some small and temporary. Some categories are simple, and some are not. In my house, for example, one of our Lego sorting bins is called the "people" bin. It includes not only Lego people, but also everything they wear and carry. That's as complicated a sorting category as stories about which people said the main characters were limited by their own arrogance.

A Lego enthusiast learns about their Lego collection, and about what they can do with it, by sorting, counting, and comparing Lego pieces. The same thing is true with stories. People who are doing sensemaking learn about the stories they are working with by sorting, counting, and comparing them. These activities create *familiarity with the body of stories* so that people can begin to think about what the stories can help them do.

Why do people need to do counting and ranking themselves? The second question I think you might have is: *Why does it matter that the participants in sensemaking count stories for themselves? Can't catalytic material do that for them? Why not just put up graphs of counts, instead of helping people count on their own?*

The answer to this question has to be, again, experiential. There is this sort of magically clarifying moment when you realize something important about answers to questions about stories you have collected. The clouds clear and a pattern emerges. I've seen many such a pattern emerge in my catalysis work.

But here's the thing with catalysis: it's never the best solution. It is *always* better if the people who care most about the project and its goals experience this moment, and experience it *together,* than if one person sees it outside of group sensemaking. A sensemaking session in which people discover *for themselves* an insight that ends up being critical to the project is a more successful sensemaking session than one in which people merely *review* such a pattern found by somebody else.

That is why I place catalysis *outside* the main triangle of the canonical PNI project: because it's helpful as an aid to sensemaking in *some* circumstances, such as when the project is ambitious, when the data set is large and complicated, and when the sensemakers don't have the time or expertise to explore patterns thoroughly on their own. But catalysis is *never* critical. It's the *sensemaking* that is critical.

I think of catalytic material as like a pair of corrective lenses. Just as glasses help people with impaired vision see the world, catalytic material supports sensemaking when unaided sensemaking is impaired by unavoidable contextual conditions. But just as any sane person would prefer 20/20 vision to the best glasses available, a sensemaking session that works without catalytic material will create the best outcome of all.

Another thing to remember about catalytic material is that it doesn't have to come from outside a sensemaking session. You can *include* catalysis in sensemaking by helping people create catalytic material themselves. The "on-paper" section of the catalysis chapter describes how you can use story cards to create bar graphs, contingency tables, histograms, and scatterplots (page 231). Any of those graphs can be produced by the participants in a sensemaking session. To use catalysis in this way, practice generating each type of graph so you are ready to help your participants create their own graphs whenever they discover a need to explore a pattern.

Relate: construct

The most exciting part of relating comes in when it's time to start building. If you skim ahead to the sensemaking exercises described in the next chapter, you will see that they *all* involve building things with stories.

Building things with stories means asking questions like these:

- If this story was told first, which of these other stories would be most likely to be told as a response?
- If three of these stories were episodes in a longer story of a journey, which stories would be the three episodes, and in what order would they appear?
- If these stories mapped a landscape of trust, which would be at the extremes of the space?

These are all larger constructions built of stories.

Sometimes, instead of building with whole stories, people build with *elements* derived from stories: settings, characters, plot points, values. That's still building, and it's still narrative building; it just uses differently-sized pieces.

To make use of my Lego analogy again: comparing and constructing complement and support each other whether you are working with Legos or stories. With Legos, the more you sort them, and the more ways in which you sort them, the more you understand what you are working with, and the better your constructions become. Also, the more varied constructions you build, the more varied ways you think of to sort your Legos. As an example, the "people bin" I mentioned above came about in part because we realized that when we put Lego people into scenes or vehicles or buildings, we usually wanted to give them something to wear or manipulate. Thus it made sense to keep those things close to the people themselves. The same thing happens when people move stories around during sensemaking. In fact, some of the questions about stories I recommend (which produce sorting categories) came from realizations of "what sort of piece we need to build with right here" during construction exercises in which we used stories to build things.

Do you need structured exercises to support people relating stories by building things? No, but if you give people a task that involves building things with stories, you'll probably end up doing a simple form of an exercise anyway. The exercises I describe in this book don't have to be complex. You can do them in such a simple form that they don't seem like exercises at all.

I do think you need to give people *some* sort of task in order to get them building things with stories. I've noticed that given a mass of stories and no task to complete, people tend to fall much more quickly into sorting stories than combining them. Maybe it's because people are used to being asked to tick off boxes on forms. Maybe a thousand years ago people were more used to combining stories into larger stories. Or maybe it's just that people a thousand years ago never encountered masses of stories at the same time. I don't know, but for some reason building with stories is something people seem to need help with.

Is catalytic material useful in the construction sense of relating stories? Yes, but only indirectly. When people are building something with stories, say a landscape or timeline, they might use catalytic material to help them find a particular type of story they need to fill a spot. But catalytic material can never be central to construction in the way it can be to counting and ranking. It's more like, if you use catalytic material to improve your counting and comparing, you'll be more prepared to begin building.

History

Shneiderman's next-to-last category of tasks people face in retrieving information has to do with helping people remember the story of their information retrieval.

Says Shneiderman:

> Information exploration is inherently a process with many steps, so keeping the history of actions and allowing users to retrace their steps is important.

I'm going to go out on a limb here and say that history is not as important for group sensemaking as it is for information retrieval. When you are navigating an information database, generally the information sits still. But in sensemaking the information changes as you interact with it. In *group* sensemaking things get even more complicated, to the point where it may be simply impossible to retrace or undo actions.

It may be useful in sensemaking to *record* what has happened, because a sensemaking session has a story of its own. It may be useful to give participants memory aids such as cameras and note paper so that they can *recall* the state of understanding they were at half an hour ago. But group sensemaking is too much of an emergent property of group interaction to be aided much by the reconstruction and replaying of history. The thrust of it is forward, and it's better to keep that energy moving forward than to help people look back.

Extract

Now we come to Shneiderman's last task of information retrieval: selecting items from a body of information to consider in isolation. When you extract something from a set of information, you can do this either with replacement (you pull out a *copy* of your selection) or without replacement (you pull out your selection). Most people think of selecting with replacement when they think of extraction during information retrieval. You wouldn't want to make information unavailable in future searches just because you pulled it out to look at it once. Making copies of extracted items is easy in a computer database, but harder when you are using physical story cards.

I can think of four ways to duplicate a story during group sensemaking: copying the whole story, copying its given name, copying a new name given to it by session participants, and copying elements of the story rather than the story itself.

Full copies. You can make a physical copy of an entire physical story card. You could accomplish this by simply bringing lots of copies of the stories to the sensemaking session at the start. If you intend to produce one deck of story cards per table, you could just as well produce two or three decks per table, so that people can draw a card and replace it. (After all, a normal pack of playing cards contains four sets of cards that are nearly identical copies of each other.)

Another option is to place a photocopier (and maybe a paper cutter) in the room and tell people they can make copies of any story cards they want to duplicate as they work. They could do this themselves, or you could station a helper next to the copier to speed up the process. Of course, making copies during the session takes time, so it would be better not to use that option if your session time is short.

Copies of original story names. You can make a copy of a story's name only, and use the name to refer back to the full version of the story on a story card. This is the option I've seen used most often. As long as all of the stories in your collection have unique and memorable names, people can quickly copy out story names onto sticky notes. This option takes little extra time; people usually don't mind doing this small amount of copying; and people are used to referring to things by titles. However, using original story names does depend on your storytellers having given their stories useful names in the first place. This doesn't always happen. If all the stories in your collection have names like "My story" and "Untitled 3" and "I don't know what to put here" and "This whole thing is stupid," the option of copying story names may not work for you.

Copies of new story names. You can ask your session participants to give the collected stories additional unique names that *they* find memorable. You could even make this part of an icebreaker exercise in getting people more familiar with the stories as they start to work with them. Say each table gets a card deck of all the collected stories. Say you ask each table to distribute the stories so that each person gets an equal number. You could ask people to read each story and decide whether the title it already has is memorable. If not, they can write an extra title on the card.

Remember to emphasize respect for the original storyteller as people do this. The extra name should not be "what an idiot has to say" or anything like that. The goal is to make the story titles more memorable, not to annotate them with opinions. Also, make sure the extra name is clearly marked as added during sensemaking. Don't obscure or change the meaning put in place by the original storyteller.

Copies of story elements. The fourth method of extraction with replacement is to copy *elements* of stories such as characters, situations, and values. You will read more about this in the chapter on sensemaking exercises (page 385), so I won't describe it here; but any activity that involves story elements involves extraction.

Now that we have thoroughly explored the facilitation of initial contact between people, project, and stories, we we need to think next about what happens *after* initial contact has been made.

FACILITATING CHURNING

To refresh your memory before we move on: churning in sensemaking is *repeated, varied contact* between people, project, and stories. Churning requires initial contact to get started, but it moves past initial contact into the consideration of multiple perspectives on the topic of concern.

Facilitating churning between people and project

People-project churning means that during a sensemaking session, people and project keep *re-encountering* each other in new ways.

People-project churning brings out the excitement of exploration, imagination, and activity. It sounds like this: *Wow! Really? I can't believe it. I never thought of that before. Did that really happen? Do they really see it that way? It's perfectly obvious now, but it wasn't this morning. How could we have missed this? This gives us a whole new way of looking at it.* And so on. It looks like people working closely together, both in mind and in body. When you hear people-project churning, you will see people increasing their physical proximity: leaning in, standing together, looking at each other and at the same things together, gesturing, moving around the room together.

When people-project churning is *not* happening in a sensemaking session, you will see and hear *withdrawal* from exploration. Withdrawal sounds like this: *I don't get this. I don't see why we should do this. This is stupid. I can't believe they are taking these stories seriously. These are lies. I'm not going to sit here and be insulted like this. What does this have to do with me? I'm out of here.* And so on. Withdrawal looks like people pulling away from each other and from the project. You might see one person sitting by themselves, pretending to be busy with something, as the rest of their group interacts; or you might see one group pulling away from the other groups in the room, or from you.

Should you try to stop people when they withdraw from sensemaking? No, for a few reasons. First, it's like spitting into the wind: can't be done without making a mess. Usually the more attention you pay to withdrawal the worse it gets.

Second, sometimes withdrawal from sensemaking is an unavoidable aspect of the project's context. If you plan to bring groups with different viewpoints or power relationships together into a single sensemaking session, you can expect some amount of withdrawal to take place. You can either plan withdrawal *out* by separating people into different sessions, or you can plan it *in* and deal with the consequences. Which is best depends on your project, your group and your own experience and facilitation style. If you are just getting started, or if you know you don't handle conflict well, you'd

better plan it out until you get your feet more securely under you.

Third, and best, sometimes withdrawal can unexpectedly turn into churning. The person who was pulling away can suddenly encounter a story or perspective that energizes them, or they can suddenly get the point of what you are doing, and the energy of their interaction can switch polarity. Don't rush to fix a sensemaking session that shows pockets of withdrawal. Just watch it. As long as the balance is on the side of engagement, you can still have effective sensemaking going on.

In fact, I would go so far as to say that a sensemaking session that shows no withdrawal from exploration (not even temporary) is not probing the issues deeply enough to make useful progress. That's all part of the paradoxical nature of stories and storytelling. We tell and hear stories as a way to push through the pain toward the understandings we need. This is as true in group sensemaking as it is in our individual lives.

Still, it makes sense to think about how you can maximize people-project churning, and minimize withdrawal from it, as you plan your sensemaking session. To do this, you need to create situations where people can come into repeated, varied contact with the project. Do you remember, way back in the chapter on project planning, how I recommended that you figure out the goals, relations, focus, range, scope, and emphasis of your project? (You can find that section on page 103.) Those are varied aspects of your project. You can plan your sensemaking session so that different aspects of the project come into play during different parts of the session.

For example, say I plan to start my session with a "getting to know you" activity where people form small groups using an association rule (like "find people who live on a different street than you do"). That aspect comes from the *range* element of the project: the juxtaposition of views from various parts of town. After the small groups have formed, say I plan to ask people to choose a theme their small group will consider within the larger topic of the session. That's the *focus* element. And so on. As you plan your sensemaking session, go back

Figure 11.20. Imagine yourself asking people to leave their original groups and form new ones. Do you think their interest in the session will be enhanced or reduced by it?

to your list of project elements and link them to your planned session activities. If the linked elements are all of the same type (say several activities link to focus but none to range or goals), mix things up a little more. Work repeated, varied contact with the project *into* your session. That way, if people find reasons to withdraw from sensemaking, they will also find reasons to remain engaged in it.

Facilitating churning among people

I said in the contact section (page 307) that the interpersonal category is all about small groups. This is also true for churning, but in this case it's about *reshuffling* small groups. Reshuffling means people leaving the groups they were in before and moving into new groups. Reshuffling brings people into fresh conversations that create new perspectives on the topic under consideration.

Reshuffling groups doesn't fit into every sensemaking session. First of all, it takes time. If you have a short time span for your session, don't plan any group reshuffling. Save this technique for when you have at least two hours to work together. It takes people some time to adjust to new groups, usually five or ten minutes for each change. If you can't afford that, don't reshuffle.

Assuming you do have enough time to reshuffle groups, whether you should do it depends on your project, people, and topic. It also depends on your own facilitation style and skills. I've found that while reshuffling leads to better churning in terms of exposure to more perspectives and ideas, it is not always something peo-

ple are willing to accept. If your participants are fearful or suspicious, or they are used to getting their own way, or your topic is particularly sensitive or personal, or *you* don't feel confident asking people to do things they might not like, reshuffling has the potential to ruin sensemaking.

How can you know whether group churning will help or hinder sensemaking in a session you are planning? Imagine it (see Figure 11.20). As you plan your sensemaking session, imagine the people you expect to attend. Picture anyone you know who shares characteristics with the people who will be coming. For example, if your session is for teachers, picture a teacher you know. Now picture a whole room full of those people. Picture them having sat down at tables with other people. Picture them having worked on some task together. Maybe they have a small, temporary feeling of camaraderie as they have worked with stories together. Picture them having a coffee break and chatting casually.

Now picture ending the break by asking your participants to move around to new group configurations. How, in your imagination, do the people respond? Some people might be energized by the idea; other people might feel put upon, uncomfortable, even angry. What do you think you will find? Of course some small degree of initial grumbling is fine, and you can't make everyone happy all the time. But if you think lots of people are likely to want to leave the session as a result of being asked to form new groups, it might be best to leave reshuffling aside.

Also, how do you think *you* might react to the reactions of your participants? Do you feel ready to handle whatever initial discomfort might come out of such a move? Maybe you've done this enough times to know it's worth doing, and you can help people over the rough spot of getting used to a new group. Maybe that sort of thing slides off you like water off a duck's back. On the other hand, if you haven't done much facilitating yet, or you have a hard time handling criticism, maybe you aren't ready for that plunge into temporary unpopularity.

You know what? It's okay. You don't *have* to do it. Shifting groups around is not an absolute requirement of an effective sensemaking session. It's a nice-to-have, and it's particularly nice to have when your project's goal has to do with generating new ideas to address old problems. But in some rooms with some people (which includes you), reshuffling can do more harm than good.

Let's say you have imagined your sensemaking session, and you see no impediment to group churning on the part of the participants or yourself. Say you are excited about using the technique to stir things up, and you think your participants will like it too. How should you go about reshuffling groups? Well, do you remember how I talked about forming groups (in the story collection chapter) using three methods: assignment, rule-based, and self-assembly? (It was on page 171.) Here, I'll refresh your memory.

1. In an *assignment* grouping, you tell people which groups to join. The assignment can be based on a previously given out identifier (such as a number on a name tag), on some attribute of participants related to the project's topic (age, street, position, gender) or on an unrelated attribute that creates random groupings (first letter of grandparent's first name, first number of street address).

2. In a *rule-based* grouping, you give people a rule and they apply it. The rule can be focusing (find people your age), ranging (find a group with nobody your age in it), or ran-

dom (find a group without the first letter of your grandparent's name in it).

3. In a *self-assembled* grouping, you give people no instructions except to form small groups.

To reshuffle people, you can simply ask them to leave their original groups and form new ones. What's the best way to do that? Different sequences of group formation methods have different uses. Let's go over all possible two-method combinations.

Assignment followed by assignment. In this pairing, you use the assignment method for the first grouping. For the second grouping you simply continue that method by creating groups orthogonal to the first set.

One way to support this is to give people identifiers that have two parts, such as letters and numbers (A3), colors and animals (blue dog), buildings and cars (fire truck in front of mall). You can make the identifiers funny or appropriate or thought-provoking, just as long as they combine orthogonally. Plan your groupings so they will cover how many small groups you think you will have. Say you expect to have sixteen people in the room; place four items in the first category and four in the second.

A double assignment maximizes interpersonal churning, because each group for the second activity will have exactly one member from each of the first-activity groups. However, don't use a double assignment unless you are sure your participants will be willing to do what you ask. An assignment is (obviously) a controlling thing, and you could lose some of your more independent-minded participants as you shuffle them around like so many puppets.

Assignment followed by rule. In this pairing, you assign people to groups at first, then ask them to take over the grouping on the second run through. This technique is especially useful if your participants are low in confidence (for example, students eager to perform but not sure how to). If you set up the first groups for them, they can gain confidence in "doing things right." By the time you get to forming the second set of groups, they can take the rule you give them (which still has *some* control in it, so they aren't left entirely on their own) and run with it.

On the other hand, if you expect people to be apathetic, don't use a rule (or self-assembly) throughout the session, because people will seize upon it as an excuse to drift off. In general the assignment-rule transition is good for groups where you expect things to warm up and get moving (so that people become both more willing and more able to do their part in grouping) as the session proceeds.

Assignment followed by self-assembly. Self-assembly never works well *after* the first grouping, no matter what came before it. Usually if you ask people to reassemble in a new way, they will just choose the same groups they had before. This is partly because they don't know *how* to form new groups (where should I go?) and partly because they would rather stay in the group they are in. I'd never put the self-assembly option in *any* place but the first grouping.

Rule followed by assignment. This is actually a pretty good pairing. You give people a rule to form groups at first, which gives them a participatory element in grouping. Then you follow up with a new grouping based on an assigned or fundamental category. Any assignment-based category you can come up with is unlikely to perfectly match the rule-based distribution (especially if you designed the rule with the reassignment in mind). So you will get some remixing, but without coming off as heavy-handed as you would with two assignments. I'd use this pairing if I had the combination of a group I knew would want to participate from the start (hence their probable engagement in the rule), plus a topic that required the meeting of multiple perspectives (which is not likely to happen unless a rule is applied or an assignment is carried out).

If you're especially fast-thinking, you can even tweak your second-grouping assignment based on your observations of the first set of groups. For example, if you happen to notice that the people clumped into age groups (even though you didn't ask them to), you can reshuffle them into groups with varied ages when the time comes. (Just don't *admit* you changed the as-signment in response to how people grouped themselves. Nobody likes to be corrected.)

Rule followed by rule. This is not the best pairing. Most people hate being asked to do the same thing twice. It *sounds* interesting to say something like, "Now I want you to choose people for a new group, and this time disregard age and find two people you live far away from." But when I've actually tried doing this, the response has most often been, "Ugh, we just did all that, why do we have to do it *again?*" Especially if you are asking people to do sensemaking exercises where they build things, you are likely to find a limited tolerance for "playing games." I'd save a rule-rule combination for only the most motivated of groups, people who understand *why* you are reshuffling and who are eager to work out a good repeated and varied mix themselves. Actually, in the case of a *very* motivated group, you can bump things up another level and ask people to come up with their *own* rule that will work well with the first rule you set. It's rare to find people that eager to participate, but you can still be ready for it if it happens.

Rule followed by self-assembly. Not a good idea. See note above (in assignment then self-assembly).

Self-assembly followed by self-assembly. Not a good idea. See note above (in assignment then self-assembly).

Self-assembly followed by assignment. In this pairing, the first groups are self-assembled, with no instructions other than "please form small groups," but the second groups form through a label or fundamental trait.

Whether this works well depends on why your first set of groups formed the way they did. If people chose groups because they knew the people in them (friends sat with friends), coming at them later with an assignment might seem like you are trying to separate people punitively. In that case I'd soften the appearance of control by using a rule instead (along with a short explanation of why reshuffling is useful to sensemaking).

If people don't know each other and self-assembled randomly, then asking them to re-form groups based on an assignment won't necessarily bother anyone. When people self-

Figure 11.21. As facilitator, you need to keep things moving so people will achieve the multiple perspectives they need for effective sensemaking.

assemble at first, whether they know anyone in the room or not, it is better to reshuffle (if they won't be upset by it) than not to. We all know that we choose people to "randomly" sit with who have something in common with us, even if it's just a similar age group or clothing style or notebook. Better to shake that up than leave it alone, *if* it isn't going to break participation.

Self-assembly followed by rule. As I explained above, it's better to reshuffle self-assemblies when you can. As to whether a rule or an assignment is better, it depends on the motivation of your participants. Motivated people given a rule can usually produce a better "shaking up" than demotivated people given a new group assignment. But when people will refuse to use a rule, won't understand it, or will see it as an excuse to drift off, it's better to stick with an assignment.

Facilitating churning between people and stories

Recall that to facilitate people-story contact you need to support overview, zooming, filtering, getting details, counting, ranking, constructing, and extracting stories and information. Churning in people-story contact is about the same things, just over and over.

I don't think there is much value in talking about how *each* of these aspects of people-story contact repeat. I don't have to tell you that people need to zoom in and out many times.

The one thing I do feel you need to know about people-story churning is to *keep things moving*. I have seen the following scenario play out many times. You ask people to do something

with stories: look at them, compare them, build something with them. The people understand what you want them to do and why, and they are willing to participate, so they set to work. They enjoy the process; they engage in lively discussion; they complete the task. Then you ask them to do a *new* thing. They don't want to do a new thing. They want to keep doing the thing they were doing before. They want to do it better and in more depth. They want to polish it and perfect it.

I don't know why this always happens, but it always does, and it always needs to be corrected. In a perfect world, people could spend a week making sense of a topic, but in this world sensemaking sessions are always half as long as they should be. Hence I have found it necessary in every sensemaking session I have facilitated to keep people "on their toes" and moving along. My guess is that you will too.

Why does this tension *have* to be corrected? Why not give people all the time they need to create one complete thing instead of three half-finished ones? Because sensemaking is not creation. Effective sensemaking requires *multiple perspectives* on a topic, and you can't *get* multiple perspectives if you use up all your time on the first one (see Figure 11.21). I said above that interpersonal churning (new group formations) was nice to have but not essential. This one is different. If you don't have enough people-*story* churning, you won't have effective narrative sensemaking.

Let me state it metaphorically. Churning between people and stories helps the rocket ship of sensemaking achieve escape velocity and rise above the atmosphere of assumptions, mis-understandings, and entrenched thinking that prohibits new understandings of your topic. It's the view from space—that sight of the big blue marble—that is the ultimate goal of sensemaking. It's up to you to build the momentum that will get everyone there and battle the inertia that will slow everyone down.

How can you tell if things are moving along well? Pay attention to the *transitions* between activities. If you planned your session well, your participants should have no problem doing what you ask them to do within the time frames you set up. When you remind people that the time for an activity is nearing its end, watch how they react. Do they finish up the activity, eager to see what comes next? Do they ask for more time? Do they complain about being pushed too hard? Do they attack your skills in setting up the session? Do they *pretend* to stop doing the activity, only to secretly keep going back to it while they are supposed to be doing the next activity? You don't have be the momentum police; some foot-dragging is fine. But if each activity falls further behind schedule, you will end up without having reached the insights you hoped to gain.

So how can you keep foot-draggers on their toes? I'll give you a few tricks. First, I like to slip in a mention of the need for speed at the start of the session. I'll say something like this.

> At some points today you may feel like we are moving too fast and that you'd like more time. But the process we are using will only work well if we keep up a good pace and cover everything that has been planned. You'll see at the end of the session why we have such a need for speed.

That sort of thing gives people a heads-up you can remind them of later.

A second thing I like to do is to write the session's time schedule very prominently on a white board or giant piece of paper so everyone can see it throughout the session. That way anyone can poke their head up from their group's huddle and say, "Guys, we only have five minutes left for this part." I also mention at the start of each activity how long people have to work.

Finally, I like to give people subtle cues about time using my own movements around the room. You'd be amazed how much people can pick up simply from your body language. When you facilitate groups, don't make the mistake of thinking people aren't paying attention to you. Any group asked to do anything unfamiliar by anybody will watch that person like a pack of wolves. If you sit down that means one thing; if you circle that means another.

So what I like to do is, I give people their task, then for the first half of the time period I pretend to get very busy with something. I stare intently at my laptop screen and type things (it's usually notes on what people are doing and saying, but they don't know that). The message is: I'm busy, and you should be busy too. You don't need my help, and you can't avoid the task by pretending you need help; you need to concentrate on doing the task yourself. Then, when the time is about half over, I look up from the computer screen and start glancing around the room. I'm checking to see if people need any help, but I'm also sending a message: I'm checking your progress, so you should be checking your progress too. Finally, when the time is close to over, I get up and start walking around the room. Again, I'm checking to see if people need help, but the message is: I'm moving, so you should be moving—to completion. Then there's the two-minute warning, then the time period ends and we start the next part.

This all sounds elaborate, but it's not. After you do it a few times the whole thing feels natural, for yourself and for your participants (see Figure 11.22 on the next page).

My last piece of advice on facilitating people-story churning is to keep it in mind as you *plan* your sensemaking sessions. When I've helped people plan sessions, I have always noticed that the less experience a person has with facilitating sensemaking, the longer times they plan for activities. They'll say, "And then we'll take two hours to build a landscape from these stories." I'll say, "That's a long time! Maybe you could cut it in half and ask them to *use* the landscape to build some constructed stories in the other half." They'll say, "Oh, no, they won't finish the landscape in time." When you write out your plans, watch out for the words *finish, com-*

Figure 11.22. Use the fact that people watch what the facilitator does to keep your session's activities on schedule.

plete, conclude, establish, and all other words that show *completion thinking.* Those are all signs that you are not keeping the pace up as much as you should to fit multiple perspectives in.

In sensemaking, *finishing* activities is not the point. Doing *lots* of activities one after another—activities that provide multiple perspectives on project, people, and stories—*is* the point. The *things* people build in sensemaking sessions don't matter; what matters is the *building* of the things. Don't slip into completion thinking, and don't let your participants fall into it either. The first time you surface at the end of an exhausting session to hear people saying things like, "I can't believe I never saw this before," and, "This changes everything!" you will understand why sensemaking has such a burning need for speed. Then all of what I wrote here will change from something you read in a book to something you know.

FACILITATING CONVERGENCE

Convergence in sensemaking is the pulling together that takes place after people, project, and stories have been mixed and remixed many times. Rivulets become streams and streams become rivers.

Convergence is partly something that happens on its own, simply because things coalesce naturally as they churn together. There are situations in which convergence will happen without any help. Maybe the people in the room are especially motivated and connected to the project's goals; or the collected stories offer excellent, revealing perspectives on the topic; or the plan set up for the sensemaking session fits very well with the goals and context of the day; or the people are familiar with the process and can "take things up a level" by moving faster; or there is ample, experienced facilitation for contact and churning. If at least some of these factors come together, you may find things converging without your having to do anything at all to help.

But spontaneous convergence is unpredictable. Sometimes it seems like everything is in place for it to happen, but it doesn't. No matter how auspicious the conditions, don't assume convergence will come naturally.

So what can you do to help convergence happen? Three things. First, *set up conditions* that make it more likely to happen. Second, *observe* what's happening to see if convergence is taking place. Third, *intervene* if convergence is *not* happening. I'll go into how you can do these things for each of the categories (people-project, people-people, people-stories) below.

Facilitating convergence between people and project

Each person in the room during a sensemaking session, including yourself, has a different idea of what the project is about. Convergence between people and project doesn't mean that all of these projects join into one grand consensus. It simply means that everyone understands better than they did before what all the projects are and how they fit together (and don't). Views on the project that were isolated connect to each other through negotiated channels of understanding.

Setting up conditions for people-project convergence

What conditions should you set in place to help people-project convergence happen? Should you establish clear goals? Should you tell people that you want them to seek convergence? That won't make convergence happen. First of all, saying "I want us to all come together on what this session is going to do" sounds like either a Beatles song or doublespeak for "you will do what I say." Secondly, goals in sensemaking are like the garden path Alice walked in *Through the Looking Glass:* the harder you pursue them, the further they recede. Narrative sensemaking deliberately *avoids* directly addressing goals by passing through the indirect medium of story. You could say it walks *away* from goals in order to reach them in a different way.

So if not goals, what *should* you put in place? I find it's best to set up *expectations* and *tasks.* Expectations help people understand the social context of the meeting, and tasks help them understand what they should do with their hands and minds. Goals for the session will be implicit in the expectations and tasks, and they'll work better that way.

Expectations. You need to create an expectation of *negotiated exploration.* Working together with stories will *negotiate* among the unique perspectives on the project people brought into the room. Through this negotiation, session participants will *explore* features of the project landscape, and those features will help your community or organization arrive at better decisions.

You can set up this expectation at the start of the session, or you can wait until you think people are more warmed up to the topic and mention it then. Obviously you wouldn't tell people what I wrote above about negotiating exploration. Nobody would listen if you did say that. It's too full of jargon. But you can say something shorter that gets the gist across.

For example, in the section above on your introduction to the session (page 314), I had these lines:

> We are not here to debate or prove anything. We don't have to reach agreement. We are here *to listen and to be listened to.*

> We are also here to *discover new ideas* about [what the project is about] so that we can make better decisions together.

The first of these statements conveys negotiation, and the second exploration.

More important than a prepared speech, though, is a thorough understanding on your part of what expectations people should have. If you understand what will happen (or what *should* happen if things are going well), you will be able to respond to any questions about what to expect in a useful way. As I've said before, the only way to truly arrive at such an understanding of "what usually happens" is to have seen it happen already. In each sensemaking session you do, you will be able to set up expectations better than in the one before.

See, I just set up an expectation for *you,* just like you will do for them. I'm not tricking you; all of this really *will* happen, if you are paying attention to what you are doing.

Tasks. What tasks create people-project convergence? For the blending of people and project, choose tasks that draw together individual perspectives on the topic and goals of the project into larger *composites.* Of the exercises described in the next chapter, timelines, landscapes, and composite stories all produce one large multi-perspective story.

If you don't want to use exercises in your session—and you don't need to—think about simpler tasks you can ask people to complete that will create a result in which every person in the room feels represented. Even something as simple as "ten useful trends we see in the stories we worked with," in which each small group contributes three trends that represent their take on the stories, can work. The important thing is to give people something to do that they can find a place to put themselves into. If the tasks you give them don't allow people to represent their own perspectives on the topic,

Figure 11.23. Small acts of imaginative rebellion are signs of convergence in sensemaking.

you won't help them reach convergence with the project. Say you asked people to list the top ten most statistically significant trends in the data. That would be a disaster, because their legitimate response would be, "What do you need *us* for?" Give people tasks they can imbue with meaning together.

Observing convergence between people and project

What does people-project convergence look like? Sometimes it looks like rebellion. If the people in your sensemaking session do *exactly* what you tell them to do, and not a bit more, or if they don't do what you say but don't do anything *else* either, you may not be achieving people-project convergence. Generally when people start finding negotiated common cause in a session, they also start getting ideas about how they can tweak the session to make it better. They say things like: "What if we build *two* of these timelines, one from each perspective?" Or you find six people in a huddle you didn't tell them to get into, frantically copying down names of stories for some new activity they want to squeeze into the schedule. Or you ask people to note three trends and then come back to find out they noted three of one type and three of another.

When you see rebellion like this in sensemaking: rejoice! It means people have found something they want to do together (see Figure 11.23). Gently guide them, yes, if they are proposing things that won't work; but don't say anything like "We have to stick to the schedule."

Because you *don't* have to. The strange thing about narrative sensemaking is that you *want* the session to get away from you. That means it's working. (You don't want it to get away from you in the sense of things moving too *slowly*, as I said above; but getting away from you in the sense of things going in a different direction than you had expected is fine.) A common purpose, and energy to reach it, are more important than strict adherence to the plan. In fact, strict adherence to the plan shows a *lack* of purpose and energy.

So, to observe people-project convergence, be on the lookout for small acts of rebellion. Even something as simple as extra margin notes on story cards or built stories more elaborated than you asked for qualify. If you *can't* find any unauthorized tweaking, see what you can do to improve people-project convergence.

One misconception you might have about people-project convergence is that there has to be only *one* convergence in the session. I've seen sessions in which different groups pursued completely different convergences, taking on different tasks and sub-goals. I've even seen sessions where groups started up (without being asked) joking competitions between different methods of carrying out tasks. Is this a problem? Not at all. As long as the competitions stay civil, and there is enough communication between groups to make sure everyone knows that the separate convergences are still contained within what the whole session is producing, things can work out fine. If I saw this sort of separate convergence taking place, I would do some quick trimming of activities planned for the session end, so we could fit in a grand final negotiation between the two or three convergences that have appeared.

Intervening in people-project convergence

Now let's say you are in your sensemaking session, and people are working away, and everything is going as planned, except for one nagging thing. You can see, in the way people are talking together, that the projects in their minds are not entering into negotiations with each other. What can you do to start negotiations going?

I would start with some quiet *reminders* about expectations. Generally all corrections in sensemaking sessions should be made quietly, usually to a small group, close in, with your head down. Stopping the whole room while you deliver a lecture on what everyone is doing wrong *might* get them to do things right, but it will stop them from converging on negotiated reinterpretations of the session.

My favorite way to remind people of something in a sensemaking session is to ask them an apparently stupid question in which a reminder is embedded. I say things like, "What theme are you guys working on again?" Or, "Where on this timeline have you written the [something they were supposed to write on the timeline and didn't]? I can't find it." And so on. This way people think they are helping the inept facilitator rather than being told what to do.

I suspect this method will not be comfortable or useful for everyone, though. You need to be self-effacing to pull it off. Luckily I'm the queen of self-effacement, if you don't mind my saying it. Your *own* style of quiet reminding may be different than mine. Jokes work well for some people. Some people set up little competitions with statements like, "See what they're doing over there?" Some people are skilled at the insider advice trick: "If I were you...." When you want to manipulate your friends and family, what works for you? Try it here too.

After quiet reminders about expectations, I like to carefully place hints that *rebellion will be tolerated*. Remember how I said you shouldn't ask for input on your session plan at the *start* of the session (page 316)? Remember how I said it might derail the session if you shared control of the plan up front? That wasn't the right time for it. This is. Why? Because by the time people and project are starting to converge, people should understand enough of how narrative sensemaking works to improve rather than hamper the process. Not everyone will, but some might.

The way I like to place these hints is, I'll explain how to do some task, like build a landscape, to the whole room. Then I'll quietly go around and watch people. If I find a group that seems ready to jump to a new level of participation, I might say something like, "You guys might want to add a little something extra to your timeline. How about an extra layer, or another scenario, or something? You seem to have a lot of ideas, and you have the time for it." As above, find your own style for hinting at gaps in your fabric of control.

Finally, practice *accepting* a lack of convergence in the people-project area. It doesn't always happen as much as you'd like it to. The success of any sensemaking session depends on a lot of things, many of which are out of your control. The particular people who came to the session, how they relate, what they had for lunch, the room, traffic outside, so many things can influence a session that you shouldn't expect every single session to come out equally well. Sometimes things just don't gel.

Facilitating convergence among people

Interpersonal convergence in sensemaking is not about group hugging; it's about group listening. It's about people coming out of the room better able to place the experiences of the other people into meaningful perspective than they could when they went in.

How much people know about the other people going in varies widely by project and session. You may find yourself facilitating sessions between old friends who complete each other's sentences, or you may find yourself with people who would never breathe the same air as some others in the room, at least not unless there were bars between them. But convergence is universally useful. There is no group of people who can't learn more about each other than they know now. In fact, in some groups the more people *think* they know about other people the less they actually perceive, because their assumptions get in the way of true listening.

Conditions for convergence among people

What conditions should you set in place to help interpersonal convergence happen?

Expectations. The same expectation I mentioned about people-project convergence applies to interpersonal convergence as well. Create an expectation of *negotiated exploration.*

You want to ask people in your session to open up as they exchange experiences, but you don't want to ask them to expose themselves completely. This is partly because too much mention of "sharing" will scare off some people, but there is also a danger in group sensemaking sessions veering too far into the confessional.

The danger in confessional sensemaking is that *individual* people may find release for their feelings, but the *group* will not discover anything useful in support of collective decision making. People need to have the expectation that they will work with others to discover insights, not just vent or express themselves. For this reason, I tend to avoid the use of the word "share" in sensemaking, because it has taken on the connotation of "confess" or "vent" rather than "work together with a common purpose." In a session devoted to *collecting* stories it may be reasonable to use the word, but the goal here is not to spill the beans but to heap them up into interesting piles together.

A second expectation to set up is one of *respect for experience.* Help people understand the differences between statements of *experience* ("I was floored by what he said"), statements of perceived *fact* ("Didn't you know the council election was rigged?"), and statements of *opinion* ("That's what's wrong with young people today").

Let's say I am participating in a sensemaking session you are facilitating. Let's say I tell a story in response to a story I've found in the collection. Let's say that within the story I tell, I express opinions that the people around me find abhorrent. Say I express the opinion that I should be able to drive as fast as I like.

If you have correctly managed expectations of interpersonal convergence, the people around me should be able to confine their expressions of distaste to the *opinions* I have stated, leaving my recounting of *experience* alone. They should be able to say, "*I see,* you felt empowered when you broke the rules." Or, "*I see,* you liked how driving fast bothered your parents." Or, "*I see,* you felt a rush of adrenaline when you drove fast." Notice how all of these "I see" statements relate to the *experiences* recounted, not the *opinions* expressed. (That's why they all mention the past tense: you felt, you liked.)

The best way to counter an offensive story is not to drown it out or refuse to hear it, but to *surround it with stories from other perspectives.* In this case, the people around me might describe how *they* have experienced speeding, perhaps as innocent victims of speeding-related accidents. I, the offender, should then be able to say "I see" in turn, because we are all following the same rules. If I am *not* able to say "I see" in return, the group should be able to *ask* or even *require* me to do so. That's how effective narrative sensemaking works: *experience meets experience.*

How can *you* as the facilitator help people understand this relatively fine point? How can you stop people from attacking *experiences* along with facts and opinions? It doesn't work to give a lecture on the difference, because most people won't get the point or won't listen. What works better is to keep an eye out for situations where people are responding to opinions or facts rather than experiences. When you encounter such a situation, *lead people back to experiences.* I could have said "lead people *away* from argumentation," but that doesn't work as well. Correcting a negative direction can come off as criticism of an opinion. It's better to give people a *positive* narrative direction to move into (see Figure 11.24 on the next page).

In my speeding example above, let's say you said to the people around me, "We should respect the fact that Cynthia thinks she should be able to drive as fast as she likes." What would be their response? Nobody would put up with that, and they shouldn't have to. The statement implies support for an *opinion* (what Cynthia

Figure 11.24. The best way to counter an offensive story is not to drown it out or refuse to hear it, but to surround it with stories from other perspectives.

thinks), not an *experience* (how Cynthia perceived what happened to her).

The better thing to say is, "Does this story remind anybody of anything *they* have experienced?" Or, "Does anybody *else* want to tell about their experiences related to speeding?" What is sure to happen in the latter case is that some stories about the flip side of adrenaline—the pain of recovery from a devastating accident, for example—are going to come out. Stories will speak to stories.

Tasks. Now some tasks related to interpersonal convergence. This one's easy: just give people things to do that no one person can do alone. Say people need to build a story that incorporates competing perspectives on a topic, or they need to build a timeline in which significant events are included from the perspectives of at least two ethnic groups in your town. If you know your participants well, you can plan tasks for them to complete which place them into a context in which teamwork is required.

As you plan your session, look at all the activities you have lined up, and think about how each activity might play out if people are inclined to work together. Then think about how each activity might play out if people are inclined to isolate themselves. Which response seems more likely for each activity? If you don't see convergence happening (in your imagination), you might want to tweak the tasks you plan so that people need to rely on each other. Every time you say something like, "Make sure your timeline has at least two competing per-

spectives on each event," you increase each group's need to *negotiate* over what they will do together. If the task can be easily broken up and done alone, people are more likely to break it up and do it alone. Don't give people tasks like that; instead, build synergism in.

There are other subtle cues you can use to help people work together. I have mentioned physical signs like giving each group only one sheet of instructions. The way chairs and tables are arranged in the room also helps; one table per group sends a message as well. Sometimes I'll give each group a wall or board to work on, and I'll say something like, "This space is for group A to build things together, and this space is for group B." Giving people things to share gives them reasons to negotiate.

You remember that joke about heaven and hell and the spoons, right? How the people in hell have long spoons and starve because they can't bring food to their mouths, and the people in heaven have the same spoons, but prosper because they feed each other? So, give people long spoons. Give them a reason to approach each other.

Observing convergence among people

What does interpersonal convergence look like? It doesn't have to look like *agreement*, but it does have to look like *connection*. To create connection, groups need *awareness, negotiation* and *representation*. You can watch people to see if they have all these things.

Awareness. When people in a group are aware of each other, you will hear them say things like this.

- Gerry, you haven't filled in the name of your story. It goes right here.
- Have we all read the instruction sheet?
- That's a great story you just told! I can relate to that myself.
- Oh, you're marking your lines with Xs? That's a good idea. Are we all doing that?

In other words, they know what other people in their group are doing. They are paying attention to each other.

When people in groups are *not* aware of each other, you will hear them say things like this.

- (to the facilitator) I'm done with my questions. What should I do next?
- (to the group) I have a story to tell. I'm supposed to tell it to *you*, right?
- (to nobody in particular) I'm putting this sticky note right here.
- (to themselves, mumbling) I don't see the point of this.

What pronouns do you see often in the first examples? You and we and us. In the second examples, it's mostly me me me. Listen to pronoun use when you want to listen to awareness. The higher the we-to-me ratio, the higher the awareness.

When people are unaware of other people in their group, they act as if they are in their own little bubbles. The fact that they are sitting *next* to other people, and that they have been *asked* to work with those other people, means nothing to them. As far as they are concerned, they are in a room with you (nobody ignores the facilitator) and with a whole bunch of cardboard cutouts. If they do address the cardboard cutouts, they use a tone of confused disbelief, like they can't make sense of the fact that they have been asked to actually pay *attention* to these people.

I sometimes see this behavior in people who are used to authority. They are most comfortable lecturing to an audience or being respectfully interviewed, so being asked to *work in a group*

seems like an insult to their dignity. These aren't bad people; they are just used to a different way of working together. Your task is help them understand what you need them to do to make the session work.

You might think the same pattern of unawareness would come up in people who are so *unused* to being heard that they don't feel qualified to participate in the group you asked them to work with. But I've watched these people. They have an *abundance* of awareness, not a lack. People who want to be included (and don't think they are) pay a lot of attention to those who *are* included, just in case the door opens for them. The door should be open for them, only you may need to help them see it.

Negotiation. When people in a group are negotiating with each other, you will hear them say things like this.

- How about we use this story for the future state?
- How many of these do we have? Is this enough?
- I have an idea. Let's take these three stories and put them into the context slot. What do you think?
- My vote would be for the 1986 election as the start for our timeline.

In other words, they don't act on their own. They talk about what the group is going to do; they ask each other questions; they put forth ideas; they discuss their collective endeavors. Listen for words like "let's" and "how about" and "what do you think."

When people are *not* negotiating with each other, you will hear them say things like this.

- I'm building my own landscape.
- I don't know what *you're* doing, but *I'm* listing three characters per story.
- I finished my part of the timeline.
- These three stories are mine, and those two are yours.

When negotiation is lacking, people tend to view the tasks you set out for them as their own tasks, not the group's tasks. They also tend to keep their own stories (whether they told them

Figure 11.25. Groups in which convergence is taking place pay attention to each other, negotiate what they will do together, and represent themselves as a unified group.

or chose them) close to their chests, almost *protecting* them from the other group members. When people do that, they are in a group of one. Usually this doesn't happen to everyone in a group at once; often you will see groups where some of the people are working together and some aren't. Maybe three people will be using we-language and collaborating, while one person is off doing their own thing.

This, by the way, is where the I'm-not-qualified-to-be-here people stand out. They don't feel they have the right to negotiate, so they don't negotiate. They just wait to be told what to do by those in charge. If you notice this happening, it might take just a nudge to empower such a person to speak up, or to remind the others to include the person in negotiations.

Representation. What I mean by representation is that people in a group that shows interpersonal convergence *call themselves something*. They represent their group, to you and to other groups, with some kind of unified description.

When people have created a group representation, you will hear them say things like this.

• Let's call ourselves "the smart group."

• Our motto should be "we know our stuff."

• It sounds like the theme of our group is "phoenix rising from the ashes."

• Look, our landscape is more populated than theirs.

The representation might be a name, a motto, a theme, a competence, a defining characteristic,

even a letter or number (we're the B's and we're proud). It is any kind of attribute applied to the whole group by the whole group.

When people *haven't* created a group representation, you will hear them say things like this.

• My stories all seem to be about dogs.

• You people have too many fictional stories on your landscape.

• Why do you keep mentioning stories about betrayal? What are you, the betrayal corps?

• You people are taking this activity way too seriously. You should be called the overachievers.

Notice how all of these statements set up the individual as *separated* from the group. Some of the statements even make up names, but with a clear understanding that the speaker is *outside* the name. The "you" in these statements isn't the you of you-*and*-me; it's the you of you-and-*not*-me.

When I hear people create names or themes for their groups when I didn't ask them to, I smile, because I know *that* group will discover useful insights. When people start thinking of their group as a team that does things together, they start doing things together (see Figure 11.25).

Sometimes I like to nudge people in the direction of group representation by *asking* them to give their group a name. I don't represent the task as a "team building" exercise, because people usually balk at that. I just say something like, "On the top of this sheet, could you please write something I can use to find your group again? It can be anything, a name or a theme or even a number, just something I can find you by when I'm looking over what we produce today." This seemingly innocent record-keeping request gives people the subtle task of negotiating what sort of collective identity they want to use to represent themselves.

You might have noticed the hint of competition between groups in the fourth statement on the positive-representation list above (our landscape is more populated than theirs). Should you *encourage* groups to compete with each other?

I have mixed feelings about group competition. For some participants, having teams compete makes the whole session more interesting. I've even heard of people giving out points for doing assigned tasks and posting a "scoreboard" with team results. Some people love that sort of thing. But for others, myself included, competition sucks all the fun out of sensemaking. The surest way to get me out of a room is to say we will be competing to gain anything by doing anything. What I love is synergism and mutual aid.

So, whether you should encourage competition between groups in order to improve group coherence depends on the people you expect to attend the session, and on you yourself.

If you can't guess how people will respond, or if you think different groups of people will respond differently, you can use hints instead of rules to leave the door open to competition for those who like it. For example, you could include a brief "walkabout" period in your schedule in which you give groups the option of either continuing to work on their creations or walking around the room looking at what *other* groups have produced. That way people who want to compete, or just wander and look and get inspired, can do that; and people who would rather hunker down and work on their own group creation can do that.

Intervening in convergence among people

What can you do if people are *unaware* of the other people in their groups? Like I said above, generally this doesn't happen to everyone in a group at once. What usually happens is that some of the people in the group try to collaborate, but one person (and usually it is just one) gives off signals that they want to be left alone. They might pepper *you* with questions instead of talking to the people in their group, or they might keep their head down and do what they see as "their part" of whatever task has been set out, or they might just sit there playing with their phone instead of attending.

I don't usually intervene when this happens. It's kind of like the advice people give about little kids fighting: as long as nobody's getting physically hurt, it's better to let them work it out on their own. The other people in the group are most likely aware of the withdrawal, and they can probably address it better than you can. Sometimes a person who started out the session withdrawn from their group will get drawn in by the others in the group, or they'll just warm up after a while. If they don't, probably nothing *you* can do will make them participate.

What can you do if people in a group are not *negotiating* with each other? What if they are not working as a team? One thing I like to do is, if one person in a group asks me a question in such a way that it's clear they want me to talk *only* to them, I don't take the bait. I give my answer to their *whole* group (and only to *their* whole group, not to the whole room). If it's necessary, I repeat the question to the group. To avoid it sounding like I'm exposing them, I say something like, "Charlie has a great question and you'll all want to hear the answer to this." Then I answer.

This sends the message to the question poser that I see them as needing information for their *group*, not for themselves. Or if I notice that one person in a group has built their own construction, I'll go over and ask a faux-stupid question about how it fits with the rest of what their group has done. I don't accuse or criticize, I just *ask for clarification*, and usually that helps people realize that they aren't pulling together.

Finally, what can you do if people in a group don't seem to be creating group representations? Not much. You can notice it and drop hints, but it's not something you can influence by addressing it directly. Representation tends to emerge in well-working groups, and you can't make groups work well together.

But I'm not sure group representation is an absolute guarantee for effective sensemaking. It's more like a nice-to-have, an indicator that things are going especially well. Of the three elements of interpersonal convergence I've mentioned here (awareness, negotiation, representation) awareness is the most important, because if people don't even pay attention to each other they aren't likely to do anything useful together. Negotiation is second in importance, and representation is third.

What I like to do with representation is to use it as an indicator of readiness. If groups aren't exhibiting signs of group representation, you might want to scale back any planned activities that require more teamwork. Or if things are going better than you expected—say each team has given itself a funny name, even though you never mentioned any such thing—you might want to pull something more ambitious out of your toolbox and see if any of the teams might want to rise to a higher challenge.

The last thing I want to say about interpersonal convergence in practice is to remember where you started. Don't expect a room full of strangers to interact in the same way as a room full of extended family members. If there are divisions in the community, watch how you set up group boundaries. Watch out for expectations in your own mind that don't match the context of your session. For example, say you've had one sensemaking session so far in your project, and it succeeded far beyond your hopes. Now let's say you come to your second sensemaking session ready to shoot the moon, but find yourself unable to get groups to even look at each other, let alone work together. Maybe the people in your second session come from different backgrounds than your first. Maybe the topic resonates with them differently. Every sensemaking session is different. Be ready to revise your expectations each time.

Facilitating convergence between people and stories

People-story convergence in narrative sensemaking is what makes it *narrative* sensemaking. You might think I would say that *story-to-story* convergence is what makes narrative sensemaking narrative, that it's the bringing together of stories with stories that matters most. Stories *do* come together during sensemaking, but that convergence is of no use to decision making unless it's part of *people* coming together with stories. Stories come from people, but stories can't build meaning by themselves, any more than clothes can get up and walk around without anybody wearing them.

Wait a minute, you say. *If it's people that matter and not stories, why bother with stories?* Because stories help people dig deeper. With their emphasis on feelings, beliefs, values, perspectives, and experiences, and with the ritualized package of social negotiations they provide, stories help people discover more about any topic than they could otherwise. In the same way that telling a story signals safety to reveal our feelings and beliefs, *building* a story together carries safety into the process of group sensemaking.

Say our group is assembling gathered stories into two larger stories told from opposite perspectives. Questions of what *really* happened, what matters, and what should be done about it do not belong to the realm of story construction, so we put them aside. *After* the larger stories have been created, we can turn to those questions, but we have already explored multiple perspectives without evaluation or attack.

Exploration of multiple perspectives without evaluation or attack is the heart of effective narrative sensemaking. It's where the plan comes together. It's also, obviously, an important part to get right. Let's talk about how.

Conditions for people-story convergence

As above, I will talk about setting up expectations and tasks for people-story convergence.

Expectations. To help people-story convergence work, build an expectation of *resonant emergence*. Emergence means that certain stories and patterns rise in importance as people work together with the story collection.

But emergence is not always resonant. Patterns always emerge when anyone examines any body of sufficiently complex information, whether it has anything to do with them or not. What makes emergence *resonant* is the personal, emotional, practical connections people build between stories, patterns, and themselves. As you help people work with stories, create an expectation of *connection to the stories.*

Of course you should never start a sensemaking session by giving a lecture on the meaning of the term "resonant emergence." Nobody would listen. Just drop words into your instructions and conversations that help people understand that you invite them to *bring themselves into the process.*

Say things like this.

- What patterns or trends do you see here that speak to you?
- Does anything in these stories call out to be noticed? What does it mean to you?
- If you were going to tell three of these stories to a friend, which three do you think you would choose, and what order do you think you would tell them in?
- What do you see here that you want to remember? Can you make a note of it?
- How do you feel these stories fit together? Are there any clusters that have meaning to you?

Don't say things like this.

- List the top ten trends in these answers to questions.
- Your task is to rank these stories by strength.
- Please take these stories and build a larger story with them using this structure.
- Next you should prove to me which stories are the most important.

Notice how these two sets of statements differ. The first set is focused on the *participants:* how they feel, what they see and hear in the stories, what matters to them, what they want to remember, what things mean to them. To *them,* not in general. The second set of statements makes no reference to the participants. Those statements refer only to the *stories,* and to universals such as listing, ranking, structuring, and proof. The people aren't *in* the statements.

When you speak to people about what they will do with stories, keep the people in all of your statements. People will pick up on what you say. Remember that the people in any sensemaking session are looking to *you* to define what behaviors are reasonable and expected. Understand what you expect people to do in your own mind, then radiate that expectation out to them.

Tasks. Do you need tasks to create people-story convergence? Yes, you do. It is a bad idea to assume this type of convergence will happen on its own. I've watched people who were working with stories together without being given direction as to what they should be doing. People tend to generate lots of *variety* in such situations, but they don't draw it together into fewer larger things without being asked to do so. It all sits there being muddled and complex, and they muddle through it until the time is up, then leave the session unresolved. You *do* need people to reach convergence on this point, because even though the muddling-through part is important in exposing people to variety (that's contact and churning), you want the session to end with some kind of coherent results that will be useful to decision making.

The one exception I've seen to this rule has been with a roomful of professionals such as scientists, doctors, or lawyers. In that case the opposite problem comes up: professionals tend to rush to *premature* convergence without ranging widely enough in their contact and churning. With that sort of room I usually have to keep saying "but have you looked at *this*" and "why not consider *this* as well" and so on. But with most people, convergence is something you need to help them achieve.

So what sort of task works to create people-story convergence? Any task in which people take lots of small things and merge them into fewer larger things will work, as long as those fewer larger things represent the perspectives of the people involved. All of the sensemaking exercises I describe in this book involve convergence, but don't think you have to use any of them in its entirety to have people-story convergence in your session. You can simplify any of the exercises until it's not much more than a single task, and you can avoid exercises entirely. Just give people something to do that draws things together in such a way that they can find themselves in what they produce. It might be stories, patterns, clusters, perspectives, plays, murals—the sky's the limit, as long as it's *one* sky and it's *their* sky.

Observing people-story convergence

I have noticed three particular categories of story that tend to come up often when people and stories are converging together. I call them *pivot* stories, *voice* stories, and *discovery* stories. When *you* watch people working together with stories, you should see the emergence of these stories taking place.

Pivot stories. As people follow threads of connection through dimensions of meaning in the stories they are considering, once in a while they will find themselves saying, "Look, there's *that* story again." Those are what I call the pivot stories of the collection. Pivot stories *just keep coming up.*

Pivot stories are not usually the most memorable or revelatory stories in the collection, but they are situated at *articulations* of the story collection: joints, junctures, hinges, points of intersection. Because of this, in pivot stories *all of the things that matter in the project happen together.* Maybe trust meets rebellion, or the official story meets the ground truth, or the reason nobody will talk about something meets the reason nobody will fix something. It's all in there. These stories are like miniaturized copies of the entire project in one recounting of events. Read them and you can see what the project is about.

To observe the emergence of pivot stories, look at *wear patterns*. People who design things to be used repeatedly, like shoes and tires, and people who diagnose the health of things used repeatedly, like feet and hands, use wear patterns to understand how things are used. You can observe wear patterns as you observe sensemaking, by looking at the physical objects people use in your session. This is yet another reason why working with physical objects in sensemaking is easier than working with computers. On a computer, you *can* get at wear patterns, but you have to know things about computers that most people don't. Anybody can look at a card to see how much it has been handled. So, as people work with story cards and other information, look to see if some cards or sheets or names are more often handled (and copied and passed from hand to hand) than others. If some story cards are being literally worn out, those are the pivot stories.

Voice stories. These are stories that sing out, that beg to be heard, that have wings and are poised to fly. They are memorable because they break through barriers of assumption, fear, ignorance, reluctance, or stereotype. They bring perspectives or experiences that are not widely known into wider awareness. Voice stories usually involve some risk to their tellers, but they also typically include relief and gratitude for "the chance to finally speak out." Voice stories, as the name implies, are especially useful in communications about the project to those less involved with it. They speak for the people and project and stories involved in the session.

Let's pretend that you are a participant in a sensemaking session and I am the facilitator. Through repeated, varied contact, you and your group have become perfectly familiar with the project's story collection. Now let's say that after the session has been going on for some time, a person comes in late and asks to be included in the session. (If that seems unlikely, let's say she has a lot of weight to throw around, so I have to let her in whether I like it or not.)

I ask you to let the latecomer join your group. The latecomer sits down at your table and takes a quick look at the story cards you have spread out on it. Then she turns to you and says, "I don't see the point of looking at these stories. Why bother? I already know about the topic. What is there in these stories that I don't already know?" This is where voice stories will stand out. If you know the stories well, some stories will leap to mind and *beg* you to use them to represent the collection.

Similarly, after a sensemaking session is over, voice stories will nominate themselves to be used in communications outside the session. If, for example, your group has decided as the result of sensemaking to do something that may be unpopular to some in the community, you may find it useful to choose voice stories that "speak for the decision" by representing some of the needs you hope to meet.

However, voice stories, as useful as they are, also have in them the potential to derail sense-

Figure 11.26. Pivot stories, voice stories, and discovery stories emerge during convergence as being especially important to the project.

making. Some voice stories attack sacred beliefs, shout taboos and disturb resting conflicts; some expose unpopular, even offensive views of other people or groups; some use hateful or abusive language. Be careful not to exclude the most useful stories in your collection from sensemaking because they are also the most upsetting.

The best way to keep the useful parts of voice stories and avoid the upsetting parts is to focus on the *experiences* described in the stories, not on the *language* used in them. When people encounter such toxic-yet-revealing stories during sensemaking, instead of dropping them from consideration, try asking groups to *redescribe* the experiences of the storytellers in their *own* words. Ask them to *replace* the names of people or groups with generic or even fictional names. (Clearly label such replacements, of course, as well as the reason they were implemented.) Ask your participants to think about the *emotions* the storytellers are experiencing in the story. What do they fear? What do they hope for? What can the group draw from the experiences described that will help in sensemaking?

To observe the emergence of voice stories, look for *retellings*. If a story wants to travel, it will find ways to be told and retold. In some sessions I've seen one story bounce its way all around a room without any one participant becoming fully aware of how many times the story was retold. You can't see retelling in wear patterns, because telling a story doesn't necessarily put any fingerprints on its card; but you can *hear* voice stories being retold if you listen.

Another way to observe voice stories is to listen for the creation of shorthand references. If you hear someone say, "Did you hear the umbrella story yet?" you've found a voice story.

Discovery stories. These stories solve mysteries. They are not particularly memorable or central, but they surprise somebody with new knowledge. You could also call them "aha" stories. When people encounter a discovery story, they say, "Oh, is *that* how it is?" Or, "I didn't know *that*."

Of course, whether a story contains a discovery depends on who is doing the discovering. A discovery for one person might be something another person thinks everyone knows and still another person thinks is an outright lie. That's fine, because these discoveries are not of *facts;* they are of *perspectives.* A discovery story reveals "how it is" not in general but *to a person in a context from a perspective.* Thus a discovery story is one in which people discover things about the experiences of others that they had not understood before.

In sensemaking, discovery stories have the potential to create new bridges of understanding between experiences, either between groups of people at the session or between the people at the session and the people who told the stories. The best discovery stories grow stories around themselves during sensemaking, stories where things change from one state of understanding (before the story) to another (after). These larger stories enter into and change the sensemaking process.

To observe the emergence of discovery stories, look for *memoranda*. What I mean is, look for instances of people making a note of something they don't want to forget. Discovery stories, because they create new understandings, cause people to say, "Let's make a note of that." Or, "Let's keep that in mind." When you see people marking up stories with "remember this" markings, or making extra copies of stories, or putting stories in a special place where they can get at them again easily, you're seeing discovery stories emerge. (Figure 11.26 on the preceding page shows some examples of pivot stories, voice stories, and discovery stories.)

Pivot patterns, voice patterns, discovery patterns. Not to complicate things too much, but for each of these types of emergent story there is a corresponding type of emergent *pattern* in data about stories. Such patterns usually appear in answers to questions about stories, but patterns can appear in other information about stories too, like how long they are or what words they use. Emergent patterns are stories, too, only they are stories about what people discovered in the session.

- Pivot patterns work in the same way as pivot stories, only instead of saying "there's that story again" people say "there's that pattern again." For example, you might hear people talking over and over about how the older the story, the less conflict is in it. When people come up with a motto based on repeated contact with a trend, a motto like "the more we look back the better things get," they've found a pivot pattern.

- Voice patterns assemble the risks and releases embodied within voice stories into larger choruses. Voice patterns can be seen in retellings, just like voice stories. You'll hear people saying things like, "Did you hear about the umbrellas-and-cats issue?"

- Discovery patterns are the closest a sensemaking session can get to the findings of an analytical study. These are patterns in the data that people notice and want to remember. Again, notice memoranda of patterns people want to get back to.

If a sensemaking session has gone well, by the end of it, some stories and patterns of each of these types should have emerged and resonated with the participants. See "Wrapping up sensemaking" (page 372) for more on using these stories and patterns as you end the session.

Intervening in people-story convergence

What can you as the facilitator do if people-story convergence is *not* happening in your sensemaking session? What if you look for the emergence of pivot stories, voice stories, and discovery stories, and you can't find any? What if people *never* say "there's that story again" or "did you hear about this" or "we need to remember that?" What can *you* do about it?

The kind of intervention I like to do in this situation is what I call a *resource offering*. If I notice that in a particular group something is not happening that should be happening, I'll walk over and quietly *give* the group something. Then I'll tell them the resource is for them to use *whenever* the thing that is not happening happens. The resource might be a notebook or a marker or a special color of sticky note I've been holding in reserve for exactly this use. I do this quietly, without alerting the whole room. I don't say there is a problem; I just give them the thing as if I had always meant to give it to them but forgot to.

For pivot stories I might say, "This is to help you remember stories or patterns you *keep coming across* as you work." For voice stories I might say, "This is for remembering stories or patterns you *want to tell other people about* later in the session." For discovery stories I might say, "This is for noting down stories or patterns you want to *remember as important discoveries* as you work." Or I might decide not to be specific, and just tell them the extra thing is for taking notes on anything they want to get back to later.

I find that by offering a resource instead of a lecture, I can help people stand back and examine their expectations about what they are doing together without making them feel that they are doing things wrong (see Figure 11.27 on the following page). In sensemaking, it's almost more important to avoid people *thinking* they are doing things wrong than it is to avoid people doing things wrong. The more attention

Figure 11.27. If people aren't reaching convergence in their work with stories, you can nudge them by offering them resources to use for convergence.

people pay to how to do things correctly, the more they twist their momentum into knots.

I know this method works because I have watched people after I offer resources to them in this way. They stare at me for a while, then they start looking at each other. Sometimes they laugh. Then they pick up the thing I gave them and start talking about what I said it was for. Then they start talking about what they should *do* so that they have a use for the thing. I don't know if this technique will work for everyone, but I find it works a lot better than going to a group and saying, "Why aren't you people finding any pivot stories? I want you to start writing down pivot stories." Not only does such a direct correction derail any exploration they had going on (maybe some useful rebellion); it puts people on the defensive. People on the defensive spend their energy building walls of justification instead of exploring their environments.

That's a small intervention, a hint really, and not all groups take it up. Other than dropping hints like that, there isn't that much you can do about people-story convergence. Sometimes the mix of stories and roles and personalities and topic doesn't cause things to draw together in the way you thought they would. Sometimes nothing emerges, or at least nothing emerges right then.

Remember to maintain humility and respect throughout the sensemaking session. You as the facilitator may have a lot riding on your session. You might have had a hard time selling

the project to your community or organization. Especially if you only have *one* sensemaking session scheduled, you may feel a lot of pressure for things to go well in it.

But you aren't a participant in the session, and you can't possibly have read the mind of every person in the room. Sometimes people need to maintain barriers that you would rather have them break down. Be careful not to pressure people to take steps they are uncomfortable with because *you* want the project to succeed. Sometimes people just aren't ready to arrive at or admit to discoveries, even when everyone in the room can see them. But just because they don't arrive there in the room in front of you doesn't mean they'll never get there. Sometimes a failure to converge with stories in sensemaking is not so much a failure as much as it is feelings at work. Sensemaking that doesn't come to a neat and tidy resolution has still happened, and it can still have an impact.

FACILITATING CHANGE

As we begin to talk about change in sensemaking, I would like to take a little time to justify the change element to you before we go on. Sometimes people don't believe me when I tell them that sensemaking is about change. They think sensemaking is just a fancy word for discussion or analysis. They don't see change as important or worth trying to create. They think I'm going all New Age on them, or trying to sell them a religion, or advocating political agitation. I'm not doing any such thing. I'm just telling you that if you want to gain the advantages of sensemaking, you *need* to understand why change matters.

Why does change matter?

To explain why change matters, I would like to tell you a story about the most powerful change I have ever seen happen in a sensemaking session. On the evening of the tenth of September, 2001, I was on my way home from a sensemaking session in Washington, D.C. Thankfully I got home the night before the attacks in New York and Washington; some of my colleagues had a much longer trip home than I did. The session was part of a three-year government-funded research project on sensemaking for decision support. Our next session, in which we had planned to experiment with new sensemaking techniques with a group of experienced analysts and historians, was set for two weeks later.

The topic of the session, like the one before it, was asymmetric conflict, that is, conflict between two powers whose resources or tactics differ widely. In the two intervening weeks, the mindset of our session participants toward the topic of asymmetric conflict changed entirely.

As we entered the room on the first morning of our planned three-day session, it was easy to tell that the room was charged with feeling. People were sorrowful, angry, blaming, defensive, and certainly not ready to consider multiple perspectives on *anything*, let alone asymmetric conflict.

Our first scheduled exercise went horribly wrong. We had planned to start the session by asking people to create and tell two composite stories from different points of view. Each story was to be presented as if a teacher was explaining recent events to their students in class. One speaker was to be a non-Muslim U.S. teacher. The other was to be a moderate yet devout Muslim teacher in a Middle Eastern country, one who been told the U.S. was "the Great Satan" but now wasn't sure what to think.

The first story, told from the point of view of the U.S. teacher, went reasonably well. Even though there was an edge of tension in the stories, they were complex and involved multiple perspectives on asymmetric conflict, some-times drawing in historical parallels such as the American civil war.

The second story, however, was remarkably different. To our surprise, the participants did *not* tell stories from a moderate point of view, as asked. Instead, the stories were radicalized. They were short and simple, not complex, and they were fueled by powerfully emotional terms like "infidels" and "evil" and "Satan," which took precedence over plot, setting, character, everything. They were not really stories at all, but diatribes, rants. The difference was striking.

Of course, the emotions people expressed in this exercise were perfectly understandable, and I don't mean to imply that they weren't. The validity of the emotions expressed is not the issue at hand. The issue is that these well-educated, open-minded, professional people were held back by circumstances in which they found themselves from formulating a complex, nuanced representation of the experiences of people with perspectives different from their own. That condition limited their ability to make sense of the situation in ways that would support effective decision making. If you translate this condition to situations *you* know of in your own community or organization, it should not be difficult to think of people finding themselves in a similar state. I can certainly think of times when I've been in such a state, more than a few.

After some discussion, my colleagues and I decided that we had better back way off the here and now. We had plenty of time, so we asked people to choose asymmetric conflicts reaching far back into the past. Being history buffs, our participants were able and willing to offer up some magnificently useful conflicts. We asked people to create detailed timelines for each conflict, specifying aspects such as turning points, surprises, interventions, dilemmas, mysteries, miscommunications, and so on. For example, in one of the most resonant conflicts considered, the War of 1812, the U.S. played the role of the small, ragged aggressor attacking the world's sole superpower. We also asked people to venture into the creation of what-if scenarios, and this they did with fervor. Eventually every wall of the two communicating rooms we had at our disposal was covered with aspects of factual and fictional events in the timelines of asymmetric conflicts going back for millennia.

Next we asked people to begin drawing together what they had created by clustering elements from all the timelines. We began to see common aspects such as power, belief, opinion, communication, strategy, technology, accelerators of change, and so on. The "clusters of clusters" that emerged gave us a set of "lenses" through which we could look at any asymmetric conflict in order to see it from all sides. We reached this state on the third afternoon after the first morning's disastrous storytelling exercise. In all the time between we avoided any direct references to recent events.

We then finally felt it was time to begin to work directly with the events of 9/11. We asked our participants to create a new time line, this time covering recent events, using the lenses we had developed as probes to help us connect events on the timeline to characteristics of similar events in the past.

The change in the room since the last time we considered the same events was dramatic. This time the participants considered, juxtaposed and made sense of *all* perspectives on recent events, whether they agreed with those perspectives or not. They didn't simplify other views. They took into full consideration the experiences, beliefs, values, and feelings of those whose actions and opinions they found abhorrent, not because they no longer found them abhorrent, but because they could consider them *even so* without feeling that their own views were in any way threatened. They spoke of power dynamics, public opinion, recruitment, networking, cultural divides, rules of engagement, expectations, options, strategies.

Sun Tzu's concept of the golden bridge, and Mao Tse-Tung's use of it, came up in discussion. The adage of the golden bridge is, "When you surround an army, leave an outlet free. Do not press a desperate foe too hard." From whatever side (or sides) you see the conflict embodied in the events of 9/11, this connection is undoubtedly relevant. As I recall it, the session participants applied the adage to *both* sides of the conflict, with insights deriving from each application.

The change in the way these participants thought about the topic under consideration, under difficult conditions, convinced me that sensemaking has the power to help people make better decisions together. You can translate the experience these participants had to *any* situation in which people begin by viewing a situation (legitimately and reasonably) from one perspective only, and end by seeing the situation from many perspectives—critically, *without* feeling their own perspectives to be in danger.

I don't mean to imply, by the way, that the participants in this session became dispassionate or disinterested in the topic as a result of their sensemaking. Nor do I want to imply that the emotions they felt in the first part of the session were illegitimate. These people didn't *discard* the intensity of their emotions as a result of sensemaking; they *transcended* them, which is something entirely different. The process of sensemaking increased their *ability* and *resources* to make sense of the situation *together with*, not in spite of, their own feelings about and opinions of it. This ability to transcend opinions and emotions is not *less* important in times when our emotions are running high; it is far *more* important.

Your role in making change happen

Assuming I've convinced you of the value of change in sensemaking, I'll now go into how you as a facilitator can help change happen. The first two elements of sensemaking (contact, churning) are events *you* choose, set up, and guide along. The third element (convergence) depends mostly on what you set up in the first two parts, but you can still observe and intervene in that element. The last element (change) is not about what you *do* but about what *happens* because of the things you do—if you do them right.

So to talk about change in sensemaking, I can talk about *expectations* that make it more likely to happen, and I can talk about *observations* you can make about what works and what doesn't. But there is no point talking about *tasks* or *interventions,* as I did when talking about convergence. Just as if you were baking a cake, you had better keep your hands out of the oven of change. You will get burned, and you'll probably ruin the cake anyway.

Am I saying you are powerless to create change in sensemaking? No, I'm not. In fact, you *are* the power that can make change happen. But to gain that power, you need to do some work *between* sessions.

Great cooks do much of their thinking between recipes. Have you ever heard about chefs making the same dish dozens of times in rapid succession, working to get the recipe just right? That's what you should do as you facilitate sensemaking sessions. I'm no chef, but my banana bread recipe sits in my cookbook as a series of about twenty sticky-note versions, starting from what I read in the book decades ago and moving forward, each recipe slightly different from the one below it, and ending with the current version on top. My sensemaking session recipe sits in my mind in a similar way. Yours will too. That stack of experiences *is* your power to make change happen. If you *don't* stack your experiences—meaning, if you don't reflect between sessions—you won't improve your power to make change happen.

I just told you that I would cover expectations and observations of change here; but actually I'm going to put off talking about observations of change until we cover the post-session review in "Wrapping up sensemaking" (page 372). In this section I'll just talk about expectations.

Facilitating change between people and project

When there has been change between people and project, the project going into the sensemaking room is not the same as the project coming out. It's that simple. But how do you make that happen?

Expectations. Helping people expect change in their relationships to your project is all about setting up *give and take* between you and your participants. This works both ways.

First, you need to give the people a voice in what will undoubtedly feel like *your* project. Be aware that you are likely to feel possessive about your project. I have noticed that the more time I put into a project, and the more unsung I feel about my contribution, the more I feel it belongs to me, by some universal right of blood, sweat, and tears. That right *does* exist, but it doesn't reach as far as you or I would like it to. It *isn't* your project, it's everybody's project. If you don't share the project, you can ruin things for everyone.

How can you set up the expectation that people are invited to share the project with you? Watch the way you talk about the project in your session. Don't say "the" project or "my" project or "the committee's" project or "the project I've prepared" or "the project I've invited you to join." Don't even say "your" project; that would be passive-aggressive, because you *have* done a lot of work on it. Say "our" project and "our" session. You'd be surprised how much a little thing like that can matter.

The flip side of the give-and-take equation is that you need to assert yourself as you ask people to share the project with *you*. You *have* worked long and hard on it, and you need them to respect that. The more put-upon or disrespected you feel, the harder it will be to carry out your plans. Don't let people walk all over you. (See Figure 11.28 on the next page.)

How can you set up an expectation that people should share the project with you? As they say in school, *show your work*. Don't make the mistake of thinking people *know* how hard you have worked. How can they, if you don't tell them? This is one of the reasons I say (in other places) to make sure the documents you give people (letters, handouts, story cards, graphs) are beautiful to look at. It's partly for clarity, but it's also a demonstration of effort. The same thing applies to the things you *say* to people. If you have a spiel to give at any point in your sensemaking session, don't wing it; practice it until you know it by heart. Bowl people over with what you have done, because that will provide them with an obligation to do their own part as well.

Which of these two sides of give and take matters more in any sensemaking session will depend on you, your participants, and your topic. If you're the dominating sort, make sure you don't dominate the project to death. If you're the self-effacing sort, make sure you don't efface yourself out of the project you've worked so hard on. If your participants are a bunch of

Figure 11.28. Don't say "my" project or "your" project, because both of those things will cause people to react possessively or evasively. Say "our" project, because that includes both you and them.

hard-headed skeptics who will argue with every word that comes out of your mouth, prepare to assert yourself strongly. If they are all so humble and timid that they will hide in the corners of the room, prepare to assert *their* right to participate. You know what you're like, and you should know what they are like. Plan accordingly.

There is one other expectation you need to set up in order for people-project change to happen: both you and your participants need to understand that they (and you) are being asked to be *open to change*. The success of the session depends on a shared willingness to examine assumptions, entertain new ideas and broaden views. You can't go on a journey together if nobody is willing to take a step.

Beware of self-delusion in this, both in your participants and in yourself. It is possible to collect stories, convene participants, and conduct exercises that follow established recommendations perfectly, creating contact, churning, and convergence, all without breaking through to *any* change. If nothing has changed as a result of a sensemaking session—if nothing feels any different than before you started, for anyone attending—you may only have gone through the motions of sensemaking. Sometimes people even do this on purpose, so they can *say* they held a narrative sensemaking session, all the while protecting themselves against any possible change. When that happens, they would be better off spending their time doing something else.

How can you set up an expectation of change? *Before* the session starts, talk about what you expect to happen *after* it's over. Explain that projects *always* change during sensemaking sessions. Say something like, "In the last period of the session we will discuss how the project has changed as a result of what we have done here today." If you are so confident that change will happen that you have set aside a time to discuss it, people will observe that confidence and internalize it. What if you're wrong and change *doesn't* happen? That's okay; you can discuss *that*. Besides, I've never seen such a thing happen. Something *always* changes.

Facilitating change among people

You may be surprised at what I'm going to say about change among people in sensemaking. Don't oversell cooperation, to yourself or to your participants. Don't pretend that everyone will leave the room in a state of post-cooperative bliss. That's not going to happen, and you don't need it to happen, and thinking it will happen or should happen could cause problems. The best expectation to set up about interpersonal change is that *we will be a working group*. We will *get things done together* in this room today, no matter how much we agree or disagree. Together we will see things we did not see before.

The goal of a sensemaking session is not to *cure* anything. It's not therapy, and you're not a therapist, so don't feel you've failed if people aren't holding hands and singing at the end. The goal is to come to new understandings and insights that will lead to decisions that better the community. The end result of your *project* might be that people in your community or organization get along better, but the end result of the *session* needn't be.

I can recall a few sensemaking sessions in which two or three groups ended the session staring at each other with arms folded. The sessions weren't failures, because those same people did find out things they didn't know before, and we could use that in the project, whose ultimate goal included bringing those people together again. In fact, I'd say that if nobody *ever* gets angry or offended during a sensemaking session, you aren't digging very deep. Don't rile people up on purpose, but don't rush to fix everything either. And don't set up the expectation that harmony will always prevail. Emphasize the synergy of discovery, not the balm of friendship.

Facilitating change between people and stories

Now we have arrived at our very last combination of elements: change between people and stories. Recall that both the people who have participated in sensemaking and the stories they have worked with should change as a result of their coming together. The people should have learned and discovered, and the stories should have become more connected (and possibly more annotated) than they were.

How can you influence change between people and stories? By setting up expectations about how people and stories will relate to each other by the end of the session. In every sensemaking session, every facilitator has to say to the participants, in one way or another, "Here are the stories." There are a thousand ways to say that. The ways in which you choose to talk about the stories in your sensemaking session have a

strong impact on the expectations people develop about their relationship to those stories.

Here are some *unhelpful* things I've seen people (including myself) say, intentionally or unintentionally, about working with collected stories during sensemaking (see Figure 11.29 on the following page).

Here are the precious stories we laboriously collected. These stories represent the true, authentic, respected voices of valued people in our community. This statement cordons off your collected stories with a velvet rope. If you describe your stories in this way, your participants won't go near them, no matter how much you contradict yourself and beg them to.

Here's some stuff people said. This statement *downplays* the importance of the stories, as if they were trash left in the room by a previous group. The stories you have collected *do* matter, and they *are* important, and people *should* treat them with respect—by putting them to good use.

These stories were told by people you have nothing in common with. Don't say that, and don't even think it, because it's *never* true. Even if the stories were told by people who share no outward characteristics with the people in your sensemaking session, there will *still* be things in the stories people can connect to. That's why stories are so important to human communication. Make sure people know that you expect them to *find themselves*, even if obliquely, in the stories told by others. Create an expectation of connection.

This is the narrative data we will be analyzing today. Don't let any *hint* of words associated with analytical research creep into your statements. Avoid the words *data, analysis, proof, evidence, measurement,* and so on. This is probably the biggest new-practitioner mistake I've seen in setting up expectations for working with stories. People new to facilitating are sometimes nervous about asking people to do "touchy-feely" things with stories. They don't want to ask people to open up and let stories impact them emotionally. So they fall into using analytical terms as a way of insulating themselves from risk. If you find yourself doing that,

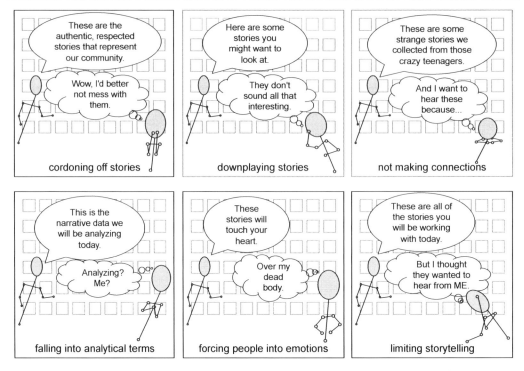

Figure 11.29. These are a few unhelpful ways to present stories for use in sensemaking.

stop. Find the courage to ask people to explore their emotions with you.

I want you to be touched by these stories. While you shouldn't present stories as data, don't bully people into feeling or expressing emotions either. If the collected stories don't resonate with them, that's not their fault. People don't have to scream and go into fetal positions for sensemaking to work. They just need to listen and respond.

Here are some stories in this spreadsheet (or some other technically complicated presentation). The message in this statement is: everyone here had better be comfortable with computers and data analysis; otherwise you might as well leave now. Don't block people off from stories. If you happen to have a group of people who all love spreadsheets and are enabled, not blocked, by them, such a statement will do no damage. But rarely is that the case.

The stories are on this wall for you to look at. I like putting stories up on walls, but only if it's possible to rearrange them or copy them or do *something* with them other than just stare at them. Putting stories up in fixed displays, as if

people were in a museum, sends a message of expected passivity.

Here are some starter stories to spark your imagination. This statement implies that people are going to be working primarily with their *own* stories in the session. Unless your collected stories are very sparse or uneven, you should aim for people to use about seventy-five percent collected stories and twenty-five percent of their own stories. Don't give people the impression that the collected stories will not be used in the session.

You must work only with these stories. While your collected stories shouldn't be presented as sidebars to sensemaking, they also must not be presented as rigid commands. The more you make working with the collected stories mandatory, the less interest people will have in them.

So what's the *right* way to present stories? There are many, but the way I like best to present stories to people is *as a resource for sensemaking.* Other useful terms are *food for thought* or *working materials.*

This is another reason I recommend the use of story cards. Most people recognize the format of playing cards right away. Nobody just sits and looks at playing cards. Playing cards are never cordoned off, nor are they trivial *or* precious to any card game. Cards in a card game are necessary but not sufficient. Cards can't play a game by themselves, but people can't play a card game without cards. That's *just* the way you want people to see the stories they use in sensemaking: useful, accessible, inviting, insufficient.

FINDING YOUR OWN SENSEMAKING STYLE

In the preceding sections I talked a lot about "your participants" in a sensemaking exercise. Now it's time to talk about you.

Any approach that is going to produce useful results in a group of people has to fit the way people think. It is not wrong to consider *yourself* as one of the people whose thinking the approach has to fit.

Let me put it this way. If the success of a sensemaking session depended on everyone taking off their clothes, and you were doing the session in a nudist colony so everyone there was fine with it, but *you* weren't anything like fine with it, would the session succeed? Of course not. If you can't make it work for *you*, you can't make it work. You can work on your skills in whatever areas give you pain, but until you do that, you need to go with your strengths.

So what *are* your strengths when it comes to facilitating sensemaking? I can think of a few strengths you might have, in the form of dimensions along which you are sure to vary.

Enthusiasm

How much energy do you typically convey to the people around you? What do people say you are? A whirlwind? A quiet person? A stick-in-the-mud? If you have a lot of energy, draw on that to get other people excited about the opportunities provided by a sensemaking session. If you don't have a lot of obvious energy in your personality, help yourself out by preparing things you can say that convey the potential of the session for you.

Explanation

How good are you at explaining complicated things to people without them getting confused or frustrated? Are you a good teacher? If you are great at this, you might be able to use more complex elaborations of sensemaking exercises than some others can. If you know you have a hard time explaining things, give yourself more time to gain experience before you try some of the more complicated sensemaking possibilities described in this book (like adding a third dimension to landscapes or building stories out of story elements).

Multi-perspective thinking

When people are thinking in a blinkered, closed-minded way, are you good at waking them up to other ways of looking at things? Do your friends laugh because you always have something to say for the "wrong" side of things? Or do they laugh because you never budge from your fixed opinions?

If you habitually see things from multiple perspectives, work on ways to incorporate that skill into your facilitation of sensemaking. Maybe you can help people look at stories from multiple viewpoints, or you can ask different groups to look at the same stories in different ways. Use what you do naturally to help other people see what you can see.

If seeing things from multiple perspectives is challenging for you, work on your own skills before you ask other people to join you in the activity. How can you work on seeing things from multiple perspectives? First of all, lots of people have written self-help books and magazine articles and web sites full of advice on how to get better at looking at things from all sides. Visit a library or a computer and see what you find. If you are the sort of person who likes to learn how your mind works, take a look at the area of psychology called "perspective taking." People have spent decades learning how people develop skills at seeing things from all sides, and there is much interesting work to read about there.

To start you out, here's a little perspective-taking exercise you could use in preparation for facilitating sensemaking. Find an article written somewhere—in a newspaper, in a magazine, on a web site. Now seek out at least two articles on the same topic but likely to disagree with it in some way. Read and compare all of the articles. The challenge is to find something you can agree with *and* something you can disagree with in *each* of the articles. Start with small differences in perspective, then work your way up to differences over which people would be willing to come to blows.

Another technique is to talk about an issue with as many people as you can find: neighbors, friends, relatives, colleagues. Make sure you find people who differ in their opinions on the topic. If everyone says the same thing, seek a wider range. Now think of another issue, but this time *imagine* the perspectives you might hear *before* you actually hear them. Then go and talk to the people. Did you guess well? If you do this over and over, you will improve your ability to envision differences in perspective without actually having to find the people who might say them. Such a skill is useful when it comes to making sense of multivocal information such as is found in a collection of stories.

Tolerance for ambiguity

Are you the sort of person who wakes up on Saturday morning with a full list of everything you plan to accomplish in your mind? Or do you just wake up and see what happens? If you are the planning sort, think about how you can keep your sensemaking sessions open for your participants. Sensemaking doesn't work as well when everything is planned out perfectly. There has to be some open space left for emergence.

For example, part of a landscape exercise involves people discovering features of their landscape (see page 406). Will it bother you that you don't know what forms those features will take? If someone comes up to you during the feature-discovery part of the exercise and asks, "What sorts of features are we supposed to find?" will you be able to tell them, convincingly, that the landscape will tell them what to find on it? Or will you need to have some sort of feature-type list to fall back on?

If you do need a feature-type list—if leaving things hanging open makes you physically sick—you don't *have* to run the exercise that way. You don't have to change your personal-

ity to facilitate sensemaking. You can give people the lists you think you would need if you were doing the exercise, if you follow two conditions. First, *test* any lists you come up with on landscapes of your own, with helpers if possible. Second, present lists as *optional resources,* never as commands. That way you and the people like you won't collapse with anxiety over uncertainty, and the people who thrive on uncertainty will ignore your silly lists and listen to the universe breathing.

PLANNING YOUR SENSEMAKING SESSION

Now that we have covered the elements of a successful sensemaking session, let's talk about the nuts and bolts of sensemaking logistics. In this section I will cover the same topics as I did for story collection sessions ("Planning your group story session" on page 166), with only a few additions that are special to sensemaking. I hope that will help you compare the two types of session.

How many people to involve

Two things can impact how many people are involved in sensemaking sessions: how many people your project *needs,* and how many people your project can *get.*

How many people you need

How many people do you need to participate in sensemaking? The answer to this question varies with the goals, focus, and scope of your project.

Goals. The most ambitious projects aim to build strong support for decision making, for example with a detailed report full of policy recommendations that will eventually impact millions of people. To support that level of output, you need a large, varied group of people doing the sensemaking work that leads up to it. The least ambitious projects have more of a meandering curiosity about their topic, or they are pilot projects meant to see what the approach has to offer. For low-key projects, you don't need as many people doing sensemaking.

Focus. A project with a compact focus covering only one topic will need fewer sensemaking participants than a project with an wide focus covering several topics.

For multiple topics, it may be best to hold separate sessions for each, then follow them up with a *blending session* in which results from the previous separate sessions are considered together. That means more people.

Scope. During sensemaking you will need people to consider a reasonable sample of the stories you collected (and answers to questions about them). The more stories you have collected, the more people you will need to consider them. Think about this when you plan your project. If you collect more stories and answers than you are prepared to deal with in sensemaking, you may unbalance the project and waste the valuable time and energy of contributors. If you feel you need to collect a large number of stories, perhaps to cover many views, expand the scope of your sensemaking to match this goal.

Taking goals, focus, and scope together, you can see that a project's need for sensemaking participants could range from as few as half a dozen to as many as a hundred people. The most typical need, in a typical-sized project with one topic and 100–300 stories, is for ten to thirty participants.

How many people you can get to participate

Participating in a sensemaking session requires more of a time and energy commitment than telling stories. Sensemaking sessions are usually longer than group story sessions, and the activities in sensemaking sessions require more concentrated thinking to pull off. You can still get good results out of a group story session if half of the people pay attention half of the time, but with sensemaking you need people to be more engaged in the process.

As a rule of thumb, the number of people who can and will participate in sensemaking (not just show up; participate *usefully*) is usually about a quarter as many as were willing to attend group story sessions. Note that I didn't say as were willing to tell *stories*. Generally more people are willing and able to fill in a form or give a brief interview than are willing to spend hours in a room doing group activities. If you got twenty percent of your community to fill in

a form, the number who will do sensemaking would probably be about a *tenth* of that number, not a quarter. Of course these are general averages based on my experiences doing this work; your community or organization might not fit the average, especially when it comes to the topic you are exploring in your project.

If you aren't sure how much participation you can expect to find, ask around. Buttonhole some people you would like to involve in sensemaking, and ask them if they think they could find the time to participate. If they look at their watches *while* you are explaining what will happen in the session, you may want to lower your expectations.

Don't deceive yourself about how much participation is out there ready to be tapped into. Remember that not everyone will have the same urgency about the project that you do. In sensemaking it's better to have fewer people paying more attention than to have more people paying less.

How many sessions to hold

A small PNI project that covers one topic and collects 100–300 stories will only need one sensemaking session. On the other hand, if your project is ambitious or complex—you have covered several topics, or the outcome of your project will be used in a major nationwide campaign, or you have collected a thousand stories—you will need more than one sensemaking session.

You could hold one very long sensemaking session to handle goals or a scope like this, but the session would have to take place over days. You can't always get that kind of uninterrupted time commitment from people. However, you can still ask the same people come to all of the sessions. Just space the sessions out in time so people can fit them into their schedules.

I've found that for ambitious projects, giving people time to reflect between long, complex sessions can actually *improve* the outcome, because they come back having had the topic in the back of their minds in the interim. For example, say you think your sessions should be no longer than four hours each, but you need to hold four of them to cover all the nuances of your topic. What about setting them up for two Tuesdays and Fridays in a row? You can ask people to participate in a "task force" to provide more coherence to the process. Some people might be able and willing to come to all four sessions; some might come to two; some only one. But overall the sessions will build momentum.

It is possible to schedule a single marathon three-day, eight-hour-a-day sensemaking session. I've helped to facilitate several of those. You need an intensely dedicated group of people to pull such a thing off, but it can be done. It's all a matter of priorities. If it's important enough to you and your participants, you can do it. Usually it isn't important enough, but there are exceptions.

What is the maximum size of a sensemaking session? That depends on the room, the participants, and you. The maximum size of a group *story* session depends on the size of the room and the number of helpers and tape recorders you can get your hands on. For sensemaking, the size of the room still matters, but you don't need tape recorders. You need *surfaces*. At some point groups will run out of wall and table and floor space to work on.

Sensemaking requires more facilitation help than story collection. Once you have given people a simple storytelling task, you can usually leave them alone; but people need more help with sensemaking. You are asking people to carry out a more complicated set of tasks. If your participants are exceptionally used to working out complex things on their own— for example, they have already done similar projects and know the drill—you can put more people into the same room than you otherwise could.

Also consider your facilitation skill and that of your helpers. I have *helped* to facilitate sensemaking sessions in very large rooms with fifty or even seventy people in them, but I have never *led* a facilitation team for a session with more than about twenty people in it. I wouldn't even *try* to handle a large session unless my helpers were at least as experienced as myself. Very large sensemaking sessions can only be tackled by experienced facilitators with experienced helpers. I'm not ready for a room like that, and I know it. If you aren't ready for a room like that,

but your project needs a lot of sensemaking participants, split up your sessions or split up your project. Splitting up your project *is* an option, you know. Sometimes two or three projects (in series or parallel) work better than one.

There is one other situation in which you will need to hold multiple sessions even if you don't have ambitious goals. In some projects, groups of people whose input you need for sensemaking won't be able to work together. They don't get along, or the groups are so different in authority that one group will talk while the other listens, or they physically can't get to the same place at the same time, or they are afraid of each other, or they just come from such different worlds that most of their energy will be spent dealing with culture shock. These are just a few of the reasons for keeping groups separated.

When groups are contentious as well as separated, it is important that you involve the groups in *perfectly parallel* sensemaking processes. You don't want anyone saying, when they see your final report or hear about the project from others, that you distorted the outcome by giving "those people" a different process than they themselves went through.

You can hold multiple sensemaking sessions as you would a sports tournament, in a tree arrangement where leaf-sessions join into branch-sessions, which join into a final trunk-session. Let's say, for example, that your project needs the sensemaking input of both doctors and patients. You don't think these particular doctors and patients would do well in the same session. You think the doctors would dictate and the patients would obey. So you plan to hold two separate sessions where you go through the same agenda with each group separately. Why not draw things together by holding a third blending session to which you have invited both doctors and patients, some who came to the earlier sessions and some who did not? This third session could incorporate previous outputs as well as generate new patterns, so that the first set of outputs gets churned back in to the process.

In the case of contentious groups, a blending session might or might not work. You could invite people at the first sessions to come to a

Figure 11.30. When you invite people to a sensemaking session, they might respond in a variety of ways based on their perception of their place in the community.

blending session afterward and see if anyone takes you up on it; but you should be ready to move forward without it if it can't happen.

Whom to invite

Now that you know how many people you will ask to participate in sensemaking and how many sessions you will hold, whom will you ask to come?

This is a more complicated question than you might think. In most communities and organizations, there are differences of power and perspective that make whom to include not just a question of logistics but of identity negotiation.

Dimensions of participation

I can think of five dimensions on which people vary with respect to how willing and able they are to participate in sensemaking sessions.

Expectations about their place in the community. People vary in how much they think they *ought* to be included in any deliberation that impacts decision making for the organization (see Figure 11.30). You might think this would apply only to people in recognized positions of power, but be careful. Whom you should ask depends on the culture and traditions of your organization or community. Sensemaking sessions are like dinner parties: it's easy to offend those you don't ask. Who has been included in decision making in the past? What are the community-wide or organization-wide norms around inclusion? Are there competing versions of these norms?

To think about this, imagine asking people from the various groups to attend a sensemaking ses-

sion. How would they respond? Which of these best matches their probable answer?

- Of course I should be there!
- I am honored to receive this invitation.
- I'm glad you asked.
- I can't believe you are asking somebody like me.
- It's about time I was asked to one of these.
- I suppose I should come.
- I can't be bothered with things like this.
- Sorry, you made a mistake.
- Please take me off your list.
- You'd better leave me alone.
- Are you trying to insult me?
- Back off!

Expectations about you. People vary in how much they expect you—in whatever identity they see you—to include them in any process that impacts decision making for the organization (see Figure 11.31 on the following page). This has as much to do with their opinions about *you* as it does on their opinions about their place in the community or organization. Who are you to them? To the masses, are you a suit, the man, the establishment? To those in charge, are you a rabble-rouser, an anarchist? To the older folks, are you an upstart trying to tell them what to do? To the young folks, are you an out-of-touch bean counter?

To think about this, imagine asking people to come to a sensemaking session, as above; but this time pay attention to the way people look at *you*. Are there looks of derision on their face?

Figure 11.31. When you invite people to a sensemaking session, they might respond in a variety of ways based on their perception of *your* place in the community.

Pleasant surprise? Attempts to uncover your evil intentions?

There are opportunities hiding in the combination of these first two dimensions. For example, the combination of people thinking they *ought* to be included but never *will* be included is one worth looking for, because those people represent untapped springs of motivation to participate. Conversely, people who think they *shouldn't* be bothered but *expect* you to bother them may actually participate more (in other parts of the project) if you *don't* ask them to participate in sensemaking. They might give a longer interview, or answer more questions, or pay more attention to a report, if you let them off the hook on something they think you are going to burden them with. If you force them to come to a sensemaking session, they might come in body but not in mind.

Motivation. People vary in how much they are *willing* to participate in sensemaking. Every project has a different resonance with every person depending on how it intersects with their many identities (see Figure 11.32 on the next page). For example, I would most likely be bored by a project about sports, but if it was about *women* in sports my ears would perk up. These connections are hard to guess at in advance, because a project might hit any particular person in a spot you can't see. I don't think you can plan for it, in terms of choosing people to ask. You can, however, ask more people than you expect to attend. That way people will self-select.

Self-selection is anathema in surveying, but there's nothing wrong with it in sensemaking.

Working with stories doesn't change the fact that the most motivated get a bigger voice, and it shouldn't, either. I always say, those who put in the most work should get the loudest voices (and it is part of your job to hear them).

Availability and capability. People vary in how much they are *able* to participate in sensemaking. This means whether they are physically able to get to the room, whether they have time for the session, and how much they are able to pay attention and contribute once they get there. Some people are a lot busier than others, by situation and by personality. Some people have physical or mental disabilities that make sensemaking harder for them. Getting twenty of your hospital's top emergency-room doctors, or their patients, to spend four hours in a sensemaking session might be a difficult task to pull off, no matter how much they would like to contribute.

Beware of forcing busy people into sensemaking sessions (for example, by getting their superiors to lean on them) when they don't actually have the time for it. They may show up, but they'll spend the whole time trying to catch up on email instead of attending. If you can't get people to put in the time you need, find ways to fit around their schedules. Maybe you could plan several half-hour sessions in which you ask the busy people to do only the simplest of tasks, then assemble results from several sessions yourself.

Watch out for filling your sensemaking sessions with people who are *available* but not *capable* of participating, for lack of interest or connection to the topic. I've seen this one happen a

Figure 11.32. When you invite people to a sensemaking session, they might respond in a variety of ways based on their interest in the topic.

lot: people don't think they can get their customers or their busy (but involved) people to participate, so they latch onto their lower-level staff, who (they think) have nothing better to do, just to fill the room with warm bodies. The problem is, people who are less involved will produce weaker, thinner sensemaking results (see Figure 11.33 on the following page). If you find yourself filling the room with warm bodies, stop and rethink your plans.

Finally, be aware of how much complication your participants are likely to be able to handle. I remember a session with cancer patients where it became quickly apparent that these extremely stressed-out people were not going to be able to achieve the vast feats of mental gymnastics we had set out for them. When you plan your session, picture the people you actually expect to attend the session doing the tasks you set out. It's a common error to think that because something is easy for *you* it will be easy for your participants. Step back and picture *them* in the task, not yourself.

Knowledge. Do you want only the people considered the most knowledgeable about your topic, or with the strongest expert credentials, to come to your sensemaking session? No. If you want to pursue analytical research, if you want to gather scientific evidence, if you want proof, then ask the experts and only the experts. But if you want to do *participatory* work, remember this: *people are the experts of themselves.*

That doesn't mean you should ask people to analyze themselves. It means you should give peo-

ple the means to work out meaning for themselves, because only then will the outcome of the sensemaking be useful to their real lives.

When you can't invite the people you should

In some projects it is possible to involve everyone in the community or organization in sensemaking. This might be true if the project is very small, say within a ten-person organization or a five-house street. But in many projects there will be three groups of people involved:

- those who tell the stories,
- those who work with the stories during sensemaking, and
- those who manage the project and prepare materials for the use of the others.

Usually the first of these groups is largest because more time and energy is required to participate in the latter groups. This means that on many projects the group doing the sensemaking will contain few if any of the original storytellers. How can you make sure you involve your original storytellers in sensemaking even when you can't?

Bring storytellers into sensemaking. You can deliberately invite some of your original storytellers to your sensemaking sessions. For example, you could add information to a handout for a group story session describing how to participate in sensemaking. If you have scheduled your sensemaking sessions far in advance, why not put that information on any papers you hand out at your group story sessions?

Figure 11.33. Don't just fill up the room with warm bodies. It's more important to find people who want to participate than it is to find lots of people.

Another option is to ask people to add their phone numbers or emails to a list if they would be willing to have you call and invite them to a sensemaking session later in the project. Their information will not be linked to any stories they told, so you won't compromise their anonymity. Then later you can go through the list and make sure you include some of your original storytellers in your sensemaking sessions.

But sometimes it is truly impossible to bring storytellers into sensemaking. For example:

• The storytellers are located far apart and can be interviewed separately but can't easily be brought to a physical location.

• The storytellers are very busy people who can manage a five minute interview but can't spare the time for a longer meeting.

• The storytellers are ill or incarcerated or disabled or otherwise physically or mentally or emotionally unable to meet in person.

• The storytellers don't like or trust some of the people involved in the project. They may be willing to tell their stories to a neutral third party, but they aren't willing to attend a sensemaking session.

• The storytellers are not motivated to participate in the project. They are just barely willing to talk to an interviewer for a few minutes. Asking them to attend a sensemaking session would be out of the question.

When one or more of these factors is in play, including the original storytellers is impossible.

In that case, what can you do to make sure your storytellers are represented in sensemaking? I know of three things you can do.

Bring sensemaking into collection. One option is to mix in some sensemaking at the time of story collection. It is perfectly reasonable to ask people in a group story session to go through some simple sensemaking exercises or tasks. They will get more out of the session, and the stories they tell will improve as a result, so the project will benefit too.

Here's what I like to do: collect a first batch of stories in a straightforward way, without sensemaking; then introduce a sensemaking exercise or task where people work with the stories they have just told; then *pump the sensemaking back in* to a second storytelling phase. The sensemaking activity will deepen the exploration of issues, and the second batch of stories will connect more strongly to the issues you are exploring. This spiraling-in technique helps everyone participate more fully in the process. Then later, even if you hold a sensemaking session in which none of the original storytellers participate, they will still have participated in a less complete, but still useful, way.

Bring collection into sensemaking. Another way to get storytellers into sensemaking is to ask the people who will be doing the sensemaking to tell more stories themselves. A typical sensemaking session involves the consideration of about seventy-five percent previously collected stories and twenty-five percent newly told stories. If you want to bring more story collection into sensemaking, you can change that ratio to fifty-fifty.

I know of two ways to increase story collection during sensemaking: with paired or unpaired storytelling.

Paired storytelling. As your sensemaking session begins, divide up the previously collected stories so that every story gets read or heard multiple times and every person reads or hears multiple stories. Give the stories to people and ask each person to choose one or two stories from those they have read or heard to *retell*. Ask them to choose stories that speak to them, that resonate with their own experiences.

When everyone is ready, divide your session participants into small groups. Ask the people within each group to take turns retelling the stories they chose. They can either retell the story in their own words or read it aloud. Here's the pairing-up part: after they retell each story they chose, they should *follow it up* with a story from their *own* experience that resonates with the story they chose.

The benefit of this pairing-up exercise is that it will instill a small nugget of responsibility in each participant. Each participant will represent the *combination* of their own experiences with those of the absent storytellers whose words they have chosen to repeat. In this way the body of stories being used in sensemaking is not a foreign object to the sensemakers; it is something they feel connected to and responsible for.

However, this is not a good method to use when there are large gaps between your storytellers and sensemakers. If no stories resonate, the exercise will fail and people will pretend to do it while actually just waiting for it to be over. No responsibility will be instilled, and the body of stories will become something worse than a foreign object. It will become something people feel has been *forced* on them, and the sensemaking will be of poor quality as a result. Therefore, paired storytelling is best used when the barriers to people participating in sensemaking are purely of a logistical nature.

Unpaired storytelling. You can simply ask people to tell some stories of their own about the topic, then include those stories in the sense-making along with the previously collected stories. You can do this before or after people encounter the collected stories for the first time (or both). This will not produce a paired-up relationship between sensemaking participants and original storytellers, but it will increase the extent to which the people at the session feel represented by the body of stories with which they are working.

Amplify the voices of the storytellers. When you cannot bring actual storytellers into the room, and you cannot inject sensemaking into collection or collection into sensemaking, you can increase the extent to which the *voices* of the original storytellers are present in the room. You can do this in how you plan your sensemaking session and how you collect your stories.

Do you remember, in the section on facilitating contact between people and stories (page 318), how I described three rooms in which sensemaking sessions were taking place? Do you remember Session A, in which dismal people peered into laptop screens? Session B, in which a half-asleep audience endured a droning presentation of stories? Session C, in which happy people bustled around carrying meaning in their hands? In which of those rooms do you think the voices of the original storytellers were most strongly present? Session C, of course. The closer people can get to stories, the better they can hear the voices of the storytellers. When your original storytellers can't be in your sensemaking session, design the session so that their voices are more strongly present. Don't diminish their voices by making people peer through computer screens or read through reams of report material. Bring the stories closer to the people who will be using them so they can hear them better.

One way to bring stories more strongly into sensemaking is by using voice recordings. Say you have 200 stories, all of which were recorded in audio form. You won't have time to ask everyone in the sensemaking session to listen to all 200 audio recordings. But that doesn't mean you can't use *any* of the audio recordings. Why not randomly choose three or five story recordings for each sensemaking participant to listen to? Or have everyone listen together to ten recordings? Or have a computer in the room anyone can use to listen to an audio recording for any of the stories they are working with, if they would like to hear the intonations of the speaker?

If you know in advance that you will not be able to include any of your original storytellers in your sensemaking sessions, you might want to broaden your collection of stories to include contextual elements like voice recordings, photographs, drawings, artifacts—whatever will help you bring the voices of your storytellers into a stronger presence in the sensemaking room.

Remember that as the planner of your sensemaking session, you have a strong influence on how the people in the session experience the stories you have collected in your project. You can use that influence to make sure your original storytellers are as present as you can make them in the session without actually being in it. It's not as good a solution as including the actual people, but it's still worth pursuing.

How to invite people

If you go back and look at the corresponding section to this one in the story collection chapter (page 166), you will recall that I said you could get people to come to a group story session by *ordering* them to come, by drawing on social *networks*, by *broadcasting* invitations to specific groups of people, by *advertising* sessions to everybody and anybody, or by *sparking* sessions by random encounters with people who happen to be somewhere. You can use all of those techniques to fill a sensemaking session as well.

You might think that the less orderly methods wouldn't work for sensemaking, because it's a more serious undertaking, but they still work. Sensemaking sessions require a higher commitment in time and energy than group story sessions, but you can still find people to come to them in the same ways. Just make sure people understand what they are being asked to do.

Paying participants

The rule for paying participants in sensemaking is the same as it is for group story sessions (page 168). If you are paying people in order to help them *find the time* to do something they

already want to do, go ahead and pay them. If you are paying them because it will *convince* them to participate, don't.

Giving gifts to participants

In the chapter on story collection, I said that giving people thank-you gifts was a great idea (page 166). For sensemaking, gifts are also useful, but they need to have a different message in them. Story collection is about sharing and revealing, so a story session gift thanks people for adding their experiences and perspectives to make the collection of stories more complete. Sensemaking is not about sharing but about *working together with a common purpose*, so a sensemaking gift should constitute *proof* that its owner was part of something, that what was created was made partly through their effort.

As an analogy, let's say you have supervised the construction of a new bridge needed by the community. Now that the bridge is complete, you want to thank the people who helped build it. Would you give the same gift to the bridge donors as you would give to the metalworkers who welded its supporting structure? No, and in fact those gifts should be very different. Both groups were essential to the project, but the two groups did different things. The donors should get beautiful framed pictures of the bridge with the sun glinting off something. Bridge workers should get little pieces of the bridge, bits of concrete or steel, or the right to put their initials on a beam hidden deep in the structure that only ten people know about. They should get something that proves *they* did what was done.

The same goes for sensemaking. Sensemaking is an effort, and people want proof of that. I said before that gifts for story session participants should tell stories. For sensemaking, the gift should tell the story of group achievement. What sort of gift tells the story of group achievement? *Proof* of group achievement.

Let's say that at the end of your sensemaking session you have arrived at a grand landscape that describes from all possible perspectives the issue around which the project revolves. This is something of which people will be justifiably proud. Why not send each participant in the session a framed copy of that landscape? Many other proof-related gifts are possible: a

Figure 11.34. Thank-you gifts for sensemaking sessions should take the form of proof, and they should be exclusive to those who put in the work of doing the sensemaking.

video recording of the session (if that's okay with the people in it); notes you typed up during it; photographs of the walls full of sticky notes; a copy of the story cards you used in the session; access to a follow-up forum to continue the discussion; the opportunity to comment on the project's final report.

Above all, a proof gift *must* be exclusive to those who participated in the session (see Figure 11.34). Part of what makes the gift valuable is that *nobody who wasn't there gets one.* That holds even for people in power. Would donors to my bridge project get little pieces of concrete from the first column poured, even if they gave lots of money? No! They didn't risk life and limb. Your participants in sensemaking are like workers on a bridge, risking embarrassment, mistakes, inadvertent revelations, group disapproval, laughter, scorn—the social equivalent of life and limb. Give them proof that they faced the challenge of sensemaking and emerged triumphant.

Where to hold your sensemaking sessions

In the section for group story sessions I said you should choose a room designed to hold twice as many people as you expect to come to the session (page 169). For sensemaking, the same ratio holds, but for a different reason. People need lots of working space, on floor and table and wall, to count and compare and build. As with a story session, avoid fixed chairs or tables. Give people the flexibility to adapt the room to unexpected needs. And never choose a room with a fixed podium or any other hint of passivity in it. It should be a work room, not a presentation or lecture room.

When to hold your sensemaking sessions

In the corresponding section on story collection, I said that the minimum time in which you could hold a group story session was one hour (page 169). For sensemaking that minimum is *two* hours. That's a very simple session with only a few tasks in it; but it can still be effective. The more typical time frame is three to six hours. An eight hour session would need a dedicated group considering a topic important to them (or it would need people paid to do the work as part of their jobs). I have seen sessions stretching over nearly a week, but that's rare.

When I was talking about collecting stories, I said that you should catch people at a time when the social context of the time frame matches what you want them to do. This is true for sensemaking too, but with sensemaking you need more mental energy than with storytelling. For example, while it may be perfectly reasonable to collect stories during the time of the evening meal, this would *not* be a good time for sensemaking. For sensemaking you need people at their sharpest, because you will be asking them to do cognitively complex tasks. For most people the hours surrounding mid-day are their sharpest, say from nine a.m. to three p.m. That timing fits the majority of circadian rhythms, and it also fits the way our society orders time.

It's when we *think* we should be doing useful things, so it's a good time for sensemaking.

Materials for sensemaking

A group story session needs little more than people, you, and a good tape recorder or note-taker. Sensemaking is different. People need physical props to work with. I have already mentioned printed story cards often enough that you should have an idea of how you can make those. A few other things may also be useful to you.

Walls

Will you be allowed to put sticky notes all over the walls of the room you plan to use for sense-making? Find out long before your session starts. Go to the room and stick some things on the walls, then unstick them and check that they won't damage anything. People who own buildings can be picky about what you stick on their walls. If you can't stick things on the walls, find other ways to create space for people to work on. You can use tables or floors as well, though walls are better. For each person you expect to attend the session, try to provide nine square feet (one square meter) of writeable space, reusable if possible. For a ten-person session, that means you will need ninety square feet, or three six-by-five-foot wall spaces ready for use. If you can't get that much space, less *will* work, but be aware that people will be a little cramped as you plan what you will ask them to do.

Whiteboards

Whiteboards and easels of all kinds are excellent tools for sensemaking. They give people canvases on which to build things, and they provide social focal points for people to gather around as they talk. If you can get your hands on any of those easel whiteboard things that create extra mini-walls, I recommend them. You can pay hundreds of dollars for these things, or you can find smaller flimsier ones for less than a hundred dollars, or you can make them yourself with cardboard or poster board on a wooden frame. You can give people dry-erase markers to write on whiteboards, or you can attach large sheets of "butcher paper" (also called "craft" or "brown" paper) to them with pins or clips. You can even buy giant sticky pa-

per sheets to stick on easels; those are wonderful because they don't fall off, and you don't get thumbtacks underfoot either. For example, I have a giant Post-it "easel pad" that has its own cardboard support structure. It doesn't have legs, so it has to sit on a table, but it's a lot cheaper than a free-standing whiteboard.

Can you use chalkboards? Yes, those work too. If you use chalkboards, I suggest making some cheap digital cameras available so people can capture their creations before they rub them out again.

Paper, paper, and more paper

Always have more paper than you can stand in any sensemaking session. Reams of paper, heaps of paper. Not because people will *use* it all; because people will *see* it all. The more paper people see, the more they will be willing to use.

Markers

There is one hard and fast rule about markers in sensemaking: no small markers, no small pens. Why? If you give people small markers, or pens, they will write small things, and you can't read small things from ten feet back. Remember the part earlier in the chapter about zooming in and out on information (page 323)? You need people to be able to do that. So give them large, fat markers. That way they'll write large, fat words that you can read from halfway across the room. (If your room is smaller, your markers can be smaller, but keep things large in context.) If you think this doesn't matter, just try it once the wrong way and you'll find out.

Sticky notes

I wrote a whole section about these things back in the story collection chapter (see "About those sticky notes" on page 211). All of the same advice applies here, only more so. Try very hard to avoid using rectangular sticky notes in sense-making. They create rectangular thinking. Look for round or hexagonal sticky notes, or make them hexagonal yourself by cutting corners off square notes. As with the markers, try it once wrong (I mean that; do it *deliberately* wrong) and you'll understand why it matters.

Craft supplies

By this I mean tape, string, thumbtacks, finger paint, crayons, blocks, poster board, cardboard, modeling clay, precut felt shapes, glue sticks, pom-poms, bendable pipe cleaners, all the amazing things you find in craft stores. I have rarely seen craft supplies used in actual fact, though that may reflect nothing more than my large experience in the corporate and government spheres, where the intrusion of anything resembling real life is frowned upon.

But in fact, craft supplies can be wonderful tools for building complicated constructions. For some groups, just having these things in the *room* can get energy and imagination flowing. They signal freedom to think out of the box. But, obviously, with some other groups doing such a thing would be courting disaster. Know your people, and give them what they need.

Facilitating sensemaking in virtual space

You may have noticed that in this chapter I have always talked about *physical* manipulation of stories, never virtual manipulation using computers. There is a reason for that, which is that I've tried it both ways and physical manipulation works better. If you *can* get people in a room together, talking face to face and manipulating physical objects together, you will get better sensemaking.

At least in the years in which I am revising this book, our options for working in groups with computers are so limited that they inhibit rather than improve group sensemaking. If you are so fortunate as to have one of those super-high-tech systems where several people can move about virtual items on a giant screen using their hands (and I have seen such systems), that's great. I believe they are called "interactive whiteboards" or "smart boards." But few people today have access to such things, so I'm not going to assume you can do that.

For most people today, computers can only be used by peering into tiny windows on which things appear at very low resolutions compared to anything we can see in physical reality. A pack of cards people can hold and trade is still better, in a room with real people in it, than a computer.

However, if you really *cannot* get people in a room together working face to face, computers can be a wonderful help in what would

otherwise be an impossible situation. If your sensemaking sessions *must* take place across a computer network, you can still have effective sensemaking. (By "across a computer network" or "online" I mean people talking over the phone or a voice-over-IP service or using video conferencing while looking at something shared on their computer screens.)

The thing I've seen happen most when people attempt to make sense of stories online is that *the stories get left behind*. It's easier to keep stories in mind when they are represented by objects you hold in your hands or see on the walls around you. When stories are on the screen, it's easier to put them aside and start talking about the topic in general. But the whole point of narrative sensemaking is to work with collected stories.

To keep your stories front and center in virtual sensemaking sessions, I suggest preparing *virtual story cards*. I've tried a few different ways of doing this, and find that the best method is to represent stories with named shapes on a shared white board. The names refer to whole stories in another location.

The reason to work with names rather than whole stories is because of the low resolutions available on computer screens. A person standing six feet from a wall of story cards can read many times more than a person looking at a seventeen-inch computer screen. It's like looking through a telescope the wrong way: everything is so tiny it has to be compressed in meaning to fit in view. If the details of each story can be accessed (on demand) by using the story's unique name as a reference, people can keep the stories in view as they work.

The other thing I've noticed about virtual sensemaking is that it tends to shift in the direction of analysis. My guess is that our ideas of what computers are for impact what we do with computers. It takes some preparation to make sure people *build things together* in online sensemaking sessions. For this reason, I think it works better to give people a structured exercise, perhaps even using a fixed template, in a virtual session.

Who should "have their hands on" the things that get built in a virtual session? It depends partly on the technology you choose and partly on your group. Some online collaboration systems allow everyone to interact with documents at the same time, and some don't. But even if the software allows simultaneous editing to a document, that doesn't mean the participants in your session will be ready for it. When people in a room work on a physical construction together, they exchange many complex and subtle negotiations over who will stand where, who will stick what piece of paper where, and who will talk about what. Online interaction reduces the bandwidth of this interaction so much that misunderstandings can quickly multiply.

I've found work on online group constructions to go better, regardless of technology, when one person is designated the group's "scribe" and tasked with making all changes to the document. That way nobody can blunder into destroying the work of someone else, because all changes to the document go through the negotiated filter of talking to the scribe. If someone has to say, "How about we merge this cluster with that one?" people can talk about the change instead of seeing it suddenly (and irrevocably) change before their eyes.

Another option is to allow entirely collaborative editing of built documents, but split people up into small groups so that you don't have ten people trying to negotiate changes to a document at once. Groups of two or three will be much better able to negotiate collaboration on construction through the thin channels of online communication. Some of the newer chat and voice applications have the ability to "move" people to and from multiple "rooms" where they can talk more "quietly."

WRAPPING UP SENSEMAKING

In every sensemaking session a time comes to bring things to a final resolution. When this time comes, there are three things you *must* do and three things you can do. I will go through these things in the order they ordinarily take place.

Mandatory: Support the after-party

In your agenda for any sensemaking session, plan some time at the end for participants to reflect on what went on in the session. You only need fifteen to thirty minutes for this activity, but don't leave it out. Even if your session is only two hours long, keep the last fifteen minutes for the after-party (see Figure 11.35 on the facing page).

Why do I call it the after-party? If you've been to any family reunions, sports matches, vacation trips, company picnics, or other socially eventful gatherings, you can recall that special time when you're on your way home and people start to reminisce about what happened. People say things like, "Wasn't that funny when Jimmy wolfed down three pieces of cake?" Or, "What about that goal in the second quarter?" Or, "I thought we were going under when we hit those rapids!" People sometimes call such an echo of a party an after-party.

After-parties happen after sensemaking too, because sensemaking is a socially eventful gathering. As the session winds down, its participants breathe a sigh of relief because nobody's asking them to do strange, impossible things anymore. They can see that the time is drawing to a close, and they can see that their efforts have produced useful insights. As a result, people will begin to slide into talking about what they have learned and how things appear on this side of the session. That's the after-party. You'll come to recognize it after you have facilitated enough sessions.

There is always a sort of glow in the room during the after-party. People speak more freely, move more loosely, laugh more readily. The greater the mayhem during the session, the more the after-party feels like a party, because there is more of an accomplishment to celebrate.

Why support the after-party? Because things always happen in the after-party, useful things, things nobody could have predicted. Someone will come out with an observation that nobody has ever made before, or people will suddenly arrive at a perfect motto that sticks for years afterward, or some other crystal of contemplation will emerge. It may seem a loss of your precious sensemaking time to let people just sit around and talk. Indeed, planning such a sit-and-chat time near the *start* of your session would waste time or derail progress. But at the *end* of the session, it's just right.

Figure 11.35. The after-party is what comes after all activities have taken place and the session has wound down. It is the time when some of the most important insights come out.

Another reason to support the after-party is because it will happen whether you support it or not. Remember, this has been an *event* in the lives of these people. They need to talk about it so they can process it while it is still fresh in their minds. The after-party will creep into the last time slot you have set up, no matter what you said people were to do in it.

I've seen what happens when well-meaning facilitators don't leave time for the after-party and keep pushing people to "produce results" right up until the last moment of the session. It's not a pretty sight. People leave the room and *attempt* to reflect about the event with people who weren't there—spouses, kids, people on the bus. It doesn't work, because nobody knows what they are talking about. They end up feeling unresolved and confused, and that impacts the progress of the project after the sensemaking session is over. Maybe they don't volunteer to comment on the report, or they dismiss the project when somebody asks them about it later, or they don't get involved in the *next* project.

Give your participants the opportunity to make sense of their sensemaking within the session itself. Everyone will be helped by it: them, you, and the project itself.

One way you can show your support for the after-party is to do something special at the end of the session that signals to people that they are done *accomplishing* things and can now *reflect* on what they have done. The signal might be bringing out some sort of celebratory food, like pizza or baked goods (food is a powerful social signal). It might be handing out copies of something people made in the session (which you had helpers furiously preparing in the last half hour). It could even be something as simple as opening doors or windows. Announcing the arrival of the after-party, instead of just allowing people to slide into it, invites people to reflect with more energy.

Optional: Draw up lists

At some point during any sensemaking session you will hear someone utter these timeless words: "Why don't we just make a list?"

You have two choices with respect to that question. You can tell the person that this isn't the kind of group work in which people make lists. Or you can say, "Just wait. We *will* make lists when it's time."

You don't have to end a session with list making, but for some projects and some participants it is extremely helpful. How much you need lists depends on how much information you need to transfer from the session to events and people outside of it.

Lists *package* the change that took place in the session into a consolidated, compact form that can more easily pass out of the session and into consumption elsewhere. In some projects that's not necessary, because the people in the session *are* the decision makers. What took place in the room can stay in the room.

But not all projects are like that. For example, say your project needs to justify its methods to a funding body, perhaps so they will green-light similar projects in the future. For that situation, having lists to show would be helpful. There are plenty of other reasons you might need lists: to support interventions, communications, reports, future discussion.

The right time to make lists in sensemaking is at the end of the sensemaking session, either during or just before the after-party. Why at the end? Because after people have been in contact with stories and with each other, after they have churned things round and round, after they have converged on meanings, after their perspectives have changed, the things people list will no longer be simply the things they *think* of. The lists will be the things that have *emerged* from the process.

If you don't believe me, try it for yourself. Insert a short list-making activity near the start of your sensemaking session, then another at the end. Compare the two lists. The first list might be *rationally* complete, but the second list will be *experientially* complete.

What to list? Table 11.2 on the next page shows some list items I've used and seen used by others.

I can imagine that you might question my "never called" column in Table 11.2. Why mince words? Why not be strong in your declaration of definitive results? Because narrative sensemaking does not support that degree of certainty, and it's risky to pretend it does. The strength of story work is in *listening to experience*. It can never be used to prove anything.

You may notice a tendency, in yourself and in your participants, to want your session to end with proof. The insights you have arrived at in the crucible of your work together will soon travel out into the hostile world of nay-sayers. You may want to clothe your insights in the armor of certainty. Don't let yourselves go there. Any such armor will fail, because it is an illusion. Narrative sensemaking cannot create any of the things I have listed in the "never called" column. That's all right, because it does such an excellent job producing the things in the first two columns. Know the strengths and limitations of the approach.

The categories of list items I've described above are just the tip of the iceberg of things you *could* list at the end of your sensemaking session.

What should you ask people to list in *your* session?

Here's a flexible approach. Arrive at the session with a fixed set of categories you plan to use to build lists. As the session begins to wind down, write each category at the top of a white board. Then ask each group to visit the white boards and *add* something to each list. (Afterwards, you can ask groups to explain their additions to the whole room.) Or ask everyone in the room to call out items as you write them down.

Here's the flexible part: prepare one or two extra lists that have *no* headings. That way you can handle categories you didn't anticipate. Maybe people want to list "wishes" or "ways we can all come together" or "disappointments" or something. It's better to say, "Let's start a new list for that!" than to say, "We don't have a list for that." Don't squelch the enthusiasm of end-session list-making! It's where people get a chance to pull things together.

Wait a minute, you say. *It sounds like list-making is an important wrapping-up activity. Why do you say it's optional? Shouldn't I ask people to make lists even if we don't need them outside the session?*

Well, you read that part above about the after-party, right? Sometimes that's all you need. Sometimes list-making spontaneously erupts during the after-party. Sometimes you don't need to *ask* people to make lists. Sometimes people will surprise you with some other method of drawing things together that you would never have thought of. Sometimes they'll tell stories or draw pictures or act out skits or put on debates or quote literature. So if you don't *need* lists to come out of your session, it wouldn't hurt to have some categories on hand. But don't *tell* people they have to make lists if you don't need them. Watch people during the after-party and see if they come up with anything *better* than lists. If they don't, pull out your categories and propose making some lists. If people come up with something better, quietly put your categories away.

Optional: Highlight stories and trends

Do you remember how, in the section on facilitating convergence (page 338), I talked about

List item	Also called	But never called	Examples
Discoveries	Insights, eye-openers, surprises	Evidence, confirmation, findings (implies proof)	We found out that.... We see that.... It surprised us to learn....
Opportunities	Options, possibilities, paths	Steps, changes, actions (implies control)	The issue of ... might be worth exploring in a future project. It looks like attention to ... might pay off. Why not explore... further?
Issues	Problems obstacles, difficulties	Misdeeds, mistakes, errors (places blame)	... is something we have to deal with. If we want to ... we will need to fix.... ... is holding us back.
Ideas	Thoughts, hunches, brainstorms	Solutions, answers, fixes, visions (implies control)	How about trying to... We could...! One idea we had was to....
Recommendations	Suggestions, proposals, trial balloons	Demands, requests, stipulations (implies control)	We think ... is worth keeping in mind. We would like the community to consider.... We ask that ... be kept in mind.
Perspectives	Points of view, viewpoints, outlooks	Disagreements, attitudes, disputes, (implies conflict)	These people see ... as ..., and these other people see it as.... There are different ways of looking at.... What seems like ... to some appears as ... to others.
Dilemmas	Decisions, quandaries, paradoxes	Predicaments, problems, difficulties (might be positive)	Much depends on the way ... turns out. ... seems to be a pivotal point for this issue. We think the issue of ... deserves some attention.

Table 11.2. Things you might list as a sensemaking session winds down.

special stories that emerge during sensemaking? Pivot stories, voice stories, and discovery stories? Do you remember how I said that for each of these categories there is a corresponding type of pattern that also emerges? Well, the time when you are wrapping up sensemaking is a good time to bring those stories and patterns out into the open.

As the facilitator of the session, you are not likely to be able to list all of these stories and patterns on your own, because they will be distributed about the room. Nor should you, because your participants can build these lists better than you can. This activity is actually a subset of the listing activity I explained above, but with a special emphasis on emergence during the event. You can do this either during or just before the after-party.

I don't like to ask for pivot stories, voice stories, and discovery stories by name. Using official-sounding labels tends to make people shift into performing and out of discovering. Instead I like to use indirect questions like these:

1. Could anybody tell me about anything they saw today that *just kept coming up?* Any stories or patterns?

2. What did you come across today that just *cried out to be heard?* What stories or patterns do you remember that were like that?

3. What *surprised* you today? What do you want to *remember* most of what you found out today?

Here are some ways you could gather answers to these questions.

• You could convene the entire room and ask each question, having people call out answers while you summarize what they say on a white board for all to see.

• You could ask each small group to come up with at least two answers for each question and appoint a spokesperson for the group. After the time allocated for that consideration, the whole room could come together, and each spokesperson could describe the answers their group gave to the questions, while you summarize the collected answers on a whiteboard.

• You could ask each small group simply to talk together about some answers to each question, then ask people to call out answers in the larger group without specifying how small groups should prepare their contributions to the whole.

• You could ask each small group to prepare a two minute presentation on their answers to the questions, then ask one presenter from each group to go "visit" the next group in a round-robin fashion (each to the next in a circle). After each presentation, the presenter could compare notes with the group they have visited, then return to their own group to report on what took place. Then the whole room could come together and assemble a common list. This method is more elaborate

and would require more time and more motivated participants, but it has the benefit of adding some extra churning near the end of the session.

• You could simply ask each small group to discuss the questions without any whole-room convergence. This would be workable if the overarching goals of the session were less ambitious and you didn't need to reach any grand set of results for the session. For a small project you may not need to draw everything together, and small-group convergence may be enough.

• You could work the questions (or similar ones) into the last exercise of the day, so that by completing the exercise people will answer the questions. For example, if people are building a timeline, you could ask them to mark surprises in yellow, elements that "cry out to be heard" in green, and things often met coming round again in blue. With a composite story, you could ask people to add relevant interjections ("Wow!", "Really!", "That needed to be said", "Again!", "Make a note of that!") that label important discoveries of the day. A well-planned exercise, especially one you feel confident facilitating, can meet these needs without sending people off to write lists.

A question you might have is: *Why wait until the last moment of the session to ask about pivot stories, voice stories, and discovery stories? Shouldn't I tell people to look for those kinds of stories up front?* No, don't do that. Emergent stories don't come when they are called, and chasing them just makes them run faster. They have to come to people of their own accord.

If you *tell* people to find pivot stories and voice stories and discovery stories, they won't be able to. Take pivot stories. The definition of a pivot story is *a story you keep coming across without meaning to.* If people go out *looking* for pivot stories, they won't find any, by definition. Similarly, voice stories are defined as stories that *call out to be heard.* If people are running around tearing open all the stories looking for voice stories, nobody will be quiet long enough to hear the voice stories calling. And discovery stories depend on surprise, which depends on being ready for surprise.

So my suggestion is: don't even hint that you want people to look for these particular kinds of emergent stories until things have begun to converge in your sensemaking session. At that point you can begin to hint at the emergence of these stories. But don't ask people to explicitly *list* these stories until the session is near its end. At that point all the emergent stories that want to be found will have been found.

Optional: Feed into non-narrative methods

There are many group methods related to decision support that start where sensemaking leaves off. Some examples are scenario planning, SWOT analysis (Strengths, Weaknesses, Opportunities, Threats), strategic planning, checklists, evaluations, scorecards, and many other popular methods. Especially if narrative methods have been a hard sell to your community or organization (or funders), *planning* to use one of these more common methods to post-process the results of narrative sensemaking can bolster support for the project. The insights that result from narrative sensemaking can create an excellent grounding for such rational techniques.

How should you connect sensemaking to another decision support method? Learn about the other method you want to use. Look for an input at the start of its process that will match what you can create in narrative sensemaking. Quite a few of these methods start with a list of factors of some kind. For example, scenario planning begins by brainstorming lists of "drivers of change" or "driving forces." If you wanted to connect a sensemaking session to a scenario planning workshop, you could design your sensemaking session so that you end by listing drivers of change. What better way to improve on brainstorming than by working with stories! The lists you create *after* sensemaking will be so much more *grounded in experience* that the work that comes after will be deeper and richer than it would have been otherwise.

Mandatory: Hold a post-session review

As you plan your sensemaking session, tack on some time at the end for a post-session review (see Figure 11.36 on the following page). Fifteen minutes per two hours of session time is a good ratio. A post-session review is nothing like an after-party. It's not for the participants; it's for you. A post-session review is about improving your facilitation methods and skills based on what took place in the session.

No matter how little time you have for sensemaking, never skimp on post-session review time. It may seem unimportant, but you'll understand why it matters after you've done a few sessions and seen your skills improve. Ask any helpers you have in the session to stick around and reflect with you. If you can't get anyone to stay, schedule the time anyway and reflect on your own. Read your notes from the session, take some new notes, talk to yourself, play act, gesture wildly.

Stay in the room if you can. Visit all the sites where things happened. Commit the session to memory. Replay in your mind what worked and what didn't. Recall every moment of disappointment, embarrassment, elation, pride, despair, mayhem. Link all of those things to the changes that took place, or didn't, or didn't in the way you expected.

Here are some things you might want to think about as you review the session.

Change

Conjure in your mind a picture of what the session looked like when it started. What did people do when they first entered the room? Where did they go? What comments did they make? What questions did they have? What looks were on their faces? What did their body language say? How did they stand or sit? How did they interact with each other and with you? What materials did they look at? Did they *avoid* looking at anything? What emotions did they express? What was the mood of the room? What did the room look like, sound like, feel like?

Now conjure up the same picture at the *end* of the session. How are the two pictures different, and what does that mean? What can you learn from the comparison?

Interactions

Consider the interactions that took place among the people in the session (not with you, among them). Did you see a change in the way people related to each other between the start

Figure 11.36. The post-session review is for you and your helpers to think about what went right and wrong in the session, so you can improve your facilitation skills.

and end of the session? How did their conversations change? Their body language? Their movements around the room? Their sharing or holding back of experiences, feelings, opinions? How were the social dynamics different from start to end?

Now consider *your* interactions with people. What did you say to people? Was it what you planned to say? Did you say anything you wish you had said differently or left unsaid? Did you miss any opportunities to say things you thought of later? Did some of the things you said work so well that you want to remember them for next time? How did people react to you? How did you react to them?

Stories

Consider the stories people told, retold, chose, moved around and built in the session. Recall the first and last few stories told (make a note of it near the start if you think you won't remember). How did the stories change as the session went on? Did they dig deeper? Did they bounce around different perspectives and topics? Did they fight with each other? Did they collaborate? What happened when people built stories, if they did? If all the stories in the room were laid out in the beginning of the session side by side, then all the stories were laid out at the end, what differences would you see?

Context

Consider the unique circumstances of the session. What was *special* about these people in this room on this day? Was there anything

about the group, the room, the time, the mood, the news on that day, anything that caused the session to exhibit unique characteristics? Maybe the room was dominated by an outspoken person, or the room was too small, or the air conditioning system was broken and people were short-tempered as a result. What is the story of the session? How would you tell it? How would a participant tell it? What will you do if you ever encounter a circumstance like that again?

Methods

Consider the methods you used in the session. What was your plan? Did you stick to it? How did it go? Did it proceed as you expected? If things changed from what you expected, which parts of *that* went well and which went poorly? Were all the ideas you presented clear to people? Which were more or less clear? Did you encounter any resistance or outright refusal when you asked people to do things? What caused it? Were you unclear in your instructions? Did you inadvertently offend people? Or did they just have a better idea than you did?

Don't miss these opportunities to improve your practice, by the way. In every sensemaking session I have ever facilitated, I have learned something new from the people in the room. They suggested a new wrinkle to an exercise, or they did something I didn't ask them to do but should have, or they interpreted something I said in a way I never meant, but liked. If you are not discovering new ideas in every sensemaking session through being with the people in it, you are not growing as a PNI practitioner. What have you learned today that you can add to PNI?

Project

Consider the project before and after the session. Write a summary sentence that describes the project as it stood at the start of your sensemaking session. Then write another sentence that describes the project at the end. Does that capture the change you saw? Was it the change you expected? Was it too little change? Too much? What can you learn about that change, for the project and for your own PNI practice?

As you end your reflections, write down your answers to all of these questions (and any more that spring to mind). Then write a list of things you want to remember, think about, experiment with, avoid, get feedback about—whatever—before your next session, whether it is in this project or another.

If you do all those things at the end of every sensemaking session you facilitate, your projects and skills will continue to improve.

Mandatory: Prepare a session record

What sort of record should you create of your sensemaking session? When you are collecting stories, answering this question is easy: just record everything everybody says, because that's where you get your stories. For sensemaking the answer is more complicated. I have seen sessions run the gamut from no record at all (people just clean up the mess and leave the room) to full video recordings of every moment of the session.

Factors that would make you want to record more of what went on in the session would be things like these.

- You want to improve on your sensemaking skills, so you plan to pore over your notes and records to see what you can learn and improve next time.
- You experimented with some new ideas, like maybe a new sensemaking exercise of your own creation, and you want to consider how that worked out.
- Some of the people you've talked to in your community or organization are not sure whether they like the idea of narrative sensemaking. They would like you to provide proof that the sensemaking session was methodologically sound.
- Your project funders or advisors want to evaluate the PNI approach before they approve any larger projects you might want to do.
- The sensemaking session is a once-in-a-lifetime event. You have managed to convene all twenty of the community's elders over one hundred years old.
- You're teaching a class on facilitation, and you want to pull out some bits from the video or audio recording to show to your students, as examples of what to do and what not to do.
- Some of the people in the session have asked to have a recording of the session for their own reflections later, and nobody else minds.

Factors that would make you want to record *less* of what went on in the session would be things like these.

- Your participants are nervous about the idea of being recorded or identified.
- Your participants don't trust you.
- Your topic is sensitive or private.
- You have no budget for recording equipment.
- Your project is too small to spend the amount of time you'd need to process any recordings.
- You just don't feel you need the recordings.

If making a record of the session will improve its utility to the project, make a record of it. If *not* making a record of the session will improve its utility more—which *is* sometimes the case— then consider that option instead.

What to include in your sensemaking record

Now let me talk a bit about each type of record you could make and why you might want to.

Lists. Above I talked about how you can wrap up sensemaking by asking people to write lists of things that came out of the session: discoveries, issues, ideas, etc. So one possible recording of a session would be simply these lists. You could record just the names people listed, or you could annotate each item with a description or story. This may seem like a small output from a large amount of work, but for some sessions it is just what you need.

Summaries. These are brief sentences and paragraphs that sum up the *major events* of the session: what you explored, what you found out, how things played out. You might write them yourself, or you might write them together with any helpers you had or any participants willing to contribute. You might write them during the after-party or the post-session review.

One way to get participants involved after the session is to ask them if they'd like to glance over your summary and add their own thoughts to it a few days after the session. Don't ask people to do major work on reporting afterward, because most won't; but you might be able to get suggestions from some participants later.

Constructions. The things people made in your sensemaking session, things like timelines, landscapes, story elements, and composite stories, are all report-worthy items. You can photograph the constructions; you can reproduce them in a cleaner-looking medium, such as a slide presentation; you can describe them; you can even save the physical objects people have assembled. I still have the rolled-up results from several sensemaking sessions in my office, and sometimes when I want to think about sensemaking I get them out and look at them. I've helped with sessions where helpers copied walls full of sticky notes onto Power-Point slides to show them to people who didn't attend the session. It took hours and hours to get all those labels typed in, but it was worth it, because ten times more people could use the constructions afterward. You can also record people describing their constructions in audio or video.

The recording of constructions is the type of recording I've seen done most often, and it's the type of recording I think is the most valuable. Why? Because people come up with some pretty amazing constructions in sensemaking sessions. Sometimes these constructions crystallize meaning so well that they reach far out past the original session and become touchstones the community or organization relies on for years afterward.

Be careful, though, not to allow too much emphasis to be put on constructions as outcomes of the session. If you do, people will concentrate too much on making their constructions beautiful and not enough on making them *meaningful*. If anybody asks, you can say that the constructions produced will be preserved; but don't make them sound too much like works of art.

Notes. You may or may not have a note-taker in your group of facilitators and helpers. Taking notes during sensemaking sessions is my favorite way to help facilitate them. Back when I worked on a lot of sensemaking sessions with colleagues, I usually got them to do most of the loud talking, while I did more of the quiet hinting and quieter watching. I took voluminous notes, on notepad and laptop, sometimes writing twenty or thirty pages of text. I wrote down everything the other facilitators said and everything the participants said. I took notes on body language, movements people made around the room, everything. We used those notes between sessions to discuss our techniques and improve them.

If you can find an accomplice who loves to take notes like this, latch on to them. Or if *you* like to take notes, find yourself a loud talker and pair up that way. Sensemaking sessions always fly by, no matter how carefully you have planned them. Taking notes helps you retain more of what you need to reflect on afterwards.

How should you take notes during a sensemaking session? Practice becoming invisible. I used to pretend I was the coffee person or secretary, or that I was doing anything other than writing down every word anybody said. I would stare at my screen as if I was paying no heed to what was happening in the room. Sometimes I would even sit down right next to a small group, making minute observations on their every word and movement, and they would barely glance my way.

One way to practice taking notes unobtrusively is to take a paper notebook or laptop into a busy coffee shop and start taking notes on everyone you see and hear around you. Practice pretending you are not doing what you are doing. Don't *look* at people; glance around the room as if you are looking for somebody (you might be), and in that sweep of a glance take in what they are doing. Also: if you can't touch type or write shorthand, learn how to do so now. Either one of these things will enable you to capture several times more than you could otherwise. Don't worry if your notes are a shambles with respect to spelling and punctuation. You can clean it up later, if you ever have to. It's not prose, it's memory.

One other thing about note-taking: keep a clear distinction between what you saw happen and what you *thought* about what you saw happen. In my notes I surround my own thoughts with square brackets. Everything not thus identified is something somebody *else* said or did. That way I don't come back later and misunderstand my own notes.

Should you *show* your notes to the participants in your session? I don't think so. They don't need that level of detail. Notes are useful primarily to improve your facilitation practice, and only secondarily to supplement any records you have of the session.

Photographs. Taking photographs of things people have made in your session is a popular way of recording sensemaking. You can do this yourself, or you can have helpers do it, or you can make cameras available for participants to do it.

Watch out, though: photographs don't always capture all the information you need. Several times I have asked people who were facilitating a session with me to take photographs of what had been built, only to find out later that the photographs were blurry or taken too far away to capture the detail we needed to reproduce the constructions we wanted to show to others. That's why I started asking people to take photographs, then roll up the papers and mail everything to me so I could fill in the gaps at home. There is also the occasional problem of photographs being ruined somehow: a camera gets broken, a memory card gets trashed, a hard drive crashes, prints get lost. If you take photographs of constructions, keep a backup of some kind.

Audio or video recordings. Should you record your entire sensemaking session in audio or video? I have done this. It's not as amazing as

it sounds. First of all, watching a sensemaking session that you are not part of is really boring. Nothing seems to be happening most of the time, especially if you have the camera set up on a tripod somewhere. People seem to scurry around talking in whispers, and not much else happens. The hours I have spent trying to find something, anything useful in these tapes has made me hate them. The better thing to do is to have recording equipment on hand during the session and record *only* during certain times that you know you will want to use later.

For example:

- If you want to work on your introductory talk for the session, or any of the times when you give people instructions, ask a helper to film you doing that. Then you can go over those films later as you think about what you want to do in the next session. If you can, film your participants as well at these times, so you can study their reactions later.

- If you want to add new stories to your story collection, place a small digital tape recorder on each table and ask people to use it when they tell a new story. People might not use it at first, but you can have a helper go around once in a while and ask if they've told any new stories. If they have, you can ask them to tell them again in shortened form into the recorder, then fill out a form with some questions about the story. (If you are just getting started facilitating sensemaking, leave this out. It adds a lot of extra complexity.)

- If you give each group a small recorder, you can let *them* decide what sort of record they want to leave. Some groups might record one minute of a story while others might record ten minutes of debate. Most groups are not going to choose to record every minute of a four-hour session.

- You might want to capture people describing a construction they have created, like a composite story or a timeline. This can be done in a few minutes.

- It is a good idea to record the conversation during the after-party. It's far shorter than the whole session; the things people say are more worth remembering; and people usually will not mind being recorded as much after they've been through the whole process and see that you're not trying to control or trick them. You still have to tell people what you will do with the recording, and you still have to maintain anonymity if that is important. But people who don't want to be recorded in general are often more willing to agree to this request during the after-party. Sometimes people even *ask* if the after-party is being recorded, because they realize that it's when the session is coming together.

Now that we've talked about all the types of recording you can do, let's talk about pulling them together into a session report. What is the formula for the perfect session report? You know what I'm going to say next, right? There is no formula. How much needs to be conveyed outside of the session varies by project. I've seen fifty-page documents describing every ten minutes of the session; I've seen PowerPoint presentations describing only the constructions created; I've seen multimedia and photo collages. Prepare as little or as much of a session report as your project needs.

But I don't know what my project needs, you say. To find out, answer this question. What do the people who *didn't* come to your sensemaking session need to know about the session for your project to create an effective bridge between sensemaking and decision support? *That's* how much of a report you need to prepare.

SUMMARY

Sensemaking means making sense of things in ways that are *pertinent* to decisions we will make or have made; of *practical* application to our real lives; and experimentally, improvisationally *playful*.

In order for people in a PNI project to make sense of its collected stories, *contact* must take place between people, project, and stories.

- You can bring *people and project* into contact with a preparatory letter, with an orienting handout, and with an opening explanation.
- *Contact between people* in sensemaking is all about small group dynamics.
- Facilitating *people-story contact* in sensemaking means understanding what people need as they work with stories. You need

to help people in your sensemaking session become aware of the body of collected stories (overview); switch back and forth between looking at one story and looking at many stories (zoom); have patterns "jump out" at them from a set of stories (filter); drill down into the details on any story (details on demand); count numbers of stories in categories (counting); order stories by answers or features (ranking); build stories with stories (construction); and draw stories out (extraction).

After contact has been established, the next important element is repeated, varied contact, or *churning*.

- *People-project churning* means that during any sensemaking session, people and project should keep re-encountering each other in new ways. To facilitate this, create situations where people can come into repeated, varied contact with various aspects of the project.
- *Churning between people* is about reshuffling small groups. Assigning people to groups can happen by assignment (you assign people to groups), rule-based grouping (you supply the rule, they apply it), or self-assembly (you simply ask people to form groups).
- Churning in *people-story contact* is about the same things as it is in contact (overview, zooming, filtering, getting details, counting, ranking, constructing, extracting), just over and over. The most important thing to remember about people-story churning is to *keep things moving*.

After people, project, and stories have come into repeated contact, the third element of narrative sensemaking comes into play: *convergence*. Convergence is the pulling together that takes place after people, project, and stories have been mixed and remixed many times.

- To set up conditions for *people-project convergence*, set up *expectations* of negotiated exploration and *tasks* that draw individual perspectives together. To look for people-project convergence, be on the lookout for small acts of *rebellion*. If people are doing only what you ask, they may not be experiencing convergence in sensemaking. If convergence is not happening, *intervene* with quiet reminders about expectations, but accept that the session will probably not go exactly as you had planned it.

- *Interpersonal convergence* in sensemaking is about people listening to each other. To facilitate this, set up expectations of *negotiated exploration* and *respect for experience*. Make sure the tasks you give people are things no one person can do alone. To look for interpersonal convergence, look for *awareness, negotiation,* and *representation*.

- *Convergence between people and stories* can help people explore multiple perspectives without evaluation or attack, and this is the heart of effective narrative sensemaking. To facilitate this, set up expectations of *resonant emergence*. Ask people to bring *themselves* into the process. Give people tasks in which many small things combine into fewer larger things. When observing people-story convergence, look for *pivot stories* (in which the threads of the project intersect), *voice stories* (that cry out to be heard), and *discovery stories* (that solve mysteries). If people-story convergence is not happening, offer people *resources* to help them achieve it.

Change in sensemaking completes the follow-through movement from story collection into decision support and into the return of stories to the community.

- When there has been *change between people and project,* the project going into the sensemaking room is not the same as the project coming out. To set up expectations for people-project change, *share* the project with your participants. Give them a voice in it. Also, develop your own confidence in the methods you use so that you can project that confidence—that things will change, and in a positive way, as a result of the session—to your participants.

- When facilitating *change between people* in sensemaking, don't oversell cooperation. The best expectation to set up about interpersonal change is that we will be a *working group*. We will get things done together in this room today, no matter how much we agree or disagree. If nobody ever gets angry or offended during a sensemaking session, you aren't digging very deep.

- Facilitating *change between people and stories* connecting people and stories in new ways. Don't present stories as precious, trivial, strange, just data, overly emotional, complicated, optional, or required. Present them as resources for sensemaking, food for thought, working materials. Present stories like cards in a card game: useful, accessible, inviting, insufficient.

As far as the *logistics* of sensemaking sessions are concerned, you need to think about how many people you will involve, how many sessions you will hold, whom you will invite, what you can do if you can't invite the people you should invite, whether and how you will reward people, where and when you will hold the sessions, and what materials you will need. Whatever details you decide on, be sure to plan to support the *after-party* (when people are relaxed at the end of the session and can reflect on it) as well as a *post-session review* (where you and your helpers talk about what went right and wrong in the session). You should also think about what sort of *session record* you want to prepare.

QUESTIONS

As you read over all the advice in this chapter on how to facilitate sensemaking, which of the tasks struck you as being easy? Which seemed difficult? For example, did helping people zoom in and out on stories seem easy to you? How about intervening when a group is not reaching convergence? Do you think you would notice if a group was rejecting the challenge of change? Where do your personal strengths and weaknesses interact with the tasks involved in facilitating a productive sensemaking session?

Now think about other people you know and work with. Would *they* find different aspects of the work easy or hard? Imagine co-facilitating a session with various people you know. How would you support each other? Where would you fall down as a team? What could you do about that?

Consider the benefits of sensemaking as described in this chapter. Imagine applying them to your community or organization. As you read the chapter, were there any parts where you said to yourself, "Yes! We need that." Were there any parts where you found yourself struggling to understand why this should matter? What does this tell you about your community or organization? For each area of good or bad fit between benefits and context, see if you can think of *another* community or organization where the fit would be better. Would the next town over get more benefit from convergence than you would? Would your lists of discoveries, opportunities, issues, and ideas fall flat at your brother's workplace? What does that comparison tell you?

Let's pretend you are facilitating a sensemaking session and I'm in it. Let's pretend that you accidentally let slip the word "sensemaking." I want to know what the word means. You don't want to derail the session, but I'm adamant, and I keep asking. *In your own words,* what do you tell me? Now keep imagining. Does it work? Does it make me happy? After you finish speaking, am I prepared to participate in the session? If my eyes glaze over, what do you tell me on your *second* try? Your third? Can you get to the point where you can imagine me (not *me* me, who wrote this book; an adamant, ill-tempered me who doesn't understand and won't listen) finally understanding what you mean and being ready to move on? (I ask this question because this scenario *will* happen to you, and you'd better practice it on me before you have to face it in real life.)

ACTIVITIES

Conduct a sensemaking session with only yourself in it. Prepare some story cards to consider. Explain the session to yourself. Present yourself with your story cards. Give yourself a task in which you encounter them. Now do something that causes you to repeatedly interact with the stories, to churn them. Sort them in multiple ways, or build multiple things with them, or come up with multiple observations about them. When you feel that you have you begun to converge on any insights, or when you feel a change in how the stories appear to you, stop your session. Now take each heading from this chapter and jot down a few notes on what happened with regard to that stage or aspect of the sensemaking process. Did you get

an overview of the stories? Did you zoom in and out on them? Did you count or rank or build with them? And so on.

Now do the same thing again, only do it with a group of family, friends, or colleagues. This time, instead of watching yourself go through the stages of sensemaking, watch (and help) them go through the stages. After the session is over, copy out the chapter headings again and write down (or just think about) what you saw happening under each heading. Did any of the parts work better than others? Do you need more facilitation practice on some parts than others? Did any of the parts surprise you? If you like, do this again, and see what you learn the second time.

After you have had some experience using the ideas in this chapter in practice: argue with this chapter. What don't you like about it? What seems ridiculous to you, or ineffective, or unrealistic, or unnecessary? Go on, find something. There has to be *something* you don't like. If there isn't, you haven't been paying attention. Make a case for your own view on the matter.

Chapter Twelve

Group Exercises for Narrative Sensemaking

This chapter contains instructions on facilitating five narrative sensemaking exercises.

1. In a twice-told stories exercise, people in small groups consider previously collected stories while choosing one or more stories from among those considered to retell more widely.

2. In a timelines exercise, people build linear progressions of events, factual and/or fictional, from a combination of stories previously collected and stories told during the exercise.

3. In a landscapes exercise, people define a two-dimensional space with meaningful dimensions, then populate the space with previously collected stories. As the stories fill the space, a landscape of features comes into view. People describe these features, discuss them, and tell stories about them.

4. In a story elements exercise, people list things they find in stories—characters, situations, themes, values, and so on—then cluster and re-cluster them into families of elements that together encompass the combined meaning of the stories. People describe and discuss the elements, and they sometimes build stories with them.

5. In a composite stories exercise, groups use collected stories as source material to build a fictional or semi-fictional story, which they tell to other groups. As they build and tell stories, people discuss the juxtapositions of meaning created.

I have written about these exercises in order of difficulty of facilitation. I suggest you start with the first, then try the others.

WHY USE SENSEMAKING EXERCISES?

Why should you use these sensemaking exercises? Can't you just get people to work through some simple tasks together, like finding patterns across stories? You can use simple tasks, and in fact each of these exercises can be reduced to a simple task (see "If you have less time" within each exercise section).

There are a few reasons I can give for working with these exercises without reducing them to simple tasks.

Direction. These exercises give your participants something to do when they don't know what to do. For many people, being led through a set of steps is easier to understand than being given a mandate to "make sense" of things.

Knowledge. These exercises were built upon experiences I and others had during years of facilitating sensemaking. They help you tell people what to do when *you* don't know what to do. Think of them as scaffolding that can hold up your growing understanding. If you keep facilitating sensemaking using narrative methods, you may not need fixed exercises at some point; you might begin to mix and match and create your own methods. But at the start it is helpful to have a plan.

Testing. These exercises have been tested. They work, and they produce relatively predictable outcomes. The basic elements of the exercises (as laid out in the stepwise directions) have been used, by myself and others, in dozens if not hundreds of group sessions. I've seen them work, and I know they will benefit your projects. (I should tell you that not every element I list here has been used in practice. Some of the "elaborations" I describe have been well tested, but others have been only lightly used, and some of the models and templates I list in Appendix A (page 589) have never been used in a narrative sensemaking session. There's no reason to assume they wouldn't work, but still, those parts of the exercise descriptions are meant to give you ideas, not instructions.)

Sources. These exercises can provide you with materials you can work with to develop your own methods. I've tried to write the exercise descriptions so you can expand or contract each exercise as your needs vary. I've tried to give you a deep enough understanding of each exercise so that you can make changes to suit the unique contexts in which you might use them. Hopefully none of these exercises will constrain your creativity. Hopefully they will inspire you to develop your own ideas.

Results. These exercises help session participants construct meaningful *artifacts* such as timelines, landscapes, story elements, and composite stories. Such artifacts can help you spread the impact of sensemaking in both space and time, supporting waves of story work yet to come. For example, you might use a set of constructed story elements to set up a story sharing space or write questions for a new story collection. It's certainly possible to create useful sensemaking outcomes without exercises; but by using exercises, you can ensure that your sessions will produce tangible results you can use in future work.

WHY NOT USE SENSEMAKING EXERCISES?

We have covered the reasons why you might want to use sensemaking exercises. Why might you *not* want to use them? Why might you put off using these exercises in favor of just helping people talk together about stories, or maybe giving them simple tasks to complete?

Difficulty. Exercises can be hard to facilitate, and they require work on your part to prepare to facilitate them. You should practice any of these exercises before you use it in a sensemaking session of high importance to a project. I explain in each exercise how you can slim it down to fit into less time or into a simpler task. But even if you do that, you will still need to think about how you will incorporate the benefits of the larger exercise into the smaller task. That's more work for you. If you are just trying out this

whole approach, or your project is very small, you might want to put these exercises aside until you decide to delve more deeply into this work.

Participation. Exercises require more intense participation than a simpler plan of reading stories together and talking about them. If you face the task of facilitating sessions where you know people will not be motivated to participate, you might want to either reduce these exercises to simple tasks or leave them out entirely.

Time. Exercises require more time than simpler tasks. If you can't get people to come to sessions long enough to include exercises, it's best to reduce the exercises to tasks or remove them from the session.

Group sizes. Exercises work better with more people in the room. If you can only get a few people to come to your sensemaking sessions, you won't have the critical mass of contact you'll need to get sensemaking exercises off the ground. Save them for times when you have more participants ready to go.

If you decide that these exercises aren't the right thing for you or your participants right now, it will still be helpful to read about them. They may give you ideas that can help your sensemaking produce useful results.

TWICE-TOLD STORIES

In a twice-told stories exercise, when it is used for sensemaking, people in small groups consider previously collected stories while choosing one or more stories to retell more widely.

When to use it

The point of this exercise is to give small groups of people a concrete yet very simple task that encourages them to consider the topic of the session together. It is meant as story work for a beginning story worker and beginning participants, or as a warm-up exercise for more complicated exercises to come later in a longer session.

What it requires

Four to fifteen people; at least an hour; a room with enough space to conduct (without distraction) as many small group conversations as there are small groups.

How to do it

Step One: Introduce the exercise and form small groups

Five minutes. Explain the exercise and its purpose briefly. Ask people to form groups of two to four people (not five or more unless necessary).

Step Two: Select criteria

Five minutes. Each small group should discuss the topic and decide on a criterion by which they will choose a story they will tell to the larger group afterward. Groups should complete this question:

Which of these stories will best _____?

What each group uses to fill that blank space can be short and simple or long and complex, but it *must* relate to the project's goals, not to any general quality of what makes a "good" story.

Some examples of utility criteria might be:

- Which of these stories will best—open our eyes to the way this issue appears to others in our community?
- Which of these stories will best—help us find new solutions for this problem?
- Which of these stories will best—help us heal the wounds of the past?

Some examples of non-useful quality criteria might be:

- Which of these stories will best—make a great movie?
- Which of these stories will best—go viral?
- Which of these stories will best—make people cry?

I hope you can see the difference. Why does this matter? Because whether a story says something *important* and whether it says something *well* are two different things. Sometimes the stories that boost a project to new levels of impact are not at all well-spoken, but are awkward, shy, painful little things. People are so used to thinking of stories as things they buy that judging stories on whether they are "hot or not" can

stand in the way of using them well in sense-making. It is up to you, the facilitator, to help people get past that limitation.

Step Three: Present and improve criteria

Five minutes. Each small group presents its criterion to the whole room. The room reacts by considering the question, "How will choosing stories based on this criterion help meet the project's goals?" If necessary, groups can rethink and present their criteria again.

Step Four: Encounter stories

Twenty minutes. The small groups read or listen to stories collected during a previous phase of the project and made available to them by the facilitator in some form: print, audio, video, or some combination. As they encounter the stories, each group chooses the one story that best matches their chosen criterion.

Step Five: Retell stories

Twenty minutes. Each small group chooses a member to retell their chosen story to the whole session. As these stories are told, the facilitator divides up the time and watches the clock so every group gets a chance to tell their chosen story. After each story is told, each teller should also explain *why* their small group chose that particular story and what the group thinks the story says about the topic.

Step Six: Wrap up

Five minutes. General discussion of all stories told and the topic.

If you have less time

You can trim this exercise down to forty-five minutes by hurrying the first two steps into five minutes (introduce the exercise and form groups, plus select criteria), dropping step three, and either cutting the retelling short or dropping the wrap-up period.

If you have more time

It is better not to expand this exercise schedule. When you use this exercise to *collect* stories, it will not hurt to add more time for story exchange; but when people are *considering* stories, they are not likely to use the extra time as well. They will probably just drift off onto talking about other topics.

Optional elaborations

You can ask the people in each small group to exchange their *own* stories in response to the stories they hear or read. They can then consider those in addition to the previously collected stories as they make their choice of stories to retell.

How you will know it's working

The encounter period is what makes or breaks this exercise. If it is working, people will be hunkered down concentrating together on which story they will choose to retell. If they are not connecting to the stories, people will not be hunkered down; they will be looking or moving around the room.

What can go wrong

People choose quality criteria

When this exercise is used for sensemaking, a quality criterion such as "the best story" or "the most interesting story" will cause more damage than it does during story collection. In sensemaking, quality criteria can push aside the most awkward, unskilled stories, even when those stories say what needs to be said. That is why an extra criterion review time slot is justified.

You get behind time

Sometimes people given this task don't get around to choosing a story because they go off on tangents of discussion. Drifting off the task is more likely when people are encountering stories than when they are telling stories. Remind people at halfway and three-quarter points that they should have a story ready to tell when the time interval is over.

You get ahead of time

Sometimes people given this task choose a story *too* quickly, just to get the task over with, and spend the rest of the time chatting. If you think that might happen with your participants, plan ahead by tightening the time schedule or giving groups more tasks in the time you have. If you didn't think it would happen but it does, you can drop a gentle hint that you expect each group to be able not just to *tell* the story they chose, but to *justify* their reasons for choosing it. If a gentle hint doesn't work, let it go. This is a low-pressure method.

Try it yourself first

The best way to try out this exercise yourself is to get hold of some stories and start choosing among them. Gather stories from the newspaper or books, or ask around, or just jot down some notes on stories you remember. Make sure the stories pertain to a common topic, though, or you'll confuse yourself because they won't hang together.

Get the stories into a format where you can play with them: titles written on sticky notes or slips of paper, printed stories on sheets of paper, shapes in a presentation file on a computer screen, anything you can manipulate. Then set yourself criteria related to your project's goals and start making some choices. Practice justifying your criteria and choices.

After you've done this by yourself for a while, ask a few colleagues or friends to do the same thing with you. You can grow your way into facilitating this exercise, first alone, then in one small group, then while helping a few small groups.

Your own style

This exercise straddles the line between task and exercise. It does that for a reason, which is to help you work your way over the boundary to the more complicated exercises available. You should think of this exercise as a simple, multi-purpose frame that can support a variety of ideas you might like to develop for your own facilitation. Once you have got some practice using the twice-told form in its simplest manifestation, think about things you can add to the framework.

For example, these are some elements you could bolt on to the basic twice-told frame.

Explore multiple perspectives. You might ask people to come up with one criterion, but apply it to multiple perspectives as they encounter stories. For example, they might choose one story that best matches the criterion and another that matches it worst.

Explore answers to questions. You might ask people to consider both the stories and the answers people gave to questions about them as they judge which stories best meet their criteria. For example, if they have decided to choose a story to tell that best "shows the double-edged sword of community development," they can use the answers participants gave to decide which story is the best example.

Explore patterns across answers. You might ask people to come up with criteria, then use them not to choose *individual* stories, but patterns *across* stories. In that case the fill-in-the-blank question would be, "Which of these *patterns* will best (blank)?" You could ask people to incorporate some materials from catalytic work in this exercise, such as graphs and interpretations.

Explore construction. You might ask people to come up with criteria, then choose two or three stories that relate to them, then *string those stories together* in some way. To explore towards timelines, ask people to place the stories in a line based on when they happened, then talk about what that means. To explore towards landscapes, ask people to arrange the stories in any kind of meaningful space. To explore towards story construction, ask people to craft the stories into a very simple tale, perhaps with a context-complication-resolution structure.

Explore combinations. You can add two or more of these elements to the basic structure at the same time. For example, people might build two short timelines from competing perspectives, choose patterns placed on a simple landscape, or explore multiple perspectives as revealed in answers participants gave to questions.

Note that I haven't included any of these elements in the "optional parts" section above. These aren't part of the exercise in its simple form, so I didn't want to imply that you should do these things. They are more like opportunities for you to grow your own methods starting with this simple form. Just make sure you keep your additions to the basic form small and simple. When you are ready to add more elaborate complications, don't keep using this form; move on to another exercise structure. The form may be versatile, but it is small, and it can't support heavy loads.

Where it came from

The basic idea of twice-told stories came from a story collection exercise I developed with my colleague Neal Keller at IBM Research in 2000 (though of course the idea of choosing something out of a group of things is more than ancient). I can't honestly say I've ever used this exercise in a sensemaking session and *called* it an exercise. Instead, I've used the twice-told form to create warm-up tasks that prepared people for more complicated work later in the session. That doesn't mean this method can't be used by itself. It just means that as you build your facilitation skills, and as people warm up to sensemaking sessions, you and they will naturally step up from it to more complicated methods.

How to find more on these ideas

It's easy to find advice on using a technique as simple as this one. Just search the internet for terms like *break into groups, form small groups, split into groups, get into groups, divide into groups*, and so on, along with the words *choose* or *select*. (Avoid the words *identify* and *determine*, because those exercises are less likely to resemble sensemaking.) You are likely to find many descriptions of simple small group methods for ice-breaking, brainstorming, role-playing, team-building, and other purposes. I find that just reading through brief descriptions of such exercises helps spark new ideas for my own facilitation. If you can find someone who often works with groups of people, ask them how they help people work together in groups. They might have ideas you can use.

TIMELINES

In a timelines exercise, when it is used for sensemaking, people build linear progressions of events, factual and/or fictional, from a combination of stories previously collected and stories told during the exercise.

When to use it

When a timeline exercise is used for story collection, it helps people remember and distinguish past events. When the same exercise is used for sensemaking, the emphasis is not on recall but on *discovery*. Thus while timelines in story collection focus on *people* and their *memories*,

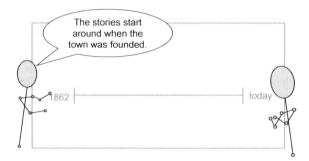

Figure 12.1. Groups should draw a line on the space and mark the starting and ending dates.

timelines in sensemaking focus on the *project* and its *goals*.

Some projects are all about time. For example, a project may focus on changes in the community's past or plans for its future. An explicitly time-oriented project is the best match for a timeline exercise in sensemaking. In such a project there will usually be only one timespan of central interest to the project, and it will probably be useful to consider that timespan from multiple perspectives.

Some projects are not explicitly about time, but there is at least one *process,* or sequence of events frequently encountered, whose consideration will benefit sensemaking. Some examples might be: an employee's first month of employment; a child's passage through the school system; the course of a community festival from planning to clean-up; the journey taken by a legislative bill; the processing of a criminal case. But not all processes lend themselves well to timelines. A timeline is useful for exploring departures from a typical process, but to do that there has to *be* a typical process. There must be some commonality across experiences. For example, if all the festivals that have ever taken place in a community have been so wildly different that no common process can be described, a timeline might not be worth pursuing.

Some projects include no time-based elements. Let's say your project is about trust in the community. You *could* think of a process by which trust is built, or broken, but trying to build a timeline of such a process would probably not be useful. The time element of such a process is too varied to make any combined sense. If that's the case, choose another exercise.

What it requires

At least three people and up to as many as the room will comfortably hold; at least ninety minutes; large sticky notes of a few different colors; large markers; places to put sticky notes (walls, large tables, clean floor).

How to do it

Step One: Introduce the exercise and form groups

Five minutes. Explain the exercise and its purpose. Split people into groups from two to eight people each.

Note that groups can be both smaller *and* larger for this exercise when used for sensemaking than they can be for story collection. Groups can be smaller because two people can work on a timeline together, and groups can be larger because during sensemaking there is no need to record stories.

More smaller groups create greater intimacy and a wider range of distinct perspectives, and are best suited to projects with sensitive topics or a need for wide-ranging ideas. Fewer larger groups create fewer but more detailed timelines, and are best suited for projects with more complicated—but not sensitive—topics and a need for depth of exploration. You can even build only one timeline (without breaking into groups) if the session is very small.

Step Two: Choose topics and dates

Five minutes. Ask each group to agree on a topic their timeline will explore. The topic should be related to the goals of the project, like

Figure 12.2. Groups should place a cluster of sticky notes with names of stories that describe the situation at the ending date.

"our town through the decades" or "firefighting through the years" or "our family's journey."

Also ask each group to choose *starting and ending dates* for their timeline (see Figure 12.1 on the preceding page). Have groups mark these dates with sticky notes (usually with the starting date on the left and the ending date on the right). In most contexts the ending date will be the present moment, but not in all cases.

Step Three: Place story titles at starting and ending dates

Ten minutes. Ask each group to choose a small number of stories, around three to five, to describe the state of affairs at the beginning and end of the timeline. They should copy the name of each story they choose onto a sticky note and place it at either extreme of the timeline space (see Figure 12.2).

Step Four: Populate timelines with stories

Thirty minutes. Ask each group to choose stories from those they have been given and place sticky notes with their titles on them along the timeline, between the start and end date (see Figure 12.3 on the next page). Ask them to build the timeline in such a way that it *tells a story* about the topic they are exploring.

Step Five: Annotate timelines with turning points

Ten minutes. Ask each group to find and mark some stories that represent turning points on their timeline, times when things changed (see Figure 12.4 on page 393). The turning-point mark can be a "T" or a circle around the name or any distinction that stands out from several

paces off. Make sure people don't mark *every* story. Things should change *more than usual*, or the distinction will not be useful.

You might remember that when I described the use of this exercise for story collection, I suggested using turning points as *prompts* to help people recall stories to tell. Should you prompt people to look for turning points *as* they choose stories to place on their timelines? No, don't do that. In sensemaking, people should look for turning points only *after* they have filled their timelines with stories. Why? Because turning points should *emerge* from the placement of stories, not shape it.

Step Six: Review timelines within groups

Ten minutes. In this period, ask each group to talk together about their timeline as a whole, including all of its annotations. What have they learned from it? What has surprised them in it? What do they like and dislike about it? What would they do if they were going to build the timeline all over again? If you have more than one group, explain that in the *next* time period people from the other groups will be visiting their timeline. What would they like to do to prepare the timeline for review by other people in the room?

Step Seven: Visit timelines

Ten minutes. Ask people to walk around the room looking over all of the timelines created and talking about the experiences described there. Have one person from each group stay at their own timeline to answer any questions or receive any feedback from visitors. (If you only have one group, leave this step out.)

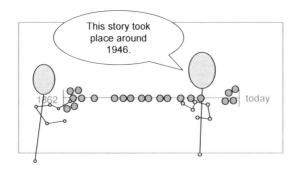

Figure 12.3. Groups should place stories on the timeline based on when the events described in them took place.

Step Eight: Finish the timelines

Ten minutes. Now ask each group to reconvene and reconsider their timeline for the last time. It is finally time to make the timelines beautiful. Ask each group to concentrate now not on adding meaning to their timelines, but on *making their meanings clear* to those who might see the timeline later.

At the close of this time period, each timeline should include a *legend* explaining the meaning of each type of marking or sticky-note color, as well as a *summary* of the timeline's major features. Summaries can be written or recorded in audio, photographs or video, depending on the project's needs and resources. (If the group received useful feedback from visitors in the previous step, they can incorporate it during this step.)

Step Nine: Discuss with the whole room

Ten minutes. Finally, bring everyone together into a large discussion of all the timelines built in the room. Talk about what patterns appear across different timelines, where there are differences of perspective, what discoveries can be gained from the events within and across timelines. (If you only have one group, use this time for general discussion of the exercise, or leave it out.)

If you have less time

You can trim this exercise down to forty-five minutes if you do only these parts.

1. Introduce the exercise and form groups. Five minutes.
2. Choose topics and dates. Five minutes.

3. Place story titles at starting and ending dates. Five minutes.
4. Populate timelines with stories. Twenty minutes.
5. Annotate timelines with turning points. Five minutes.
6. Visit timelines. Five minutes.

To convert the exercise into a fifteen-minute task, forget about topics and dates; forget about annotations; forget about visits. Just ask people to "grow" a timeline as they encounter stories. This will give them a bit of insight into when things happened as they consider stories, but that is all.

If you have more time

To add more time to this exercise, include one or more elaborations, or add time to the steps in this order:

1. Populate timelines with stories
2. Annotate timelines with turning points
3. Review timelines within groups
4. Visit timelines
5. Place story titles at starting and ending dates
6. Discuss with the whole room
7. Finish the timelines
8. Choose topics and dates
9. Introduce the exercise and form groups

The maximum time I would suggest for this exercise would be about four hours.

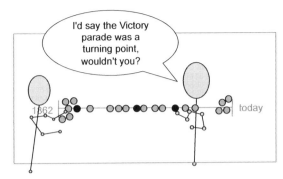

Figure 12.4. Groups should choose some stories already placed on the timeline to be marked as turning points.

Optional elaborations

Use whole stories instead of story titles

The basic instructions for this exercise say to write story titles on sticky notes and place them on timelines. If you have printed story cards, and they are not very large, you can have people place *whole* stories—with entire texts and answers to questions—on their timelines. If you use a wall you will need some way to affix the cards to it, but that's easily done with tape stuck to the backs of things. (You can even buy *partially* sticky tape that works like whatever is on the back of sticky notes, and stick it to the backs of your story cards. If there is text on the back, you can plan "tape spots" where you don't print anything.)

The advantage of using whole story cards is that people can zoom in to compare stories in detail while finding turning points and looking for patterns. The disadvantages are two: patterns might not be as visible from far away (keep those title font sizes large), and people might get too drawn in to reading story cards and take a long time to do the exercise.

Use vertical space to annotate stories

The aspect ratios of most walls and tables are rectangular, like a book turned sideways. That leaves a lot of space above and below a timeline that runs horizontally through the center line of the space. So why not use vertical space to add meaning to the timeline? I mentioned this technique when I talked about using timelines for story collection, as a means of fitting more stories onto the timeline and opening up gaps people could fill to balance the story collection. I said people could *displace* stories so

that they rise up and fall down like balloons and plumb bobs. During sensemaking, you can use the same vertical space, but for another reason: to reveal patterns in previously told stories.

Let's say a group is placing stories along their timeline. Using this elaboration, instead of simply placing each story *on* the line, they place the story above or below the line ("sliding" it on its "string") according to how strongly positive or negative its storyteller rated its emotional tone (see Figure 12.5 on the next page). In this way the timeline will show the ebb and flow of emotions as events unfolded. This will help the group discover patterns in the timeline as they work.

Distinguish multiple perspectives

A different way to use the vertical space on a timeline is to use it to separate perspectives (see Figure 12.6 on the following page). Say there are two perspectives important to your project, like people who were born in the area and people who moved in later. You could place one set of stories above the timeline and the second set below. (Just be careful to avoid introducing a subtle bias through the universal up-is-best connection. Put the underdogs on top, or flip a coin to see who should get the up side.) Contrasting perspectives in space often reveals patterns, such as that one perspective saw a situation as hopeless while the other was optimistic. If you want to distinguish three or more perspectives, you can do that too: just draw multiple timelines across the same space.

Mark multiple types of turning point

When it comes to marking turning points, the instruction given above is the simplest option.

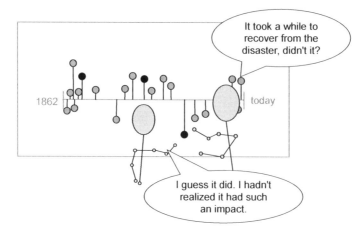

Figure 12.5. Groups can displace stories from the timeline to denote some axis of difference, like outcome or emotion.

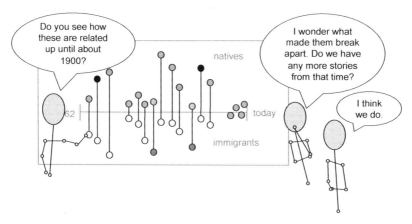

Figure 12.6. The top and bottom areas of the timeline can be used to contrast different perspectives on events.

The more complicated option is to have people mark more than one *type* of turning point (as in Figure 12.7 on the next page). Using multiple turning-point types deepens the exploration. Examples of turning point types might be problems, decisions, dilemmas, "aha" moments, times of joy or despair, times of solidarity, times of conflict, breakthroughs, accidents, and surprises.

If you add this elaboration, expand the turning-point time slot to fifteen or twenty minutes. You can choose types yourself based on the project's needs, or you can ask groups to choose from a list of types you present, or you can ask groups to come up with their own types, or some combination of these. In any case, keep the number of turning point types small, no higher than three or four.

To annotate stories with multiple turning point types, people can write letters or symbols on their sticky notes (D for dilemma, S for surprise, etc), or stick some tiny colored label dots onto them (hot pink for surprise, neon green for solution, etc). Just make sure people mark their annotations large enough to be seen from several feet away, because you want annotation patterns to stand out. That's why single letters or dots are best, because if people write something like "these stories all have conflict in them" nobody will see those patterns from afar. A big red "C" for conflict works better.

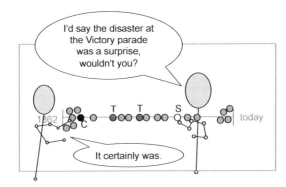

Figure 12.7. Marking multiple types of turning point can help people talk about why things happened the way they did.

Annotate timelines with story sets

In this optional activity, you can ask each group to find and mark *sets of stories* on their timeline. (Put this after turning point annotation and before timeline reviews, and allocate fifteen or twenty minutes to it.)

A story set hangs together for a complex reason that may have nothing to do with what happens in the stories or what types of stories they are.

Story sets might have names like these:

- stories we wish we had heard last year
- stories nobody in the community wants to hear but everyone needs to know
- stories that should never have happened the way they did
- stories that show where this community could be five years from now

Where should people get these types of story sets? They should come up with them on their own. Don't tell people what sorts of story sets to create. If people ask you what their story sets should be, tell them that the sets should *emerge* from their timelines. Ask people to mark sets of stories they want to remember or tell others about as being particularly important to consider *together*. You can give people a quota for the number of sets they should create, if you think they need one, or you can just ask them to create as many sets as they think matter.

There are two ways to annotate story sets. The first, which I call *spidering,* is to place a sticky note of a special color somewhere near the set of stories to be annotated, write the name of

the set on the sticky note, then draw lines or attach strings from the sticky note to all relevant stories (see Figure 12.8 on the following page). People can only do spidering when the stories in their timelines are not too spread out or numerous. But it's a quick method, and it's easy to see where the spiders appear on the timeline.

A second method of set annotation is to mark each story in the set with a special symbol or letter (Figure 12.9 on the next page). So for example all stories marked with a "5+" might be stories that show where the community could be five years from now. This *scattered* set annotation method has the advantage of working across large or spread-out timelines, but it has the disadvantage that set patterns are harder to see than spiders, especially if turning-point annotations and set annotations are overlaid.

You can also use combinations of color and symbol to clarify distinctions. Let's say your group has three letters marking turning point types (D, S, P). Those are written in red, while the story titles are written in black. You have also marked three *sets* of stories with shapes (square, triangle, circle), and these are drawn in blue. Both the colors and the number-shape difference help people filter out either turning-point or set annotations as they look at the timeline.

Include newly told factual stories

You can ask people, as they populate their timelines, to tell some of their *own* stories in response to the stories they are placing, then give those stories titles and place them as well. Just ask people to denote newly-told stories with

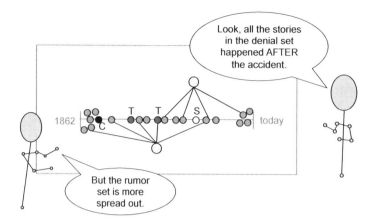

Figure 12.8. "Spidering" is marking a set of stories by connecting them to a descriptive label with lines.

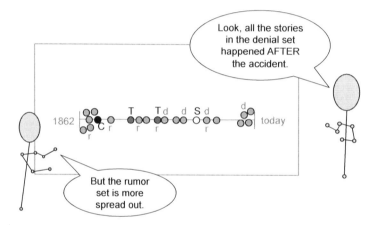

Figure 12.9. The "scattered" method of marking story sets is more useful when timelines are complex and it's hard to create spidered connections.

a special note color, marker color, or symbol. (If you want to add these new stories to your collection, have a helper come by with a small audio recorder or notebook and some answer sheets.)

Include newly told fictional stories

Fiction in narrative sensemaking widens the scope of imagination. It draws out elements of the topic that are hidden or hard to articulate. Moving into fiction is particularly useful if your project aims to find new ideas to address old problems. If your project has come to narrative sensemaking seeking depth, fiction might be the way to get it.

Place this elaboration after all annotations and before timeline reviews, and allocate twenty to forty minutes to it. Ask each group to de-

scribe an inconceivably utopian, perfect, heavenly state of affairs by telling some fictional stories about that state (see Figure 12.10 on the facing page). Ask them to place this cluster of story names *above* their factual timeline, either at the end point (describing an alternative ending) or beyond it (describing an alternative future). After the end state of the utopian timeline has been described and placed, ask people to fill it in, moving backwards, and finish it by connecting it at some point to the factual timeline (but *not* to the ending date).

Groups can repeat this process *below* the timeline with an inconceivably dystopian, horrible, ruined state of affairs. Both fictional timelines can then be annotated with turning points,

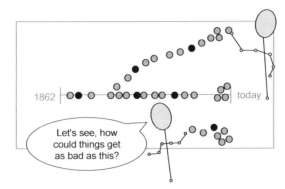

Figure 12.10. Groups can move into fiction, adding counter-factual utopian and dystopian timelines to the timeline created by considering the stories collected.

story sets, and phases. Either utopia or dystopia can go first.

Expand timelines or construct new ones

If you have more time, you can ask people to go back to their timelines and extend their start or end points, adding more stories. Or you can ask them to think of another timeline the first one suggests to them.

Annotate timelines with phases and boundaries

In this optional activity, you can ask each group to find and mark phases on their timeline (see Figure 12.11 on the next page). Put this after turning-point or story-set annotation and before timeline reviews, and allocate five or ten minutes to it.

You can call phases periods or chapters or spans, or even eras or epochs or ages if you want to make them sound more interesting, but *don't* call them stages or steps. Those words describe plans, not events.

To mark phases, groups should stand back and consider how they might describe the *state of affairs* in different parts of the timeline. They should name their phases with meaningful titles, like these:

• the time of anxiety
• before we knew
• after the new people came
• while we still held out hope
• the time we ran the experiment

They should also mark the places where one state no longer applies and a new one does. Groups can mark and name phases with sticky notes or markers, and they can mark boundaries between phases with tape or string or marker lines. Phases can be short or long; they can overlap; they can vacillate; they can fade away. It doesn't matter how the marking of phases plays out, as long as it helps to tell the story of what happened. Some boundaries between phases will be at turning points, but some will mark broad, slow "sea changes" between phases. Ask people to describe both the phases and the boundaries between them.

Compare timelines to published models

Juxtaposing what *did* happen in a timeline with what *usually* happens or *should* happen can provide a new perspective on events and help people make better sense of them (see Figure 12.12 on page 399).

A model is simply somebody's idea of what usually happens or should happen in some context. Models are bundles of expectations and assumptions. Departures from models are valuable because they can lead to explorations of why things happened the way they did and what could have happened had events flowed differently. You can find models in textbooks and in other educational materials about any topic. Models that are useful in the timeline exercise describe *phases* or *stages* in some progression.

Introduce models into the timeline exercise only *after* all timelines have been built and fully annotated. I'll repeat this part because it is

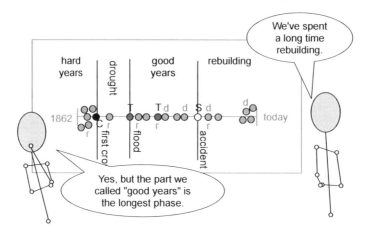

Figure 12.11. Marking phases of the timeline, and boundaries between them, is a good way to transition a timeline of scattered events into a coherent story.

important. *It is imperative* that you introduce models only *after* timelines have been built. Introducing models too early can limit sensemaking instead of enhancing it. Depending on how much you think this activity will add to the session, you can allocate anywhere from five to twenty minutes to it.

To introduce models, after all planned annotations have been added to timelines, briefly show groups the model or models you have chosen and ask them to *compare* the model(s) to their timelines. Always present models as *perspectives* to be considered, never as *corrections* to be applied or *standards* to be met. Be very careful about setting up this expectation. Models can be perceived as only for prescriptive use even when *you* say they are not. This is doubly true for models normally used for planning actions rather than describing events. Explain that the places where models *don't* fit the timelines are as useful as the places where they *do* fit.

Models don't work well for all groups and all topics. As you plan your session, think about how your participants are likely to react to the presentation of models within the timeline exercise. If you think they will attempt to conform to any model you show them, no matter what you say about it, either leave this elaboration out or change it to suit your needs. For example, you could show people two or three models and ask them to choose the one that provides them with the greatest insight. Or you could ask

them to use two or three models in succession, then think about the differences between them as they apply to the timelines. These changes to the basic activity might help people understand that it is not *conformity* to models that matters, but the addition of new perspectives to the story told by the timeline.

Where can you obtain models to use in this activity? Just look around. Every field of inquiry has some models written down somewhere. You can use general models that apply to many situations, or you can use models that focus very specifically on the topic you want to consider in the session. Scan through textbooks or other books; search the internet; ask around. The challenge is not likely to lie in *finding* models but in choosing from the abundant ones available.

Here's an example: there's a time-based model in the chapter before this one. Its four phases all start with a "c." I call the phases elements, but that's because I don't want you to take their order prescriptively. Still, you probably noticed that I described contact, churning, convergence and change as taking place roughly in that order during sensemaking. That's right, they usually do happen in that order. They don't *have* to, but they *usually* do. That's a model.

In Appendix A (page 589) I describe some examples of the sorts of time-based models you might find useful for timeline exercises.

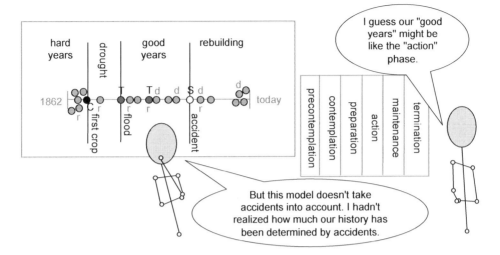

Figure 12.12. Comparing a built timeline to a model of how things usually happen or how things should happen can provide insights about the unique features of the timeline.

How you will know it's working

When a timeline exercise is used for sensemaking, it doesn't matter how full or balanced the timelines are. This was not true for story collection, because one goal of that exercise was to balance the story collection. So to find out if this exercise is working for sensemaking, don't watch the *timelines;* watch the *people.*

When people are building timelines, you should hear them making sounds of discovery. They should say things like, "Look at *that!*" or "I never noticed *that* before." If people are talking about nothing but the *placement* of stories ("this goes before that"), the exercise may not be helping them as much as it should.

But this process does takes time. Don't rush to fix things during the early parts of timeline building. If most of the time has been used up and you *still* don't see people discovering things together, you might want to offer some help, or just watch and learn how you can improve your methods the next time.

What can go wrong

People throw stories onto their timelines without paying attention to them

Be careful not to give the impression that people should fill their timelines in a mechanical way by simply sorting stories into time periods.

A timeline is not just a catalogue of events. It is a *story* built for a purpose and with a goal. At every location in a timeline, there are likely to be several candidate stories that *could* be placed to represent that moment in time. Those choices, taken together, create a story. Tell your groups that their timelines should both *explore* their topic and *tell a story* about it to the rest of the room.

One condition that can cause people to throw stories onto timelines is too much space. When I wrote about using timelines for story collection, I said you should give people lots of space to build timelines in, because you want them to tell lots of stories. I said, "Don't make the mistake of having people run out of space before they run out of stories." For sensemaking, this advice is reversed. If you give people *too much* space for their timelines, the need to choose stories for it will go away, and they'll just throw stories onto it without thinking. There must be *some* kind of selection process during the creation of a timeline to prevent it being nothing more than a catalogue of stories the group has encountered. A space limitation creates such a selection process.

People are talking, but they don't seem to be doing anything

If you were to map the progress of any two random groups of people building timelines, you would be likely to see differences in how

Figure 12.13. Emergence in sensemaking is like growth in seedlings: the most important parts of the process are often the least visible.

each group moves through the task. I remember once watching two groups build timelines at the same time on different walls of a room. One group populated their timeline with stories in a tick-tock fashion, one story per so many minutes with great regularity. The other group seemed to do absolutely nothing but sit and chat for nearly half the time they were given for the task. Then suddenly one of the people in the second group jumped up and placed a handful of stories on the timeline in rapid succession. I guess they *had* been working on their timeline the whole time, only it didn't seem that way from across the room.

So if you see a group that seems to be ignoring the task, eavesdrop a little to find out what they are talking about. If the topic of discussion is dinner, you might need to nudge them to pay attention to the work at hand. But if they are saying things like, "why don't we" and "then we'll" and "so this is all about" and "wait a minute, what about" then my advice is to leave them alone. They are negotiating meaning.

Sometimes it's not *you* that gets anxious about groups that seem to be making no progress; it's the people in the groups themselves. Sometimes people get so upset about the fact that their timeline has too few items, or doesn't say anything big or important, or looks amateurish, that they stop making sense of the topic. It is your responsibility to help people get past these feelings.

Emergence in sensemaking is like growth in seedlings: the most important parts of the process are often the least visible (see Figure 12.13). If you've ever planted seeds, then watched them with disappointment as they seemed to be doing nothing for weeks, you can remember the moment when a fully formed cluster of seedling leaves suddenly sprouted up from the empty soil. The same thing happens in sensemaking. Watch people as they are building their timelines. If they are saying the things that indicate to you that they are negotiating meaning, and if they tell you that their timeline is "not coming together," you can feel confident in assuring them that *something* is growing, whether they can see it or not.

But what if you're wrong? What if their timeline *doesn't* come together? Well, of course, sometimes planted seeds don't emerge. The ground is too wet and they rot, or it's too dry and they die, or it's too cold and they freeze. But you are the gardener of the sensemaking session. You have prepared the soil as you planned and facilitated the session. The more your confidence grows in the process of sensemaking and your ability to guide it, the more you will be able to help people push through to emergence.

People are doing things, but they aren't talking

A narrative sensemaking session should be a lively place, full of energy and movement. If a group has gone quiet, find out what they are up to. This is especially important during the crit-

Figure 12.14. Voting is a way of collating meaning, not of negotiating it.

ical time period when groups are first placing stories on their timelines. Check to make sure that they are *negotiating meaning together*, not simply assembling their individual opinions.

If you are used to facilitating non-narrative group processes, you may have to adjust your expectations as you prepare to facilitate narrative sensemaking. It's *louder* than other methods of group work. Narrative sensemaking requires negotiation, and negotiation makes noise. If you are facilitating narrative sensemaking and you *don't* hear noise, find out why.

You may have heard of a group decision support method called "dot voting" in which people vote on items by placing colored label dots on them. Each participant is given three to five votes, which they place on whichever items they think best meet some criterion. Individual voting does not belong in a narrative sensemaking session. Voting may be fine for non-narrative group work, but it doesn't work as well with stories. Why? Because voting is a system for *collating* meaning, not for *negotiating* it.

I've watched dot voting. What I've seen happen is that the most opinionated or powerful people stride up to the white board and confidently place their dot or label or whatever, while the meek and powerless watch, and either fall into line or rebel against authority. What ends up getting created is not so much something the group has *negotiated* as it is a portrait of power as it flows through the group.

You might argue that dominant people can dominate story work too. Yes, they can. But this is where the fundamental nature of stories comes into play. You *can't* collate stories; they won't allow it. Why? Because stories *are* nego-

tiation devices. Their intricate internal structures (story form), far-reaching external linkages (story function), and participatory conveyance methods (story phenomenon) draw people into complex interactions that cannot be represented by a simple counting of votes. For this reason, working together with stories stands in the way of power having as *direct* an influence on what a group creates together as when what is "built" is simply a compilation of votes. Stories have been used for millennia for exactly the reason that they move people past collation and into negotiation.

Sometimes you will come across a group that has decided to vote instead of negotiate, even though you specifically asked them to talk through the task together. When you find such a group, my advice is to ask them to describe their voting system. If the group simply fell into voting because they didn't understand the instructions, they will describe their voting system without enthusiasm. However, if the group chose to vote in order to *avoid* negotiation, they are likely to describe their voting system in a defensive and emotionally stressed way. When that happens, I've found that the person who describes the voting scheme with the greatest zeal is usually the person with the greatest need to avoid negotiation (see Figure 12.14).

When you come across the defensive use of voting, you probably aren't going to help if you correct the group's choice of method. But you can be *aware* that at least in one group people are trying to avoid the more difficult parts of narrative sensemaking. If the person who presents the voting system is different in some way from others in their group, you will know that mixing people in those roles isn't working out very well. (It is common to find out only during a session that people you thought would work well together actually have barriers between them.)

In that case, you might look at the remainder of your session schedule and see if you can fit in more time to reflect quietly on the stories (to become more comfortable with them), reshuffle groups (to see if other combinations of participants will be able to explore better together), or explain a bit more about the nature of narrative sensemaking and the goals of the session.

If you see voting but it's not defensive, review your instructions after the session is over and see if you can improve the way you introduce the exercise the next time you do it. Avoid words people might associate with voting, like *decide, determine, resolve, elect, specify, set, fix, assign, designate, establish,* and *choose.* Instead, use words associated with negotiation: *discuss, talk, talk about, talk over, talk through, work out, arrive at, agree on, settle on.* Help people understand that they are to produce a collaborative creation, not a set of assembled elements.

The timelines are not meaningful

In this situation, people have created timelines, and the timelines have lots of stories and annotations on them. But the larger patterns created by the stories and annotations are superficial. Timelines like this have a "just the facts" flavor. They seem more like empty recitations of lists than they do living stories. Meaningless timelines are almost always the result of *distance:* between participants and the stories they are working with, between participants and each other, between participants and the project. Sometimes distance comes about because of poor project planning, but sometimes it's just an unavoidable condition in a particular group considering a particular topic.

If you are planning a sensemaking session and you think people might create meaningless timelines, try to reduce distance by collecting more stories from more people, inviting more or different people, or planning the session so that people go through more warm-up tasks that help them connect to the stories and to each other *before* you ask them to build timelines.

What can you do about meaningless timelines *after* they have been created? Not much. By the time people have created them it's probably too late to reduce the distance. Just learn from what happened and move on.

People can't or won't go into fiction

Moving into fiction brings many benefits to sensemaking, but it is not always possible. Don't ever *force* people into fictional exploration. As you plan your use of timelines, think about whether the people you expect to attend the sensemaking session will feel safe enough to "make things up" about the topic they will be exploring. Picture their reactions to such an instruction. Are they energized? Enabled? Confused? Disdainful? Afraid? If you aren't sure how they will react, make the fictional part of the exercise optional.

Try it yourself first

Building a timeline by yourself is a great way to find out what obstacles other people will have when they build theirs. The first thing you need, of course, is some stories you can work with. Not every set of stories is a good set for timeline practice. For example, it's probably impossible to build a timeline from a folk tale collection, because there is no shared time scale in them. Find some stories that center around the same event or cover the same historical period.

Themed oral history collections are good places to get timeline-ready stories, because typically everyone interviewed in the collection is talking about the same time period. You can draw out brief anecdotes from such collections and write them on story cards, or just write their names on cards or notes. One example that comes to mind is the series of American Slave Narratives collected by the Works Progress Administration in the 1930s. The major event of the U. S. Civil War is so prominent in those stories that mapping anecdotes from the narratives onto the various periods surrounding the war is easy. These interviews are readily available in several places on the internet, as well as in print. Similar archives exist for World War II and for various other periods in history. If that seems too distant, your local library may be able to help you find oral histories you can use that pertain to topics closer to home.

When you try building timelines on your own, you are guaranteed to come across some of the same difficulties that people will come across in your sensemaking sessions. You will find yourself placing stories on your timeline without thinking; stop and consider why you are placing each story and what it means. You will feel anxious that your timeline won't "add up" to anything in the end; take your time and build trust in the process. If your timeline *doesn't* add up, think about why it didn't and what you can change the next time. Make your mistakes now, when you can use them best.

After you've built a few timelines of your own, move on to participating in the creation of timelines in a group. Working in a group adds a whole new world of complexity to the process, and it's useful to experience that before you facilitate it.

Your own style

When you think of time, do you always picture it as a straight line? I ask because for some people, in some times and places, time is more naturally represented by other spatial arrangements. Some alternative representations of time are as a series of circles, a spiral, a branching tree, a matrix of layered elements, a series of comic-book-style panels, a meandering path laid out in meaningful space. All of these are legitimate representations of a timeline, and all of them can be useful in sensemaking. Which works best for you and for your participants in any sensemaking session depends on cultural backgrounds and thinking styles.

There is a benefit in matching your time representation to the way people think, but there can also be a benefit in *breaking* expectations about how time is laid out. Particularly if your project wants to find new ways to look at old problems, asking people to represent time in a new way might help them see the same events through new eyes. You could even draw inspiration from fields of endeavor that have a need to represent time, for example in musical notation or historical diagrams or train schedules. (Searching the internet for images related to the word "timeline" will provide you with many ideas.)

You aren't going to break the timeline exercise if you change how you lay it out. Why not explore your options and find a style that suits you, your project, and your participants? Just try out whatever ideas you have on your own and with a small group before you put them in front of a room full of sensemaking participants.

Where it came from

Of the five exercises I describe in this book for use in sensemaking, this one is the oldest and the one in widest use. I described the basic history of timeline use in the corresponding section for story collection (page 197), but what I didn't talk about there was the history of timelines for sensemaking.

The use of timelines for anything other than the authoritative presentation of facts is fairly recent. A few trends led the way toward their use in sensemaking.

In the mid-nineteenth century, games and puzzles with a chronological basis began to grow in popularity (though some of these games, like Pachisi or Parcheesi, Figure 12.15 on the next page, originated centuries earlier). Timeline games were usually races of some kind where people competed to advance along a course. Timeline puzzles were disassembled sequences people put back together. The use of timelines in education became popular around the same time. The American author Mark Twain even created his own timeline game as part of his system for helping people (especially himself and his children) remember the dates of historical events.

In the twentieth century, timelines began to be used more widely as means for conveying persuasive arguments. For example, R. Buckminster Fuller used timelines to illustrate his views on how technology and society might interact in the future. Gordon Moore and Ray Kurzweil used timelines to illustrate their predictions about the capabilities of future computers (see Figure 12.16 on the following page).

Timelines have grown past their factual origins and have become available for speculation, learning, and discussion. Today, visionaries from all fields use timelines not simply

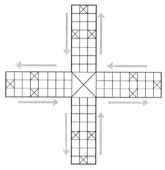

Figure 12.15. A diagram showing how the time sequence in the game Pachisi plays out. (Public domain image from Wikipedia.)

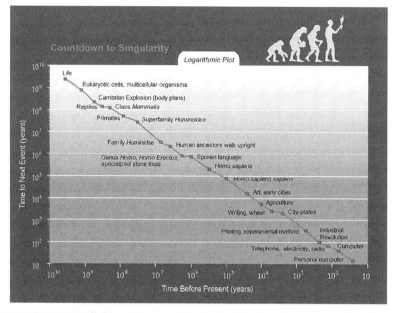

Figure 12.16. Ray Kurzweil's "Countdown to Singularity" timeline. (Image from Ray Kurzweil and Kurzweil Technologies, Inc. Creative Commons Attribution 1.0 Generic license. Retrieved from Wikipedia.)

to represent what has happened but with a variety of intents ranging from illumination to confrontation.

The use of timelines specifically for making sense of events together combines all these uses of timelines: as historical records, as mnemonic devices, as games, and as expressions of worldviews. I haven't found any definitive histories on the use of timelines for group work in sensemaking, decision support, brainstorming, or planning, but my sense is that the practice started in the 1950s and 60s as work on group facilitation in all of these fields progressed. Today, using timelines to think together through issues is a widespread practice in a variety of fields, such as family and community therapy, health care, social work, change management, and urban planning. Particulars may differ, but the basic structure is stable. This means that the timeline exercise is also the least likely to appear strange to a random group of people assembled in a room. That makes it a good choice for wary participants or a fledgling facilitator.

How to find more on these ideas

The age and widespread use of timelines means that you can tap into a wide cultural repository of ideas about ways to use them. If you search the internet for "timeline exercise" you

Figure 12.17. Ask each group to define a rectangular space using labels for dimensions and corners.

will find hundreds of descriptions of exercises you can use. Not all of these descriptions will work with stories in exactly the way they are described, but you should be able to get ideas to enhance your practice. Just picture using each described exercise with stories told from multiple perspectives (not simply events) as the elements being placed.

LANDSCAPES

In a landscapes exercise, when it is used for sensemaking, people define a two-dimensional space with meaningful dimensions, then populate the space with previously collected stories. As the stories fill the space, a landscape of features comes into view. People describe these features, discuss them, and tell stories about them.

When to use it

Landscapes and timelines are complementary because space and time are complementary. Both are essential elements of our lives. We move in time as we move in space, so these two ways of arranging things come about naturally. The story-time connection is the more obvious one, so the timeline exercise is easier for inexperienced participants and facilitators to work with. Mapping stories onto conceptual space is a more abstract activity.

What it requires

At least three people and up to as many as the room will comfortably hold; at least two hours; large sticky notes of a few to several different colors; large markers; places to put sticky notes (walls, large tables, clean floor).

How to do it

Step One: Introduce the exercise and form groups

Five minutes. Explain the exercise and its purpose. You can split people into groups of anywhere from two to eight people each. More small groups means more perspectives; fewer larger groups means more depth. Show people the walls, markers, and sticky notes you have prepared for their use.

Step Two: Present dimensions and corner points

Five minutes. Ask each group to mark each axis of the space using dimensions you chose to connect to your project's context and goals, such as trust and leadership. Then ask people to label each corner point with descriptions of how the two dimensions come together at that corner: low trust and strong leadership, high trust and weak leadership, and so on. Don't allow people to label quadrants or sections or any other *areas* of the space. Only label corners and sides. (See Figure 12.17.)

Figure 12.18. Groups should place each story as they consider it where they think it belongs.

Step Three: Populate landscapes with stories

Forty minutes. Ask each group to consider the stories they have been given in light of the space defined by the dimensions. Groups can use *all* the stories they have or some *subset* of stories they think apply especially well to the issues they are exploring. For each story they want to place, people should copy its name onto a sticky note and place the note where they think the story best fits in the space (see Figure 12.18).

If groups can't decide or don't agree on where a story belongs, they can copy its name onto two or more sticky notes, adding what aspect or perspective of the story the note refers to (e.g., "The cat came home: Neighbor's perspective").

Step Four: Discover and annotate features

Twenty-five minutes. As people place stories in their defined spaces, patterns will naturally appear. Perhaps there are many stories in one spot but few in another, or the stories in one area form a line that divides one condition from another, or all the stories in one area mention city building sites.

After people have populated their spaces, ask them to mark and discuss *features* of the landscape (see Figure 12.19 on the next page). They can use marker, tape, string, sticky notes stuck

to each other and arranged into chains, whatever works to make the discovered meanings clear. Ask people to annotate their landscapes *until the stories are no longer needed* to describe the major patterns in the space. They shouldn't *actually* remove the stories; but such a goal will help people better understand the task.

Step Five: Review landscapes within groups

Fifteen minutes. Ask each group to work together on the *story* their landscape tells. What does the whole thing mean to them? What have they discovered? What has surprised them? What do they want to tell *others* about? If you have more than one group, explain that in the next time period people from the other groups will be visiting their landscape. What would each group like to do to prepare the landscape for review by other people in the room?

Step Six: Visit landscapes

Ten minutes. Ask everyone to walk around the room looking over all of the landscapes that have been created. Have one person from each group stay at their own landscape to answer questions. (If you only have one group, leave this step out.)

Step Seven: Finish the landscapes

Ten minutes. This is the time in which groups should make sure that the understandings they have developed in the exercise are available to

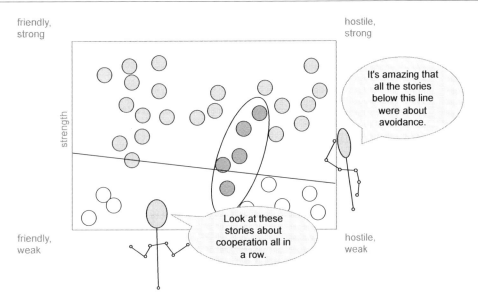

Figure 12.19. After all of the stories have been placed, groups should find and mark features created by the distribution of stories in the space.

those who did not participate in the session. They should add a *legend* explaining all annotations to their landscape as well as a *summary* of its major features (a few sentences will suffice). Summaries can be written or recorded in audio, photographs or video. Feedback from visits by other groups can also be incorporated in this step.

Step Eight: Discuss with the whole room

Ten minutes. Bring everyone together into a discussion of all the landscapes. Talk about what patterns appear across different landscapes, where there are differences of perspective, and what discoveries can be gained from the patterns within and across landscapes. (If you only have one group, use this time for general discussion of the whole exercise.)

If you have less time

You can trim this exercise down to forty-five minutes by doing only these parts.

1. Introduce the exercise and form groups. Five minutes.
2. Present dimensions and corner points. Five minutes.
3. Populate landscapes with stories. Twenty minutes.
4. Discover and annotate features. Ten minutes.

5. Visit landscapes. Five minutes.

To convert the exercise into a fifteen-minute task, present the dimensions simply (no corner points), then ask people to place stories on them as they consider them. This will give people only a brief glimpse of patterns, but it will help them prepare for more work with the stories afterward.

If you have more time

To add more time to this exercise, include one or more elaborations, or add time to the steps in this order:

1. Populate landscapes with stories
2. Discover and annotate features
3. Review landscapes within groups
4. Visit landscapes
5. Discuss with the whole room
6. Finish the landscapes
7. Present dimensions and corner points
8. Introduce the exercise and form groups

The maximum time I would suggest for this exercise would be about four hours.

Before you start

To facilitate a landscape exercise, you need to prepare some dimensions of meaning beforehand. This is true even if you plan to ask your participants to come up with their own dimensions, because some people might not be willing or able to do this on their own.

Coming up with dimensions for a sensemaking landscape exercise is quite different than when the exercise is used for story collection. For sensemaking, let your collected stories be your guide. Look for ways in which stories *vary in meaningful ways* across the collection. Don't look for commonality; look for diversity. For example, you might notice a range of expressions of trust and distrust in your stories. Even if you didn't think trust was important to your project going in, you might choose trust as a dimension for a landscape exercise because *you find it in the stories.* Catalytic work might also suggest useful dimensions to explore.

What about examining your project's goals and context? You need to look at that, right? Well, yes, but *afterward.* You can look at your project's goals to *evaluate* whether dimensions you find in your stories will address the project's goals well, but don't set up dimensions for sensemaking based on project goals alone. Put the stories first. Why? Because if the dimensions can't be *found* in the stories, the exercise will fail. The stories collected in story projects are not always the stories the project planners thought they would collect.

Let's pretend that your project was supposed to examine "conflict in the workplace." But in fact nobody told stories about conflict in the workplace. All the stories are about other things. Maybe the barrier to admitting conflict was stronger than you expected, or the method you chose for collecting stories didn't allow people to feel safe enough to talk about it, or people needed more anonymity than you gave them, or there wasn't as much conflict as you thought there was. For whatever reason, people didn't tell the stories you thought they would. In that case, setting up a dimension for this exercise called "conflict in the workplace" would be a bad idea.

Stories coming out differently than you expected doesn't always mean people refused to participate in the project. Sometimes it just means people addressed the topic in ways you hadn't anticipated. If I found myself in this posi-

tion, I'd spend a few hours reading stories to get a sense for what dimensions stories *did* range across. There are *always* dimensions in stories, and useful ones too, if you look for them. Maybe people told stories with more or less hypocrisy or deception or coalition building or cooperation. Maybe people didn't exactly *avoid* the topic of conflict, but came at it in an oblique way *that would be obscured* if you blundered into sensemaking based only on your project's stated goals. *The stories know* what dimensions you should use. Ask them.

I mentioned *orthogonal dimensions* in the section on landscapes in story collection (page 202), but I'll repeat it here because it's even *more* important in sensemaking. Any two dimensions you use together in a landscape exercise must be independent of each other, meaning that they are not likely to co-occur by definition. For example, pairing the age of the storyteller with how long ago the story took place would not be likely to reveal useful patterns, because older people are likely by definition to tell stories ranging over a longer time period. Pairing storyteller age with something that might or might not be related, like fears about strangers, would be more useful to the project.

Using dimensions from a published model

Another option is to use a set of "canned" dimensions from a model or framework that relates either to the topic you want to consider or to decision support in general.

Published models work better in sensemaking than they do in story collection. It's not that they don't work at all in story collection—they do, when used with care—but they work better and more reliably in sensemaking. Why? Because by the time people are doing sensemaking, the stories have already been told. Previously told stories can't be influenced by a model they are being placed on and compared to. Stories can still be ignored and misunderstood and distorted, but those are lesser problems than self-censorship during story collection.

The most important factor in the success of using published models as landscape dimensions is *how you present them* for use in sensemaking. Can you guess what I'm going to say next? It's the same thing I said about presenting catalytic material. If you use a published model in any sensemaking exercise, present it as a *resource,* not as an *authority.*

The word "model" has two uses in common speech: as a description of what *usually* happens, and as a prescription of what *should* happen. Stay away from all language that might hint at the prescriptive should-happen meaning of the term. Avoid words like *example, blueprint, design, mold, template, guide, instruction, theory, standard, paradigm,* or *ideal.* Instead, use terms like *perspective, view, angle, frame of reference, interpretation, aspect, element,* and *facet.* Do you see the difference? As long as published models multiply perspectives, they enhance sensemaking. As soon as they provide instruction, they diminish it.

Now, where can you get landscape-ready models? You can find them in any textbook on any subject. Just be careful to find a model that describes *continuous* space (from this to that), not *discrete* categories (this or that) or *phases* (this then that). Category and phase models are useful in sensemaking, but they fit other exercises better. Phase models work with the timeline and story construction exercises, and category models work with the story elements exercise. For landscapes, use only models that lay out *continuous dimensions.*

You can sometimes convert discrete models to landscape models. For example, say you find a model that seems useful, but it defines three categories instead of one range. Say it describes ways in which teams work together: with rigid *hierarchy,* with semi-flexible *roles,* and with open *tasks* anyone can take on. Since these three categories can be considered—without distortion—as taking up three portions of a scale from greater to lesser structure in group work, you could use this as one dimension in a landscape exercise. Quite a few models that don't *look* continuous can be converted to continuous use in this way.

Check that any dimensions from published models you want to use connect with dimensions of variation you find in your collected stories. If the models don't fit the stories, you can't use them.

In Appendix A (page 589) I describe some examples of the sorts of models that work well for landscape exercises.

Optional elaborations

Rename, choose, assemble, or create dimensions

I went over these options in detail when I described the use of landscapes for story collection (page 204). Since the options are identical when the exercise is used for sensemaking, I will only summarize them here and refer you to that section for details.

Briefly, you can:

1. Give groups one set of dimensions to use, but ask them to *rename* the dimensions and corners with terms they find more meaningful.

2. Present groups with two or more sets of dimensions and ask them to *choose* a set to use.

3. Present groups with *unpaired* dimensions and ask them to *pair up* dimensions they will use together.

4. Ask groups to *create* their own dimensions (possibly after spending some time becoming familiar with the collected stories in a previous exercise).

5. Any combination of these elaborations.

If you choose any option after the second one on this list—that is, if people are doing anything other than using or choosing a dimension set—add a review period in which each group presents to the whole room the dimension set they have put together and receives feedback. The review period should include consideration of whether the proposed dimensions can be found in the stories.

Add a third dimension

This elaboration is the same as for story collection, but it's more useful for sensemaking. Using a third dimension in a landscape sensemaking exercise is deeper, more complicated, more difficult, and more revealing. The instructions for adding a third dimension for sensemaking are the same as for story collection (color is the easiest way to set it up), so I won't repeat them here.

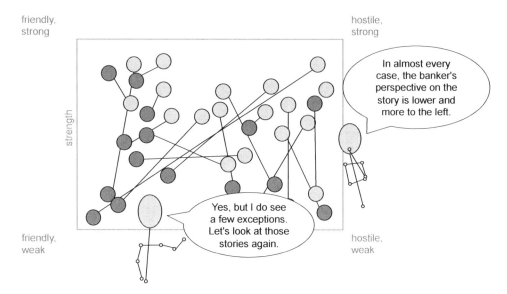

Figure 12.20. Interpreting each story from multiple viewpoints can help groups discover useful patterns in the stories.

Consider multiple perspectives

You can ask people as they place stories to represent each story from at least two *competing* viewpoints (see Figure 12.20). You can even ask people to connect the perspectives within each story with lines, to look for patterns across perspectives.

Let's say you have collected two hundred stories about the dangers and opportunities of starting small businesses in your city. Say you are in a sensemaking session in which people are working together with the stories, and they are doing a landscape exercise. Say they place—that is, interpret—a story about managing small-business finances from the perspective of a banker, a local official, and an entrepreneur. Their entire landscape will gain a greater depth of understanding when it begins to come together.

This elaboration does require quite a bit more patience and care, but for some highly motivated groups the effort will pay off.

An even more complex form of this elaboration, one you should reserve for the most motivated and capable groups, is to generate two or three *parallel* landscapes. As before, each story generates three sticky notes, one per perspective. But in this case the story-perspective notes should be placed on three *separate* landscapes.

Thus a group could end up with the banker's landscape, the official's landscape, and the entrepreneur's landscape, on three adjacent wall spaces, working from the same stories.

Place story elements

If you have derived story elements in a previous exercise (see the "Story elements" exercise on page 419), you can place these on your landscape, instead of or in addition to stories. You can intermingle different types of story element (e.g., characters, situations, themes) on one landscape, or you can build separate landscapes per type.

Place official statements

Your organization or community might have some officially documented statements relevant to the topic of the session: mission statements, sets of proclaimed values, operating principles, rules of conduct. You can ask groups to place those on their landscapes as well. If you add this elaboration, do it after the stories have been placed and before any features have been found. That way the official statements won't influence the placement of stories (attracting or repelling stories around them), but they will contribute to the features.

Use geographic landscapes

Some approaches to community development work combine the use of space with partici-

Figure 12.21. Using a geographic landscape as a backdrop can help groups think through issues affecting their town or work location.

patory sensemaking, but in *real* space. Participatory mapping (also known as community-based mapping, grassroots mapping, and ethnocartography), uses cartographic representations of actual geographies to help communities represent local knowledge and perspectives. When geography is important to the context and goals of your project, you can bring these ideas into your narrative landscape exercises.

This elaboration is more useful for communities than it is for organizations, because communities *are* spaces. For organizations, whether a real-space elaboration is useful depends on what sort of work is done in the organization and how much space matters to that work. A project about cooperation in a train yard or assembly plant, or in a service organization that covers a geographical area, would benefit more from this elaboration than a project about collaboration in an office building full of dimensionless cubicles whose locations are irrelevant.

To use real landscapes, present as your primary dimensions the real dimensions of space: north to south, east to west. At the start of the exercise, ask each group to decide where the center point and outer boundaries of their landscape will be located. Then ask them to place some points of interest before they start placing stories. Remember that people don't need to place stories simply by where they happened; they can consider more interpretive elements, like where the

story had the greatest impact, where it might have the greatest impact in the future, where it was collected, where it should be told, where it *cannot* be told, and so on (see Figure 12.21).

By incorporating perspectives as well as facts into the placement, the landscape produced adds meaning to geography to create something more than "just a map." If people cannot agree on where a story should be placed, as usual, it can be split and written multiple times. If you like, you can ask people to incorporate a *third* dimension into the landscape: not height, but some element of negotiated meaning such as trust, cooperation, conflict, hope, and so on.

Tell stories

After the landscapes are complete, and after they have been reviewed and summarized, you can ask people to use the landscapes as *substrates* on which to build stories (see Figure 12.22 on the following page). This mixes a bit of both timeline and composite story exercises into the landscape exercise.

The least complicated form of this elaboration is to have groups choose from among the stories they have already placed in the space some stories that, taken together, tell a larger story. For example, say a story about a new bridge design sits in the upper right corner of the space. A group might choose that story, then *link* it to another story about the start of bridge construc-

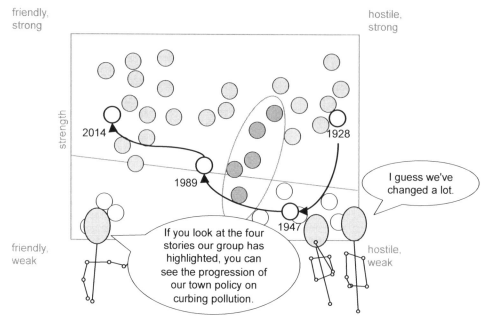

Figure 12.22. Overlaying time series on the landscape can create new views of how events unfolded.

tion in the lower right area. Next they might draw a line up to a story about an accident during construction way up at the top of the space, and so on. The way the larger story plays out in the space—the path it takes—will help people think about what the space means in the context of the project.

A more complicated option is to overlay a *historical* story onto the space, in a sort of layer floating over the stories placed there. Such a story can be drawn from the general history of the world or country, or the specific history of the organization or community. Episodes in the history can be placed at points in the space with a path laid between them. The relationship of the historical story-as-path can be compared to the stories placed in the space to find patterns of coincidence.

The most complicated option is to overlay a *fictional* story, perhaps about the future. This can be done in the same way as with the historical story, and the comparisons are the same as well.

How you will know it's working

This exercise is all about flow. Things should keep moving. There should be action in the room. When people are placing stories, you should see people walking back and forth with sticky notes in their hands. You should see spaces filling up, even if they fill up unevenly. When people are finding features, you should see people talking, gesturing, drawing, proposing, writing, sticking notes here and there. If you don't see movement, find out why.

What can go wrong

People categorize

Even though this exercise depends on the continuity of gradients, sometimes people can't help drawing lines in the space *before* they have placed their stories (see Figure 12.23 on the next page). When you see people doing this, drop in and quietly ask them to refrain from drawing any lines until *after* they have placed *all* of their stories. Don't tell people they can't draw lines *ever*, because obviously they want to. Just ask them to *wait until the right time* to draw their lines. Then, when they do get to the point where it is reasonable to draw lines on the space (when they are annotating features), the lines will aid in the sensemaking, not limit it.

Figure 12.23. If people draw lines to divide up the space *before* they place their stories, they won't be able to find very many patterns in the placements.

People pay too much attention to precise placement

When you see people coming up with "metrics" and "plans" and "yardsticks" and "protocols" for placement of stories, or when you see people talking about "evidence" and "rankings" and "levels," it is best to step in and help them understand the exercise better. Building a landscape with stories is not a compilation of scientific measurements. It is a process of discovery, yes, but discovery of *meaning,* not of facts.

Let's say, for example, that you are helping a group of people build a landscape with stories about religious tolerance in your community. Through this process these people are not likely to find out precisely how many visitors to church, temple, or mosque live in the community. Nor will they find out how likely a person is to live next to a person of a different religion. Those are things people find out in *quantitative* research, where people build representations that are compilations of measurements. In sensemaking, people are more likely to find out things you can't measure. For example, they might find out about some unexpected benefits and detriments of living in neighborhoods with intermixed versus separated religious groups. Or they might find out some reasons people visit or avoid houses of worship of other faiths. These discoveries cannot be precisely measured, but they can be explored and made meaningful.

It is your job to help people understand that the point of building a landscape together is not to "pin down" stories to precise locations but to *weave together threads* that will build a tapestry of understanding. Watch people to make sure they are placing stories based on what they mean in context, not based on how much of this or that quantity can be found in them. If someone says, "We placed this story here because it shows strong evidence of tolerance," or, "We placed this story here because its level of tolerance is low," that's measurement. If they say, "We placed this story here because it says a lot to us about what happens when religious tolerance is lacking," or, "We placed this story here because we think our community could benefit from this sort of tolerance," that's meaning in context.

People pay too little attention to precise placement

This situation is the opposite of the one before it. Sometimes people aren't too *careful* in placing stories; they're too *casual.* This sometimes happens when people don't want to think about elements of stories that are unpleasant or taboo, or when they got dragged into the session and don't want to be there, or when they're being paid to be at the session and are trying to do as little as possible to get something for nothing. You might see people placing stories based on relatively trivial things, even though you purposefully gave them dimensions that have the potential to dig deep into meaning.

An example might be that you asked people to consider how much trust is apparent in stories, but instead of actually *thinking* about whether the people in the stories trust each other, they simply place the stories based on what sort of trust might be expected given the relationships of the people in the stories. So a story about a parent and child might be placed higher on the trust axis than one about co-workers, but without actually considering the content of the story itself.

When this sort of holding back happens, you can't always fix it. You can't remove emotional blocks for your participants, and you can't make people care when they don't. But you can notice the problem and drop a few quiet hints as people are working. It wouldn't work to mention the issue in a blaming way ("You didn't really consider trust when you placed these, did you?"). Instead, call attention to contrasting stories. You can ask faux-naive questions, like "I'm curious about why you saw more trust in this story than this other one. Can you explain this to me?" Doing this will cause people to reexamine how they are placing items, but it won't cause them to defend their methods.

Another method (suggested by a reader) is to ask people who seem disconnected from the placement of stories to place a few of their *own* stories in the space. This might increase the participants' connection to what they are building and their motivation to finish it.

People are hesitant to place stories on the empty space

This situation is like writer's block. People don't want to place wrongly, so they hold back and invent excuses for leaving the space blank. We don't have enough markers. The coffee pot is empty. Our table leg is broken.

There are a few ways to help people push past an empty landscape. One method is to give people time pressure by repeatedly mentioning how much time is left in the segment allocated to placement. Another method is to break up the placement period into two time periods. In the first time period (say five or ten minutes out of forty), ask people to place only the first five or ten items. Because they have lots of time to place each item, so they can approach the task cautiously. Then in the second time period (the rest of the forty minutes), pick up the pace and ask people to place all the other items. This slow-then-fast method helps people warm up to the task, then gets them moving so they can get some real work done.

People think you are asking them to be rocket scientists

When you define dimensions in a space using labeled axes, some people respond with a wide-eyed stare of panic. To some people, anything that hints of scientific procedure is frightening.

If this situation is happening, you might hear people making comments like these:

- These are supposed to be *dimensions?* And those are *what* again?
- How are we supposed to *figure out* where these things should go?
- Have I got this in the *right* place? I'm not sure this is where it is *supposed* to be.
- I haven't made a graph since I was twelve. How are we supposed to *measure* a story?
- This is all over my head. Are you following this? It's too *complicated*.

This is mostly an identity issue related to what people think people like themselves do. People who think of themselves and their lives as far removed from mathematics, science, and measurement think they are not *qualified* to do what you ask. Of those people, some feel unqualified but still *try* to do the exercise. The people who try usually find out that the process is not scientific at all. Other people feel unqualified and refuse to try, though they might *pretend* to try for a while and hope nobody notices.

You can help the science-phobic by explaining that the space is not a space of measurement but of composition, like a box full of blocks ready to be stacked into interesting patterns. This is *play*, not science.

People think you are asking them to be creative artists

In contrast to the previous issue, some people feel unqualified to perform the task in another way: they don't think they are *creative* enough to carry out such a loosely defined activity.

If this situation is happening, you might hear people making comments like these:

- You said we are supposed to "place" these stories in this space, but you didn't say *how*. We need a *method* here.
- What are the *units* on this dimension? Why didn't you tell us that?
- So what are we doing? Making some sort of *picture?* Of what?
- We just put these somewhere based on … what? The way we *feel* about them?
- I'm not very good at this sort of *psychobabble*.

People whose identities are involved with science, the law, medicine, and other professions of careful, meticulous expertise sometimes react in this way. They think you want them to take up paint and brushes and produce a masterpiece, and they see themselves as "only" scientists. They like to work from logical, precise instructions, and they aren't getting any. To them, your saying "place the stories where they seem to fit" sounds pretty much like "align the story with your third chakra crystal." The whole thing seems too dangerously free of structure to be approached.

You can help the creativity-phobic by explaining that while the process is one of creation, it's the sort of creation that emerges from the coming together of many small placements. In other words, you aren't asking people to build a house from a blueprint; you're just asking them to put boards here and there, and all by itself, something will emerge from the activity. It might be a house, but it might just as well be a boat or a fence or a sculpture of a sleeping cat. People don't need to fret about whether they are *capable* of building anything worth looking at, because the thing will be build itself, if they follow the directions they've been given.

Of course, scientific types are the worst possible audience for this sort of "it will build itself" statement, since they are likely to be skeptical of any such claims. If you get a negative response to a claim of emergence, you can simply admit, in truth, that working with stories is a leap of faith into the unknown. To scientists, paradoxically, your willingness to note their concerns and *admit* that the process is unscientific will help them take the leap of faith

with you. You *can't* offer certainty, but you can speak from experience. If you don't have experience, you can speak from the experiences of others. Speak from my experience if you like, I don't mind. You can truthfully say something like, "We can't know *exactly* what will happen today, but I'm confident that *something* interesting is going to happen as we do this work together. Let's give it a try and see." Presenting the exercise as an *experiment* rather than as a measurement can help lovers of structure come around.

People argue about where to put things

Arguing is not actually a problem. The problem comes in when people don't have any way to *resolve* arguments. You should explain that if there is disagreement over where an item should go, people can simply put it into multiple places. They should add some extra text that captures the reason the item was split up. These will come out in pairs or trios or quartets, such as "if you think of it as fact" versus "if you think of it as emotion," or "from the teacher's perspective" versus "from the student's perspective" versus "from the parents' perspective."

If you expect the people you have invited to your session to be especially argumentative, plan for smaller groups. That way you will get a wider variety of perspectives *across* landscapes and less contention *within* them.

The dimensions don't fit the stories

This can happen if you or the participants chose dimensions based on goals or first principles without paying enough attention to the stories. If a group tries and tries, and still can't place very many stories, it is not unreasonable to restart the exercise with new dimensions. Doing this won't eat up as much time as you might think, because the stories are still the same, and considering them a second time will not take as long as it did the first time. My advice is that if you need to reboot your landscape, fall back to simpler axes than you used the first time. Having a few very simple sets on hand as you start the session (like strength versus friendliness or responsibility versus outcome) will help struggling groups find an easier path.

Some stories fit the dimensions and some don't

This can happen when the stories collected are very diverse, such as when they cover multiple topics or were collected from very different groups. I can think of two ways to deal with partially fitting dimensions. The first is, as above, to jettison the dimensions and start over. The second is to ask people to put stories that don't fit the space into a special *unplaceables* pile. After all the stories that can be placed have been placed, people can come back to the unplaceables and see if they fit into the populated landscape. If a lot of stories are still unplaceable, people can either put them aside, talk about what unifies them, or come up with two *new* dimensions that *would* work for the unplaceables. Ending up with two landscapes instead of one can be a reasonable and useful outcome to the exercise.

People don't like the dimensions you have given them

Here's a what-if situation to consider. You have worked long and hard over your preparations for the sensemaking session you intend to facilitate. You have read every story; you have deeply understood the goals of your project; you've read everything you could find on how to facilitate participatory sessions. For the landscape exercise, you have carefully chosen the one perfect set of dimensions that will best suit the stories and the project. Now you are in a room with your participants. You start the exercise. You give your carefully prepared instructions. You present your carefully chosen dimensions. *They fall flat.* The people don't like them. They don't understand them, are irritated by them, find them meaningless, demand a change. What should you do?

Give in. Give up. Ask your participants to *help you choose something better*. However, do not give in without any conditions! If the participants in your session have not yet had significant contact with the stories, tell them that they *can* choose different dimensions *if* they first spend some time gaining more exposure to the stories. Fifteen minutes of concentrated work should be enough. Explain that the stories and the dimensions *must* match for the exercise to work. Once they are familiar with the

stories, then go ahead and let them come up with their own dimensions.

It is better in sensemaking for people to do something you hadn't planned than it is for people to do nothing at all, which is likely if you force your own best ideas onto them. This is true even when your ideas are *better* than theirs. Participation matters more than perfection. Don't let people use nonsensical dimensions, but work with them to find something they can use.

People place items too slowly or too quickly

I list these together here because I already considered analogous situations for the timeline exercise (go back several pages and look for "People throw stories onto their timelines without paying attention to them" and "People are talking, but they don't seem to be doing anything"). The dynamics are the same here, so rather than write the same thing over again I'll refer you back to that part.

Only some people place items

I've seen this situation happen a lot in this exercise. Building a landscape, or building anything on a large space, requires people to shuttle back and forth between some sort of central repository where the items are piled up and a surface on which they are being placed. As people do this shuttling back and forth, what typically happens is that some people shuttle and some don't. Some of the non-shuttlers are just pondering. But some reluctant people usually seize upon this opportunity to say "I can't, because *they* are." That's why wallflowers grow on walls; it's away from where the action is.

But here's the problem. For sensemaking to work you need the full *diversity of thought* within the group to come into play. If only the most active people in the group build the landscape, it will be less meaningful and less useful than one built by everyone in the group (see Figure 12.24 on the facing page).

The best way to deal with this type of holding back is to head it off with a rule or instruction given at the start. Say something like this:

> We want this process to result in new discoveries and new ideas. To make that happen, your landscape must represent

 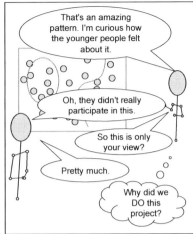

Figure 12.24. Watch out for partial participation in this and other exercises. You and your participants share a responsibility to make sure the full diversity of thought is represented by what is created during your sensemaking session.

all of the perspectives present in your group. That means that everyone in the group must agree about the placement of each item. If everyone *doesn't* agree, you must *split up* the item to represent the different views present. *Don't leave anyone out* of what you make.

In other words, set things up so that success in the exercise is *impossible* without the inclusion of every view. This will enlist the active people in drawing out the passive people, because you've shown the active people that they can't succeed alone.

If you expect partial participation, make your group sizes smaller, say of four or fewer people. The fewer people in each group, the greater the impact non-participation will have on group success, and the better the inclusion rule will work.

People write too small

I've mentioned this issue in other places, but I'll repeat it here because it is especially important for the use of landscapes in sensemaking. When people are writing things on sticky notes to build the landscape, *make sure* they understand that they must write them large. If they don't write things large, no features will stand out when they step back to consider the whole landscape. The usual advice for this is to give people large markers. But watch out. Sometimes people switch to using their own

pens to get more onto each sticky note. Some people can be hopelessly pedantic about their great need to write a paragraph of explanation on each note. Here's how to fix that problem. Let them write small—but ask them to confine their treatises to the backs or bottoms of the sticky notes. Set up a rule that at least two-thirds of each sticky note *must* be written in large print. That'll work.

People guard their work

Sometimes you will come across a group whose solidarity is very high. Such high-solidarity groups work together intensely, and what they have produced has strong and deep emotional meaning to them. That's great. But when you get to the point of the session where people are supposed to *share* their work, these groups hold back. They barely participate in mutual reviews; they don't do much cleanup; their summary is superficial. They don't really *want* everyone else to know what it is they have found out. "What happens in the group stays in the group" is their motto. This is a problem, because the point of sensemaking is for everyone in the room, and everyone *not* in the room, to gain benefits from what has been discovered there.

How can you as the facilitator deal with guarding? This is a tricky one, because people guard only when strong emotions are involved. You can't barge in and police transparency. But you can remind people of their responsibilities as participants in the project. Everyone in your session should have some kind of *hope* that the project will create positive change for the *whole* community or organization. Call on that hope now. Ask the people in guarding groups to share *as much as they can* with the goal of making their hopes for the project come to reality.

If you know before you start your session that your participants are likely to have guarding tendencies, you can plan a defense against guarding into your review (visiting) period. For example, you might ask each group to collaboratively answer three questions about the other groups' landscapes. One of these questions can be about how well each landscape, as it is presented, seems open to understanding by people outside the room. This will give groups the feedback they need to correct their own guarding, but indirectly.

People pay too much attention to sharing

This is the opposite of the guarding situation. Sometimes you will come across a group for whom the fact that their landscape will be shared with others, inside and outside the session, is the only fact worth considering. They see themselves more as a group of travel journalists preparing a television series than as a group of explorers traveling together. To these groups, the map matters more than the territory. Landscapes created by journalistic groups are *sensational*. They surprise! They amaze! They shock! But they don't *mean* all that much.

How to deal with journalism? Keep bringing the attention of these groups back to *utility*. Pop over to their table and quietly say something like:

> So, based on all the work you've done here, which I can see is huge, what strikes you as being the one thing most likely to *create lasting change* in the organization? I'm just curious what you think. Ooops! I have to [go do some made-up thing] but I'll come back in a few minutes.

Then walk away and let them chew on that. If they don't *have* anything in their landscape with the power to create lasting change—which they won't, if it's superficially sensational—a little nudge like that might help them look at

what they have built in a new way. And as I said for the guarding issue, you can insert a utility question into your review process if you think journalism will be an issue for your participants (for example, if they happen to *be* journalists).

To finish this "what can go wrong" section, I suggest you go back and review all the things I said could go wrong when this exercise is used for story collection. With the exception of "People don't fill up the whole space," all of the things that can go wrong there can go wrong here as well. (Don't be discouraged: a lot of things can go *right* as well! You don't my help when things go right, so I haven't listed any of those things. You'll find out about all the good things on your own.)

Try it yourself first

To try this exercise yourself, you need some stories. Find at least thirty or forty stories, then try placing them into a space. Even better, place the same stories into two or three different spaces. Pay attention to your thought processes as you decide where things should go on different dimensions.

Then ask a few people to do the same thing you did by yourself and observe how the process changes. Your observations of how variation in the dimensions and the participants change the process will help you understand some of the variations you will see as you help people build landscapes for themselves.

Your own style

This exercise is one you have to try out in practice to find out how it fits your thinking. It's good to read about the exercise, and it's fun to watch my stick people have their stick-people insights, but until you actually try this exercise in real space and time, you won't know how well it works for you.

So here's an idea. Go through the exercise once or a few times on your own, then read over the "what can go wrong" section above and think about whether you experienced any of those issues. If you did, what does that mean about your own ways of thinking? Where do you need to improve your facilitation skills, or change the exercise, or both, to make the fit between your facilitation and the exercise work better?

Where it came from

I wrote about the origins of mapping ideas in space, and about my own introduction to it, in the corresponding section on this exercise when used for story collection (page 209). Not only is the use of conceptual space thousands of years old, it is in widespread and varied use today.

How to find more on these ideas

I wrote about fields related to mapping ideas in space in the corresponding section on this exercise when used for story collection (page 210). Rather than write more I'll save us both some time by referring you back to that section. The same fields are just as useful to explore (perhaps even more so) when considering the use of this exercise for sensemaking.

Story Elements

In a story elements exercise, people list things they find in stories, then cluster and re-cluster them into families of *elements* that together encompass the combined meaning of the stories, usually in ways that reveal useful discoveries about the topic of concern. People describe and discuss the elements, and they may build stories with them.

When to use it

The story elements exercise works primarily with aspects of story form such as character, plot, and setting. It does therefore require stories that *have* coherent forms. If your story collection misfired in such a way that few of the stories are true stories—that is, they are scenarios or situations or lectures or opinions or facts—this exercise will not work as well as some others will. For this exercise to work, the stories have to be about actual things happening to actual people, about which the actual people actually cared. If that is the case, you will be able to use this exercise to draw meaningful resources from the stories for sensemaking.

The story elements exercise is a good one to use with participants who have less formal education. It is not elaborate or technically complicated. It does not require people to understand narrative form in detail. It does not require people to understand abstract spatial representa-

tions of meaning. It just asks people some questions (such as, "What is going on in this story?"), then asks them to think about which of the answers belong with other answers. On the other hand, because the exercise is so simple, those who are *used* to elaborate technical complications may find it difficult to think as simply as is required. But you can guide people to the right place to make this exercise work.

What it requires

At least three people and up to as many as the room will comfortably hold; at least ninety minutes; large sticky notes of a few different colors; large markers; places to put sticky notes (walls, large tables, clean floor).

How to do it

Step One: Introduce the exercise, form groups, and present a question

Five minutes. Explain the exercise and its purpose. Split people into groups from three to six people each.

Note that the recommended range of group sizes is smaller for this exercise than for timelines or landscapes. When people draw elements such as characters out of stories, they need to consider the *insides* of the stories more intensely than they do while placing stories on a timeline or landscape. This inwardly-focused attention to stories is closer to telling and retelling stories than it is to anything else. Thus group sizes should be similar to those used for telling stories in the first place. Two-person groups will stifle creativity (you'll get shoe examination instead of story examination), and large groups will create partial participation and self-inhibition.

Before you started the exercise, you should have selected a type of element you want people to draw out of their stories, such as characters, situations or values. I'm not going to describe all possible element types in this section, because there are several to choose from. See the "Before you start" section below (page 425) for a full explanation of all the element types you can use. To keep this part brief, let's use an example case of working with *situation* elements. For situations, you will ask people to answer the question, "What is going on in this

Figure 12.25. The story elements exercise starts with answering a simple question, in as many ways as possible, about each story.

story?" Present the question simply and without elaboration. If you can, write it in a place where everyone can see it and refer to it afterward.

Step Two: Gather answers from stories

Twenty minutes. During this part of the exercise, each group should consider each story they have to work with and draw answers to the question from it (see Figure 12.25).

Where should the stories come from? Typically they will be randomly assigned or chosen in a previous task or exercise. How should people consider the stories? They can read texts silently together; they can read texts aloud (having one designated reader or taking turns); they can listen to audio recordings; they can watch video segments.

As each group considers each story, whenever they come across any answers to the question they were given, they should briefly write down the answers on sticky notes. Groups should aim to draw three to five answers from each story. Make sure people understand that the answers should be *brief*. Give them large markers and ask them to write only a few words per note. They have to be able to read all the notes from six feet back.

How should they write the notes? A group can have one designated "scribe" write all their sticky notes while others call out answers; or they can have everyone but the story reader

write down answers as they occur to them. It doesn't matter how each group carries out the task, as long as the people in the group do it together.

How many stories do people need to make this exercise work? Each group should end up with five to seven groups of answers with seven or eight answers in each. That means they will need anywhere from 5x7=35 to 7x8=56 items to cluster. If we make a conservative estimate that people will be able to draw out two answers per story, on average (it's always best to plan for lack of enthusiasm), that means each group will need at least twenty stories in order to create a well-populated field of answers for clustering. If groups can start with thirty stories, that's even better.

Does thirty stories seem like too many? Remember that these are not *long* stories; most are only a paragraph or two. Also, in most story collections individual stories vary in how well they support sensemaking. Some stories are profoundly meaningful while some are trivial, and this does not correlate with story length. So to make sure groups have enough meaning to work with, it is best to give them enough stories to make up for any weak spots in the set. It's better to run out of time than it is to run out of stories.

Because this idea of "drawing out" answers is probably not clear to you, I'll give you a made-

Figure 12.26. The starting question can be about situations or characters or a number of other aspects of stories.

up example so you can see how it works. Let's say you and I are in a group of four people, and we are taking turns reading stories out loud. Let's say I am reading this story.

> Why did they install those stupid *speed bumps* in the parking lot? Do they think the adult employees here will run donuts and have drag races in the parking lot? And here's the thing that really gets me: at the same time they expect us to work long hours and do competent adult things. These contradictory messages are insulting and demoralizing. I put in an anonymous comment about that. As if *they* care.

While I'm reading the story, you are looking for answers to the question, "What is going on in this story?"

You write:

- Double bind
- Contradictory messages
- Lack of respect
- Nobody cares what I think

All of these things are legitimate, if opinionated, answers to the question, "What is going on in this story?"

Now let's enter into a parallel universe in which everything is the same as in this one, except that now our group is listing *characters* instead of situations (for the same story, on the same

day, with the same coffee and everything). The question this time is, "Who is doing things in this story?" (See Figure 12.26.)

This time you write:

- Irresponsible teenagers
- Competent adults
- People who put other people in double-binds (special place in hell)
- Clueless contradictory message senders
- Out-of-touch managers

These are all legitimate, if opinionated, answers to the question, "Who is doing things in this story?"

You might argue that the statement "irresponsible teenagers are in this story" is incorrect. You might say the story involves no teenagers at all. But I tell you, the teenagers are in there. They are in the storyteller's perception of the managers' perceptions. The storyteller thinks the managers think he is nothing but an irresponsible teenager, so the "irresponsible teenager" character is in the story, and it is important to the story. This exercise has nothing to do with facts and everything to do with perceptions.

Notice something else about all of these answers you are writing down. They are emotional. They are reactive. They are far from objective. They are even sometimes funny. They represent a *perspective*, maybe a blinkered or wrong one, but a real one. *This is all good.* When

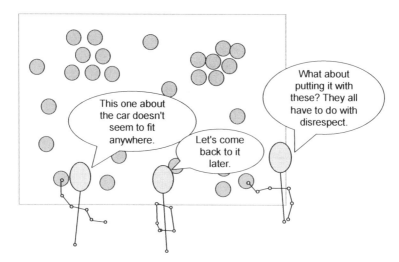

Figure 12.27. Groups should place their answers on a wall and start moving them so like goes with like.

you facilitate this exercise, you are not asking people to catalogue or dissect stories. You are asking them to *react* to stories. Answering questions about stories is a great way to make sense together of what matters in the stories *to the participants,* not to some disembodied general audience. So don't worry if people are putting their emotions into the exercise. It only works if they do.

The first few stories each group considers will take a long time. Let them take their time and work their way up to a more efficient process. After a while they will be speeding through stories.

Step Three: Cluster the answers

Fifteen minutes. At this point people should have anywhere from thirty to a hundred or more sticky notes with answers on them. Now ask each group to put away the stories and consider *only* the answers, all mixed together regardless of what story they came from. (Why mixed together? To move beyond individual stories into the meaning represented by all of the stories together.)

Each group should bring all of their sticky-note answers to a large blank space and begin sticking them on it. (Each group should have its own space in which to work.) Here's the simple rule for clustering: When two answers seem similar to each other, people should place them close together. When two answers seem dissim-

ilar, people should place them far apart. Another way to say it is: *put like with like.* (See Figure 12.27.) As more and more answers are placed, *clusters* of answers will begin to appear. Eventually each group should aim to arrive at five to eight coherent clusters, with no "orphan" answers between them.

After all the answers have been clustered, ask the groups to give each of their clusters a brief name (see Figure 12.28 on the facing page). They should write the cluster name on a differently-colored sticky note and place it in the center of the cluster. These names need not be things of beauty; they are only meant to help people remember what the cluster was about and have a quick reference to it so they can talk about it.

Finally, ask people to clear a little "halo" of space around each cluster name, because they are going to be putting something there in a minute (see Figure 12.29 on page 424).

Step Four: Describe the clusters

Ten minutes. Now each group should look at each cluster and ask themselves the question, "What is good and bad about this cluster of things?" Groups should try to come up with two to four good answers and two to four bad answers to this question (see Figure 12.30 on page 425).

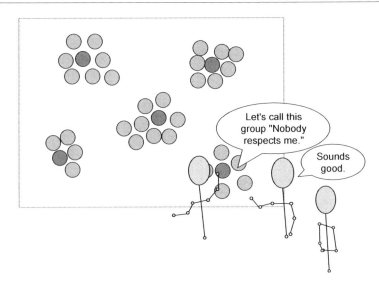

Figure 12.28. After all of the answers have been clustered, groups should come up with reference names for each cluster.

For example, if a cluster is named "Double bind," a group might come up with these "good things" about it:

- Sharpens the mind
- Weeds out the easily frustrated
- Makes for good jokes

And these "bad things" about the cluster:

- Creates tension
- Wastes time and energy
- Breeds mistrust

Each good or bad attribute should be written on a sticky note of a third color and placed inside the little halo of space around the cluster name. The whole cluster should end up looking like a flower, with a name center point, a circular ring of attributes, and the original answers on the ragged outside.

Step Five: Cluster the descriptions

Ten minutes. Now ask each group to either *remove or copy* the good and bad attributes from the little halo around each cluster's name. Ask them to carry those attributes over to a *new* space and start sticking them to it. Now they are going to cluster the attributes in exactly the same way in which they clustered the original answers. Ask them to *ignore the original memberships* of the attributes (remember, they should *not* take the cluster names with them

to the new space) and cluster the attributes by similarity.

When the attributes have been clustered into five to eight groups, and there are no stragglers left over, groups should name the new clusters of attributes. These names are the final story elements (see Figure 12.31 on page 426). Ask groups to come up with names that *anyone* in the community or organization would be likely to understand. The names can be unique to the community or organization, but they should not be cryptic outside the sensemaking session.

Step Six: Review story elements within groups

Ten minutes. Now ask each group to talk together about what they have discovered. Are the story elements they found the ones they thought they would find? If they compare their story elements with the names of the original clusters, what is different? How did things change when they moved up to a second level of abstraction by clustering their attributes? What have they learned about the stories, and about the topic, by doing this? If you have more than one group, explain that in the next time period people from the other groups will be visiting their story elements. What would each group like to do to prepare the elements for review by other people in the room?

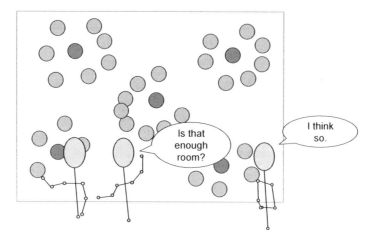

Figure 12.29. Groups should clear a little "halo" of space around each cluster name.

Step Seven: Visit story elements

Five minutes. Ask everyone to walk around the room looking over all of the story elements that have been created. Have one person from each group stay in their own space to answer questions. (If you only have one group, leave this step out.)

Step Eight: Finish the story elements

Five minutes. This is the time in which groups should prepare their story elements for viewing by people outside the session. Groups should make sure that the understandings they have developed in the exercise are available to those who did not participate in the exercise. They should create a *summary* that describes, in their own words, what each story element means to them and what they have learned from it. Summaries can be written or recorded in audio, photographs, or video. Feedback from visits by other groups can also be incorporated in this step.

Step Nine: Discuss with the whole room

Ten minutes. Bring everyone together into a discussion of all the story elements. Talk about what patterns appear across different groupings, where there are differences of perspective, and what discoveries can be gained from all of the elements taken together. (If you only have one group, use this time for general discussion of the whole exercise and what came of it.)

If you have less time

You can trim this exercise from ninety minutes to one hour by doing these steps only:

1. Introduce the exercise, form groups, and present a question. Five minutes.
2. Gather answers from stories. Twenty minutes. (Don't skimp on this part.)
3. Cluster answers. Fifteen minutes.
4. Describe clusters. Ten minutes.
5. Cluster attributes. Five minutes. (Clustering takes less time the second time around.)
6. Discussion. Five minutes. (No visits, no cleanup.)

To convert this exercise into a simple task that takes up fifteen to twenty minutes, give people only a small number of stories—say ten—and ask them to simply *talk about* some of the answers that come up when they consider a question like, "Who is doing things in this story?" Don't ask them to cluster anything; just ask them to think together about the question in relation to the stories they are considering. Doing so will give people a peek inside the stories, and this will help them do more with the stories later in the session when you ask them to delve deeper into detail.

If you have more time

To add more time to this exercise, include one or more elaborations, or add time to the steps in this order:

Figure 12.30. After the clusters have been named, groups should come up with two to four good and bad attributes of each cluster.

1. Gather answers from stories
2. Describe the clusters
3. Cluster the answers
4. Cluster the descriptions
5. Review story elements within groups
6. Visit story elements
7. Discuss with the whole room
8. Finish the story elements
9. Introduce the exercise, form groups, and present a question

The maximum time I would suggest for this exercise would be about three hours.

Before you start

Before you consider using this exercise in a sensemaking session, take a good look at the stories you have collected. If your story collection didn't go all that well, you might have few actual stories (recountings of events) and many half-stories (scenarios, situations, states of affairs) and non-stories (opinions, lectures, facts). You can't draw story elements out of things that are not stories, and drawing them out of half-stories is difficult, especially for people who are not used to the idea. If you know as you plan your sensemaking session that your story collection is weak, you can still use this exercise, but you need to do some extra preparation.

To prepare a weak story collection for use in a story elements exercise, annotate your collected stories with a tag that marks them as actual stories (something happened), half-stories (a situation was described but nothing happened), or non-stories (only opinions or facts were stated). If you have relatively few collected stories, say two hundred or less, mark every story. (It doesn't take that long.) If you have more than 200 stories, you can extract a random subset of 200 and mark only those. After your marking is done, select only the actual stories for use in this exercise. You can do this by preparing a special set of story cards which are duplicates of the cards participants are given in other parts of the session, or you can simply mark in an obvious way which are the actual stories, then ask participants to use only those stories for the exercise.

You need at least twenty or thirty stories for this exercise to work. So if you marked your stories as actual stories, half-stories, or non-stories, and you only end up with ten actual stories, you can either use the half-stories as well—knowing the exercise will not be as well supported—or you can drop this exercise from the session and wait to use it until you have a better story set to work with.

Questions to ask

I said in the "How to do it" section above that there are different questions you can ask for

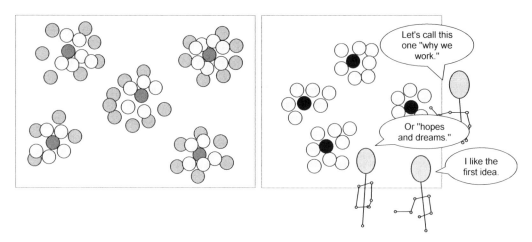

Figure 12.31. The final clusterings of attributes should be named; these names are story elements.

each type of story element. Now let's look at those questions. As you might expect, questions that draw out story elements depend on ancient and universal concepts of story form. Every story has a setting; every story has characters; every story has an ending. It is these universal properties of stories we can rely on as we draw story elements from stories.

The element types I have used in this exercise are as follows.

Situations. Story situations describe what is going on in a story (see Figure 12.32 on page 428). They are like scene summaries in descriptions of movies or plays; for example, "In this scene, the two brothers work out their anger over a game of basketball."

To create situation story elements, start by asking: What is *going on* in this story? What is happening?

Some situations I've seen derived from stories in this exercise have been *on the ropes, wartime footing, safe haven, sucking the life out of us, where do we go from here, between a rock and a hard place, when it rains it pours,* and *constant concern.*

Themes. Story themes are not about what is happening but what it *means* (see Figure 12.33 on page 428). Themes are like headlines or advertisements for movies or books; for example, "In a world where there is no order, one man brings peace."

To create theme story elements, start by asking: What is this story *about?* How would you describe its subject matter?

Some themes I've seen derived from stories in this exercise have been *can't get no respect, violation of norms, excuses,* and *power grabs.*

Characters. Story characters are about who is doing things in the story (see Figure 12.34 on page 428). You can think of characters as like lists of actors in movies—only they should be actors nobody has heard of, so the qualities of the character come out; for example, "Starring an unknown prodigy from the slums of Rio."

To create character story elements, start by asking: *Who* is doing things in this story? Who is taking action?

Some characters I've seen derived from stories in this exercise have been *unscrupulous opportunist, worker bee, winner, devil, double dealer, showboat, Mother Teresa, justice league,* and *figurehead.*

Values. Story values are about what in the story matters to the people inside and outside it (see Figure 12.35 on page 428). Values are like marketing slogans that try to attract people to movies based on perceived similarities; for example, "If you've ever wished you had lived a different life, you need to see this movie." Values are things people want or don't want, value or don't value.

To create value story elements, start by asking: What *matters* to the characters in this story? What do they like and dislike?

Some values I've seen derived from stories in this exercise have been *we're all in the same boat, innovation is king, bluebird of happiness, freedom, perseverance, time is money,* and *get it done.*

Note that I list *two* questions for each element type. I suggest giving people the first question only and keeping the second question unspoken but ready to give to those who want (or seem to need) clarification. For some people an additional question is a hindrance, and for some it's a help.

More questions to ask

While thinking about this exercise, I have thought of more element types that *should* be present in stories and that *should* be useful in this exercise. But I can't tell you how to use them with confidence, because I've never actually used them. I would *like* to use them, but the opportunity has not yet come up to try.

The potential elements I have in mind are as follows.

Relationships. Story relationships are about connections between characters in the story. Some stories are defined not by what happens in them or who acts in them but by how a relationship between characters plays out through the story. I can imagine using story relationships in this exercise for a session on business partnerships or neighborhood conflicts.

To create relationship story elements, start by asking: How are characters *related* in this story? What dynamics do you see going on between characters?

Some relationship elements might be *cat and mouse, servant and master, innocent and confidence man, opposites attract,* and *planet and moon.*

Motivations. Story motivations are about *why* people do what they do in stories. You could imagine a movie advertisement highlighting a motivation like this, "He was a man driven to succeed, whatever the cost to those around him." Or, "She knew she was breaking all the rules, but breaking the rules was the only rule she knew." Asking people to list motivations in stories, disregarding the characteristics of those who displayed them and concentrating only on the motivating forces, might be useful in projects about understanding why people act the way they do. I'm thinking of projects about things like crime, deception, cooking the books, or the reverse: volunteerism, life-saving.

To create motivation story elements, start by asking: *Why* do people do what they do in this story? What moves them?

Some resulting motivation elements might be *stairway to heaven, fame at all costs, fear breeds anger, if I don't look it will go away,* and *nobody can say I didn't do what was asked of me.*

Beliefs. Story beliefs are about the assumptions people build about the world around them. Beliefs are connected to motivations, but they dig deeper into more essential explanations of actions. A movie line for beliefs might be, "To Genevieve, a man was nothing more than a bank vault. And she had a skeleton key." I can imagine this type of story element being useful when you want to enter into the worldview of people unlike yourself through their stories. Say your group wants to support former child soldiers in their reentry to society, and you can't wrap your heads around their experiences. If you hold a sensemaking session with this exercise in it, and you draw elements of belief from stories told by the child soldiers, you may get some way towards understanding what sorts of assumptions you need to deal with.

To create belief story elements, start by asking: What do people *believe* in this story? What assumptions do they make about the world?

Resulting belief elements might be things like *nothing we do will make any difference, only the strong survive, compassion is peril, keep your eyes open,* and *never say no.*

Conflicts. Story conflicts are about tensions that appear in stories. These are similar to situational elements, but with a sharper focus on contradiction. The standard story-form view of conflict is that it can be of three types: *internal* conflict (between "warring" drives or motivations within the story's main character), *external* conflict (between the main character

Figure 12.32. Situational story elements describe what goes on in stories.

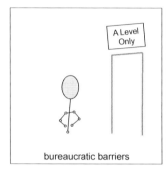

Figure 12.33. Theme story elements describe what stories are about.

Figure 12.34. Character story elements describe how people behave in stories.

Figure 12.35. Value story elements describe the values people hold (positive or negative) in stories.

and some larger force such as nature or death), or *interpersonal* conflict (usually between two characters, but possibly between cultures and worldviews). These are all useful types of conflict to consider in this exercise, either separately or intermingled. Projects for which conflict elements might be worth creating might examine divisions within the community or organization or difficult decisions made by organization members.

To create conflict story elements, start by asking: Who or what stands in *opposition* in this story? Where do you see tensions?

Some conflict elements might be *arms race, scorched-earth policy, cold war, simmering discontent, war of words, damned with faint praise, one-upmanship, chest-beating, emotional blackmail, confidence men,* and *rat race.*

You might also consider conflicts between *options* or possibilities if you want to think about how people make decisions or why they choose the paths they choose. Conflict elements of the option type might be things like *Catch-22, chicken-and-egg problem, vicious circle, muddle, no-win situation, opening a can of worms, the lesser of two evils, between a rock and a hard place,* and *endless loop.*

Transitions. Some stories are not defined by setting or character or relationship or motivation but by change. Coming-of-age stories are like this, as are stories of decline and decay. I can imagine this type of story element being useful in projects whose goals include making sense of change, say for example in a community adapting to new technologies or new memberships or new conflicts. Using this exercise you can work through the characteristics of changes in stories to understand better what has happened in the community.

To create transition story elements, start by asking: What *changes* take place in this story? What is different from beginning to end, or from one part to another?

Resulting transition elements might be things like *the busy streets are so quiet, where are all the hard-working people, neighbors were once friends, sixteen miles was far then, do you remember quilting,* and *no more hunger winters.*

So, as you plan your story elements exercise, decide which of the four established or four experimental element types best suit your stories, participants, and project. Then memorize the question you need to ask.

Optional elaborations

Use more than one element type

If you have more time and think your participants will be willing to explore more fully, you can ask them to work with two or even three types of story element at the same time. As people consider stories together, ask them to fill out notes in answer to two or three questions instead of just one. Use different-colored sticky notes for the different element types. One way to do this is to ask groups to assign one person to each type of element: one does characters, one does situations, for example. Or you can give groups the requirement that they must generate at least two answers to each question per story, and leave it to them to figure out how they will do that.

When all the stories have been considered, give each group one space for each element type they will be creating, and ask them to go through the whole process in series, choosing one element type then another. When they are finished, they should be able to see the two or three spaces next to each other and compare them. Within-group reviews, visits, and overall discussions should then take the multiple element types into consideration.

Have different groups do different element types

This is a similar elaboration to the one above, in that you will end up with two or three element types. But in this case each type of element is derived by a different group. This elaboration is useful when you want to explore your stories from as many angles as possible. However, don't use it when there are strong differences of opinion among people in your session. People won't be able to make useful juxtapositions with the story elements created if any "us-them" component will be present in their interpretation.

Carrying out this elaboration is simple: just present the questions you have chosen beforehand, and either allocate them to groups yourself or ask groups to choose which they would like to address. You can do this by printing the questions on cards, then either handing them out to groups or asking groups to grab them from your hand (in the "take a card, any card" manner you would with playing cards). Then after the story elements have been created, allocate some extra time to the visiting period and to whole-room discussion, because each group will only experience the other types of elements after their own work is complete.

Have different groups cluster together

In the basic instructions I said that each small group should have its own space in which to work. Optionally, you can ask people in small groups to *merge* their answers and create combined sets of story elements. You could have pairs of groups work together, or you could ask people to create only one set of story elements for the whole room.

Whether this elaboration is useful to you depends on your topic and the energy in your session. When groups work alone, things are more intimate, intense, and quiet; this is better for sensitive topics or when you think people won't be willing to put forth much energy or take chances. When groups merge their work, you can get more creative results, but there will be more pockets of stillness for reluctant participants to hide in. Also, merged group activities might be chaotic enough to frighten off nervous people who would be more willing to participate in a quieter interaction. And of course, don't ever ask groups to work together if they are very different from each other in their identities or power expectations (managers with workers, teachers with students, doctors with patients).

To carry out this elaboration, start in the same way as usual, but when people have generated their answers to the original questions, ask multiple groups to come together and cluster *all* of their answers together into one space. When the time comes to describe clusters with attributes, you could have people break up into their original groups again and come up with another set of things to cluster, or you could have the merged group work together. If the larger group does split up for attribute creation,

have the groups merge again for the final clustering and story element naming.

Give different groups the same stories

Normally you will start this exercise by having groups consider stories that have been randomly assigned or used in a previous exercise or warm-up task. Groups might overlap a bit in which stories they are using, but will for the most part have varying selections of stories from the same overall collection. You can, however, set up the exercise so that all the groups start with *exactly* the same twenty or thirty stories.

Why start groups with the same stories? To see what will happen. It is by no means sure that different groups considering the same stories will come up with the same story elements. Nor is it certain that different groups considering different stories will come up with different elements. The exercise is more complex than that. I've seen amazingly similar sets of story elements created by people working with different stories in different organizations in different countries and different years. I've also seen two groups from the same organization working in the same room at the same time start with the same stories and end up with element sets so different that you'd never guess the groups had *anything* in common.

Why all the uncertainty? Because this exercise has more to do with *people* than it has to do with *stories*. The process of drawing out answers to questions crystallizes each group's perceptions and experiences of the stories they consider into pure streams of concentrated meaning. Those streams of meaning are unique to the people in each group; but at the same time, different groups can discover surprising points of agreement.

So when should you use this elaboration? When you think it will be helpful to people to find out what happens when different groups work with the same stories. To choose, ask yourself this question. After the exercise is finished and people are looking at all the results together, would you rather say, "Look, we all started with the same stories and this is what we created." (Whatever that is.) Or would you rather say, "Look, we all started with different stories and this is what we created." (Whatever that is.) You can't predict what people will do, but you can choose which comparison you would like them to make.

To carry out this elaboration, have everyone start with an identical set of story cards as the exercise begins. Make sure people understand that you want them to use only the stories they have been given, even if they liked other stories they encountered earlier in the session. Tell them they'll find out why you want them to do this later.

Cluster your clusters

This elaboration only makes sense if you have a large session. Let's say you have fifty people in your sensemaking session (rare but possible). Let's say you have them broken up into ten groups of five people each, and you ask each group to create their own set of situational story elements. Usually the exercise ends in the production of five to eight story elements. With ten groups, that works out to between fifty and eighty elements. What can you do with so many elements? Why not cluster them? Copy the names from each group's space, then go to a special space you saved just for this, and ask *everyone* in the room to participate in making one grand clustering of the story elements created. Comparisons of group and overall clusterings should provide some interesting insights into the topic.

Can you do this with fewer groups? Yes, but I wouldn't try to do this unless you had at least twenty-five or thirty story elements (of the same type) to work with throughout the room.

Use other attribute-addition methods than the "halo" method

The way I describe of adding attributes to answer clusters, which I call the "halo" method, is only one of several ways I've seen used for this (admittedly complicated) step in the process. I put forth the halo method because I think it's the most foolproof, but you can try these other methods as well.

Removal. You can ask people to remove all answers after the cluster is named, leaving only the name behind to be described with attributes. This has the benefit of leaving lots of space on the wall, which encourages people

to write lots of attributes. However, it has the detriment of making it hard to remember what the cluster name means. Keeping the answers that make up the cluster in place makes it easier to think of attributes. I rarely use this option, mainly because people tend to get upset and confused when you take away what they have created. I don't blame them! I wouldn't want my workspace erased halfway through an exercise either.

Having said that, the removal option is very useful in one particular situation: when people have come to the session with exceptionally rigid mindsets. When you think your participants will not be able to move past the obvious, for example if their attribute lists will be nothing more than copies of answers in the original clusters, then this stripped-bare option sometimes works to help people wake up and start thinking. For most sensemaking sessions you won't need to jolt people like this, but save the idea in case you ever need it.

Copying. You can ask people to leave their original clustering in place and copy the cluster names to another wall where attributes are added. I like this option because it maintains the original clustering for reference. But it does require more space than other options, and sometimes, physically, that isn't possible. If you do have the space I would suggest using this option. People like it; it works.

Overlay. You can ask people to just lay their attribute sticky notes, in another color, right on top of the answers in each cluster. Orderly people will hate this option, but it does work in less space, and people should be able to see most of the answers. Personally I find this option ugly (I guess I'm orderly), but some might not mind it.

Outside. You can ask people to add attribute sticky notes to the *outside* of the cluster instead of in the middle. This option doesn't erase any work, and it doesn't take up too much space. But to make it work, you have to ask people to keep their clusters well away from each other as they work, to leave room for the attributes. That means more instruction at the start and more poking your nose in while people are working. If your participants are not particularly willing to listen to what you say, you might not want to try this option.

So as you can see, I've thought a lot about where to put everything in this exercise. It is a weak point of the exercise that the sticky notes have to jostle for room; but with practice you can get used to working out solutions. I find the halo option to be the least intrusive and confusing and the most conserving of memory and space. But it doesn't much matter how you work out the issue. You may have better ideas than I have had.

Use different questions for the cluster description part

When you get to describing the clusters of answers, there is another elaboration you can add. Instead of asking the same "good and bad" question about each type of cluster, you can use *targeted* questions that help people zoom in on more detailed consideration.

For the four element types I have used, these questions work.

1. Themes: What would someone who has had good experiences with this say about it? What about someone who has had bad experiences with it?

2. Situations: How would an optimist describe this? How would a pessimist describe it? (Or: What are the opportunities here? What are the dangers?)

3. Characters: What would this character's best friend say about them? What would their worst enemy say?

4. Values: What would someone who loves this say about it? What about someone who hates it?

For the four element types I think *should* work but haven't yet tested, these questions seem like they would work.

1. Relationships: What in this relationship helps and hinders its members?

2. Motivations: What are the benefits and detriments (to all parties) of having this motivation, or of not having it?

3. Beliefs: What about this belief is correct? What is erroneous? (Or: What about this belief is safe for the community, and what is dangerous? Or: What about this belief is helpful to the community, and what is harmful?)

4. Conflicts: What in this conflict brings energy to its participants, and what drains their energy? (Or: What is helpful and harmful to the community?)

5. Transitions: How does this change make things better and worse?

Using this elaboration will deepen the level of sensemaking, but it will also require more careful, precise thought on the part of your participants. Think about their level of education, energy, and patience in deciding whether you should use a more detailed question in the exercise.

Create association trails

I didn't mention this above because it can get complicated, but you can ask groups to annotate their sticky notes in such a way that you can trace back story elements through all the stages of the exercise and back to the original stories (see Figure 12.36 on the facing page). Doing this gives you additional insights into what led to what as the process went on.

I'll give you an example of why this elaboration is useful by telling you a true story about a sensemaking session one of my colleagues held. (I wasn't there; I heard this second-hand.) The session was with police officers, and they were considering stories about crime. Two of their answer clusters were called something like "Lifesaving officer" and "Master criminal." When they clustered their attributes, one of the story elements they created was called "Hero." Because they had noted where each attribute came from, they were able to find out that the Hero story element was defined by as many attributes from the "Master criminal" cluster as it was from the "Lifesaving officer" cluster. This was a great revelation to the police officers, who were forced to consider the fact that criminals could have courage. Coming to that sort of breakthrough insight is exactly what sensemaking is for. Association trails can help people work their way back through their own thinking to discover surprising things.

Here's how to create association trails.

1. When people are writing answer sticky notes while considering stories, ask them to write a brief *identifier* of the story the an-

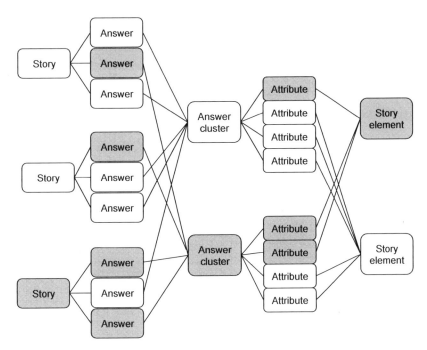

Figure 12.36. In this (impossibly simple) example, the first story element is more represented by the second answer cluster, which is more represented by the third story. Seeing patterns like this can help people observe their own work and learn useful things by it.

swer came from, in small print (using a pen or pencil) somewhere on the sticky note. Make sure your stories have short identifiers, such as numbers, to make it easy for people to do this.

2. When people cluster their answers, have them give each cluster name a letter or number, then write it on each answer next to the story number. Use some convention like 23/B means that an answer to a question about story 23 was placed in cluster B.

3. Do the same with the attributes. Ask groups to write the cluster number or letter described by each attribute somewhere on it. (So B/5 means attribute 5 describes cluster B.)

4. When groups cluster their attributes into story elements, ask them to add a clustered story element identifier to each attribute. Thus each attribute will have two cluster assignments on it: where it came from and where it ended up. (23/B/5/D means that an answer to a question about story 23 was placed in cluster B, whose attribute 5 formed part of story element D.)

5. When you have finished the second clustering, all of your answers and attributes should have annotations. Then you can look at those annotations and count them to find out what led to what.

That all sounds pretty confusing, doesn't it? It will get easier to understand once you've tried it. If you want to use this elaboration, I strongly suggest trying it once or twice on your own before you use it with people.

How can you make this work in a room full of people? Here are three ways.

1. You can add the annotations yourself. Of course, you can only add answer-to-story annotations if you are *in* the group as the notes are being written. So if you have multiple groups, drop the story annotation part and just do the cluster annotations. To do the cluster annotations yourself, plan a five-minute break just after the attributes have been added to the clusters. While the participants get a cup of coffee, rush in and annotate all of their sticky notes before they move on. Then do the same thing again af-

ter the final clusters (the story elements) have been created.

2. If you have a motivated and capable group of participants, they might be able to do the annotations themselves. This option is much simpler for you (no scurrying around with a pen), but it does require you to spend more time up front making sure people understand what annotations they are being asked to write. Some groups can pick up a complicated task like this and run with it; but with some groups, the attempt to add this elaboration will reduce their interest or confidence in the session. Know your people before you ask them to do this.

3. You can have helpers do the annotation. I've been in sessions where we had three or four people running around writing annotations on all the sticky notes. You need one helper per small group (to write the answer-to-story annotations, if you want to do that). For this option you should also plan breaks after attributes are added, but it will be the helpers rushing to write things instead of you (and you can have a break). However, if your topic is very sensitive, don't use helpers to write story annotations. In that case, use the first or second option here, drop the story annotation part of this elaboration, or drop the entire elaboration. You should never appear to be scrutinizing too carefully what people are doing when they are exploring sensitive topics.

Building association trails is complicated and tedious, and it's not always worth the effort. But in some circumstances it can make a sensemaking session come together.

Find exemplar stories

After story elements have been created, during the within-group review period, you can ask groups to go back to the stories they started from and find a few stories they think illustrate the meaning behind each story element. They can either write the story names on sticky notes (of a new color) and stick them near each story element, or they can take whole story cards and stick them up on the wall with tape. If a group can't find at least one story to exemplify a story element, they may want to look at their clustering again and see if they are missing something.

During the visiting and discussion periods, exemplar stories can enter into the discussion about the meaning of the story elements. If one group has created more than one type of story element, they can find stories in which the elements appear separately or together.

This elaboration deepens negotiation around story elements, because each element needs to be "backed up" by stories that illustrate it. It is also useful if you want to use story elements after the session, perhaps in an intervention or return phase of the project. Having some stories the element creators chose to illustrate their creations helps to convey the meanings they found.

Another use of exemplar stories is in the situation where you are helping a group of people prepare to communicate with another group of people outside the group. You might, for example, be helping a group of aid recipients work with their own stories to explain to outside aid agencies where their strongest needs lie. Or you might be helping a group of factory workers explain their safety concerns to management. Or you might be helping a town prepare a proposal of cooperation to another town with which there have been disputes over water rights. In the case of communicating with outsiders, the group may not want to share *every* story outside the room (or even with *you*). Surrounding created story elements with exemplar stories can help people explain what they mean to outsiders without revealing more private details than they feel comfortable with. To use the elaboration for this purpose, ask groups to choose exemplar stories they don't mind being told outside the community, and ask them to tell the stories (that is, write or record them) in such a way that private details are hidden.

Compare story elements to official statements

After story elements have been created, groups can compare them to established statements of the community or organization, such as a mission statement, official history, or set of values. Where do the two sets of statements agree or disagree? Do they cover the same ground? Are they pointed in different directions? How can you explain the differences and similarities you see?

Compare story elements to published models

As with the timeline exercise, it can sometimes be helpful to compare created story elements with elements in a published framework. For this exercise the most useful frameworks are those that set up *categories* to compare. To introduce model categories, after all the groups have finished their story elements and are discussing them, briefly show groups the model or models you chose to use (before the session) and ask them to compare the model(s) to their story elements. As with any other use of models, present them as *perspectives* to be considered, never as *corrections* to be applied or *standards* to be met. In Appendix A (page 589) I describe some examples of the sorts of category-based models you might find useful for story element exercises.

Illustrate story elements

Groups can draw pictures of what they mean by their story elements. Illustrations don't need to be elaborate or artistic. For most story elements, all you need is some kind of depiction of people acting or interacting in some way, like the cartoons of story elements I drew above (see for example Figure 12.32 on page 428). Participants can use stick people or even dots with speech bubbles. The important thing is to capture the essence of what each story element means to the participants.

By the way, some practitioners I know who use this exercise bring in professional cartoonists to help people illustrate story elements. I'm not a big fan of the practice, for a few reasons.

1. It's expensive and hard to set up, so it can't be used on all projects. Learning to rely on something you can't always use makes you less flexible.

2. Having a cartoonist do the drawing makes it seem like the drawing has to be professionally made to be meaningful. That's not true, and in fact, that's usually the opposite of the truth. The least artful drawings sometimes have the deepest meanings.

3. When the issues being explored are sensitive, having to explain story elements to an outsider can make people less willing to explore the issues as deeply.

4. When drawings are shown outside the session, the fact that they were not drawn by the participants gives them less power to communicate. People say, "Sure, but that's just what a *cartoonist* drew. It's not what the *people* thought." It's true that when people do this they have the participants go back and forth with the cartoonist refining the representation. But still, there is a mediating influence, and the cartoonist's goal cannot be the same as the participants' goal.

I don't think there's anything *wrong* with bringing in a cartoonist to help with illustrations, and in some high-ambition, big-budget projects it might be justifiable. But in the majority of sensemaking sessions I don't think it's necessary. I'd rather see homely illustrations created by participants, because they will be full of meaning to those who went through the process.

Perform story elements

This option is similar to illustration, only in this case people play out their story elements in little skits. If you use this option, change the review period so that instead of people milling around the room, all the groups stay in place while each group puts on a presentation illustrating some or all of the story elements they have derived. Even a minute or two is long enough to play out a little skit in speech or pantomime showing the events or behaviors drawn from stories. I probably don't need to tell you that this elaboration is only possible when people are motivated and open to trying socially risky things.

Tell stories with story elements

An optional task you can add, both in the within-group and whole-room discussion periods, is to ask people to *tell stories* using the story elements. The point of this storytelling is not to collect more stories but to enable more complex narrative sensemaking.

There are four ways to do this, ranging from simplest to most complicated, as follows.

One-element storytelling. In this simplest and most open option, groups can use the story elements they have created to spur the telling of stories, either from experience or from their imaginations. The instruction here would be simple: just look at the elements created and see what sorts of stories come to mind. This option is useful if you don't think people will follow complicated directions.

Two-element conversations. Groups can use their story elements to make up situations in which two elements have a conversation, then role play as if they were the elements personified. This doesn't have to depend only on character elements; any of them will work. A group could have a person in a situation element talking to a person with a character element, or a person with a value talking to a person with a belief, or a person in a relationship talking to a person in a situation. This option is useful when the project is about understanding how different forces interact to produce conditions of interest; say, what makes small businesses succeed or fail, or why some community groups hold together and some fall apart.

Historical re-enactments. Groups can compare their story elements with a well-known story of historical importance to the community or organization, like how the organization got started or how the community weathered a storm. The way they should do this is to talk about the real events in the history, and find places where they think their story elements come into play. They can annotate these connections with more sticky notes, or they can even draw out a brief timeline of the historical progression and copy story elements onto sticky notes and place them on it.

Juxtaposition card games. This option only works if groups have created more than one type of element, or if multiple groups with different element types want to work together. In this option, groups should copy the names of story elements (of two or more types, such as characters and situations) onto index cards. Then they should place all the cards into a pile and shuffle it so the order is random. The game is for each team to draw out two or three cards at random and build a story with them. The story can be based on real experiences or it can be imagined. (See Figure 12.37 on the facing page.)

You might come up with more options for adding storytelling to story element creation than I have. The great thing about story ele-

ments is that because they *come* from stories, you can put them back together to make *more* stories, which will deepen your sensemaking.

How you will know it's working

When people are considering stories, it's working if they are writing. If people are not writing, they will not have enough items to cluster. If you see a group looking at stories and talking, and nobody is writing anything, keep an eye on them. If each group doesn't get at least twenty or thirty answer notes to cluster, they won't be able to complete the exercise.

When people are clustering, it's working if they are negotiating. If you see a group mechanically placing notes on a wall, and nobody's ever taking any notes back *off* the wall and placing them somewhere else, they aren't really clustering. Clustering is a trial-and-error process. There should be a lot of false starts, a lot of oh-wait-how-about-this discussions, a lot of how-about-we-try-it-this-way proposals, and a lot of differences of opinion. Watch for negotiation, not just construction.

What can go wrong

People write too few answers to questions about stories

Sometimes it takes a while for people to get started on this exercise. They sit in their groups, and they look at their stories, and they look at each other. Sometimes they get into long discussions about what is and isn't a character or a situation. Sometimes they just give up and talk about the weather. It is your job as the facilitator to ease this transition. How can you do that? Use the power of the self-fulfilling prophecy.

Say something like this.

> As you encounter these stories together, answers to the question written here will occur to you. When they do occur to you, write them down on these sticky notes. Don't worry about whether they are right or wrong. If they occur to you, they are right.

Framing the task as a task of *reception* rather than *creation* takes the pressure off. It also stops people debating what is and isn't a valid answer,

Figure 12.37. If groups have story elements of more than one type, they can use them to play a game in which random combinations of element "cards" suggest stories to recall or imagine.

because the definition of a valid answer is: *what occurs to you*. If it springs to mind, it's valid.

People categorize instead of clustering

Sometimes you will hear people in a group saying things like this to each other.

- How about we write an "officer" note every time a story contains a police officer?
- These three stories all have to do with traffic intersections, so let's write three notes for that.
- This one takes place in a public space, right? So let's label all the ones in public spaces "public."

Watch out for people using general words like *every* and *all* or categorizing words like *label* and *type* and *category* and *class* and *group*. When you hear talk like this, intervene. There should be no categories in this exercise. Answer notes should be *unique to each story and to each group*.

There's a simple reason to avoid categorization in this exercise. The *stories* are not what people are meant to be examining. The stories are a *means* of examining their *own* assumptions, feelings, and imaginations. The more people put *themselves* into this exercise, the more the exercise will do for them.

What should you do if people start the exercise by categorizing stories? Redirect their attention to *observing their reactions* to stories. Ask them to pay attention to what *jumps out* of the sto-

ries at them: what *springs to mind*, what they *notice*, what *matters* to them, what they find *memorable*, how they *feel*. Explain that what you are after is not a classification of *stories* but an accumulation of *reactions*. For example, if you see someone writing down "a man," ask them what it is about that man that they want to remember, or what strikes them as most important, or what they like or dislike about him. Is he tall? Kind? Misunderstood? Brave? Those are the sorts of things they should write down and use in their clustering.

Nothing jumps out at people

If you facilitate long enough, you are guaranteed to come across a person who, when you say, "Write down the answers that occur to you," tells you that nothing occurs to them. Usually these are people who are very used to following rules and procedures in their lives. They are not stupid; they are just not accustomed to *waiting for things to happen* in their minds. But they *need* to wait for this exercise to work.

A helpful tweak to the exercise in this case is to have people break down stories into smaller pieces. In a group of diehard nothing-occurs-to-me participants, one group member might read a story out loud one sentence at a time. After each sentence has been read, the group can ask itself: Can we think of any answers to this question based on the sentence we just read? If they can think of an answer, they should note it down. If they can't think of an answer, they should move on to the next sentence. After they have read a few stories in this step-wise manner, answers might start occurring to them without breaking stories apart. (The observant reader will have noticed that this method is similar to the way in which unaccustomed storytellers can be helped to tell stories; see page 49.)

People blur distinctions between element types

People often don't get the distinctions right between types of story element. You ask them for situations and they come up with values; you ask them for values and they list characters. Don't allow yourself to care about this. It doesn't matter all that much. As long as the things people are writing down are meaningful to them, the exercise will still work.

People argue about distinctions between element types

Sometimes groups doing this exercise get into arguments about what constitutes a legitimate answer to the question they are supposed to be answering.

If this is happening, you'll hear people saying things like this:

• That isn't really a who, it's a what. You can't put that down for the "who" question.

• What do you mean, what's going on is "an angry man?" An angry man can't be something that's going on.

• We're supposed to be saying what matters to people in the story, not what they're feeling.

When you hear this, first, wait and see how long people argue about it. If the argument passes over quickly, ignore it. However, sometimes people get so mired in "doing things right" that they use up all their time without getting anything done. If you think that is happening, step in and quietly explain that it doesn't really matter if the answers to the question fit it perfectly. Some sloppiness in the answers won't break the process.

Clusters are too big

As a general rule, any cluster (of anything) should contain no more than seven or eight items, maybe ten at the most. Sometimes you will find groups who have clusters of fifteen or more items in them. Usually this happens when people are hesitating to explore the meanings embedded in the cluster (see Figure 12.38 on the next page).

Should you step in and help people break up large clusters? Not in a direct way, because people may take it as criticism. What you can do if you notice too-large clusters is to make a general announcement to the room, as though you hadn't noticed anything but forgot to mention one part of the instructions before. You can say something like, "By the way, you should aim to have no clusters with no more than eight or ten items in them." Particularly if you say this while *not* looking at the giant cluster one group has been hoarding, they may take the hint and break it up. If they don't take the hint, let it go. Maybe they just aren't ready to break through to that level of insight right now.

People think they are done after the first clustering

Quite often, people doing this exercise think it is over after the first set of clusters is finished. I don't blame them; it *looks* done. They have created a neat and tidy group of clusters with names. They feel ready to rest and enjoy the results of their hard work. However, you cannot let them do this. For reasons I will explain in the "Where it came from" section, stopping after the first clusters are complete will ruin the benefits of the exercise. Don't let people rest at this point. I wouldn't even schedule a coffee break just after the first clusters are complete, because it will give people the wrong idea that the exercise is over. A better place to schedule a break is after the descriptive attributes have been written, because it will be clear that *something* will follow from this. Keep people moving past the part where it looks like things are finished. You don't want to lose momentum just when you need it to build.

People write too few attributes

After people have created their initial clusters, sometimes they have a hard time describing them. They might list few descriptive attributes, or they might copy words from answer notes to attribute notes. If this happens, explain that the quality of the exercise outcome will depend on these attributes. If people are getting tired, you might let them take a break in the middle of writing attributes, because they might find

Figure 12.38. Very large clusters usually mean people aren't willing to address an uncomfortable issue.

more to add after they've had five or ten minutes to rest their imaginations.

People can't or won't write attributes on both good and bad sides

Coming up with silver linings to obviously bad situations or bad things about revered heroes takes imagination. Sometimes people can't or won't do it. Unbalanced descriptions will decrease the utility of the exercise. If this happens, issue a room-wide instruction to include equal numbers of positive and negative attributes for each cluster.

People spend too much time making clusters beautiful

If people are rearranging their sticky notes not for meaning but for beauty, making their clusters symmetrical for example, this is a sign that the exercise isn't moving fast enough. There shouldn't be enough time to think about beauty. If you see a lot of sticky-note fidgeting in any time period, check to see if all of the groups are doing it. If they are, say something like, "I see things are moving along well, so let's cut this time period short and move right into the next step." It's better to save time for discussion later than it is to lose attention because people have burned through an instruction faster than you expected.

People come up with confusing story element names

I didn't want to burden you with this in the step-by-step instructions above, but you might need to give people some help naming their story elements so that they can be understood outside the sensemaking session.

Some types of names I've seen people create that don't work include the following.

Proper nouns. Names of actual people, cities, towns, sports teams, and so on have the problem of being too specific. It is highly unlikely that people in any sensemaking session will arrive at any story element that means *exactly* a real person, place, or thing, no more and no less. What is more likely is that the person, place, or thing will have been *evoked in context* by the sensemaking. But using the name *outside* the sensemaking session will not carry that context with it, so such a name could be damaging to understandings after the session.

If people insist on using a proper noun as a story element name, ask them to add at least one or two words to the name that give an idea of *why* that name applies to the topic. For example, if a character element is named "Michael Jackson" people might add something that says "great dancer" or "tortured genius" or "style setter"—so other people have at least some hope of understanding what that name meant to the people who chose it.

Names that could mean anything. In one sensemaking session I helped with, one of the character elements created was "mom." Another was "self." Those names are not enough, all by themselves, to travel outside the session. Why does the word "mom" or the word "self" have meaning in that context? As with proper nouns, ask people to add a few words more to describe what is mom-like or self-like about the cluster.

Buzzword names. Sometimes people choose names they know to be completely safe because they are buzzwords (commonly used jargon used to impress) for the topic under consideration. Some examples might be "positive mental attitude" or "education is key." You will see this more often when participants feel constrained to speak within accepted boundaries about a topic, perhaps one on which they feel judged. This problem is easy to fix. If you notice any buzzword names, just shout out, "Forgot to say: you may not have any story element names that anyone would recognize as buzzwords." Then the people who have been hiding in the safety of buzzwords will find them dangerous (breaking the rules), and they'll rename their elements in a hurry.

Names from movies or books only some have seen. Quite often people choose names for their story elements based on movies or other things in the mass media. That's fine if everyone in the community or organization can be expected to know what those things mean. But it's not fine if not everyone has access to the same information. Sometimes these difficulties come up in age differences: a group of teenagers will give elements names that are unintelligible to seniors in the same community. When this happens, ask people to add a few more words to clarify what that reference means to the group.

Inside jokes. Here's a story element name from a real project: "to bee or not to bee." That is evidently some sort of joke about bees, or stinging, or something, but it won't travel. Just the simple addition of "ouch!" to this name would help people outside the session understand that the story element has something to with unexpected pain.

The ultimate test of any story element name is: would everyone in our community or organization know what we mean by this name? No story element should ever have to travel *outside* your community or organization, but it should make sense to everyone *inside* it.

Try it yourself first

This is the easiest exercise in the world to try by yourself. Just find some stories—twenty or thirty will do—choose your question, and get to work. I suggest using real sticky notes on a real wall, because that is what you will be asking other people to do. Even if you think it's silly to do all that by yourself, you really should spend some time with the actual pieces of paper to understand the task. First go through the process with only one question, then do two questions at once (it's a lot harder). Then ask a few friends or colleagues to do the exercise with you. Once you have gone through the exercise several times, adding more complexity to the mix each time, you will be ready to facilitate the exercise.

Your own style

This exercise, more than any other I've described here, is very loose in its definition. Because the exercise is based on the simple acts of listing things and lumping them together, you can imagine all sorts of elaborations that could add to the simple plan. Why not explore some of these ideas yourself?

- What would happen if you asked people to look at each story from multiple perspectives? What could they do with what they wrote down?
- What would happen if two groups worked from the same stories, then swapped clusters for the second round?
- What would happen if groups presented their clusters to other groups before and/or after clustering the second time?
- What would happen if groups used fewer stories, say only five or ten, but fully exhausted every possible answer they could come up with for them?
- What if each group could only give *one* answer to each question for each story?

- What if everyone in the room wrote the initial answers together (by shouting out answers while you read the stories), then each group got its own copy of the whole-room answers and went through the double-clustering process with them? How would that turn out?

Can you add more exploratory questions to this list?

Where it came from

This exercise might seem complicated, but really it's not, because it's just the same process repeated twice. Something is described, and the descriptions are clustered into groups. Then something is described, and the descriptions are clustered into groups.

Clustering things into groups is both very old and in very widespread use today. Nothing about that is new. But clustering things *twice* is unusual.

The question is: why cluster twice? There's a reason for that, and it's also a story of discovery. This story has nothing to do with me. The method was developed by Dave Snowden and Sharon Darwent (and possibly one or two other people I don't know about) just before the time I started working with them. They had been using a one-step clustering process, just like this exercise except stopping with the first set of clusters. But they were disappointed with the results. People seemed to come up with only the most superficial descriptions of stories. They wanted to help people dig deeper into their *reactions* to stories.

So they thought, what would happen if we turned the wheel round another time? They tried a simple repetition of the process, and voila, things got a lot better. The second round of clustering helped people move further away from the concrete details of the stories into a more abstract consideration of the feelings and beliefs embodied in them; and this allowed people to work more with their *own* feelings and beliefs. Essentially, the stories started the sensemaking going, but the exercise needed to move *beyond* the stories before it really worked well. The exercise has been in use in this two-stage manner ever since that discovery.

By the way, Dave Snowden calls the things that come out of this exercise "archetypes." You may see the exercise described as the "extraction" of archetypes from stories. I never liked calling them archetypes because people kept mixing them up with Jungian archetypes; and I never liked calling their creation "extraction" because it seemed too clinical a procedure. For a while I called the things "emergent constructs," because they emerge and they're constructed, but that name never caught on very well. It was confusing, and it left people unsure of what they'd made and what they could do with it. After many hours of thought I finally came up with the name of story elements.

The reason I chose the name "story elements" is because it tells you what you can *do* with the things you've created. *You can build things with them.* Elements are the building blocks of matter, and story elements are the building blocks of stories. When you create story elements, you create a *symbolic language* you can use to feed new levels of sensemaking.

Story elements are not meant to be created and then put aside; they are meant to be combined and recombined into new stories, during and after the sensemaking session in which they arose. They can be used as inputs to the time-line, landscape, and composite story exercises. They can be combined in simple ways, such as by having elements "talk" to each other.

Story elements can also be used in the intervention and return phases of story projects. For example, people could anonymize stories in an ongoing story exchange by taking on the "voices" of character elements drawn from the originally collected stories. All of the exercise outputs created in sensemaking sessions have the potential for use outside the sessions; but story elements are the simplest outputs, so they can travel best to new phases of your projects. For more on using story elements in other sensemaking exercises, see the "Combining exercises" section later in this chapter (page 463).

How to find more on these ideas

The act of clustering like with like appears in many facilitated group exercises in a variety of fields. Essentially, if you can find a field that involves people thinking or talking together for any reason—to design a product, to come to a decision, to get new ideas—you will probably find clustering somewhere in what they do.

Clustering has two other well-known names you should know about if you want to find more exercises that use it.

The K-J method

This method is named after Jiro Kawakita, who developed the idea in the 1960s. It is also sometimes called *affinity mapping* or creating an *affinity diagram*. The K-J method is similar to what I've described here, but with a few differences.

1. The K-J method starts by having people list brainstormed answers to questions, like this exercise. But the questions are not about stories or any other texts; they are *direct* questions, like, "How do you feel about the downtown revitalization project?"

2. The K-J method places answers together, like with like, as does this exercise. But it only does so *once*. There is no second clustering.

3. The K-J method specifies that while clustering, participants should be *silent*. This is meant to make the process more egalitarian and creative. I don't believe silence actually makes things any more egalitarian (power signals move into body language very well) or creative (some people get more creative when they talk, some less). So I encourage people to discuss and debate placements instead—although I certainly don't think it would *hurt* anything to try silent clustering, if a group wants to do things that way.

I'm not saying, by the way, that I think the K-J method is flawed because it doesn't work from source materials or cluster twice; its structure is appropriate for more direct discussion of straightforward issues. In story work there is a need for greater obliquity and penetration, which is why my colleagues developed the double-abstraction elaborations of this method.

Card sorting

This method is widely used in cultural anthropology and in information systems design. As with the K-J method, answers are written to direct questions, and clustering takes place only once. I don't believe there is a requirement of silence in card sorting, but otherwise it's fairly similar to the K-J method.

As far as I can tell, there isn't any meaningful difference between card sorting, affinity mapping and clustering, which is a good thing because it means you can use ideas from all of these methods to enhance your own explorations of facilitating narrative sensemaking. There might even be other names for the same activity of placing like with like that I'm not aware of. I wouldn't be the least bit surprised to hear it. Grouping things by similarity is a universal human tendency, which is one reason it's so powerful.

By the way, if you start looking up "mapping" in your search for more information about clustering, you are likely to come across *concept mapping* (also called *mind mapping*). Concept mapping is *not* clustering. The process may be participatory and egalitarian, but concept maps tend to be *hierarchical* diagrams, not clusters of like with like. There are many free or cheap software solutions out there that support participatory concept mapping, but I would avoid using them *unless* you can work out a way to create clusters and move things around (a lot) without having to name the clusters too early. If you can adapt concept mapping solutions to loosen the suggestion of hierarchy, it might not ruin the exercise; but tread carefully. Hierarchies create categories.

COMPOSITE STORIES

In a composite stories exercise, groups use collected stories as source material to build a purposeful story, fictional or semi-fictional, which they tell to other groups. As they build and tell stories, people discuss the juxtapositions of meaning created.

When to use it

The composite stories exercise is the most complicated one in the book, which is why I put it last. You should not use it on your first sensemaking session, nor should you use it if you have not practiced it beforehand. It does not require any particular types or qualities of col-

Figure 12.39. The first step in the composite stories exercise is to fill in each template slot with at least one story.

lected stories, but it does ask more of your participants and of yourself. Some people will eat this exercise up and ask for more; others will find it unappealing for various reasons (see "What can go wrong" for a full catalogue of misperceptions and fears). This is a high input, high risk, high commitment, high engagement, high output exercise. When all the indications are right, this exercise is the most powerful in the toolkit. But when anything is off, this exercise has more potential to go wrong than any other.

What it requires

At least nine people and up to as many as the room will comfortably hold; at least two hours. This exercise does not require the use of paper or markers. However, because building a story with stories requires people to go somewhat deeper into understanding, I do not suggest placing this exercise first in any sensemaking session. It should be done *after* people have had some prior exposure to collected stories, even if it was just a fifteen-minute first-contact task.

How to do it

Step One: Introduce the exercise and form groups

Five minutes. Explain the exercise and its purpose. Split people into groups from three to six people each. Make sure you have at least *three groups* in total. (That's why the exercise requires at least nine people.)

Step Two: Choose a message

Five minutes. Each group should agree on a message they want their constructed story to deliver. It should be related to the goals of the project and of the session. What do they want the audience hearing the story to take away from hearing it? What do they want people to remember?

Step Three: Fill in a story template

Twenty minutes. At this point in the exercise, you should introduce a *story template*. This is a set of slots into which chosen stories will be inserted to create a composite story (see Figure 12.39). You should have decided which template to use before the session. See the "Composite stories" section in Appendix A (page 589) for a list of templates you might want to use. A simple example is Aristotle's three-part template: beginning (context setting), middle (creation of tension, reaction to tension), and ending (resolution of tension).

To fill the story template, each group should consider the previously collected stories they have been given, looking for stories that fit the characteristics of each slot *and* fit the message they want the story to deliver.

Taking the Aristotelian template as an example:

1. For the "beginning" slot, groups should choose a story that gives the audience an understanding of "what it's like" to be in the chosen situation.

Figure 12.40. Once the template slots have been filled, groups should use them to create a coherent story that delivers the agreed-upon message.

2. For the "middle" slot, they should choose a story in which tensions are created and in which people react to the tensions.

3. For the "ending" slot, they should choose a story in which something is resolved.

You might say that in *every* story these three things happen, and you'd be right. So how can groups choose stories that fit the slots, if they all have all the slots? Ask people to find stories in which whatever should be going on in that slot (context, tension, resolution) is particularly *dominant* or *memorable* in the story.

So for example:

1. A group that needs a story for the "beginning" context slot might choose one where an arthritic patient describes a typical morning. In that story, *context* is the dominant element.

2. For the "middle" slot, they might choose a story in which someone finds out they have cancer. In that story the *creation* of the tension is the dominant element.

3. For the "ending" slot, they might choose a story in which someone finds out that their skin condition has been caused by a food allergy all along. In that story, the *resolution* of a tension is the dominant element.

What does it mean to *put a story in a slot?* At this point, it literally means just that: groups should take a story card or sticky note and lay it down on a table or stick it on a wall where they have already written "beginning" or "middle" or whatever part of whatever story template they are using. If more than one story seems appropriate for a slot, groups can place them both, then choose which fits best after all the slots have something in them. The group doesn't have to do anything more than that in this step of the process. Just *filling in the slots* with stories that seem to work there and fit the chosen message is all that is required right now.

Step Four: Form the story

Twenty minutes. In this step the focus of each group should move from *assembling* stories to *creating* one new fictional story *inspired by* the assembled stories (Figure 12.40). Groups should choose one person who will be the storyteller for their story-building team. That storyteller should now practice *telling* the larger story that combines the stories the group has slotted into their template. (Make sure groups understand that even though one person will *tell* the story, the entire group should *build* it together. All of the group members should be active in negotiating the form and substance of the story.)

In this period, the group should work out how their assembled stories will merge into one *coherent* story that effectively delivers their chosen message. They will need to figure out how they can fit the separate settings together into one coherent setting. Taking our medical example above, the group would need to find a way to merge the conditions of arthritis, cancer, and a skin condition into one coherent illness: perhaps one of those, or something en-

Figure 12.41. One person from the group should tell the story to another group, then ask for feedback.

tirely different. They would also merge the three characters (maybe an old man, a teenager, and a middle-aged mother) into *one* fictional person. Making composite characters and settings fictional is important, because it avoids any blame being directed at *specific* individuals or groups. Groups can incorporate other fictional elements, even fanciful or impossible ones—like alien interventions or time travel—as long as the elements serve to *deliver the message* the group has chosen.

At the end of this time period, each group (and each group's storyteller in particular) should be ready to deliver their story to others outside their group. Some groups will practice telling their story only once within their group, discussing its details as they go. Other groups might tell the story three or four times, adding more detail in each telling. That doesn't matter, as long as all the groups end up with a story they feel ready to pass on at the end of the time period.

Step Five: Tell the story

Ten minutes. Now each storyteller should visit another group and tell their group's story (see Figure 12.41). They should keep the telling to about the first seven or eight minutes of the ten-minute period. The people in the other group should listen respectfully and should avoid interrupting the storyteller.

After the story has been told, the people in the other group should answer questions like these:

• What did you take away from this story?

• What did it mean to you?

• How do you feel about it?

The storyteller should listen to what the group says, taking notes if they think they might forget. If there is time and they think of more questions to ask, this is the time to ask them.

Step Six: Prepare for the second telling

Fifteen minutes. Back in their groups, storytellers should report on how the storytelling went (see Figure 12.42 on the next page). The storyteller should recount how the audience reacted during the storytelling and answered questions about the story afterward. Then the group should evaluate what happened. Did the story fulfill its purpose? Did it deliver its message?

Then the group should go back and improve on their story in preparation for a second telling. They can practice telling it again. They can replace a slotted-in story with another one. They can think about nuances like conflict, empathy, intensity, and memorability.

Step Seven: Tell the story again

Ten minutes. Now the same storytellers should proceed to *another* group (*not* the one they told the story to the first time) and tell the story again (see Figure 12.43 on page 447). To keep this orderly, you can ask groups to go first one group clockwise then two. The same rules apply again: the story should take seven or eight minutes, followed by two or three minutes of discussion; the other group should listen quietly and not interrupt; the storyteller should at-

Figure 12.42. After the first telling, groups should work to improve their story's delivery of its message.

tempt to capture (in memory or in notes) what the other group said so they can report back.

Step Eight: Finish the story

Fifteen minutes. Again the storytellers should return to their groups. Again the groups should discuss how the storytelling went (see Figure 12.44 on page 448). Again the groups should improve their stories. Any improvements made the second time through will probably be minor, but groups may want to tweak their delivery of the stories based on their second round of feedback.

This is the time to make a record of the built stories, if that is a goal of the session. You don't *have* to record stories in this exercise; you can just let them linger in the memories of the session participants. If your topic is very sensitive, recording may not be an option.

If you *can* record the stories built in this exercise, *should* you? Is it worth doing? That depends on what you expect to happen after the session is over. The most valuable outcome of this exercise isn't the story; it's the sensemaking that goes on while people are building the story. However, for projects where you need people who didn't attend the session to learn about what went on there, hearing someone tell a story a group has prepared can create a deeper understanding of what went on in the session. Even if only the people who attended the session will receive copies of the recordings,

having such a recording will help people recall the "story of the session" later.

In contrast with timelines, landscapes, and story elements, there will be no physical artifacts left behind after this exercise is finished. So if you want to keep the built stories after the session—for anyone inside *or* outside the session—you will need to ask people to record their stories. The simplest way to do this is to have each storyteller tell their group's story a third time, either within their group or by visiting a third group, while recording audio or video.

Step Nine: Discuss the story within groups

Ten minutes. Now that each story has been told, retold, and possibly recorded, it is time for groups to discuss what they have learned by *building* the story (see Figure 12.45 on page 449). What surprised them: about the story, about the process, about the reactions of the other groups? What did they like and dislike? What discoveries have they made? How do they see the topic differently now? What would they like to tell the other people in the room about their story or about the process they went through? What would they like to tell people *outside* the room?

Step Ten: Discuss with the whole room

Ten minutes. Now bring everyone in the room into one large discussion about all the stories and the entire process. Talk about patterns that appeared across stories. Were any similar? Did

Figure 12.43. The second telling should have a different audience from the first, so that the storyteller can get new feedback on the improved story.

any argue or present different perspectives on the same issue? What do people feel is different now than it was before the exercise? What did they find out by doing this exercise? What do they want to remember?

If you have less time

It's hard to find much you can trim out of this exercise. Groups need to fill slots in a story template with stories; they need to work the assembled stories into a coherent whole; they need to tell the story and gather reactions to it; they need to discuss what happened. If I had less time, I wouldn't remove any whole step of the process; I'd just slim down all of the pieces. For example, you can introduce the exercise, form groups, and have groups choose messages, all in five minutes, especially if you keep the same groups as you formed in a previous exercise. You can reduce the storytellings from ten minutes down to seven, with five for the story proper and two for discussion. And so on.

To convert this exercise into a simple task that takes only fifteen minutes, do only the very first two steps: choose a message and put stories into slots. Just talking about which story would work where to build up a larger story that delivers a message (even though nobody will actually *do* that) can help people think through the issues. It can also introduce the idea of building stories with stories, which you could return to later in the session, or in another session on another day.

If you have more time

To add more time to this exercise, include one or more elaborations, or add time to the steps in this order:

1. Fill in a story template
2. Form the story
3. Prepare for the second telling
4. Discuss the story within groups
5. Discuss with the whole room
6. Finish the story
7. Choose a message
8. Tell the story
9. Tell the story again
10. Introduce the exercise and form groups

The maximum time I would suggest for this exercise would be about four hours.

Before you start

Before you start this exercise, you need to decide what sort of story template you will use. In Appendix A (page 589) I list several candidates worth looking at, but it's easy to find more. Just look for books and web sites that have something to do with story form or plot or fiction writing.

Two more words about preparing to facilitate this exercise: folk tales. The more folk tales you read before you facilitate this exercise, the better it will go. Reading books full of hundreds of stories helps you internalize story structure in a way that reading books and academic papers about story structure cannot. Soak yourself in

Figure 12.44. After the second telling, groups should finish and optionally record their stories.

stories, then look at the story templates listed in Appendix A. You should feel the templates becoming more meaningful to you. And don't *stop* reading folk tales after you've facilitated the exercise for the first time; keep doing so between sessions. You will find that your ability to keep this exercise exciting and productive will be enhanced by maintaining your exposure to story form.

Optional elaborations

Add more up-front story choices

After groups have chosen their messages, they can make more choices, each of which deepens the complexity of the story building task.

Topic. A story topic narrows the field of what the story can be about. This is not the same as a message. It is more like the subject matter of the story. Adding topic choices is particularly helpful if people are dealing with a large number of stories and might have a hard time choosing among the many possible candidates for inclusion.

Genre. A story genre is just like the genre of a movie or book: a well-known category. Some examples might be Westerns, war stories, spy stories, buddy stories, road-trip stories, superhero stories, epic sagas, satire, farce, parody, romantic comedy, situational comedy, science fiction, documentaries, mockumentaries, edutainment, detective stories, courtroom stories, police stories, gangster stories, musicals, fantasy, legends, historical stories, counterfactual histories, ghost stories, thrillers, horror stories,

disaster stories, and finally, apocalyptic stories and end-of-the-world thrillers.

To use genre in this exercise, give groups a printed list of genres (like this one, which I drew mostly from a Wikipedia page, or your own). Then give people the option to choose a genre to guide their story work. Genres specify to some extent what should happen in a story. For example, in a buddy story two people will probably come closer together as the result of some shared experience. Using genres can make the experience more engaging and creative, which is useful if you are dealing with people who don't start out enthused about the session. If you know your participants well enough, you might be able to build a shorter, more targeted list of genres that will engage people without making them feel bored, threatened or insulted. But if you think people will respond negatively to the elaboration as a whole, put this one aside.

Subtext. A story subtext is a deeper message, one more subtle and emotional than the explicit message chosen at first. After people have heard the story, they should be able to identify the message easily. But the story's subtext should be difficult to express; it will manifest itself more in how people *feel* after they have heard the story. Choosing a subtext adds another layer of complexity to the story and makes groups work a little harder at crafting their story well. Some groups will eat up this elaboration, eager for more complex detail to build into their story. Other groups will find it confusing and distracting. Consider how inter-

Figure 12.45. After finishing their stories, groups should discuss what they've learned.

ested your participants will be and how used they are to dealing with nuance when deciding whether to add a subtext.

Time frame. Should the story take place in the past, present, or future? When exactly? Covering what period of time? Ten minutes? Ten years? If you don't explicitly give people the option to think of a time frame, they will probably tell a story set in the present, even if some elements of the story are fictional. However, you can suggest that people explore the idea of setting their story in the past (perhaps as a counter-factual what-if scenario) or the future (perhaps as a utopian or dystopian vision).

Outcome. Should the story end well or badly? If you don't mention this option, most stories will end well, just because that's what people are used to. However, if you give people the option of building a story on any point along the wonderful-to-horrible spectrum, this might give some groups new ideas about how to explore their thoughts and feelings.

Fact-fiction blend. Groups will need to step at least lightly into fiction simply so they can blend stories with different settings and characters together into one coherent account. However, there is a wide range of blends between fact and fiction, from "it mostly happened this way" to "it *could* happen this way" to "imagine if it happened this way" to "it could *never* happen this way"—and beyond. Asking groups to choose a point along the line blending fact and fiction might nudge some of them to explore further than they would have without any mention of the possibilities of fiction.

Metaphorical displacement. Groups can *displace* the setting of their story to a setting obliquely connected to the real setting they want to consider. For example, if a group wants to tell a story about dangerous conditions in factories producing low-cost goods, they might choose to displace the setting and tell a story about fishermen being forced to go out on stormy seas because of low prices in the fish market, or (displacing the setting even further) about beavers wandering into the suburbs, looking for streams they can dam. When groups use metaphorical displacement, they should *translate* each story they choose so that its foundational elements of tension and conflict stay intact, but the specifics of who, what and where shift to the new setting. Such a metaphorical device can help people surround their story with a message of safety in disclosing strong emotions (it's not about us, it's about beavers).

All of these elaborations to the basic story-message choice are meant to help groups explore more fully in their sensemaking. It doesn't matter what type of story a group chooses to build, but it does matter whether people are fully engaged in the process and ready to explore the topic together. You might think of more elaborations to the basic story-forming options yourself. Why not try them out? If an elaboration helps people get excited about the process and dig deeper into their sensemaking, it's worth using.

Tell the story three times

The basic outline of this exercise has groups telling their story to another group twice. Ex-

Figure 12.46. Making any part of the template hold an episodic series makes the story-building task more complex.

tending the exercise to three tellings is helpful in some situations but useless in others.

When is it helpful? When people are going through the process mechanically or superficially, or when they have been warming up slowly to the idea and are just getting into the process when it's time for it to be over. Generally if groups are moving at a slow pace or exploring at a shallow depth, it will improve the exercise to tell the story a third time.

However, if the first two tellings came off well, having groups tell the story a third time will not be helpful; it will just waste time. People will polish their stories instead of delving deeper into sensemaking. In that case, it would be better to use the time for another elaboration of the exercise, or for another exercise, or for more discussion.

Deepen stories with repetition

Story templates specify what sort of event should fill each slot. But in the telling of folk tales, a *series of episodes* often fits into each part of the story template. Typically the episodes in these series escalate in intensity, building to a climax as the series turns over into the next part of the story. If you've read a lot of folk tales you'll recognize this pattern immediately. The hero might encounter three giants, each stronger than the last. Or she might meet three poor old women, each more shrunken than the last (and each more shrill in her demands for charity). Or three young men might step forward to fight

for the princess's hand, each stronger than the last; and so on.

Sometimes the last episode in the series is special and different, which makes the escalation even more intense. The last giant is monstrous but kind. The last old woman is magical. The last young man has a heart of gold. Escalating repetition is a technique often used in oral storytelling to make stories more compelling for the audience (and easier for the storyteller to remember).

As it happens, repetition is also useful in sensemaking. Why? Because including more than one story inevitably includes more than one *perspective*, which deepens exploration of the issue. There are three ways you could use repetition to add complexity to this exercise.

1. You could alter the story template you've chosen so that in one or more of the slots there are places for a series of episodes.

2. You could keep the story template the same, but include in your *instructions* the direction or option to choose one or more slots of the template to expand to include multiple episodes.

3. You could refrain from mentioning the option in your general instructions, but hang around and *listen* as groups get started filling their templates. If any groups leap through the task quickly and start looking bored, you could quietly mention the possibility of making the exercise more chal-

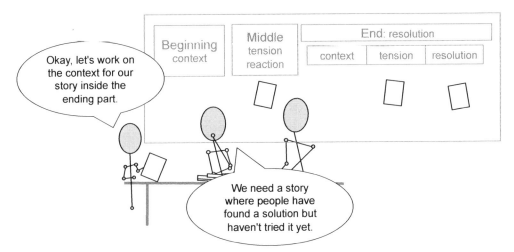

Figure 12.47. Making any part of the template hold an entire embedded story makes the story-building task even more complex than using repetition.

lenging (and productive) by expanding one slot into a multi-part episode.

Whichever option you use, remember to tell groups that the intensity within each episodal series should escalate. If the slot prescribes context, the stories should reveal more. If the slot requires challenge, the challenges should increase. If the slot describes resolution, the relief should become greater. (See Figure 12.46 on the preceding page.)

Deepen stories with recursion

Another trick often used in folk tales is the inclusion of whole stories within other stories (see Figure 12.47). This is often done through reported events, such as when the old woman met on the road tells the story of her adventures in early life, or when one of the young men vying for the princess' hand has a vivid dream in which he learns of the maiden's secret history. Some of the great Arab tales (*One Thousand and One Nights*, for example) embed stories within stories within stories, sometimes to a dizzying extent.

Between repetition and recursion, recursion is the more difficult option. Stories within stories are hard to keep track of. So it is best used for only the most motivated, creative, and energetic groups (or if you have lots of time and a very pressing need to make sense of things). In the same way as with repetition, you can include this elaboration by altering your template

to include other, smaller templates inside it; by instructing people to include a whole story inside one part; or by pulling the elaboration out of your hat to engage a bored group who have already filled their slots and want more challenge.

Deepen stories with dramatic elements

If you like, you can add a complication to the preparation for the second (or third) telling, and that is to give people a list of *dramatic elements* they might want to consider adding to their story. You can find lists of these things in any book on fiction writing; I'll just throw out a few.

- Stories in which the audience can *identify* with the protagonist in some way are more memorable.
- Stories that feature *conflict* at more than one level (within the main character, between the main character and other characters, between the main character and "the world" or "the system") pack a bigger punch.
- Stories in which expectations about how people typically behave are *upended* deepen interest.
- Stories in which the stakes of success or failure *grow* larger and larger keep people paying attention.

And so on. You can introduce a few of these dramatic elements with a few words—

identification, conflict, surprise, escalation—and suggest that people pay attention to them as they improve their stories. This will complicate the task and give people a stronger challenge. It will also cause them to think more deeply about the issue they are exploring through building the story.

Send an observer with the storyteller

If there are enough people per group, say four or more, you can send an additional person to visit other groups along with the storyteller. This person will not tell the story, but they will ease the storyteller's burden by *watching* the audience and making their own notes on how people react and what they say in response to the discussion questions afterward. This can help to give groups more feedback on how their story went over with the audience, which can deepen their exploration of the story and the issues it explores. However, if doing this means groups won't have at least two people *left* in each group to hear the story being told, don't add the elaboration. You don't want to end up with nobody reacting to the stories, because that won't turn the wheel of reflection.

Have two people tell the story

If there are enough people per group, you can have two people tell the story together. Doing this eases the burden on one storyteller. It makes the story more interesting to everyone, and it removes the possibility of one forceful person taking over the group and drowning out other views than their own.

Here is a question you might have: If you can have exactly two people go round for visits, is it more useful to send around one storyteller and one observer, or two storytellers? I'd say one storyteller and one observer. The observations are as important as the storytelling in this exercise. The observations help each group gather reactions to their story from other perspectives, and that's more powerful than a better-told story.

Play out the story

With this elaboration you again send around more than one storyteller, but this time the story gets played out, not told, in a sort of little skit. Groups might have to simplify their stories so that the "cast of characters" can be minimal, or people might have to play multiple parts; but having the story "take place" instead of being told can inject more creativity into the process. As you can guess, you wouldn't want to use this option when you think people will be very unwilling to leave their comfort zones; or at least, you wouldn't want to use it at the *start* of the session, but should wait until people have warmed up and feel that they can trust the other people there.

Ask more questions about the story

Do you recall, way back in the parts of this book about collecting stories, the sections about asking people questions about stories as they were being collected? (See page 133.) You can use all of those same questions now, when people are telling stories to audiences in a sensemaking session (see Figure 12.48 on the next page).

For example, groups could tell their stories, then ask their audiences questions like these:

- In this story, would you say that people trusted each other?
- What surprised you about the events of this story?
- Are there any people or groups you think particularly need to hear this story?
- Does this story ring true?
- Who was responsible for the events that took place in this story? Who *should* have been responsible?

Before your session, you might want to look through the lists of questions in the story collection chapter (page 137) and find a few, or even several, that you think will help people use their audience reactions most fruitfully in making sense of their stories as they build (and rebuild) them. I wouldn't go past five questions in this period because it would take too long. But the more feedback groups get on their stories, the more churning and convergence (remember those?) they will achieve during the exercise.

You can even have storytellers give out paper forms to audience members with three to five questions about the story. Because this method is anonymous, it might be more fruitful than open discussion when the topic is sensitive. After each storytelling, groups can look over the

Figure 12.48. For sensitive topics or for deeper exploration, storytellers can hand out paper forms for audience members to fill out.

forms audience members filled out as they discuss how to improve their story.

Build follow-on stories

Another elaboration which deepens sensemaking (but requires more time) is to run the whole process again with a second story. The second time through, things should move much more quickly, because people will have grasped the basic process. There are many ways to go further with a second story. Here are just a few ideas to get you started.

The opposite view. Groups could challenge themselves to build a second story whose message counters the message of the first story. Can they make a case, using different stories as sources, for the opposite point of view? For example, say a group's first story is about injustices committed by officials working in the court system. After that story has been built, told, retold, and recorded, the group could then build a story about court officials serving the public interest with integrity. If the story collection is sufficiently diverse, they should be able to find stories that support an opposing message. Just *looking* for opposing-view stories to work with will help people think more deeply about the issues.

A different perspective. Groups could choose a character who played a minor part in their first story and build a second story in which events are seen from that character's point of view. Critically, they should not use the same source stories to build the second story; they

should find new stories that convey how that character (in the first story) might have experienced similar events. For example, say the project is about apartment housing, and in the first story the main character is frustrated by the inattention of their busy, hands-off landlord. A second story could be built about the difficulties of *being* a landlord, continually belabored with requests and complaints. This is somewhat similar to the opposite-view story above, but it uses the mechanism of seeing the world through the eyes of different characters instead of looking only for the opposite view. If you've ever heard of *Wicked*, the story of *The Wizard of Oz* told from the perspective of the wicked witch of the West, you'll understand why this sort of exploration can be fruitful.

Group to group response. Groups could create stories that *respond* to stories they heard from other groups. They might be reminded of a story they'd like to put together. Or they might want to counter a story told to them with one that shows the same issue in a different light. Or they might want to take another group's story further and build a story about what might happen next. When groups respond to each other, the degree of complexity in the entire sensemaking session rises above what can be achieved with visits and discussions. This is a more complex and difficult task, but for motivated or energetic participants it could be just the task they would like to tackle.

You can probably think of some other ways in which a second story could deepen the sensemaking started by the first story.

How you will know it's working

When people are building a composite story, they may or may not be moving physical objects. Some groups might build their story literally, by placing story cards or story-name notes in various locations on a table or wall. (I've shown that approach here in my stick-people pictures, but that's just so you have something to look at.) Other groups might write story names on a single small piece of paper. Still others might write nothing and talk their way through filling the slots in their template.

Those differences don't matter. What matters is that people in every group should be putting their heads together to work on their story. I mean this literally, not figuratively: people's heads should be close together.

Because this exercise includes a stronger component of performance than any other, groups should *want* to hide their preparations from other groups to some extent. People should be saying things like, "We're working on our story, but we're not ready to show anybody yet." So look for huddling and hiding in this exercise. Groups that huddle together like what they are making. Groups whose members show wandering attention are probably not doing very well in the exercise and may need some help.

What can go wrong

The chosen message doesn't fit the stories

The first part of this exercise involves choosing a message the built story will convey. But when people start looking for stories from the collection to fit into slots in the story template, it does sometimes happen that the message and the available stories don't fit well together. Usually this happens when there is some sort of barrier between the session participants and the stories. Maybe the stories were collected from people the sensemakers have little experience with, or the questions used to collect the stories pointed people in a different direction than people want to take now, or the participants were insufficiently familiar with the stories be-fore the exercise started to choose a message the stories would support.

The remedy for all of these problems is to give people more time to consider the stories they have to work with as they assemble their larger stories. If people are telling you that they can't tell the story they want to tell using the collected stories they have to work with, extend the time period for putting stories into slots in the template (say from twenty minutes to twenty-five or thirty). Ask people to negotiate a compromise between their message and the stories they encounter. They might need to change their message to work with the stories; but that's better than ignoring the mismatch and charging on with a story that doesn't hang together.

People say the stories don't fit the template slots well enough

This happens often when people are just getting started fitting stories into template slots. The fit between collected story and template slot doesn't have to be perfect; it just has to be reasonable. If the slot says a challenge should appear, any story in which *any kind of challenge* appears will do for the slot. The goal of the story assembly process is not to find the *best* stories for each slot; it's just to find an *acceptable* story for each slot so the process can move on.

People say that all of the stories fit all of the slots

If you tell people to choose stories for template slots based on the dominant elements of stories, and they don't understand what you mean, provide examples from some books or movies or folk tales you know and can expect your participants to know. Whatever template you choose to use, have a few examples ready to show how a story might fit one slot in the template better than another. Don't use these examples if people *don't* need them, because examples can be leading. Just have them on hand in case you need to give people some help.

If well-known examples don't help, sit down with the struggling group and look at some of the collected stories *with* them. Point out a few stories that seem to you to feature one part of the template, and ask the group members to find more stories that share the same characteristic feature. Ask the group to look at their stories and answer these questions:

- In this story, where does the *emotion* lie?
- What do you *remember* best about this story?
- What is the most *surprising* part of the story?

Highlighting the answers to these questions will help people see which aspect of each story is prominent, and finding the prominent aspects will help them see where each story might fit into the larger story.

People don't understand the template

Let's say you have chosen a template—from those I've listed in Appendix A or from your own research—that you think will best suit the participants in your sensemaking session. You have taken into account their educational backgrounds, their maturity levels, their worldviews. But when you get to the part of this exercise where people are supposed to be filling in the template with stories, they complain. They say, "We don't understand this thing. What are these words supposed to mean? What's a 'denewment?' Why do we have to use this? Can't we just tell a story?" Sigh.

You can respond to this problem in any or all of three ways.

Explain. You can explain what the template's words mean. If you've been doing your research, you should know that the word "denouement" comes from the French word dénouer, or untying, as in a knot. In the denouement of a story the knot of tension that gives the story its forward motion is untied, and the story relaxes to its end. Whatever story template you choose to use, prepare yourself to explain what its words mean. You can also prepare some alternative, less strange words people can use instead, and offer them up if people are confused.

Demonstrate. You can apply the template to a story. Have an example ready from a well-known book or movie or folk tale so you can explain how that story fits the template. Make sure the reference is well known, or have two or three references ready in case people aren't familiar with your first choice.

Offer alternatives. You can offer a selection of templates instead of just one. Any time you want to give people a fixed structure to use in an exercise, whether it's a story template, a set of landscape axes, or questions to form story elements, it's a good idea to have one or two other structures on hand in case people don't understand (or don't like) what you've chosen. That way, if people say, "We don't understand this thing," you can just pull out another one and say, "How about *this* one?"

Always remember that *the template doesn't matter*. It's just a way to get people to think about the issues as they play with stories, fitting them into the slots and taking them out again. Don't let yourself get seduced by the advice of important people about proper story form. Proper stories are not the goal here; proper *sensemaking* is. Listen and be flexible, and things will get moving.

People don't like the idea of making up stories

Sometimes people react to this exercise by thinking you are asking them to tell lies. They might be wary of manipulation; they might think you are asking them to disrespect the collected stories; they might think you want them to build a propaganda machine.

Is it lying to merge several true stories into one fictional story in which issues common to all of the stories are explored? It's a matter of interpretation. On the one hand, it is unlikely that events could possibly have unfolded in *exactly* the way any composite story lays them out. So technically speaking, any composite story has to be a lie. On the other hand, the *deeper* truths behind a composite story remain when the details of what exactly happened to whom are changed. You've probably seen movies made of famous novels in which minor characters have been merged. Usually this is done simply because there isn't enough time in two hours to include every word spoken by twenty people. Some people find this an abomination; others just laugh and enjoy the movie.

As you plan your session, think about how your participants are likely to respond to the idea of building a story out of stories. If you think they will be sticklers for literal truth, get ready to avoid the words *fiction, creation,* and *performance.* You don't need those words for the exercise to work. You also don't need to include any of the more imaginative elaborations, and you don't need to record the built stories. Instead, introduce the exercise as a means of understanding the collected stories by working them into composites.

If people still find that too close to lying, tell them that they can include side comments in their story that identify which original story lies behind each episode of the built story. Or they can tie the stories together in some other way than by merging the characters and setting. They might create a multi-threaded story in which real events come together without ever crossing the line into fiction. There are more ways to be creative than making up stories.

People think the whole thing is silly

Oh yes, this is bound to happen. For some people, the moment you say the word "story" you have identified yourself as a buffoon. They will immediately fear that you will drag them into a world of clown noses, big shoes, and pink tutus. Of all the narrative exercises in this book, this one is the most likely to trigger the silliness reaction.

Two groups of people are most likely to react to a story building exercise as something out of clown school. First are those who are insecure in their positions of power or status, who don't believe they can afford to take any risks with so-called "creative" methods in front of other people. Second are those who believe that the topic they have come to discuss, and perhaps their work or life itself, is so ponderously serious that any approach not strictly analytical-statistical-empirical-logical must inevitably offend them to their deepest core.

I know of two ways to get past the idea that going through this exercise will involve wearing funny hats. The first is to highlight the serious nature of narrative sensemaking. Story work can be and is used for serious topics, and it can have serious impacts on serious situations. Building stories with stories is not a joke; it is a serious method in the body of serious story work.

How can you get this point across? Keep a few deadly-serious stories handy, like the one I told in the previous chapter about the analysts grap-

pling with the events of 2001 (page 353). If you don't have a story of your own yet, tell one you've heard from someone else. When you hear a group trading comments that include the words *ridiculous, inane, trivial, absurd, childish, frivolous,* and so on, step in quietly and drop a serious story into the group. Then ask the group to check their story's message to make sure it "cuts to the heart" of the issues at hand. A story building exercise can be as serious or playful as people want it to be. It can even be serious and playful at the same time.

The second way to remove the silliness barrier is to talk about return on investment. Point out to people that they are already in the room; that they want to make progress on whatever the goals of the project might be; and that they might as well use their time doing *something* other than nit-picking about methods. Explain that you've seen this method work for other people with real needs. If you *haven't* actually seen the method work for real people with real needs, shame on you, because you should have. Even if the "people with real needs" have been yourself and two friends trying out the method, you should *still* have seen results using it.

I put this method last in the sensemaking chapter because it is the hardest to facilitate. Don't use this method with real participants in a real sensemaking session until you have tried it and seen it work in practice sessions. If you've done that, you can tell groups who are complaining that you *know* the method works and you're *sure* they will benefit from it. But explain that they need to give the method their full attention and work at it: or it will be their own fault if it fails.

People go through the process mechanically

Sometimes you will see people doing this exercise as if they were on auto-pilot. They fill the template slots with stories, and they prepare a story to tell. But the story they tell is wooden and empty of feeling. They haven't invested themselves in the exercise. This can be because they think the exercise is silly (see above), or it can be because they don't think they know how to build a story (see below) or tell a story (see below). It can be because they don't really want to explore the topic deeply and are holding themselves back from it. Or it can be because they just don't see where the exercise is going.

Sometimes when groups are going through the motions on this exercise, you'll notice that they complete all their tasks early. They'll say things like, "Okay, we put five stories in the slots. We still have five minutes left, so we're going out for a coffee." What this really means is: We aren't doing the exercise, really. We're just doing the minimum so we can pretend we're doing it.

What can *you* do when this happens? Raise the stakes. Make the exercise more challenging. Sometimes adding a colorful elaboration like story genre, recursion, or a he-said-she-said debate performance can engage people who aren't getting excited about the exercise as it was presented.

It also helps to highlight the fact that the built stories will be *evaluated* during the exercise. If a group is dragging their feet, ask them things like, "Are you sure the stories you picked for these slots are the most useful ones?" Or, "When you tell this story, the other group will be listening to hear whether you've made it engaging and memorable. Do you think it is?" If you have chosen some questions to ask audiences about stories, show reluctant groups the questions and ask if they are prepared for them. You might even want to engage unenthusiastic groups in a bit of friendly competition: not for the "best" story, but for the *most useful* story.

Remind people of why they are doing the exercise. Keep the goals of the project in their minds. Ask them to do their best to carry out the exercise so that it advances those goals. Challenge them to succeed.

The stories come out fake or superficial

The emotional intensity of this exercise is high, at least as high as that of the story elements exercise. Sometimes when people feel unable to handle that level of intensity, they create *fake* stories (see Figure 12.49 on the following page). This isn't the same as going through the process mechanically, because people don't work mechanically when they make fake stories. They pay very close attention to what they are doing. The problem lies in the fact that the purpose of all fake stories is to conceal and avoid, no mat-

ter what message the group *said* they would work on delivering.

You can spot fake stories in two ways. First, watch the storytellers. People who are telling fake stories exhibit signs of tension and anxiety. They sweat and stammer and look at the floor and talk rapidly to get the ordeal over with sooner. Second, listen to the stories. Fake stories sound like television commercials. They are short and full of clichéd, over-the-top, absolutist phrases like "we will succeed because we have strength" or "the government is behind everything" or "we will rise again" or "this is wrong in every way." Do you remember the post–9/11 session I told you about in the "Facilitating change" section on page 353? The stories participants created at the start of that session were fake stories. They were bizarre, strained and weirdly cheery, like the hysterical laughter of people in distress.

When you see and hear fake stories being told during this exercise, you might be able to help. It depends on why the stories are fake. Sometimes fake stories happen because people try too hard to contribute at first, then realize they are in too deep and can't find a way out of revealing things too intense to talk about. If you think this has happened with a particular group, you can mention to them (in the usual quiet "forgot to say" way) that they are free to change their message or anything they like about the story at any time during the process. This gives them the freedom to retrench and find another story they are more willing to tell. Normally in this exercise the message shouldn't change. But if people are clearly telling a story with the intent to avoid telling a story, it's better to change the exercise than to let it fail entirely.

On the other hand, sometimes people just can't handle the whole exercise. They might have known this from the start, but they didn't feel able to say so, and now they're just trying to make it through the day without a disaster. Their feelings about the issues might be more intense than you anticipated. There may be power elements in the room that you had not understood. They may not trust you or their fellow participants as much as you thought they would. If telling people they can retrench doesn't work (and you'll usually be able to tell

Figure 12.49. When people tell "fake" stories created to conceal rather than reveal, pay attention and prepare to give those groups some help.

if that works right away, by the looks on their faces), I would suggest shortening the exercise (claiming poor planning on your part) and moving on to something less threatening.

This situation, in which a deeply probing exercise has to be curtailed because it is more threatening to your participants than you expected, is a perfect example of why you should prepare your session schedule with some flexibility built in. It also explains why you should practice facilitating every exercise you will ever want to use (including some not in this book), even if you don't think you will need them. You never know when you will have to scrap your whole plan and put something else together to suit an unplanned-for contingency. If you get used to thinking of sensemaking sessions not as wholly scripted events but as packages built of scripted portions, you can shift those portions around as the situation requires.

People pay too much attention to story quality

Sometimes people misunderstand this exercise and think you want them to write a screenplay for a critically-acclaimed blockbuster movie. There are two common responses to this misunderstanding: excitement and despair.

When people think they *can* write a great screenplay, they get so excited about making their story perfect (from the perspective of narrative form) that they forget about using the story to make sense of the issues. You'll know this is happening when you hear people debat-

ing which novelist is "the best ever" or which are the "top ten" films of all time. Or when people want more time to practice their story, or more "takes" to polish it.

When people think they *can't* write a great screenplay, they sometimes drift away from the exercise, using up the time discussing issues without building anything. Or they try to learn screenwriting in five minutes, entering into long debates about what Aristotle meant by "poetics" and searching the internet for hot tips on writing screenplays or novels.

If either of these things happens, it will be nobody's fault but your own. When you introduce the exercise, be very careful to avoid any impression that people are creating stories for consumption. Don't even mention that the stories will be recorded until it's time to do that. (If you need people to sign a release form to be recorded, make it a blanket permission; don't mention that they will be recorded *telling a story*. Legally there's no difference, but socially there is.)

I can hear a question you might have right now. In a previous section on people doing the exercise mechanically, I said that you should raise the stakes and tell people that their stories will be evaluated. Now I'm telling you to say that the stories don't matter. Isn't that contradictory advice? No, it isn't.

What you need to communicate to the people who do this exercise is this: the stories they cre-

Figure 12.50. If you frame the selection of the group's storyteller as one of ability or opportunity, people will be more willing to step forward and perform.

ate will matter, but not *as stories*. The stories will matter only if the *process* of building them, telling them, and improving them helps their tellers discover something useful.

I've said elsewhere that stories are both nouns and verbs. The noun part of stories isn't what this exercise is about. It's the *verb* part that matters. If you can get that point across, you will help people understand what they need to do to make this exercise work. *Practice* getting that point across.

If you do experience this reaction to this exercise, you might want to review your introductory remarks after the session to see if something you said led people up the wrong path. (Taping your introductions and reviewing them later, after you know how the session turned out, is a useful way to improve your skills at facilitating sensemaking.)

Nobody wants to tell the story

This is related to people thinking they can't create a story, but it has to do with the actual *performance* of the story. Some groups might put together useful, thought-provoking stories, but when it comes to *telling* the story in front of an audience, they all fight for the right to be silent. Then, when one poor soul has drawn the short straw and is thrust before the audience, they hesitate and stammer and mumble, and even the best story comes across as a muddle. Because the audience can't hear the story or make any sense of it, their reactions are muted, so the group reconvenes with little to think about for the next iteration. This is not conducive to sensemaking.

If you notice groups spending all their time arguing about who "has" to tell the story, here's a little trick that can help move things along (see Figure 12.50). Quietly explain that even though everyone in the group will benefit from the exercise, the people who tell the stories will contribute the most to—and *gain* the most from—from the exercise. This is not a lie. As anybody knows who tells stories a lot (either professionally or because they can't help it), telling a story to an audience and watching the reactions on their faces is extremely beneficial to making sense of things. That's why people go around telling stories all the time, because it helps us think about the challenges we face. Telling stories in this exercise is no different from telling stories in daily life: *it helps us think better*. It follows, then, that the person who tells the story will get more "help thinking better" than anyone else in the group. Looked at in that way, is telling the story a chore to be avoided or an opportunity to be seized?

You can affect the way people see being chosen as their group's storyteller by carefully managing how you talk about the selection. When you introduce the task of choosing a storyteller, don't say, "Next you should choose somebody from your group to tell the story." That sentence sounds like it would work as well for "to walk the plank." Say something more like, "Next you should decide who among you is most suited to tell your story and observe the audience's reactions to it." Or, "Next you should decide who among you gets to represent the group by telling its story." Framing the selection as one of either ability or opportunity (or both) helps

Figure 12.51. Even if you don't plan to use printed question forms for this exercise, it's a good idea to have some on hand in case any particular audience is unresponsive.

get across the message that the storyteller is central to the process and will benefit from that position.

This will also have an impact on the way the storyteller tells the story. A storyteller who is grateful for the chance to represent the group and make discoveries on its behalf will not stammer and mumble. They will be alert to the opportunities before them and make the most of their place in the limelight.

The audience has no response to the story

This problem is related to people thinking they can't build a story, but this time it's the audience who has the wrong idea. Sometimes people become intimidated by the task of responding to a story and can't come up with anything to say about it. After the story there is a dull silence, and when questions are asked, people respond by saying things like, "I thought it was all right?" or "I liked it, I guess." Often this happens because people don't feel qualified to judge a story without being experts in narrative form. As with the above situation with the mumbling storyteller, this situation results in too little thought power to turn the pump of sensemaking.

The best way to get past this problem is to move the audience's thoughts away from performing an evaluation and towards observing naturally occurring phenomena. Everyone reacts to stories, no matter how educated they are about narrative or anything else. Everyone has feelings. Everyone knows whether they have been "struck" with a story or not. Everyone can say whether what they have heard has surprised them. As Lance Bennett famously said, the ba-

sic facts of narrative form are "everyday equipment for living." Make sure you convey to the people acting as audiences that their task is to report not on the story itself but on their *reactions* to the story. How did it strike them? What surprised them? How did it make them feel? Sad? Angry? Confused? Amazed? What did they get out of the story? Did it remind them of any other stories? And so on.

This problem can come up for another reason, which is that the story is an emotional one and the audience feels unable to respond to it out of concern for the storyteller or fear of repercussions if they honestly reveal their feelings about the story. If your topic is sensitive or people with different levels of power will be participating in the session, you might get better results if you give storytellers paper forms for their audiences to fill out (see Figure 12.51). Another method is to have a second person from the group (an observer) ask the questions *after* the storyteller has finished the story *and left the room*. Even a facilitator or helper might be easier to talk to than the person who told the story, especially if it was an emotional one.

The storyteller tells the story but doesn't notice the audience's response

I could have said that having two people visit each other group was a requirement of this exercise. But if you do that, you have to have groups with at least four people in them, so that somebody is still left to be the audience (two people visiting one seems ridiculous). That would mean the minimum session size to use this exercise at all would be twelve people, or fifteen if you want to have three-person audiences. I hate to have to suggest such a limit, because this is such a great exercise for deep exploration of issues.

Still, it *is* better to have two people do the visiting if you can. That way one person can concentrate on telling the story while the other person handles the task of watching the audience's reactions and gathering answers to questions. If you don't have enough people in your session to have observers visit with storytellers, and you notice that the storytellers are having trouble gathering responses, you can extend the discussion period after the storytellings to allow more feedback to come out.

Gathering written answers to questions can help too. Even if you haven't prepared paper forms, you can ask people to write down short answers to questions as they are read out loud, like this: "1. Not really. 2. The cat. 3. Because it was blue." That sort of thing can give groups more to work with after each storytelling, even if the storyteller remembers nothing from the episode.

People don't want their stories recorded

This is a simple one. If people don't want you to record their stories, don't. And don't plan a sensemaking session that will fall apart if people suddenly decide they don't want to be recorded. They have the *right* to withdraw.

However, there are several steps you can take back from full recording which might help you get past an unexpected need for privacy. Maybe people will be willing to *summarize* their story instead of telling the whole thing in detail. Maybe they would be willing to write it down, or write down a summary of it. Maybe they would be willing to let you take some notes and show those outside the session (especially if you let them read and change the notes, and promise not to change them afterward).

Ask people if they can meet you halfway. Tell them about the role the sensemaking session will play in the project. Tell them how their stories will help other people understand the insights they have achieved in the session. Ask them what they can do to help the project succeed without endangering their privacy.

Try it yourself first

This is the hardest of all the exercises in this book to try out on your own. There's no point telling the story to yourself, obviously, because you'd already know what you were going to say in response. And you need two *different* audiences to tell the story twice. Still, you can start practicing the exercise by building the story yourself, then cornering one person after another, telling them the story, and watching their response.

When you're ready to start practicing helping *other* people do the exercise, see if you can get nine people to practice this exercise with you. Maybe they'll do it for donuts or pizza. If that's impossible, you could get away with using only six people. To do this, have two groups of three people, and ask one of the two audience members in each group to sit out the first telling. They should leave the room entirely so they won't hear anything of the story. That way for the second telling, one person listening will have never heard the story before. Doing this, especially if you can do it a few times with different people, will help you understand the process of revision and deeper discovery that makes the exercise work. Look for mini-projects to do where you can help people think while developing your own skills.

Your own style

I was trained as a scientist, and I'm sure to some readers of this book my description of this exercise will come off as dull. That's only *partly* because I'm dull. The other part of it is that I've spent a lot of time trying to get corporate types in corporate meeting rooms to accept this exercise. *Your* style in using and developing this exercise for your own use, and the styles of the participants you help to use the exercise, might vary so much from the way I've described it as to be unrecognizable. That's a *good* thing.

Even though this exercise is the hardest in this book to facilitate, the *idea* behind the exercise is very, very simple. You build stories, drawing inspiration from collected stories; you tell stories; you learn from what happens. What you do with that simple plan is up to you. You could encourage your session participants to play out their stories using costumes, props, and sound effects. You might have them do old-time radio shows, write short stories, or create mime shows. You might even have groups direct other groups to perform stories, or bring in a troupe of professional actors to do the play acting.

On the other hand, you may be even more dull than I am (hard to imagine, but I'm trying to be even-handed here). Or your participants may not want to take even a baby step out of their comfort zones. So you may decide you need to tone down even the small amount of creativity I've described here. That's okay too. Whichever way you change this exercise, just remember to make sure that the storytelling is in the service of the sensemaking, not the other way around.

Where it came from

I first came into contact with the idea of helping people build stories in my work with Dave Snowden and Sharon Darwent. They were using the exercise, in a somewhat more elaborate way, in their narrative consulting for corporations looking to solve problems. I'm not exactly sure where *they* got it from, to be honest, but they were certainly not the first people to help other people create stories. Quite a few facilitators in a range of fields use similar (but not identical) techniques to help people work through issues together. See the next section for some places you can look to find similar methods. I do know, however, that Sharon and Dave improved the method through repeated usage in projects.

In my use of the exercise later on, and in my description of it here, I have made some changes to the exercise I learned from Dave and Sharon. To begin with, I slimmed down and shortened the exercise for use in smaller projects and in smaller time frames. It originally took at least a half-day to complete. I dropped the fixed, fairly complex template we originally used in favor of a variety of templates to suit a variety of needs and backgrounds. In short, I made the exercise simpler, more flexible, and more adaptable to suit a wider range of purposes, because I think that will suit *you* best.

How to find more on these ideas

Every time I think I've found all of the fields that use group storytelling exercises to support sensemaking, I find another one. So I'm not going to pretend I can give you an authoritative list of places to look for more information on group storytelling exercises. I'm just going to point you to what I've found so far.

The field of *participatory theatre* involves people in building stories together that help them think about their communities. In fact, if you read Augusto Boal's book *Games for Actors and Non-Actors*, you will find many of the same ideas as you found in this description of story building. The methods of participatory theatre are more geared toward playing out stories as they are built, but the sensemaking element of them is the same. Viola Spolin also has an excellent book called *Theater Games for the Classroom* that describes many useful theatrical activities, all of which—when used with real stories about one's own community—can aid in sensemaking. (See page 501 for more on participatory theatre.)

The field of *family and community therapy,* especially *narrative therapy* or *drama therapy,* includes exercises in which people build stories. The book *Narrative Therapy in Practice* (edited by Gerald Monk and others) gives several examples of therapists helping people in families talk through the creation of stories to make sense of a situation. Reading some material on narrative community therapy might give you ideas for improving your facilitation of story building using this exercise (or whatever you develop from it). (See page 495 for more on narrative therapy.)

Life coaches and people who help other people write *memoirs* know how to help people build stories from their real experiences. Some professionals even give classes and lessons in how to write one's memoirs. I've had some thoughtful conversations with Jerry Waxler, who gives classes like this, and I've found out that his methods have a lot in common with the exercise I've described here. Jerry's book *Learn to Write Your Memoir* is a good reference for learning more about how life-story methods can aid in sensemaking. Says Jerry on his web site, "Writing your memoir is not only about the past. It provides creative rewards now and in the future." That sounds like sensemaking to me.

Similarly, Yvette Hyater-Adams, a life coach I met who also helps people build stories, says on her web site, "There is power in writing personal stories as a way to fully understand what is unclear within us." Clearly these methods have much in common, and we can learn from finding out more about all of them.

Getting Help Facilitating Sensemaking Exercises

When you are conducting story collection exercises, the best help is logistical, because during story collection you need to focus on getting your stories and annotations recorded. For sensemaking, I would place instructional help (answering questions) first, observational help (taking notes) next, and logistical help (making sure things get done) last. Sensemaking exercises are more cognitively complex than story collection exercises, even if they start with the same basic form. So people are likely to need more help making their way through the tasks. Besides, you can substitute automated recording (audio or video) for note-taking, but you can't automate instructional help.

I suggest taking any helpers you have through their own version of the exercise days or weeks before your session, then quizzing them to make sure they can answer the questions people are most likely to ask during the exercise. Once you have enough instructional help, you can turn to note-taking help next.

Combining Exercises

Once you become comfortable with facilitating each type of sensemaking exercise, you can begin using them *together* to create more complex and productive sensemaking sessions. Because all of the exercises deal with essential narrative forms, they can feed into each other. Figure 12.52 on the next page shows how the inputs and outputs of the five exercises can work together.

I'll go through how each exercise connects with the others.

Twice-told stories

The twice-told stories exercise takes as input all of the collected stories. It produces as output

selected stories from the collection. Thus the "Selected collected stories" box acts as input to all of the exercises *except* the twice-told exercise that created it. All of those exercises can use the main body of collected stories as well, but putting the task of selection first can *focus* the other exercises on stories that will work best to consider the topic chosen.

Timelines and landscapes

The timeline and landscape exercises can take as input all of the collected stories; a selection of collected stories (coming from the twice-told stories exercise or the story elements exercise); or story elements. They produce as output a space filled with meaningful patterns. These spaces can be used for creating story elements and for building composite stories.

Story elements

The story elements exercise can take as input all of the collected stories; a selection of stories chosen using the twice-told stories exercise; a sensemaking space filled by a timeline or landscape exercise; or a complex story built using the composite stories exercise. It produces as output story elements, and it may produce exemplar stories selected from the collected stories to represent story elements. Story elements and exemplar stories can be used as input in any of the building exercises (timelines, landscapes, composite stories). This is another method of selection by which the building exercises can be focused and strengthened.

Composite stories

The composite stories exercise can take as input all of the collected stories; a selection of collected stories (coming from the twice-told stories exercise or the story elements exercise); story elements (which can slot into the story as characters, situations, themes, etc.); or a space filled with meaningful patterns (on which the plot of the composite story can be played out). It produces as output complex built stories. These stories can be used to fuel the process of story element creation.

As you can see, you can focus and strengthen your sensemaking session by building within it a complex of exercises in which each output feeds into another input.

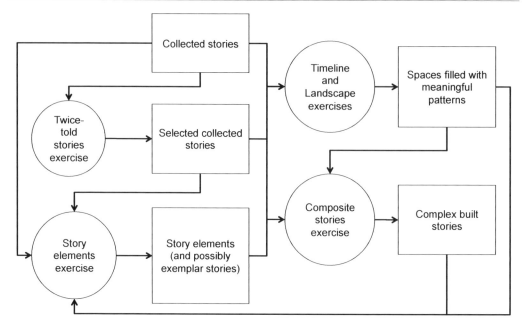

Figure 12.52. The five narrative sensemaking exercises described in this book can be used together, with output from one feeding input to another.

This is not simple work. It requires time, intense facilitation and strong motivation—not to mention help with transferring information from one exercise to another. However, if your needs for sensemaking are great, and you and your participants are motivated, there is much you can achieve by building your session in this way.

I'm not going to explain *how* to link these exercises together, because by the time you have enough experience with the exercises to begin to think about linking them together, you'll have so many great ideas of your own that you won't need my help.

MERGING STORY COLLECTION AND SENSEMAKING

Because story collection and sensemaking are described in separate chapters of this book, you might get the idea that these activities are far apart. They are not. People who are telling stories for collection always do some sensemaking, and people who are considering stories for sensemaking always tell some stories. That's a good thing, and it's something you can use. Injecting a little sensemaking into story collection leads to better collected stories, and injecting a little storytelling into sensemaking leads to better sensemaking.

Sensemaking in story collection

To introduce sensemaking into story collection, wait until your small groups have told some stories prompted by eliciting questions. Give people at least one quarter of the time you have planned for the session to just trade stories without any explicit sensemaking taking place. Then *pause* the storytelling and ask people to participate in a brief sensemaking task of fifteen to thirty minutes. Ask people to string together some of the stories they have just told into a simple timeline or composite story. Give them a few predefined dimensions and ask them to place their stories on a landscape. Have them draw one type of story element from their stories.

After the sensemaking task, people should return to telling stories, only now they should *refer* to whatever they made during the sensemaking *as they tell stories*. How should you ask people to refer to what they built? There are two options, one simpler than the other. The simple option is to ask people to *consider* their creations as they return to telling stories by answering eliciting questions. This is the easiest option for inexperienced facilitators and participants to use.

Constructed artifacts as story elicitation devices

The more complicated option is to ask people to use their creations as story elicitation devices.

Composite or selected stories. A composite story or a selected (twice-told) story can be a launching pad from which people can explore other stories they remember. If the built or selected story doesn't remind people of any stories just as it is, you can help them remember by highlighting themes or goals of the project.

You might say things like:

- When you think of trust in the community, does this story remind you of any experiences you've had?
- Does the level of cooperation in this story remind you of anything you've experienced?
- Do you know anybody who has responded to a crisis the way the doctor responded in this story?
- That man must have really cared about his friends to do that. Have you ever seen friendship like that?

Timelines. Some aspects of timelines that might bring experiences to mind include:

- Gaps: What can you remember happening during this time?
- Turning points: Where in this timeline did things change? Do those changes remind you of any experiences?
- Multiple perspectives: How do you think the immigrants saw this event? Have you heard any stories about their view of it?
- Patterns: Do you notice anything about these stories, and does that remind you of any other experiences?

Landscapes. Some aspects of landscapes that might bring experiences to mind include:

- Clusters: Why are there so many stories about danger here? Does that remind you of any experiences? How about stories of safety?

- Boundaries: Do you see any differences between these stories and those? Do those differences remind you of any experiences?
- Gaps: Why is there nothing in this area? Can you think of any experiences you would place there?
- Official statements: Where on this space would you put the town's motto? Does that bring any experiences to mind?
- Multiple perspectives: Where in this space would this story fall if it was told from the point of view of the criminal? Does putting another note there remind you of any experiences?

Story elements. Using a set of story elements, people can follow up with activities like these:

- Juxtapose elements: What would happen if the Gossip-Mongerer met the Selfless Soul? Does that remind you of any experiences?
- Contrast elements: How is the Hero different from the Worker Bee? Does that remind you of anything that has happened to you?
- Role-play elements: I'm the Opportunist and you're the Unsung Workhorse. What would I say and what would you say? Does that remind you of anything?

Whichever way you move people back into storytelling, you should see stories told after the sensemaking task that probe more deeply into the issues being explored.

Limit the intrusion of the sensemaking task to a quarter or less of the total session time. Also, manage your own expectations about what will happen during the task. Don't expect people to discover anything useful to the project. That's not what the task is for. Its purpose is to help people consider their experiences about the topic in a broader and more insightful way. This will lead to stories that better support sensemaking later on.

You might be wondering where the benefit lies in having people do a sensemaking exercise when you could just have them do a story collection exercise. After all, three of the exercises I've listed here work for either story collection or sensemaking. Why not just build a timeline *as* people tell stories?

When people participate in a story collection exercise, they know *as they tell each story* where it fits into the overall scheme of the timeline or landscape they are building. But when they tell each other stories *before* the exercise is introduced, the stories were not formed in reference to anything. Looking at how previously told stories fit into a sensemaking structure helps people think about the stories told, whether they were told months ago or ten minutes ago. When people have an opportunity to explore the stories they have told, they can think more deeply about the *issues* they are exploring. This in turn helps them tell more useful stories as the session continues. Interleaving storytelling with sensemaking, instead of blending them with a story collection exercise, is most useful when people need extra help thinking more deeply about the issues they are exploring.

Could you have people tell some stories, then start a timeline or landscape exercise with them in sensemaking mode, and then *switch* to filling in the spaces in storytelling mode? Sure. If your groups are motivated and you feel ready to help them do this, switching modes midexercise would be fine. It would only work with timelines and landscapes, since these are the only exercises that lay out spaces to be filled. But for those two exercises you should be able to switch between exploration and elicitation. Just practice the switching process with helpful friends or colleagues before you try facilitating it during a project.

Can you *always* inject sensemaking into storytelling? Not always. It requires strong facilitation experience on your part. Don't try this insertion technique until you have facilitated at least a few group story sessions and sensemaking sessions. When you do try it, remember this: your participants *don't need to know* you've injected anything into anything. Plan the session well and present it to them as a coherent whole. Don't say, "And now we're going to insert some sensemaking into our process." Just say, "Now I'd like you to look at the stories you've just told." They won't know you're splicing together methods; they'll just tell better stories.

Story collection in sensemaking

I talked about *why* to collect stories during sensemaking in the section called "When you can't invite the people you should" (page 365), so I won't repeat the reasons to do so here. You can bring story collection into sensemaking even when everyone who told the original stories is present, but the reasons to do so are less pressing in that case.

How should you mix storytelling into a sensemaking session? Expand the time allocation for any part of the session (or any exercise) in which people are considering stories from the collection. Tell people that as they read or listen to stories, they should feel free to tell stories from their own experiences. When they tell a story, they should give it a name and mark the name down on a sticky note or sheet of paper. That way they'll be able to refer to the story later as they place or use stories. If people are building something with paper, make sure they mark their own stories with a special color or symbol, so patterns that involve "right now" stories stand out in the final creation.

If you want to add the newly told stories to the collection permanently, ask people to tell their stories into small audio recorders, and give them answer sheets to fill out. This is a great way to improve on your story collection if you can pull it off. I wouldn't try recording new stories during sensemaking unless I had one or two reliable helpers I could give the task to (and ignore it afterward). Managing the technical details of recording on top of guiding people through sensemaking can be overwhelming.

Do you need strong facilitation experience to insert storytelling into sensemaking? No, not at all. In fact, I'd say it takes more facilitation skill to *stop* people telling stories during sensemaking than it does to support it! This is an "elaboration" anyone can do from the start. Hold off on *recording* new stories until you feel more confident, but by all means let people add their own stories and use them in their sensemaking. The session will run more smoothly if you do.

BUILD YOUR OWN SENSEMAKING EXERCISE

The five sensemaking exercises I've described here were developed over the course of dozens of sensemaking sessions. All of them came from ideas that have been floating around for millennia, but all of them had to be planned, tested, and improved (and improved, and improved) before they really started to work reliably. But *please* don't think these are all the sensemaking exercises you could do! Many other exercises are possible. I encourage you to develop your own sensemaking exercises.

Here's how to do it. Start with an idea. Get some people together and try it out. Afterwards, think about what worked and what didn't. Try it again. Keep doing that for, well, pretty much forever. That's all there is to it. You don't need to be a "methodologist" to develop methods; anybody can. It just requires patience, thought, and lots of opportunities to work with participants eager to make sense of things. You almost certainly have some unique ideas the world of sensemaking needs; so why not develop them?

What does a good sensemaking exercise need? I can think of four things (see Figure 12.53 on the following page).

Value-free structure

In a sensemaking exercise, people need some kind of framework or form or scaffolding to work with. In the timeline and landscape exercises, this structure is built of spatial dimensions. In the story elements exercise, it is built of similarities and differences. In the composite stories exercise, it is built of named slots in a story template. All of these structures provide a way for people to arrange and combine the meanings they find in stories into larger meanings.

What structure will you provide for people to use? What form will it take? How will it help people assemble meanings? Will it be approachable? Will it make sense? As you test the structure, evaluate whether its use is helping people to arrive at new insights. Have they found out anything using the structure that they couldn't have found out without it? Has it added value to their sensemaking? Or has it stood in the way of understanding?

In addition to being sturdy, a structure for sensemaking must be *value-free*, meaning that no part of the structure should be obviously better than any other part. Sensemaking depends on the *emergence*, not calculation, of meaningful patterns in the things considered. If the placement of items into patterns is predetermined, no sensemaking can take place.

To illustrate the difference between value-laden and value-free sensemaking structures, let's consider two group activities you might conduct in a gymnasium full of people. Let's say you first ask everyone to stand in front of a large marked scale of heights. This is a predetermined placement. Doing the exercise brings no additional insight that could not be gathered from, say, measuring each person independently and collating the responses on paper.

Now consider what would happen if you asked each person to stand in a location that best fits their agreement with a series of statements posted around the room, such as "People should rely on themselves" and "People should depend on each other." The patterns resulting from *this* exercise could not be predicted in advance, even if you knew the people in the room very well. If you asked each person to answer a set of survey questions, you would not get the same result. Why? Because the people in the room wouldn't be human if they didn't negotiate meaning by continually monitoring where they and the others are in the room (while everyone else was doing the same thing). A value-free structure creates a space in which people can negotiate meaning without constraint. In my gymnasium example, if the posted statements had obvious value dimensions to them (such as "People should behave morally" or "People should commit crimes"), it would not be necessary to ask people to go through the exercise at all. The outcome would be predetermined.

Check your sensemaking structure for hidden value determinations. Don't rely on your own instincts here, because you may not see value axes others can. Test the structure by showing it to people and noting how they respond. Are

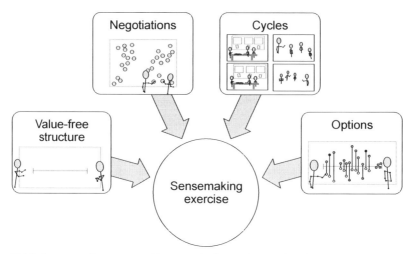

Figure 12.53. Any narrative sensemaking exercise has to have *value-free structure* to support building, *negotiations* to give people something to do together, *cycles* to come back to the topic with new views, and *options* to customize the exercise to many contexts.

they attracted to one part or another? Do they avoid any parts? Why do they do that? What impact might that have on their sensemaking?

Negotiations

In a sensemaking exercise, people need decisions they can make together. They need ranges of possibility that can be narrowed down. They must be able to choose together: Should we do it this way or that way? How far up or down? How much of this or that? How shall we build this?

To create these decision points, there must be some *ambiguity* to be resolved. If all the decisions have been made before the process starts, there won't be anything to negotiate. In the exercises I've described here, the decisions are mostly ones of fitness for placement into structures (or parts of structures), but you can imagine other decisions in other contexts.

In *your* exercise, what will people decide together? What will they negotiate? How will those negotiations have meaning for them? When you test your exercise, pay attention to the things people are talking about. Are they negotiating the things you thought they would? Are they making the decisions you expected?

Cycles

In a sensemaking exercise, people need to circle back and approach the task over and over. If

you look back at the stepwise instructions for the exercises described in this chapter, you'll see that the various portions of the exercises bring people back to consider the same structures again and again. For example, in the building of landscapes, people start by considering the dimensions alone. Then they come back and consider stories on the dimensions. Then they come back and look for patterns in the stories on the dimensions. Then they might (optionally) come back and build new stories using the patterns, stories, and dimensions. Then they get into the "visiting" part of the exercise, which is all about seeing their constructed artifact in a new way through the eyes of others. This pattern of cycling around the central structure is an important part of any sensemaking exercise.

Consider the exercise you are building. Where in the process do people circle around? How many times do they circle around? What is different in each iteration? When you test the exercise, notice how people act during each cycle. Do you see changes? Do people come back to the structure and see it in new ways?

Options

I have presented the exercises in this chapter with many optional elements. That's because every sensemaking session is different. No sensemaking exercise should require people to follow the same steps every time. You might have an hour or a day to work with. Participation might range from engaged excitement to mere toleration. You might be facilitating the exercise for the first time or the hundredth time. The topic might be trivial or life-changing.

Design your sensemaking exercise with expansions and contractions in it from the start. How can your exercise be trimmed down? How can it be expanded? What can facilitators do if they have less time or more time? What can they do if their participants are more or less engaged? Which parts of your exercise are required and which are optional? What would happen if each part was dropped out?

As I said in the "Build your own story collection exercise" section (in the Story collection chapter, page 211), the best tools you can use for developing a sensemaking exercise are a notebook and a tape recorder. While you are working on your new exercise, record or take notes on everything that happens. Capture especially the parts where you tell people what to do next and they respond and start to work. Later, review what went well and what didn't. Every time you do the exercise you should change something, and you should learn from what happened. In this way the exercise will keep growing as you continue to use it and begin to rely on it.

Finally, make sure you tell other people how to do your new exercise! Don't keep it bottled up. Send it out into the world so it can help other people make sense of things too.

SUMMARY

Sensemaking exercises are packages of activity you can ask participants in your sensemaking session to carry out to focus and strengthen their sensemaking. Five exercises are covered in the chapter: twice-told stories, timelines, landscapes, story elements, and composite stories.

1. In a *twice-told stories* exercise, people in small groups consider previously collected stories while choosing one or more stories from among those considered to retell more widely.

2. In a *timelines* exercise, people build linear progressions of events, factual and/or fictional, from a combination of stories previ-

ously collected and stories told during the exercise.

3. In a *landscapes* exercise, people define a two-dimensional space with meaningful dimensions, then populate the space with previously collected stories. As the stories fill the space, a landscape of features comes into view. People describe these features, discuss them, and tell stories about them.

4. In a *story elements* exercise, people list things like characters, situations, themes, and values, then cluster and re-cluster them into families of elements that together encompass the combined meaning of the stories, usually in ways that reveal useful discoveries about the topic of concern. People describe and discuss the elements.

5. In a *composite stories* exercise, groups use collected stories as source material to build a purposeful story, fictional or semi-fictional, which they tell to other groups. As they build and tell stories, people discuss the juxtapositions of meaning created.

You can combine exercises by using the output of one exercise as the input to another. You can bring storytelling into sensemaking and sensemaking into storytelling. You can build your own sensemaking exercises by creating a *value-free structure, negotiations, cycles,* and *options* for people to use.

QUESTIONS

(These first three questions are identical to the ones in the "Group Exercises for Story Collection" chapter, for the simple reason that they have the same utility here as they do there.)

Are you familiar with any group exercises from work in other areas? Have you ever used an icebreaker exercise, for example, or started a group game, or ran a debate, or got people to brainstorm about something? How do the exercises in this chapter differ from what you have done before?

Do any parts of the exercises in this chapter seem particularly challenging to facilitate? Do any parts seem like they will be interesting or motivating to you? Do any parts seem trivial or dull? If you were to customize these exercises so that they perfectly fit your style of doing things, what changes would you make?

Think about people who might be involved in a sensemaking session you might facilitate in your community or organization. How would these exercises go over with them? What parts might they find exciting, empowering, boring, worthless? If you were to customize these exercises so that they perfectly fit your community or organization, what changes would you make?

(Now some questions that pertain specifically to sensemaking exercises.)

In the chapter before this one, I described four essential elements of narrative sensemaking: contact, churning, convergence, and change. In this chapter I described five sensemaking exercises. But I never brought the two chapters together, did I? I never said how each exercise creates contact, churning, convergence, and change. Why don't *you* do that? How, in your opinion, does each of these five exercises create contact, churning, convergence, and change?

Did you find this chapter overwhelming? Does it seem like you will never be able to facilitate such complicated exercises as these? If so, which parts of the chapter did you find most daunting? Which parts of the "What can go wrong" sections do you think would be the worst disasters? Conversely, if this chapter seemed simple and easy to you, what do you think you could *add* to it? How could you make these exercises even more productive of effective narrative sensemaking?

ACTIVITIES

(These first three activities are identical to the ones in the "Group Exercises for Story Collection" chapter because they have the same utility here as they do there.)

Go back to each "try it yourself" section in this chapter and do what it says there. Gather some stories to work with, then select a story to retell, build a timeline, create a landscape, derive some story elements, and build a composite story. Then go back and reread the sections on each exercise. How does facilitating each ex-

ercise seem different now? What would you like to try next?

After you have tried each exercise yourself, try helping a small group of friends or colleagues carry out each exercise. What happens differently in a group than by yourself? What do you need to do before you will be ready to facilitate these exercises in a story session that is part of a project?

In the questions above, I asked what you might do if you were to customize these exercises for your own style and for your community or organization. Choose one of the exercises, make some changes to it, and try it out with some people in your community or organization. Take notes on what you learn from doing this.

(Now some activities that pertain specifically to sensemaking exercises.)

Do you remember, in the section of Chapter Five called "Meeting challenges," how I mentioned a study done by David Boje in which he identified "functional patterns" in organizational stories at an office-supply distribution firm? (You can find the section on page 67.) Go back to that section now and review the story types Boje found. Can you match each of his story types with a sensemaking exercise covered in this book? (Extra: Find a copy of Boje's paper, read his descriptions of his story types, and think some more about connections between the stories as negotiated in conversation and the organized exercises described here.)

In his book *Sensemaking in Organizations*, Karl Weick lists seven "functions of stories for sensemaking" thus:

1. Stories aid comprehension because they integrate that which is known about an event with that which is conjectural.
2. Stories suggest a causal order for events that are originally perceived as unrelated and akin to a list.
3. Stories enable people to talk about absent things and to connect them with present things in the interest of meaning.
4. Stories are mnemonics that enable people to reconstruct earlier complex events.

5. Stories can guide action before routines are formulated and can enrich routines after those routines are formulated.

6. Stories enable people to build a database of experience from which they can infer how things work.

7. Stories transmit and reinforce third-order controls by conveying shared values and meaning.

Consider each of these seven functions in relation to the sensemaking exercises described in this chapter. For example, in which exercises do stories help people integrate fact and conjecture? If your answer is "all of them," build a "top three" ranked list of exercises for each function.

Are there any of Weick's story functions you *can't* find considered in these exercises? If so, think up a sensemaking exercise that might work to bring that function of stories into sensemaking. What would people do?

Write out schedules for two fictional sensemaking sessions, one without exercises and one with exercises. Describe how you plan to achieve the sensemaking goals of contact, churning, convergence, and change within each schedule.

Design a schedule for a fictional sensemaking session in which these exercises are combined, with the output from one feeding into the input for another. Include at least three exercises in your schedule, and make sure some are more elaborate than others (perhaps using one as an icebreaker to get people warmed up at the start).

Find at least three group exercises described in books or on the internet that seem like they will work for narrative sensemaking. Try looking for things like brainstorming, affinity mapping, concept mapping, participatory theatre, theatre games, and so on. Compare those exercises to the exercises described in this chapter. What can you learn from the comparison? If those exercises and these exercises learned from each other, how could each group come away working better?

Come up with a plan for your own sensemaking exercise. It can be simple, and you don't have to actually use it. Just try making a plan. Come up with something that meets all the requirements for a sensemaking exercise (value-free structure, negotiations, cycles, and options). Write a brief set of instructions for how to use the exercise. Include a "what can go wrong" section in which you imagine the exercise failing. If you like, ask some friends to help you try out the plan, then describe what happened.

Chapter Thirteen

Narrative Intervention

This chapter covers the intervention phase of a PNI project, which comes after sensemaking is complete and before (or as) stories return to the community or organization. Because intervention is an optional phase, it will not take place in every project. For the same reason, it is more likely to include the help of outsiders than the internal phases of collection, sensemaking, and return. The chapter starts with thirteen ideas on narrative interventions you can carry out, and ends with three interviews with colleagues experienced in narrative intervention.

Intervention is about spreading the change that started in your PNI project throughout the whole community or organization, and maybe even beyond it. Many interventions might come about as a result of carrying out a PNI project. Policies might be changed; laws might be passed; data might be gathered; funding might be approved; groups might be formed; permissions might be granted. I will not write about any of those things in this chapter, because those things are beyond the scope of this book. I will only speak of *narrative* interventions, that is, *actions whose purpose is to intervene in the flow of stories*.

What does it mean to intervene in the flow of stories? It means doing something that changes the way stories are told and heard and retold. Note that a narrative intervention does not necessarily involve *telling* stories. There are many other ways to have a positive impact on story flow, as I hope to show you in this chapter.

IDEAS FOR INTERVENTION

In the sections that follow are thirteen ideas for narrative interventions you can carry out in your community or organization. These are not detailed sets of instructions, just ideas to inspire you. I *can't* give you detailed instructions on narrative intervention, because I have done far less work in this area than I have done in project planning, story collection, catalysis, sensemaking, and return. I haven't *avoided* intervention; I just happened to end up doing other things.

A few of the thirteen intervention ideas I list here I've worked on myself. Some I've helped other people carry out behind the scenes. Some I have discussed and even planned but never implemented due to limited time or participation or resources. Some I have suggested to clients but don't know whether they followed my suggestions, did something else, or did nothing at all. Some describe projects colleagues have told me about. Some I have read about in books and journals and on the internet.

This chapter, more than any other, brings in ideas from fields you might not realize are connected to PNI, like community theatre and narrative therapy. I don't consider myself a practitioner in those fields, but I'm confident that learning a bit about them and getting pointers to where you can learn more will improve your PNI practice, as it has mine. I hope this chapter will inspire you to expand the scope of your imagination when it comes to working with stories.

I have divided the thirteen intervention ideas into three groups: listening to stories that need to be told, getting stories to where they need to go, and helping people work with stories.

INTERVENTIONS FOR LISTENING TO STORIES THAT NEED TO BE TOLD

Interventions in this category involve targeted listening to stories. They are useful when your project has identified situations in which people need to be heard after the project's main story collection phase has ended.

Narrative ombudsmen

A common outcome of sensemaking in PNI projects is the identification of *crisis points,* or places where people face situations too difficult to resolve alone. Often the stresses created by these crisis points radiate out to affect many other people in the community.

The idea of an ombudsman or advocate as a representative of people in crisis arose thousands of years ago. Today ombudsmen in many communities and organizations help people register complaints, find help, and mediate disputes. When ombudsmen know how to listen to stories, they can help those in need feel *heard* as well as *helped.* This is especially true when people believe that "nobody cares" about the particular problems or people involved. In addition, an ombudsman who has been trained in listening to stories will be able to arrive at deeper understandings of problem contexts than they will if they only collect statements of fact.

When is a narrative ombudsman a useful intervention in a PNI project? When you discover needs that can be met or problems that can be averted with a small amount of help given to the right person at the right time. For example, say people *should* theoretically be able to work their way through a complicated process, like starting a small business or choosing a long-term care facility for family members, but in your project you learned that people often get lost in the process and give up, causing larger problems later on. In such cases an ombudsman can help to resolve problems as they start. A *narrative* ombudsman can also gather *experiences* related to the problems so that other people can be helped before they need the attention of an ombudsman—perhaps with better informational resources or changes to an unwieldy process.

As I was writing this section, I wondered whether ombudsmen *already* elicit stories. So I did a little survey. I searched the internet for the words "ombudsman form" and looked at the first fifty forms I found.

A form used to explain a problem to an ombudsman typically has three parts, which taken together tell a story about the past, present, and future of the problem, thus.

1. What is the problem? (What happened?)
2. What attempts have been made to fix the problem? (What have you done? What have others done?)
3. What is your desired outcome? (What do you want the ombudsman to do to help you?)

For each of the fifty ombudsman forms I found online, I marked whether there were questions in each section about:

1. facts ("Describe the problem" or "Who was involved?")
2. feelings ("How did the problem impact you?" or "How do you feel about the problem?")
3. opinions ("What do you think the office did wrong?" or "Who was at fault, in your opinion?")
4. stories ("What happened?" or "What did you do?")

I should tell you that this little survey has some unique characteristics that make it far from reliable as to proof. First, I looked at only the first fifty forms that came up on Google, for whatever reason. Second, I passed over descriptions of advocacy that told people how to contact an ombudsman in person, without a form. Third, I wasn't able to survey any forms that proceeded in a step-wise fashion (enter your name, then click Next) since I was not actually intending to use the forms. Fourth, I only looked at forms written in English. So the best story elicitations might have remained undiscovered by my search.

Still, looking only at forms I could review in full, Figure 13.1 on the next page shows what I found. The percentages on the graph are for each section separately. In total, people were asked about the problem sixty-three times; about attempts at fixing it twenty-seven times; and about desired outcomes thirty-four times. (The reason people were asked about the problem sixty-three times in fifty forms is because

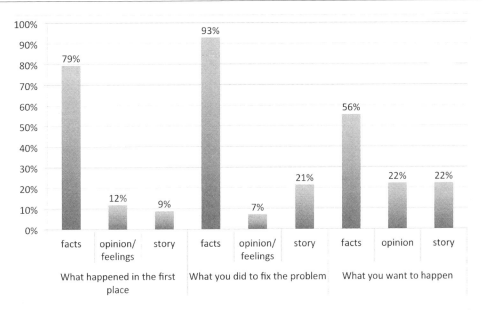

Figure 13.1. Elements present in fifty ombudsman help web forms. Relatively few forms elicited stories about the original incident.

some forms asked for multiple things within one section, like both facts and opinions.)

In the part of the form that asked people to describe the problem, only nine percent of the questions asked for a story. However, when people were asked about attempts to fix the problem or about desired outcomes, almost a quarter of the elicitations were narrative in nature.

This lack of openness to up-front storytelling was easy to see in many of the forms I read. I'll show you one example of a pattern I saw over and over. Here's an excerpt from an ombudsman form for a city health department.

- Describe the reason(s) for requesting a formal complaint. Please be specific by including names, dates, and times, whenever possible.
- Have you tried to resolve the problem(s) before requesting the Formal Complaint? If yes, please describe what you have done to try to resolve the problem and include the results.
- What would you like to see happen to resolve this complaint?

The participant is asked to tell a story about what happened when they tried to resolve the problem ("describe what you have done"). They are asked to tell a story about what might happen in the future ("What would you like to see happen"). But when they are asked about whatever it was that *started* the whole problem, they are asked only for a "reason" and for "dates." The admonition "please be specific" almost reads as "please don't tell us *what actually happened.*"

My guess is that the people who wrote these forms were more comfortable asking for stories when the topic wasn't what happened in the first place. They probably didn't even realize they were censoring storytelling. But you see, allowing people to describe what happened to them in the first place is *just* what can have the strongest positive impact! The chance to tell someone *what happened and how it felt at the time* is a big part of what people are looking for when they go to an ombudsman, whether they can admit it or not. Not only does asking what happened help people feel heard, it helps the ombudsman understand contextual details surrounding the incident that can help them bring more appropriate help to the situation. Forms that ask people to "be specific" and "describe your reasons" often collect everything *but* the real story.

You might say that a "just the facts" question might be used to route the problem to an appropriate office in a large bureaucracy, but I saw the same pattern in organizations and communities of varying sizes.

Here's another ombudsman form that puts the story elicitation in the wrong place. It's from an environmental department in a U.S. state. The form asks:

- Against which [department] employee, program, practice or process do you wish to complain?
- When did it come to your attention?
- What is the decision or matter about which you complain?
- What result do you hope to achieve with your complaint?
- Have you already contacted [the department] in order to resolve the problem?
- If so, whom did you contact? When? What happened?

There is story elicitation here (the "what happened" in the last question), but it is situated in the "why haven't you fixed this yourself" section, and there it sounds more like an attack than an elicitation. It's not fair to ask people to tell a story about what *they* did but not allow them to explain *what happened to them*. And it's certainly not helpful.

This form, from an Australian government office, is the closest thing to a truly narrative ombudsman form I found in my (admittedly brief) search. It asks:

- What happened?
- Where did the events take place? When? Who was involved?
- Were there any witnesses to these events? Have you included their details?
- Do you have any medical evidence, photographs or documents which may be relevant?
- Have you taken any action already in relation to your complaint? What happened?
- What action or outcome would you like to see as a result of your complaint?

This is a story-eliciting form at all three points of importance: initial event, steps taken by the applicant, desired outcome. Granted, that last question could have read, "What would you

like to happen?" but this is pretty close to perfect. I would guess that this particular ombudsman's office has an easier time helping people than many of the others whose forms I looked at. That first, simple, open-ended question, sitting all by itself, vulnerable, inviting, reassuring, probably results in a higher satisfaction level for anyone using this form than for people using any of the other ombudsman forms I surveyed. It takes courage to ask people a simple question like *what happened*. But it works.

Narrative suggestion boxes

Many communities and organizations already have suggestion boxes, but few use them to give people permission to talk about *what has happened* to them and what they'd like to see happen. Making just that small change to the way in which suggestions and complaints are collected is a valid intervention in the flow of stories. Suggestion boxes, like ombudsmen, are used by people in need, and people in need *always* have stories to tell.

Whether physical or virtual, suggestion boxes are particularly useful in projects which have suggested but not quite surfaced tensions (and resolutions) running in undercurrents in the organization (see Figure 13.2 on the facing page).

Using narrative suggestion boxes to listen to stories does three useful things. It opens up richer channels of communication, so that whoever is reading the suggestions can understand better what people truly need. It helps the people who are complaining or suggesting to do a little bit of sensemaking as they communicate. And it creates new stories about the nature of the community's response to complaints and suggestions.

Let's pretend that during the sensemaking phase of your project you discovered five needs important to your community or organization. Say that two of the needs are strong and focused. They are needs people are willing and motivated to solicit help in resolving. For those needs you might appoint an ombudsman who listens to stories in order to help people.

But let's say the other three needs you have uncovered are less obvious. Perhaps they are represented by vague rumors or mentioned

Figure 13.2. Giving people permission to tell stories as they register complaints and suggestions helps those in charge understand their needs better, helps people think through their problems better, and helps to spread the word that the suggestion box is not just a trash bin.

only obliquely. Still, you think there may be something worth looking into. Setting up an ombudsman for those needs might result in skepticism or distrust rather than resolution of any problems. So instead, you set up an anonymous story suggestion box specifically related to those three "undercurrent" needs. It might be a web form or phone number or paper form people can use to speak out about the issues without having to supply identifying information.

The form might read something like this:

- Which of these things would you like to tell us about? Something that *has* happened? Something that *could* happen? Could *never* happen? *Should* happen? Should *stop* happening?

- What was it that happened? (Or that could or couldn't or should or shouldn't happen?)
- How do you feel about what you've just told us?
- Who do you think needs to hear about this?
- If you told us about a problem, who do you think should solve it?
- If you told us about a solution, who do you think can make it work?
- Is what you described something common, or is it unique?
- (and so on)

Your intervention has now become an interim mini-project whose next step will be sensemaking around the stories collected. Say you gather so many stories about one of the three needs, and those particular stories cry out so loudly to be heard and considered, that you decide to conduct another full-blown project around the need, with an aim toward bringing it out into the open and getting ideas on how to meet it.

Has your anonymous suggestion-box story collection done anything more than give you information about potential projects you might carry out in the future? Of course it has. The very fact that you have established and advertised a story listening device specifically for the needs you tentatively discovered has altered the stories people are telling each other about it. People who have seen notices about the narrative suggestion box have spoken to those who haven't. People who have told stories have told others about their experiences. If your questions on the suggestion box web form or phone interface have been respectful and open, people have noticed that. If your questions have been defensive or dismissing, people have noticed that.

Your solicitation of stories through your story suggestion box has been an intervention in the flow of stories. The return phase of your project (and the planning phase of the next) will be influenced by it. If you've done the intervention well, it should have had a positive impact on the needs you discussed, whether you follow up the intervention with another project or not. Not only that, but your ability to carry out a follow-up project will be affected by how you carried out the intervention. For example, it will affect whether you can get people to participate in storytelling or sensemaking sessions. Such interventions can make projects possible that would have failed without such preparation, and they can alert you to dangers you would never have seen otherwise.

Story-sharing spaces

The third type of listening intervention I want to mention is that of setting up a space in which people can tell the stories they need to tell, but *not* for the purpose of collection. In a story-sharing space, people tell stories simply *because they need to tell them to somebody.*

Why should your community or organization invest in helping people tell stories if the stories won't be used for future projects? Because some of the needs that surface in PNI projects can never be met. Sometimes there is no fix to be found, and nothing can be done but to help people cope with the difficult situations they face. When that happens, giving people a place to share their experiences with each other provides a different kind of help than solving their problems or changing policies. The ability and permission to share stories with people who have similar problems helps people feel that they are not alone. It helps them process what has happened to them. It helps them find emotional support and internal strength. It helps them cope.

You can find stories like these all over the internet: just type in the name of any medical condition and "tell us your story." The Christopher and Dana Reeve Foundation has such a site at christopherreeve.org (under "Success stories"). The blurb on the site explains exactly what a story-sharing space is for:

> Telling your story is one way to let anyone touched by paralysis know that they are not alone.

> We've created a place where you can share your journey for your benefit, and the benefit of others. Your story matters. Share it.

The most important thing to remember in setting up a story-sharing space to help meet an unmeetable need is to *keep your hands off it.* You will probably do a lot of work on the setup of the space, but afterward you should back off. Make it possible for people to share stories in a way that is both safe and meaningful to them. Ask people meaningful questions about their stories, then make it possible to search on the answers to those questions. That will help people find the stories they need to hear as well as tell. Then *stay out* of the space.

I don't mean you can't look at the stories or observe what people do, but don't force people into complex sensemaking about the stories they are sharing. Let *them* decide how they want to use the space. You can *offer* help in doing mini-projects with sensemaking in them, but don't make it seem like people are doing anything "wrong" or "not good enough" by simply using the space to share their experiences.

And don't limit the storytelling by calling the stories "Success stories." Let the people who need the space define what it will be for them. I'll say more about supporting meaningful story exchange in the return chapter (page 565), but *creating* such a story-sharing space in the first place fits into the realm of intervention.

INTERVENTIONS FOR GETTING STORIES TO WHERE THEY NEED TO GO

My second category of narrative intervention is about taking some or all of the stories you have collected in your project and bringing them to the attention of someone: either everyone in your community or organization, or some groups of people who most need to hear them.

Narrative orientations

When people enter your community or organization, or when they enter into some group or activity within it, they don't know what to expect. Presenting people with collected stories that help them understand ground rules can help ease transitional difficulties. A narrative orientation is an effective intervention in projects where difficulty getting started with some process or in some group comes up often as a barrier.

Narrative orientations don't have to be fancy. A sheet of paper with "the ten stories you need to hear as you join our community" can be as useful as a documentary with high production values. What is important is that the stories represent real experiences recounted by real people in the community or organization, not engineered fantasies of what you want people to think about the community or organization.

Here's an example of such a narrative orientation from a web site that provides news related to the legal profession. (I've removed some identifying details.)

> [We] will be hosting an "Unofficial Orientation to Law School" [over video chat]. This three-part series will help [new law students] navigate the application process and the first year of school and hopefully steer them towards an actual

lawyer job, without the crippling debt. Confirmed guest panelists for the Hangouts include professors from [two law schools], [law firm] hiring partners and associates, and current law students.

> We are looking for help from those of you who have already cleared the major hurdles of a legal career: by getting into law school, by succeeding academically, and by landing a job.

> We are looking for three categories of stories:

> 1. What was your law school application strategy? Did you retake [the entrance exam]? How did you decide where to apply? How did you choose which school to attend? Did/do you plan to transfer?

> 2. What was your strategy for academic success? Did you join a study group? Did you buy commercial outlines or [textbooks]? Did you use a tutor or coach?

> 3. How did you find a job? [Interviewing?] Networking with student groups? Random luck?

> So this goes out to all the success stories out there in Lawland: Share your stories with us.

> Your stories may be used in the hangouts anonymously, or with the submittor's permission.

If these people were to ask *me*, I would beg and plead with them to include stories of failure as well as success. And not just from lawyers! Also from people who wanted to be lawyers but gave up trying. Telling half the story isn't even half as useful as gathering all perspectives on the endeavor. The goal of a narrative orientation is not to sell anything to anyone. It is to prepare people to participate fully in the community or organization. To do that they need to know the peaks *and* valleys of the landscape.

You can work preparation for this type of intervention into your sensemaking sessions. Once people have spent enough time with your collected stories, ask them to choose some that "every newcomer needs to hear to understand our community." Make sure they consider the community's weaknesses and faults as well as its successes.

Narrative learning resources

A narrative learning resource is just a learning resource with real stories from real people in it. Combining how-to information with stories grounded in the reality of experience can help people get a better start on building their own bases of experience.

This type of intervention is most useful in projects in which a lack of information or knowledge is a barrier, or when people face difficult tasks for which information may be available but questions remain. To test whether a narrative learning resource is a good intervention for your project, consider whether you heard people say anything like this in your story collection or sensemaking phases.

- I knew what I needed to do, but I wasn't sure how to put it all together.
- This topic is so overwhelming! There is information everywhere, but I haven't been able to figure out how to get started.
- If only I could sit next to somebody who has really *done* this, I'm sure I'd be able to pick it up. But it's hard starting from nothing but the facts.
- I know what I'm doing *now,* but at first I floundered around for a long time not knowing what to do.
- I thought I knew how to do this already, but I learned so much from this story session!

These kinds of statements imply an excess of information combined with a lack of understanding. That last example in particular, of people expressing gratitude for what they have learned during a story collection or sensemaking session, is a sure indicator that a narrative learning resource would be a helpful intervention. When you ask people to tell you stories and they tell you how much they've learned from the *other* people in the session, you've found a need to learn.

I worked on a project like this once at IBM Research. We collected stories about the patent process from researchers who pursued patents for IBM. We used the stories both to improve

institutional support for the patent process and to enhance a learning resource about it. In the learning resource, each page of how-to information was linked to a number of real-life stories that related to it, and each story was linked to several how-to pages. From what I heard, people using the resource found that the stories added depth to their understanding of the process. (This project is further described as "Incorporating narrative into e-learning" in the "PNI Stories" section in *More Work with Stories.*)

Sometimes the stories you already collected will suffice to help people learn what they need to know. Sometimes a small extra collection is needed to bolster the collection in some areas. But the project itself often paves the way toward building such a learning collection. One strategy is to keep a look out for people in your story collection and sensemaking sessions who have had a lot of first-hand experience with the topic. At the end of the session, ask them if they would be willing to help out with an additional interview or group session in which you focus on the lessons they've learned about the topic. Make sure you ask them about the mistakes they've made as well as their successes, because those will be just as important to the learning resource.

Narrative simulation

This category takes participation one step further by not just telling stories but *immersing* people in them. Narrative simulation is called for when you uncover a need for the development of skills around a complex task. It is especially called for when you have found a dangerous excess of confidence around existing skills, meaning that people *think* they know how to do something but don't, in a way that creates danger for themselves and others (see Figure 13.3 on the next page).

Simulations can help people learn to do complicated yet dangerous procedures in safety. Adding stories to simulation engages people in the learning task and helps them remember what they learned afterward. There is a large academic literature on the creation of narrative simulations for education and training in a variety of applications. Search for the terms "serious play" or "serious games," the "gamification"

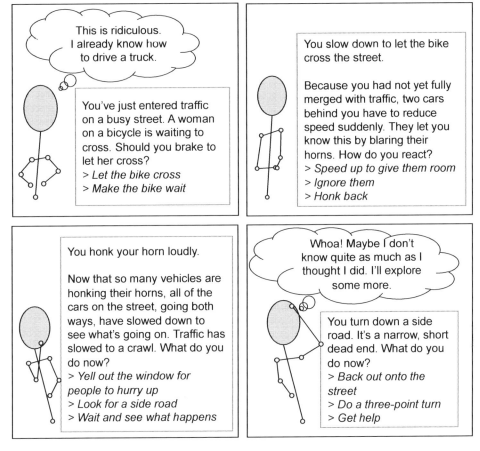

Figure 13.3. Narrative simulations are useful interventions when people think they know how to do something (usually something complex) better than they really do.

of learning, and "case-based" or "story-based" simulation to find out how to create participatory narrative training experiences.

An example is the STAR-LITE simulation created to help students learn about laboratory safety. Says the STAR-LITE web site:

> Work with your colleagues (some humanoid, some not) to complete quests in a lab. The STAR-LITE laboratory can be chaotic and safety violations will occur. You will make critical safety decisions to ensure that you and your colleagues work safely in a lab. STAR-LITE (Safe Techniques Advance Research — Laboratory Interactive Training Environment) is an innovative and groundbreaking method to learn about laboratory safety techniques.

My husband and son went through this simulator together. The combination of silly alien blob-people and true-to-life laboratory safety procedures helped my son learn important facts about laboratory safety in a memorable way. This might seem like your typical educational resource, but the STAR-LITE program is more like a PNI intervention than you might think. The simulation was developed in memory of a young woman who died after contracting a deadly virus in a laboratory. Thus the impetus to develop STAR-LITE grew out of sense-making about real events within the community of research scientists.

I can tell you about another narrative training simulation that had an impact on my work. When I worked at IBM more than a dozen years ago, I met several people who used narrative in their work. One of these people was Peter Orton. Peter builds educational resources for IBM employees. He came to IBM after writing television screenplays and studying narratology. One of the many things Peter created for IBM was a narrative training simulation whose goal was to help people develop better management skills.

When I heard about this simulation I wanted to try it, because I was eager to learn about all possible uses of stories. So I tried out Peter's creation. In the simulation, you took on the role of a manager in charge of several employees. At that time I had never tried to manage anybody, but I was pretty sure I knew how. I *didn't* know how. In the simulation, I failed to make the right choices over and over. An employee needed encouragement and I didn't give it; an employee needed more autonomy and I micro-managed them; an employee needed my support in a dispute and I didn't notice until it was too late to help.

I learned something unique and irreplaceable by playing that little game: that managing people isn't as simple as I thought it was. I don't think I would have come to that realization as fully if I had read about management in a book. That's what narrative simulations are best at: giving people new experiences that overturn what they *think* they know about something.

So let's say you have decided that your community or organization is badly in need of a narrative simulation built around a set of critical skills. How should you go about building it? Here's what I'd do.

1. Gather some people in a room for a sensemaking and design session. Make sure some of them know a lot about the skill set and some know very little. If some of the people have already participated in a general sensemaking session for the project, that's even better.

2. Before the session, go through your collected stories and pull out those that have to do with the skill set you want to help people develop or improve. You should have at least thirty stories, preferably fifty or more, for the session. If you don't have enough stories, see if you can do a few interviews to add more stories you can use.

3. As the session starts, manage the contact between people and stories as you usually would for a sensemaking session. Encourage people to tell their own stories in response to the stories they see.

4. Now get people talking about the *skills* they see people using, or not using, in the stories. Ask them to list some skills, or needs for skills, on sticky notes. (Use different colored sticky notes for skills and needs.) You can guess what's coming next, right? After people have written down all of the skills and needs they can find in the stories, ask them to cluster them. Those clusters will become the parts of your simulation.

5. In some cases you might want to cluster twice, as you do for story elements. Whether you need this depends on how much emotion and nuance are involved in learning about the skill set. If there are people skills involved, such as for example in management, you might want to turn the clustering crank round again to get past simple responses. To turn the crank, ask people to describe their clusters with attributes, then cluster the attributes into a second set of clusters.

6. Ask the group to discuss each cluster they have created. Ask them to find some stories from the collection that exemplify each cluster well. Ask them if those stories remind them of any other stories. Ask the experienced participants to reflect on what obstacles they faced in learning the skills described in each cluster. Ask the novices to reflect on what challenges they face now, what they hope for and what they fear as they look forward to learning the skills. Record this conversation.

7. Take all of what you have recorded from the session and use it to build a series of scenarios in which people find themselves as they go through the simulation.

A simulation doesn't have to involve actors with scripts or computers with programs. You can build one on paper. Have you ever seen a "choose your own adventure" story? They were popular when I was a teenager. They came in paperback form. Every few pages they had a question like, "Should Nathaniel charge at the dragon or run away to get help? If he should charge, turn to page 28. If he should get help, turn to page 125." That's all you have to do to create a narrative simulation. Use the stories from your session to build vignettes in which participants find themselves in situations where they need to use the skills you want them to develop.

After you describe each situation, give participants a choice of two or more options. Have each option deliver them to a new location in the resource: a card or page or screen. The simplest such resource will have only one level of situations, with each choice dead-ending in a resolution. But if you work at it you can create a branching tree of choices. If Nathaniel runs to get help, should he ask the distant fairy queen for help, or should he take his chances with the nearby evil sorcerer? As he runs towards the house of the distant fairy, should he stop to pick some magical herbs? And so on.

Once you've built your set of story dilemmas and resolutions, test it by asking people who came to your design session to play the game. If you can, create and test the game in the session itself. That requires more time than people may be willing to give you, but it can't hurt to ask. Even if you plan to create a multimedia resource later with cartoons and voice-overs, testing a paper prototype can help you improve what you have built before you start spending money.

When you release the game to the entire community or organization, be sure to provide plenty of options for sending feedback, including encouraging people to tell their own stories about learning the skill set. Those new stories can fuel an even better version of the simulator in the future.

A narrative simulation that grows out of stories collected in a PNI project will be grounded in the reality of experience both in its content and in its intent. This will help people come to understandings that are relevant to the challenges they face.

Narrative presentations

This type of intervention is about bringing selected stories from a story collection to the attention of people in the community or organization. Narrative presentations can feature stories that surfaced during sensemaking as being particularly important to the project, because they bring together important issues (pivot stories), highlight views people need to hear (voice stories), or explain things about the community or organization (discovery stories).

Narrative presentations can vary widely in scope and complexity. For example:

- You might post some stories on your community bulletin board. Maybe you replace the stories with new ones from the collection every week or month, and people get into the habit of checking to see "what people have to say" lately.

- You might enlist local young people to work with an artist on a mural that incorporates excerpts from some of the most important stories into a "who we are" reminder of what draws the community together.

- You might hire a documentary team to create "the people say" videos in which actors read out selected stories (exactly as they were told) while montages of contextually appropriate images play out and music sets the tone. The documentaries might be placed on a web site, shown at meetings, or referred to in discussion forums. (It would be better to have the original storytellers speak than to use actors, but if you have guaranteed anonymity you won't be able to find the original storytellers.)

- You might hire a professional storyteller to coach your leaders in telling stories inspired by collected stories at various formal occasions. It is important if you use this method not to have the leaders simply *tell* collected stories. They should review all the stories available for retelling, choose one that appeals to them, then practice telling a story from their *own* experience that resonates with the one they read. In this way the story they tell will be genuine.

These are just a few of many possible ways of telling stories from your collection. As I've said before, telling stories is not my area, so I can't offer you advice on how to do these things beyond saying that the original stories should be respected and not "cleaned up" or changed.

You're in luck, though, because plenty of other people have written advice on how and why to tell stories in organizational and community settings. The field is called "organizational storytelling." If you look up those words you will find many books and other resources on how to tell stories for a variety of reasons.

I'm not going to recommend any books to start with in organizational storytelling, because I don't feel I can. I have *started* to read a few books about telling stories, but I've never been able to *finish* any. Those and the books on narrative inquiry sit mostly unread on my bookshelves. I understand that there are good reasons to try to influence people, I really do. When telling stories is done with respect and care, it can work wonders. When you need to communicate something deep and complex, telling a story is the best way to do it. But the power of purposeful storytelling comes with a price, and that price is danger.

When you engage in purposeful organizational or community storytelling, the biggest dangers are manipulation and distrust. These two are like twin giants smashing their way through the land of purposeful storytelling hand in hand. When I see titles of books and blog posts like "how to use stories to get your audience right where you want them" and "how to hack cultures with stories" and "how to win with stories" and "how to use stories to motivate people to follow your vision for the future," I cringe because I know the twins are near.

While I don't like visiting the land of organizational storytelling, I do know some intrepid souls who live and work there. The three interviews that make up half of this chapter are with people who work much more on the "telling side" of organizational and community narrative than I do. I chose these people for these interviews because even though they live in the land where I fear to tread, they all do good work, work that respects the power and danger of stories. You can look up things they've written, some of which I have read and know to be worth reading. As I finish this book, Karen Deitz is finishing her book *Business Storytelling for Dummies* (with Lori Silverman). I haven't read it yet, but I've seen the table of contents, and I like what I see so far. (Karen got her initial training as a folklorist, so she knows better than

to believe telling stories will get you something for nothing.)

Even though I can't point you at specific resources (beyond those written by the people interviewed here), I do think I can help you sort through the many options available based on what I have read. Here are some things I think you should look for. (See Figure 13.4 on the facing page for a summary.)

- Look for resources that help you tell stories *grounded in the reality* of your community or organization. You don't need to know how to write a blockbuster movie, but you do need to know how to communicate an important story to those who need to hear it. Look for resources centered on you and your needs, not abstract definitions of what a story should be like outside of any context. Look for sections about understanding your audience, finding your voice, and building a resonant connection.

- As you look at a resource, find its *definition of story*. (There is *always* a definition of story, even if it's not explicit.) Considering the dimensions of story form, function, and phenomenon, where does the definition fall? Is it wide or narrow? How does that definition match what *you* feel a story to be? If the resource's definition doesn't feel right to you— for example, if it portrays stories as nothing but emotions, or nothing but machines, or nothing but power plays—look for a better resource.

- As you look at a resource, see if it has a section on *listening* to stories. All good storytellers are good story listeners. A resource that tells you how to tell stories should also cover listening to stories so that you know which stories to tell, how to tell them, and what impacts they might have. If the resource doesn't mention listening, it's not looking at the whole picture, and its advice will be flawed.

- Look for resources that *give you things to do*. You probably don't need to be convinced that storytelling is useful, or that people remember stories well. Look for practical activities and ideas you can use.

- Look for resources that *tell stories!* You need to read about the experiences people have

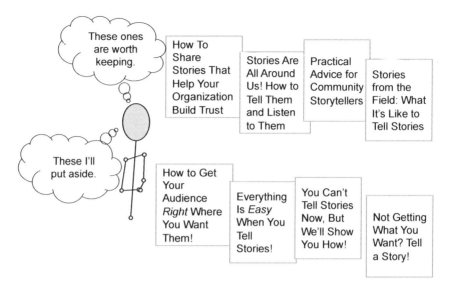

Figure 13.4. When evaluating resources about organizational storytelling, look for those that address your needs, consider listening, and give practical advice. Avoid resources that promise the impossible.

had telling stories. You need to find out what has happened to people who have done what you want to do. And look to see that there are some negative stories included, because anyone who has had experience telling stories should be able to tell some tales of failure you can use.

Here are some things to avoid.

- Avoid resources with *manipulative terms* like "get your audience right where you want them." Respect for stories and for audiences should radiate through the writing. The emphasis should be on the communication of perspectives, not the manipulation of beliefs. Remember the twin giants of manipulation and distrust, and plan your path to avoid them.
- Avoid resources that present storytelling as a *risk-free, fool-proof* option. If there is no mention made of the dangers that come with telling stories, look for advice that comes from deeper experience. The last thing you need in the land of purposeful storytelling is a guide who doesn't know where the giants live.
- Avoid resources that artificially *narrow their scope* of what qualifies to be a story. The little things we tell each other every day *are* stories,

and nobody has the right to say they aren't. Don't let a resource draw you into the trap of thinking that only polished, prepared, professionally delivered stories are allowed to be called stories. Look for resources that respect all of the stories we tell, no matter how well-spoken they are.

- Avoid resources that say you will get *magically abundant benefits* from the use of storytelling. Some books say that by telling stories you can seize power, create motivation, change cultures, dissolve resistance, and get people to follow you anywhere. None of that is true. Telling stories doesn't make you into the Pied Piper. It just makes you human. Sometimes people need some help remembering how to be human, but they don't need people telling them that stories will get them anything they want. Even today in this everything-right-now age, patience, forgiveness, and the hard work of building trust are still more important than *any* story you can tell. Stories can help with that task, but they can't replace it.

An example of narrative presentation: *Material World*

To complete this section, I'd like to describe a narrative presentation that I think has much to tell us about presenting stories as a narrative intervention. It's a book called *Material World: A Global Family Portrait* by Peter Menzel.

Here's Menzel describing the impetus for his book in an interview with photo.net:

> Freelancing in Somalia during their civil war and in Kuwait right after the first Bush War, I had some rather intense experiences that made life in the U.S. seem rather shallow and superfluous. … Sitting in my office early one morning, listening to NPR, which is the way I like to start every day, I heard an amazing piece on the marketing of Madonna's autobiographic book called *SEX*. The book was a sensation in the U.S. The radio report ended with Madonna singing, "I am living in a material world and I am just a material girl," or something close. I thought it was spot on. We live in an idiotic capitalist self-indulgent society where the sex life of a pop star is more important than impending starvation, land mines and child soldiers in Africa, or more interesting than the world's biggest man-made natural disaster in oil fields of the Middle East.

So Menzel decided to show people what the "material world" is *really* like. He says it took "about a minute" to come up with the idea that would make his project famous: he would go to the homes of "statistically average" families from thirty countries, rich and poor, and photograph their material possessions.

The resulting book is a masterpiece. Each family is represented by a large photo spread showing everything they own, taken out and arrayed in front of their house. Smaller photographs illustrate descriptions of the families' daily lives, along with comparative information such as incomes, hours worked, schools attended, and typical meals. The differences in income are in some cases stark, but what is amazing is the sense of dignity on each page. These are real people, not caricatures of "the rich" and "the poor" we have heard so much about.

Has the book had an impact? Judging from the abundant comments on the internet, I'd say it has. I've been reading hundreds of these comments, and I'd say the reactions in them fall into these categories:

- I started leafing through the book, and suddenly it was hours later. ("I checked this out from the library thinking I'd get some enjoyment flipping through it over the next couple of weeks. Fast forward to me sitting on the couch ignoring everyone for about 5 hours straight so I could read this cover to cover.")

- Soon after I read this book, I bought copies of it for all of my friends. ("I have given this book to about 10 friends as gifts and all of them always are amazed and love the book just as much as I do!")

- I used this book to help my kids understand that we're not "poor" just because they don't have things their friends have. ("Within 10 minutes, my 9-year-old "material girl" zoomed in on the large, glossy cover, and asked about the book. … Were the darling kids in the picture the anonymous "poor people" they heard about so often at school? They don't look unhappy in the photos… they look just like a regular family. *Yes! Connection!*")

- I've been re-evaluating my needs and wants because I've found this book. ("This book has haunted me since my first encounter with it years ago. Even to flip quickly through its pages and witness the stark contrasts so powerfully and immediately revealed in images is heartbreaking, sobering, staggering. And life-changing, if one allows it to be.")

- This book made me rethink what it means to be rich and poor. ("Though [some of] these families own little, many of them are smiling. Maybe what you own is not what makes you happy.")

- These families are just like my family, and yet they are not. ("I especially like the photos of people cooking and eating. Meat, potatoes, bread and peppers are revealed as near-universal. Several shots had me salivating. But when I read about the sanitary conditions surrounding the shots I felt a confusion of emotions. Leaving in these and other contradictions is part of the book's fascination and strength.")

Aren't those like reactions you'd like to hear following a narrative intervention you've carried out?

By considering the elements that made *Material World* an effective narrative intervention, we can think about how you can apply similar ideas to your own narrative presentations.

Discovery. One phrase that comes up often in comments on *Material World* is "eye-opening." This is because the book brings information to people that they cannot get in any other way. Says Menzel in the book's afterword:

> We all have an understanding of what our own lives are like, but even as the countries of the world become more interconnected, we know very little about the lives of people in other societies.

As a photojournalist who had spent time in over fifty countries even before starting his book project, Menzel was in a unique position to know exactly what was waiting to be discovered by the people he knew back home. This understanding helped him build a book that focused only on what people were missing: not statistics about economies or news stories about famines and floods, but an understanding of what life is simply like for people in other places.

In your community or organization, *you* are a world traveler. You have listened to the stories of people from all over your world. What do you know that the people "back home" need to know? What information can you present to them that they cannot get in any other way? In what ways are their eyes closed, and how can you help to open them?

Reality. Quite a few of the comments on the book mention surprise at learning how "real" people live around the world. This makes me wonder—if people don't know how real people live, what sort of people *do* they know about? People in movies? People in the news? People they made up based on the little information they had? Probably all of those.

In your community or organization, how do people build their assumptions about what is real around them? Do they have the information they need to understand reality, or do they cobble their understanding together from inad-equate, even perhaps skewed, information? If you think about the stories you have collected, which of them would surprise people? Would learning about some of those stories help people put together better pictures of reality?

Juxtaposition. The fact that each family in *Material World* is treated in exactly the same way, with the same photos, the same answers to questions, and the same facts, makes the book a tool for comparison. It seems that many of the commenters used the book by "flipping" back and forth from one section to another. If the book had been formatted in a less structured fashion, for example as a story about the photographer's visits (though "photographer notes" are included), the resource would not have been as useful a tool.

In your community or organization, what do people need to compare? If you were to create a narrative presentation that juxtaposed things, what would the things be and how would you juxtapose them? If you consider your collected stories, which do you think would help people most if you brought them together and presented them side by side? What impact do you think that might have?

Immersion. Many of the comments on the book mentioned the "couldn't put it down" aspect of the presentation. One librarian even mentioned that his library had to buy a new copy of the book because it had fallen apart from heavy use. The presentation of photos in the *Material World* book is personal and intimate, never clinical or detached. This is partly because the project was set up so that the photographers lived with each family for a week while taking pictures of them. If the photographers had just shown up, took their pictures, and left, the book would have been far less compelling. It was the immersion of the photographers, and the book's readers through them, that made the book so difficult to put down.

In your community or organization, who needs to be immersed, and in what? How can you bring about such an immersion? What will it take to get past the facts into the heart of the issues? Who needs to go where, live where, see what, do what, to make that happen?

Dramatic action

The last type of narrative intervention that falls into the category of "getting stories to where they need to go" is not about *telling* stories at all. It's about making stories happen by doing things people tell stories about (see Figure 13.5 on the next page).

People make stories happen every day, in all of the things they do. The great majority of stories people make happen are small and quiet. They live small, quiet lives within a family or group of friends. But the life of a small, quiet story can change in an instant.

Consider what happens when somebody gets noticed by society. They run for office or start a company, or they are in the right or wrong place at the right or wrong time, or they do or create something interesting or wonderful or horrible. Suddenly all of their small, quiet stories come flooding out into the public sphere, from teachers, classmates, neighbors, colleagues, friends, family members, people who met them on the bus. The public uses these small, quiet stories to check the new, big, loud stories for veracity. Perhaps the person running for office has a history of dishonesty, or the person accused of a crime has been a pillar of the community, or the whiz-bang inventor has been accused of plagiarism in the past.

This is how people make sense of things. A narrative intervention based on making stories happen uses this natural process to fuel positive change.

The idea of making stories happen is nothing new. I first encountered it in the work of Alan Wilkins, who in a 1984 paper called "Organizational Stories as Symbols that Control the Organization" described how managers who want to create organizational change through storytelling cannot simply rely on telling stories. They should also (or instead) make stories happen by taking what Wilkins called "dramatic action in the name of values." (I like to call it "dramatic action *based on* values," because "in the name of" still sounds a bit fake.)

Wilkins tells this story:

> [M]ost employees at one company I researched have been told the story about how the company avoided a mass layoff in the early 1970s when almost every other company in the industry was forced to lay off employees in large numbers. Top management chose to avoid a layoff of 10 percent of their employees by asking everyone in the company, including themselves, to take a ten percent cut in salary and come to work only nine out of ten days. This experience became known as the "nine-day fortnight" by some and is apparently used as a script for the future of the company.
>
> In 1974 the company was again confronted with a drop in orders, and it went to the "nine-day fortnight" scheme for a short period. When other companies in the industry began layoffs, the old-timers used this story to quiet the anxiety of concerned newcomers.... Employees occasionally tell [this] story to communicate that this is the "company with a heart." Everyone I talked to in the company knew the story, which is used both as a symbol and a script.

Now *that's* effective narrative intervention. Those managers could have told a beautifully crafted story about the poor economy and their sad need to lay off employees. But instead they took an action, and that action made stories happen that strengthened the organization for years to come.

The paradox of it is, the most effective narrative interventions happen when the people taking the dramatic actions have no intention of telling a story. They are just doing what needs to be done, and they have good reasons for doing it. The narrative intervention is a result, not a cause, of the action.

When is dramatic action called for in a PNI project? When everything else isn't good enough. Sometimes listening to people is enough; sometimes informing or persuading people is enough; sometimes helping people work out issues is enough. But sometimes needs are uncovered for which all of these things will fall flat because the need is too great, or the layers of mistrust are too deep, to be solved by any amount of talking. Only action will do.

Figure 13.5. Dramatic action based on values can create positive change in the flow of stories around a topic. The most effective dramatic actions happen when the people doing them have no intention of telling stories.

At the end of your sensemaking sessions, when you are looking at the concentrated essence of what is going on in your community or organization, you can find such needs by playing through fictional scenarios of what might happen if you responded to each problem using every intervention you can think of. Would educating people help? Would connecting people help? Would giving people resources help? If your answers to all of these questions are negative, consider what might happen if dramatic actions were taken. Play out *those* scenarios and see where they lead you.

The dangers of dramatic action

As you might guess, making stories happen is not without danger. One danger lies in making stories happen without knowing it.

When soldiers descend to the ground in helicopters, they often ride with their booted feet hanging off the sides. When U.S. soldiers first went to Afghanistan, this innocent practice generated many local stories, because showing the soles of your feet is considered a deeply offensive (and usually deliberate) insult in most Arab countries. Soon the military started training soldiers about this and other insults, but the stories remained. Similarly, at one point Israelis were offended by a photograph of U.S. President Obama talking on the phone with Israeli Prime Minister Benjamin Netanyahu—with the soles of his feet prominently displayed on his desk. In both cases nobody told a story, and the actions may have been inadvertent, but the actions made stories happen nonetheless.

Another example of unconscious story creation happened in 2008 when three CEOs of U.S. automobile makers flew in private jets (at the estimated cost of $20,000) to ask the U.S. Congress for taxpayer money to bail out the car companies. To make matters worse, a statement from a Chrysler spokesperson said that they flew in private jets for "safety" reasons. The stories that flew around this incident surfaced many feelings about class and money and humility in the United States.

A few quotes randomly selected from the web:

- "Heads they win, tails we lose again!"
- "They really, really, do not get it."
- "Are their lives any more valuable than yours or mine?"
- "$20,000 is more than a lot of hard-working people see in a year."
- "Not even *they* will drive a US built car."
- "I will never buy or recommend another American auto again."

Now imagine that you are trying to *sell* the cars made by these companies. Puts you in a bad spot, doesn't it? Makes it harder to pull off a "we care about you" sort of advertising campaign, doesn't it?

Another wrinkle to the private-jet story was reported in the magazine *Washington Monthly*:

Alan Mulally, CEO of Ford, understands the importance of symbolic gestures and public relations. Yesterday, for example, when he arrived on Capitol Hill, hat in hand, hoping to convince lawmakers to help bail out American auto manufacturers, he arrived in a new Ford Fusion Hybrid. Ford's media team, of course, made sure reporters knew about this.... If only Ford's p.r. team had thought about the other leg of the trip. How one gets to the Hill from the hotel isn't quite as interesting as how one gets from home to D.C.

So the people at Ford had *not* been making stories happen without knowing it. They had been *trying* to make a positive story happen. But they hadn't thought it through well enough (or couldn't?), and a negative story happened instead. The story they made happen (of failure to make their *preferred* story happen) was the worst story of all.

Backflow and dramatic action

Like viruses that lie dormant for years, stories you make happen can come back to bite you long after you have forgotten them. Sometimes stories can turn into what I call "backflow" stories. A backflow story is one of my favorite kinds of story to read or see, but living through one can be unpleasant. In a backflow story, the very last part of the story flows back over the previous parts and changes them into something different than what they were. (I talk more about backflow stories on page 543.)

Say a person runs for political office. Everything seems to be in order. They have built their career slowly and carefully, making many friends and few enemies. They have mastered the art of public discourse and built a deep understanding of policy. They are well loved for prominent actions that have helped many people. Many good stories have been told about them. Their story seems destined to continue with their taking on the mantle of public authority. But then something happens that not only derails their political future, but retroactively changes the perceived story of *everything* that happened in the past. Now the fact that they led their high school debating group seems sinister instead of stately. Different stories start to come out, about how they kicked a neighbor's dog, or

didn't show up for a job, or snapped at a customer. In the end the whole story gets rewritten, from start to finish, and they are a different person than they were—possibly even to themselves.

That sounds scary, but the good thing is that *positive* backflow works the same way. Former heads of state often actively create positive backflow by devoting the remainder of their time to earning their place in history.

Communities and organizations can do the same thing. Do you remember how, at the end of the chapter on sensemaking, I talked about things you might list when you are wrapping up sensemaking? (See page 372.) One of those things was "ideas." Among those ideas will be actions people in your organization or community could take. Among those actions, some will be dramatic, meaning that they will cause new stories to flow around them. Among those dramatic actions, some will cause stories to flow *back* into the past, helping to heal old wounds. If one goal of your project is to resolve problems from the past, my advice is to work on bringing out as many ideas for action as you can, so you will have more options for narrative intervention.

Fake dramatic action

I want to make a special warning about publicity stunts as dramatic actions, because when I say "make stories happen" it may seem that I am talking about this. I am not. Publicity stunts have two inherent problems, one for each word. The first is that a publicity stunt is done to get publicity, meaning for the sake of effect. People are pretty good at sussing out the intent of actions, especially when the people doing the actions are leaking signs of intent without realizing it. People have a lot of ways of talking about the gap between what people do and what they say—not walking the talk, not leading by example, do what I say not what I do, and on and on. And it's very easy to let your real intent slip out. (You know what they say about lying: you need a good memory to do it well.)

The second problem with publicity stunts is with the "stunt" part of it. By making your action deliberately exciting or provoking, you run the risk of the story-of-the-story taking over and becoming the story that happens. Nobody cares what a talking dog has to say. The fact that the dog is talking is the story that happens, and nobody asks what story the dog might have been trying to tell. This often happens when somebody wants to tell the world a story, finds it difficult to be heard because they are not in a position of power or authority, isn't willing to build an audience slowly and patiently, and grasps at an extreme way of telling their story, perhaps using the power of voyeurism (always a sure bet). These people usually provide only a temporary spectacle to a public that rushes off to the next shiny thing without ever noticing what the person had been trying to say. The sad thing is, an entire industry centers around exploiting these poor souls and making stories happen at their expense.

Effective dramatic action

So what is an organization or community to do if they want to make a positive story happen? How about this? *Do good stuff.* It's amazing how refreshing that is nowadays. In a world where everybody is spinning, standing still stands out. Find things you can do in which your community's or organization's values are apparent. Make sure they are big enough to get noticed, but be careful not to artificially expand them. Find them, then *do* them, and don't make too big a to-do about it. Make sure your values soak all the way through the action and aren't just painted on the top of it. People will notice, because they are looking for it. They are hungry for it. And they will tell the stories *for* you.

I buy a lot of my clothes from the Land's End company. I like their clothes and their policies, but I also remember a dramatic action they took decades ago. When I was in graduate school, one of the students I knew lived in a rented house that burned to the ground. He lost every single thing he owned. Another student sent a letter to Land's End saying how this guy and all of us loved their clothes, and could they send him a few shirts to help him out.

Land's End didn't send a few shirts. They sent a huge box filled with clothes, a whole new wardrobe. We guessed that the clothes they sent would have cost at least several hundred dollars. Given the fact that our graduate-school stipends at that time came to a whopping eight

thousand dollars a year, and we lived on expensive Long Island, this was incredibly memorable. I can still remember how exciting it was when the huge box came and the guy opened it.

Even more amazingly, Land's End didn't seek to publicize the incident. They didn't make the poor guy do a commercial or anything. They just helped him out. The very fact that they didn't seek to publicize what they did proved to us that they must do this sort of thing all the time. I'll just bet that everybody who knew about that incident (and it was dozens of people) has told the story of it many times. I just told it to you. That's what I mean by dramatic action based on values.

It's not that hard to find opportunities to make positive stories happen. Just listen. Listening to stories about needs and fears and beliefs is a great way to find opportunities to take dramatic action based on values. But you can't find such opportunities by asking people to tell you "success stories." You need to find out things you aren't sure you want to know, like why people don't trust you, and why they choose others over you, and what they think your values are, and what nasty rumors they have heard about you. This requires a degree of self-awareness, honesty, and courage that is not always available at all levels of every organization or in every house in every community. And then, when you find out what dramatic actions you could take based on values, it requires another layer of courage to actually *do* them, because some of them require you to give up some control or safety or freedom. But the rewards can be great.

INTERVENTIONS FOR HELPING PEOPLE WORK WITH STORIES

The third category of narrative intervention I want to cover is helping people in your community or organization continue to work with stories after the main part of your project is finished.

Spaces for sensemaking

This intervention is about making everything created or collected during the first phases of your project—your planning questions, collected stories, catalytic patterns, and constructed artifacts—available to everyone in the community or organization for continued sensemaking. Just making the information available is a start, but you can go much further than that. You can actively promote continued storytelling and sensemaking after the main part of your project is over by creating a special space in which support is concentrated.

Let's imagine that you build an "experience room" in a side room of your community's town hall. The walls of the experience room are covered with story cards, and more copies of these cards sit on tables, just as if the room were about to be used for a sensemaking session. Visitors can read stories and rearrange cards. Printed indexes to the stories, by name and by answers to questions, are also available to help those looking for stories they want to think about or retell. Wall spaces, materials, and instructions are available for groups who want to use the room for ad-hoc sensemaking around an issue of concern. The project's planning documents, catalytic material, and outcomes of sensemaking sessions can also be found in the room. Also prominent are rules for use of the room, including the need to respect the experiences of others and the need to keep the room in good condition for the use of all.

The experience room can be used for storytelling as well. Visitors can fill out story cards and drop them into a box for inclusion in the collection. Groups can use peer interview scripts and instructions for group storytelling exercises. Every so often, volunteers check on the experience room and process any new stories, constructions or reports of sensemaking sessions. Planning meetings for new story projects take place in the experience room, because just being in the room helps people think about the narrative life of the community.

That's a physical experience room, but you could do the same thing in a virtual space with support for storytelling, story listening, and sensemaking. You can also create hybrid physical-virtual sensemaking spaces, with physical space for in-person sensemaking but with computers available for listening to audio or video stories, visualizing patterns in answers, and learning from video instructions.

When is a sensemaking space called for? That's a complicated question, because a sensemaking space can meet many needs. Here are just a few.

- A space for sensemaking can improve *transparency*, both in the project and in the community or organization in general, because it proves that nothing collected has been kept hidden. This aspect of the intervention is particularly useful when people have been distrustful about the story collection up front.

- If there wasn't enough *time* during a sensemaking session to address a problem or opportunity, participants can return to the sensemaking space after the session to explore the issue more on their own. This aspect of the sensemaking space is particularly helpful when there has been a history of people claiming that their views have not been represented. It's also helpful if your facilitation skills are just getting started and your sessions didn't go entirely as planned—for example, if you think people might have sensemaking needs that weren't met.

- If someone participated in a story collection or sensemaking session and wants to show friends or colleagues the stories they worked with, or wants to work with friends or colleagues on issues of mutual concern, they can *return* to the sensemaking space to conduct their own sensemaking sessions. This aspect is particularly helpful when recruitment for sensemaking sessions has been difficult, but interest in the project has grown afterward.

- If *new issues* arise after the project has ended, people can return to the sensemaking space to support unanticipated sensemaking needs. This aspect is useful when the project was wide-ranging (thus the collected stories can address many issues) and when a community has many needs of which your project had to select only a few to address.

- People who *join* the organization or community after the project has ended can use the sensemaking space as a resource to find their way around the culture and to understand where the community or organization is going. This aspect is especially useful when the rate of new arrivals to your community is high.

- Groups that were poorly *represented* in the project proper (through limited planning or low participation) can visit the sensemaking space and find representation through storytelling and sensemaking after the main sensemaking phase of your project has ended. This aspect is useful when you weren't sure what groups to invite at first, or when some groups were less willing than others to participate.

- A well-tended sensemaking space can form a *bridge* between projects, supporting the return phase of one project (so participants have somewhere to go to think about the last project) and the planning phase of the next (so planners have somewhere to go to think about the next project). This aspect is most useful when you would like to plan a series of projects, each building on the insights from the last.

A sensemaking space takes time and resources to set up and maintain, so it requires more investment than some simpler interventions. And once you've set up such a space, if people notice it and use it, they will want it to continue to exist; so there is a higher level of commitment to setting up a sensemaking space as well. It's not an appropriate intervention for a small or short-term project. But if your project plans are ambitious or you want to plan multiple projects that cover years instead of months, a space for sensemaking might provide you with a good return on your investment.

Sensemaking pyramids

Let's say you just finished the sensemaking phase of your project. You engaged a few dozen people in lively, productive sensemaking sessions. The sessions took a while to warm up, but by the end people were ready and willing to keep going. So why not *help* people keep going?

I've noticed a sort of bell curve of interest in sensemaking sessions. There are always a few people who barely tolerate the session from beginning to end. A large number of people are confused or reluctant at first, but get the point eventually and start enjoying the process by the time it's over. But there are always a few people who find the process fascinating and want to

know more about it. That little glowing seed of fascination is an opportunity for your community or organization.

Here's what you can do to seize the opportunity (see Figure 13.6 on the following page).

1. As each sensemaking session winds down, ask if anyone in the room is interested in learning more about the process they've been using. If some say yes, tell them that if they give you some contact information you'll send them information about the process. (If the session is anonymous, make sure you explain that their contact information will not be connected to anything they said or did in the session.)

2. A few days later, contact the people who said they were interested. Give them the information you promised, which will be a brief explanation of the methods you used and why you used them, along with some pointers to resources on story work. Also ask the people if they would be willing to learn more about how to conduct sensemaking sessions like the one they participated in, so they can help the community or organization as you have done.

3. If anybody responds to your second level of inquiry, invite those people to an hour-long mini-course in which you explain to them in more detail what you know about narrative sensemaking and PNI in general. Give them copies of some resources to review.

4. At the end of the mini-course, tell the people that if they are interested in doing some small projects on their own, you would be glad to help them based on your own experiences.

5. If anybody does do a small project (and remember, a PNI project can fit into an hour-long meeting), support them by answering questions and making suggestions.

6. If anybody does more than one small project, or moves up to do a larger project, encourage them to seek out more people who might want to learn how to do narrative projects and pass on the knowledge again.

By spreading the word about sensemaking (and PNI), you can amplify the impact of your origi-

Figure 13.6. Creating a sensemaking pyramid means asking participants in your sensemaking sessions if they'd like to learn how to conduct their own sensemaking sessions—and so on, and so on.

nal project and improve the sensemaking skills of your whole community or organization.

Of course, you can't build a sensemaking pyramid in every community or organization. Sometimes random people can't just start up story projects without the approval of authority. Sometimes people won't tell stories to just anybody. Sometimes nobody is willing to step forward to find out what they can do to help. Sometimes people are just too busy to help, no matter how willing they are. You may even find an obstacle in your own feelings of proprietorship about your projects and methods, especially if this sort of thing falls under your job description. But under the right conditions, that is, when people have the freedom and motivation to explore, a network of narrative sensemaking could spread throughout your community or organization. It won't work everywhere, but it will work somewhere, I'm sure of that.

When is a sensemaking pyramid called for? When you finish the project and wish you could start all over again, because there is just so much more out there waiting to be done. When you are surprised at how much interest you find in your sensemaking sessions. When peo-

ple hang around at the end of your sessions asking questions about the methods you are using. When people envy you your role in the project, because they want to do what you're doing. When your collected stories show pent-up energy waiting to be released to solve problems of universal concern. When people show you that they are hungry for solutions. When people have the freedom and motivation to explore.

Narrative mentoring

You already know what mentoring is, I think. People who have lots of experience in some area get paired up with people who have little experience, and mentors help mentees find their way. As I'm sure you know, mentoring is a great way for any community or organization to improve its collective resilience. So what is *narrative* mentoring? The same thing, only with both participants receiving instruction and support in listening to and working with stories. Instruction and support could take the form of printed instructions, training sessions, coaching, and possibly even a distinct layer of mentoring between those more and less experienced in listening to and working with stories.

When is narrative mentoring called for? Let's first consider the case in which your community or organization already has a mentoring program in place. Adding narrative support to an existing program is called for when people say they have mentors and have learned from them the facts about something complex they are struggling to learn, but they don't seem to understand the deeper essences of the matter, the "what it's *really* like" stuff. In such a case, their stories will show that while mentors are listening, giving advice, and providing helpful tips, and while mentees are asking useful questions, neither mentors nor mentees are *sharing experiences*.

Mentoring without storytelling can happen for several reasons. Mentors and mentees might never feel they can take the time to get to know each other, so their conversations remain fact-laden, unable to break through into disclosure. Mentors might feel that telling mentees stories about mistakes they've made might damage their reputations or even livelihoods if word gets out. Mentors and/or mentees might feel that telling stories wastes time, so every time they begin to drift into telling a story they feel an urge to "get back to work." If mentors are particularly high up in some hierarchy, mentees might feel that mentors' time is so precious that it would be disrespectful to ask them to simply talk about what has happened to them. And finally, mentors and/or mentees might just not be used to telling stories in the contexts in which the mentoring relationship exists.

When you have a mentoring program in place, giving mentors and mentees instructions on how to improve the productivity of their mentoring relationships with narrative gives them ideas and, more critically, permission. Instructions on how to do something imply permission to do it. They imply that the activity is *qualified* to take place within the mentorship, and that time will not be wasted doing it. If the instructions are complicated, and if people have to attend a training session to learn how to follow the instructions properly, that's even more proof that story work is allowed, well regarded, and worthwhile. Thus people will begin to tell and listen to stories, and to work with stories together, even if they never follow any of the instructions properly. If you can get mentors

and mentees doing this, I am sure your mentoring program will improve in its impact on your community or organization.

What if you have no mentoring program in place? When is it worthwhile to set up a narrative mentoring program from scratch? In the same situation as before: when you have discovered that people understand how to do something complex and difficult at a superficial level but not at a deep level. Actually, starting a narrative mentorship program from scratch might be easier than adding narrative to an existing program. Just include instructions on narrative in your instructions on mentoring. As long as the information on narrative methods is clearly indicated as being a bona fide part of the instructions, not some "fluff" addition meant only for people who like touchy-feely stuff, people will take it, rightly, as proof that story work is allowed, well regarded, and worthwhile.

Narrative therapy

In 1998 Erik Sween published a short paper called, "The one-minute question: What is narrative therapy?" In the paper, he defines the term from seven different perspectives. I find the last definition the most useful. It goes like this:

> A person's life is criss-crossed by invisible story-lines. These unseen story-lines can have enormous power in shaping a person's life. Narrative therapy involves the process of drawing out and amplifying these story-lines. Questions are used to focus on what has been most meaningful in a person's life. Common areas of inquiry include intentions, influential relationships, turning-points, treasured memories, and how these areas connect with each other.

Drawing out and amplifying hidden story lines sounds a lot like sensemaking in PNI, doesn't it? It is similar, but not identical. Narrative therapy is participatory, and it's narrative, but it goes beyond inquiry. I said in the chapter on sensemaking that sensemaking encompasses change, but I was referring to change that flows naturally as a result of sensemaking. Change created by therapeutic story work is *deliberately* created by

Figure 13.7. Externalizing conversations help people consider problems as separate from their identities.

a therapist, and that puts it outside the bounds of PNI (at least as it stands right now).

In PNI there is no therapist, only a facilitator, someone like you. That's deliberate. It's to keep PNI as close to participation, and to participants, as possible. Having said that, during the intervention phase of the PNI cycle, the help of a skilled and experienced therapist may be useful. You could bring one in, or you could read enough about narrative therapy to bring some *elements* of it into your PNI work yourself. When should you consider bringing narrative therapy into your PNI project? When you have discovered an issue about which people need to start telling themselves new stories.

To give you more of a sense of what narrative therapy entails, I'll describe a few of the techniques commonly used in the approach.

Externalizing conversations

When people have problems, they tend to associate the problems with some aspect of their identity, as being *situated* in themselves. He's a drunk. She's a control freak. He's a workaholic. This makes the problems harder to approach because they are too closely intertwined with the people to consider separately. Externalizing conversations change the way we talk about problems by giving them their own identities, almost as characters in stories. He is burdened with alcoholism. She has difficulty with control issues. He struggles with a compulsion to overwork. A narrative therapist uses externalizing conversations to help people find better ways to talk and think about problems. Narrative therapists say that externalizing conversations help people see that "the problem is the *problem*, not the person." (See Figure 13.7.)

Says Michael White, one of the founders of narrative therapy, in his book *Maps of Narrative Practice:*

> Externalizing conversations employ practices of objectification of the prob-

lem against cultural practices of objectification of people.

To give an example, a child who has a learning disability might be encouraged to speak about the disability as a mischievous imp who stands in the way of the child achieving goals. The child can then be asked questions about the imp: what it looks like, when it's awake and asleep, how it disrupts things, what its motivations might be, and what we might be able to do to reduce the imp's damage to the child's learning. This might help the child (and parents and teachers) find new ways to improve the situation.

You can see how this sort of re-imagining of problems could work in a community setting. By engaging people in externalizing conversations, a narrative therapist might help people build new stories in which the embodiment of problems is shifted to the problems themselves. This could help people think more clearly and productively about the problems and the people.

You might have noticed a similarity between this practice of seeing a problem as a character and drawing character story elements out of stories. In fact, I believe—though I have not done this in practice—that you could bring a bit of narrative therapy into PNI by asking people to create characters that explicitly represent problems as distinct from people.

Let's make up an example to explore the possibility. Let's say that homelessness is a problem in your community. Let's say you have just finished the sensemaking phase of your PNI project. During sensemaking you found out that different people talk about the problem differently, depending on the experiences they have had. Some see the homeless as lazy beggars, some as victims of an unjust society, some as free spirits whose rights of independence should be respected, some as dangerous misfits who should be institutionalized. But those are all characterizations of *people*. What if you asked people to characterize homelessness *itself*? Let's say you hold some sessions advertised as additional sensemaking sessions ("to learn more") but actually meant as interventions (because you want to include those who *don't* want to change the way they think). In

those sessions, you ask people to draw characteristics of the behavior of homelessness (*not* the homeless) out of stories. How might the way people think about homelessness change after such a session has taken place?

As I said, I've never actually done this in practice. But if you find this idea appealing in the context of a project you are planning, perhaps one where you know you have this sort of "people are the problem" perception in your community, you might want to follow this trail of opportunity and see where it leads.

Re-authoring conversations

This practice involves the construction of larger stories out of smaller stories. People do this every day as they piece together experiences to make sense of their lives, and communities do this as they piece together stories to create a narrative of the community.

Says Michael White, again in *Maps of Narrative Practice:*

> When people consult therapists they tell stories; they speak about the history of the problems, predicaments, or dilemmas that have brought them to therapy, and they provide an account of what led to their decision to seek help. In doing this, people link the events of their lives in sequences that unfold through time according to a theme or plot. These themes often reflect loss, failure, incompetence, hopelessness, or futility.

There are often other stories people *could* be telling but are not: stories of strength, success, competence, and hope.

Michael White again:

> Re-authoring conversations invite people to continue to develop and tell stories about their lives, but they also help people to include some of the more neglected but potentially significant events and experiences that are "out of phase" with their dominant storylines. These events and experiences can be considered "unique outcomes" or "exceptions."

By discovering neglected stories and bringing them into greater prominence, re-authoring

Figure 13.8. Re-authoring conversations help people highlight previously neglected stories in order to change the larger story they tell themselves.

conversations invite people to compose new stories with new themes. (See Figure 13.8.) Eventually this new composite story can replace the original composite, providing people with the strength to face problems.

Re-authoring conversations sounds a lot like building composite stories in a PNI sensemaking exercise, doesn't it? It's not as structured an activity, but a re-authoring conversation could be seen as a composite story exercise with a template whose slots have people actively searching out stories for inclusion that highlight strengths and successes and hopes. You could imagine that this small change to PNI's composite story exercise could constitute an intervention in the narrative life of your community or organization. You could imagine discovering the need for such an intervention during sensemaking, then planning new "action" sessions that incorporate the change.

I'm not saying that adding a new story template to a PNI exercise constitutes narrative therapy. Far from it. I've briefly mentioned only a few of the practices involved in narrative therapy here, and I'm sure any narrative therapist would tell you that tweaking an exercise is not the same as having a therapeutic conversation. But adding narrative therapy to PNI intervention does not have to be a binary choice. Learning more about narrative therapy will help you bring some of its ideas into your PNI practice, whether you enlist the help of (or become) a professional narrative therapist or not. I can see people adding just a few therapeutic elements to a PNI project, and I can see people using a PNI project to prepare for a therapist-supported narrative therapy project. It's all good.

A good source of information about narrative therapy is the Dulwich Center in Adelaide, Australia. Their comprehensive web site (dulwichcentre.com.au) contains many free and inexpensive resources for learning how to get started in narrative therapy. Start there, then branch out.

An example of narrative therapy (by another name): Fambul Tok

As you begin to learn about narrative therapy, keep your eye out for approaches that build on the same therapeutic ideas but use other names.

One compelling example of such a differently-named approach is Fambul Tok, developed in Sierra Leone as a revival of age-old traditions after a devastatingly brutal 11-year civil war. During the war, many ordinary people, including child soldiers, were forced to perpetrate unspeakable crimes on their neighbors, friends and family members. Legal procedures in the aftermath of the war indicted only a handful of high-ranking offenders, issuing a blanket amnesty to all other combatants. There was a Truth and Reconciliation Commission, but it was limited to relatively brief hearings held only in the major cities. The war devastated the whole country, but most ordinary Sierra Leoneans could not participate in the hearings. In many rural villages, life several years after the war found victims and perpetrators living near each other, unable to speak, wary of each other, unable to move on with their lives.

John Caulker was involved in the Truth and Reconciliation Commission, but he was frustrated at how few Sierra Leoneans were involved in the process. Not only could few people travel to the cities, but few perpetrators were willing to talk. So the whole story of the war could not be told, and people could not move on to rebuild the country.

Caulker remembered traditions from his rural childhood, called *fambul tok,* or "family talk" in the Sierra Leone Krio (creole) language. He remembered how people used to gather around bonfires at night to talk, gossip, joke, resolve disputes, and sometimes apologize and forgive. Caulker began to visit rural communities and ask them about these traditions and whether they might help people restore their communi-

ties. Thus the Fambul Tok approach grew where need met tradition.

From a 2008 interview in the *Christian Science Monitor:*

> "It's like they [the international community] have this postconflict checklist: Truth commission, tick. Military assistance, tick. Trials, tick. Next. Go on to the next country," Caulker says. "But the people have answers. They have their cultural values." Caulker wants to put those values on that checklist.
>
> It's a tradition with a long history— before the war; before, even, the white man—and a range of meanings. Villagers sat around nightly bonfires, telling jokes and recounting the day's events. Sometimes, fambul tok resolved disputes, adjudicating everything from petty theft to matrimonial discord. The practice made villagers more than neighbors; it united them as a fambul.

So Fambul Tok began to help rural communities bring back their ancient traditions of restorative justice. Of course, such deep transformations of ravaged communities could not happen without preparation. Before anything happens in any community, Fambul Tok staff negotiate, sometimes for months, with community leaders and members to prepare them for the process and agree to certain principles.

The day of ritual begins with community dances and religious observances unique to each community. At the heart of the Fambul Tok process is a storytelling session held around a huge bonfire. Surrounded by all members of the community, each victim and perpetrator tells the story of what happened to them during the war without interruption. Finally each perpetrator apologizes to the victims and the community and asks for forgiveness, and the victims and the whole community publicly forgive the perpetrators. After the bonfire there is a feast, and all celebrate the first step in making the community whole again.

The Fambul Tok process continues long after the bonfire. There may be religious ceremonies that cleanse and heal places where atrocities took place. Communal activities may be planned in which perpetrators contribute to the community through participating in new activities like football matches, the creation of community farms, the building of new community resources, and so on. So the Fambul Tok process starts with apology and forgiveness, but continues as the community heals. One follow-up activity is the designation of a peace tree, a place where people can gather to deal with any conflicts that take place in the future. Another activity is the creation of "peace mothers" groups who work together to continue the peaceful momentum started by the bonfire. All of these things can be seen as narrative interventions, because they create new stories that define the community.

The Fambul Tok approach has begun to spread outside Sierra Leone. It is being used by groups around the world to resolve longstanding problems. It is a therapeutic process, and it is a narrative process, and it's one anyone can learn from and use in a situation of conflict.

Few people reading this book will have experienced the degree of devastation encountered by the people in Sierra Leone, but these methods can help people dealing with any kind of conflict that has created rifts in communities or organizations. If we think together about the factors that have made Fambul Tok a success, you might find ways in which you can use similar methods in your own community or organization.

Local solutions. Unlike the Truth and Reconciliation Commission, Fambul Tok traveled directly to the remote villages that needed help. Because the Fambul Tok ceremonies took place in familiar, comfortable places, people were more willing to take chances than they would have been otherwise. Where are the familiar, comfortable places of *your* community or organization? In what locations do you think people would feel safe enough to take chances on reconciliation?

Rootedness. Fambul Tok didn't bring a set of unknown methods into the communities they approached; they brought back a practice familiar to all of the community elders. If they had brought a foreign solution, it would probably have been rejected. Are there ways your community or organization has resolved conflicts in the past? Is there a local history you can call upon? If there isn't a unified history of conflict resolution, think about how the methods of Fambul Tok, or the methods of *any* approach to therapeutic narrative, mesh with the culture of your community or organization. What do the words *justice, forgiveness, reconciliation,* and *peace* mean in your community or organization? What will it take to make these things work for you?

Equality. Victims and perpetrators at Fambul Tok gatherings were given equal opportunities to tell their stories. Everyone around the bonfire was asked to listen with patience and respect to every story. If one group had been favored over the other, say if victims had been allowed to tell their stories but perpetrators had been shouted down, the approach would not have worked. What are the challenges to equal storytelling rights in *your* community or organization? Does everyone have a chance to speak? Is everyone listened to with patience and respect? What can you do to negotiate agreements about equality in storytelling as preparation for a Fambul-Tok-like gathering?

Security. One of the agreements insisted on by Fambul Tok staff before every ceremony was that everyone who spoke, victim or perpetrator, would be *safe*. "Do not be afraid," was the message of the ceremony, "we will hear your story." If perpetrators had been asked to tell their stories while being threatened with retribution, they would not have come forward and admitted their guilt. What barriers to security in storytelling exist in your community or organization? Who is afraid to tell their story? Why are they afraid? Are there community assets or traditions you can draw upon, or agreements you can create, to help everyone feel free to speak?

Future orientation. Several of the victims who forgave perpetrators during Fambul Tok ceremonies stressed the fact that they were not forgiving their attackers because they had forgotten what happened. They could never forget the horrors they lived through. But they forgave because they had *hope* that through forgiveness they could help their community move forward to a better, safer, more prosperous future. Their forgiveness was not a capitulation but a gift—a gift they gave to themselves and to their communities. If the victims of violence had not been able to find those common hopes for their communities, the reconciliation would have failed. What hopes for *your* community or organization might help people forgive each other and work together towards a better future?

Narrative. All of the perpetrators and victims at Fambul Tok ceremonies were encouraged not to just report the facts of their experiences, but to tell the stories of what happened to them from their own perspectives. If people had been told to "stick to the facts" the solution would have failed, because it was the *stories* that needed to be told. What stories need to be told in your community or organization? What would it take to get people telling and listening to those stories?

Preparation. Every Fambul Tok ceremony depends on months of preparatory consultation with village elders as to exactly how the ceremonial events should play out in the community. On the day of the bonfire, the gathering starts several hours before the bonfire is lit, with dances, meals, and other events of social significance. When the time has come to begin the storytelling, people have already been participating in a unique event for long enough to feel committed to the process. They know what is coming next, and the mood is expectant. If such a bonfire was entered into quickly, with no consultation and no preparation, people would not be ready to come forward with their stories. What sorts of preparations make sense for your community or organization? What sorts of social events are significant to the people in your community? What will help bring participants in your gathering to the place where they are ready to speak and listen?

Follow-through. The bonfire is never the last thing that happens in a Fambul Tok process. For months afterward, Fambul Tok staff help the community plan activities people will participate in together. If there was nothing to do together after the ceremony of forgiveness, the spirit of change might die away and people might slide back into the old resentments. Instead, people lay down new layers of experience working together toward common goals. What sorts of follow-through activities make sense for

your community or organization? What would lay down new layers of experience for your community members? What will keep the momentum for change going?

To learn more about Fambul Tok, its origins and methods, and how you can use these methods yourself, look at the Fambul Tok web site (fambultok.org), movie, and book. This is only one example of story work that has therapeutic value; I'm sure you can find many more to inspire you in your own work.

Theatre of the Oppressed

Theatre of the Oppressed (commonly abbreviated as TO) is a body of methods that use participatory theatre to help people work with stories to create social and political change. The approach was created by Augusto Boal, a Brazilian director, writer, and politician. Boal was himself inspired by the work of the educator Paulo Friere. Friere's best-known work, *Pedagogy of the Oppressed*, argues that educators should treat students as respected co-creators of knowledge rather than empty vessels to be filled. Boal brought Friere's ideas of co-creation into the realm of theatre.

If you're put off by the name, don't be. It's not necessary for anybody to be oppressed for these techniques to work. It's true that TO was originally created for use in situations where one group of people was oppressed by another, mainly during a time of harsh military repression in Brazil. But TO is now used in many situations in communities and organizations around the world. The general understanding of the name today is that we are *all* oppressed in some way, even if only by our own assumptions.

Says the TO web site (theatreoftheoppressed. org):

> The Theatre of the Oppressed is based upon the principle that all human relationships should be of a dialogic nature: among men and women, races, families, groups and nations, dialogue should prevail. In reality, all dialogues have the tendency to become monologues, which creates the relationship *oppressors-oppressed*. Acknowledging this re-

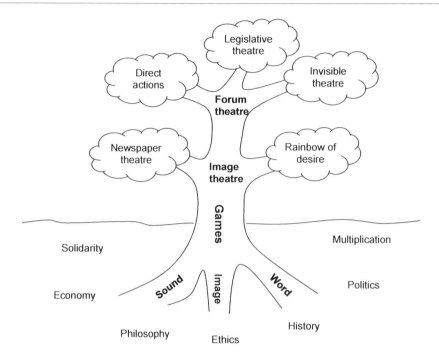

Figure 13.9. The tree of Theatre of the Oppressed methods, redrawn from Boal's illustration in his 2006 book *The Aesthetics of the Oppressed* (and from various sources on the internet).

ality, the main principle of Theatre of the Oppressed is to help restore dialogue among human beings.

Thus every person can be both oppressor and oppressed, and TO exists to help those who are oppressed in any situation find ways to alleviate their oppression. It does this by helping people participate in the creation and re-creation of stories in a theatrical setting.

TO makes a critical distinction between *spectators,* who remain isolated and confined in the audience of conventional theatrical performances, and *spect-actors,* who in TO events both observe *and* take action. According to Boal, this makes TO "a collective rehearsal for reality."

Some TO methods

Theatre of the Oppressed places its categories of methods into a tree that shows their relationships (see Figure 13.9).

The tree's roots are labeled *sound, image* and *word,* and the element of *games* is added as you move up the trunk.

Says Boal about games (in *The Aesthetics of the Oppressed*):

> On the trunk of the tree grow, first, the *Games,* because they bring together two essential characteristics of life in society; they have rules, as does society, which are necessary in order for the *Games* to be enacted; but they also require creative freedom, so that the *Game,* or life, is not transformed into servile obedience. Without rules, there is no game, without freedom, there is no life.

That sounds like TO agrees with PNI, doesn't it? Coming out of the trunk above games are two large groupings of methods under the headings of *image theatre* and *forum theatre.* I'm going to cover each of those and one "branch ending" for each, and I'll let you look up the others.

Image theatre. In this category of game, people in a group consider a theme by using their bodies, and the bodies of others in the group, to create images. An "image" in this context means a person or persons holding a position as if frozen in time. Images are created quickly, without time for thought, and in silence. People may work on their own or in pairs or larger groups to create the images. For example, a group considering the theme of homelessness might create the image of a man sleeping on a bench, of a woman knocking on a door, of a child looking through a window, and of a man shivering in the cold. The group might then discuss what these images mean to them, allowing for differing interpretations. Then they would discuss what images they would like to see instead, or what images might present solutions to the problems represented by the initial images. Several variations on the exercise further ritualize negotiation of image creation.

One method within the category of image theatre is *newspaper theatre*. People read articles out of a newspaper, with theatrical interpreted performances interspersed into the reading.

For example:

- In *parallel action,* group members silently play out actions as the newspaper text is being read. Their pantomimed actions can either match what is being read or can be based on reactions to the text, or to what people believe it avoids saying or obscures.

- In *crossed reading,* two news items are read in an interleaved fashion so that each changes the way the other is read. The selection of the two items to read, and how and when to interleave them, is an interpretive event in itself, which can be discussed.

- In *text out of context,* the newspaper text is deliberately read in an acted-out context that doesn't match the one in which it was originally published. It might be historically displaced (read as if it was written hundreds of years ago), spatially displaced (read as if it was written in another country), socially displaced (read as if it was written by someone much richer or poorer), and so on. The choice of what context to displace the newspaper text into constitutes an interpretive performance, which can be negotiated and discussed.

That's only three of about ten suggested variations on the newspaper theatre exercise. (I thought these three were the most connected to PNI.) You can find the whole list in Boal's book *Games for Actors and Non-Actors.*

Forum theatre. In this type of game, people in a group start by creating a short scripted play in which some kind of oppression plays out (and remember, the same people can be both oppressor and oppressed). Some of the people in the group act out the script while others watch (see Figure 13.10 on the following page). After the play has been performed, there is a short period of discussion. Then the play begins all over again; but this time through, anyone watching the play can shout "stop" or "freeze," and the play has to stop.

Next, the person who stopped the play steps onto the stage and takes the place of one of the play's characters. There is an important rule in this replacement: a character being replaced must *want* the situation to change. Participants may not replace actors who like things the way they are, because the solution of magically replacing people who are causing problems is not realistic. Violent solutions are also ruled out. The original actor is asked to step aside and observe the change created by their replacement, although they may support the new actor with advice (about the character's personality and so on).

Now the drama resumes, with the new "spect-actor" acting out their own solution to the problems and dilemmas faced by the character they have replaced. In this way the play might start and restart several times as the group works through multiple solutions to the problems presented. By going through this process, groups rehearse the change they want to create.

A type of forum theatre that takes things one step further is called *legislative theatre.* This game starts out like forum theatre, with a play repeated and stopped by spect-actors who step into the roles of characters. However, in legislative theatre, the game continues as participants recommend laws that address problems explored in the play. Proposed laws are written down and clustered; the clusters are discussed; and some are chosen to become "bills." Spect-actors take positions for or against bills and debate their merits and demerits. Finally, the whole assembly votes on the bills.

Legislative theatre is most often used today either by an official decision-making body as a way to involve the public (but not to share

Figure 13.10. Forum theatre creates situations, then challenges people to come up with alternative solutions to them.

decision-making power completely) or by an opposition group as a way to protest policy. But there is no reason this method could not be used in a community or organization as a bona fide way of making binding decisions together, as long as everyone in the community or organization can participate in the game.

Boal's book *Games for Actors and Non-Actors* contains short descriptions of well over a hundred games people can play together, some under these categories and some under others.

When to use TO

I think you might be able to guess by now that I like Theatre of the Oppressed. I like how its techniques empower people to bring about real change.

Says Boal (in *Games for Actors and Non-Actors*):

Theatre of the Oppressed creates spaces of liberty where people can free their memories, emotions, imaginations, thinking of their past, in the present, and where they can invent their future instead of waiting for it.

What's not to like about that?

However, as you and I both know, the methods of TO won't fit into *every* PNI project. PNI's methods may be dull in comparison to the theatrics of TO, but PNI works in areas of low motivation, low interest, low trust, and high fear that TO may not be able to enter into, at least not without expert facilitation. I'd like to think that PNI and TO are complementary approaches, each working at a different band in a spectrum from low to high risk and low to high potential for transformation.

So when is it worth using TO as a narrative intervention in a PNI project? I could say the same thing I said about narrative therapy: when you have discovered an issue about which people need to start telling themselves new stories. But having said that, there are significant differences between the two methods in context.

Like narrative therapy, TO goes beyond inquiry into creating change. But unlike narrative therapy, TO does not require or even *allow* dependence on expert help. In fact, facilitators in TO are called "jokers" because the joker in a deck of playing cards does not belong to any suit. Jokers guide interactions from the side but remain neutral at all times. This is similar to the role of a PNI facilitator, who stays out of the way as much as possible during storytelling and sensemaking. Thus it will probably be *easier for you* to incorporate elements of TO into your PNI projects than it will be to incorporate elements of narrative therapy.

On the other hand, TO is *riskier to your participants* than narrative therapy, so even when it's useful it may not always be possible. Narrative therapy places a lot of the weight of the transformation on the expert therapist. The therapist shapes the interaction, asking the right questions, making the right nudges, guiding the conversations. Those who are being helped come to new realizations, but sometimes they don't realize how they were helped to get there. You could say that the narrative therapist works with stories more than the patient does. This is not necessarily a bad thing. It's safer to the participants, and that makes it a complementary option, useful when riskier methods will fail.

The methods used in Theatre of the Oppressed ask more of participants than either PNI or narrative therapy. TO won't work unless people step out of their comfortable places in the audience and assert their rights to make change happen. There will always be some people who will not be ready to take that step. I've read some records of forum theatre sessions, and it seems that often there are a few people who refuse to participate or leave the session. TO methods accept a loss in the number of participants in order to give the people who remain greater power over their own work with stories.

The question is, how many participants will remain?

If you think the people in your community or organization need to start telling themselves new stories, and you want to plan a narrative intervention to make that happen, the next question to ask yourself is: Would it be better to include everyone at a moderate level of intensity, or would you be willing to risk losing some people to engage those who remain in a more intense process that creates deeper change—for those people? The more inclusive you are, the less powerful the change will be; and the more powerful the change, the fewer people will be engaged in it. Which is more important to your community or organization?

How to use it TO with PNI

As you may have noticed, some of the TO techniques I described above resemble those used for sensemaking in PNI. As I said when I wrote about narrative therapy, I've never actually done this in practice, but I can think of some ways you might be able to incorporate aspects of the TO games listed above into narrative sensemaking sessions.

Image theatre in PNI. Instead of drawing images from open-ended reflection, people could derive images from stories they've encountered. The stories could be randomly selected or chosen based on answers to questions, such as the ten stories with the highest values of memorability and conflict. Grounding images in stories might surprise people with aspects of the theme they wouldn't have thought to consider otherwise.

For newspaper theatre, instead of reading from a newspaper, people could read stories from the collection. You can imagine the impact of interleaving two stories told from opposite points of view, or of acting out scenes from a story as it's being read, or of reading a story out of context.

Forum theatre in PNI. Instead of writing the original play from consideration of a theme, it could be based on stories from the collection. After all, writing the play in forum theatre is similar to a composite story exercise in PNI. Then, when people stop the action and insert themselves as characters, they could draw on other stories they've encountered to propose alternative endings. This would ground the performance in real stories people told, both in its original situation and in its solutions.

Legislative theatre might be a good way to finish up a PNI sensemaking session (or maybe a PNI-TO sensemaking-intervention session). Instead of writing up lists of suggestions, people could propose laws, choose bills, debate their merits, and vote on resolutions. If the community or organization is small and everyone is present, the resolutions could even be binding.

If you read more about Theatre of the Oppressed, you are likely to find even more connections between TO games and PNI exercises. You might come up with more ideas on how to integrate these two bodies of work. You can find information on how to carry out TO games in Boal's books and in many places on the internet. Two notable resources are the International Theatre of the Oppressed Organisation (theatreoftheoppressed.org) and Pedagogy and Theatre of the Oppressed (ptoweb.org).

Participatory theatre outside TO

The last thing I want to say about Theatre of the Oppressed is that it is not the only way of bringing theatrical methods into narrative intervention. I chose to write about TO because it is more coherent, more widely used, and more thoroughly tested than any other approach to participatory theatre I've seen. However, there are other methods for helping people work with stories in theatrical settings.

I must admit to some confusion here. I've followed trails through terms like participatory theatre, development theatre (also called theatre for development), intervention theatre, interactive theatre—and I always get lost in the blurry line between performance, intervention and just plain spectacle. For example, is a flash mob (in which hundreds of people descend on a space, do something nonsensical, then leave again) a form of sensemaking? Or is it just a fad, a joke? I don't know. All I know is that there is more in the space where narrative intervention and theatre come together than Theatre of the Oppressed. *The Applied Theatre Reader* (profiled in the "Further Reading" appendix on page 617) is a good place to start your explo-

ration; it gives you a sampling of approaches from all over.

An example of participatory theatre: Matt Harding's dancing videos

Here is an example of a theatrical intervention I found by accident on the internet. I would like to tell you this story at some length, because I think it explains a lot about the opportunities and uncertainties inherent in creating effective narrative interventions.

Matt Harding started out his work life building computer games. He liked some of the games he worked on, but some were less exciting to him. In 2003 he was told by his employers to abandon work on a family-friendly game he liked because customer tastes had "matured." In response, he came up with a fake pitch for an over-the-top killing game called "Destroy All Humans!" Surprisingly, his employers didn't get the joke and actually developed and sold the game. That was the last straw for Harding. He quit his job, gathered up his savings and began to travel.

Since he was a kid, Harding had danced the same silly little dance. He did it at work when it was time for lunch, to get his co-workers to put their work aside. A few months after he quit his job, while he was traveling in Vietnam, he asked a friend to videotape him standing on a street in Hanoi. The friend said, "Why don't you do that little dance you do?" Harding did, and it turned out funny. So he made a compilation video of himself dancing his silly dance at lots of famous places, in front of monuments and tourist spots. He made a web site in 2005 to show his friends where he'd been, and he called it wherethehellismatt.com. At this point in the story, Harding had no other intention but to record his travels.

Later that year, Harding discovered that a teenager had uploaded his dancing video to a new internet site called YouTube, and that 600,000 people had seen it. The video had turned into a "viral" sensation.

Soon after, the Cadbury-Adams company, which was launching a new chewing gum and looking to get in on the new viral marketing, asked Harding if they could sponsor him on another tour of the world. So Harding made another video of himself dancing in many places and released it on the internet in 2006.

Halfway through his 2006 tour, something amazing happened. Harding didn't have many planned locations in Africa, so he stopped off to visit a friend who lived in Rwanda. He couldn't find any well-known landmarks to dance in front of there, so he just went to a little village and started dancing. There were lots of children in the village, and as soon as he started dancing, they started dancing with him. This had never happened before, and it gave Harding two fundamental insights: first, people are a lot more interesting than landmarks, and second, he might have something he'd like to say to the world about travel and about people.

Says Harding in an interview on the Australian television show *Enough Rope with Andrew Denton:*

> I saw a bunch of kids playing and I just started dancing. I just did this and within seconds—you saw the footage—within seconds they were dancing as well. There was no explanation; there was nothing that needed to be understood; it just looked like fun. And they joined in, and when that was over I just thought—wow, I should have been doing that all along. I've been wasting my time, because it's so much more interesting to see other people and to see the joy on their faces and, honestly, watching *me* dancing really isn't that interesting after a while, or even at all.

So Harding went back to Cadbury-Adams and asked them to sponsor another video. Harding's 2008 video doesn't feature Harding dancing in front of landmarks. It features Harding dancing with people. Around the world, people in lots of different countries are doing Harding's funny little dance with him. Again, the video took the internet by storm, this time with a different message.

But Harding was not entirely happy with the 2008 video. His sponsors had asked him to avoid traveling to a number of countries they considered too dangerous (for example, those in which dancing is frowned upon). And he was unhappy with the dancing too. Even though his

second sponsored video showed him with people, he wasn't dancing with *them*; the people were dancing with *him*. That wasn't what he wanted to say about travel and about people.

Then another amazing thing happened, and again it taught Harding something about what he was doing. Here he is in an interview with the magazine *GeekWire.*

> I was in India and I got some Bollywood dancers to teach me how to dance. They showed me a couple of Bollywood moves, which at that point I figured I wasn't going to be able to actually do, but what the hell I'll try. I found it's a lot more representative of what travel is about, or should be about, which is talking to people and engaging with people, and learning from people in the places that you go to. I thought that was a whole lot more interesting than doing the same thing in the places I went to.

So, using his savings from the sponsorship, Harding decided to fund himself and make another video on his own. This one took him longer to complete (partly because he had a child) and he released it in 2012.

The 2012 video is different from the others. In it, Harding dances with a lot of people, but this time he's doing lots of different dances. He's dancing with the people, not the people with him. Some of the dances are based on ethnic traditions and some are made up on the spot, but in each case Harding asked people to help him find a way to dance with them, experimenting with moves until the people in the group liked what they were doing. (Groups were gathered through notices on the internet and through connections.)

In the 2012 video, Harding's message comes through loud and clear. Says David Pogue in the *New York Times:*

> This time, it's not Harding just swinging his arms, stepping in place. This time, he actually learned to dance, often in the style of the country he was visiting. As a result, there's a feeling of collaboration, of immersion, that wasn't in the earlier video.

The kicker is the final shot. After all those joyous, wordless clips from 50 countries, the final scene is Harding, his baby son on his shoulders, dancing simply with his wife in their own back yard. It's perfection. And it's hard not to tear up.

Harding explains in an interview with the *Smithsonian* the significance of that final shot.

> The last shot … is me, in one sentence, saying, "This is really important to me." A lot of people watch the video and they are sort of waiting for the other shoe to drop, waiting for a sponsor's logo to pop up in the end, to see who paid for this. I funded the video myself and I wanted people to know that there's not a corporate message here—this matters a lot to me. It's an expression of what I believe is important and what I want to pass on to my kid and my family—this is what I think *really* matters.

Speaking personally, I've watched the 2012 video several times, and I can't get through it without crying. A lot. The reason Matt Harding made that video is the reason I wrote this book.

In the *GeekWire* interview, Harding says:

> I think we all really want to feel a part of something and we feel really isolated as of now. I think there's this exuberance and enthusiasm that I experience when people come out to these big mobs in Slovakia or South Korea, and they're really excited to be part of this thing that connects them with people all over the world. I think that's a really powerful and really positive thing that we all have. It's great to find any way you can to cultivate that and make it into something worthwhile.

To see Harding's videos, go to his web site (wherethehellismatt.com) and watch them. They're all there. The best way to view the videos is to watch them in chronological order, because you can follow the progression in Harding's thinking. If you're watching for it, you'll see the clip from Rwanda—it's only a few seconds long, so keep your eyes peeled—and you'll see how it changed everything.

I wanted to tell you this story for a few reasons. First, it's an inspiring example of an effective narrative intervention. As of this writing, Harding's 2012 video has been watched on YouTube thirteen *million* times. In the video's comments on YouTube, Harding asks people to state their locations, and the comments show that people all over the world are watching.

Here are some comments I found particularly interesting:

- If aliens ever come to the earth, this is what we should show them.
- Show me a better video. Go ahead.
- This is some of the most important work anyone has ever done.
- Thanks for letting me know I'm not alone.
- Why am I crying?

The second reason to tell this story is that Harding's video project fits into the category of participatory theatre—all those people making stories happen together—but it falls outside the bounds of any defined approach. This doesn't surprise me! When it comes to participatory work, there are usually more examples outside the bounds of any defined approach than inside it. Participatory work is, or ought to be, participatory in its methods as well as in its content. That's why I say that if you don't make PNI your own you are not doing PNI. The participatory part of PNI isn't just for the people you involve in your projects. It's for you too. Don't be afraid to start your own journey of discovery.

The third and most important reason I wanted to tell you this story was that Harding *himself* didn't know what he was doing when he started making videos. His approach, and his message, evolved through exploration, happenstance, and discovery. That doesn't make his project's impact any less powerful; in fact, I'd say it makes it even more compelling. So in your own work with your community or organization, I suggest you do what Harding did. Start doing something, but don't plan it out too carefully. Harding describes himself in various interviews as "lazy" and "the opposite of a perfectionist," but I think he's being modest. What I think is essential in Harding's approach is that he didn't box himself in by doing things in a prescribed way. He let the work show him how to do it. Your work on narrative intervention should show you how to do it, no matter how much you learn from established approaches (including this book).

COMBINING INTERVENTIONS

I hope I've shown you that narrative interventions can be useful in your community or organization. Now I'll try to explain how you can make them even more useful. Narrative interventions can have synergistic effects with each other. If you are planning one narrative intervention, you might get better results if you split your budget and support two smaller interventions that address the same issue in different ways.

Why do narrative interventions add up to more than the sum of their parts? Because combining interventions creates a diversity of options that helps you draw on a variety of motivations to participate. If there's one thing you should know by now about people and stories, it's that different people in different situations want to do different things with stories. Some people will participate in a narrative intervention to the point of reading some stories or watching a video, but they won't go any further than that. Some people will want to trade stories in conversation. Some will want to play with stories but won't want to build anything. Some people will want to build elaborate constructions. Some will want to spread sensemaking to others. The more options you provide, the more people you can involve.

Let's explore an example of synergism between three fictional narrative interventions.

1. Let's say your PNI project has revealed that your organization needs to change how it thinks about something. Say you begin your intervention by creating a narrative presentation in which stories from your original project collection are posted, very simply, on the walls of your office cafeteria for a month. Visitors to the cafeteria sample the presentation as they like (with low commitment of time) during that month.

2. At the end of the month, let's say you hold a participatory theatre session with people who indicated their interest on a sign-up sheet at the cafeteria. During the session, people work with the stories they have already seen on the walls as they create and act out plays. The energy in the room is high, and the session exceeds all expectations.

3. After the session is over, you place photos and excerpts of transcripts from the plays on the cafeteria walls, right next to the original stories. Visitors to the cafeteria again sample the enhanced presentation, again with low commitment, for another month. The people who participated in the theatre session can see the impact of their participation.

4. After the second presentation phase, you open a new sensemaking space in a room down the hall from the cafeteria. The materials from the original presentation and the theatre session are placed into it to seed the space. A sign in the cafeteria directs people to the new space. People start visiting the new sensemaking space and using it to hold their own events.

5. As people start interacting in the new sensemaking space, you can see that the interventions of presentation, theatre, and space have worked together to spread the impact of the combined interventions both deep and wide.

Now consider what the intervention would be like if it only contained one of those parts.

1. With only the narrative presentation, people would notice and ponder, but the intervention would stop there. Maybe some people would *want* to do more, but they wouldn't have anywhere to put that energy, so the opportunity would die off again.

2. With only the theatre session, you'd have a hard time recruiting people to participate. The session might end up being populated only with people who were already committed to change—say members of the committee that started your PNI project in the first place. Because a less varied spectrum of people participated, people who felt the project had nothing to do with them would feel left out. Rumors might even begin to make the rounds about who gets "chosen" to make new plans.

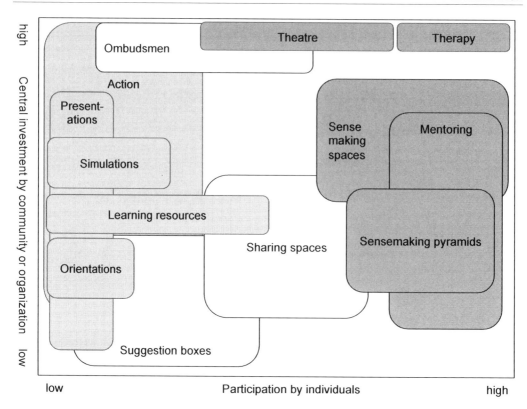

Figure 13.11. How much time and energy I think different types of narrative intervention require from the organization or community as a whole and from its individual members. Items in white have to do with listening to stories; items in light gray have to do with getting stories to where they need to go; items in dark gray have to do with helping people work with stories.

3. With only the sensemaking room, people might walk by it for months without noticing it. Or people might visit, feel no connection to what's in the room, and walk out again. There would be no force drawing people in. Again the room might be populated only from the group of people already invested in the project, and again the impact would be smaller, less varied, and less familiar to everyone.

By meeting people at more levels of participation, you can improve the impact of the intervention on your community or organization. And don't think you can't do multiple interventions if you're operating on a shoestring. Any of the interventions I've mentioned in this chapter can be done very cheaply, with nothing but patience, paper, and pens.

Figure 13.11 shows how much investment I think each type of intervention requires from the community or organization as a whole and from individuals. The interventions that involve people working with stories require relatively high investments of time and energy from individuals. That's why you need to diversify your interventions whenever you can. Planning a pair or trio of interventions that cover the spectrum of individual participation levels can hedge your bets when facing uncertain participation.

THE INTERVENTION INTERVIEWS

In this section are interviews with three colleagues who work on both the telling and listening sides of organizational and community narrative: Shawn Callahan, Karen Dietz and Thaler Pekar. These interviews complement what I've written above by giving you a broader view of experiences in narrative intervention. What makes me happiest about these interviews is that each person responded to my questions in different ways, so the interviews complement each other as well.

The interview questions

I asked each interviewee to ponder five questions before we talked. To avoid us just "talking shop" throughout the interview (a serious danger), I asked my colleagues to speak to me as if I was a member of a community or organization that had just finished its sensemaking phase and was ready to think about intervention. Here's what I sent them before the interview.

1. Building and telling

Our group has been carrying out a PNI project in our community or organization. We have collected stories and used them in sensemaking sessions in which some (but not all) community or organization members participated. The sensemaking has resulted in two things: a set of constructed artifacts that describe our understanding of the issues most important to the community or organization (timeline of events and landscape of perceptions); and a prioritized list of concerns, opportunities, and ideas related to those issues.

We have decided to create and tell some purposeful stories to the larger community or organization in hopes that they will create a positive spiral of storytelling. We have our sensemaking outputs and collected stories to work with. Can you give us any advice on *building* and *telling* these stories?

2. Action

We have changed our minds. Instead of building a purposeful story, we would now like to take dramatic *action* that produces ripples of storytelling in the community or organization. What is your advice on taking such action?

3. Divided

Our group is in the intervention phase, like the previous group, but unlike them we face a significant *division* in our community or organization. Our project group includes people from both sides. We have discovered some amazing insights and opportunities among ourselves, and now we want to spread them to the entire community or organization. Do you have any special storytelling advice for our *divided* situation?

4. Powerless

Our group is in the intervention phase, like the first group, but unlike them we are all in one group: the group *without power* in our community or organization. We carried out our project without the involvement of those above us, though we invited them to participate. We would like our intervention to reach our *entire* community or organization, even though some of them did not participate in our project and may not believe a word we say. Do you have any special storytelling advice for our *bottom-up* situation?

5. Outsiders

We are outsiders who were *paid* to study certain issues by those in power, who genuinely want to improve the situation for everyone in the community or organization but have their own perspective on things. We did get people from all parts of the community or organization to participate in portions of the project, but we are not sure our attempts to spread participation will be sufficient to convince everyone our project is not simply a tool of those in power. Do you have any special storytelling advice for our *outside-in, top-down* situation?

Shawn Callahan

Shawn Callahan, founder of the narrative consulting firm Anecdote, is a management consultant who has been designing and implementing organizational change initiatives for the past fifteen years. His specific skills and interest lie in anthropological techniques such as the collection and interpretation of workplace stories and in helping leaders be better storytellers. In more recent times Shawn has focused his attention on how organizations create and embed their strategies.

Cynthia Kurtz: Hello Shawn. I'm going to ask you the first scripted question I wrote up for our interview. Here it is.

> We have decided to create and tell some purposeful stories to the larger community or organization in hopes that they will create a positive spiral of storytelling. We have our sensemaking out-

puts and collected stories to work with. Can you give us any advice on *building* and *telling* these stories?

Shawn Callahan: I guess one of the things that I've learned doing these types of projects is that in the early days we thought the story approach was all about *insight*. That you would get a group of people together to look at stories, and you would go through a process, and they would draw out new patterns that they weren't aware of. And that's *true*, you absolutely *do* get amazing insights. All sorts of things come out.

I remember one of the really early projects we did was with the Defense Department—I've told this story lots of times before—but essentially we had two teams. One team did a structured interview; another team collected stories. After a period of time of going out and doing that, we decided to get the two teams together to compare results. It was all around occupational health and safety training.

And the structured interview guys said, "Yep, they're more or less doing the right thing. Not much we have to change here. All looks good." And the three of us doing the story work looked at each other and said, "So, you didn't hear about the soldiers who all wear protective footwear because some poor chap had his toes knocked off, but they don't wear protective *eyewear*, because they've never had an *eye* accident before?"

So, we had heard all these stories of major transgressions that didn't actually come up in the structured interviews.

Cynthia: By structured interviews you mean they said, "Which of these answers to this question do you choose?"

Shawn: Yes, that type of thing. And, maybe even more openness than that, but it more or less elicited an opinion rather than a story.

So we got all excited about the fact that you've got these insights. And when we did the sense-making workshops people could really *see* these insights, and they said, "Oh my god, is this *really* happening?" It was a new view for them.

But over the years we started to realize there's actually something *more* important in this process. The more important thing—and this is the thing that drives the intervention—is that when people work with stories, they get engaged *emotionally* with the issue. And then they're *inspired* to take action. So it's not just a rational thing, a cognitive thing, like, "Let's think it through and get the insight." It's a *gut*-wrenching, knot in the stomach, "Oh my god, is it like that, we've got to *do* something" thing.

And that's why that whole participatory approach is so important in this. Because you want to get a group of people who are influential in the organization, all with a similar feeling, who want to do something. That's sort of like a preliminary, if you like, before I jump into the actual question here.

The intervention of building and telling stories is something we don't do very often. Except in one circumstance, which is around the use of *strategic* stories. The way we see a strategic story is it's like a broad *narrative* that reflects the organization's strategy. I like to think of it as the original score from a musical. Each leader needs to create their own arrangement when they share it. If you are a country and western kind of guy you'll do a country and western arrangement. The jazz guy does a jazz arrangement and so on.

If you were working with a group, and they decided that they wanted to take a certain approach—for example, in this situation where you've got a group that's come to some sort of conclusion about what they need to do—they might say, "There are three initiatives we want to put in place." One of the things you'll hear in an organization after someone says that is, "*Why* are we putting those initiatives in place?" The *strategic* story explains why.

The strategic story is simply, "In the past it was like *this*, then something *changed*, and as a result of that we're going to do *these* three things, so that in the future it can be like *that*." It's just a simple *story spine* approach to helping people understand the reason why you're doing something. [Note: You can read about Kenn Adams' story spine in Appendix A on page 613.]

Now, on the telling side, one of the things that we've started to work out in helping leaders be better storytellers is that the first thing they have to learn how to do is develop the ability to *spot* stories. They need to understand what is a story. We've got now probably a couple of thousand people, maybe three thousand people, have done thestorytest.com, and it's quite a normal distribution in terms of the results. There are lots of people skewed to the higher end of the score...

Cynthia: Because they're interested.

Shawn: Yes, because they're interested. This is not a randomly selected sample. So you get a small group of people who get ten out of ten. And the people who get ten out of ten e-mail me, and they say, "I don't get this story test thing." It's so *obvious* which are the stories to them. And then I'll get other people who get five out of ten. They just cannot see the difference between a story and an opinion.

In my mind you can't really take advantage of story techniques unless you know what a story is. That's the premise. So part of helping people develop story-related initiatives and interventions is building the *narrative intelligence* in the organization so that they can at least simply spot and tell a story. Of course, spotting a story and telling a story are quite different.

And the other thing that is related to this is that most people in organizations don't see themselves as storytellers. Whenever I start a workshop—I had one just yesterday, I had about sixty people in the audience, and I asked people, "So who here believes they're a storyteller?" I always get about three or four hands up, always. And then I tell them about Robin Dunbar's research on gossip, and how he more or less eavesdropped on peoples' conversations. And it turns out that something like sixty percent of the time we're speaking, we're talking about who did what to whom. And the only way we can do that is to tell stories. So if sixty percent of the time we're speaking informally we're storytellers, we're telling stories. So I take this idea that we're *all* storytellers, but what we have to do is be more *purposeful* and *systematic* in how we do it. How we find the stories and how we go about telling those stories.

I don't particularly go through any other process for *building* stories. But we might have interventions. Say, for example, you've recognized that there's a particular value that's stated

in your strategy. Pick a value like integrity. Say you've discovered that maybe people are not acting with as much as integrity as you would like that they would act. So one of the interventions that we have applied was essentially inspired by the Ritz Carlton, and how they embed the value of customer service.

The way they do that is that they invite every staff member out of all their hotels to submit stories of great customer service. This happens every month. Then they pick one story, and then they push that same story out to every team leader, and the team leaders read it out to their team just before their shift. They have a quick conversation about that story. They ask questions like, "So, what's *significant* about this story?" And people say things like, "Oh, well, you know, that person obviously has the confidence to jump out of their normal role, and actually jump over there to help the customer out." And then someone else will jump in and say, "Yeah, obviously they've got the support of their high-level managers." And someone else will jump in and say, "Oh yeah, you can see they've gotten the proper training."

So they embed what customer service means, and the people work it out for themselves. And then they have a series of other questions to even further embed, and maybe even *inspire* people in that team to try something out like that. It's a lovely intervention, because you essentially have all these *concrete* examples going around the organization of what the value means.

So we've done that with helping teachers be more innovative, for example, where we worked with a government department. We wanted to improve innovation among teachers. They first started off by trying to *define* innovation. And you know what that's like, it's a hard thing to do. You end up getting to the philosophical level of what is innovation. And they went into a bit of a spiral and couldn't quite make progress.

So when we got involved we said let's forget about the definition. Let's just go out and collect stories of teachers being innovative. So we did that, and then we took one story at a time, and instead of pushing it out to team leaders, people called in on a teleconference, and I read the story out, and did exactly the same thing.

And it was, again, giving this concrete specific example of what innovation really means.

Cynthia: How did you pick the story?

Shawn: It was just to do with trying to break some of the perceptions of innovation. So for example when we asked teachers what innovation was, the things they would say would be things like, "Oh, that's using wikis, and Twitter, and Facebook." But when you've got *stories*, the stories are about turn and talk techniques, and principals coming up with new funding models to get different types of teachers on board.

There was this one lovely story of a teacher in a suburb in Melbourne. She started a Vietnamese language program for third graders, and then eventually expanded it to the whole school. So they had Vietnamese being taught throughout the whole school as a second language. And then that became the *model* for second language Vietnamese teaching throughout Victoria. So people picked up all these ideas and thought, why not try things small and get something going.

Cynthia: So you chose the stories to meet the needs you perceived.

Shawn: Exactly. Instead of telling them this is what innovation was, we just picked stories which had it embedded in them. So those types of interventions work really well.

Now this probably jumps into the next question a little bit.

Cynthia: Yes. The question was:

> We have changed our minds. Instead of building a purposeful story, we would now like to take dramatic *action* that produces ripples of storytelling in the community or organization. What is your advice on taking such action?

Shawn: It was interesting that you used the words dramatic action, because the approach we've taken is "small things can make a big difference." So we're after *non*-dramatic action.

Cynthia: I don't mean it in the way of dramatic meaning big, I mean it in terms of being a drama, an action that tells a story. It could be a small action, but it creates a story because it is linked to circumstances in such a way that

it's dramatic. I got that from a research paper by Alan Wilkins from thirty years ago, about the fact that when actions are dramatic, that is, linked into the drama of the organization or community, they have an impact out of proportion to their size.

Shawn: It's a good point. It's doing those things that will actually trigger a story of some sort.

It was very nice reading Teresa Amabile's latest book, called *The Progress Principle*. It's an interesting story-related research project. She did this daily diary exercise, where she asked 250 employees across seven or eight different companies, across three or four different months. Every day they had to write down something about an event that was significant for them for the day. She didn't mention stories, but essentially the question was such that it got them talking about something that *happened*.

One of the major findings of the research was that, yes, big things had big impacts, and also many small things have very small impacts. But there was something like twenty-five or thirty percent of small things that actually had *big* impacts. And that's the mantra that we use in intervention designs. Let's not try to do the big rollout. Let's not try to work out every specific detail. We're going to experiment. We're going to try things out; we're going to kill things off that don't work; and we're going to expand on things that seem to be working. Which is very influenced by Cynefin-type thinking. [Note: Shawn is referring to the Cynefin framework, which can be used to support decision making in a variety of situations. According to the framework, in situations where complex interactions are important, it is useful to try many things and keep only those that work.]

And the other thing, which is also related to this, is that we give people the instruction of, "Don't try to fix the problem." Which is one of these paradoxical phrases, I think. We find that when people get into the mindset of, "We're going to fix the problem," they start to believe that they actually *know* what all the different actions will result in. They start to believe that we'll do X and then Y, and then Y will lead to Z, and then we'll do A and B, and this will happen over a twelve-month period, and they start project planning...

Cynthia: Because if you can fix something, it must be fixable. If you *say* you're going to fix it, you have defined it as fixable.

Shawn: Indeed. And this really gets them thinking quite differently when you give that instruction, "Don't try to fix the problem." It's about trying to create new behavior, trying to create new ways of working in an organization. So there are two principles.

And then what we would tend to do is, we would give people a *framework* for changing behavior. One of the ones that we're using at the moment is by the guys who wrote the book *Influencer*. It has a framework which is based around this idea that people can only change if they have the motivation to change and also the skill to change. And they look at three levels, the individual level, at the social level, and at the infrastructure level. [Note: The book's full title is *Influencer: The Power to Change Anything*, and it is written by Kerry Patterson, Joseph Grenny, David Maxfield, Ron McMillan and Al Switzler.]

So you've got these six boxes of places where you can create certain types of intervention. One might be individual motivation-type intervention: how can we get people motivated to do this? The individual skill stuff is basic training, and different ways of building skills and knowledge. The social part is about peer pressure, and how do you get people understanding what other people have done? This is that whole area of social proof, Cialdini's work, who's an influence researcher. [Note: Robert Cialdini's (excellent) book is called *Influence: The Psychology of Persuasion*.]

The last two, one is around individual motivation at the structural level, which is rewards and recognition, and things related to that. The idea being is that you don't try to do anything in that space until you've done stuff in the others. It should be a point of last resort, reward and recognition. Maybe reward more than recognition. Recognition actually can be very useful for you. Reward can screw you up totally.

Cynthia: That reminds me of the project I did on the future of volunteering. There were two different sets of motivations for volunteering. The same action that would motivate one group of people would de-motivate the other group.

Shawn: Is that right? Wow. We've just done a big sensemaking project for KPMG, and the big learning out of that was just how important *unanticipated* recognition is in terms of motivation. It really came out as a top thing. And when people *cared*, the person who provided the recognition really cared, and did something to illustrate the level of caring, that made a difference.

Cynthia: And that is a perfect example of where the insight and the intervention come together. Because the insight leads you to the proper intervention that will have the positive change you want.

Shawn: Exactly.

Cynthia: That doesn't always happen. Sometimes your insight is that we have this problem we didn't know we had, but the insight does not tell you how to *address* it. But sometimes you're lucky, and the insight does connect to it.

Shawn: Actually, did I ever tell you about our example of, in sensemaking, what I call "The bitching story"? You ever heard our bitching story? Does it ring any bells?

Cynthia: I'm not sure. Why don't you tell it?

Shawn: I've just written this up as a paper, and it was just one of the little vignettes. Essentially we were doing a project for a library. The library was moving buildings, and they wanted to have a look at their culture, and maybe think about how they might better improve their culture moving from one building to the other. So we collected all the stories around a sensemaking workshop. In that sensemaking workshop we had a group of librarians standing in front of a wall of sticky notes and clusters, and we asked them what did they make of that? What were the key patterns in all that? And what might you do about that? And they said, "Oh, it's clear, we've got a *training* problem."

We *knew* they didn't have a training problem. That wasn't what was on the wall. But we knew we couldn't *tell* them that, because you've got to learn it yourself, right? So we said, "Okay, why don't we try something? Why don't we use a story spine, and you tell the *story* of what you see on the wall." So they went off in groups to use the story spine.

So they went off and they made up this story. And they came back and told it. The story was essentially about this woman, I can't remember her name, we'll call her Sue. And Sue had joined the library, and was renowned for talking behind peoples' backs about them. And she eventually got promoted, and promoted, and she was very good at managing up, but everyone else she would bitch about behind their backs. And then eventually after a while people started bitching about *Sue*. Until one day Sue went out for lunch, and she stepped off the curb, and got run over and killed by a car.

It was a much better story than what I've just told you there, but essentially when they told this story I was shocked, because some people had almost tears to their eyes hearing that story. And almost in unison, they looked at each other, and they said, "We don't have a *training* problem. We have a *bitching* problem." And right then and there they committed to addressing this issue of bitching in their library.

Well, they put in all these different initiatives around bitching, mainly about calling the behavior, and not being tolerant of that behavior. And when they opened the new library, the CEO stood up, and all the librarians were there, sitting in rows of seats. And she got them to look under their seats, and underneath their seat was a tag which had "bitching" written across it. And she got everyone to rip the tag off, come up to the front, rip the tag up, and throw it into a bin. It was like a ritual cleansing. And now, by all accounts they're very happy with their new ways of working in the new library.

Cynthia: That's amazing.

Shawn: Yeah. And so again you have that connection between insight and intervention, it's very close. But you had to do a little bit more work where you had to use a different story technique to actually draw out the insight, which then had the feeling—they really *felt* it. And as a result of that they were going to fix it.

One of the paradoxes that you face in doing this sort of work is that, on the one hand you don't want to lead people to a solution, because it becomes *your* solution rather than *their* solution, and it loses motivation for them to do something about it.

I had one example where I helped this group of bankers. And I had six groups of five, and each group of five was a little team, and it was working on interventions. And I was going around to each of the teams, and I was asking what they were doing, and making suggestions for improvements. And this one team wanted to improve the effectiveness of their sales force. I mentioned to them that maybe they want to think about a community of practice for salespeople. And they went, "Oh, that sounds like a great idea, fantastic, really love that."

We then got all the groups together to review all the different interventions, and the guy who was leading that group that I suggested the community of practice started off his overview by saying, "Oh yeah, and for our sales force we got this great idea from Shawn about communities of practice, and it works like this, this, this, and this."

Well, the rest of the group around the table sort of rounded on the initiative, saying it wouldn't work, it was a bad idea. And I jumped in and said, "No, no, no, it's a *good* idea, and here are the reasons why it's a good idea." And it just got worse and worse. And then it just *dawned* on me, and I thought, oh, you *idiot*, Shawn. It's *my* idea. I'm the outsider. I'm not the banker. I don't understand this world. I'm not like anyone else around this table. So I backed off. And of course by that stage it was dead in the water.

That's on the one hand. They don't want to accept stuff that's more or less given to them by someone outside. But on the *other* hand, the people who are developing the interventions—because I've discovered you get more traction if you can get people *in* the business lines actually developing interventions, and not in the HR [Human Resources] department, because they've got real connections to how the organization works. But they're not experts in change interventions. They don't know what's possible. They don't have a lot of patterns of different types of interventions that they can put in place. So you're always treading this fine line between making little suggestions, but not wanting them to feel that your idea is better than their idea.

I think that's always big. I have to bite my tongue. When I suggest something they take it in their own way, and can take quite a different approach to it. I now think of it as, well, that's innovation. They're just sparking on something and applying it into their particular world. The most important thing is that something actually *happens*. Some action takes place. So I guess that's another lesson.

We should get into question three.

Cynthia: Okay, here it is.

> Our group is in the intervention phase, like the previous group, but unlike them we face a significant *division* in our community or organization. Our project group includes people from both sides. We have discovered some amazing insights and opportunities among ourselves, and now we want to spread them to the entire community or organization. Do you have any special storytelling advice for our *divided* situation?

Shawn: Yeah, there are a couple things that spark some ideas. Like in that question, if you had these divided groups, how do you get them to come together in some ways?

I did a little project for IBM ages ago where we got a group that was divided, and had real different views on things, but they weren't hearing each other. So we recorded a session that we had, and it was a pretty robust session. And after the session had finished I got the session transcribed, and then I sent the transcription to all the participants. And I said, "Before our next meeting I want you to *read* the entire transcription, and where the people who've got the opposite view as you, I just want you to make some notes about their views." Anyway, they came back, and it was a totally different feeling, because when they were reading through the transcription, they were doing it in a *cold* state rather than a *hot* state. And they were actually able to see and hear the other person's point of view.

Cynthia: And this was a transcription of all the different people telling stories, or…?

Shawn: Yeah, it was mostly stories, but a lot of it was argument, and opinion. So I guess what it got me thinking about is the importance of *listening*. How do you actually help people listen?

I guess the thing that we also learned in this space is, it's not like we don't know *how* to listen. We all know how to listen. But do we *want* to listen? It's an issue of motivation rather than skill. We may not listen to someone because we might have a low opinion of them. We might think, oh, they're a garrulous person, and they're just going to go on forever. So we just cut them off. Or they're from a different part of the organization, and they don't add value. We just have these labels. They don't add value, so we won't listen to them. And a lot of it's about just helping people recognize this. It's how you build that motivation to listen.

Cynthia: And it sounds like you changed the context in that example.

Shawn: Yeah, and it was an accident. It wasn't one that we tried to design up front. It just *happened* that I was recording it. It just *happened* that I transcribed it and sent it out to them. And then they reported back just how much they learned about what the other person was saying. So I wish I could say it was this brilliant idea, but it was a discovery that we've since used again, so it was a happy discovery.

Cynthia: The fourth question is:

> Our group is in the intervention phase, like the first group, but unlike them we are all in one group: the group *without power* in our community or organization. We carried out our project without the involvement of those above us, though we invited them to participate. We would like our intervention to reach our *entire* community or organization, even though some of them did not participate in our project and may not believe a word we say. Do you have any special storytelling advice for our *bottom-up* situation?

Shawn: I suppose on that question, in terms of if you're a group that's seeking to have influence, you're a group that doesn't have a lot of power in the organization, it's a sort of a bottom-up situation.

I'm actually doing something like this for a mine site at the moment. They're implementing SAP [a resource management system]. It's bigger than Ben Hur, this SAP implementation.

They're spending two billion dollars on it, and it's just crazy, the money, two *billion* dollars. And at one of the mine sites, they're getting all of the corporate guff on what to do and how to do it. But what they *know* is that that doesn't influence the guys at the mine site. The guys at the mine site just want to see, how's it going to affect *us?*

So they were being very smart. They decided to take one machine—they call them *assets,* these big dredging machines—and they're going to have a scheduled maintenance period, I think it takes about two months to do maintenance on these things. And during that time they're going to use nothing but the SAP system to do the maintenance. And it's going to *force* them to do it, and it's going to teach them all sorts of things. But they've engaged us to collect the success stories of what happens when they do this very detailed specific pilot, if you like, of the SAP system at their mine site. Because they know if they can get the successful stories, they can then use that from the bottom up to influence what the rest of the organization does with the actual implementation of SAP.

So they're being very proactive in doing it, so they're having multiple benefits. One benefit is they're actually going to get the people at the mine site more interested in the SAP system, rather than the sort of guff they're getting from corporate. And secondly, they're going to have an influence on the rest of the organization, based on the stories that they're going to collect.

So that would be another way of having influence when you don't have that power.

The other one that I mention in these types of organizations, is that we suggest to them that they avoid the "s" word, *story.* Because especially in mining companies, or a lot of other organizations, they attach story with spin, and they manipulate it. Whereas what *we* want to do is, we just want to share *experiences,* and say how it actually works at the coal face.

Cynthia: I think that when you work with stories you need to know something about stories, but that doesn't mean that you should *use* that word.

Shawn: Oh, absolutely.

Cynthia: And that advice applies up and down and sideways.

Shawn: Yeah, absolutely, definitely.

I didn't really understand the fifth question, that was the one that sort of stumped me a little bit.

Cynthia: It was:

> We are outsiders who were *paid* to study certain issues by those in power, who genuinely want to improve the situation for everyone in the community or organization but have their own perspective on things. We did get people from all parts of the community or organization to participate in portions of the project, but we are not sure our attempts to spread participation will be sufficient to convince everyone our project is not simply a tool of those in power. Do you have any special storytelling advice for our *outside-in, top-down* situation?

Cynthia: That one's more of when the project involves outsiders coming in, and you say the project is participatory—this comes up a lot in development work—that the people at the bottom, or the people who are mistrustful of authority, because it's been authorized by authority, they won't accept it. They don't want to accept it. It smells. What do you do in a situation like that?

Shawn: Yeah, that's a good question. Nothing springs to mind for me on that one.

Cynthia: I think some of your stories about, like the library one seems to me to resonate with that. Because there might have been all kinds of initiatives that told these people who made up that story about Sue what to do, but it didn't resonate with them. It wouldn't have resonated with them the way that that thing did, the bitchiness did. Because it bubbled up.

Shawn: Yeah, I think you're right.

I think the other thing, too, is who do you get *involved* in these sort of changes in organizations? Say, for example, the top has decided we want to make some sort of change. Well, the smart ones will say, "Okay, if you look at the informal networks in our organization, where are some of those nodes of influence? They can either be for this approach, or against it. So maybe we should get them involved really early, and get them involved in the process of working out how this thing's actually going to *look*, and the actual detailed approach we're going to use." Now, that requires a bit of *letting go* by the top in the design of the initiative, but these sort of things only work if you have that willingness to let go.

Cynthia: This is great. Thanks a lot for your help, Shawn.

Shawn: It's very exciting, and you're doing a terrific job in getting the word out about different ways of using stories in the world, which is what we want. And I'm trying to write something as well, so I'll be coming on your heels. Build on top of what you've got there.

You can find more on Shawn's work and writing on his web site at anecdote.com.

Karen Dietz

As the owner of *Just Story It*, Karen Dietz's passion is to help companies grow their business through the power of storytelling and organizational narrative. In addition to her corporate work, she is a trained storyteller and the former executive director of the National Storytelling Network. Her clients include Fortune 500 companies, business leaders, and community advocates. Industries include financial services, travel, entertainment, technology and non-profits. For more information on Karen's work, visit her web site at juststoryit.com.

Cynthia Kurtz: Hello Karen. I'm going to ask you the first scripted question I wrote up for our interview. Here it is.

> We have decided to create and tell some purposeful stories to the larger community or organization in hopes that they will create a positive spiral of storytelling. We have our sensemaking outputs and collected stories to work with. Can you give us any advice on *building* and *telling* these stories?

Karen Dietz: I'm going to respond globally, and then work down to specific things.

So, the way I interpreted your question was, I said to myself, what do you really want to know? It seems like what we're stepping into now in this implementation phase is: how do you take the stories that you have collected, stimulated, shared in that body of work now from your research—how do you use them in this phase you're calling intervention? For me, what that's really all about is: how do you change something? How do you move from one place to another and use stories as the *fuel* as you go along?

There are a couple of things that we do know in this implementation piece, this intervention piece, is that there are *stages to the change cycle*, moving from launching the change, to overcoming obstacles, to making adjustments, to celebration. You start here, and you end up over here. And you go through different phases of it. Most people think of change as, "Oh, let me just *launch* the change, and then that's all I have to do. It will take care of itself. Because we have our plans in place, and now we're going to implement the project." But even that sometimes gets lost.

So there's change, and then there's adding stories into the mix of it. And this is where story *telling* is really the worst way to think about stories during a change initiative. Because it's really not about just *telling* stories, it's about, in addition to sharing your story, listening for, and allowing *others* to share *their* stories, as you go along each phase of the change cycle. So it's that interaction back and forth. Because we know storytelling is a co-created experience. In that phase every story I tell on launching change is going to stimulate stories in you. If we don't *allow* for that story sharing to happen in each phase, then we oftentimes lose engagement, and lose involvement, and lose that *fire* that keeps us going.

So we need to be very thoughtful and conscious about what we're doing with stories in this intervention phase. That's above and beyond, "How do you tell it?"

At each cycle of the change process, you have to tell *different* stories. I'm happy to share with you a chart that I made years ago and that I've used. [Note: You can find Karen's chart of stories to tell and listen to during a change process on her web site at juststoryit.com/story-resources.htm.]

Once you launch a story, there's a set of stories which are what you need to do to launch change—why the change needs to happen and what your commitment is to it. And it is listening to the stories from others in the organization on the same topics.

Once you tell those sets of stories, and you've launched the project, then the *next* set of stories comes into play. Those stories are about gathering resources: if this group over here has this work to do, and another group has different work to do, but they all have to be part of the change effort, then what's the story of *your* work that you're going to contribute to this change effort? And, I have resources over here, you have resources over there, we need to share resources, so *how* are we going to share our resources? And how are we going to collaborate, and how are we going to make this happen? What are *those* stories?

We think of implementation and planning for change as a flow chart, but how it becomes *alive* is in the stories we share as we go along. So we have to put our story listening ears on, and our story sharing ears. We need to evoke from others *their* stories, and what *they're* going to be doing in this piece to launch the change effort. We need to listen to the actual work they're going to be doing to make it a reality. We need to *broadcast* that story outside of the group, because then you're also building *tendrils of accountability*.

Cynthia: I like that phrase. Tendrils that grow out.

Karen: Right. Get people invested, get people involved.

Cynthia: I guess that's accountability and commitment.

Karen: Right, right. There is a little story that needs to happen *before* that, that I forgot, so let me step back a step.

One of the things that's very effective when you're launching change is to elicit stories from others about when they have *gone through change and survived*. And what the *qualities* were that emerged from that, what qualities

saw them through that change. And then what were the untold, unseen benefits: stuff that they never could have imagined before, when they were in the middle of it, and it was so ugly and awful.

But you get *through* it, and then you have the *boon*—the prize at the end of the successful outcome, some lesson that enriches your life. So, what's the boon? What did they experience in terms of a boon that they were able to bring back into their lives having survived that change? Because you *want* people to *remember* that, oh yeah, this is familiar, I've done it before, and good things happened.

Cynthia: Yes, and it's more complicated than, "Oh no, change is terrible."

Karen: Right. So, you really have to consciously build the sharing of those stories into the intervention.

Cynthia: I like that.

Karen: Then after that you can start growing into, "This is what I'm going to do, this is what this group is going to do, this is the resources we're going to share, this is what we need, this is what we're short of, this is how we are going to get it." And then, "This is how we have solved our problems." You'll recognize that this whole thing is a *journey*. It's a story journey, with a typical story structure.

The next piece is how we overcome obstacles, and how we persevered. Life got tough. Every organization hits this spot, and in most organizations the change effort just kind of falls apart at this place. This is where storytelling becomes really, really critical.

Often projects end up out of sight, out of mind. There was a change project, but it doesn't matter. The launch was great, but you never hear about it again, because everybody gets busy doing regular work. Unless you're consciously evoking, collecting and broadcasting these stories, you're not saying, "Oh no, we're *continuing* on this change, by the way. This is our progress in this change. This is how we are overcoming the obstacles. This is how we're persevering. And yoo-hoo, we're winning." So that's really critical.

Then there's *another* set of stories that comes right behind that. Which is, "Ooh, you know, we've overcome these obstacles, we've persevered, and we've *learned* things in the process. And now we're having to shift and adjust as we go along. So, maybe our original thought about doing all this blah, blah, blah—hmm, maybe not so. We *thought* what we were going to do is redesign our customer service platform. And what we *ended up* doing, because we learned along the way by talking to our customers about what they *really* needed, was something *else*. So, we didn't *abandon* the change project. We shifted and changed, and we *met* the new learning."

So, there are all kinds of stories to share about that. This is what I *personally* learned about this process, this is what we're learning about the *entire* process, and how we shift and change. It can happen at the individual, the group and the organizational level.

Cynthia: This is fascinating, because instead of saying you're going to craft *one* story, and you're going to tell it, you're saying you *can't* do that, that's not enough. There are a series of stories, there are a series of stages and conditions and contexts, and you have to think about all of them as you lead through this process.

Karen: Yes. I can't tell you how I sick I am of people who say, "Oh yes, it's your vision story, that's change, woo-hoo, tell that." And I say, that will only get you so far. It will last about two weeks. And then things start falling apart, or not go along as expected. And the *end* result is that storytelling gets a bad name.

Cynthia: Right, because obviously it doesn't work.

Karen: Right, "I told the story, got everybody engaged, rah-rah." But what happened with the follow through? I'm not saying that *nobody* follows through, but we know companies that don't follow through. We know companies that do follow through, and yahoo for them. The point about storytelling is that it makes the follow through just that much easier, and more *powerful*, and it's a lot easier to stay on track.

So we've gotten to the place of what we've learned, shifted, changed, adjusted our path as we've gone along. We're at the place now where it's really about: we've made it, and these are our successes, and—the *celebration*. And *then* you want as many stories as you can collect about, "It was tough, we persevered, this is what we've learned, and here's what we were able to do, and it's the coolest thing since sliced bread. Here is this person over here, the unsung hero; here's this person over here, toiling away; and *look* at what they were able to do."

Cynthia: Would you recommend that all these stories that are being told be authentic, in other words collected, or do you think it's reasonable to craft some of them from—I don't want to say from nothing, but not from direct experience.

Karen: No, they all have to be from direct experience. Authenticity is a big deal here.

Cynthia: Because I have seen some things where people will make up sort of fairytale stories, and try to use that for change—so you don't like that…

Karen: It's crap. And I'll tell you why, in my own humble personal opinion. If you want to get the biggest bang for your buck out of leadership, then *tell your own personal stories*. Tell authentic personal direct stories. You can tell a tale that's helpful, but it's not going to get you really what you need. I *never* work with clients on helping them tell a *tale*. The hard work is, can you stand and deliver your *own* personal story?

Cynthia: I guess you could argue that building these tales of the way our organization's going to work five years from now, a tale that's ridiculously made up, is almost a way of *avoiding* doing the hard work.

Karen: It is. And it's putting people in a fantasy land. And you're going to get *buy-in*? I'm sorry. People are jaded enough. Why go there? Why risk it? It's dangerous.

And yet there is a role for a Future/Vision Story, but it must be *grounded* in the present. People must be able to see themselves in the story in order for them to bring their current selves into the future. This creates a story then that people can relate to and bring into reality.

One of the stories early on in launching the change—I said that there was a little set of core stories that needs to happen just in the launching of the change. One of those stories that everybody *never* realizes they need to tell, but they *need* to tell it, it is essential, is that the leadership needs to get up and tell the story about their *personal commitment* to the change. "This is why we need to change. These are the problems we're encountering. If we don't change *now,* the future's pretty bleak. If we *do* change, this is the vision that we have for the future. These are the opportunities that we could reach. And, oh, by the way, I'm not gone tomorrow. This isn't just a bunch of puffery to get you hyped up. This is *my* commitment to the change. This is what *I* will be doing every single day, because I'm committed to it."

Cynthia: I would say that they shouldn't tell their story *about* their commitment to the change, but it should be a story that *proves* their commitment to the change. The events in the story prove it.

Karen: Yes.

Cynthia: That reminds me of a story I heard once fifth-hand about a guy who was an executive in some corporation. He had just implemented some plan of cost savings where nobody was allowed to fly business class. The very next day he went to fly, and he had bought a ticket on coach. But the airline recognized him and said, "Oh, we'll bump you up for free."

So, he had this dilemma. It's not actually going to cost the company anything, and I can ride in business class. But he said, "No, I said coach, I'm flying coach."

And he gets into the coach section of the airplane, and there are five people from his company there. And they all *see* him there. And the word spreads that he really did fly coach. So he made the right choice. And then he could now go and tell everybody that story. But he didn't *have* to tell it, because everybody told it to everybody.

So if he had taken the option the airline offered to him, even though it didn't actually break his agreement, he would have lost the opportunity to provide proof. So that's the kind of story you're talking about, I think.

Karen: That is.

It can also happen in another way. I was coaching a global Fortune 500 company. They had different regions across the globe, and these different regions all had different performance review procedures. Well, they were implementing a new standard across-the-board performance review process. You can imagine that some people didn't like it. How can Germany be evaluated the same way as Asia? But, that's what was happening.

So, the executive had to launch this big change initiative. And when we were working on the stories that she could tell to launch this change effort and have it be successful, one of the questions I asked her was, why are *you* committed to this? When in your life have you had something similar happen to *you,* where you saw the benefit, and you decided to persevere and do it anyway? And what happened as a result?

So we worked on that story, and she had all of her division heads in a meeting. And she said it went really well. She could see people nodding their heads, they were getting it, and they were getting her commitment through that story. It was also a story that was hitting a couple of things at the same time. They also were realizing that, yeah, you can survive change, because it was a change story *and* it was a commitment story kind of all rolled into one. When we were in the coaching session, she asked me, "Why are you asking me that question? Why do I even need to tell that story?" And I said, "Because they need to *trust* you."

Cynthia: They need to see that it goes all the way in, it's not just painted on the top.

Karen: Right. They need to know that they can trust you, they need to know that they can depend upon you, and they need to know that you're not launching this and then leaving them in the lurch. Because that's what many people's experience is about change at the project level, at the big corporate level. And so they're jaded. So you *have* to tell that story.

Cynthia: I did a work life balance project once, and one of the stories that came out was, they said, "The manager gave this big speech about how we have sane work hours, and [whispering] by the way, can you come in on Saturday?" At the end of this big speech they were turning aside in a whisper and contradicting it. And of course *that* story got out and went all over.

Karen: Yes, that's true.

So that kind of goes through the change cycle, and briefly explains the kind of stories that you need to tell and listen for and share in each phase.

Cynthia: That's your unique thing, because I haven't heard that from anyone else.

Karen: Thank you.

Now, there's another piece to add. A great example of this added piece is Gaylord Hospitals, and Alicia Korten and I wrote about this in our chapter in the *Wake Me Up* book. Gaylord Hospitals is a fabulous example of dramatic change that needed to happen, and their ability to use stories effectively, and turn around an entire organization. [Note: The book chapter referred to is: "Who Said Money Is Everything? Story Is The New Currency In Financial Management," pp. 78–92 in *Wake Me Up When The Data Is Over: How Organizations Use Stories To Drive Results*, edited by Lori Silverman.]

They were bleeding so badly, they were in the red millions. They were on the verge of closing. And they needed a financial turnaround. So they did two things. They set measures in place so that they could measure their progress. For example, they needed dramatic savings in all areas of the company. So they were asking people, as you're going about your daily work, how would you do it differently to save money? And, they were getting all of these ideas coming from the grassroots, the ground up, the janitors sweeping the floors, the nurses changing bedpans. And those ideas would be evaluated by their department, and if those suggestions helped the department meet those financial savings measures, the funds that they needed to cut from their department, then they'd implement the idea, and then they would watch the money that they saved.

Then they would take that story, and they would *broadcast* it throughout the organization. "This is how this janitor, this is how this nurse saved the hospital fifty thousand dollars in one month. This is the annual savings that we will have. This has made us more efficient, because

we're cutting out waste." And, they would be brought on stage at a monthly meeting, and given an award, and have the opportunity to have their story told with their permission.

Cynthia: Wow. That's quite different from, "We, as this department, have decided this," and no word about where it came from.

Karen: They were able to turn around a bleeding red situation to a profitable black situation within a year, or year and a half. Very dramatic financial turnaround.

Cynthia: And it probably had a cultural impact as well. You couldn't implement a thing like that, and not have a positive impact on the way people feel about their work.

Karen: Absolutely. So, this is where Gaylord Hospitals effectively married measurements with stories, and did it supremely well, and had huge results.

Cynthia: And they probably had to follow all those stages that you described.

Karen: Yes, they did.

Cynthia: They didn't tell *one* story on that, they bled it through.

Karen: Different stories all the way along. But it was all about the little successes that they were having along the way. Just like if we go back to the chart, it's these little successes, "Yes, we persevered, yes we had this obstacle, we persevered. Yes, we were missing this resource, and this other team came in and helped us out to success. Yes, we were working on this particular part of the project, we were learning that, oh, maybe it's not really about this, so we shifted, we changed, and now we have success. The little mini successes all the way along." But, I don't *language* it as mini successes, because then it almost *cheapens* it, and then you're in, "Oh, all I have to do is collect my success stories," and then you're right back into invalidating a whole range of human experience.

Cynthia: So, you're saying that you have to give the attention to the actions, and the motivations, and things like that, not to the stories themselves. Is that what you're saying?

Karen: Yes.

Cynthia: Or the performances. Because then it just brings in the whole invitation to embellish.

Karen: Yes. It becomes more bragging, and a performance, "Look how good *I* am," as opposed to, "The shit hit the fan, and look at what we did, in spite of it. And this is how we kept it going. We are the heroes." It's a very different feel to it.

Cynthia: And what about the negative stories? What about where we tried to do something, and this part failed?

Karen: Well, you do need to find a place for those. You do need to have those stories shared and told.

Cynthia: They're still learnings.

Karen: Yes, in terms of learning. You see, it's all how you *frame* it. And you need to be very conscious about keeping the momentum going. So when you stumble upon, "Oh, this is *not* working," then you have to help people find the story that allows them to see the path through. It's okay if parts of the change are abandoned. That's normal, and we sometimes forget that. But extreme care needs to be taken in that those negative stories don't become pervasive.

Cynthia: I guess it's a balance. They don't become pervasive, but they also don't become locked out, because then you lose the authenticity.

Karen: That's right. And it invalidates people. And you don't ever want to invalidate people. You don't want to invalidate their experience. It's a *valid* experience.

Cynthia: But you also don't want to participate when they want to wallow in it.

Karen: Yes. I call that *story interruptus*. We need to require people to complete the story. There are a couple of simple techniques that allow people to do that. They're in a pattern of, "Oh woe is me," or, "Ain't it awful?" What we need to do for those people when they are in the middle of that, or when they finish that ain't-it-awful or woe-is-me story, is that we need to ask them, "Well, what *decision* did you make because of that? What do you think you *learned* from that? How are you going to conduct your work now because of that? What do you think

that all *means* to you?" You need to ask those kinds of reflective questions that allow them to *finish* the story.

Cynthia: Rather than leave it interrupted and stuck.

Karen: Right, because then it goes back to your sensemaking. It just becomes a stuck story, and there's not the opportunity to make the *sense* out of the story.

Cynthia: Do you feel like you've addressed the first question fully?

Karen: No. I just want to make it really clear that we are talking about story *strategy* right now. We're not talking about how to *tell* stories.

Cynthia: Right.

Karen: So, there's a whole other component to story work that we cannot address here, but I think it should be acknowledged. And, that work is how do you build story skills, story confidence, personal inspiration, personal motivation, listening skills, and those types of things, in actually being able to tell your story. That's at the personal, individual mastery level.

We're just talking about story strategy. This is also about leadership. A lot of what we're talking about is really about leadership. So we could have a discussion about leadership in successful change, and the stories that a leader needs to tell, and how somebody needs to be a leader to work with stories in this kind of environment. That's a whole other conversation, but I wanted to raise it so you know this *is* what we're talking about; we're talking about story strategy and change, and *referencing* leadership, but not really talking about it head on, that's a whole other chapter.

Cynthia: I think that leadership in PNI has to do with supplying the energy to participatory story work. I think of it as leading from behind. It's supplying fuel and helping people participate in doing something that helps everyone. The element of leadership, when you come to spreading a message, or motivating people, I haven't done much work on, which is why I've asked you to talk to me about this.

Karen: This is about looking at the archetypes of leadership, and thinking about leadership during change as being more of a magician, as opposed to a cowboy leading the charge.

Cynthia: An enabler.

Karen: An enabler, but somebody who is an *empowerer*, actually. Somebody who can see the vision, and help the community get to that vision over a period of time. And, that's a different way of thinking and working that some people have an innate ability to do, and others do not.

Another dynamic that's here is that change is usually thought of as a plan and a flow chart. And when you marry change with storytelling, it actually becomes a *creative act*. It's a dance between creativity, planning and action. You're constantly moving between the creative and analytical worlds, and the creative and analytical processes. I think that bears understanding. Because all too often in our wonderful business world where we're trained in "just tell me the facts ma'am," we apply analytical thinking and processes to things that are actually *created acts*, and then we get all screwed up. And we don't understand why they work.

What we're really talking about here with marrying stories to a change initiative, to an intervention, to engaging the community to move from one place to another, there is actually a great deal of *creativity* that's required.

Cynthia: That's a great point.

Karen: You can build all the plans that you *want*, but you're going to miss a whole dimension to what's actually going to make the change work, and that's in the creative realm. Is this making sense?

Cynthia: Yes. An intervention isn't a plan, and then you carry out the plan. It's more like a garden that you grow. And gardens don't always grow the way you plan them. You adapt, and you discover, and it isn't exactly what you expected, but it's beautiful anyway.

Karen: Thank you. I love that metaphor, please use that, because it really does frame what I'm talking about very well.

Cynthia: You tell me when you're ready to move on to any other questions.

Karen: I am ready.

Cynthia: Now, I think you've actually covered question two, the one that was about action. The question was:

> We have changed our minds. Instead of building a purposeful story, we would now like to take dramatic *action* that produces ripples of storytelling in the community or organization. What is your advice on taking such action?

By the way, I took that part about dramatic action from a paper by Alan Wilkins in the 80's, where he talked about dramatic action in the name of values. That paper said you shouldn't always tell stories, but you can sort of *act out* stories. You can do things that create stories that are in the direction that you want to go. You don't always have to do an advertising campaign. You might have someone do something as a leader. It's like when you were talking about the leader who told her story. She might *tell* that story, but she might also *do* something, like the guy on the airplane. He did something based on principles, and that created stories.

I think a lot of times when people are thinking of stories and change, they think of *telling* stories, but they think less of creating stories *through their actions*.

Karen: Right. It goes back to leadership, which is all about modeling. Particularly in a change effort, when you're trying to change behavior and the way people think, well, you've got to model that. That's part of the leadership journey that we're talking about here. So, it's about authenticity, it's about personal connection, it's about embodying your story—walking your talk. But to go back to modeling, you're saying, well, what do you want to model? Once a leader understands what values and messages they want to model, they need to embody those principles and embody the stories being told.

Cynthia: The other thing I like to ask is, "What stories are you telling *now* that you don't realize you're telling?" Because *you're never not telling any*. Every day you make decisions, and you take action, and other people notice that, and that turns into stories.

Karen: Right. It's all about being hyper-aware of both the stories you are telling, and those that you are not. Truthfully, this is a balancing act. There are times you go through when certain stories are dominant. As that time fades and you face new challenges, then the stories you've told for a while fade into the background and other or newer stories become dominant. That happens at least for those who are aware of the nature of stories, and who are also self-aware.

For me it's all about deep listening. A leader—or anyone involved in storytelling—needs to listen for the story that needs to be told at that particular time with that particular audience. That's a skill to develop. I'm sure we've all groaned when someone tells the same stories over and over again, not realizing it's a new day and other stories need to be told. On the flip side of the coin are folks who also know when a story has lost its juice and needs to retire. That means the teller experiences the story going stale when telling it, and has the wisdom to know it's time to let that story go and find new stories to tell—even if it is a favorite story that's been told for over twenty years. That's hard, but necessary to do—both for our own growth, but also for the growth of others around us.

The most aware leaders and storytellers are those who also reflect periodically on the stories that are being told, and wondering about the stories *not* being formally told. And if those stories *not* being told need to surface, they go find those stories and tell them.

Cynthia: I can see that when you talk about story strategy it *encompasses* dramatic action. It's not a separate thing, it includes it.

Karen: Right.

Cynthia: The last three questions are all sort of—after covering the sort of standard question of how do you do this, I was thinking of special conditions that people might be in, and there were three that I came up with: a divide, coming up from the bottom, and coming down from the top.

Karen: I loved these questions, they were great.

Cynthia: I don't know if you want to take them one at a time, or if you want to just pick one, or whatever you want to do.

Karen: We'll start with number three, and see where we end up.

Cynthia: Okay. Question three is:

> Our group is in the intervention phase, like the previous group, but unlike them we face a significant *division* in our community or organization. Our project group includes people from both sides. We have discovered some amazing insights and opportunities among ourselves, and now we want to spread them to the entire community or organization. Do you have any special storytelling advice for our *divided* situation?

Karen: So, this is about division. The only real process I know of that's effective here is that when you have people on different sides, that when you sit them down and each of them shares their story with each other, walls start breaking down. Or at least cracks in the walls start emerging. Sometimes, depending on the people and situation, a lot of that division can actually go away.

Now, that sounds a little Pollyanna-ish ... [Note: Pollyanna is a character in a best-selling 1913 book by Eleanor H. Porter, adapted for film several times, about an orphaned girl with a strongly optimistic outlook.]

Cynthia: The differences in *opinion* aren't going to disappear, but the differences in *understanding*. . . .

Karen: That's exactly true. When we share our stories we humanize each other, and we automatically start finding some common ground.

I think the best way to set it up is with appreciation and deep listening. Not listening with an agenda, but listening to understand. So you have to do a lot of preparation before you can get two people who are divided to sit down and actually work. You can't just bring two people who are divided into a room, and say, "Okay, tell me your story." You have to do a lot of preparation about, "This is how we're going to listen, this is how we're going to ask questions, this is how we're going to share." Then the chance of success is a lot greater. So it's possible. It's important work to do. I think Paul Costello in Washington, D.C. is the master of this.

[Note: Paul Costello is the Executive Director of The Center for Narrative Studies in Washington,

D.C. He works with people in areas of conflict (such as Israeli and Palestinian youths) to help them share stories that build peace. You can find out about his work at storywise.com.]

Cynthia: Yes.

I think it's important to, like you said, not think that this means any conflicts are going to go away. It means that they're going to change so that they—it's just a greater perspective taking, a better understanding of the different perspectives that changes the nature of interactions. But it doesn't make the conflict go away.

Karen: Right, it builds bridges. The likelihood of being able to stand on the bridge together and find some solutions is greater.

Cynthia: Right, but if you think it's going to do more than build bridges, if you think it's going to fill in chasms, that's too much, and you'll fail.

Karen: Right, you need to be underwhelmed by this one. And, if you're pleasantly surprised, yahoo, but be underwhelmed, let it come from the place of *very modest gains*.

So, then let's talk about question number four.

Cynthia: Okay. Here it is:

> Our group is in the intervention phase, like the first group, but unlike them we are all in one group: the group *without power* in our community or organization. We carried out our project without the involvement of those above us, though we invited them to participate. We would like our intervention to reach our *entire* community or organization, even though some of them did not participate in our project and may not believe a word we say. Do you have any special storytelling advice for our *bottom-up* situation?

Karen: I think what's important to remember here is that when you tell a story, and you listen to others, and you get story sharing going, that that's where the *real* power lies. Even if it's an awful woe-is-me story, I tell you, just *telling* a story is not going to get you very far in terms of being able to create a bottom-up revolution. You need a vision with a problem and an urgency, and a clear picture of—this is

how it *could* be. You need a key message in that. You need to have stories with actions to take about your commitment, and there needs to be listening appreciations all along the way.

Cynthia: Right. Because I think that when you're out of power, it is particularly difficult in this one, because all you can hear is the conditions of your different status drowning out anything they could possibly say. It's hard to listen to someone who's, for example, rich, talk about how unhappy they are. And it probably takes a lot of integrity, or—I don't know what the right word is—but something to *admit* that maybe they don't have as much power as you think they do, or that your caricature of them might be wrong. I think it's easier to do that when you're *in* power, because then you have the freedom to play with it. But, when you feel as though you're a supplicant to those in power, I think your ideas of them get harder to change.

Karen: Right.

So, here's a story I can share with you. This was many years ago. I'm sitting here in California. The consulting firm that I was a part of was one of two consulting firms that was hired on this project. The two consulting firms worked together on the project. And, this was a town in California that was really concerned that they had a good vision for the future, for the coming century. This was in the 1990's, and they were looking forward to the millennium. They wanted to create a vision for the city that would be a guide for all the players in this city, to help them create what everybody wanted.

So they realized that this needed to be a community-wide project. They needed to get all the people from the community in. Now, they weren't handing out invitations to just anybody off the street, they were looking at who are the people in all the different communities who could come in and help guide us, and then go back into the communities with the message.

I was the only woman, and everybody was white. So I wasn't very well thought of because I was a woman. And all the guys actually were racist, also—didn't know it. So they said, "Karen, *you* get to go into the ethnic communities, and...."

Cynthia: *We* don't want to think about it.

Karen: Right, we don't want to think about it, we don't want to talk to these people, but we'll let *you* do that. That's your job. And, I was laughing, because I was kind of going, well, yeah, *you* could never do it, frankly, and I know I can.

And, they said, okay, we're going to set you up in an office in the town hall, and you can conduct your interviews there.

And, I said nope, see ya.

Cynthia: You wouldn't get the same interviews there.

Karen: Well, I wouldn't get anybody. Nobody is going to travel to downtown to sit with a white woman consultant.

Cynthia: In a place that's pretty close to the authorities.

Karen: Right, and this was also a town that had had severe racial problems over the years. So trusting the powers that be was not high on anybody's list.

So I had to go interview, and talk to people in the black community, Asian, and Hispanic communities. So, what I did was I found somebody in each community who could act as an introducer and gatekeeper for me, which is standard ethnographic procedure. They told me who to talk to, and I called up those people, ministers mostly, school principals. And if there was a Chamber of Commerce, like the Hispanic Chamber of Commerce, and the Asian Chamber of Commerce, that's who my initial in-roads were.

I was in communities where there were gang wars, crack cocaine, prostitution, homelessness, poverty—it was really ugly, and that's where I worked. I would have four or five interviews a day. I would just drive around the community from one interview to the next, and I'd meet them on their home turf.

I remember this one black minister sat down in his church, he was dressed in a suit, everything. Before we got into the interview he said to me—he was very somber—he said, "Well, I dressed for you," and I said, "Oh!" and he said, "Well, and I dressed for *you*." And, he said, "As a white woman coming here I did not want you to be afraid." And, I said, "I appreciate that. Now, let me talk to you about this…"

And the interview I gave was never an interview, it was always, "Well, we had this invitation for you," and the conversation went something like this, "You know what? I don't know what's going to happen. We'd like you to come. If you think it smells rotten and you are just being taken advantage of, and it's just another racist thing that's going on, then my advice to you would be hightail it out of that room, and not look back. But we would really like you to participate, because we really value your opinion."

That was the end of the interview. For the hour before that they all had to share with me stories about how they had been abused, and the stories about racism.…

Cynthia: When you say *had* to, did you mean they asked, or they just did it?

Karen: No, I just had to sit quietly while it happened. By the end of the day after you hear four or five of those stories, and they're awful stories, and I would go away feeling quite beaten up. But I share this story with you because what worked—and, by the way, every single person that I contacted showed up at the weekend event.

Cynthia: And if you hadn't spent that hour listening.…

Karen: It never would have happened. That's a point. Let them tell their story. This is not about me sharing my story, it's about offering an invitation, but *just shut up,* Karen. So, at the very bottom—and, this is where I was, I was at the *bottom* of the social economic cultural ladder—you have to *listen*. It's all about story sharing.

Cynthia: Here's the amazing thing. Even if you *are* at the bottom, I mean if you *live* at the bottom, you *still* have to listen. And that's hard, because you need to be heard, but you need to listen if you want to be heard.

Karen: Right. So to answer your question, what's my advice for bottom-up? Well, you'd better have a clear vision about what you want changed, and how you're going to get there, and the opportunity that's ahead of you. But you damn well better just sit and listen first.

Cynthia: That's a great story.

Karen: And, by the way, *no one* expected these people to show up. No one *wanted* these people to show up. Really.

Cynthia: What was the impact of their showing up?

Karen: It was fabulous. They got to know people, they got to build on their teams, they got to build their vision. It was really interesting. And, what was even worse is that in order for everybody to participate, and defray the cost of this whole event, everybody was being *required* to pay a hundred dollars. So some of these poor churches, these poor communities, they'd get together in their churches, and everybody would donate a little bit so that their minister could go. Now, that has got to be the worst—talk about an economic hurdle, and a power hurdle.

Cynthia: Yes, because for some people that hundred dollars was trivial.

Karen: Yeah, to the white people who were putting this on.

But we're getting off-track.

Cynthia: Yes. We're down to the last question. Actually, this one is a bit of a weakness of my whole book, which is that it's called Working With Stories In *Your* Community or Organization. The problem is, I'm a consultant, and while I would like to do this sort of thing in my own community, you know, prophets are without honor in their own countries. So all of my *actual* experiences are as an outsider coming in. This question addresses the issue of that, how does your status as an outsider change things. And *you* would be able to talk about this too.

> We are outsiders who were *paid* to study certain issues by those in power, who genuinely want to improve the situation for everyone in the community or organization but have their own perspective on things. We did get people from all parts of the community or organization to participate in portions of the project, but we are not sure our attempts to spread participation will be sufficient to convince everyone our project is not simply a tool of those in power. Do you have any spe-

cial storytelling advice for our *outside-in, top-down* situation?

Karen: The only thing that really comes to mind is that it's all about facilitating other people sharing your stories. *I* have no power. Even if they pay me I don't have any power.

Cynthia: I love that.

Karen: You can't make people do anything because they paid *me* a lot of money!

Cynthia: And I suppose it's probably important to make that clear to everyone involved.

Karen: Yeah. So it really is about facilitation. How do I facilitate people finding their voice, sharing their story, and listening to other peoples' stories? And then once they share their stories, once they hear those stories, then I go about helping them craft those action steps. That's what I know how to do well. But ultimately I have to ask everybody this, which is, "What's your *personal* stake in it? Do you *have* one? If yes, what is it? If not, why not?" And then we can go on from there.

Cynthia: Does that aspect of the personal stake extend to the outside helper, the consultant? How does that apply to them?

Karen: The consultant is there because they either have an *extrinsic* motivation, because they're being paid, or they have an *intrinsic* motivation, because it's some kind of work that they enjoy, and they want to do some good work, they want to see some change happen. Now, any consultant who's worth their weight in gold has that intrinsic motivation pretty strong. And they get paid for it, which is really cool. So, always the consultant has a stake in the game, and it's not just financial.

Cynthia: I came to a realization about a year ago, when I was talking to somebody about the role of a consultant as an outsider in projects, and I suddenly had this flash of insight that the role of the consultant is a trickster.

Karen: Oh yes, very much so.

Cynthia: When I wrote about this [Note: it's in *More Work with Stories*: look for "PNI Skills"] I went through four qualities of the trickster, and how it applies to being an outsider in projects. There was shape shifting, and the role of being half in and half out of multiple worlds. There was being a game player, where you set up games, and you sort of jump around, and you invite people to play games, you entice them with charm. The last part I called hungering, which is that you feed people hunger. What I mean is that you don't satisfy them, you get them excited about the hunt.

Karen: Right, you stoke their hunger.

Cynthia: Yes, exactly. If you're a good outsider in any project like this, you should be doing those things. And, if you are slipping into going too far into the group, or staying too far out of it, you're not doing it right. You have to find a place between. If you sink too far in, and become part of an opposition group, you aren't doing your job, because you have to be a resource for *everybody*.

Karen: Right. I would agree completely. The other thing that I would add to that is that to get all people, and all parts in the community or organization to participate in portions of the project, you have to find a balance between the inspirational, the motivational, and the intrinsic what's-in-it-for-them stuff, and the guidance about how do we do it. People can get all hepped-up and excited, and if you don't give them the steps of *how*, then they are completely lost, and nothing will happen.

Cynthia: I think I wrote that the true mark of a trickster is that they know when to stop tricking. The complement of game playing is what happens when it's time to get serious and just provide information or support, or whatever is needed that *isn't* jumping around, when it's standing still that is needed. I think that's what you're saying, that it's not all fun and games. There has to be a time when you have to be rock solid so they can rely on you.

Karen: Right. Particularly I see this with storytelling. People *love* storytelling. They say, "Yes, let me tell stories!" And then they scratch their heads and say, "But how am I going to *use* it? And how does it actually *work*? Like, as I'm thinking about my daily work, *when* do I tell stories? Is it at ten o'clock?"

Like the trickster, we think of storytelling as entertainment, or comic relief, or of less consequence than other competencies. But under-standing the vital role of storytelling, like understanding the vital role of the trickster, is sophisticated leadership. Storytelling is not something to play with. As you say, it's not all fun and games. People, through their experience of you embodying your stories—walking your talk—can depend on you because you are rock solid. And part of experiencing that "rock solidness" is because you are competent in the dynamics of storytelling—in understanding how hungry people are for stories that enliven us, feeding that hunger, respecting their stories, listening deeply, and being flexible with their stories. And they also know when *not* to tell a story.

Cynthia: Now, when you're working on a project and somebody says, "I want you to take over and create some kind of magic for me, and create this story that's going to change everything," how do you respond to that?

Karen: You say, "It's *your* story, so *you* have to tell it. I'll *help* you tell it, I'll help build some skills so you can tell it, but it's your story."

There was one project when I *didn't* do that, but it was the nature of the problem. This was a non-profit that was wanting an advocacy campaign, to send a short story in an e-mail to state legislators on a monthly basis, so they would understand the results that this non-profit was producing, so that would help guide the legislature when they were crafting policy. So I had to evoke the stories from members of the organization, and then take those hour-long interviews, and get it down to a 250-word text, the core essence of the story, laden with multiple meanings, multiple messages. I knew I was the only one who could do that, particularly for the amount of money that they had. And they didn't have any resources. They were actually hiring me to take their stories and craft them for this very specific advocacy campaign. And *that* worked.

Cynthia: Because you weren't actually *writing* stories, you were just doing a bit of clean-up.

Karen: I was doing a *lot* of clean-up, and focusing the message, targeting the message, and layering meanings within the story.

Very often people don't understand about which communication channels to use and how to layer meanings in very simple stories.

They'll think, "Oh, let me just tell the story," and it's a nice story, no doubt about it. And yet if they had worked on the story a little bit more the depth of it could have really increased. But that's just knowing the *craft* of story. And sometimes people are able to pay me for that. And sometimes when I'm coaching people, if they have that opportunity I get to work *with* them on layering meaning. But that's kind of advanced story work.

But that's when it's okay. In a situation like that I think it was perfectly acceptable to craft their stories like that.

Cynthia: You were almost like a tool for them, really.

Karen: Yes. I think we've pretty much covered....

Cynthia: Yes, this is going to be really great. Thanks so much, Karen.

You can find more about Karen's work and writings at her web site, juststoryit.com.

Thaler Pekar

Thaler Pekar, a consultant specializing in persuasive communication, helps smart leaders and their organizations find, develop, and share the stories and organizational narratives that rally critical support.

Cynthia Kurtz: Hello Thaler. I'm going to ask you the first scripted question I wrote up for our interview. Here it is.

> We have decided to create and tell some purposeful stories to the larger community or organization in hopes that they will create a positive spiral of storytelling. We have our sensemaking outputs and collected stories to work with. Can you give us any advice on *building* and *telling* these stories?

Thaler Pekar: As I see it, you have two options. One is sharing some of the stories that have been gathered. In that case you'd want to make sure that the group is figuring out in an ethical manner which ones they want to share. Certainly some stories are better than others just merely in that they have stronger story elements of character, and conflict, and setting.

And some stories might be stronger in that they yield the more immediate insight, or they help you get to the insight much more quickly.

And then the other option would be to create a new *composite* story, which is a story that would be, "The story we most often hear is such-and-such." And that would be a story that, again, very ethically *represents* the bulk of the stories that have been gathered. So it's a fair and equitable composite story that in no way manipulates all of the stories that have come in, but rather condenses them, and creates the composite.

Now, my assumption is that the community, in gathering the stories, has been very good about looking for stories that they *weren't* hearing. So, in other words, as they've gone through this PNI process they've actually said, "We're not hearing a lot from this one group. Let's make sure we hear that."

My other assumption is that they've looked for stories that were indicative of the *opposite* of what they were hearing, to make sure that those are either heard, or that they *truly* don't exist. That they've given respect to the full sphere of stories that *could* be gathered.

Cynthia: How do you advocate that they choose these stories that will represent the story collection?

Thaler: I think it would depend on the numbers of stories. There are a lot of different ways to do this. It could be done electronically with people favoring certain stories. It could be done through discussion, where people actually weight the stories as having the characters and the settings that are most representative of the community. They may wish to choose different stories for different audiences. You can't say, "Oh, we want *everybody* to hear."

Cynthia: I like the point you made in one blog post you wrote, about how you had to reach the audience to resonate with their experience.

Thaler: Since a goal is to "create a spiral of storytelling," the group may choose stories for their ability to prompt recollections from specific community members.

Or let's say that the group has now decided that they want to advocate for a specific policy-related action, if not a policy, but then a policy action. It might be anything from, we want a new stop sign on this particular corner, or it could be that we want a state law enacted. You can't just say "policymakers." Try to be as specific as possible. *Which* policymakers do we really need to get to? *Which* members of the Board of Education?

Cynthia: And understanding that audience. That's a key to crafting the message.

Thaler: It's a key to figuring out which story, because we're not talking about crafting a message here, we're talking about which stories to share?

Cynthia: It could be choosing stories, or it could be choosing stories and then choosing how to build them into something that is not exactly what they were before. Say you're going to make a commercial, or a presentation, you might merge several stories into a composite. You know, like there was that famous insurance couple who sat around their table talking about health insurance?

Thaler: Ah, "Harry and Louise." Because now that you have your audience in mind, you want to share a story that best resonates with them. You want to make sure that the protagonist in the story is somebody to whom they can relate. You want to make sure that the benefactor in the story is somebody whom they won't dismiss out of hand.

Because of privacy concerns, and the complexity of individual cases, I often work with medical clients to create composite stories.

I'll tell you about a project that is related. This is very business-oriented. I spent three days with different stakeholders in a corporation, interviewing management, factory workers, bankers, people inside and outside of the organization at all different levels *about* the organization. And then I did an analysis of all these stories that were elicited, to come up with an organizational narrative. So based on everything that I heard, I said that the organizational narrative was about *creation*. It was the story of creation. And then I shared many of the stories that supported that. And then I spent another three days working with the top management of the organization on how the creation story

can influence their internal communications, and their external communications, and their branding, and their marketing efforts.

Cynthia: So, you helped them sort of....

Thaler: I don't know if you like that story, because that's about *me* doing the analysis, not the group doing the analysis. It's not participatory.

Cynthia: I'm not a purist.

Thaler: But if your thesis here is about participatory narrative, and I just shared a story that was *not* participatory...

Cynthia: I don't think of participation as a binary thing. There are many levels of participation. Besides, you didn't tell these people what story to tell. You didn't *give* them a story. You gave them advice on how to incorporate that element into the stories they tell. And you worked with them to develop their skills in incorporating that.

Thaler: Yes. Shawn Callahan of Anecdote calls that the "big S" story. In my work I'm referring to that as the *narrative*. It's the big story of the organization, the big organizing story. Whether it's organizational, or whether it's about an issue, there's a big story. And then you find what Shawn says are the "small s" stories, and you can come in and support that. My background being communication, that's what creates your brand. Whether it's a personal brand or an organizational brand, it's that *authenticity* of making sure that the small stories that you're sharing support the big narrative. And that creates solid, strong, sustainable identity.

Cynthia: Okay. So, you've talked about choosing stories, you've talked about sort of building stories into the communications that you do. Do you want to address the dramatic action question? It's this one:

> We have changed our minds. Instead of building a purposeful story, we would now like to take dramatic *action* that produces ripples of storytelling in the community or organization. What is your advice on taking such action?

By dramatic I mean part of a drama, that they mesh into the drama of the organization or community, in such a way that people tell stories about them. If you are planning to take action, there are ways to anchor the action in the drama of the organization based on what you've learned about it.

Thaler: Yes, let's do that. Here's a story that hasn't come out yet, but it's going to come out in a few weeks in an article. [Note: The link is at ontheissuesmagazine.com/2011fall/2011fall_pekar.php]

The Children's Health Fund is an organization that was founded by the doctor Irwin Redlener and the singer Paul Simon. It's an organization that provides health care to underserved children around the country. They do that by bringing mobile pediatric clinics to the patients. For instance, in the South Bronx in New York they bring mobile medical units to homeless shelters, because people are in medical deserts, and they can't get care, and it's very difficult to go out and get the care. In migrant farm camps in Florida they bring health care to the migrant workers. In Appalachia they bring these mobile units into these incredibly isolated hollers, to provide pediatric care to children who otherwise wouldn't get it.

The big story about that organization is about innovation and tenacity. There are lots of organizations that are providing health care to underserved children, and there's a lot of organizations that can say that they provide charity care to poor kids who can't afford it. What was unique about this organization is that they said, "We're going to do *whatever it takes*. We're going to outfit these vans to make them state-of-the-art vans. And we're going to bring this incredible high quality care to people."

So there was one doctor who drove the mobile medical unit—she didn't *literally* drive it, but she was in charge of the mobile medical unit—in Anacostia, D.C., in the nation's capitol, an incredibly poor neighborhood. And she has an incredible story of having rocked so much as a child that her teacher actually tied her to her chair in the classroom, in Bed Stuy, Brooklyn, where she grew up. She fought like heck to get a good education, graduated at the top of her high school, got a scholarship to Howard University, got a Master's Degree, and then got a scholarship and went on to medical school at

Georgetown. And then she decided she wanted to give back to the community that she grew up in, to make sure that no kids had to face what she faced as a poor child. So she went back, and after getting her degree decided that this was the kind of health care she wanted to deliver.

That story was a really authentic story, because it reflected the "big S" story. It was a "small s" story that reflected the "big S" story in the organization. So that's the kind of story—again, you can tell lots of stories about kids not getting health care, and lots of stories about being charitable, about providing that care, but when you can *weave in* the tenets of the "big S" stories of tenacity and innovation, then you're really supporting your brand.

It's not just the brand support; it's this *cacophony* that you want. We share stories so that we hear other stories back. That's why I refer to story *sharing*, and not storytelling. When we share a story, we elicit similarly themed stories. These small stories are then *repeated*; people in the community go out and retell the story, whether that community is a consumer community, or whether it's a local community.

You want people to repeat the same story. You want that kind of authenticity. Small stories that support the big narrative being consistently shared. You want people to be hearing the same thing from the same people over and over.

Cynthia: Right, you want the story to grow and travel.

Thaler: Yeah. And unless you're consistently sharing stories with similar elements, then you're not going to reach that kind of *critical cacophony*. You're not going to reach that kind of *repetition* of the same elements that, in turn, results in the repetition of the same emotion.

Another thing that you want to do—one of the reasons why you would *find* this one story after the community does the sensemaking exercise—is let's say there's an issue, or a dramatic action that you want to have taken. You want to make that *bearable* to the listener. And I mean bearable in two ways. One, that it's *cognitively* bearable, that the context of the story will make it easier to understand the complexity of the situation.

And it's also bearable in the sense that it's a *story*. It has a clear beginning and middle and end, and everything we know from science, we know that we remember things in story form much more easily than we do as a list of disparate facts.

So you want it to be bearable, as in being able to be carried around, to be repeated.

And you want it to be *concrete*. So that's another thing that you're looking for as you're choosing that *one* story to go out and share. You want to make sure that it's a story that really does capture and simplify all the complexity in your issue.

Cynthia: If you tried to be extremely faithful to what you had collected, and you went out and told a very complex story with too many nuances, it wouldn't go where you need it to go.

Thaler: And my guess is that if you've done enough story collection, the majority opinion will lead towards finding the *simple story that captures that complexity*. That's what people like.

Cynthia: This is great.

Thaler: People talk about Hemingway's short story: *For sale: baby shoes, never worn.*

[Note: Interestingly, attribution of that story to Hemingway is apocryphal. It appears to be an urban legend that Hemingway wrote the story, which only goes to show how powerful it is.]

I don't really believe that that's a story, and my guess is Shawn would say that that's not a story either, because you're not watching something happen to somebody. But I thought of that this morning.

Somebody tweeted, "Crying while flipping through my passport. I need a vacation." And I was like, wow, that's story right there, crying while flipping through my passport.

Cynthia: Actually, I would disagree in that case. I think that that shoes thing *is* a story, but it's what I call a backflow story. It blooms backwards.

Thaler: Because you're filling so much in?

Cynthia: Yes.

Thaler: How interesting.

Cynthia: What I call the "bloom" of a story is that moment when the shape of the story becomes apparent to you. In a well-crafted story the moment of bloom, that moment of enjoyment, dawns on you in a natural way that's enlightening and engaging. That shoes story has a backflow bloom. You read it, and *then* you go, "Ah," and then you fill in the rest of it.

Thaler: I like this idea of back-flowing bloom.

I find that because my work is about communication, and my work is about helping people find and share stories that help them communicate better, and more persuasively, more efficiently, that the one place that I need to be fairly didactic is in what a story is.

So I don't want to teach people who are beginning to think about applied story sharing strategy about the more nuanced things like that. I want them to focus on, "Something's happening to someone, and I can see it."

So my purpose, and my task, is always communication. I am doing some knowledge sharing work, and knowledge sharing, of course, *is* about communication.

Cynthia: So we've covered the first two questions, and you've talked about some great insights that give people ideas. Do you want to address the other questions?

[Note: We then talked a bit about the goals of the book, and we wandered into the topic of people not feeling their own stories are "good enough" to tell without fancy interventions from story experts.]

Thaler: Do you remember, I wrote a piece that you liked, and I don't know if it fits in at all with the book, but you're welcome to use it, and that was the piece on how everybody wants to be a hero.

Cynthia: I think that's the one I was thinking of when I said the thing about knowing your audience, and knowing what will resonate with them.

Thaler: You're welcome to quote from that for the book.

Cynthia: Oh, that would be great.

[Note: Here is Thaler's essay, which she has graciously given me permission to include here.]

Everyone Wants to Be a Hero

by Thaler Pekar

Much of my work is focused on helping smart leaders and organizations find and develop stories to share with their audiences. To that end, I'd like to share two anecdotes that may help you achieve greater clarity in your communications.

Everybody wants to be a hero. Smart leaders and organizations know that. You also know it's natural for people to align themselves with solutions rather than to associate themselves with problems. You want the audiences for your stories to relate as much as possible to the protagonists in the stories you choose to share and to empathize with the protagonist's heroic journey.

Here's an example from the private sector, in which the target audience—the potential customer—was cast as the hero. Recently, I helped North America's largest provider of emergency response software share the story of a county emergency services director. Wanting to provide more value to the residents of her community—and convinced the software would save lives—the director took a risk by going before her budget-constrained county supervisors and advocating for a state-of-the-art emergency response system. In preparing to share this story, the inclination of my client, the company that designed the software, was to focus on the battered woman whose life was saved because she was able to text emergency services from the closet in which she was hiding from her abusive husband.

Certainly, a compelling story. My client's customers, however, are public-sector employees in a position to purchase my client's software. And because these public sector customers wish to see themselves as making smart and effective decisions, I urged my client to focus the story on the emergency services director who fought for and secured the purchase of the life-saving software. Again, this story is not simply about one saved life, but is instead about one person who fought to save many lives—a protagonist to whom the customers can relate.

Here's another example of what I'm talking about, this time from the nonprofit sector. America's largest creator of affordable housing has been sharing stories of formerly homeless men and battered women who are now living safely and happily in homes the organization helped build. These are heartfelt stories that showcase men and women whose lives have been transformed. The wealthy bankers and real estate moguls from whom the organization receives financial support, however, are more likely to relate to stories about the community developer who built the housing with support from the organization and thereby helped reclaim a neighborhood from despair. The story of the developer shares his or her journey from original idea through challenges overcome and frames the developer as a hero who made a key contribution to the organization's proffered solution. It ends with not just an individual but an entire community transformed.

Stories about systemic solutions are crucial to persuasive communication. That's because people can more easily imagine themselves as the hero of a solution story than they can picture themselves in a near-hopeless situation. In "Wanted: Master Storytellers," an engaging 2009 article in *The Nonprofit Quarterly*, Susan Nall Bales wrote:

> When the narrative is all about problems, and no solutions, people have little recourse to ideas of prevention and intervention. If what is asked of us are tears and charity, it is unlikely we will find our way to pragmatic action....

Or, as screenwriter and best-selling author Robert McKee teaches, "Empathy is necessary. Sympathy is optional."

So focus on solutions when sharing your stories. Solutions invariably inspire optimism and engagement. If the solution is still a work in progress, focus on the aspirations behind the solution. The idea is to present your organization as offering a solution in which the listener has a heroic role to play. If you do that on a consistent basis, you'll be pleasantly surprised by the results.

Cynthia: I love that piece. In fact, that is exactly the kind of insight I'm lacking for this chapter, because I have thought so little about persuasion and influence. I get to the end of the sensemaking, and when it comes to reaching out, I can't find any interest in going further. I think maybe it's from being a scientist. You can't persuade mice to do anything. There's a barrier in my mind that I just don't cross. And that's why I felt I needed help in this section.

Thaler: I think of how skeptical you were of *me* when we first met. It was like, oh, wait a minute, she's doing *persuasion?* She's *telling* people what to *say?* And then I think you've learned to trust me and my understanding, I'm helping people be the best they can be. I'm helping them say what *they* want to say in the most efficient and effective way possible.

Cynthia: I've never thought persuasion, or attempts to communicate, were *wrong*. Obviously I'm attempting to persuade people of something in this book. I have very specific messages that I want to get across. I guess I've just got a healthy skepticism about deception, and underhanded ways of getting power out of people.

Thaler: Right.

I worked with a government organization last week, and it was a workshop in helping leaders find and develop and share stories. Through the course of the day I heard so many stories that the big story seemed obvious to me. But I wasn't hired to go in there and do a narrative analysis, to do an elicitation and find their big story. But little by little, everybody was sharing stories about being able to make a mistake and learn from it. Being able to take a far-out creative chance. To present a report in prose. To draw a painting to accompany a presentation that was being made. To use cupcakes as an analogy for a big data presentation that the person was doing.

And it was just really obvious that the big story of this government office was about being able to be innovative and take a chance and do what it takes to get through to the audience. It was just really interesting that the leader in that organization had done a wonderful job of articulating what I later heard, which was that she

believed in *failing forward*. That was incredibly apparent, because everybody in the organization was sharing small stories that supported that big story.

Cynthia: How do you think that happened? That her belief translated into the stories they told?

Thaler: I think she communicates it often, through both her words and actions. I think she allows people to fail forward publicly. It's not just writing on a wall. People are seeing their colleagues doing this. It's a fairly social organization, so stories are shared. It's an organization where there are some terrific storytellers in high positions. And obviously they had invited me in, so it's an organization that respects the idea of story as a management and leadership tool.

Cynthia: That's a good example, because you have marked out a whole bunch of things that they did to make—not necessarily on purpose, but because they believed in them—to make these stories ripple out, as opposed to dying off.

Thaler: Right.

I had another organization come to me, a charter school management company. They came to me and said, "We came up with seven values that guide our organization, and we want to hire you to message those values. We want you to write them up in a way that people are going to remember them and act on them."

And I said, "Great! Can you tell me some stories that support the values?"

"Oh yes. Two of our values are tenacity and having fun. So here's a story. Real estate's really really expensive, and our vice president of real estate was trying to acquire space for us to build a new school, and of course it was expensive, so she and her team worked around the clock for a week, 24/7. Some of them even slept in the office. And when they closed the deal they saved us $100,000. That's *huge*, $100,000. And we were so excited that we forced her to go out for a drink that night."

And I said, "Your story about tenacity and having fun is *forcing* somebody to go out for a drink after they slept in their office for a week?" I was like, "I can message these all you want, but unless you're *living* those values...."

Cynthia: My third question is about division, and it's related to what you've just said. It's easy to put out a message, but how do you put out a message when there are divisions? So the question is:

> Our group is in the intervention phase, like the previous group, but unlike them we face a significant *division* in our community or organization. Our project group includes people from both sides. We have discovered some amazing insights and opportunities among ourselves, and now we want to spread them to the entire community or organization. Do you have any special storytelling advice for our *divided* situation?

Thaler: Right. So this is where sort of that "everyone wants to be a hero" comes in, right? You're looking for points of empathy. From a strict communications standpoint, there are people who are going to be opposed to you, and they're *always* going to be opposed to you. If you are an advocate, you really shouldn't waste your physical, mental, and financial resources on fighting the people who are always going to be opposed to you. You just can't do it. I do a lot of work in the reproductive justice field, and that's a real example of a place where when somebody believes abortion is murder, that person really believes abortion is murder, and you're not going to change their minds on that.

Cynthia: I was actually wondering if you could mention that group, I forgot the name of it, and what their approach is.

Thaler: Oh, the Exhale Group? Great, I'm happy to talk about Exhale. Exhale is a pro-*voice* organization. I now am a special advisor to them. Exhale really believes that by having people share their stories, having men and women share their stories about abortion—whether they're good or bad or ambivalent or ambiguous—that *all* of those stories deserve to be heard in a nonjudgmental place. Only when we can have people sharing those stories and *not* being judged will we actually be able to bring peace to a contentious issue. [Note: The Exhale web site is at exhaleprovoice.org.]

Cynthia: That's an excellent answer to those questions. Exhale is a situation in which some-one found a way to reach divided people. Their approach is to say, "We will suspend judgment and we will listen."

Thaler: Yes, that's exactly what it's about. And it's incredibly powerful. I think Exhale has incredible lessons for many organizations that are working with stigmatized communities to hear. And they are very much a learning organization. They are learning from other organizations like GLBT organizations, African refugees, other groups that are doing work with groups that are often unheard, or stigmatized, or where there's only one story that's normally associated with those groups.

And pro-voice is exactly that, it's about letting *all sorts* of stories be heard. And it's saying that there's no right or wrong, there's no sides to the issue, and that can be incredibly difficult in organizational work. It's very scary, it's saying that we're going to be open to chaos.

Cynthia: Yes. It actually reminds me of a book called *Terror in the Name of God*, by Jessica Stern. In the book she was talking about how she has spent a lot of time talking to people she disagrees with—people most people could not disagree more with, like white supremacists, and people who want to blow up all Americans, and things like that. She spent a lot of time sitting with these people and listening to them. Not going into their world, but just opening her mind enough to hear what they're saying. And she has derived amazing insights that she's now passed on to other people, because she schooled herself in learning how to listen to things she really didn't like, but without judging and without being taken in. She said that this is a difficult task to pull off, but it can be done.

Thaler: Right. It's not our tendency. It's not the tendency even for incredibly benevolent people, because we want to jump in, and we want to say, "Oh, I understand *that*," or "I agree with you on *that*," or "I had a similar experience." So it's even hard for the *nicest* of people to shut up and just listen. But you need to do that, because often where a story goes at the end is very different than where it might end if you interrupt, where you might artificially end it by interrupting it.

Cynthia: Sometimes you have to keep listening past the story you *thought* you were going to hear, to find out what they were going to say. I find that often in story workshops, that the useful stories only come out in the last quarter of the time. The first part is camouflage, and jumping up and down to try and give you what they thought you wanted. But then eventually you break through to something else. If you don't have the patience to break through to that, if you don't have faith in the process, you will think the process has failed.

Thaler: Now, I know that David Boje talks about counter narratives. He talks about for every story that rises there will be a counter story. I've talked about the stories that aren't heard, and our ethical obligation to seek out the stories that we're *not* hearing. I also think that what *you're* getting at is that there are stories that are shouted, and there are stories that are whispered.

Cynthia: Yes, that's a good way to put it.

Thaler: As facilitators of story work, we need to stay with it long enough so that the whispers can be heard at a speaking level. We need to listen really carefully, because we need to hear what's being whispered. I've been meaning to write about this, because this came up at a program I was doing the other day for an organization where they were asking about culture. They were asking me if the narrative of the big story equaled culture. And I said no, because culture also encompassed the whispered stories as well as the shouted stories.

Cynthia: And the "big S" narrative is often the shouted stories.

Thaler: Yes. Now, ideally the "big S" narrative will be authentic. The biggest narrative *is* authentic enough that it covers both, and it covers almost everything. I thought that the big story, the "big S" story, the *narrative* of 9/11 is that three thousand people were killed that day, hundreds of thousands or more have been killed since in two wars, and we've bankrupted a nation because of paying for these wars, and we've lost our civil liberties. Everybody knows what the big story is, but in this rush to create this day of remembrance, these small stories were being told that seemed so flat and inauthentic, because they were not being authentic to the big story that was told.

Cynthia: I guess the problem is that there are different big stories about 9/11. That's the big story *I* think of; it's that the tragedy is much bigger than what happened on that day. But for a lot of people that much bigger part [about the wars] has to be tucked away, has to be denied, because it hits a vein of, "We may not say that." It gets into the whole thing that, "Those aren't really people," or that they don't matter. I find that hard.

I remember a conversation I had with my mother when I was twelve. At that age I had gotten into a lot of thinking about human suffering. I was reading all about Hiroshima, and the Holocaust, and awful things. I was dealing with death, basically, and what humans can do to humans. So one evening we were in the kitchen, and she was washing dishes and I was drying. And I said how awful it was about Hiroshima. Right away, she said that Hiroshima was a *wonderful* thing because it saved the lives of many American soldiers. I didn't say anything else, but I just thought, "Wow, that's a *really* different way of thinking about it."

Because to *her* those Japanese people didn't count, or didn't count as much, as the Americans. They were on a different level, a different plane of existence or something. It's hard to get past those differences in ways of thinking. I find that in a lot of people I know, that if it's not an American life, it's not a life, it's not a full life. That way of thinking is foreign to me, but it is very comfortable and familiar to a lot of people, and not just in the U.S.

Many years later, in another conversation, I mentioned to somebody about how when I was twelve I read all about the Holocaust and Hiroshima. He said "The Holocaust *and* Hiroshima?" In his mind those were totally different events—one justified, one not, I guess—but I saw them as undifferentiated suffering.

Another time I mentioned to somebody that I thought this way of partitioning suffering was a strange way of thinking. And she said, "It's *not* strange. Why *shouldn't* I care more about people in my own country? I think that's completely natural. *You're* the one who's unnatural."

So I don't know what to do with that.

Thaler: Yeah, this might be a little heavy for the book. But it certainly gets into the issue of insiders and outsiders. And the idea that values are non-hierarchical.

Cynthia: But see, that's a valid question. How *do* you work with stories around a divide like that? That's why I like this Exhale group so much. They don't say, "This is right and this is wrong." They say, "Listen to everyone. Just listen. Don't judge, don't think, just listen. You can condemn *after*, you can categorize *after*, but for a *moment*, just *listen*."

Thaler: I would say we're *all* inside and outside. We're all in something, and we're all out of something else.

Cynthia: For every person you have irreconcilable differences with, in some *other* dimension you agree wonderfully.

Thaler: That's why I had difficulty with that inside and outside question. I'm not being Pollyanna-ish, I'm not being stupidly optimistic, but I *do* think that story can enable points of connection on that continuum in a way that other forms of communication cannot. Especially when the stories are shared—and by sharing I mean giving the story as a *gift* to the listener, being willing to hear what the story elicits back in response, and creating the physical and cognitive space to hear that that response back.

I think of story "telling" as incredibly pedantic and didactic. I think the power of story comes from understanding that you share a story to receive a story back. If it's done in that way, it can be a very powerful communication tool. And communication is a tool for *humanity*, and showing our humanness, and creating better societies.

Cynthia: Thanks so much, Thaler.

Thaler and I didn't get to the rest of the interview questions (I broke my rule about not talking too much during the interview—oops), but I think you'll agree that the interview was a success regardless. You can find more about Thaler's work, including several excellent articles like the one she shared with us above, at her web site, thalerpekar.com.

SUMMARY

Intervening in the flow of stories means doing something to change the stories people tell in your community or organization, hopefully in such a way that the change you have envisioned in your project is more likely to come to pass.

We can categorize narrative interventions in three groups: listening to stories that need to be told; getting stories to where they need to go; and helping people work with stories.

Interventions that listen to stories include:

- creating a narrative ombudsman who can help people solve problems—and listen to their stories
- creating narrative suggestion boxes where people can tell stories about what they'd like to see change
- creating spaces where people can share stories to help each other cope with difficult conditions

Interventions that get stories to where they need to go include:

- creating narrative orientations that bring new members up to speed
- creating narrative learning resources that intersperse how-to information with "what it's really like" stories from real people
- creating narrative simulations that challenge people to test their knowledge by playing out scenarios
- creating narrative presentations that bring stories to people who need to hear them (for their own good or for someone else's)
- taking dramatic actions that create ripples of storytelling

Interventions that help people work with stories include:

- creating sensemaking spaces where people can keep the momentum of the project going
- helping people learn how to conduct their own sensemaking sessions
- creating networks of narrative mentoring (or adding narrative to existing mentoring networks)

- using therapeutic narrative to help people learn how to tell themselves new stories
- using participatory theatre to help people rehearse the change they want to create

Carrying out more than one narrative intervention at once increases the diversity of motivations able to participate, creating synergies between interventions.

The chapter ended with three interviews with people whose work includes both telling and listening to community and organizational stories.

In his interview, Shawn Callahan talked about how insights derived from sensemaking need to be met with *emotional engagement,* so that people can find not just the *reason* but also the *motivation* to create change. He explained that a strategic story can help people understand *why* a planned change is worth getting behind. He said that before people can gain benefit from stories, they need to develop their ability to distinguish stories from opinions and statements of fact. Shawn mentioned two principles in designing interventions: that small changes can have big impacts, and that it's important not to slip into believing all problems are fixable with a plan. Facilitators of story work, says Shawn, should help people understand what is possible but stay out of idea creation, so that people can come up with their own solutions. Finally, Shawn explained that helping people work with stories means helping them find the motivation to listen as well as tell.

In her interview, Karen Dietz presented the idea that creating change with stories is never about telling one story. There are *stages* to the change process, and each stage requires telling and listening to *different* stories. Karen explained that it is a mistake to tell only one story and think change will happen as a result. Great leaders, said Karen, are acutely aware of the stories flowing around them, and this helps them tell—and listen to—the right stories at the right times. Karen talked about how listening to people as they tell their stories is a mark of respect. She said that no initiative can succeed that does not plan to listen to the stories that need to be told. Finally, Karen told us that people who help other people work with stories must find a bal-

ance between getting people energized to work with stories and giving them practical advice on how to go about it.

In her interview, Thaler Pekar mentioned the importance of listening for stories that are not being told, and of checking to see if opposing stories are still out there waiting to be told. She talked about how a "big S" story that creates change must align with the "small s" stories people are telling every day, or the effort will misfire. Thaler looks for a *critical cacophony* of stories being shared in many directions rather than the quiet of an audience listening to one performance. She suggests that when finding stories to share, people look for *simple stories that resonate,* because those stories will be passed on and will reverberate through the community. Thaler believes a story is not likely to move people unless it gives them a protagonist they can identify with and through whom they can see *themselves* making a difference. Thaler recommends listening to stories from all sides of a contentious issue without judgment. Finally, Thaler would like us to remember that story sharing is about telling a story and hearing a story back, and that story sharing is far preferable to the didactic performance of storytelling.

QUESTIONS

As you read about the thirteen narrative interventions described in this chapter, which of them engaged you—you personally—the most? Which do you think you'd like to participate in? Which interventions had the opposite effect on you? Did some sound boring? Dangerous? Frightening? Too good to be true? Why do you think you feel that way? What is it about the interventions you like most and least that makes you react in that way? How does that connect to your personal strengths and weaknesses?

Now think about facilitating the thirteen intervention types, either thinking of you yourself or of your project team. How would you go about supporting interventions of each type? Which types would come easiest to you? Which would pose greater challenges? Which might you need help with? Where might you get help? What would happen if you did get help?

If you think of the thirteen intervention types in general, that is, not in reference to any particular goals, which of them seems to hold the greatest *utility* for your community or organization? Which would you (collectively) be most *capable* of carrying out? What do you see if you compare utility with capability? Is there anything you would *like* to do that is beyond your reach? Why is it beyond your reach? What can you do to change that? (One way to think through these questions is to create a table on paper or in a word processor or spreadsheet. On the row and column labels of the table, write the thirteen types of narrative intervention. In each cell of the table (actually half of them, above or below the diagonal), consider each pair of interventions for utility or capability. Which intervention of each pair "wins" the contest? When you have gotten through all the pairs, count up how many "wins" each intervention got, and you'll have a ranking of interventions. Do that once for utility and once for capability, and you'll have two rankings you can ponder.)

Let's you and me have a little externalizing conversation about your use of PNI in your community or organization. What challenges have you faced so far in your work with PNI? If those challenges were a person, what would they be like? How have you and they interacted? How have they helped and/or hindered you? How might things play out if you changed your behavior towards your challenges?

Let's continue our little talk and have a re-authoring conversation about your use of PNI. What is the overall theme of the story of your use of PNI? Now tell me about some unique outcomes, some *exceptions* to that theme. How does paying attention to those exceptions change your perceptions of the overall story? What sort of story do you *want* to be able to tell about your use of PNI? What will it take to make that story happen?

If someone made a Theatre of the Oppressed play based on your actual use of PNI in your community or organization (or if you haven't done any yet, your imagined use of PNI), where would you shout "stop" and change the action of the play? How would you like to rehearse your use of PNI? Where might that lead you?

As you read the three interviews in this chapter, what surprised you? What did you like, and what didn't you like? What would you like to do with what you read there? What inspires you to learn more or do more? Can you list three ideas brought up in the interviews that you would like to find out more about?

ACTIVITIES

Tell three stories for each intervention type covered in this chapter. The first story should end impossibly well; the second should end normally, as expected; and the third should end impossibly badly.

1. Tell three stories in which people are helped (or not) by telling their stories to a narrative ombudsman.
2. Tell three stories people "drop into" a narrative suggestion box (and that makes things go well, normally, or badly).
3. Tell three stories people share with each other in a story sharing space (and that leads to healing, the status quo, or pain).
4. Tell three stories new members read in a narrative orientation (and that help them a lot or a little, or confuse them or turn them away).
5. Tell three stories people find in a narrative learning resource (and that help them learn a lot or a little, or confuse them).
6. Tell three stories that surprise people in a narrative simulation (and that teach them a lot or a little, or confuse them).
7. Tell three stories that open eyes in a narrative presentation (and that improve conditions a lot or a little, or make things go horribly wrong).
8. Tell three stories a dramatic action creates (great, okay, and downright ugly).
9. Tell three stories people tell when using a sensemaking space (I think you get the great-okay-ugly thing by now).
10. Tell three stories people tell when teaching others how to do sensemaking.
11. Tell three stories a mentor tells to a mentee, or vice versa.
12. Tell three stories in which stories that constitute "unique outcomes" or "exceptions"

to the larger story of the community or organization are surfaced and explored.

13. Tell three stories in which someone shouts "stop" and changes the flow of events in a play depicting events in the community or organization's history or daily life.

What do those stories tell you about the needs and capabilities of your community or organization? Which stories do you like best? Which ring the most true? Which are the most interesting? Which feel the most intense? Why is that?

I described thirteen narrative interventions in this chapter. Come up with some more. Think of things I haven't mentioned that you could do in your community or organization to intervene in the flow of stories. Don't worry if your ideas are crazy; just brainstorm, don't judge. Now pick the intervention you like best and describe it, in speech or in writing, as if you were writing it up for your own textbook. Describe what might happen if someone carried out the intervention you have created.

Choose one of the narrative interventions in this chapter, or one you came up with, and carry it out on a scale so small it can fit within an hour-long session. Create a temporary story-sharing space, or make a narrative presentation, or hold a narrative "clinic" to help people with problems (like a narrative ombudsman would do), or carry out a very brief dramatic action over lunch. What have you learned about yourself and your community or organization by trying out a narrative intervention?

Interview yourself for this chapter. Find my interview questions at the start of the interviews, then sit down and pretend I've just asked *you* to answer them. What would you say, based on your own experiences? If you like, find a few people you know and ask them the interview questions. I suggest simplifying the questions to avoid references to PNI or jargon (e.g., "What's a good way to do things people tell stories about?" or "What can I do to help people who disagree tell each other stories?"). What surprised you in what you said and in what other people said? What have you learned from exploring a wider range of answers to the questions?

Chapter Fourteen

Narrative Return

What happens in a PNI project after the stories have been collected, sensemaking sessions have been held, and decisions have been made? People go back to what they had been doing before the project started, which includes telling and listening to stories. But the stories told after a PNI project has taken place are never the same as the stories told before the project started. This is why I include the return of stories *within* the scope of a PNI project, because it's a natural part of what happens when you start the PNI wheel rolling. In this chapter we will talk about what happens during the return phase and how you can support it.

WHY SUPPORT THE RETURN PHASE?

Some people reading this chapter will be skeptical that there is *any* reason to put energy into supporting the return of stories to the community or organization. *What does it matter*, they will say, *what people say about our project after it's over? Why should we help people talk about the project, and why should we listen to what they say? Our project goals are to find out things and make decisions. After those goals are met, why should we put more investment into the project?*

That question reminds me of a similar question about follow-through in racket sports like tennis, racquetball, and squash. Why is it necessary to consider the movement of the racket *after* the ball and racket have parted company? The racket can't possibly have any impact on the ball as it flies away. Why keep the arm mov-

ing in good form when it is too late to impact the ball? What possible benefit can come from that?

Backflow

Tennis experts speak of attention to follow-through as having two benefits. One of these works backwards in time. If you plan, or even expect, to pull back your arm after you hit the ball, you will hit the ball differently than you would if you planned to act as if you were still contacting the ball. Even thinking about *when* to pull back can disrupt the racket's impact on the ball. So, say the experts, it's best to plan your swing as a fluid motion before, during *and* after impact. This means that one of the two benefits of follow-through is gained before it even happens.

The idea of follow-through working backwards in time reminds me of a backflow story (which I mentioned briefly in the Intervention chapter, on page 490). That's my name for a story whose ending flows back to change the parts of the story that came before it. A backflow story sets up an expectation of a certain state of affairs, then at some point the story upsets that state of affairs in a way that recasts the story—backwards—in a new light. You could say a backflow story splits itself into two stories: the one it appeared to be before the revelation that changed it, and the one it became afterward.

I can think of three novels I've read that relied on such a backflow device: Thomas Mann's *The Magic Mountain*, Toni Morrison's *Beloved*, and Edith Wharton's *Ethan Frome*. The movie *A Beautiful Mind* has such a device in it as well. The apocryphal Hemingway story "For sale: baby shoes, never worn" (which Thaler Pekar mentioned in our interview in the Intervention chapter, page 531) is another classic backflow story (see Figure 14.1 on the following page).

Mann's *The Magic Mountain* is the best example of backflow I've found, because the second story begins on the last few pages of the 700-page novel and ripples backward to change everything that came before it. The first time I read the ending of *The Magic Mountain*, my mouth hung open in shock as I discovered the second story embedded in and entangled with

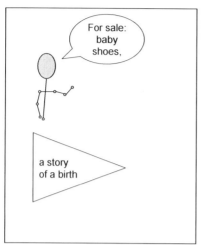 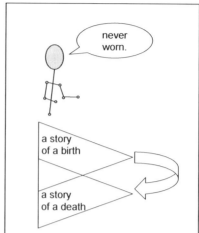

Figure 14.1. A backflow story starts out one way, then at some point wraps back around itself to reveal a second story hidden inside.

the first. Mann knew this would happen, because he famously recommended that readers of *The Magic Mountain* read it twice.

Says Mann:

> I believe that the peculiar construction of the book, its composition, results in a heightened and deepened pleasure for the reader if he goes through it a second time—just as one must be acquainted with a piece of music to enjoy it properly. … On that account you have my presumptuous suggestion to read it twice. Only then can one penetrate the associational musical complex of ideas. When the reader knows his thematic material, then he is in a position to interpret the symbolic and allusive formulae both forwards and backwards.

Mann's "musical complex of ideas" that works "both forwards and backwards" lies in the interplay between two related, contraposed stories, one of which only appears *after* the first reading of the book. He couldn't *say* all this, of course, because if he said the story was going to flow back on itself at the end, he would have ruined the reading experience. People would have spent the whole book wondering what was going to change. (Oops! Hope I haven't ruined it for *you*. Forget everything I said. Nothing changes. I made the whole thing up.)

Now let's imagine two intertwined stories in the form of nearly identical PNI projects. In the first project, you have thought about the return phase from the start and planned to follow through your work *as if* you were still in contact with the people and stories you worked with during the main parts of the project (when the ball was touching your racket, so to speak). In the second project, everything is identical *except* that you have broken off attention to the project (pulled back your arm) by "wrapping things up" on the day of the last sensemaking session. Would both projects come out the same? Not at all. That seemingly small difference in the last few pages of the project's story would ripple back through the project and result in something entirely different. Such intertwined stories would make a fascinating novel, but I think you'd rather your project turn out useful than fascinating.

Backflow reasons to support the return phase

Here are some reasons to support the return phase that fit into the category of backflow effects on earlier phases of the project.

Risk management. There is a return phase in *every* PNI project, whether you support it or not. If you don't support the return phase, what happens during it will be entirely out of your control. I don't mean to imply that the return of stories will ever be entirely under your control even if you *do* support the return phase.

But the more involved you are in the return phase, the greater the influence you will have on how it plays out. This influence will ripple backwards to impact your influence on how the sensemaking plays out and how the story collection plays out. You are making an investment in your project in order to create positive change, so it makes sense to protect your investment by remaining involved in the last part of the PNI cycle.

Closure. Even well-planned PNI projects can expose painful emotions. Your project may anger some people; it may bring people into contention; it may bring memories people want to keep hidden into the spotlight. This is not because PNI methods are flawed; it is because these are the sorts of issues narrative methods excel at handling. After the sensemaking phase of the project is over, people may feel a need to bring the emotional level of the discussion back down to a normal, calm, everyday level.

The return phase is a time of resolution and closure, a return to safety, the *denouement* of the project. By supporting the return phase, you can help people process what happened in the project and find closure so they can move on to new things in the future. If people *don't* find closure during the return phase, the lack of it will ripple back and affect their memories of what happened during the sensemaking and story collection phases, changing the story of the entire project.

Listening. In every PNI project, people should feel that their voices have been heard. As you plan your project, consider the possibility that even after the story collection is complete, and even after sensemaking sessions have been held, some people might not feel that the project has adequately listened to their experiences. Pay special attention to this prospect when there are strong differences of power in your community or organization.

Supporting the return phase helps those who felt their voices were left out or overpowered in the previous phases to finally feel heard. It also helps those who think they *might* have been heard but lack confidence in the process. They might worry that the whole project was a trick created to make them *believe* they have been heard but actually to shut them up by tucking away their experiences into a place nobody ever goes. You can show people that you not only encourage everyone in the community or organization to continue the conversation, but are offering material support for the discussion. This will prove that all voices have truly been heard and respected, and the proof will ripple back into perceptions of what happened during the previous phases of the project.

I've said elsewhere that a good indicator of a successful PNI project is gratitude. If you've finished your sensemaking sessions and have not yet heard people thank you or the project for the chance to speak out, use the return phase of your project to improve on this situation. Give people a voice to speak out once more about the project and the issues it explores.

Memory. Let's say you've worked long and hard planning, supporting and facilitating your project. How soon do you want everyone in your community or organization to forget it ever happened? Not soon, I would guess, and maybe not ever. The best projects remain in the collective memory of the community or organization long after they have been completed. Supporting the return phase will help people remember the project by talking about it after the visible, official parts of the project are over. If you *don't* support the return phase, memories of the earlier phases may fade faster than you would like, changing the story people tell themselves about what happened.

Your own skills. Few people are able to be completely honest with themselves about the flaws in something they've worked long and hard on. Listening to the people who participated in your project (and to those who didn't) in its return phase will help you see the project with new eyes. This will help you develop your facilitation skills better than if you relied only on your own reflections about the project. It may not be fun to hear people talk about what went wrong in a project you threw yourself into, but your next project will surely benefit from the experience. If you *don't* talk to people during the return phase of your project, your memories of the earlier phases may become misaligned with what happened to others, causing you to plan badly in the future.

Future health

I said above that tennis experts give *two* reasons to follow through. The second reason puts its emphasis not on the past but on the future. Tennis players who pull back instead of following through are more likely to injure their racket arm. Abruptly stopping the arm's motion can injure the arm's muscles, tendons, and ligaments, especially if it's done hundreds of times a day. Here are Mark Kovacs and Todd Ellenbecker in an article for the journal *Sports Health:*

> The follow-through phase is the most violent of the tennis serve, requiring deceleration eccentric loads in both the upper and lower body. Continued glenohumeral internal rotation and forearm pronation occur during the acceleration stage and continue after ball contact during deceleration.

I have no idea what that means, but it sounds like it could hurt. So following the analogy again, another reason to support the return phase is to maintain the narrative health of your community or organization going forward.

This also reminds me of something that happens in stories. As you might recall, when people are telling each other stories in conversation, the stories don't end abruptly when the narrated events end (see page 35). Instead, each story ends with a ritual (the coda) in which the storyteller and audience negotiate the return of the conversation to its usual rhythm. A story without a coda is like a tennis swing without follow-through. Each may damage the health of the system in which it occurs.

It is a small step from imagining a story told without a coda to imagining a PNI project conducted without attention to the return phase. Return is all about negotiation between those who initiated, funded, and carried out the project (probably you and some others), those who participated but did not provide the project's central force, and those who did not participate in the project but still belong to the community. If you do not support the return phase of your PNI project, your community or organization will return to its usual conversational rhythm, but in a way that could damage its future health.

Future health reasons to support the return phase

Following are some reasons to support the return phase to ensure or improve the health of a community or organization.

Better ideas. By the time you finish your sensemaking sessions, you might have some good ideas for projects you'd like to conduct in the future, maybe in another year or two. That's great, but there may be even *better* ideas for a new project out there in the community. After all, you aren't the only one who experienced the project's events. In fact, you may be in the worst position to come up with new ideas, because you were so enmeshed in project support that you couldn't see the forest for the trees. By supporting the return phase of your project, you can tap in to the ideas of everyone in the community. This may help you find better ways to build on what you have done in the project. You could say that supporting return leverages the effort you put into the project to achieve better outcomes in the future.

Common language. A common outcome of sensemaking is a set of short-hand *references:* phrases or story summaries people use to refer to complex understandings about the community or organization. These maximally compressed stories have no meaning to people outside the community, but intense meaning to people inside it. People might say things like, "You're about to do a Kevin," or, "This is just like harnessing the ostrich," or, "Don't you remember the dirty boot?" and so on. Sometimes such references survive far longer than the project itself, coming up in debates years later. Support for the return phase can help keep references alive, and this can help your community build on the sessions you've held instead of falling back to talking in the old ways.

Early warning. Your project will undoubtedly open up some issues for ongoing sensemaking. By observing what happens during return, you can continue to monitor the situation and detect emerging problems before they grow larger.

Crowdsourcing. Think of the return phase as a very long after-party for the whole project. The momentum created by organized project activities tends to echo forward into the return phase, prompting people to continue working together on the issues raised, if at a lower intensity. By supporting the return phase, you can build on that energy to address problems without additional project work. In effect, the story collection and sensemaking phases of a PNI project recruit community or organization members to participate in finding solutions. Why not continue to make use of that participation as the project ends?

HOW RETURN HAPPENS

In this section I would like to give you an idea of what typically happens during the return phase of a PNI project. To remind myself about this, I went back through my list of projects and reflected on what happened in each of them at the end of the project, to see if I could come up with some general observations about return.

I have to admit to a pretty severe limitation here. As an outside consultant, I have not often been told much about what happens during the return phase. I always ask people to tell me what happens after the official parts of projects are completed, but often I don't hear much beyond "everything has gone well, no problems." In only a handful of projects have I been able to see for myself what happened as events wound down. Still, I hope these outsider observations can be useful to you as you build your own base of experience.

The dynamics of return

My first observations have to do with the ebb and flow of reactions during the return phase.

Silence

One thing I've noticed about the endings of projects is that there is often a sort of silent time, when people need to reflect quietly on what happened during the project, or not reflect at all but let the project "sit on the back burner" as they do other things. I find this pattern of silence similar to the silence that happens when people are telling stories to each other, those lulls in the conversation when people are thinking quietly about what has been said and what might be said next. When you are collecting stories, it's best to let these silences

happen and not rush to end them artificially. The same goes for the return phase of projects.

If people have gone quiet, it does not necessarily mean they have forgotten about the project entirely. They may return to thinking about it later. Let's say you plan a follow-up activity of asking various people for their perspectives on the project's impact. What does it mean if nobody answers? Does it mean they will *never* answer? Not necessarily. You might just need to wait a little while—a week or two, maybe—and try again. Let the silence play out, then see if people are ready to talk to you.

Face saving

The highly interactive parts of PNI projects—the group story sessions, the sensemaking sessions—can be retroactively stressful. During group sessions, people get swept up in collective energy, step outside of their comfort zones, and do things they normally would avoid. But afterward, those same people may feel overexposed or embarrassed by what they said and did in the heat of the moment, even if it led to useful outcomes. I've found that after people have participated in PNI projects, they sometimes need a little time to reflect *alone* on what has happened, especially when projects have explored sensitive areas.

Let's say you have finished your project's sensemaking phase, and you've written up detailed reports on all of your sessions, with plenty of photos and verbatim quotes of what people said. Should you bring your participants back into a room together and give them the reports to consider together? Not yet. People might need some time to reflect on the reports *alone*. Later you can ask people to come together to talk about the project's outcomes. But give them a little time to ponder sensitive issues without anyone watching them. If you respect people's need to save face on sensitive issues, you will probably get better participation from them the next time you want to ask them to explore.

Recovery

If your PNI project succeeded in finding new solutions to important problems, be aware that people might need to recover from the solutions. Especially if your project has surfaced

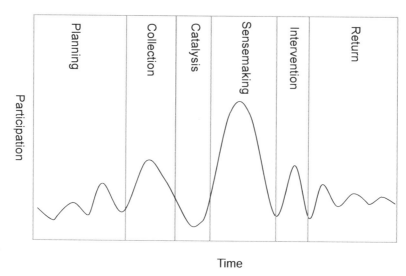

Figure 14.2. The intensity of participation at both the start and end of PNI projects tends to come in waves.

and explored difficult emotions, there might be a backlash in which people refuse to participate in solutions, attack your methods or intent, deny the utility of solutions they themselves helped to create, or just don't want to talk about the problems, or solutions, at all. This does not necessarily mean people think the project was a mistake or the solutions won't work. It might just mean that people need some time and space to process what happened and to recover their balance. Try to keep an open mind and develop a thick skin as you support the return phase of your project. You might hear some things you don't like as people express their feelings about the issues you brought to the surface.

Waves

As you might have guessed from what I've already said, the strength of participatory interest in the return phase of a PNI project tends to come in waves (see Figure 14.2). Similar waves take place in the planning phase as people consider the benefits and risks of the project. In some projects, participation in the return phase is strongly positive at first, but dies down as people think through the difficulties or implications of the solutions arrived at. Or the first response might be negative and people might withdraw, but then a slow wave might rise as people realize the potential for positive change. Expect to see some waves of rising and

falling interest and evaluation during the return phase.

You can find out about these waves by periodically asking people about the project and seeing how they respond. When you find a wave of rising interest, the time might be right to engage people in thinking about new projects or about solutions the project has put in place (possibly in an intervention). Also, if people seem to hate the project one week, don't despair; they may see the good side of it soon after.

The rights and responsibilities of return

This next set of observations has to do with rights: who has responsibility for what, who owes what to whom, who owns what.

Promises

One thing I have noticed in the projects I've helped with is that the more participation a project has included, the more important the return phase has been. This makes sense. Think about a time you filled out a survey that took two minutes. Did you pay very much attention to the project it was part of? Now think about a time you spent hours working with people towards some end. Did you pay more attention to that project than you did to what was done with your two-minute survey? Of course you did. The more involved you are in a project, the more you want to know and influence how it comes out.

Participatory research, unlike extractive research, makes *promises* to the people in your community or organization. Once you've made a promise of participation, you can't just cut it off when the main part of the project is over. People will expect to be informed as the project winds down, and they will expect to have the *opportunity* to participate during the return phase, even if they don't expect to use it.

If you break the promise of participation at the end of your project, you may find people less willing to participate in future projects. Even something as simple as a way to comment on the project—what it was like to participate in it, what people liked and disliked about it, ideas they have for future projects—will help people stay involved to the end.

Ownership

When I designed the diagram of PNI phases, one reason I felt it was necessary to separate intervention from return was that they have different profiles of activity. Interventions, while they may attract the participation of many, are centrally planned and supported: by you, or by your team, or by your organization's or community's infrastructure. That's why I place intervention outside PNI's central triangle, because it is not driven by the entire community or organization.

The return phase belongs to the people, and only the people can decide what will happen in it. You can provide support for the return phase, but your support must be low-key. It cannot be controlling or even enticing. During the return phase you can observe and respond, but you cannot direct. If you try to control the return phase, all you will do is create another intervention phase, which will inevitably be followed by another return phase you cannot control. The return phase is like an echo, and an intervention is like a call. Try as you might, you cannot create or control an echo. You can only call again.

I remember a time when I first encountered this need for ownership as a project wound down. After a sensemaking session, I asked people to answer some questions about the session and

the project. In one question, I asked people to estimate their interest in hearing more stories like the ones they'd worked with, on a scale from one to ten. One person responded, "Ten if uncensored." The message was clear: facilitation is nice, and projects are great, but when it's time for us to go back to simply sharing stories, keep central planning out of it. That's worth remembering.

Perceptions

Another thing I've noticed in the projects I've worked on has been that how a project plays out and what it means in the long term is different to different people. To some people the project has been ground-breaking, opening up new vistas of possibility, inspiring them to apply themselves to new challenges. To some the same project has been a mildly interesting blip in a humdrum year, but nothing worth getting excited about. To some the project has been insipid, an exercise in going through the motions without accomplishing anything. To some it has been misguided, an embarrassing misstep, something to be tucked away. And to some the project has not happened at all, as far as they can recall (which project did you mean?).

I don't think there is anything anybody can do about this state of affairs. It's just the way things are. I've seen it happen on many a project. Don't let yourself get upset about this. I know you've put your heart and soul into your project, but people have the right to give the project whatever meaning it has to them, even if it's far less meaning than you hoped. You can't change how people see the project as it ends, but you can *find out* how they see the project, and you can *use* that information to improve your methods and plan your next steps. Sometimes what you learn about how the project was perceived by people in various positions in your community or organization can turn out to be as useful as the stories you collected.

Processing during return

My final set of observations has to do with how people make sense of a PNI project as it ends and recedes into memory.

Stories

As people move further away in time from the main events of your project, the project will become a story for them. It will become compressed into something tighter and less detailed. It will conform to a universal plot shape. Some events will be highlighted, while others will be sidelined or forgotten. The story will develop an overall theme, which may be expressed as a catch-phrase or slogan.

All of this is as it should be. A story is what you *want* people to remember, because a PNI project is above all else *something that happens*. It's not a fact or opinion or evidence or proof. It's a story. We started out; we made plans; we tried this; we encountered these obstacles; we succeeded; we failed; we were surprised; we changed; we learned; we arrived at a new place.

References

If your project has had an impact on your community or organization, it is likely that there will be some changes to the way people talk about the issues it explored. Terms that came up during sensemaking sessions may bounce around afterward, and you may hear them in places and times far removed from what you might consider the project proper. A reference that ties together the project story's theme may be repeated until people only need to mention the reference and everyone knows what it means. People might say something like, "It's a get-rich-quick scheme" or "we need to finish what we start" or "keep the heat on" or some other penetrating truth that came out of the project. Listen for these.

Wishes

Another thing I've noticed about the ends of projects is that when all the project events are over, people sometimes communicate a feeling of disappointment or letdown. This usually happens because people temporarily experienced something during the project that they don't usually have in their work or home lives, and they wish they could have it back.

Here are some examples of wishes I've seen people express when a project has ended.

- I have had a brief glimpse of what life is like for other people. I've *learned* more about those around me. That has been something new, and I'd like to see more of it.
- It was great to have the opportunity to *compare* notes, to learn how my experiences have

been similar to and different from the experiences of others.

- I valued the chance to *reflect* on my own life and experiences. I have seen myself through new eyes.
- I feel that I've *connected* to other people in my community in a new way. We have shared more than just facts and opinions. I feel more deeply rooted in the common life of the community than I felt before.
- It was nice to feel like I was *responsible* for the problems that face the whole community. I've felt involved in finding solutions and making them work.
- I was so glad to have a chance to tell my story. I felt *heard* for the first time in a long time. Somebody wanted to know what I've gone through.
- This project was so *interesting!* I looked forward to every activity I participated in. I'd like to do more of what we did then.

When people wish they could have something back, that's an opening, an opportunity, something you can use to get people to participate in future projects.

IDEAS FOR SUPPORTING RETURN

Assuming I've convinced you that it's worth the investment to support the return phase of your PNI project, here are some ideas on things you can do. Because return looks different to different people, I've separated the ideas by whom they help: you and your team, those who gave you permission or funding to carry out your project, and the entire community or organization.

Supporting return in your PNI practice

This first set of ideas has to do with supporting return within the group of people who supported the project: you yourself, and your project team.

Celebrating the project

You worked hard on your project. Pat yourself on the back. Do something special for yourself. If the project turned out wonderfully, celebrate your success. I don't know why, but for a while

I got into the habit of buying myself a small piece of furniture every time I finished a big project. I've had to stop doing that because my house filled up with end tables and step stools and things; but my point is, don't just trudge back to work after you've finished a PNI project, especially if it was a large one. Do something special to mark your accomplishment. Doing so will help you sustain your effort in the most difficult parts of the next project.

What if the project *didn't* turn out well? What if people whose good opinion you value were not satisfied? What if you were not satisfied? In that case it's even *more* important to reward your hard work. Sure, you made some mistakes. You can see them clearly in retrospect. Sure, you failed to anticipate some conditions that changed everything. But you still worked hard, and you still did your best. I doubt you'd have read this far in this long book if you weren't the kind of person who does your best. There will be a time to reflect on your mistakes, but right now just take a rest and reward yourself. Go out and get that end table anyway. You deserve it.

Always remember that it is entirely possible in story work to do your best on a project and *still* fail to satisfy people. That's why I say story work is high input, high risk, and high output. You will not always succeed. I haven't, and while I still cringe at the memory of projects that failed to satisfy, I value the lessons I learned as a result. You will too.

If you are working in a team, make sure everyone in the team participates in the celebration during the return phase. Have a party, go out to dinner, do something *together*. Don't celebrate alone. You worked hard on the project as a team, you struggled and strove as a team, you succeeded and failed as a team.

What if you were not a productive team? What if you argued the whole way through? In that case it is still important to end the project as a team, if you can. You all *tried* to work together, even if you failed. Finish the story of your project together. If you mark the project's end separately, it will be harder to make sense of what happened and learn from it later on. Even if it's awkward, try to mark the end of the project together.

Gathering perspectives on the project

This next idea is probably the most important part of the return phase for your own personal and professional development. During the return phase, not only do stories need to return to the community; they also need to return to *you*.

There is a danger when completing projects of believing you know what happened in them. You don't. You can't possibly know how your project appeared to everyone involved (and uninvolved) in it. If you think your project has been a resounding success, you're wrong. If you think your project has been a dismal failure, you're wrong. Every project succeeds and every project fails. If you don't know where your project has succeeded *and* where it has failed, you don't know what happened in your project. You need to ground truth your project as it winds down; you need to climb off your satellite and walk around on the ground of perception. If you don't, you run the risk of creating a rift between perception and reality that will cause you to make errors of misalignment in future projects (and worse, *you won't know why*).

In a perfect world, every PNI project would have an echo that collected stories about how the project went, and that echo would have an echo, and so on *ad infinitum*. But in the real world that would be ridiculous as well as impossible. You have other things to do, and so does everybody else. So what can you do to find out what happened in your project without burdening everyone with another formal story collection?

Do you remember how, in the "How return happens" section above (page 547), I talked about how people process the events of the project? Do you remember how I said people develop *stories, references* and *wishes* related to the project? One of the most useful things you can do during the project's return phase is to simply listen to these stories, references, and wishes. They are out there; just listen.

Give people some time to process the project's events—days or weeks, depending on the duration of the project. Wait until talk about the project has died down and people have gone back to their normal routines. Then ask some of the people who participated in the project to tell you what happened in it from their perspective. If your project was small, ask just a few people. If it was larger, ask more, say ten. You don't have to do this formally; just start conversations and get an idea of what people are thinking.

Ask people questions like this:

- What surprised you about this project?
- What moments of the project were best and worst for you?
- What did you get out of participating in this project that you wouldn't have got if you hadn't been involved?
- What's different for you now than it was before the project started?
- Have you heard anything interesting from other people about the project? Any rumors?
- Is there anything about the project you'd like to keep going?
- Is there anything you wish *hadn't* happened during the project?
- Is there anything you think I should know about the project?

Don't ask *all* of these questions; just choose one or two you think will be most useful to you. You don't have to record the responses. Just take notes on what people say, either while they're talking or afterward.

Involving the uninvolved. In addition to asking participants questions, find some people who *didn't* participate in the project and ask *them* what happened in it.

In some ways, asking non-participants about the project is even more important than asking participants. There are many special-reality bubbles you can develop as you go through a project (see Figure 14.3 on the facing page). You can have your own bubble, within which everything looks different than outside. Your team can have one. Your team and your funding or steering group can have one. A bubble might contain everyone who participated in the project in any way. And finally, there can even be a bubble enveloping everyone who even knows that the project exists. You've got to break *all* of those bubbles to find out what *really* happened in your project.

Oh, come on, you might be saying. *Why is it so important to find out what the people who haven't even noticed my project think of it?* Because those might be the very people your *next* project depends on. If they belong to your community or organization, you need to know what they think.

The most direct way to hear from the uninvolved is to simply stand in some place where people often walk by and try to engage them in conversation. You might ask them things like this:

- Have you seen this project that has been going on? (if yes) What do you think of it? (if no, describe it, then ask) What do you think of that?
- Have you heard about the project that went on last month? (if yes) What did you hear about it? (if no, describe it, then ask) What do you think people would say about that?
- I heard this story the other day. (tell a story from the project) What do you think of that?

When you're asking non-participants about the project, don't let on that you spearheaded it. Just ask as if you had not participated in it either, or as if you had a tiny role in it, because if people know the project was your baby they won't answer honestly. Try to gather as many stories from non-participants as you do from participants. Draw your sample from the *entire* community or organization, not just from those who took part.

If you think it will be difficult to ask people who were not interested in your project to talk to you about the project, you can find other ways to ask. Here's one. Find a place where people congregate, like a community room or lunch room or library. Make sure it's a place where people are used to talking to each other in public, not a place they expect to be alone. Display some of the things generated in the project there, like quotes from important stories, sensemaking constructions, bits of transcripts from sensemaking sessions. Make your display large and eye-catching, and not too detailed, so people will stop and glance at it. Then hang around pretending to do something else but *actually* listening to people as they notice the display and talk to each other about it.

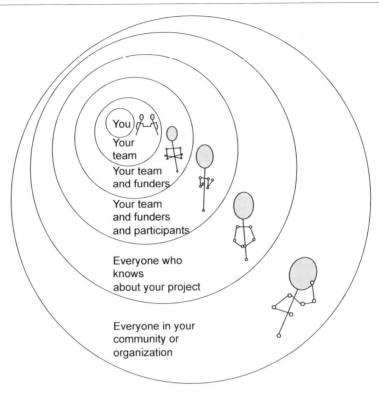

Figure 14.3. There can be many reality bubbles about your project. You've got to break them all to find out what really happened.

If you think people are amenable, try to engage them in conversation about the display, as if you had just discovered it along with them. If you think people will suspect you of listening in, find something you can do nearby that seems legitimate, or just walk back and forth through the space all day looking like you're on your way to somewhere else. It might not take more than a few hours to gather enough reactions to what you've displayed (see Figure 14.4 on the next page).

Another way you can gather information from the uninvolved is to create a display, just as above, but this time don't stand around listening. Just design the display in such a way that it tells you what people do by the wear patterns they leave behind. Place several carefully-chosen stories or sensemaking constructions in several locations in a public place, then note how much dirt is left before each one as people stop to look at it. Or write up mini-reports with various significant project results on them, and leave them on a table in a public place. Vary the contents of the different reports, then wait

a week and count how many of each type are left on the table. (You can do all of this virtually as well, by putting things on the web and observing click patterns.)

References and wishes. As you gather stories and reactions from participants and nonparticipants, listen for *references* to things (stories, patterns, themes) that seem to matter to people. You are likely to hear the same references from different people. When you hear a reference that seems important to the person who is saying it, note it down. Keep a list of these references, and look for patterns in them. Also, listen to conversations where people come together and see if you hear any of the references on your list being mentioned. Are the references coming up in conversation? Which ones, and how? Do they come up everywhere, or only in some places or with some people? And if not, what *are* people talking about?

Also be on the lookout for expressions of *wishes*. Listen to see if you hear people missing anything or wishing they could have anything back.

Figure 14.4. You can gather reactions to your project from people who did not participate in it by putting up displays with project outcomes and seeing what people do and say in front of them.

If they say something like, "I've been thinking, I've never heard so much about how people see our community as I did on that day," that's a wish. What do those "it was nice for a while" feelings tell you? What do people hunger for? Where is there energy waiting to be released? What does that tell you about what sorts of projects people might be eager to support in the future?

Using what you have heard. After you have heard a variety of stories and references and wishes about your project, use them to revise and widen the story you tell yourself about the project. Review the whole landscape of perception about the project. You might find out that some of your participants didn't enjoy or value the project as much as you thought they did. You might find out that there are non-participants who saw the project as a problem, not a solution. You might find out that some non-participants *would* have participated if the project had been set up differently. Use the return phase of your project to open your own eyes about what happened, so you can learn and prepare for future story work.

If you are working in a team, ask everyone in the team to gather stories, references, and wishes

from participants and non-participants. Ask them to take notes on what they find out. Then get together as a team and review what everyone has found. You might want to use sense-making methods to map out what you have found, for example by clustering perceptions or building a landscape. Talk together about what surprised you in what you heard. Develop your group's story of what happened during the project, considering all views.

Reflecting on and recording the project

Okay, so now you've marked the end of your project with a celebration of your effort, and you've listened to hear the full story of the project from all perspectives. Now it's time to make sense of it all, reflect on what you've learned, and wrap up the project so you can move on to new things.

Here are some things to ponder.

1. Reflect on what you've learned about *stories*. I've said in other places that the best way to learn about stories is to experience stories. You've experienced some stories in this project. What have you learned from them? What in them surprised you? Is your definition of story different now than it was

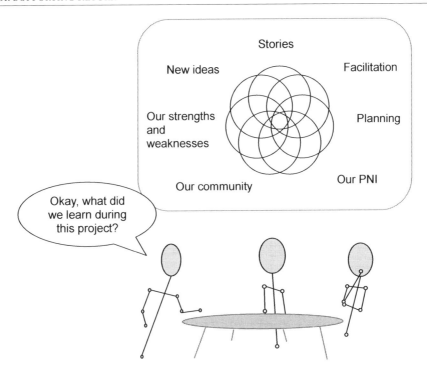

Figure 14.5. Wrap up your project by considering what you learned about stories, facilitation, planning, your version of PNI, your community or organization, your strengths and weaknesses, and ideas for new projects.

then? Pull out some stories that taught you things. What did they teach you, and how can you use that going forward?

2. Reflect on what you've learned about *facilitation*. Think back on every interaction with participants in your project, whether it was collecting stories or helping people work with them. What were the high and low points in your facilitation? What surprised you? What moments will you remember for a long time?

3. Reflect on what you've learned about project *planning*. Did your plan turn out the way you thought it would? Did you ever panic because things seemed to be falling apart? Did you ever discover a new opportunity you could not have seen coming? What does this project make you want to do differently in projects you might do in the future?

4. Reflect on *your own version* of PNI. How did this project challenge the way you do PNI? How will the way you do PNI change after it? Did you try any experiments during the project? What happened? What new ideas

did you get? What do you want to remember about your own PNI practice when you start your *next* project?

5. Reflect on your *community or organization*. What do you know about it now that you didn't know before the project started? What about its culture, or unwritten rules, or strengths and weaknesses, is newly apparent? How will this knowledge impact any future projects you might do?

6. Reflect on your own *strengths and weaknesses*. Did you find yourself (personally or as a team) stuck in an area you thought you had strength? Did you find skills you didn't know you had? If you are working in a team, reflect on your collaborative strengths and weaknesses. How does your team work differently now than it did then? How can you use that going forward?

7. Reflect on *ideas* that came up during the project. Write a list of ten follow-on projects you'd love to do, if you had the time and help and participation. What are your ideal next steps?

If you are working alone, set aside some time to reflect, review your notes, and write up some new ones. If you are working in a team, plan a meeting (or extend the meeting where you go over what you heard from people) for a final wrap-up (see Figure 14.5 on the preceding page).

While you ponder all of these things, *write down* what you think. *Please* write things down. Especially if you work in a team, make sure things get written down and not simply discussed and forgotten. Even one page of notes will seem like it's written with golden ink months or years later. You'd be amazed by how easy it is to forget, in a matter of months, so much useful information about a project that has wound down.

It's a good idea to keep a list of all the projects you've ever worked on, with notes for each. Start doing this with your very first project. I keep a list of projects, with notes, for all the projects I work on. However, I didn't realize I should do this until I had reached about the twentieth project. By that time all I had left from my earliest projects were dream-like snippets of memory: an image here, a word there. Thank goodness I did start taking more notes as I went on, because without them I could never have written this book. I've relied heavily on my notes in every chapter of the book. Who knows, maybe someday you'll write your own book about story work. Start taking notes for it now.

Supporting return with your steering committee

In larger communities and organizations, projects are often authorized and funded by a steering committee, funding group, executive office, council, board, or other body of people in charge. If you have received permission to conduct your project from one of those bodies of people, you will need to make sure they are informed and satisfied during the return phase of your project. You want them to understand what happened, approve of what you did, and hopefully support you as you think about future projects.

What if you *are* the steering committee? What if you have nobody to answer to but yourself? It's still a good idea to prepare to inform and satisfy *yourself*, in your role as the person in charge, during the return phase of your project. You don't need to convince yourself of what the project has accomplished, but you might need to convince somebody someday. It won't hurt to present the project to yourself so you can improve your own confidence in what you've done.

So, what does your committee need during the return phase of your project? I can think of three things: information, evidence, and records.

Essential information

First, you need to inform your committee about what went on during your project. This is another place where gathering diverse perspectives about the project comes in handy. The last thing you want to do is go to your committee ready to tell them about your great success, only to have them tell you they've heard a negative rumor about the project. It should be your business to find out what people in your community or organization are saying about the project *before* you talk to your committee. So it's a good idea not to present your project to your committee until *after* you've done the return steps listed above for yourself or your team. If the committee wants to hear from you sooner, tell them you are doing some wrap-up work and will be ready to talk to them soon.

When you inform your committee about the project, give them the whole picture, but don't make it too detailed. Give them the bird's eye view of the project, with only its major results highlighted. Here are some things you should show them.

Stories. Show your committee some of the stories that had the biggest impact on the project. Make sure they get to see the authentic experiences of some of the people who told the stories. That's how they'll know the project reached real people and gave them the chance to speak.

But be careful here. You are likely to be tempted, as you approach the people who allowed you to conduct your project, to show them the *best* stories, the most compelling, memorable, well-told—maybe even the most shocking stories. Don't do that. Show them the stories that *mattered* most in the project. Do this for two rea-

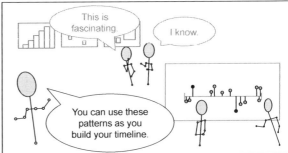

Figure 14.6. Don't present catalytic patterns to your committee as results, because they aren't results. Present them either as a record of what resonated during sensemaking or as catalytic material for sensemaking at the meeting itself.

sons. First, you don't want the committee to get the idea that the purpose of your project was to collect amazing stories, because that's not what you said you were going to do. Second, you need to communicate to them the project's meaning. Even if the stories that best represent the project's meaning are not well put together, those are the stories you should share. Put the Hollywood blockbusters away, and show them what matters.

Constructions. If your sensemaking sessions resulted in the production of any significant constructions, such as timelines or landscapes, show those to the committee. Don't show them in a rough format, say in out-of-focus photographs from a sensemaking session. If you truly need the support of these people, clean up and simplify the constructions until they convey their essential meaning well and simply.

Lists. If your sensemaking sessions resulted in the production of lists of things (discoveries, opportunities, issues, ideas, recommendations, perspectives, dilemmas), this is the time to bring them out. Only don't present *every* detail that was generated. If you know you'll need to present this sort of information to your committee, ask people in your sensemaking sessions to choose the top three items in two or three lists (discoveries and ideas, for example), and just present those. Be ready to reveal more list items if the committee wants you to, but don't present too much information at first.

Patterns. Here's a question for you. Should you present catalytic patterns, that is, graphs of how many people said this or that about your sto-

ries, to your committee? You can, but only if the patterns were important to exploration during sensemaking. Your presentation to the committee is about the *sensemaking* that took place in your project, not the patterns that catalyzed it. Remember, catalytic work is not a *replacement* for sensemaking; it's simply an aid. Presenting catalytic patterns *as results* is not participatory, and it's not very useful either. Catalytic patterns can never be sound empirical proof, because they are based on a mountain of complex perceptions about stories and intent and social negotiation (yes, even if they were collected over the magical internet). If you present catalytic patterns to your committee as analytical results, you will run the risk of the whole meeting turning into an attack on your methods and expertise. That's not useful to anybody.

The one situation in which it is legitimate to present catalytic patterns to your committee is when they are engaged in sensemaking of their own. This is actually an excellent idea. If you can involve "the powers that be" in sensemaking, you won't be presenting the "results" of "analysis" to them. You'll be engaging them in exploration alongside all of the other project participants (see Figure 14.6).

Why not consider your committee meeting one more sensemaking session? It will certainly add another dimension of perspective to the project. You might not be able to get your committee to spend hours walking around with sticky notes in their hands, but you might be able to get them to do a few simple exercises with the stories and patterns you have collected. I've tried this, and I have to tell you that "powers that be" are often pleasantly surprised to be included in, and not just informed about, participatory projects.

That's a general rule about participatory work. Don't assume that *anyone* wants to be left out of participation. They might not admit it, to you or to themselves, but usually everyone wants to be included in some way, even if they are too important to be bothered.

Q&A. Be ready to answer any questions your committee might have. Bring all the materials you have with you, so you can delve into detail when it is wanted. I've found that people sometimes want a capsule view when they are in a project-ending meeting, but later want to peruse something longer. You can prepare a project report that incorporates all of the information I mentioned above (stories, constructions, lists) and give it to committee members to look over at their leisure.

Evidence

The second thing you need to show your committee is *proof* that their money or permission was not wasted. You need to show a return on the investment they made in the project. This is different information than the stories, constructions, lists, and patterns I mentioned above, because it features what people *said* about the project rather than what they *did* during it.

To prepare for your committee meeting, hunt up some verbatim comments people made, during your story collections, sensemaking sessions, and ground-truthing afterward. Find times when people said what the project meant to them. For example, during one of your story collection sessions a person might have said, "I never really thought about this before today." Or during a sensemaking session you might have seen two people discovering a new opportunity together. Or afterwards a person might have told you, "I wish we could do ten more projects like this. It would be good for us."

Come to your committee meeting armed with evidence that the project has borne fruit, both in addressing the *specific* issues it was meant to approach and in the more *general* sense of improving the community's collective ability to make sense of things. Prove that the project has not just skimmed the surface but has reached

deep down and changed something about the way people think and talk about the issues you addressed. Look for expressions of gratitude, excitement, revelation, discovery.

What if you *can't* find proof that your project has succeeded? What if there *are* no expressions of anything positive you can bring to your committee? What if people just did what they were told, and nobody discovered anything or got excited about anything? What if the whole project was a flop? Well, first, I've *never* seen this happen, not even once, so it probably won't happen to you. Somebody *always* finds something out, and it's always something useful, even if it's not an earth-shattering thing. The likelihood of your not being able to find even a few favorable comments on the project is vanishingly small.

Secondly, even if the project failed in the sense that people didn't get fired up or discover anything new, *you* certainly learned a lot by doing the project. So tell the committee what you learned. Go through your notes and find some aspects of growth in your own understanding of your community or organization and in your methods. Show the committee that your ability to fit available techniques to your community's unique needs has grown. Show them that you will be able to carry out more fruitful projects in the future. Have confidence in your own learning, and present that confidence to your committee. They'll see it and respond.

Records

The third thing your committee needs from you is project records. Don't let yourself become indispensable to the success of the project. Give someone copies of all the records you have from the project, including all of your notes, and make sure your steering committee knows where those copies are. This will help the committee ensure the continuing success of the project. It will also convince them of its value. Only things of value are worth keeping.

Supporting return in your entire community or organization

Do you remember, in the section on rights and responsibilities during the return phase (page 548), how I talked about *ownership*? Do you remember how I said return belongs to the people and not to you? We will now be explor-

Figure 14.7. Be prepared to help each person who comes to you with a request during the return phase. If you do, you will increase participation in the next project and also encourage the creation of new projects.

ing the aspect of return in which ownership matters most.

Your interactions with people during all previous phases of your project were *active invitations*. You asked people to tell stories; you invited people to make sense of things together; you may have intervened in the life of stories in your community. The return phase is different. During the return phase, your support must be *passive:* available and ready, but not asking or inviting. Now it's time to let the *people* do the asking.

So let's say you have made it clear to everyone that, as the person or team responsible for your PNI project, you are available and waiting for any expressions of need. Let's say somebody comes to you with a request. Based on my experience, these are the types of requests you are most likely to hear (see Figure 14.7).

1. This was a great project. I'd like to help you do *more* projects like this. How can I help out?

2. My friends and I have been talking. This project has *inspired* us to do more about the issue the project addressed. Do you have any ideas for things we could do together?

3. I really enjoyed the opportunity to share stories with people. I wish there was some way to keep that *conversation* going. I'd be willing to put some time into making that happen, but I don't know how to start. Could you help?

4. I participated in the project, but I wasn't really aware of everything that went on. I'm interested in the topic, and I'd like to *explore* more about the issue using what was collected. Could you help me do that?

5. I find the approach you used on this project fascinating. Could you help me *learn* more about story work?

I'll go through each of these requests in turn.

Supporting people who want to help you

Interested helpers are one of the fruits of a successful PNI project. By being there to help people find out how they can help you, you can grow your base of support for future participation.

In my experience I have found that there are three levels of interest in any community or organizational project:

1. people who want to stay informed;
2. people who want to be consulted; and
3. people who want to collaborate.

The usual proportions of these groups are something like sixty, thirty and ten percent respectively. Each group requires a different type of support (see Figure 14.8 on the next page).

Supporting people who want to be informed. It's a good idea to give participants in story collection and sensemaking sessions the opportunity to declare their interest in staying informed about the project. The best way I know of to do this is to end each session by showing people forms on which they can write their

want to stay informed   want to be consulted   want to collaborate

Figure 14.8. Three types of interest generally appear as a project winds down. Some people want to hear about what you are doing, some people want to be asked what they think, and some people want to work with you.

contact details to indicate that they want to be informed about further developments in the project and about new projects coming up. (If the topic is very sensitive and anonymity has been preserved, you can instead give people a way to submit their contact information *after* the session. In that way they will be absolutely sure that their expression of interest in the project will not be connected with the stories they told.)

Supporting people who want to be consulted. At the end of each session and publication related to the project, make it clear that you are not just willing but *eager* to hear any opinions, complaints, or suggestions people might have about the project. Don't hold back; *embarrass* yourself with your enthusiasm for feedback. *Plead* for it. I did this in pre-publication versions of this book. I wrote, "Constructive feedback is encouraged, appreciated, lauded, embraced, hoped for, dreamed about." Every word I wrote there was true, and people responded, and the book improved as a result.

When anyone does contact you, give them *plenty* of your attention and time. Listen to anything they have to say, even if it's rambling or uninformed. Put aside everything else and listen to them. Feedback on your project is like diamonds. Never underestimate its value.

Sometimes people *want* to be consulted about a project but aren't willing to take the first step. If you think people might hold back like this, you can reach them by attaching a question to your keep-me-informed form. It should say

something like, "Would you be interested in answering some questions about the project in a month's time?" When people check that box, it means they would like to be consulted, but they want you to reach out first.

Supporting people who want to collaborate. Some people, not many but some, will want to do more than just talk to you after the main part of your project is over. They might want to brainstorm with you about designs for future projects; they might want to participate in quick story collections or sensemaking sessions; they might want to help you collect stories; they might want to catalogue or organize collected stories. My advice is to welcome these people with open arms. They will be your new friends, and someday they might be your new team.

It is important to maintain a barrier between the first two groups I've described here and this last group, the collaborators. Those who want to be informed or consulted might come to you by filling out a form or checking a box, but people who want to collaborate never indicate their interest in such a timid way. Collaborators always jump some kind of barrier in order to indicate their strong interest in the work you are doing. They might send a well-thought-out letter; they might ask you when they can call or visit; they might offer to carry out some task; they might tell you about an idea they've had for a future project (and about their willingness to make it work). When someone contacts you not with a *request* but with a *proposal*, you have found a collaborator. Collaborators *create* the barrier they jump, because they need it. The barrier is proof that they are in a special group with special access and special power. This is what they want: not to be notified or listened to, but to stand *with* you and create change.

You can help to erect the barrier collaborators need, and you can give collaborators useful things to do to help. For example, you can create special places that only collaborators can visit. These can be simple: an online discussion forum, a monthly meeting or phone call, a special "project table" in a little-used room of your library. What you want to do is create an *interface* where collaborators can help your project team, and possibly eventually join your project team, with intense, time-consuming help only they want to provide.

Of course I should mention the possibility of collaborators wanting to take your projects in directions you don't want to go. There are always negotiations in project teams about directions, and those negotiations will inevitably extend outward to the collaborators that surround your project team. A rule I like to use when I collaborate with people is: whoever does the most work gets the loudest voice. If you have ten people in your collaborator group and one does ten times the work of the others—real, substantive work that gets things done, not just standing around arguing—that person should have more of a voice about the team's direction. That might not be your rule, but you will need *some* rules to govern your collaboration.

Are collaborators worth having? Of course they are, if you plan on doing many projects or large ones. Not only will you need to grow your team and replace members who have left, but you also need to keep in touch with a handy group of available critics, so you can keep your project plans grounded in reality. If you've planned any projects, you already know that plans tend to drift off like balloons if nobody is holding onto them. Collaborators can help you hold on.

Supporting people who want to work together (but not with you)

Sometimes people will come to you during the return phase full of enthusiasm to address issues raised by the project. But unlike the collaborators in the previous group, these people don't want to *help* you. They want to *become* you. They may have already put together their own team, or they may have ideas about recruiting people to join them. They may want to use methods exactly like those you used; they may want to use different methods; they may want to mix methods; or they may have no idea what methods they want to use. Sometimes people just want to *do something*. I call these people *task-force people*, because they have force (or energy or enthusiasm) and they want to apply it to some task. All they need is a little help getting started.

When you meet task force people, applaud their effort and provide advice where and when it is asked for, but don't overdo it. Later on we'll talk about people who come to you wanting to learn about story work. When you meet *those* people you can download your entire body of knowledge onto them; but these aren't those people, and they don't want that.

Watch your own feelings when you meet task-force people, because meeting them may cause you to feel defensive or proprietary about your project. It's reasonable to feel ownership for the project you've worked so hard on. But it's not reasonable to dampen someone else's enthusiasm because you need to own everything. Don't pretend to help task-force people so you can control them; don't avoid them so your secret methods will be safe; don't dump the entire contents of your brain onto them; don't criticize their ideas because you know better; just give them a boost and wish them well on their journey.

Supporting people who want to keep talking

Another thing that typically happens as a project ends is that somebody tells you they wish they could keep sharing and working with stories the way they did during the project. Some people might mention such a thing casually, but other people might actually come to you asking for help making better story sharing happen. That's an expression of need, and it's one you can be ready to support.

How can you help these people? Well, if you happened to have set up any kinds of story sharing or sensemaking environments during the intervention phase of your project, you can direct people there. If you haven't set up any spaces like that, you should still learn enough about them to give people who want to create them some tips. The last part of this chapter is about what you or anyone else can do to support ongoing story sharing in your community or organization. If you've read that part of the chapter, you should be able to give people who want to keep talking some ideas they can use. If they need help getting the community or organization to fund or permit such a space, you might be able to help them get support from those in charge.

Supporting people who want to explore

If you've ever participated in a project and then wondered what became of it, you will understand this next need. Most of the participants in your project will have had a limited view of what went on during it. Sometimes people will come to you in the return phase with a desire to find out more. They might want to read or listen to more stories than they had time to encounter during the story collection session they attended. Or they may want to build another landscape with the stories they used in their sensemaking session. Or they may just want to explore what has been collected and created on their own. These people don't want to help you do more projects, and they don't want to do projects themselves. They just want to make use of the resources they helped to create. Or they may not have participated in the project, or they may have joined the community or organization too late to participate. In any case, they are interested in the project now.

How can you help these people? I can think of a few ways in which you can support project explorers.

Show them your stories. Let explorers have access to all of the stories you've collected, with full support for searching and comparing. This is not story sharing, so you don't need to help them tell their own stories. Remove details that might compromise any privacy agreements you have in place. Also remove details you needed during your work on the project but that might be in the way now, like dates of collection, interviewers, and so on. Format the stories in as simple and accessible a way as possible, just as you did for your sensemaking sessions. If it's not against your privacy agreement, help people make copies of stories they want to remember or use for their own projects.

Show them your patterns. In addition to looking at stories, people may want to explore patterns in the accompanying data on their own. As far as you can, make it possible for people to look at patterns across stories. If access is physical, give people a space where they can sort, count, and lay out story cards. If access is virtual, give people tools to build visualizations of patterns, such as for example providing the data in spreadsheet format.

Show them your records. Your project will have generated some records beyond the stories collected. There might be planning documents; tapes or transcripts from interviews or story collection sessions; things built during sensemaking sessions; notes taken during sessions; notes taken during after-session reviews; tapes or transcripts of sensemaking sessions; catalysis results or reports; notes from your return-phase review; and a final report that summarizes everything that went on during the project. You can allow explorers to see some or all of these records. Just make sure to remove any details you don't want everyone in your community or organization—and really, the whole world—to see. Make sure you are aware of what is in every document you release. Check your privacy policy to see if you promised to hold anything back from public view. Obtain permission from your steering committee, your team, or whoever has the right to keep secrets about your project.

Give them space, tools, and help. As you provide all of these resources to people, give them a place to work and tools they can use in their exploration. For example, if you provide access to stories on story cards, set aside some tables people can use to sort the cards and walls people can use to build new constructions with them. Make sure explorers know you are available to help if they have any questions, but otherwise don't bother them as they do their research.

You may have noticed that providing these elements of support sounds a lot like setting up a sensemaking space, as I suggested in the chapter on narrative interventions (see page 491). Yes, the two situations are similar. The difference is in the *intensity* of the effort. An intervention sensemaking space involves active help in the form of abundant handouts, training sessions, and helpers posted in the space ready to jump in when there is the slightest confusion. Such a space will be heavily promoted, with advertisements, contests, or other means of spreading the word and getting people in the door. The space itself will be carefully designed to maximize its attraction to people who have only a slight interest in exploration.

By contrast, support for exploration of project resources outside of narrative intervention should be low-key and passive. The space is not likely to be beautiful or large; more likely, it will be nothing more than a spare table or shelf in a room already used for other things. The space will not be promoted; indeed, few people might even know of its existence. In the space, resources will be laid out simply, without attention to enhancing interest. Help using the space will be provided by people who already have other responsibilities but are willing to find a half hour now and then to help. In short, if a sensemaking space built for intervention is like a fancy restaurant, a sensemaking space built for exploration is like a kitchen. Its purpose is purely utilitarian.

Why should you create a place for people to explore your project? Isn't this a waste of time and effort? Not at all. To begin with, you and your team are likely to want to explore the project's documents yourselves. Secondly, if people do come and visit the space, you can pay attention to what they look at and how they use the space. That will tell you a little about what people care about as you think about participation in future projects. If people come to you having heard about the space from others, you'll get an idea of what the grapevine is saying about the project. And finally, people who get help exploring the project you've finished might be more interested in participating in the next project, or even joining your project team someday. Keep your project's doors open to the future, and good things might happen.

Supporting people who want to learn more about story work

This last request is from people who found the methods you used in your project interesting enough to think about learning more about them. They might have a project in mind they'd like to carry out, or they may just want to know more about what's possible.

Here are some ways you can support people with this request.

Give them an introduction to PNI. If I were impossibly arrogant, my advice in this section would simply be "give everyone who asks copies of my book." *Please* don't do that. I know this book is far too long and complicated. It will probably scare off all but the most determined readers (which by definition you are, and that's a compliment, you know).

Instead I'd like to create a challenge for you—call it a pre-chapter-end activity. *Write your own* introduction to PNI, and give *that* to people who come to you to find out more. What in your own PNI work has resonated most with you? What essential elements of your knowledge have you found most indispensable to your PNI work? You should be able to write a one-page introduction even if this was your very first project.

Your introduction should be brief, say, no more than several pages long. It should contain a manageable number of pointers to detailed resources you've found useful in your work. It should be approachable and relatively free from jargon; it should be interesting; it should draw people in. You should be able to read it out loud to your grandmother or neighbor or grandchild and not feel like an idiot or a pompous dogmatist.

Now, if you are one of those people, like me, who reads things in books that exhort them to go out and do things, and thinks they will jump up and do them ... for about three minutes, I have one other solution for you. At the end of each chapter of this book I have written summaries of what has been covered in that chapter. I tried to make the summaries work as stand-alone mini-documents in case people are skimming. If you took all of the summaries from this book and pasted them, in order, into a document with the chapter names for headings, you'd end up with a super-compact version of this book. Why not start out with *that* as your introduction to PNI? Then you can edit what

I've written and add your own insights to it. If you like, you could also look over the activities I propose for each chapter and choose one to add to each chapter summary, or come up with your own (possibly easier) activities.

What if you don't like to write? Don't write. Talk. Develop a ten-minute presentation on getting started with your own version of PNI. Practice your talk until it's automatic, then reel it out anytime anybody asks to learn more. You could also ask people to carry out some activities in the room just after you've spoken (for example: listen to a story from your neighbor, then identify the abstract, some evaluative elements, and the coda). This is just another way to deliver the same information: no better, no worse, just different. Do what works for you. Obviously I like writing, but you might find other ways of delivering information more useful. If you want to be of maximal assistance, develop *both* forms of information delivery at once. Write up a five-page introduction *and* develop a ten-minute talk and training session.

Whichever way you deliver it, you need to find some way to give people their first small pill of understanding. Until we really do have those knowledge pills the science fiction books keep promising us, writing and talking are the only options we have.

Show them your process records. In the previous section, I mentioned showing project records to people who want to explore the project during the return phase. This time I mean something different. With people who are interested in narrative work, you can show them things you don't show other people, things that reveal the *processes* you used as you carried out your project.

I do this when people want to know how I do some aspect of narrative work. As I carry out my work for clients, I keep many versions of files I'm working on. I do this partly out of fear that something will get garbled by the computer, but I also do it to retain a *process record* of how I did things in each project. When somebody wants me to coach them through doing something they've never done before, I go back to my process records and use them to help people understand the processes I use. I did that for

you too. I've leaned on my process records from dozens of projects as I've written this book.

You can do this too. Keep *everything* you generate in your project, even things that seem unimportant. Keep all of your meeting notes, records of discussions and decisions, multiple versions of planning documents, ideas you didn't use, everything. You'd be amazed how important little things can become months or years later when you're struggling to remember just how you did something before. That's right, keeping detailed process records is not just for interested people; it's for you too. Prepare now to inform yourself later, because believe me, you'll need it.

Coach them. Even though giving people information is important, the *most* important thing you can give to people who want to learn more about story work is *help doing story work*. Here's what I propose. Tell anyone who's interested that their first PNI project can fit into an hour, and that you'll talk to them for half an hour before *and* after their first project. They ought to experience your introduction to PNI first, of course, but they shouldn't absorb much more information before they get out there and start trying things. For example, they might collect twenty stories from five people in a room, then engage them in building one simple timeline, then talk about what they have built. That's a PNI project right there. Later, as people go out and start trying longer projects, you can offer to keep in touch to provide them with a sounding board for their own PNI ideas. And of course you should encourage anyone who has learned from you to help others learn in their own turn.

You might have noticed (as in the section on explorers) that what I've been saying here seems eerily similar to what I said in the intervention chapter about a sensemaking pyramid (page 493). You're right, this *is* another sensemaking pyramid. Again the difference is in the intensity of the effort. When you are creating a sensemaking pyramid as an intervention, you will polish your presentations perfectly; you will offer a variety of training and coaching options; and you will advertise your effort with energy.

Spreading the word about PNI work outside of an intervention is a simpler and slower-moving process. It could end up having the same effect in the end, but its energy will come from the people who are interested, not from you. They will choose the process; they will guide it; they will pass it on. That's a good thing, and it's something I hope you experience. There's nothing like finding out that more people are listening to stories because of what you did.

IDEAS FOR SUPPORTING ONGOING STORY SHARING

One of the things that often happens in the return phase of PNI projects (one of my favorite things, in fact) is that people begin to wake up to the benefits of sharing stories. You might not see much of this awakening if you aren't looking carefully. People might talk about it quietly with friends, or they might not talk about it at all; but they'll be *thinking* about it. During your project, people have shared stories in groups with a stronger intensity than they normally do in everyday life. That's what you asked them to do, after all. But sometimes, after the story sharing is over, people realize that it would be nice to have more story sharing in their everyday lives. Such an awakening represents another of the opportunities inherent in the return phase.

What follows are some ideas for things I believe anyone can do to increase the strength and vitality of story sharing in their community or organization. I doubt all of these ideas will appeal to you, and some of them might seem like nothing but common sense; but I hope that at least one of the ideas will be useful to you.

Where do the ideas come from? Partly they come from my experiences observing story sharing in communities and organizations I have belonged to or consulted for. Partly they come from books and papers I've read in the area of organizational and community narrative. Partly they come from my experiences designing, building and using Rakontu, a research-prototype web application for online story sharing (of which more later).

IDEAS FOR SUPPORTING IN-PERSON STORY SHARING

Supporting story sharing differs quite a lot depending on whether people are speaking di-

rectly or through mediating words and images. When stories are told face to face, they exist entirely as events, verbs. After a storytelling event has ended, no trace of the story remains except in the memories of those who participated in the event.

When a story is told through mediating words and images, asynchronously (not at the same time), a story-as-noun comes into existence. This is both a benefit and a burden. It's a benefit because the original storyteller and audience, as well as others who did not participate in the event, can come back to noun-stories to explore and compare. It's a burden because anyone who creates a lot of noun-stories has the task of keeping them in order so that their utility remains intact over time. You could think of it as like the difference between talking to somebody and leaving them lots of little notes. You can look at the notes later, but you need somewhere to put them.

Because these ways of supporting story sharing are so different, I've written two different sections to cover them. This section covers ideas for supporting face-to-face story sharing, while the next considers story sharing through a mediating device. The following six ideas (waves, circles, times, places, permission, safety) all have to do with helping people tell stories face to face.

Create waves of story sharing

You could think of a PNI project as a wave that moves through a community or organization, creating temporary change for the sake of permanent improvement. You can follow up a PNI project with wavelets—mini-projects that fit within an hour or take place over weeks but at a very low intensity. As you think about how you can help people share stories in your community or organization, think about mini-projects people might want to participate in. Would people like to trade stories about the new road over lunch? Would they like to get together at the museum to talk about their favorite exhibits there? Would they like to find out how others use the new intranet?

Here are a few ideas for setting up low-key, on-going wavelets of story sharing.

1. Hold monthly or weekly gatherings where people share stories about topics important to them. Allow people to submit topics they'd like to explore. Make it like a book club, only instead of talking about a book, people talk about their experiences.

2. Write a page of instructions for holding a mini-PNI project (choose a topic; share some stories; do a simple sensemaking task; discuss, reflect). Distribute the instructions in places where people gather. Put your contact information on the bottom of the sheet so interested people can ask for help.

3. Write a page of instructions for setting up regular story sharing gatherings. Encourage people to contact you if they'd like help supporting story sharing in their group.

4. Keep exploring your story collection and putting up stories on a wall in a place where people gather. Change the stories once a week or month. Under the stories, post a telephone number people can call to share their own stories. Make sure some newly submitted stories make it up onto the wall, so people can see that somebody is listening.

These are just a few ideas. There are many ways to create story sharing wavelets, at many levels of length and intensity, after the wave of a PNI project has completed its course.

Promote circular story sharing

Christina Baldwin and Ann Linnea, in their book *The Circle Way*, make the point that when people sit in a circle, physically or metaphorically, they can achieve more mutually agreeable solutions than when they are arranged in other configurations.

Say Baldwin and Linnea:

> Once upon a time, fire led our ancestors into the circle. It made sense to put the fire in the center and gather around it. A circle defined physical space by creating a rim with a common source of sustenance lighting up the center. These ancestors needed the circle for survival—

food, warmth, defense—and they discovered that the circle could help design social order. ... It is the nature of circle to invite in, to provide both access and boundaries, to provide a participatory process, to set social expectations, and to absorb diverse, even opposing, views through the alchemy of a symbolic central "fire."

When I read this part of Baldwin's and Linnea's book, I was struck by the fact that *every one* of these things—inviting in, providing access and boundaries, creating a participatory process, setting social expectations, absorbing diverse views—is also a function of story sharing. You couldn't ask for a better match. Clearly the circle and the story are related. (I'm sure Baldwin and Linnea know this, because at least Baldwin has other books specifically about story sharing, such as *Storycatcher*.)

But here's where the problem comes in. If you've just started learning about stories, a circle may not be the first shape that comes to mind. If I asked you to give me an archetypal image of someone telling a story, you might more readily think of a *stage* than a circle. After all, storytelling is a performance, isn't it? Baldwin and Linnea call a performance sort of arrangement a *triangle:* one person speaks while the others listen.

So which is it? Is storytelling a circle or a triangle? It's both, but which shape *dominates* depends on context. When professional storytellers speak to professional audiences, the triangular performance of storytelling anchors itself in the storyteller and sweeps round and round the circle like the hand of a clock, and the story flows uniformly outward. An expert storyteller watches the audience and is keen to pick up on reactions, but the audience generally does not initiate interactions, because they know their place.

When people speak among themselves, especially if they know each other well, the storytelling triangle may be *connected* more to one person than to others, but it could never be seen as *anchored* to any one person. Sometimes it dances around the circle, appearing, disappearing, and reappearing in new configurations as storyteller and audience merge, separate, col-

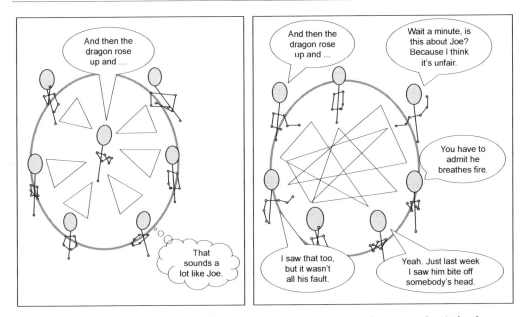

Figure 14.9. In professional storytelling, the triangle of performance dominates the circle of sharing. In everyday storytelling, the circle dominates the triangle, which appears and reappears all over the circle.

laborate, and even switch places. In everyday storytelling, the triangle comes and goes, but the circle remains (see Figure 14.9).

But everyday storytelling is not the same as it once was. Professional storytelling in the form of theatre has been with us for thousands of years, and novels for hundreds, but those forms of storytelling involved people speaking to people face to face. (Early novels were often read out loud to small groups of family and friends rather than alone.) The way stories come to us today on television and in movies is unprecedented. Now we interface directly with the stories, and the storytellers are pushed to the side, barely noticeable in the credits at the end of the show. The ubiquity and impersonality of this experience has a dampening effect on story sharing in many communities and organizations. Not only is our time and attention taken up by it, but our own story sharing seems boring and clumsy by contrast. Even the layout of our living rooms has changed from the circle of sharing to the triangle of performance.

So let's say you want to support story sharing in your community or organization. To which shape should you give your support? You might think you should help people learn to tell "good" stories, to create memorable impressions in the minds of their audiences, to perfect their storytelling skills. What I've found is that *any* support for triangular storytelling kills story sharing. Why? Because we all live in the triangle already. We are all professional audiences, and we know our places. Most people in what *Where There Is No Doctor* calls the "overdeveloped" countries live on a steady diet of commercially prepared, perfectly triangular stories. Things might have been different a hundred years ago, but today you can't support circular storytelling without making an effort to guard *against* triangular storytelling.

So how can you favor story sharing over storytelling? It's all about emphasis and modeling. Watch the words you use, and watch what you say and do as you tell and listen to stories. For example, I always caution people not to say "thank you" after someone tells a story. Why? Because people thank people for *things*. If you met someone on the street and said, "How are you today?" and they said, "I'm all right, can't complain," would you say "Thank you!" in response? Of course you wouldn't. That would be ridiculous, because they didn't *give* you anything. They *talked* to you. Don't say thank you when someone tells you a story either. Saying thank you transforms a circular communication into a triangular transfer. Many little hints and nudges like that can add up to favor the circular or triangular experience in story sharing.

Here's another hint: don't stand up when you tell a story. If you stand and everyone else sits, you've created a triangular story experience. Since *you* did that, everyone else will too, and the story sharing will shift slightly more towards performance.

Here's one more: don't *rate* the stories you hear. Don't say, "Can anybody top that story?" or, "That's a better story than Joe told!" or, "That's the most amazing story I've heard today." Again, rating stories will subtly favor the triangular over the circular. What should you do *instead* of rating stories? Continue the conversation. Keep the wheel rolling. Say something like, "So you *never* went back, huh? Did you ever regret that decision?" Or tell a story of your own in response. Rolling the wheel of story sharing strengthens the circle and weakens the triangle.

Support occasions for story sharing

When I think about times when I've seen strong story sharing, I come up with three general categories: common quiet simple tasks, after-parties, and milestones. Let's think about each of those in turn.

Common quiet simple tasks

This first one is something people used to do a lot more than they do today, and it is a major reason for the decline in story sharing in most communities. Many of the things people used to do for themselves were tedious, quiet, simple, and easier to do in groups. Sowing, harvesting, and processing crops; spinning, weaving, knitting, and sewing cloth; snaring and hunting animals and processing meat; building and maintaining houses and furniture; even repairing cars: these were once things people did together, and for the most part, quietly. While using their hands, people had nothing else to do, so they talked, and while they talked they told stories.

Do people still get together over common quiet simple tasks? Of course they do. Not as much as they once did, but not *never* either. On any given day, any given person does do some simple, quiet tasks with somebody else. For one

thing, we still need to eat. That at least can't be done in a factory far away. People tell stories during meals with family, friends, neighbors, and co-workers. In organizations, people often eat lunch together in the cafeteria or at a favorite café. We still need to stay healthy. People often walk or jog together, and as they walk they share stories. Driving or taking mass transit together is also a common quiet simple task. And there are still some common quiet simple tasks to be done: people paste labels on envelopes, sort papers, prepare for and clean up after parties, put up signs, rearrange furniture. In short, whenever people have something to do together that's quiet and not too complicated, they still talk, and they still tell stories.

Some of the common quiet simple tasks people do today don't *have* to be done together, but people come together to do them anyway, just because it's nice to talk while you're working. People get together to knit, spin, quilt, whittle, carve, cook, build, and so on. All the things we used to have to come together to do because we couldn't get them done any other way, people still do. Only now we *choose* to do them together because life is more interesting that way. Most people aren't ready to jettison all of their modern conveniences, but a surprising number of people choose a few traces of the old ways to revive so they can have something to do while they talk (see Figure 14.10 on the next page).

Long ago we shared stories because we needed something to do while we worked together with our hands. Now we work together with our hands because we need something to do while we share stories. Some people even call a local knitting group a "stitch 'n bitch." The name is perfectly appropriate, because bitching, or complaining, is one of the best reasons to share stories.

Every community and organization has the potential to develop more common quiet simple tasks, both to get things done together and to support story sharing. What I'm not sure people realize is how much power such tasks have to support all the things story sharing can do for a community or organization.

Figure 14.10. People used to share stories while they did things with their hands. Now they are more likely to do things with their hands while they share stories.

After-parties

The second occasion I want to mention in which people naturally tell stories is right after something organized has ended. This is the same phenomenon I talked about when I was describing sensemaking sessions. In communities, after-parties happen after church services, school or community plays, club or society meetings, sports games, festivals, parades, music jam sessions (which are not quiet), and so on. In organizations, after-parties happen after presentations, project reviews, planning sessions, sensemaking sessions, and so on. Any time people meet for a purpose to do a cognitively complex task together—the kind of task that *isn't* simple and quiet, even though it's common—they will want to hang around for a little while afterward to reflect on what happened. Story sharing almost always goes on during those times.

It's not necessary to help people create or maintain after-parties, since they happen naturally. But it may be necessary to give after-parties the resources or time they need to occur naturally. If you are planning an organized event, for example, you might make the mistake of planning to close the office or community center as soon as the event is over, instead of allowing people to keep using the space to swap stories during the after-party (see Figure 14.11 on the following page). After-parties always happen, but if they don't have the time and space and permission to happen for everyone together, they happen in patchwork ways, among two people here, three people there, a day later, a week later. Planning to allocate time and space for after-parties is a simple thing any community or organization can do to improve story sharing.

Milestones

People share stories during times when they gather to mark changes in the lives of individuals, families, communities, and organizations. These can be momentous rites of passage such as baptisms, weddings, and funerals, or they can be simpler markings of time like birthdays, anniversaries, and annual reunions. In many communities, seasonal events take place throughout the year: coloring eggs in the spring, celebrating the fall harvest, lighting up a holiday tree in the dark of winter. In organizations there are also such milestones, but they mark passages through work tasks. There are project kick-off events, end-of-project celebrations, new employee orientations, and promotion and retirement dinners. When work has a seasonal component to it, there are seasonal milestones as well: the start and end of the school year, the end of the dreaded holiday shopping season, the closing of the fiscal year, annual performance reviews, and so on.

Figure 14.11. If you don't allocate time after events for an after-party, the story sharing that might have gone on will be lost.

As I said at the start of this book, we tell stories because they, like us, are made out of time. So it makes sense that as we mark the passage of time in our lives we tell stories about what has happened to us. You could say that milestones are a natural point of intersection between time as we experience it and time as we make sense of it through storytelling. At milestone gatherings, people tell stories about what has happened to them since the last such gathering, about similar events in their own lives (their own weddings, for example), and about what the future might bring.

What can you do to improve the sharing of stories at milestone events in your community or organization? When people gather to mark significant occasions, do they have enough time to share stories, or are they too rushed? Do they feel they have permission to "hang around" and share stories casually during the gatherings, or are the gatherings too well organized to allow them to do that? Are the gatherings performances rather than story sharing events? If a gathering needs to be a performance, can some time be added to allow people to share stories before and after the performance? Is the place in which people gather to celebrate milestones conducive to story sharing? Are the chairs laid out in circles, or do they all face a podium? Is there something to eat and drink? Is the atmosphere welcoming? Can people mix and mingle? Would *you* want to tell stories there? If not, why not, and what can you do about that?

Support places for story sharing

We've gone over some special times in which people are likely to share stories, but there are also special *places* in which more story sharing happens. Let's go through those next.

Places of relaxed purpose

I can't come up with a better name for what I mean by places like this, but let me explain a bit and I think you'll understand. People go to places of relaxed purpose for a reason, but while they're there, they don't mind doing other things. Every community or organization has some places like this. Public libraries, community centers, parks, and popular coffee shops are some common examples.

Take a library, for example. People generally go to the library with a purpose in mind: to read, check out, and return books. But while they are at the library, they might do any number of other things as well. If they see a friend, they might sit and chat quietly with them. They might look something up on a library computer. They might sit down with a magazine. They might browse the "new books" section. They might check out what's new on a community bulletin board. Some large libraries even have cafés where people can grab a cup of coffee and a pastry. The opportunity to carry on all of these peripheral activities makes the library a place with a relaxed purpose.

In contrast, consider a police station, courtroom, or hospital. When people have to go to any of these places, they do what they have to do, then leave. It would seem strange to linger in a police station or to sit chatting with a friend there. If you did happen to meet a friend in such a place, the natural thing would be to suggest moving the conversation to a place of relaxed purpose like a park or café. Nobody would go to a police station or hospital just to see who they might run into, at least not if they didn't work or volunteer there. But people *might* go a library or café just to see who might turn up.

The people who run places of relaxed purpose usually know that people use their spaces to talk. Some coffee shops even create an entire business model from the idea of a place of relaxed purpose, where people go to get food and drink, but also to socialize and check in. People share stories in these places because the atmosphere is encouraging. Visitors are not rushed by any mandate to get out quickly; their activities are not strongly organized; they are not given complex tasks to perform; they have freedom to move around. Colors, sounds, and lights are muted, not glaring; quiet music covers quiet conversation so people can be heard without being overheard; comfortable chairs are arranged in circles, or movable to form circles. The intrusion of commercial storytelling is lessened by removing televisions and magazines or keeping them in cabinets or on easily ignored side tables. All of these cues tell people that the place invites casual, lingering conversation, the kind of conversation in which stories get shared.

Consider the places of relaxed purpose in your community or organization. Where are they? Are there very many of them? What are they like? Are they conducive to story sharing? Who comes to them, and how do they use them? Who *doesn't* come to them? Why not? Does everyone have a place of relaxed purpose to share stories in?

If some people don't have such a place, what could you do to either create new places of relaxed purpose or make existing places more welcoming? How might you design such a place? Where might you put it? How might you draw people to it? Remember, a place of relaxed purpose does need a purpose, or nobody will have a reason to go there. People might be

willing to visit a place for a variety of reasons: to play sports, use equipment, eat and drink, learn, and so on. If a place has a purpose that draws people in, and its tone is casual and welcoming, people will share stories there.

Multi-purpose places

A second place in which people typically tell stories is a place designated for use by groups for a variety of purposes. Most communities and organizations have at least one of these places, and they are often called exactly that: *multi-purpose rooms*. Typically there is a sign-up schedule on which people claim such rooms for blocks of time and hold meetings in them. Some multi-purpose rooms accommodate story sharing nicely, and some don't. What follows are some tips on making a multi-purpose room work well for story sharing.

First and foremost, a multi-purpose room that supports story sharing should be open to use by any group of people, even if they don't have an organized activity to carry out in it. There should be no lower limit on the size of the group—even two or three people should be able to use the room. If people can simply walk in and use the room (if it's not already in use) that's even better. If the room has to be locked between uses, it should be easy to check in with somebody who can quickly get people access to the room. The higher the barrier to use of the room, the less often people will be able to come together for purposes that don't seem all that purposeful, like doing a common quiet simple task together, or having an after-party, or celebrating a small milestone.

When I worked at IBM Research, I saw many people use the large, often empty cafeteria as an impromptu meeting space. People would run into each other in the hallway, start a conversation, then say, "Let's go and talk this over in the cafeteria." Thus the space served as a ready-made forum for thinking and talking together, for any group at any time. Just keeping the cafeteria open between meals had an impact on story sharing.

A multi-purpose room that supports story sharing should ideally be small. Some large libraries, universities, corporations, and other institutions have huge multi-purpose rooms designed to hold hundreds of people and fitted out with fancy light fixtures, podiums, and support for multimedia presentations. That kind of multi-purpose room isn't conducive to small group story sharing; it's too imposing, meaning that it imposes a fixed, formal purpose on people entering the space. It doesn't seem right to sit around swapping stories in such a grand, impersonal chamber. If you can find a smaller room, perhaps one that's not so clean and perfect, that would make a better place for small-group story sharing.

If you have a large multi-purpose room, you might be able to put up dividers or temporary walls to block off smaller spaces for more intimate conversations. The cafeteria at IBM Research, which I mentioned above, was subdivided by walls, planters, and other obstacles that created small islands of privacy in various nooks and crannies of the large space. If the cafeteria had been one giant echoing expanse, I doubt so many people would have used it as an impromptu meeting place.

A multi-purpose room that supports story sharing should be filled with cues that lead people toward casual, lingering conversation. It should send the message that people are welcome to relax there. Chairs and tables should be in circles or easily movable to make circles. Colors, sounds, and textures should be soft and muted, to fade into the background. Real house plants always help a place feel more natural. A scuffed-up ping-pong table and some old board games and playing cards can do wonders for helping people unwind and start talking.

In case people start to relax *too* much in the room and leave messes behind, the multi-purpose room should have a clearly posted set of rules about keeping the room clean for others. When people see such rules prominently posted, especially if the rules say something about "keeping the room clean for everyone," they will develop a sense of shared ownership about the space. This will lead people to tell *more* stories, because instead of the room being an anonymous, generic place, like a hotel room cleaned by invisible employees, it will become something comfortable and familiar, a place people feel a connection to, a place people can share stories in.

You might have a room like this in your community or organization right now. Do people use your multi-purpose room to share stories in? Have you spent much time in the room? Do you remember sharing stories there? Ask some people who have used the room what they have done there. Does anyone mention doing any common quiet simple tasks there? Getting together after an organized event? Marking a milestone? Having casual, lingering conversations? If people don't seem to share stories in your multi-purpose room, why don't they? What *do* people do in the room? What do you think might prevent people from sharing stories there, and what could you do to make the room more available and welcoming to people who want to share stories?

Edges

The architect Christopher Alexander, in his influential book *A Pattern Language*, speaks of the importance of edges, or places of transition, in community life. He contrasts a modern building whose featureless slab walls "cannot support any life" with an older building whose complex walls feature "benches, galleries, balconies, flowers, corners to sit, places to stop." (See Figure 14.12 on the next page.)

In his advice to builders, Alexander says of edges:

> Make sure that you treat the edge of the building as a "thing," a "place," a zone with volume to it, not a line or interface which has no thickness. Crenelate the edge of the buildings with places that invite people to stop. Make places that have a depth and a covering, places to sit, lean, and walk, especially at those points along the perimeter which look onto interesting outdoor life.

Why am I showing you quotes from a book on architecture? Because when people stop and linger where edges are inviting, one of the things they do there is share stories. So it follows that the more inviting edges you have in your organization or community, and the more inviting they are, the more story sharing will go on. A place where nobody can ever "bump into" anybody coming or going and stop to have a

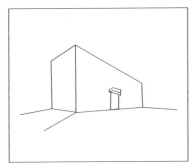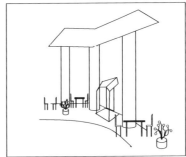

Figure 14.12. These are my redrawings of Alexander's examples of a lifeless edge ("The edge cannot support any life") and a "crenellated" edge ("An edge that can be used") from *A Pattern Language*.

quick chat is not a place where people will share as many stories.

An edge doesn't have to be a *literal* edge. It's just a place where people habitually run into each other and stop to chat as they move between other places. Some well-known edges are porches, entryways, "pocket" parks tucked in between buildings, and waiting rooms in bus or train stations. Even a corridor or sidewalk can be an edge, it if is marked out in some way: wider than usual, with a bench or chairs, near a window, under a shelter.

When any boundary between places is inviting, people tend to use it for quick conversations as they move around. People usually know where the edges are and how to use them in the places they live and work. They might not be able to *articulate* the rules of edge use, but if they bump into somebody going somewhere, they know where it makes sense to stop and chat and where it doesn't. If they meet near an inviting edge, they will move to it. And where edges cannot be found, people tend to create them.

Here's an example of an edge built entirely of ritual. In the rural community where I live, every road is an edge. When people are out driving and bump into anybody they know on the road, whether the other person is walking or driving, it is acceptable country custom to stop and chat for a few minutes. But not every part of every road is available for chatting; everybody knows that. People never stop to chat near an intersection or a blind curve, or at night, or when it's raining or snowing. Whoever is in a car is expected to keep an eye on the road and on the mirrors to make sure nobody's coming.

People who come upon other people chatting on the road know what to do as well. The general rule is, when you drive up behind people who are chatting, you wait a bit to see if they are done talking. If they are, they'll say their goodbyes, and one or both of them will drive on to let you get on your way. If they want to keep talking, they'll wave you around them, or they'll move their cars temporarily to let you through, and then get back to their conversation. It's just part of living "out here" to respect the road as a meeting place.

I don't have any hard data on this, but I think this practice is pretty widespread in rural communities. In suburban areas, where you can't just stop in the middle of the road, I've seen parking lots and sidewalks serve the same function. None of these places are wonderful places to chat, but they are illustrations of the fact that people will find edges even where there are none to find.

If you want to improve story sharing in your community or organization, then, one suggestion is to assess the edges people use to connect as they move from place to place. Where do people stop and chat when they bump into each other on their way from one place to another? To look for edges, walk or drive around your community or organization. Look for situations where people bump into each other and seem to want to find a place to stop and chat. Every time you see that happening, pay close attention to what happens next. In each place you see people meeting by happenstance, how do they behave?

Inviting edges. Do the people who meet in the place simply stop and chat right there, taking advantage of a space that invites them in? Are they comfortable there? Do they linger? Do they relax? If so, you've found an inviting edge.

When you find inviting edges, watch who uses them, because maybe not everyone does. Some people might feel they are not *qualified* to use these impromptu meeting places because their status or involvement in the community or organization is too low. If only some people stop and chat in your inviting edges, what keeps others from stopping? What can you do to make your inviting edges work for everyone?

Near-inviting edges. Do the people who meet in the place refrain from talking, but move together to a *nearby* place where they feel they *can* stop and chat? Near-inviting edges often occur at doorways and other bottlenecks where people are more likely to meet because they have to go through a narrow passage. Stopping to chat in such a narrow passage is generally difficult, but if an inviting space is close by, people will often make the effort to go there together.

When you find near-inviting edges, first consider if they can be made inviting. Can the bottleneck be loosened? Just opening a hallway wide enough to add a few chairs on the side might be enough to transform the space. If the edge can't be made inviting, can you make the nearby inviting space closer and more obviously inviting, so that moving over to the space to talk will be more attractive to people who bump into each other?

Improvised edges. Do the people who meet in the place stop and chat *even though* the place is not inviting? Do they keep their conversations brief? Do they maintain vigilance, ready to stop talking at a moment's notice? Do they glance around a lot? Do they stop under some conditions and not others? My rural road traditions fall into the improvised category, as may traditions in your community or organization around particular unsuitable-yet-still-used sidewalks or corridors.

Improvised edges have the special quality that people are *already* using them and may have built up a bank of commonly-known rituals surrounding them. So they are particularly amenable to use for improving connection, if they can be converted into inviting edges. For example, rural roads that have pull-off sites transform from improvised to near-inviting edges, since people can move into pull-offs to linger without impeding traffic. What can you do to turn your improvised edges into inviting edges? Could you offer protection from the weather, a place to avoid traffic, benches to sit on? What would help people use the spaces they are already using more comfortably?

Lifeless edges. Do the people who meet in the place glance around, then say something like, "Well … I guess I'll see you later," and move on? These are lifeless edges, places where people run into each other but feel they have no option that allows them to speak. They can't stop and chat in the place, even with vigilance. They can't move a short distance to another space that's more inviting, because they can't find any such space to move to. All they can do is hope to run into each other in a better place the next time they meet.

Like Alexander's ugly-big-box building example, these are the worst edges you can have. If you find lifeless edges in your community or organization, think about what you can do to transform them into *any* of the other kinds of edge I've mentioned here.

Small changes to the places in which people come across each other can have large impacts on the way people interact and on the stories they share. By paying close attention to where people meet and what they do when they meet, you can improve story sharing in your community or organization in small, simple ways that don't involve training anyone or providing anything other than perhaps a few chairs or an awning.

Support permission for story sharing

Of all the types of support for story sharing we are exploring here, this is the only one that I think differs significantly between communities and organizations. In communities, permission to tell *particular* stories has to do with social status, group membership, and all the complexities of social life. But permission to

Figure 14.13. Even when they have gained important insights through trading stories, people often don't appreciate the value of story sharing when they are in work contexts.

share stories *in general* is not usually something anyone can withhold. Sharing stories is a basic right of human life.

In organizations, the picture is different. Sharing stories is an activity many professional people see as foreign to the work environment. You can see this when people share a story, then say something like, "But we'd better get back to work." The fact that people say this even when the story sharing has been useful to everyone involved—has been more work than the work they have to get back to—shows that in many organizations people don't fully understand the benefits of story sharing (see Figure 14.13). People call times when they are standing around "at the water cooler" sharing stories "slack time" and try to reduce it so they can be more productive. But if you rephrase the concept and call it "connection and learning time"—because that's what it is—things look different.

If your organization is willing to invest in such things as training, team-building exercises, collaborative learning systems, and other ways to connect people and help them share knowledge, you will be surprised by the benefits that can be obtained by simply allowing people to share stories in conversation. Any organization in which people are given permission, time, and space to share stories will be more con-

nected, more productive, and more resilient in the face of unexpected challenges.

You might think that people in your organization have permission to share stories because your culture tolerates a reasonable amount of "slack time" as people go about their work days. But as long as you're hearing the "let's get back to work" line, people still need some convincing that sharing stories *counts* as work. One way to convince people that sharing stories counts is to tell stories about telling stories. If you publish an internal newsletter, or if your leaders give talks, or if there is any comfortable and familiar way you normally reach people in your organization, look for a way to slip in some stories in which real work benefits come from the sharing of stories. This will help people understand that sharing stories is not only permitted but encouraged as a bona fide work activity.

Support safety in story sharing

Even though sharing stories has great power to make your community or organization a better place to live and work, it comes with its own dangers. Each community or organization arrives at its own complex set of unwritten rules for sharing stories, and the purpose of those rules is largely to ameliorate the dangers of story sharing. You can't write those rules, no matter who you are in the community or organization, but you can observe them and use that knowledge to support story sharing.

Do you remember the section in Chapter Five where I talked about Shirley Brice Heath's study of two different story sharing cultures (Trackton and Roadville), and how what was acceptable in one place was taboo in the other (page 69)? Your community or organization also has its culture of story sharing, and you can carry out your own study of it. Watch people as they tell stories until you can describe your culture as Brice Heath did for Trackton and Roadville. You are not likely to be able to *change* your story sharing culture, but the more you know about it, the more you will be able to help people share stories within it.

IDEAS FOR SUPPORTING MEDIATED STORY SHARING

My ideas about mediated story sharing come mainly from my experiences building and using Rakontu, a prototype web application for story sharing and sensemaking in small groups. But by "mediated story sharing" I don't necessarily mean this has to take place on computers. Mediation can happen with pencil and paper. My subject in this section is what has to be taken into account when story sharing is supported by *any* intervening medium.

I could write pages here about how I first got the idea to build Rakontu (in 1999), why I wanted to build it (because existing social media applications do a terrible job of supporting story sharing and sensemaking), how I built it (in 2009, quickly, in some months I had free between paying projects), what it was built to do (support everyday story exchange and sensemaking), its design (members, with volunteer roles; stories, with answers and comments; views, with search filters and patterns), how I used it (with a small group of volunteer testers), why the project ended (I needed to get back to other projects, like this book) and what I'd like to do with it next (build it all over again with improvements based on what I learned). But I'm not going to burden you with all of that. You can read all you'd like to read about Rakontu on its web site (rakontu.org).

What I think I should show you here is an essay I wrote about Rakontu, called "Steal These Ideas." I wrote it in response to some people who asked me for general advice on supporting online story sharing. I think this should tell you all you need to know about what I learned from Rakontu. Here is the essay, pretty much as I wrote it then. I invite you to "steal" these ideas and use them in your own community or organization.

Steal These Ideas

In my Rakontu lessons-learned document I said that I'm more interested in the *ideas* from Rakontu moving on than the actual *software* surviving. Since then a few people have asked me to elaborate on that statement. So I've reviewed and thought, and I've come up with some advice for anyone who would like to incorporate ideas from Rakontu into their own effort to support online story sharing.

Support sharing over performing

One of the biggest challenges in supporting online story sharing today is countering the performance problem. The web has developed into a grand marketplace for self-expression and self-promotion, and people shape their behavior on it accordingly. There is nothing wrong with self-expression, and surely all storytelling contains an element of performance. But I'm interested in supporting the kind of storytelling that leads to conflict resolution, perspective-taking, mutual learning, strong communities, and effective decision making. I call this story *sharing* to distinguish it from storytelling, in which performance is a larger force.

Over about a decade and a half of observing storytelling and story sharing on the internet, I've developed a kind of loose metric for story sharing. I look at the comments posted in response to told stories, and I divide the number of comments that express gratitude or support (thanks, helpful, sympathy), or that ask follow-up questions, by the number of comments that express value ratings (amazing, well put, ridiculous). From this I get a sharing quotient, or how much story sharing is going on relative to performance (see Figure 14.14 on the next page).

The highest sharing quotients I've seen on the web have not been in the "tell us your story" col-

Figure 14.14. When people respond to stories with statements of support and questions rather than ratings, story sharing is going on.

lection sites, or the "I've got a secret" confession sites, or the "budding novelist" self-expression sites, or the "I just had sushi for lunch" updating sites. They have been in the still, quiet pools where long-term, somewhat coherent social groups meet, and in which people help each other through difficult conditions and decisions.

The interactions in such high-sharing-quotient settings have a few consistent components. They are repeated many hundreds or thousands of times over periods of years as trust gradually accumulates. They are comparatively rich in content and context. And they are goal-oriented. Sites about everything or nothing, or about connecting for no reason except to connect, seem to lead to more story performing and less story sharing. The best story sharing seems to happen, at least on the web, when people know *why* they are talking.

How did Rakontu support this, and how well did it succeed? To begin with, I was not able to address this issue well enough to find out that much about it. Because of time constraints, I had to make an "ugly" version of Rakontu first. It had almost no hover-drag-type interactivity and no support for the near-conversational elements I think would work best, like facilitated story sharing sessions using voice and chat, with story capture and question answering afterward. I was forced to use the standard, boring fill-in-this-form version of story sharing,

which was pretty much guaranteed to produce performance from the start.

I could find no way around this, and the outcome was predictable: even I, the staunch advocate of natural story sharing, performed most horribly. I found myself perfecting my prose on a daily basis. So any future efforts in this direction should make at least some attempt to get past the fill-in-a-box form of story sharing, in any way possible. In some ways I wish I had not even tried to use a basic fill-in-your-story form but had gathered stories only from chat sessions and the like. It might have been a better test of the ideas.

My other attempt to keep story sharing natural was to reduce performance rating by using a utility-based rating system. This failed miserably. The fact that I myself was the greatest failure at this is clear evidence that it could not work, because I was strongly motivated not to succumb to performance storytelling (and I knew it when I was doing it). I've now realized that if you set up a rating scale, it doesn't matter what you call it. Your pitiful protests that it is all about utility, not popularity or quality, are simply lost in the massive explosion of instincts you have invoked. People evaluate everything, every minute of every day. It is what keeps us alive, and we can't stop doing it. It doesn't matter what you *say* about evaluating. It only matters if people *can* evaluate things and can see the evaluations of others.

So, if I were to try this again, I'd keep the evaluation for utility, but I would remove it from view. I'd pull it deep down into the plumbing of the system and place it only in the questions about stories, which provide the same utilitarian mining capability but without the visibility. If you want to use these ideas, my suggestion is to build in utility tagging (through questions) but build *out* visible ranking and popularity.

Even the reputation-building system I put into Rakontu didn't work out that well, because it became another system of ranking. People could see who posted the most stories and comments and so on, and that became another form of evaluation.

Don't get me wrong: for some online communities, doing some things, reputation and ranking are essential elements. They work well when people are sharing opinions and building encyclopedias. But for story sharing, ratings are damaging because they cause stories to compete. When stories compete, the experiences in them do not accumulate into useful aggregations. In some contexts, like the Olympics, experiences should separate and compete. But making a goal-oriented story sharing site work is more like *building* an Olympic stadium than using it. Everyone succeeds together or fails together.

Build a café in a library or a library in a café

Possibly the most important things I learned by designing, building, and using Rakontu are that online story sharing is both a verb (storytelling) and a noun (stories); and that neither matters more than the other; and that they must intermingle for story sharing to work. I picture these as a café where people meet and recall their experiences, and a library where people browse through experiences previously recalled. Any software that supports story sharing needs to support both activities well, and it needs to support frequent and easy transitions between them. I had originally thought of this as a café and a library with lots of doors between them, but then I realized the metaphor was potentially damaging: there should be no wall between them to have doors in. The space should be multiple-use, and the café tables should sit among the library shelves, or vice versa.

In fact, I'll be so bold as to say that any story sharing system in which the telling and the keeping are not intermingled will not succeed. How do I know this? I guess it's an intuition gathered from years of watching people tell stories in person, in email, on the web, and now (for a short time) in Rakontu. In off-line (formerly called "normal") conversation, people are the cafés and the libraries in which stories live, and stories move fluidly from telling to remembering to retelling. When an old woman remembers a story she heard in 1923 and tells it to her great-grandchild, she doesn't type search terms into a web form or traverse a taxonomy tree. The passage of the story from memory to event is effortless and natural.

In the online world, however, the wall between event and memory is high and strong. It's between your starred and recent emails and the rest of your massive "inbox"; between the "latest activity" and other posts in your discussion group; between the first page of your social media "wall" and the stuff you forgot about last month; between the content and the context of Wikipedia articles. These walls reduce the capacity of the collective narrative ecology to churn its content, which is critical to useful story sharing.

I knew about this duality of event and memory before I created Rakontu, and indeed addressing it was part of the design from the beginning. In my 1999 presentation on the topic, I included this quote from a 1993 paper by Larry Masinter and Erik Ostrom, which still applies.

> The primary technology elements proposed for funding in the development of electronic libraries are in the areas of input (scanning, character recognition), retrieval, and presentation. The entire technology emphasis is on collecting material and making it available to individuals.

> However, a library is more than just a pile of books. Libraries are also social spaces. Treating the 'electronic library of the future' as an information repository ignores many of the roles played by current institutions, where library users interact with their friends, colleagues, and

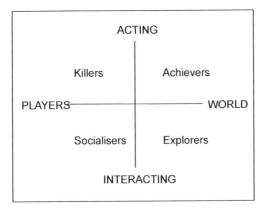
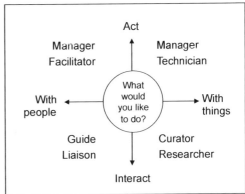

From Bartle's 1996 paper   Roles in Rakontu

Figure 14.15. The volunteer roles in Rakontu draw their inspiration from Richard Bartle's observations of volunteer activities in on-line multi-user role-playing games.

professionals to [find] material that is relevant for them.

A story sharing site cannot be just a pile of stories, but that is what I see happening on most sites that say they are for story sharing. What I see on the internet is either stories entirely absorbed in events and never transferred to memory, or stories stacked up in memory and never returned to the world of events. This is one of the central ideas of Rakontu and should be stolen as widely as possible.

One of the ways I tried to support intermingled event and memory in Rakontu was in my creation of *roles* as packages of commitment. I stole the idea from a 1996 paper by Richard Bartle ("Hearts, Clubs, Diamonds, Spades"), and it's still so interesting I'll repeat it here. The paper was about what people do in multi-user dungeons (MUDs), and it presents a framework to explain motivations of MUD users.

The vertical dimension of Bartle's diagram (shown in Figure 14.15) compares *acting* (changing something) with *interacting* (coming into contact with something without changing it). The horizontal dimension compares social with environmental focus.

When I first encountered this diagram in 1999, I got very excited about how it related to the roles people might take on in a story sharing environment. MUDs and story sharing sites have much in common, because people are both building something and living in it. (It also reminds me

of my favorite quote from Stephen Crites, that people live *with* mundane stories and *in* sacred stories.) So Bartle's framework has unique applicability for this purpose.

The roles I designed for Rakontu deliberately populate Bartle's spaces. Facilitators are the—well, let's call them the social achievers—who run story sharing and sensemaking sessions, acting to shape story sharing among people. Technicians are achievers who keep the site running smoothly. Managers straddle both upper-quadrant roles, helping to shape the story exchange and configuring the story sharing environment. Guides are the socializers of Rakontu, answering questions, helping people get started, leading tours. Liaisons bridge on-line and physical worlds, interacting with people across the digital divide. Curators and researchers are the explorers of Rakontu, mining the collection for stories, finding patterns, fixing tags, keeping the story museum in order.

Even though I was the only one who really used the roles in the beta testing of Rakontu (the other people who did assume the roles didn't actually use them much), I did feel that they matched the activities I carried out while using it—the hats I put on, if you will. They helped me set a frame for whatever I was doing in the system as I approached it each time, whether it was cleaning up tags, answering questions, adding collected stories in batches, or encouraging people to tell stories. So I think this is an idea worth keeping and using.

Technologically, supporting both a library and a café at once proved to be a challenge. One of my strongest technology lessons was that I spent way too much time reinventing wheels related to social media. I had to implement many things that already exist in many web platforms, such as groups, permissions, private messaging, notification, management control, removing offensive material and spam, and so on. So one possibility in doing more with these ideas is to start with a platform that already supports much of what is required for social media.

However, that is only the café part of the equation. Few social media solutions provide much support for library functions. For that you need semantic indexing, taxonomy or folksonomy, simple and advanced search, typed linking, and all the other things that make a library work.

I have yet to find any system I can build upon that combines the café and the library in equal proportions. Everything I see favors one strongly over the other. Wikis and other collaborative creation software favor the library, and discussion and social media software favor the café. In any system you choose as a foundation you will most likely need to reinvent some of the wheels of the other system. My advice is to think about your strengths: what do you know well how to build? If a café is something you can build in your sleep, look around for pre-built library components. If your experience is in library building, see what you can find to complement it in café packages. I'm used to library building myself, which is probably why the café building parts were onerous for me.

Embody knowledge about narrative

One of my favorite discoveries about story sharing is that people vary in whether they tell stories and in whether they *think* they tell stories. Another dimension to the variation is whether people understand why people telling each other stories matters, and how to do that. I learned before I started Rakontu not to explain any of that, or at least not to make explanations into barriers. Systems that force people to understand something before they can enter them are empty places. The better solution is to shape the experience itself so that it *embodies* knowledge about stories and story sharing. The best tools teach you how to use them.

Probably the best successes of Rakontu so far have been in this area. For example, one thing that seemed to work well was Rakontu's system of typed, annotated links between stories. In Rakontu, when someone sees a topic, they can respond to it with a story, and that link, and their annotated reason for it, is kept and can be reviewed and searched. When someone reads a story, they can tell another version of the events it recounts, tell another story it reminds them of, or explicitly link it to another story for any (annotated) reason. As we built a base of stories using Rakontu, I found these links an essential tool for "getting around" in the library we were building. I often found myself clicking through the web of connections among stories to follow a sort of thought-path around. I can see how this sort of web-building could be much more powerful as the story collection grows and its interlinkings intensify.

By the way, I got this web-building idea from Roger Schank's work on case-based expert knowledge databases. More specifically, I got it from an interesting essay by Jorn Barger, who worked on Schank's team and revealed in it more about how these story databases were constructed. When I read this sentence back in 1999:

> All the links from story to story in the Ask-Tom casebase had to be 'hand-crafted' or hardwired, which ultimately meant looking at every possible pair of clips and asking whether either would make an interesting followup to the other, and which of the eight CAC-links it made most sense under.

I realized that the human creation of such typed links (which the AI researchers working on expert systems found a burdensome task and seemed embarrassed to admit was being done by clerical help) was a *perfect* sensemaking activity for people telling each other stories. Building a web of typed, annotated links helps people understand their stories as they tell them, *and* it creates something they can use later to explore the same issues when they have a need for them. That idea is a definite "keeper" out of what makes up the Rakontu design.

Rakontu's question-asking system also worked out very well. When anyone tells a story in

Rakontu, and when anyone reads a story, they are presented with several questions that capture their interpretation of the story.

For example:

- How do you feel about this story?
- Why do you think it was told?
- To whom did this story happen?
- How long will you remember this story?

Some stories will only collect one set of answers, but controversial stories are likely to collect many sets that represent varied interpretations. This question-answering mechanism has several benefits to the group using Rakontu. It gives people a way to voice their opinions about stories that can accumulate into useful patterns. Thus offending stories do not require a power structure to remove (though Rakontu has one anyway) because they can be dragged down by the power of collective voice.

The reason I wanted this was because in natural story sharing, offensive stories can never be "deleted" from the community; they are just weighed down with so many annotations that they sink into oblivion. If anyone attempts to dredge up the offensive story again, it is immediately attacked with more attachments and sinks again. This is a closer analogue to what should and does happen to damaging stories "in the wild," and I think it's effective. I have no proof of this, of course, as there were only a small number of people answering questions in the tests of Rakontu so far. However, even in that tiny test, I did notice differences in answers between storytellers and story readers in ways that would be instructive if they accumulated further.

One important component of the question-asking system, and this may be special to questions about stories, is that it has to be flexible. Many systems are available to attach metadata to collected items; but rarely can you change indexing schemes attached to live data. In Rakontu such after-the-fact redesigning turned out to be critical. When a group is forming, they can only guess at what questions will best serve their needs. Even in the small tests I did, I found myself mucking about with the questions often as the story collection began to form and newly obvious questions and answers emerged. Supporting flexible questioning means that it must be possible to modify existing answers—very carefully—to match a new indexing scheme. For example, if you find that people rarely choose the how-do-you-feel answer "stymied" but often choose "frustrated," you might decide that "stymied" is close enough and would make searching easier, so you may want to lump together the two answers. Or you might find that nobody ever picks "thwarted" and you have too many answers and just want to remove it.

Supporting this functionality also requires mechanisms for reviewing large numbers of answers and looking for gaps where metadata is scarce. Clipping and pruning the collection takes work, both on the part of the system builders and on the part of those maintaining the story museum. But it's worth it. I'd say that the ability to keep your questions relevant and useful as your participants and understandings and goals change is a requirement for a useful living story museum.

You might say that such flexible organization can be accomplished through tagging. Somewhat, and in fact I loved the tagging aspect in Rakontu and used it often. But tagging narrows the source of interpretation and reduces the utility of the story collection to support multi-perspective sensemaking. Few people (mostly curators) have the time and attention and willingness to tag stories. It's a nerd thing. Tags are tasks, but questions are conversations. Questions bring everyone in and increase the diversity of response and thus the strength of the story collection.

One thing I think Rakontu needs much more work on is diverse visualization of the collected stories and other data. The timeline view of stories I used as Rakontu's main interface was adequate for the café (though it had its problems, mainly related to the performance point above). But as soon as we got up over a few dozen stories I found myself wanting to see many other views of the data: link maps, bar charts, tables, sorted lists, and so on. Granted, if I had been able to make the fancy high-mouse-interaction interface I had mocked up, some of these things would have been included. But still, I found that I wanted lots of ways to stroll around in the stories when I needed different things. So that is an area that would, I think, reward exploration.

But having said all that, and even though Rakontu strongly featured widget-based question answering and other methods of tagging and so on, I'm not sure it needs to be as idiot-proof as all this. Do you know those emails you get from friends where you get a page of questions about yourself, and you are supposed to insert your own answers? Those are essentially semantic indexing sheets. I've been amazed by how few mistakes people make in doing this. Even people whose eyes glaze over when you try to explain flexible semantic indexing can paste their answers over Uncle Joe's and send the email around.

It's possible that a motivated group could run an entire Rakontu-like story sharing system through email or in a discussion group. All it needs is somebody putting some time into pulling apart messages with hand-filled templates in them. It would be a pain, but it wouldn't require any special software. For example, say you send out an email to your group that says, "Does anybody remember eating at that old restaurant on the corner, you know, the one that burned down last year?" And then when people tell stories about it, they remember to take the list of five questions and paste them in at the end along with their answers. Then some long-suffering secretary of the group takes all the stories and answers and puts them into a spreadsheet, and at the next meeting of the group everybody looks at the bar charts they printed out. Or everybody takes the printed stories-and-answers and puts them into little piles, which is the same thing.

What I'm trying to say is that you don't need fancy software to do useful things with information, and you don't have to wait until you get the fancy software (or the creator of the fancy software gets a big grant) to do what you want to do. Fancy software helps, but you can do the same things with pen and paper, and I think people might be starting to forget that. (If you don't believe me, look at old records from a church or factory or port. We had complicated metadata long before we had computers.) Computers are useful for managing metadata, but they are still the smaller part of the equation.

The important thing in supporting story sharing is to keep its connective tissues intact. When we speak through computers, our conversations get broken up and put into little boxes, and the connective tissues don't get laid down as they should. Story sharing, and especially the interplay between event and memory, depends on connection far more than other conversation does. You can maintain connective tissue using fancy software, but you can maintain it using norms and practices too. In fact, the best fancy software doesn't supplant human norms and practices; it gets its power from them. The great advance that is Google came from a realization that the way people link up their web sites—by hand—is a resource that can power fancy software. You can do that with stories too.

Build for commitment

In the 1999 presentation that held the idea that eventually became Rakontu, I said that "stories thrive in groups of people in frequent and persistent contact in a shared culture." I of course know that stories also live in other environments, like in vast marketplaces where people choose products and services, and in the shifting sands of coalition building in discussion and debate. What I probably should have said was "the types of stories *I* am most interested in supporting thrive in groups of people in frequent and persistent contact in a shared culture." I'm still interested in supporting the same types of stories, and I still think they live in the places where small groups of people come together often. That is why I built Rakontu for small groups of people who already know each other, at least a little. It's where the gear-turning stories, the change-making stories, the life-improving stories, thrive.

The tests of Rakontu bore this out. Rakontu worked best when it was being used by people who knew each other. With strangers such things as responding to one story with another story, interpreting the stories told by others, and looking at patterns in stories together didn't happen as much, or they happened in a high-school-dance way in which most of the people watched as a few people started to dance. Of course, this same thing happens on all discussion groups, which may form for months before the interesting conversations take place. But with something created for the express purpose of story sharing, the most fruitful interactions might have to be put on hold until the necessary trust is established. I'm starting to think that a dedicated story sharing site like Rakontu can't work unless one of two things happen: the Rakontu is "seeded" with stories gathered from conversation or a special in-person or chat story session, or the Rakontu is used for an existing group that can jump into the commitment-requiring elements without hesitation. Even in the latter case it may be necessary to supplement lower-intensity fill-in-the-form story collection with higher-intensity conversational elements periodically.

I've seen many story collecting web sites go up in which complete strangers post stories, and I've never seen one of these succeed—in the ways I would like to see story sharing succeed. They do sometimes succeed in the sense that people looking for information find what they need. I myself have received much needed help reading stories of medical conditions and life challenges. But for working towards a common goal that will benefit everyone in a group, this sort of story collection lacks the connective tissue to build something larger.

In general I think web software has been wonderful for people finding and meeting people. It has been wonderful for people trying to draw more people to a cause. It has done a dismal job helping people who already know each other do anything but bring the most basic information together. In my opinion, Margaret Mead's small groups of thoughtful, committed citizens trying to change the world are still waiting for their internet. If there is one thing I think could not be stripped away from Rakontu without ruining it, it would be its emphasis on helping small groups achieve common goals. Why? Because it's unique, because it's needed, and because it's what stories do best.

Build roundabout paths

To finish off this section: I was looking back over the few pages I had written to cover supporting mediated story sharing in the first edition of this book, and I found a little gem I'd like to bring forward.

People often say that supporting knowledge sharing means helping people find the right information at the right time. Right? But it's not always that way with stories. There are times when it is more important to surprise and even provoke people with stories than it is to get them exactly what they are looking for.

Here's a fictional example of a mediated story collection that made that point brilliantly way back in 1857. It is from George Eliot's novelette *Janet's Repentance*.

> Mrs. Linnet had become a reader of religious books since Mr. Tryan's advent, and as she was in the habit of confining her perusal to the purely secular portions, which bore a very small proportion to the whole, she could make rapid progress through a large number of volumes. On taking up the biography of a celebrated preacher, she immediately turned to the end to see what disease he died of; and if his legs swelled, as her own occasionally did, she felt a stronger interest in ascertaining any earlier facts in the history of the dropsical divine—whether he had ever fallen off a stage coach, whether he had married more than one wife, and, in general, any adventures or repartees recorded of him previous to the epoch of his conversion. She then glanced over the letters and diary, and whenever there was a predominance of Zion, the River of Life, and notes of exclamation, she turned over to the next page; but any passage in which she saw such promising nouns as "small-pox," "pony," or "boots and shoes," at once arrested her.

Notice how Mrs. Linnet chooses stories by steps: first by message (the secular portions); then by the climax of the story (what the preacher died of); then by plot points (whether he had fallen off a stage coach, etc); and finally by environmental elements (boots and shoes). What is funny about this passage (and why Mrs. Linnet serves as the comic relief in the story) is that she thwarts the purpose of the religious books entirely: she goes straight for the elements she values most.

In developing methods for supporting mediated story sharing, normally one would expect to help people quickly meet their particular needs. But on the other hand, there *may* be cases where there is a message the story collection wants to get across, such as getting along with people from different groups, and one might not want to make thwarting the central point of a collection as easy as Mrs. Linnet found it. That's a point worth remembering.

SUMMARY

The return phase of a PNI project is like the part of a tennis swing after the racket has lost contact with the ball. Supporting the return phase is like *following through* during a tennis swing. In tennis, follow-through works backwards in time to improve the racket's impact on the ball. Similarly, a PNI project that supports return is more likely to succeed even before the return phase begins.

Some working-backwards reasons to support return are *risk management* (there will be a return phase whether you support it or not), *closure* (people need to bring the emotional level back down), *listening* (people need to feel entirely heard), *memory* (people need to process the project so they'll remember it), and *your own skills* (you need to learn from the project).

Also, follow-through in tennis keeps the arm moving to avoid injury from a rapid pull-back. Similarly, a PNI project that supports the return phase avoids damaging the community's or organization's culture through an abrupt withdrawal of participation.

Some health reasons to support the return phase are to *gather ideas* (leveraging your effort in the project), to help create a *common language* (as outcomes of sensemaking become part of the culture), to *listen* for early warnings (of emerging problems), and to *crowdsource* (the return phase as after-party for the whole project).

The return phase has some typical characteristics you can expect to find. There is a *dynamics* to return: people need a time of *silence* to reflect; people need to *save face* and may need to process the project's outcomes alone; there might be a *backlash* in which people are less eager to participate than previously; and in general, the return phase happens in *waves* of interest and evaluation that rise and fall.

During return, *rights and responsibilities* are important: you must continue to honor your *promises* of participation; you must respect the fact that the people, not you, *own* the return phase; and it is best to accept the fact that *perceptions* of the return phase (and of the whole project) will differ as the project ends.

As people *process* the project during return, you can expect to observe people doing these things: forming the project into a *story* in their memories; trading *references* to insights that came up during the project; and expressing *wishes* about aspects of the project they would like to see continue.

To support the return phase in *your own PNI practice,* you should expect to: *celebrate* your effort in working on the project (even if things didn't go as well as you hoped); *gather perspectives* on the project from participants and nonparticipants; *reflect* on the project; and complete your project *records.*

To support the return phase with your funding or *steering committee* (or yourself if you don't have one), you should expect to: communicate essential *information* such as stories, constructions and lists of discoveries; supply *evidence* that the project succeeded in creating positive change (or at least taught you a lot); and provide *records* so that others can learn from the project after you.

To support the return phase in your *entire community or organization,* you should expect to *respond to requests* as people bring them to you. These requests are generally likely to come from people who want to: *help* you (by staying informed, being consulted, or collaborating); *work* on new projects; keep *sharing* stories; *explore* what the project created; and *learn* more about story work.

You can support *ongoing story sharing* during and after the return phase of a PNI project. Face-to-face story sharing differs from story sharing through a mediating device (such as written words or images) because mediation creates a story-as-noun which persists after the story sharing event is over.

To support face-to-face story sharing, you can do these things: create *waves* of story sharing; promote *circular* (sharing) over triangular (performing) story sharing; support *times* for story sharing, like common quiet simple tasks, after-parties, and milestones; support *places* for story sharing, like places of relaxed purpose, multi-purpose places, and inviting edges; provide *permission* for story sharing; and help people find *safety* for story sharing.

To support mediated story sharing, you can do these things: support sharing over performing by favoring goal-oriented cooperation over competitive ranking; *intermingle* conversational events (as in a café) with exploration of memories (as in a library); *embody* knowledge about narrative in the support system so people learn about stories by using the tools they are given; and build tools to support *committed groups* working toward a common goal.

QUESTIONS

At the start of this chapter I said that some people would be skeptical about the benefits of putting energy into supporting the return phase. Even if you're not skeptical, this chapter was probably not an exciting one for you. It's natural to get bored during the tidying-up parts of a project. The cookies are out of the oven and you've already sampled a few, but the cookie-making dishes are still sitting in the sink, and we all pretend they aren't there, at least for a little while. As you read through this chapter, which sections seemed the most tedious to you? Asking people about the project? Cleaning up your records? Helping people who pester you with requests? Conversely, which parts of the chapter appealed to you most? Are there ways you can help yourself get through the tasks you find less appealing? For example, can you find somebody who finds different tasks appealing than you do?

As you read through the types of requests people might have during the return phase of a PNI project, which struck you as those you are most likely to hear in your community or organization? Do you think a lot of people will want to help out with future projects, or none at all? Will people want to continue the conversation? Will they want to explore? It may be impossible to guess in advance, but if you were wrapping up a PNI project right now and people came to you with requests about it, what sorts of requests do you think they would be? Which requests are you the most ready to handle? Is there a good match between what you can expect and what you can support? If not, what can you do about that?

Do you remember the "reality bubbles" I mentioned in the "Supporting return in your PNI practice" section (page 552), of people more and less involved in PNI projects? How big are the bubbles for your community or organization, in terms of how many people are involved at each level? Can you draw them? Now consider the strength of the bubbles. How likely are people at each level to show you their view of reality? Are some bubbles likely to pop easily, and are some hard to break? (For example, will people uninvolved with the project be willing to talk to you about it?) What can you do to prepare to break through all of the bubbles so you can learn from every view of the project?

What are the common quiet simple tasks people get together to do in your community or organization? Can you list them? If you can think of few such tasks, why is that? What can you do to encourage the creation and maintenance of such tasks?

Where are the edges in your community or organization? Where are the places of transition? How do people behave as they come together in those edges? Which edges are inviting, near-inviting, improvised, and lifeless? How could the non-inviting edges be made more inviting?

If your community uses the internet to connect, how do people share stories on it? How do people comment on each other's stories? How do they negotiate elements of truth? How do they make sense of the stories together? Do people perform as they tell stories, and how does that impact the exchange? As you read about my experiences with Rakontu, which elements of them seemed like they would be helpful for your community? What can you do to use those ideas in your community or organization?

ACTIVITIES

Do a very small PNI project, say one lasting a few hours. Make sure it has a long enough after-party—say fifteen minutes for every hour of session—and follow up by talking with participants a few days or a week later. Take notes on what you observe during the after-party and in your follow-up conversations. Then read back over the "How return happens" part of this chapter (page 547) and check to see whether what I wrote there matches what you saw. Did you miss anything, and did I miss anything? What does that tell you about your methods, your skills, your team, and your community or organization?

After your very small PNI session is over, pretend to present the project to a steering committee. Provide information, evidence, and records to prove that investment in your project has paid off. If you can, get some friends or colleagues to pretend to be the committee and act the part by being skeptical of your work. Practice justifying your methods and efforts so you'll be more ready when real support (and possibly real money) is resting on the outcome.

After your very small PNI session is over, make up some pretend requests for help in each of the five categories I covered in the "Supporting return in your entire community or organization" section (helpers, task-force people, story sharers, explorers, learners; see page 558). Write brief requests on sticky notes or in fake emails. If you're in a team, challenge each other in per-

son. Then pretend to respond by thinking up, and maybe writing, responses to the requests. Practice helping people in the return phase so you'll be more ready when people actually do want your help.

Assuming that you did the test for assessment of story sharing earlier in the book (page 72), create a table with the four assessment categories (freedom, flow, knowledge, unity) as rows. On the columns of the table, place this chapter's ideas for supporting story sharing, either in the in-person category (waves, times, places, permission, safety), mediated (sharing, intermingling, embodiment, commitment), or both. Now think about each cell. How does the level of story-sharing freedom you found have an impact on, for example, times when people share stories? How does the level of unity impact safety? Which ideas might help your community or organization improve its story sharing in the most effective ways?

Do your own survey of story sharing on the internet. Find a web site in each of the categories I mentioned in the section called "Support sharing over performing" (page 576). Find a "tell us your story" collection site, an "I've got a secret" confession site, a "budding novelist" self-expression site, an "I just had sushi for lunch" updating site, and a "still, quiet pool" where a coherent social group meets. Compare the story sharing you see going on in each of those places. What are your own conclusions about story sharing on the internet?

Part III

Appendices

These appendices include models for use with group exercises; a reading list; a bibliography; and a combined biography and acknowledgements section.

Appendix A

Example Models and Templates for Group Exercises

In this appendix are thirty descriptions of published models for use with the timeline, landscape, story elements, and composite stories exercises. They are primarily for use in sensemaking, but can also be used in story collection. See Chapters Nine (Group Exercises for Story Collection, page 187) and Eleven (Group Exercises for Narrative Sensemaking, page 385) for details on how to use the models for each exercise.

TIMELINES

Here are brief descriptions of six time-based models you might find useful in your timeline exercises (see page 397 on instructions for use). Note that I'm not saying these are the models you *should* use. These are just *examples* of the sorts of models that work well in the timeline exercise. If you look through these you should get an idea of what works.

For most of these models I list references you can find to learn more about them. Where I don't list explicit references, the models are so well established that you can find information about them on the internet or in standard textbooks and reference works in any library.

Bruce Tuckman's stages of group development

This model describes how groups of people come together and work on projects together. The model's five stages are:

1. Forming: The people in the group learn about each other and start thinking of how they will relate to each other.
2. Storming: Different ideas about how the group should work together arise and negotiate. This stage might be short or long, and it might involve many nuances of conflict and cooperation.
3. Norming: The group comes to an agreement on common goals and responsibilities. (In some groups this stage is never reached.)
4. Performing: The group does what it set out to do, working as a functioning team.
5. Adjourning: The group finishes its task and breaks up.

Tuckman's stages might be useful in a timeline exercise if your project involves looking back over a time (or planning a time) when groups of people came together (or will come together), say in forming a community or organization, dealing with a crisis, or planning a change.

The Transtheoretical model of behavioral change

This model, developed by James O. Prochaska and colleagues, describes how individuals change their behavior. It is primarily used in the health care field and is called "transtheoretical" because it aims to bring together ideas from multiple theories about behavior.

1. Precontemplation (Not ready): The person knows that they ought to change something, and they think vaguely about doing it in the future, but they don't feel ready to take any concrete steps yet.
2. Contemplation (Getting ready): The person has started to think about why they should change and what the change might bring to them, but they have not actually started to *plan* the change yet.
3. Preparation (Ready): The person is actively planning the change, and may be taking

small steps to prepare the way for larger steps later.

4. Action: The person has actively changed their behavior from what it was before. They have taken large steps and are doing new things.

5. Maintenance: The person continues to act in a new way while trying not to slide back into old ways.

6. Termination: The change has been made. The person doesn't need to make an effort to avoid backsliding anymore. Sometimes this stage slides into relapse, in which the person goes back to old ways, returning to an earlier stage of the process. From there they either advance again or remain stuck.

The transtheoretical model might be useful in a timeline exercise if your project involves examining a time in which people make a change to the way things have always been done, especially if the change involves tradition or culture, say in gender or class relations.

The Kübler-Ross model of grief

This model describes how individuals deal with loss. The model was originally applied to the terminally ill, but it was later expanded to apply to other types of loss, such as bereavement, job loss, divorce, or incarceration.

1. Denial: The person doesn't want to face the reality of the situation.

2. Anger: The person concentrates on the unfairness of the situation.

3. Bargaining: The person attempts to negotiate with someone to change the situation.

4. Depression: The certainty of the situation sinks in and the person experiences sadness and regret.

5. Acceptance: The person comes to terms with the situation.

Note that Kübler-Ross was adamant that her model not be considered a complete or perfectly ordered description of the process of grief, which is unique to each person going through it.

Kübler-Ross' model might be useful in a timeline exercise if your project involves talking through the aftermath of some kind of catas-

trophe, like a natural disaster, or readiness for such contingencies in the future.

Everett Rogers' theory of the diffusion of innovations

This model describes how new ideas are communicated through a culture. It describes successive waves of actors who play dominant roles as the innovation spreads.

1. Innovators: This tiny group of people, amounting to only about three percent of the population, adopt innovations the moment they are available. Innovators are tolerant of risk as they seek the benefits new ideas might bring. These are usually the youngest and most social of the groups.

2. Early adopters: These people (14%) adopt innovations after a short time has passed. They are somewhat tolerant of risk, but they choose more carefully from among the innovations they think will help them most. In general, financial liquidity (ease of spending), social status, and social connections tend to decrease, and age tends to increase, as each group comes forward to adopt the innovation in its turn.

3. Early majority: This group of adopters (34%) waits longer to take up the innovation, but is still in the forefront of its adoption.

4. Late majority: This group (34%) lags behind the early majority, watching and waiting to see how the innovation will play out before they take it up.

5. Laggards: This group (16%) brings up the rear of innovation adoption. They prefer not to change the way they do things, even if they might benefit from the change.

Rogers' theory might be useful in a timeline exercise if your project involves considering how people in your community or organization have taken up or might take up some kind of new idea, like a new farming method or educational approach.

Kurt Lewin's three-stage change model

This model describes how organizations and communities change the way they do things. Lewin, who coined the term "action research," was concerned with how groups of people change, mainly from the view of helping them do this in a positive way.

1. Unfreezing: The community recognizes that change is necessary and that things can't go on as they have been, overcomes its inertia, and weakens defense mechanisms that keep things in their current state.
2. Change: The old ways are challenged, but the new ways are not yet in place, so this is a transitional state of uncertainty, confusion and possibly conflict.
3. Freezing (sometimes called "refreezing"): The new ways are firmly in place, and the community begins to stabilize.

Lewin's model might be useful in a timeline exercise if your project involves making sense of some kind of major, far-reaching change in your community or organization, either past or possible, like building a mass transit system or passing significant legislation.

John Kotter's eight steps of leading change

This is not a model of how change happens; it's a model of how people can *make* change happen. (Prescriptive models like this one can be just as useful as descriptive models, as long as their application is one of comparison, not judgment.)

1. Establishing a sense of urgency.
2. Creating the guiding coalition.
3. Developing a vision and strategy.
4. Communicating the change vision.
5. Empowering employees for broad-based action.
6. Generating short-term wins.
7. Consolidating gains and producing more change.
8. Anchoring new approaches in the culture.

Kotter's model might be useful in a timeline exercise if your project involves any kind of planned change program, whether in the past or future, and whether it has succeeded (or will succeed) or not. In particular, finding places where reality doesn't match this stepwise pattern could open up useful discussions about the nature of the community or organization. Maybe multiple visions and strategies compete for dominance, or instead of short-term wins there are short-term disasters.

LANDSCAPES

These are six examples of the sorts of published models that work well for landscape exercises (but they are *examples*, remember, not suggestions or requirements). By looking over these you should be able to understand what makes a model useful for landscapes, and you should be ready to find more like them. See page 203 (story collection) and page 408 (sensemaking) for instructions on using models in the landscape exercise.

The Interpersonal circumplex

This model, developed by Mervin Freedman, Timothy Leary, and others in the 1950s, describes aspects of individual personality and motivation. It is used in psychological evaluation.

The vertical axis of the model (see Figure A.1 on the next page) describes the perception of *status* (or dominance or power or control) on the part of the person being evaluated. This is not necessarily the person's *actual* status. It is the status the person perceives themselves as having in relation to the person or people they are interacting with. The same person might have different feelings of status or control in different social contexts.

The horizontal axis of the model describes the person's degree of *friendliness* (or solidarity or warmth or love) with respect to the social context they find themselves in. Again, this is as it is perceived by the person, and in a particular context, not in general.

Putting the two axes together, a person whose perceptions place them at the lower-right edge of the space would be considered exceptionally trusting (friendly, high perceived status). A person on the opposite corner (hostile, low perceived status) would be considered exceptionally *mistrusting*. As the model is defined, its exact center describes the most well-adjusted human being possible, and all deviations from

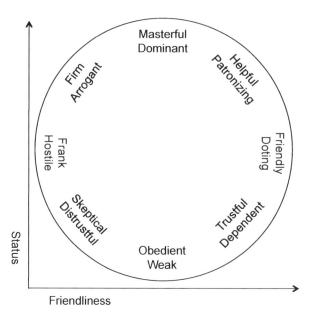

Figure A.1. The Interpersonal circumplex. Redrawn from various sources. Many examples of states around the circle have been published. Here I've included one positive and one negative aspect of each location.

the center point represent pathological conditions (to a greater or lesser degree).

This model is called a "circumplex" because it is usually drawn as a circle, with names given to pie-slices of the space. But it's really a two-dimensional landscape model with the corners sawed off. Why people turn squares into circles like this I don't know, but it could have to do with the scarcity of pure states in complex human behavior. If you want to use a circumplex model for sensemaking, I would suggest *not* presenting it as a circle, just to keep open the options of exploring extremes. This is especially important if you are considering fictional as well as factual stories. It's better to let empty spots emerge during sensemaking than it is to fence them off in advance.

This model might be useful in projects where people need to think about the perceptions of storytellers and of characters in their stories, for example in a project about people choosing to use or avoid drugs. For a historical view of the interpersonal circumplex as well as its current uses, see the book *Paradigms of Personality Assessment* by Jerry Wiggins.

The Circumplex model of marital and family systems

This model, created by David H. Olson and Dean M. Gorall, is used to consider how families relate to each other.

The vertical axis of the model (see Figure A.2 on the facing page) describes *flexibility* (adaptability, changes in roles and rules) in the family, from low to high. Named states along the axis are: rigid, structured, flexible, and chaotic.

The horizontal axis of the model describes *cohesion* (emotional bonding, interdependence, togetherness) in the family, from weak to strong. Named states along the axis are: disengaged, separate, connected, and enmeshed.

The center area of the circle is defined as the most *balanced* condition, which is considered the most healthy state for a family to be in: neither too close nor too distant, neither too rigid nor too chaotic. The further a family moves to the outer corners of the space the less balanced, and less healthy, the family becomes. Note that even though this model is called a circumplex model, it is *not* generally drawn with its corners cut off. The corners indicate extremely unbalanced (usually pathological) states.

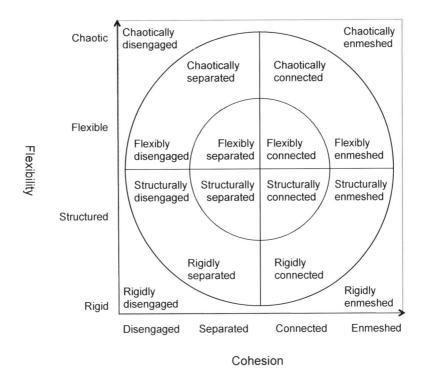

Figure A.2. The Circumplex model of marital and family systems. Redrawn from various sources. Locations in the inner circle are considered balanced; locations in the outer circle are considered mid-range; locations outside the outsider circle are considered extreme.

This model includes a third dimension: *communication,* moving from positive (empathy, listening, clarity) to negative (criticism, double binds, hiding information). The third dimension is considered a "facilitating" dimension in that it influences the other two. It is not generally drawn on the model itself. You could easily incorporate communication into a landscape exercise by color-coding or adding symbols or dots to sticky notes to indicate whether communication in each story was more positive or negative. The third dimension does not work in the same center-balancing way, of course, because more positive communication is always better. Generally communication is expected to be better in balanced than in unbalanced families, but departures from expectation could occur.

This model might be useful in projects where dynamics within small groups of people is of interest, such as in projects about families or work teams. For more information on this model see Olson and Gorall's 2003 paper "Circumplex model of marital and family systems."

The Four Rooms of Change model

This model, created by Claes Janssen, is a perfect example of a category-based model that can be converted to a two-dimensional continuous model and used in a landscape exercise. The model examines how people and organizations make changes in their lives, and uses the metaphor of journeys through rooms. Note that you could also use this model for a timeline exercise, since it has a time element (a cycle) as well as two orthogonal axes. Few models can do double duty in this way, but this is one of the few.

The vertical axis of the model (see Figure A.3 on the next page) describes *motivation* for change: to what extent is the person willing to change their behavior? The extremes of this axis are fully "yes" (the person is motivated and eager to change) to fully "no" (the person is dead set against change).

The horizontal axis of the model describes *satisfaction* with current conditions: to what extent is the person happy with things the way they

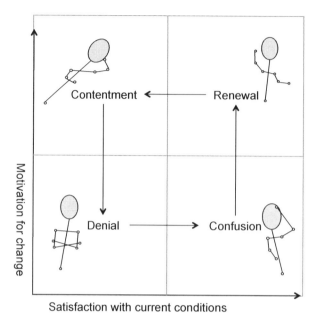

Figure A.3. The Four Rooms of Change model. Redrawn from various sources.

are? Again the extremes range from a strong "yes" (the person is perfectly satisfied) to a strong "no" (the person is entirely unhappy).

These two axes come together to create four named quadrants of the space, as follows:

1. Denial: The person is dissatisfied, but is not willing to change. They refuse even to *admit* that they are unhappy.
2. Confusion: The person is dissatisfied *and* willing to change. They try to change but don't know how, so they become confused.
3. Renewal: The person is satisfied with the state of affairs, but is still willing to change. They want to move onward to an even better state.
4. Contentment: The person is satisfied and has no motivation to change. They prefer to keep things the way they are.

To use a category-based model like this one as a landscape model, you must present it carefully. *Do not* present the quadrant definitions listed above (contentment, renewal, denial, confusion) at the *start* of the exercise. *Only* present the axis names (motivation, satisfaction) and the characteristics of the corners of the space (motivation strong yes with satisfaction strong yes, and so on). If your participants have heard

of the model, explain why you want them to put away its quadrant names *until you tell them* to pay attention to them. If they have not heard of the model, don't even let on that any such quadrants exist at first.

After groups have placed their stories on their landscapes, and *after* they have discovered and discussed emergent features—that is, during the within-group review period—you can tell people about the model's defined quadrants. Even then, don't present the quadrants as corrections to be applied or standards to be met. Present them only as *perspectives* to be considered. Any discrete model used as a landscape model must be used in this holding-back sort of way, if it is to be useful in the landscape exercise. Presenting bounded spaces first will stop sense-making and start categorization. If you cannot be *sure* that your participants will be able and willing to keep all predefined boundaries off the landscape space during most of their work with it, either disguise the model by renaming or moving axes, or don't use this type of model at all.

This model might be useful in projects where change is a dominant feature of the stories, for example in projects about recovery from illness or addiction. You can find more information

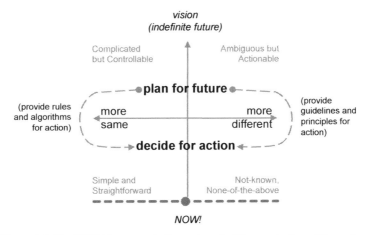

Figure A.4. The SCAN framework. Reproduced with permission of the author.

about the four-rooms model at Claes Janssen's web site, claesjanssen.com. He has written a book on the topic, but it is only available in Swedish at the time I am writing this. Many other blogs and web sites offer descriptions of the model.

The SCAN framework

This model, created by the enterprise architect Tom Graves, is used for sensemaking and decision support in a variety of contexts within organizational and community work.

The vertical axis of the model (see Figure A.4) describes the amount of *available time* as perceived in the situation, from "now" (no time available, such as in a crisis) to "infinity" (infinite time available, such as in long-range planning). The more time available for making a decision, the greater the array of options available. When we have lots of time to think before we act, we can rationally consider options, draw up checklists, conduct experiments. When we have to act quickly, in "real time," emotions and "gut feelings" become more important. Sometimes we may plan to plan, that is, *think* we have made a decision by rationally considering options, but find at the last moment that the decision we made is not the decision we *actually* have to make in the end. In this way one story (taken as a whole) could cover the entire spectrum as it plays out.

The horizontal axis of the model describes the degree of *uniqueness* as perceived in the situation, or how likely it is that if we do the same

thing we've done before, we'll get the same result as we did before. At the left-hand extreme of the uniqueness dimension, the same action *always* produces exactly the same result. This is like what might happen if we approached a grandfather clock we've long owned (and are sure is in good repair) to wind it. After we finished winding the clock, we would barely even look to see if it was still working, because it always does. The closer we get to the always-the-same end of the uniqueness axis, the more we rely on *rules* and *algorithms* (like our clock's mechanism and the way we wind it) because they reliably produce the outcome we want to achieve.

At the right-hand extreme of the uniqueness axis, it is simply *impossible* to get the same result by taking the same action. This is like what might happen if we attempted to redirect the waters of a swirling flood during a hurricane. Even if we did manage to divert such a flood *once*, it would be insane to believe we could follow the same procedure to divert the *next* flood. Each flood is unique due to interacting particulars of land use, soil makeup, erosion, flood control measures, rain, wind, waves, and even human error. In fact, some well-known failures of engineering have occurred precisely because what worked in the past failed to work in a new and different situation. The closer we get to the entirely-unique end of the uniqueness axis, the more we rely on *guidelines* and *principles* (like "avoid river banks during rainstorms" or "inspect levees frequently for leaks"), because no matter what happens they will help us adapt to the circumstances we find.

At the midpoint of the uniqueness axis, you might find an activity like raising a child. Every child is like other children in some ways and unique in other ways. We can use our experience with one child to show us how we might be able to act with another child, but it would be dangerous to assume that *everything* that works with one child will work with another. In the middle of this axis both rules and principles have bearing, but we must be mindful of their limits in context.

This model might be useful in projects having to do with the consideration of decision making in situations of interest, for example in projects about crisis response or urban planning. Thinking about how people in your collected stories have made decisions under varying conditions can help you make sense of how things happened the way they did and how things might need to change in the future. There is a lot more to SCAN than I've described here; you can find out more about it in Tom Graves' book *SCAN: A framework for sensemaking and decision making*.

The I-space (information-space) framework

This model, created by Max Boisot, describes the use of information as it flows among people. The model has three dimensions, of which you can use two or three.

The vertical axis of the model describes the degree of *codification* of information, or how much *structure* is embedded in its articulation. The dimension ranges from vague, easily misinterpreted information, such as "it's a nice day today" (nice to whom? nice in relation to what?) to highly structured, detailed, impossible to misinterpret information such "the temperature as measured by this particular type of thermometer is this many degrees Celsius; the wind speed as measured by this type of anemometer is this many miles per hour" and so on. Fully codified information is not open to interpretation. As a result, the more codified the information, the less effort is required to understand and use it. Story structure is itself a method of

codification, though it is one that deliberately goes only part of the way to full specification.

The horizontal axis of the model describes the degree of *abstraction* of information, or how general or specific, abstract or concrete, global or local it is. This dimension ranges from the very *general* statement, such as "in the temperate latitudes, snow generally falls in winter" to an intermediate statement, such as "the weather in the Northeast United States is following seasonal patterns this year" to a very *specific* statement, such as "the town of Middle Grove received two inches of snow within the past hour, especially on the North side of town." Note that codification is independent of abstraction. Information can be structured yet general (as in precise measurements of changes in average global temperature) or vague yet specific (as in the statement, "it's snowy outside my window").

The third axis of the model describes the degree of *diffusion* of information, or "the speed and the extent to which particular types of data and information spread within a target population." If information once discovered flows quickly and widely, diffusion is high; if it flows slowly and locally, diffusion is low.

This model might be useful in projects where you want to improve your community's collective adaptability in situations where information flow is critical to safety or efficiency, such as on factory floors or in coordinated volunteer efforts. Another aspect of the model which I have not described but which you might find useful is the *Social Learning Cycle*, a phase-based model of how knowledge flows in organizations and societies. The best reference on I-space is Boisot's book *Knowledge Assets*.

The Confluence Sensemaking Framework (CSF)

This is my very own framework for use in sensemaking for decision support. I developed it with some help from colleagues Sharon Darwent and Dave Snowden.

In Figure A.5 on the next page a central directorate (the seeing eye at the top) exerts control over the constituent elements under it, like a

Figure A.5. In this situation a central directorate *organizes* the constituent elements under it.

Figure A.6. In this situation there is no central force, and the constituent elements *self-organize*.

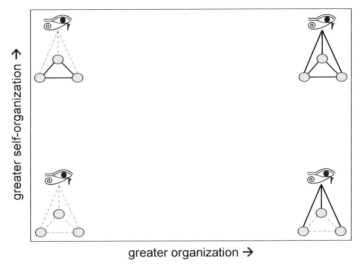

Figure A.7. The confluence framework describes all combinations of organization and self-organization.

big gear turning little gears. The elements are *organized* by the actions of an organizer.

In Figure A.6, by contrast, there is *no* seeing eye, no central force. The constituent elements interact with each other like fish swimming together. Here we say the elements are *self-organized*.

Every situation is filled with organized and self-organized connections like these, which shift and sift like grains of sand at the beach. We can draw the combinations of organization and self-organization as in Figure A.7. Between the four corners of extreme conditions are many mixtures of the two states.

Now we have defined a sensemaking space. Working with stories on these dimensions to think about what caused what to happen can help people think about why things are the way they are.

(For the seeing eye I like to draw the Eye of Horus, an Egyptian symbol associated with myths of order and reason overcoming chaos. Diagrams of the Eye of Horus were carefully constructed using a standardized system of measurements, and this also matches since organization is all about standards.)

Some examples of situations on the sensemaking space:

- A dictator likes to keep things in the lower-right-hand corner, where they have complete control and the public has none. They like it when there is no self-organizing going on, so they try to break bonds that form between people under them.

- In an emergency, many connections break and nobody has control; that places the situation in the lower left.

- In a flock of birds, each bird looks to its neighbors to get its bearings, but nobody calls out, "Fly to the right for thirty more feet!" This places the situation in the upper left.

- A waterwheel combines elements of centralized force (in the design of the wheel and water channels) with constituent connection (eddies and flows in the water caused by localized differences in temperature and viscosity, and objects and organisms in the water). This places the situation somewhere in the middle of the space.

- A hermit living in a cave might be said to live close to the lower right-hand corner defined by this space, since they rule their tiny world; but on the other hand they might be said to inhabit the lower left, since they have no constituent elements to rule. Which is it? Perhaps both? There are no easy answers here, which is as it should be.

You can also use the CSF to consider change as a situation moves around in the space. Some examples:

- Consider a car sitting in a driveway. As a driver approaches the car, opens the door, gets into it and starts it up, the situation is primarily one of organization. The many mechanical and electronic components in the car depend entirely on the oversight of the driver. As the car begins to move, self-organization increases as fluids move within the car, air moves around it, and the road surface contacts the tires. As the car turns onto a busy road, the proportion of self-organization increases again as the driver begins to interact with other drivers.

- Consider a teacher in a classroom. At some times the teacher is a central directorate, holding the attention of every student as a demonstration is made or a concept is explained. At other times the teacher may fade into the background as the students self-organize to discuss problems and find solutions together. Sometimes the teacher switches rapidly between direction and observation as the students begin a new self-organized activity.

- Consider a corporation. It has an organizational chart, a hierarchical control system that makes sure someone in authority signs off on all decisions. It also has informal networks, people who see each other at lunch or on the tennis court, and those people connect and talk. Sometimes the two networks come together, like when a manager asks her tennis partner who might be able to help her team meet an organizational goal. Sometimes the two networks conflict, like when the executive team raids the pension fund and raises the ire of the twenty-year-plus club, which alerts the tennis club, which causes one of the executives much embarrassment.

This model might be useful in projects where people are trying to make sense of complex events in which many factors may have had an influence, and they want to think about why things turned out the way they did. For example, it might be useful if you are trying to make sense of a conflict that grew out of a misunderstanding, or trying to find solutions for an ongoing conflict that seems impossible to resolve because it is too deeply entrenched.

There is more to the CSF: four nested subframeworks support sensemaking about situations that blend organization and self-organization in various ways. At the time of this writing, you can find out more about the confluence framework on my blog at storycoloredglasses.com. (If you can't find it there, search on the internet and you'll find it somewhere.)

STORY ELEMENTS

Following are some published models and frameworks you can use in the story elements exercise (see page 435 for instructions). In this case there are two types of models you can use: models to *compare to* your story elements, and models to *evaluate* your story elements.

To make the compare-evaluate distinction more clear, I'll use an analogy. Suppose you are a car racing enthusiast. Suppose you are *such* a racing enthusiast that you have built your own race car. Once you've finished the car, what might you want to do next? You might want to *compare* it to established brands of race cars—Ferrari, Lamborghini, Porsche, etc—to see which brand yours resembles most and least. And you might want to *evaluate* your car by referring to some sort of racing-car guide book, to see where your car meets or exceeds "industry standard" expectations.

Apart from not going anywhere and being made of paper, a set of story elements is not that different from a custom-built race car. Each creation is unique to its creators, purpose, and context; each has its own style and flavor; each is like and yet unlike named types in its category. So the two types of models I present here are like brand-name cars (element packages) and industry-standard car guides (evaluation packages).

Remember to introduce these models only *after* story elements have been created. Otherwise you risk putting forth the message that these models represent elements that *ought* to exist rather than generalized descriptions of elements that *often* exist. The utility of the comparison lies in the opposite of prescription: understanding what is unique, and uniquely meaningful, about the world from which the collected stories were drawn.

Situational story elements

Situational elements are created in response to the question, "What is going on in this story?" A set of situational story elements can help people make sense of what is going on in their organization or community today and what has happened in the past.

Comparing situations with the Native North American medicine wheel

The medicine wheel has nothing to do with medicine as we typically define it, but it does have a lot to do with health—emotional, spiritual, collective health. This ancient ritualized process has many forms and methods, but at its simplest, it is a set of situational story elements.

East. The East is the direction of the dawn, spring, and *new beginnings*. The color of the east is red, like the rising sun. There is some risk in the East, because situations are unformed, spontaneous and chaotic; but there is much opportunity in the East as well. In the East we adapt quickly to new circumstances and seek sources of hope and potential.

South. The South is the direction of mid-day, summer, and *growth*. The color of the South is yellow, like the sun overhead at noon. In the South, situations are forming, changing, and complex. Situations in the South can be managed if we establish relationships within them, but they cannot be controlled. The South is a place of transformation.

West. The West is the direction of the setting sun, autumn, and *maturity*. The color of the West is black, like the gathering darkness. In the West, situations cohere and coalesce into understandable yet complicated patterns. In the West, we learn from the wisdom and knowledge of experienced elders or experts as we develop our own maturity.

North. The North is the direction of night, winter, and *rebirth*. The color of the North is white, like the moon and the snow. In the North, situations are simple and stark, quiet and still, waiting. In the North, we reflect, solve problems, bring events to completion, sort things out, and preserve order.

Center. The Center is the direction of balance and of *self*, individual and collective. From the center, we embark on journeys toward all the other directions, but where we go and why we go depends on what we find in the center.

To compare a set of created situations to the medicine wheel, groups can place sticky notes with each of these labels (East-beginning, South-growth, West-maturity, North-rebirth, Center-self) in a compass-like circle around their story elements (with the "Center" note in the center, of course). Then they can move each story element nearest to the medicine wheel directions it seems most connected to. For example, a story element called "Safe haven" might be placed near the North (winter, rebirth) direction. (For people in the Southern Hemisphere, the North-South direction should be reversed to make more sense.)

Groups can add annotations to the diagram marking why they think any story element belongs where it was placed. After the group has connected everything they think connects, they can stand back and look at the overall pattern.

What have they learned about their situations by comparing them to the medicine wheel directions? Where do their situations lie? Is there any part of the medicine wheel they have left empty? Why did that happen and what does it mean?

There is much more information available on the medicine wheel and its many forms and uses. Some versions of the medicine wheel have more elements specified, such as animals, minerals, and plants. Some have more directions specified, such as other compass points (e.g., Northwest, Southeast) plus up (sky) and down (earth). I particularly like two books as references: *The Medicine Wheel: Earth Astrology* by Sun Bear and Wabun Wind, and *Leadership Lessons From The Medicine Wheel* by Gary Lear. *Dancing with the Wheel: The Medicine Wheel Workbook* (written by Sun Bear, Wabun Wind and Crysalis Mulligan) includes detailed instructions for using the medicine wheel in group exercises very similar to the ones described in this book.

Evaluating situations with SWOT analysis

SWOT stands for Strengths, Weaknesses, Opportunities, and Threats. This method was created by Albert Humphrey in the 1960s and is a popular method of decision support.

Using SWOT analysis as part of the story elements exercise is very simple. After the story elements have been created, each group should lay out a table with situational story elements as rows and SWOT elements as columns, and talk about the strengths, weaknesses, opportunities, and threats represented by each story element. You can use SWOT analysis with any type of story element, but it fits with situations best.

Since this method is so well known, it is easy to find out more information about it on the internet or at any library. A similar method you could also use in this place is PEST analysis (PEST meaning Political, Economic, Social, Technological), or its longer-acronymed cousins PESTLE (adding Legal and Environmental) and STEEPLED (adding Ethical and Demographic). All of these methods are useful for evaluating situations drawn from stories.

Starting with stories creates a more grounded version of SWOT analysis. So even if you end up with what looks like a conventional planning output, you'll know that it is built on a firmer foundation than one built by asking these questions without having worked your way through stories first.

Theme story elements

Theme elements are created in response to the question, "What is this story about?" A set of theme story elements helps people make sense of the issues people care about in the community or organization, from multiple perspectives.

Comparing themes with the Tipu Ake ki te Ora Lifecycle Model

This model is used to help organizations and communities think about and plan for the future. In the Maori language the full name of this model means "growing from within ever onwards and upwards towards a place of well-being."

The story of this model's creation is fascinating. In the 1950s Peter Goldsbury had been a student at a small rural school in New Zealand. Many years later he returned to find the school thriving. This surprised him, since he knew that not long before his visit the school had been doing badly, its students falling far behind their peers elsewhere. Peter asked the school's leaders what they had done to turn things around so completely.

The school leaders described their ways of thinking, which were based largely on ancient Maori teachings. Having spent many years working in organizational development, Peter realized that these ways of thinking might be useful to others. So he and the school leaders collaborated to produce the Tipu Ake model, which they called "a project leadership model for innovative organisations." The model is now being used by organizations and communities around the world to create positive change.

The central metaphor of the Tipu Ake model is that of a tiny seed growing into a giant tree in the forest. Each element of the model is a theme that interacts with the other themes in the same way that the forces of life interact in the forest.

This is not a stage model, which is why it is a good match for comparison with themes derived from stories. The Tipu Ake themes, like themes from stories, cut across all possible time scales as they interact and intermingle.

For each theme, the model includes an essential definition; a metaphorical connection to the forest tree; a time-worn saying that illustrates the theme; "birds" that sow seeds (create new ideas) related to the theme; and "pests" that destroy, but also recycle and diversify.

The themes are as follows.

Undercurrents. For the theme of undercurrents, the metaphor is of the soil in which the tree grows. In the chaos of birth and rebirth, what matters is the courage to change. We are birds when we face the issues. We are pests when we base our convictions on false assumptions. The saying for undercurrents is, "The greatest enemy is the one within us—conquer that and the rest are easy."

Leadership. For leadership, the metaphor is of the seed from which the tree grows. True leadership leads without controlling, inspires without censoring. We are birds when we share our knowledge. We are pests when we pay too much attention to ego and credit. The saying for leadership is, "A kumara [sweet potato] never calls itself sweet—that's for the eaters to say."

Teamwork. For teamwork, the metaphor is of the roots that feed the tree and keep it stable. Teamwork is about working together to get things done. We are birds when we develop trust and support each other. We are pests when we struggle over power. The saying for teamwork is, "We leave our hats at the door," meaning that our external powers have no say over the team's work together.

Processes. For processes, the metaphor is of the trunk of the tree, keeping it strong. Processes must work without elaboration or obstruction. We are birds when we improve our effectiveness. We are pests when we develop rigidity in our processes or slow things down with avoidable delays. The saying for processes is, "Own your own processes; keep them simple and effective."

Sensing. For sensing, the metaphor is of the tree's branches, reaching out. Sensing means becoming aware of everything that is going on in the organization or community. We are birds when we listen. We are pests when we use only predefined measures. The saying for sensing is, "Keep your ears open. Sense what is happening around us; reflect on it together to learn."

Wisdom. For wisdom, the metaphor is of the flowers of the tree. Wisdom means sharing and protecting the essential collective wisdom of the community or organization. We are birds when we live our values. We are pests when our values clash. The saying for wisdom is, "We have no room around here for Matapiko [stingy] gatekeepers—we share our knowledge."

Well-being. For well-being (also called Ora), the metaphor is of the fruits of the tree. Well-being is about developing a vision of the future that is worth working towards. We are birds when we focus on outcomes. We are pests when we become smug and complacent. The saying for well-being is "When we focus on outcomes, nothing becomes a barrier."

Finally, the model includes two other elements or themes: *sunshine*, which represents external energy, and *poisons*, which stop the process of germination. Because these are external to the tree image, they don't have bird and pest elements, nor do they have sayings, but they are part of the model as influencers from outside the tree itself.

To use the Tipu Ake model in a story elements exercise, after groups have created their theme story elements, they should create sticky notes representing some or all of the Tipu Ake themes. They should use whichever representations of the Tipu Ake themes hold the most meaning for them. For some groups this will be the name and description of the theme, for some the metaphorical association, for some the saying, for some the birds and pests.

Then groups should connect their story element themes to the Tipu Ake themes in some way—by drawing lines, by placing things together, by adding annotations, by arranging the two sets of themes in a way that represents relationships. For example, a group might place the Tipu Ake themes along one vertical line and their own themes along another, then shift the themes around until they feel the two lines connect well across horizontal "rungs" of a "ladder." That's one way to visualize the connections, but there are many others.

You can find out more about the Tipu Ake ki te Ora Lifecycle model on the internet at tipuake.org.nz, where the group of volunteers who put together the model have assembled a large number of useful papers, presentations, and videos. According to the Tipu Ake web site, "acknowledgement [of the model] is by *koha* (a gift in return based on its value to you)." So if you use the Tipu Ake model, make sure you find a way to return a gift to its creators, as I have done by telling *you* about it.

Evaluating themes with Causal Layered Analysis (CLA)

Causal Layered Analysis comes from the field of futures studies, but in its outlook it has a lot in common with narrative work; so it's not surprising that it works well in a narrative sensemaking session. According to its creator, Sohail Inayatullah, CLA "is concerned less with predicting a particular future and more with opening up the present and past to create alternative futures."

CLA describes four layers of meaning in any situation, all operating at the same time, as follows.

Litany. The litany is the body of well-known statements about the situation as they are presented in public, by the media and in popular knowledge. The situation at the level of the litany is apparently obvious, lacking depth and requiring little thought. Things are hopeless, or already solved, or somebody's fault.

Systemic causes. The second layer of meaning is concerned with social systemic causes of the situation, such as technological factors, political movements, and historical events. At this level research is conducted, data is collected, and interpretations are put forth (sometimes as facts); but deep assumptions are rarely challenged.

Worldview/discourse. At the third layer of meaning are deeper assumptions about the situation, things everyone knows and nobody questions—"positions that create notions of collective identity." At this level worldviews clash, ideologies define, stakeholders support their interests, and cultures see the world differently.

Metaphor/myth. At the deepest layer in the stratum lie "the deep stories, the collective archetypes" of societies. At this level we have "gut-level" emotional reactions to situations based on the deepest experiences of our existence.

CLA does not claim that any of these layers are superior to others, only that all of them will be present in any situation people consider and define. This makes CLA a perfect model with which to more deeply consider thematic story elements drawn from stories: because all themes have layers.

To use Causal Layered Analysis in a story elements exercise, after each group's thematic story elements are complete, ask them to copy their theme element names onto new sticky notes. Next groups should create a layered view (in a new space) by marking out lines to separate the four CLA layers (like a layer cake) on the paper. Their story elements should be placed along the top of the space like candles on the cake. Then for each story element, groups should fill in the layer cake with at least one *aspect* of each theme that fits best into each CLA layer. Table cells can be filled with sticky notes or by directly writing on the paper; but remember to keep people writing in large print so that they will be able to see larger patterns when they step back.

Some questions that will help people find these aspects are as follows.

1. Litany: What newspaper headlines might be written about this situation? What is well known about it? What is obvious?

2. Systemic causes: What events or actions caused this situation to happen? What solutions are available in this situation? What factors are in play in it?

3. Worldview/discourse: What are some of the explanations different people might have for this situation? What would different groups say about it? How many of these positions can you describe?

4. Metaphor/myth: What's the *real* story of this situation? What's going on deep down? How do you *feel* about it at the gut level? Can you think of any proverbs, folk tales, or stories that fit this aspect of the situation?

After the layers have been filled in for each story element, groups should stand back and look at the larger patterns that appear.

This is not the only way to use CLA in a story elements exercise; it is just the way that seems most useful to me. I have never actually *done* this, mind; this is just how I think I *would* use CLA if I had the chance to. So you should experiment with your use of this model (and with all of the models I have listed here, and any others you might find) and figure out what works for you.

You can find out more about Causal Layered Analysis on the internet or in *The Causal Layered Analysis Reader*, a book edited by Sohail Inayatullah which includes case studies of the model's use, as well as more information about its history and theoretical underpinnings.

Character story elements

Character elements are created in response to the question, "Who is doing things in this story?" A set of character story elements helps people make sense of the behaviors and motivations behind the actions people take in the stories.

I'd like to make a special note on character-type models. I had a very hard time choosing models to recommend for comparison with and evaluation of character story elements. This was not from want of choices; it was from want of *clear* choices. There have been abundant attempts to categorize the way people behave. Many of these derive from the work of Carl Jung.

I thought about including Jungian archetypes here; certainly they represent a set of elemental character "packages" that describe behaviors and motivations. But I decided not to include them, for two reasons. First, it's difficult to find any one definitive set of Jungian archetypes. Many different people seem to have interpreted Jung's writings in many different ways (which is probably what he wanted). Second, some of Jung's archetypes are difficult to use in group

work without large facilitation experience (or so it seems to me). When people are talking about improving their community or organization, I would not relish asking them about their anima (female soul of a man) or animus (male soul of a woman) in relation to the behavior of the people around them. All sorts of differences in worldviews related to gender roles would get mixed up into the sensemaking, which might simply cause the process to stall.

I always say that stories go deep, but Jungian archetypes go perhaps *too* deep—and too *personally* deep—for use in the contexts PNI envisions. PNI is about community, not about the depths of *individual* psyches. I haven't found Jungian archetypes used much in organizational work, though I'm certainly no expert on all of their applications. If *you* want to use Jungian archetypes in PNI exercises, by all means do so, and please tell me and everyone else how you used them. *I* don't feel capable of telling you what I think is the best way of using Jungian archetypes in a sensemaking session, because I'm not sure I *could* use them well. My guess is that the majority of my readers couldn't either. So instead of describing Jungian archetypes here, I've chosen two other approaches that I think will have more practical utility in the sensemaking sessions you might actually facilitate.

Comparing characters with Belbin team roles

This model, created by Meredith Belbin in the 1970s, describes how people in a team take on complementary roles as they work together. The model does not represent personality types, but *complementary behaviors* people tend to assume in groups. One person might take on different roles in different groups depending on their memberships and purposes. The model was created based on research into how people work in teams, specifically looking at what clusters of complementary behaviors lead teams to succeed in collaboration.

Nine team roles are defined by Belbin. The first three are oriented towards *action*.

Shaper. Shapers are all about challenge. They enjoy stimulating the team to do better, to explore further, and to question assumptions.

Shapers can help the team get past obstacles by drawing out enthusiasm, but they can also push too hard and come off as aggressive.

Implementer. People in this role get their work done with great discipline and order. They are highly motivated, but they may be closed-minded and unwilling to consider making changes.

Completer/finisher. These perfectionists like to see things done, done well, and done on time. They work hard, take deadlines very seriously, and set high standards for their work and everyone else's. However, people in this role can frustrate team members who don't want to worry over details, and they are not good at delegating (because they don't want anyone else doing things wrong).

Roles in the second group are oriented towards *people*.

Coordinator. Coordinators are excellent delegators, confidently handing out tasks to those most suited to carry them out. However, some may see coordinators as manipulative, delegating not for efficiency but to avoid doing the work themselves.

Resource investigator. These are the explorers of group work. They pursue contacts and opportunities with enthusiasm, gathering ideas from their broad networks. However, resource investigators may be sloppy with details, and they may lose enthusiasm for the work once they have explored all they believe there is to be found.

Team worker. The work of teamworkers can seem unimportant, but they keep the team working smoothly by listening to everyone and negotiating disputes before they get out of hand. The down-side to teamworkers is that because they listen to everyone, they may have difficulty coming to decisions and taking definite positions.

The final three roles are oriented towards *thinking*.

Plant. Plants come up with new ideas and new ways of thinking. They work best alone, don't take criticism well, and keep disrupting structured processes with their innovative ideas. But plants also serve an important function in the group because they bring new "seeds" of thought into discussion. (I don't know about you, but I'm plenty confused about the name "plant." The other names all make sense, but this one leaves me wondering. The Belbin web site says the role "was so-called because one such individual was 'planted' in each team." But what does *that* mean? *Why* was one planted in each team? I've seen other references to these roles say the name "plant" refers to the tendency of these people to keep to themselves, like potted plants apparently (*do* potted plants keep to themselves?). Some people call the "plant" the "ideas person" or "innovator." I think those names work better, but I'm keeping "plant" here so you won't be confused if you look up Belbin roles yourself.)

Monitor/evaluator. A person taking on this role sees things impartially and from all sides, carefully weighing the pros and cons of all ideas. However, people in this role can be critical, and they can place a drag on group enthusiasm with their cautious and careful analysis.

Specialist. Specialists know one thing very well, and they are happy to educate everyone else in the team about it. However, whenever the work called for falls outside of the specialist's field of expertise, they lose interest in the work.

Most people naturally gravitate towards some of these roles and away from some others, but rarely is anyone only able to fulfill one role in a group. This is good, because the original research from which this model was developed found that when any of these roles was missing from a group, or when there were too many of any role, the group was less likely to be successful.

You might think this set of characters won't work for story projects. You might say that if stories were collected from people in a diverse community, perhaps from different groups who don't see eye to eye, how could elements derived from those stories match up with a set of roles taken on by members of successful teams? But you see, that's just where the utility comes in: in the comparison with success. If your organization or community *were* a successful team, it would have elements of these behavioral roles in it, even if the roles weren't situated in actual individual people. Somehow new ideas would be brought to the table; somehow the pros and cons of decisions would be analyzed; somehow deadlines would be kept; somehow disputes would be negotiated; and so on. Comparing sets of behaviors drawn from stories with an ideal portrait of a well-functioning team can help people think about what is happening in their community or organization.

To use Belbin team roles in a story elements exercise, ask each group to line up the nine Belbin roles alongside their character story elements and simply look for connections. How they portray those connections can vary from annotation to placement to connecting lines. Just ask people to build something that visually explains where the character story elements and the Belbin roles overlap, and where they don't.

You can find out more about Belbin team roles on the Belbin web site at belbin.com, or in Meredith Belbin's book *Team Roles at Work*.

Evaluating characters with the "Big Five" personality traits

Also called the Five Factor Model, the "Big Five" personality traits are based on five questions about individual personalities. The questions were developed through the combined work of several psychologists, including Warren Norman, Lewis Goldberg, Paul Costa, and Robert McCrae.

The five questions are as follows.

1. How *open* is the person to experience? At one end of this scale are people who are insatiably inventive and curious, always ready for a new adventure. At the other end are the ploddingly consistent and cautious, uninterested in anything new. The degree of "preference for novelty" is another way of phrasing this question.

2. How *organized* is the person? At one end of this scale are people who are highly efficient, with a place for everything and everything in its place; dutiful, conscientious, with strong self-discipline. At the other end are people described as easy-going or careless; unpredictable, ready to jump to action—or not, as the mood takes them.

3. How *outgoing* is the person? At one end of this scale are people who vastly prefer the company of others, to the degree that they become drained when alone and are always looking for company. At the other end are people who get their energy by writing books that grow far too long in the quiet of their country offices, surrounded by nothing but trees and rainfall, then snowfall, then rainfall again. (Ahem.)

4. How *agreeable* is the person? At one end of this scale are those who trust easily, are compassionate and warm towards others, and are ready to cooperate. At the other end are those who are habitually suspicious and slow to trust—not necessarily malicious, but slow to warm up.

5. How *neurotic* is the person? At one end of the scale are those who could be called sensitive or nervous, who take everything personally, have thin skins, and are easily roused to anger, fear, and anxiety. At the other end are those whose feathers never get ruffled, whose emotions are stable, who are secure and confident in all circumstances.

Groups can use these "big five" questions in a story elements exercise by placing each character element at some point (or area) on each scale. One way to do this is to draw five vertical lines in a space; copy the character element names five times; then place the sticky notes on each scale, sliding them up and down until they seem to be in the right places. As the character elements are considered, patterns of gaps and concentrations should appear. For example, maybe none of the character elements created are outgoing; or all of them are neurotic; or only the ones that have to do with planning are organized. Annotations can be added in another color to highlight interesting patterns among the elements. Finally, groups can discuss what they have learned from asking these questions about their character elements and what that means about the project and the community or organization.

You can find out more about the "big five" personality traits—well, all over the internet, to begin with. I would suspect you would find these described in many recent psychology textbooks as well. This body of research is so well-known that it is fairly easy to find manifestations of it in many textbooks of psychology and even in popular self-help books about psychology. I'm not going to suggest a particular book, but that's just because there are so many out there that you don't need my help choosing one.

Value story elements

Value elements are created in response to the question, "What *matters* to the characters in this story?" A set of value story elements helps people think about what matters, and what *doesn't* matter, to different groups of people in the community or organization—and how those values might come together or clash.

Comparing values with the Rokeach Value Survey

This model, which is really just a list of values, is used to survey people about their values in empirical psychological work. It was developed by the psychologist Milton Rokeach in the 1960s.

The values are grouped into two sets of eighteen values each: *terminal* values (things people would like to achieve by the end of their lives) and *instrumental* values (ways people would like to be, or see in others).

The terminal values are:

1. A comfortable life (a prosperous life)
2. An exciting life (a stimulating, active life)
3. A sense of accomplishment (lasting contribution)
4. A world of peace (free of war and conflict)
5. A world of beauty (beauty of nature and the arts)
6. Equality (brotherhood, equal opportunity for all)
7. Family security (taking care of loved ones)
8. Freedom (independence, choice)
9. Happiness (contentedness)
10. Inner harmony (freedom from inner conflict)
11. Mature love (sexual and spiritual intimacy)
12. National security (protection from attack)
13. Pleasure (an enjoyable, leisurely life)
14. Salvation (saved, eternal life)
15. Self-respect (self-esteem)

16. Social recognition (respect, admiration)
17. True friendship (close companionship)
18. Wisdom (a mature understanding of life)

The instrumental values are:

1. Ambitious (hard-working, aspiring)
2. Broadminded (open-minded)
3. Capable (competent, effective)
4. Cheerful (lighthearted, joyful)
5. Clean (neat, tidy)
6. Courageous (standing up for your beliefs)
7. Forgiving (willing to pardon others)
8. Helpful (working for the welfare of others)
9. Honest (sincere, truthful)
10. Imaginative (daring, creative)
11. Independent (self-reliant, self-sufficient)
12. Intellectual (intelligent, reflective)
13. Logical (consistent, rational)
14. Loving (affectionate, tender)
15. Obedient (dutiful, respectful)
16. Polite (courteous, well mannered)
17. Responsible (dependable, reliable)
18. Self-controlled (self-discipline)

Usually the best method when you want to compare two sets of things is to draw a table in which one set comprises the rows and the other the columns, the cells representing combined pairs between the two lists. In the cells some kind of annotations are made: letters such as "A" for agree and "D" for disagree, sticky-note explanations of how each pair holds together or doesn't, or simple dot marks in cells where agreement occurs (and nothing otherwise). After the table is complete, patterns should appear in which some areas of the table are busy with markings while some are empty. If the rows and columns are sorted in some way (say from positive to negative, or personal to societal, or common to rare) the patterns can be even more revealing.

Building a patterning table with a set of story elements against the thirty-six Rokeach values is somewhat daunting, though it does have the highest probability of revealing interesting patterns. If reflecting on a set of created values is important to your project, you can set aside the time to do this well.

If you can't spare that much time or attention, I can think of three alternatives to using the entire list of Rokeach values.

Trimming. You could prune Rokeach's lists of values to remove elements you think would be less likely to come up in the context of the sensemaking session. For example, "Mature love" is not likely to come up in a project about weather forecasting, and "Salvation" is not likely to be useful in a project about a town park. You can do this before the session, or you can ask groups to remove some values from the Rokeach lists before they start using them.

Ranking. Instead of thinking about how every story-element value pairs up with every Rokeach value, groups could quickly pick out the *top three* Rokeach values for each story element and mark only those in the chart, leaving the rest of the pairs unexamined in detail. This is still a pairwise comparison, but it's a faster one, more like skimming than fully considering the values.

Clustering. Instead of making a table at all, groups could write each value (their own and those from Rokeach's system) on a sticky note, then move both sets of values around so *proximity* means similarity. This might be more or less difficult to accomplish, depending on how many cross-connections there are between values. Still, this method is faster than making pairwise comparisons in a table, and it might draw more imagination from groups who need to range more widely in their thinking.

You can find out more about the Rokeach values and their history and uses in Rokeach's 1973 book *The Nature of Human Values*.

Evaluating values with the Competing Values Framework

This model was developed by Robert Quinn and John Rohrbaugh in the 1980s, as part of a study on the indicators that distinguish effective organizations. The framework sets up two axes, each describing a tension between two values: *stability* competes with *flexibility*, and *internal focus* competes with *external focus*. Effective organizations, say the framework's authors, manage these competing tensions by achieving paradoxical mastery over all four values at once (becoming, for example, both stable *and* flexible).

The two axes come together to describe four ways of looking at values, called "models," thus:

1. Human relations model: Flexible, internally focused. In this view, what matters most is that people work well together, get along with each other, enjoy their work, and reach their *potential* individually and collectively.
2. Open systems model: Flexible, externally focused. In this view, what matters most is that the organization is *dynamic,* agile, fully informed, ready to seize opportunities as they appear, and prepared to grow rapidly.
3. Rational goal model: Stable, externally focused. In this view, what matters most is that the organization is effective, competent, and above all *productive* in meeting its goals.
4. Internal process model: Stable, internally focused. In this view, what matters most is that the organization works perfectly, like a *well-oiled* machine, with excellent information and knowledge management, internal communication, and stability of process.

Later, in work with Kim Cameron, Quinn used the original two axes of tension to define four organizational culture types based on how the tensions are resolved. The types are:

1. Clan: Flexible, internally focused. Like a family, this culture is based on trust, teamwork, and participation. People look forward to becoming involved in synergistic achievements, looking to be part of something bigger than themselves.
2. Adhocracy: Flexible, externally focused. This risk-taking culture is focused on innovation, freedom, and growth. People are curious and inventive, and they hope to surprise everyone by discovering the next big thing.
3. Market: Stable, externally focused. This competitive culture values high expectations, rapid development, and toughness. People are driven to succeed, outperform-

ing all previous scores and leading the market.

4. Hierarchy: Stable, internally focused. This bureaucratic culture is rule-bound and proud of it. People are careful and cautious; teams run smoothly; errors are quickly detected and fixed; processes are under perfect control; results are guaranteed.

To use the Competing Values Framework in a story elements exercise, ask each group to lay out the two dimensions of the framework on a space, as if this were a landscape exercise. Don't mention the four quadrants yet (if people know about the quadrants, ask them to leave them off the space for now). Then ask each group to place their value story elements into the space based on where they think each fits on the two dimensions. Is the value more closely related to stability or to flexibility? Does it have more of an internal or external focus? As with a landscape exercise, any values that could arguably be in two places can be split into two sticky notes with the two aspects that cause the split placement noted.

Once each group's value story elements have been placed into the space, groups can then apply labels to the four quadrants (from either of the two lists above, or from others—there are more quadrant labels available if you look around the internet). Then groups can talk about what their placements mean. Are any of the quadrants empty? Are there similarities between the values in each quadrant? What can groups learn about the values they drew from the stories by looking at them against this framework?

To find out more about the Competing Values Framework, see the original paper by Quinn and Rohrbaugh ("A spatial model of effectiveness criteria: Towards a competing values approach to organizational analysis"). By the way, Quinn and Rohrbaugh also came up with personality-trait mappings for the Competing Values Framework, which you could use for comparison with character story elements. Look for the CVF and roles, and you'll find it.

COMPOSITE STORIES

These are some story templates I've found by poking around in books and on the internet. See page 447 for instructions on using them. As I've said with every other exercise, these are not the models you must use; these are the *sorts* of models that work. It's easy to find more of these; why not look around and see what you find?

Aristotle's plot points

The Greek philosopher Aristotle wrote in his *Poetics* about the structure of dramatic plays around 330 BCE, and his three-part drama has been used for centuries.

However, if you read what Aristotle *actually* said about plays having three parts, you'll find it is not all that meaningful. What he actually said was this:

> A whole is that which has a beginning, a middle, and an end. A beginning is that which does not itself follow anything by causal necessity, but after which something naturally is or comes to be. An end, on the contrary, is that which itself naturally follows some other thing, either by necessity, or as a rule, but has nothing following it. A middle is that which follows something as some other thing follows it. A well constructed plot, therefore, must neither begin nor end at haphazard, but conform to these principles.

That isn't very different from what the Red King said to the white rabbit in *Alice in Wonderland:*

> "Begin at the beginning," the King said gravely, "and go on till you come to the end: then stop."

I almost wonder if Lewis Carroll was making a joke about Aristotle. It's hard to find a less useful statement about stories than this. *Anything* that has duration can be said to have a start, a finish, and something in between, but that can't help anybody build a good story.

The useful parts in the *Poetics* come later on, like this one:

> Every tragedy falls into two parts, Complication and Unravelling or Denouement. ... By the Complication I mean

all that extends from the beginning of the action to the part which marks the turning-point to good or bad fortune. The Unravelling is that which extends from the beginning of the change to the end. ... Many poets tie the knot well, but unravel it ill. Both arts, however, should always be mastered.

Now *that* we can use. In any story, things get complicated, then things get resolved. That is a very simple story template with only two slots in it: *complication,* or the tying of the knot; and *unraveling,* or the untying of the knot. We can use that. And we can ask people to think about things like: What *is* the knot? How does it get tied? How does it get untied? That's a nice and simple, but thought-provoking, story template. It is also easy to add elaborations to it, such as repetitions (increasingly intricate complications, for example).

Aristotle also hints at a story template with more pieces to it, thus:

> Plots are either Simple or Complex, for the actions in real life, of which the plots are an imitation, obviously show a similar distinction. An action which is one and continuous in the sense above defined, I call Simple, when the change of fortune takes place without Reversal of the Situation and without Recognition. ...
>
> A Complex action is one in which the change is accompanied by such Reversal, or by Recognition, or by both. ...
>
> Reversal of the Situation is a change by which the action veers round to its opposite, subject always to our rule of probability or necessity. ...
>
> Recognition, as the name indicates, is a change from ignorance to knowledge, producing love or hate between the persons destined by the poet for good or bad fortune. The best form of recognition is coincident with a Reversal of the Situation...
>
> Two parts, then, of the Plot—Reversal of the Situation and Recognition—turn upon surprises. A third part is the Scene of Suffering. The Scene of Suffering is a destructive or painful action, such as death on the stage, bodily agony, wounds and the like.

The people who wrote Monty Python's "Spanish Inquisition" routine must have read this part of the *Poetics* (the two important things—the *three* important things) about complex plots. Supposedly this document was not actually written by Aristotle, but was a set of lecture notes jotted down by his students. When you understand this, the hesitations in the text make sense. Aristotle knew there were three plot points he wanted to talk about, but his students didn't. (The funniest thing about Aristotle's *Poetics* is that you can now find student-written—wait for it—study notes about it on the internet.)

So we can add to the complication and unraveling three more elements: *reversal* of the situation, *recognition* of the state of affairs (by the story's protagonist, presumably), and a scene of *suffering.* The next question is, *where* should these things be added? Should they be between the complication and the unraveling? Within them? Aristotle didn't say, so your guess is as good as mine.

Here's an idea. Why not offer up these additional plot points as free-floating elements your participants can use in their simple story template wherever they think they work best? This would give people some "spices" to make their story more engaging, but allow them to choose where—and if—they want to apply them.

To find out more about Aristotle's *Poetics,* which I highly recommend reading, just look in your local library for classical documents or search the internet, where free copies abound.

Gustav Freytag's pyramid

Freytag was a playwright and novelist who in 1863 proposed a five-part "dramatic arc" for stories. The structure is called a pyramid because it is usually drawn in a triangular shape, as in Figure A.8 on the following page.

The parts of the pyramid are as follows.

1. Exposition: The setting and characters are introduced. There may be hints of conflict in this part, but they are muted.

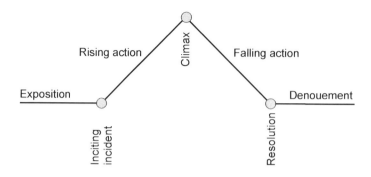

Figure A.8. Freytag's pyramid is a popular model for story structure.

2. Inciting incident: The story's central conflict is introduced, and this sets the plot in motion. This event can also be called the inciting moment, the precipitating incident, or sometimes the story's "hook" (as in, the hook that draws people into the story).

3. Rising action: A series of events builds the story's tension and excitement as the conflict introduced in the inciting incident plays out. This is sometimes called the complication.

4. Climax: Also called the crisis, this is where the story turns and things change, for better or worse. In a tragedy things usually get worse at this point; in a comedy things usually get better.

5. Falling action: The conflict begins to resolve itself, in one way or another. The protagonist might solve the problems created by the conflict, or they might be saved by someone else, or they might simply be defeated by the situation.

6. Resolution: The conflict is fully and finally resolved.

7. Denouement: The conflict and its resolution are explained and reflected on, and all loose ends are tied up.

To find out more about Freytag's pyramid, you can read his original book (*Freytag's Technique of the Drama: An Exposition of Dramatic Composition and Art*), in German or in English. The English translation is out of copyright and freely available on the internet. Or you can search the internet, on which you will find dozens of slightly varying descriptions of Freytag's structure.

Syd Field's Paradigm

Field is an American screenwriter and teacher of screenwriting. His 1979 book *Screenplay* lays out a three-act structure he calls "the paradigm." His ideas have been widely taken up in screenwriting. This structure, like Freytag's pyramid, comes with a diagram. The diagram is used in a few different forms. I'll show it to you in four versions, from simplest to most complex.

In its simplest form (Figure A.9 on the next page), Field's paradigm divides a story into three acts, as follows:

1. Setup (Act One): Introduces the setting and characters.

2. Confrontation (Act Two): The protagonist of the story struggles with something.

3. Resolution (Act Three): The conflicts in the story are resolved.

In this version, the model is very similar to Aristotle's beginning-middle-end structure.

A slightly more complex version (Figure A.10 on the facing page) adds three surprising plot points.

The three circled plot points are as follows:

1. Plot point 1: This point, near the end of Act One, is a surprising event that changes the protagonist's life. It is not the same as an inciting incident (that comes in the more complex form of the model); this is more like something that changes things so completely that there is no going back to the way things were in the first act.

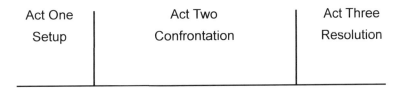

Figure A.9. The simplest version of Field's paradigm of story structure.

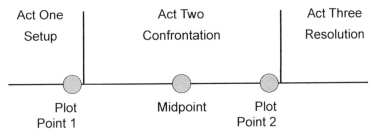

Figure A.10. The second of four increasingly elaborate versions of Field's paradigm of story structure.

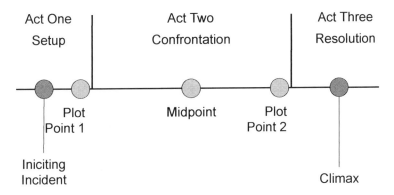

Figure A.11. The third of four increasingly elaborate versions of Field's paradigm of story structure.

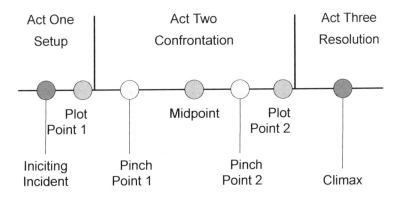

Figure A.12. The last of four increasingly elaborate versions of Field's paradigm of story structure.

2. Midpoint: This part of the plot, usually midway through Act Two, keeps the confrontation phase of the story full of energy by putting forth a surprising reversal.

3. Plot point 2: This point, near the end of Act Two, adds another dramatic surprise. This time the surprise ends the period of confrontation and begins the period of resolution.

A third version of the model (Figure A.11 on the previous page) adds two more incidents to the setup and resolution phases.

The two new points are:

1. Inciting incident: Also called the catalyst, this is the point in the setup in which events are set in motion.

2. Climax: Here is where the main conflict or problem of the story is completely and finally resolved, and the protagonist succeeds or fails in the attempt.

Finally, there is one more level of complexity in the full paradigm (Figure A.12 on the preceding page), and that is to add two "pinch points" which serve to keep the progress of the confrontation phase compelling. The pinch points are events that give the confrontation complexity and remind the audience of the central conflicts underlying the story.

You could use this story template at any of its levels of complexity. Or you could use it in stages, where groups work their way through the four levels of complexity. Or you could introduce all of the levels of complexity at the start and ask groups to choose which level they would like to build into their story.

You can find out more about Field's paradigm by reading his book *Screenplay* or by reading any of the interpretations of it on the internet.

Stein and Glenn's story grammar

Starting around the 1970s, several researchers have studied how children learn to tell stories, what sorts of stories they tell as they learn, and how they remember and retell stories. In 1977, Jean Mandler and Nancy Johnson created a detailed "story grammar"—a set of expectations about the structure of stories, which children learn from their elders—based on an analysis of orally transmitted folktales. In 1979, Nancy Stein and Christine Glenn simplified the grammar for use in instruction.

When Mandler and Marsha Goodman tested Stein and Glenn's model in 1982, they found that when people were told stories that did not conform to the model (due to events being out of order or omitted), they *altered* the story as they retold it in such a way that it conformed to the model. Educational specialists have since recommended that children be helped to understand this "universal" story grammar, so as to improve their comprehension of learning materials.

Stein and Glenn's grammar is as follows.

1. Setting: The characters and other elements of setting are introduced.

2. Initiating event: Something happens that starts the story moving with a problem or dilemma.

3. Internal response: The protagonist reacts to the initiating event. The response is called "internal" because the protagonist's feelings about the event are important in the response.

4. Attempt: The protagonist takes action to resolve the dilemma or solve the problem.

5. Consequence: The protagonist's action has some outcome, good or bad.

6. Reaction: The protagonist responds to the consequence.

The benefit of using this story template is that because it was developed with the instruction of children in mind, it is relatively simple. It has no stage directions or plot twists. It just follows the feelings of a protagonist attempting to solve a problem.

You can find out more about this story grammar by looking up the references mentioned above (see the Bibliography for details; look under Mandler and Stein). I don't see this model used much outside of the world of primary education, but if you search for terms like "story grammar" and "story schemata" (schemata are sets of expectations) you are likely to find out more about it.

Kenn Adams' story spine

Adams is a playwright with much experience in improvisational theatre. In his book *How to Improvise a Full-Length Play* he outlines his "story spine" structure, which he calls a "tool" for improvisation. The story spine goes like this.

The Beginning (or Balance)

- Once Upon a Time…
- Every day…

The Event (or Catalyst or un-Balance)

- But one day…

The Middle (or Quest for a Resolution)

- Because of that…
- Because of that…
- Because of that… (etc)

The Climax

- Until finally…

The Resolution (or New Balance)

- And ever since then…

To use the template, ask groups to fill in each of the ellipses with inspiration from a collected story. Note that this model includes some repetition in it ("Because of that…"), which is in the nature of a quest.

The benefit of this template is its absence of categories. You don't even have to use the names for the parts of the story (like "The Beginning"). You can just use the conversational prompts (like "But one day…"). If you need something very simple and quick, this template may be perfect.

To find out more about the story spine, look for Adams' book *How to Improvise a Full-Length Play: The Art of Spontaneous Theater*, or search the internet for the term "story spine."

Joseph Campbell's Hero's Journey

Campbell was an expert in comparative mythology and religion. His "hero's journey" story structure claims to capture the fundamental pattern of myths around the world. The hero's journey has seventeen stages broken up into three larger phases, as follows.

Separation

The separation phase of the journey involves the hero's transition away from the normal world.

1. The call to adventure: The hero begins in a normal situation (normal to the hero, that is) with life going on as it always has. Into this world comes some kind of message or challenge inviting the hero to enter into a new adventure.

2. Refusal of the call: The hero at first ignores the call, possibly through fear but possibly through an obligation to others. Eventually the hero has a change of heart and takes on the challenge.

3. Supernatural aid: Some sort of magical or supernatural helper (human, animal, or object) arrives to help the hero on the quest. The helper may seem weak or insignificant at first, but later turns out to be critical.

4. The crossing of the first threshold: The hero begins the adventure by taking leave of normal routines and surroundings.

5. Entering the belly of the whale: The hero enters fully into a dangerous situation. There is no going back, and the story's tension increases.

Initiation

In the initiation phase, the hero endures tests and trials, and emerges changed.

1. Road of trials: The hero passes through a series of tests in order to begin the transformation into what they will become. During these tests the hero's allies and enemies become apparent.

2. Meeting with the soul mate: The hero encounters someone or something that symbolizes love, birth, and creation. This could be an actual person or supernatural being, or it could be an idea or even a memory, but it represents positive energy. (In some versions of the hero's journey this is called "Meeting with the goddess" but I find that too limiting; it doesn't have to be an *actual* goddess.)

3. Overcoming temptation: The hero encounters someone or something that symbolizes temptation, in the form of short-term relief. If the hero succumbs to temptation, the quest will fail. The hero must pass through this ordeal in order to continue the quest. (This stage is sometimes called "Woman as temptress." Speaking as a woman: excuuuse me?)

4. Atonement with power: The hero discovers and confronts the true source of power that controls the hero and the journey. By grappling with this power, the hero takes full responsibility for the journey. This stage ends when the hero defeats, reconciles with, or gains the support of the power. The hero and the power reach a state of atonement, or balance, between them. (This stage is sometimes called "Atonement with the father," but it doesn't mean a literal father; just the father as a *symbol* of power.)

5. Apotheosis: The hero ascends to a god-like state (which is what "apotheosis" means), achieving power through the deeds in the initiation phase. The hero may change in appearance through gaining new understandings and abilities. (Glowing is common.)

6. The ultimate boon: The hero achieves the goal of the journey and receives a boon or reward of some kind, thus resolving the most important tension of the story.

Return

The return phase of the story is all about what happens *after* the goal of the quest has been achieved.

1. Refusal of the return: Having achieved the goal, the hero faces the responsibility of bringing the reward back to the ordinary world. But the hero does not *want* to go back to the life they led before. They want to stay in the excitement of the adventure.

2. Magic flight: The hero decides to return home with the boon. Pursuit is sometimes involved (generally by whoever had the boon before the hero got it) to keep up the excitement.

3. Rescue from without: The hero is rescued from pursuit by an unexpected helper. The

hero may need help with their return because they have been weakened by the quest; or the journey back may be long and difficult. In any case, the hero's ego, which had been inflated by success, is corrected by their realization that even a returning hero needs help.

4. The crossing of the return threshold: The hero returns to the ordinary world and attempts to integrate the exciting journey with the banalities of daily life. This may be even more difficult than crossing the first threshold, since the hero must find meaning in ordinary life that they never needed to find before. This is the hero's final challenge.

5. Master of the two worlds: Having overcome the final challenge of reintegration into ordinary life, the hero can claim mastery of both ordinary and quest worlds, able to exist in both and move freely between them.

6. Freedom to live: Having faced the ultimate challenge and succeeded, the hero becomes free of the fear of death, thus free to live without fear and enjoy every moment for what it brings. The hero may become a teacher or leader. They may not be judged fairly by others in the ordinary world, and they may not stay there, but they have the freedom to choose where and how they will live because of what they have achieved.

Heady stuff, huh? This is a complex story template. I would only use it in a long session with highly motivated participants. Still, it could help people think deeply about change in a community or organization.

Campbell's original structure has since been modified by several authors into simpler models with eight or twelve stages, but I find that the simpler versions leave out some of the most interesting aspects of the original scheme. You can find out more about Campbell's "monomyth" (as he called it) in his book *The Hero with a Thousand Faces*. If you look around on the internet you can find this structure (and the simpler ones) applied to explain many popular movies (including *Star Wars*, which George Lucas edited based on Campbell's book). Another benefit of using this template, though it is complex, is that a lot of people know about it, and some will be excited to have the chance to use it.

Labov's and Waletzky's model of conversational story structure

You might recognize this one; it's from the "How do stories work?" chapter of this book (page 35). There I called it the "iceberg" model of conversational story. It's just as good a story template as any, and it's a nice simple one. (See Figure 4.2 on page 38 for a reminder.)

The three parts of the story "above water" are pretty much exactly the same as those in any of the simple three-part story structures you've read about so far.

1. Orientation: The setting is introduced.
2. Complication: Things get complicated.
3. Resolution: Things get resolved.

You can use this as a very basic story structure for this exercise, especially in cases where you think people will be reluctant to do anything more complicated.

As a second step or combined with the basic three-part structure, you can ask groups to deliberately plan out *conversational* elements of their stories that will aid in the oral delivery of the story. Ask people to add these things:

1. An *abstract:* Before the story starts, the storyteller gives the audience a quick up-front idea of what the story will be about.
2. One or more *evaluation* statements: During the story, the storyteller reassures the audience that the story is worth listening to.
3. A *coda:* At the end of the story, the storyteller explains why the story mattered in the context of the sensemaking session.

As with the three parts of the story above the water line, these conversational elements should be inspired by stories from the collection. If not inspired by an actual plot, they can be inspired by a phrase, an image, a metaphor, or any other allusive element. For example, if a group is building a story about civic duty, for their evaluation they might find a phrase that rings true in a collected story—say it's some-thing like, 'If I want to get what I want from this town, I'd better do my part."

Algis Budrys' seven point plot structure

Algis Budrys was a science-fiction author and critic. He came up with a simple plot structure that is easy to fill in, thus.

1. A character
2. in a context
3. has a problem
4. and tries to solve it
5. and fails—and tries and fails some more, in bigger and bigger ways
6. and finally succeeds or finally fails, in the biggest way of all
7. and the story is over.

I've actually simplified this a bit; Budrys calls step six "victory or death" and step seven "affirmation." But I like the simple nature of the first few parts, so it seems useful to extend those throughout. What I like about this structure is its simplicity: no fancy words, no goddesses, just the bare bones of people facing challenges. It may be too simple for some groups in some settings, but for people you think would be daunted by some of the more fancy-sounding schemes, this might be the right fit.

You can find out more about this structure in Budrys' 2010 book *Writing to the Point.*

Tzvetan Todorov's narrative theory

Todorov is a philosopher who developed his "theory" of narrative form through analyzing the structures of classic fables, primarily those in Boccaccio's *Décaméron.* As seen by Todorov, stories have more of a circular than a linear structure. Central to his view is the concept of equilibrium or balance, which is disrupted and restored in every story.

Todorov puts forth five stages to a story, thus.

1. State of equilibrium: Everything in the world of the story's protagonist is as it has always been.
2. Disruption of the equilibrium: Some event or action throws everything off balance.

3. Recognition that the disruption has occurred: The story's protagonist becomes aware of the disruption.

4. Attempt(s) to repair the damage: The protagonist makes one or more attempts to return things to a state of balance.

5. Restoration of a new equilibrium: Things return to a state of balance, though not always in a positive way; final failure can lead to an equilibrium of loss.

Within one story there can be one repetition of this departure from and return to equilibrium, or there can be more than one disruption. Multiple disruptions generally build to a climactic last restoration.

You can find out more about Todorov's theory by reading his 1969 paper, entitled "Structural Analysis of Narrative."

Phase models

All of the models described in the timelines exercise section (page 589) will also work as story templates. Models for timelines are models for stories, after all. *Any* phase-based model can work as a story template, or as the inspiration for building one. If you look back at those models now, you'll see that many of them bear some resemblance to these story templates.

Using story templates

Enough with all the story templates already! That's what you're saying, isn't it? I thought you would. But I *did* have a good reason for putting so many templates in front of you, and it isn't just my usual reason of being annoyingly thorough. I wanted you to *notice* a few things.

First, I hope you noticed the *fundamental similarity* in these story templates. Even though they were created by people from a variety of fields, in a variety of centuries, and for a variety of reasons, they never contradict each other. They just offer slightly different views on what makes up a story.

Second, I hope you noticed the interesting *variety of flavors* in these story templates. Maybe one seemed accessible to you, another was logically sound, and a third struck you as particularly engaging. That's why it's a good thing that there is no one canonical story structure I can hand down to you on tablets of stone. Diverse views of story form suit themselves to diverse contexts of use.

So why does it matter that these story templates are the same and yet different? What does it mean to *you?* It means that you have the freedom to use whichever of these templates you like, or to tweak one of these templates, or to find another not on this list, or to blend two or more of these, or to make up your own entirely new story template. As long as what you use substantially agrees with what I've listed here, it will work to help people build stories.

As you think about what story template you would like to use for the composite stories exercise, think first about the educational backgrounds and experiences of your participants. Choose a template that's simple enough for them to understand yet complicated enough to be interesting and challenging to them.

Think about *your* readiness to use the template as well. If you have chosen a template but don't feel ready to explain it, learn more about story form in general. Read more folk tales, then come back to the template you've chosen and think through it again. You need to understand the template very well, because you need to be able to explain it to other people. So if there is a template you think looks interesting, but you can't quite get it into memory—the words seem strange or the order seems wrong—choose another one, or change it. Make sure you can draw or recite the template from memory before you use it in a sensemaking session.

Remember to test any story template you want to use by running through the exercise with real people considering real stories. Ask people lots of questions about the template as they work, and be prepared to make small changes as the experiment proceeds.

Appendix B

Further Reading: Your PNI Bookshelf

To choose the set of books annotated here, I asked myself a question: if one of my readers decided to provide themselves with a PNI support library, within a reasonable budget, what would they need in that library to improve their PNI skills and projects?

I considered the topics of the books, removing any potential contributors that cover only partially the information you need. If two good books covered the same area, I chose only the one I think you will get the most out of. I culled autobiographical book selections, including only books that I think will have utility to *you*, regardless of how much *I* like them. I considered clarity, removing some books otherwise useful but overly encumbered with academic jargon. And I considered cost, removing some books that pertained but could not justify a high cost when another option was just as good and more cheaply obtained.

In summary, I recommend these books to further your studies in participatory narrative inquiry.

Story Fundamentals

Narrative: A Critical Linguistic Introduction

Toolan, M. 1988. *Narrative: A Critical Linguistic Introduction*. London: Routledge.

Author: Michael Toolan, academic narratologist. Audience: college students, mostly. Style: academic, though more approachable than many such works. Length: 272 pages. Price: expensive new ($45) but perfectly comfortable used (as little as $2).

Why you might want to read it: I used to recommend Mieke Bal's *Narratology* textbook, but (with all due respect to Bal) Toolan's work covers the same territory while being both more comprehensive and more readable to the layman. Toolan's work is like a *Gray's Anatomy* of stories, illuminating in painstaking detail the internal structures of narrative and how they join together. All relevant ideas on story form are covered, going back thousands of years. Surprisingly in a narratology textbook, a section on stories in society includes some elements of story phenomenon such as story in conversation (though not in as much detail as in books dedicated to that topic). Story in cognitive *function* is not much considered here, but the deficiency can be remedied by reading some function-oriented works in addition. Overall, however, this is an excellent reference work for those looking to understand more about narrative form.

An example quote:

> In at least implicitly seeking and being granted rights to a lengthy verbal contribution, narrators assert their authority to tell, to take up the role of knower, or entertainer, or producer.... Any narrator then is ordinarily granted, as a rebuttable presumption, a level of trust and authority which is also a granting or asserting of power. But this trust, power and authority can be exploited or abused....

Story: Substance, Structure, Style and the Principles of Screenwriting

McKee, R. 1997. *Story: Substance, Structure, Style and the Principles of Screenwriting*. New York: HarperCollins.

Author: Robert McKee, screenwriting guru. Audience: aspiring screenwriters. Style: clear; authoritative; confident, perhaps a little too confident, yet useful enough to overcome this. Length: 480 pages. Price: $22 (also available in audio format for the same price), $16 used.

Why you might want to read it: If Toolan's narratology textbook is the *Gray's Anatomy* of stories,

McKee's *Story* is *The Way Things Work*. *Story* takes stories apart and tells you how to put them back together again in ways that convey powerful, memorable messages. Much of what is in *Story* is intuitively obvious, but only *after* you have read it. Some have criticized McKee for repackaging what Aristotle said about story form, but he admits this; and even if he does repackage the obvious, it works. It's impossible to deny the utility of this book to anyone who wants to understand how stories work.

An example quote:

> "Event" means *change*. If the streets outside your window are dry, but after a nap you see they're wet, you assume an event has taken place, called rain. The world's changed from dry to wet. You cannot, however, build a film out of nothing but changes in weather—although there are those who have tried. *Story Events* are meaningful, not trivial. To make change meaningful it must, to begin with, happen to a character. If you see someone drenched in a downpour, this has somewhat more meaning than a damp street....

Tell Me a Story: Narrative and Intelligence

Schank, R. 1995. *Tell Me a Story: Narrative and Intelligence*. Evanston, Illinois: Northwestern University Press.

Author: Roger Schank, cognitive scientist. Audience: general public. Style: clear; authoritative yet accessible. Length: 254 pages. Price: $18 new, $12 used.

Why you might want to read it: This is a wide-ranging introduction to stories from the consistent point of view of cognitive function. If this were the only book you ever planned to read about stories I would *not* recommend it, because the cognitive-science slant is strong and limiting. But if you read it along with books that consider story as form and phenomenon, Schank's book has much to tell you about the way people think about stories.

An example quote:

> When people learn to speak, they learn what each word means because they have heard the stories connected to these words first. Children learn complex words because these words are used to describe situations that they have observed or taken part in. When children are told that they have been "inconsiderate," they have no idea what that word means. They only know what they have done. In order to learn that word, they must construct a story that describes their own actions to themselves. Then, when they hear the word again, they must compare the former story with the new story that is unfolding before them. So they learn the skeleton story that underlies the word "inconsiderate" by comparing the two versions.... The understanding process, however, involves constantly misunderstanding one another to the extent that the words we use refer to skeleton stories that we don't quite agree upon. Consequently, my version of "inconsiderate" is probably different from yours.

Sources of Power: How People Make Decisions

Klein, G. 1999. *Sources of Power: How People Make Decisions*. Cambridge, Massachusetts: MIT Press.

Author: Gary Klein, decision making expert. Audience: general public. Style: friendly; persuasive; anecdotal. Length: 348 pages. Price: $18 new, somewhat less used.

Why you might want to read it: This book is not actually about stories; it is about how people make decisions. Gary Klein started a field of inquiry called *naturalistic decision making*, which examines how people make decisions in real life, as opposed to how they *ought* to make decisions, or how they make them in artificial laboratory conditions. In his research, Klein set out to find out how people in time-critical situations, such as firefighters in burning buildings, decide what to do next. He thought he would find out that expert decision makers draw up lists of options and compare them, as previous decision-making theory said they ought. But he found, to his surprise, that the most experienced experts essentially told themselves stories about previous experiences.

What got me excited about this book when I first read it was that Klein didn't go looking for stories: they came looking for him. While Schank's book starts with stories and looks for manifestations and applications, Klein's book comes from the opposite direction. Taken together, the two books give you a pretty good idea of how stories help us think.

An example quote:

> Before we did this study, we believed that novices impulsively jumped at the first option they could think of, whereas experts carefully deliberated about the merits of different courses of action. Now it seemed that it was the experts who could generate a single course of action, while novices needed to compare different approaches.

Story, Performance, and Event

Bauman, R. 1986. *Story, Performance, and Event: Contextual Studies of Oral Narrative.* Cambridge, Massachusetts: Cambridge University Press.

Author: Richard Bauman, folklorist. Audience: folklorists. Style: academic, but with many examples taken from the field that provide illumination. Length: 144 pages. Price: $36 new, far less used.

Why you might want to read it: Unlike the narratologists and screenwriters and cognitive scientists cited above, in this little book Bauman explores stories as embodied contextual aspects of "deeply situated human behavior." Through the careful examination of several long, complex, and fascinating examples of situated story exchange, Bauman explores the lives of stories in human society. He dives deep into the paradoxical ambiguities of story exchange; he speaks of truth, lies, and expectation; he destroys any possible conception of stories as "disembodied superorganic stuff" by showing them living and breathing. There is a joy in the complexity of situated storytelling here that infects you with an eagerness to hear and work with

stories yourself. This is not a reference work about story as phenomenon; it is more like an exercise in listening to stories and making sense of the way they move around in people.

An example quote:

> When we juxtapose the personal narrative and the tall tale, actually two dimensions of "lying" become apparent. First, the unusual but not impossible events of the former are transformed into the exaggeratedly implausible events of the latter. Thus tall tales are lies, insofar as what they report as having happened either did not happen or could not have happened. There is more, though. The tall tale presented above is told in the third person, which distances it somewhat from the narrator, and contrasts with the characteristic use of the first-person voice in the personal narrative.

Memory, Identity, Community: The Idea of Narrative in the Human Sciences

Hinchman, L. P. and Hinchman, S. K. (Eds.) 1997. *Memory, Identity, Community: The Idea of Narrative in the Human Sciences.* Albany, New York: State University of New York Press.

Editors: Lewis and Sandra Hinchman, Professors of Government. Authors: academics from a wide range of fields from political science to social science to psychology to philosophy to law. Audience: academics of all kinds. Style: varied, but mostly academic and complex. Length: 328 pages. Price: $32 new, as little as $6 used.

Why you might want to read it: This edited volume contains fifteen thought-provoking essays and papers about stories in use. Of all the books on my shelves, this one wins the sticky-note prize, with over fifty passages marked as particularly noteworthy. Here you will find Stephen Crites' seminal work "The Narrative Quality of Experience," W. Lance Bennett's exploration of storytelling in criminal trials, and chapters by Alasdair MacIntyre and Walter Fisher that summarize the major points of their important longer works.

I think one of the reasons this book is so valuable to the person studying stories is that none of the authors represented in this book study only stories. Each comes at narrative from a different oblique perspective.

An example quote (from David Carr's chapter "Narrative and the Real World: An Argument for Continuity"):

> ...I am the subject of a life-story which is constantly being told and retold in the process of being lived. I am also the principal teller of this tale, and belong as well to the audience to which it is told. The ethical-practical problem of self-identity and self-coherence may be seen as the problem of unifying these three roles.

An example quote (from Edward Bruner's chapter "Ethnography as Narrative"):

> Narrative structures organize and give meaning to experience, but there are always feelings and lived experiences not fully encompassed by the dominant story. Only after the new narrative becomes dominant is there a reexamination of the past, a rediscovery of old texts, and a recreation of the new heroes of liberation and resistance. The new story articulates what had been only dimly perceived, authenticates previous feelings, legitimizes new actions, and aligns individual consciousness with a larger social movement.

An example quote (from Walter Fisher's chapter "Narration, Reason, and Community"):

> The point I would stress is that embedded in some local narratives are narratives with potential universal application. For instance, in the example MacIntyre cites of protesters arguing past one another, they also participate in a story about how dispute in a democratic society should be conducted. The basic plot line of this story is respect for the dignity and worth of all people. Acting in accord with this story would transform the dispute into dialogue. And, it should be noted, this story, regarding the dignity and worth of all people, like other meta-narratives, began as a local narrative.

Conversational Narrative: Storytelling in Everyday Talk

Norrick, N. 2000. *Conversational Narrative: Storytelling in Everyday Talk*. Amsterdam: John Benjamins Publishing Company.

Author: Neal Norrick, linguist. Audience: the book says it "aims to advance narrative theory" so I think the audience is mainly academic. Style: authoritative yet personable, and absolutely full of examples. Length: 245 pages. Price: $50 new and not all that much less used.

Why you might want to read it: This is the most expensive book in this list, but it is the best work I've found on stories as they are actually told, retold, and negotiated in conversation. (If the cost is prohibitive, Toolan's book covers the same territory in less fine detail; so you could do without this book if you choose that one.) Norrick pulls together all of the relevant research in the area and adds in his own extensive (and fascinating) research. The detailed examples provide plentiful insights into the way people tell stories. They also make you want to go out and record some conversations yourself so you can start looking deeply into them like Norrick does.

An example quote:

> Further, tellability is tangled up with the notion of telling rights.... After all, a potential teller must assure listeners not only that a story counts as tellable, but also that she or he is the proper one to tell it. Telling rights depend in large part on knowledge of the events related. ... A narrator with first-hand experience of an event will generally have a better claim to storytelling rights regarding the event than another participant who learned about the event only from the accounts of others. ... Storytelling rights depend on many contextual factors beside the matter of who has knowledge of the events reported.

WORKING WITH STORIES IN GROUPS

The Oral History Reader

Perks, R., Thomson, A. (Eds.) 1998. *The Oral History Reader*. London: Routledge.

Editors: Robert Perks and Alistair Thomson, oral historians. Authors: lots of oral historians. Audience: students and oral history practitioners. Style: thorough; dense; careful but readable. Length: 496 pages. Price: no longer available new, but many used copies available for as little as $6.

Why you might want to read it: Several well-respected textbooks on oral history exist, but this anthology of important writings (past and present) gives the most "bang for the buck" in terms of bringing together many voices on the topic. I said above that *Memory, Identity, Community* won the sticky-note prize on my bookshelf, but when I counted the notes in this volume, the total came out nearly identical.

There are a few important balances covered in this book. First, approaches are included from around the world, not just from one dominant culture. Second, theoretical concept and practical advice are counterposed. Third, a balance is struck between oral history as historical documentation, as participatory sensemaking, and as political movement.

The most important thing I think you will get from this book (and possibly more than from any other in this list) is *what it's like* to collect stories from people for a reason.

An example quote (from Alessandro Portelli's chapter "What makes oral history different"):

> The importance of oral testimony may lie not in its adherence to fact, but rather in its departure from it, as imagination, symbolism, and desire emerge. Therefore, there are no 'false' oral sources. Once we have checked their factual credibility ... the diversity of oral history consists in the fact that 'wrong' statements are still psychologically 'true' and that this truth may be equally as important as factually reliable accounts.

An example quote (from Hugo Slim's and Paul Thompson's chapter "Ways of listening"):

> ... the interview form has a tendency to put unnatural pressure on people to find ready answers, to be concise and to summarise a variety of complex experiences and intricate knowledge. It may also mean that researchers and interviewers unwittingly violate local communication norms relating to turn-taking, the order of topics for discussion or various rituals attached to storytelling. In some societies, individual interviews are considered dangerously intimate encounters. In others, the recounting of group history can be a sacred ritual and certain people must be considered before others. Sometimes a number of clearly prescribed topics should be used to start proceedings, while other topics may be taboo, or should not be introduced until a particular level of intimacy and trust has been achieved.

An example quote (from Shaun Nethercott's and Neil Leighton's chapter "Out of the archives and onto the stage"):

> From these same voices we learned that the strike was not a monolith. It was hated and loved, endured and created, exciting and painful, foolish and wise. It was the strategic manoeuverings of the leaders, the manipulation and counter-manipulation of the press, the boredom of those who stayed in the plant, the endless drudgery of those who ran the strike kitchen and rounded up picket lines. It was young wives with little kids wondering how they were going to eat with no money coming in. It was blacks joining the union despite the protests of some whites. It was women using blackjacks and breaking windows, defying the police. It was unlooked-for victory, and crashing defeat. It was all those things and then some. It just depended on where you happened to be.

Narrative Therapy in Practice: The Archaeology of Hope

Monk, G. et al. 1997. (Eds.) *Narrative Therapy in Practice: The Archaeology of Hope*. San Francisco: Jossey-Bass.

Editors: Gerald Monk, John Winslade, Kathie Crocket and David Epston, all family and community therapists. Authors: generally more of the same. Audience: mainly family and community therapists looking for help adding narrative methods to their practices. Style: friendly; full of examples; practical. Length: 352 pages. Price: expensive new (over $50) but reasonable used ($20 to $30).

Why you might want to read it: In the introduction to *Narrative Therapy in Practice*, the editors describes its topic as "the narrative approach to therapy." This tells you that the book is centered not in narrative but in therapy (it could have said "the therapeutic use of narrative"). You may not be all that interested in becoming a therapist who uses narrative; but put that aside. This book has much to teach you, not about stories, but about dealing with *people telling stories*, and people not knowing they are allowed to tell stories, and people not wanting to tell stories, and people not knowing what their stories mean, and people wanting *you* to tell their stories for them. I am no therapist, but I found in this book several almost uncanny parallels with my own experiences in helping people tell their stories.

For example, the authors explore power relationships that develop in interview settings, where people attempt to perform for whatever authority they think the interviewer represents. They talk about the importance of careful wording of questions to control the messages contained therein (empowerment, not belittlement; hope, not helplessness). They talk about the paradoxical nature of participation: how it liberates but can be difficult to achieve in people long accustomed to being prodded for information. So while this book won't tell you all that much about stories *per se*, it will definitely help you improve your skills at helping people work with their own stories.

An example quote:

> Curiosity can be seen as one safeguard against the use of counselor expertise to steer the client in the direction that the counselor deems appropriate. ... Genuine curiosity opens space for the client and the counselor to observe what is taking place in greater breadth and depth. It is a specific kind of curiosity giving rise to questions that highlight new possibilities or directions for the client to consider. ... An attitude of curiosity allows the counselor to live with confusion and ambiguity and to avoid moving too quickly to a therapeutic fix. ... [In our therapist training] We have found that people need practice in being curious. Some people find this approach natural to them, whereas others feel initially very uncomfortable. We give participants in our workshops plenty of practice in being respectfully curious and persistent.

Narrative Methods for the Human Sciences

Kohler Reissman, C. 2007. *Narrative Methods for the Human Sciences*. Thousand Oaks, California: SAGE Publications.

Author: Catherine Kohler Reissman, sociologist. Audience: sociologists and college students. Style: very readable actually, probably because of the many detailed examples. Length: 264 pages. Price: $40 new, somewhat less used.

Why you might want to read it: As you may have noticed, I have an irrational bias when it comes to narrative inquiry. I own several books on the subject, but they are the abject losers in the sticky-note contest, not a single one of them well-marked, well-thumbed, or even thumbed. They are, however, the winners in the times-thrown-down-in-disgust contest. I hate it when narrative analysts call people "informants." I hate it when they consider themselves more competent to interpret people's stories than the people themselves. I hate it when storytellers are never given the chance to see or talk about or think about the stories they tell.

However, having said all that, it is impossible to deny the fact that narrative analysts have developed some very useful ways of looking at the stories people tell in great detail. There is no doubt that *including* these methods in a participatory practice can be enabling to everyone involved. So if you want to do participatory narrative inquiry, it will definitely help your practice to read a book on *extractive* narrative inquiry, even if you end up throwing it down a few times in the process.

I chose this particular book to represent the field of narrative analysis for a few reasons. First, the writing is perfectly readable for the non-academic. It is based on a lecture course, so it has been time-tested. Second, the quantity and variety of examples described, based on real research projects, is commendable. Very little in this book speaks in the abstract. In fact, you could say it's a book of stories about working with stories. Third, Kohler Reissman covers four ways of working with stories (thematic analysis, structural analysis, dialogic/performance analysis, and visual narrative analysis) that all lend themselves to useful inclusion in participatory work. Fourth, Kohler Reissman's tone is much less arch than some of the other books I've read on narrative analysis. Even though she does call people "informants" she does so with more respect than I find in some other places. If you take care to keep an open mind, you should find these methods useful in your own PNI work, as means of supporting collective sensemaking around stories and storytelling.

An example quote:

> Stories don't fall from the sky (or emerge from the innermost "self"); they are composed and received in contexts—interactional, historical, institutional, and discursive—to name a few. Stories are social artifacts, telling us as much about society and culture as they do about a person or group. How do these contexts enter into storytelling? How is a story coproduced in a complex choreography—in spaces between teller and listener, speaker and setting, text and reader, and history and culture? Dialogic/performance analysis attempts to deal with these questions.... As a kind of hybrid form, the approach pushes the boundaries of what is and is not included in narrative analysis.

Designing and Conducting Mixed Methods Research

Creswell, J. W. and Plano Clark, V. L. 2011. *Designing and Conducting Mixed Methods Research*. Thousand Oaks, California: SAGE Publications.

Authors: John W. Creswell and Vicki L. Plano Clark, researchers (and researchers of research). Audience: college students and research practitioners. Style: methodical; well-organized; practical; perhaps a bit dry, but enabling nonetheless. Length: 488 pages. Price: $40, slightly less used.

Why you might want to read it: If you do not plan on including narrative catalysis in your PNI practice, this book will probably be overly detailed for your needs, and you can just look up "mixed methods research" on the internet to get a quick idea of the topic. However, if you do want to add the depth catalysis brings to sensemaking, this book will help you understand why and how a mixture of qualitative and quantitative approaches gives catalysis its power to support sensemaking.

The highlight of the book is a typology of approaches to mixing qualitative and quantitative data in research designs, including a detailed example of a study of each type. I spent a long time trying to figure out where narrative catalysis fits in Creswell and Plano Clark's typology of mixed methods approaches, and I never arrived at a satisfactory answer. Sometimes I think it best fits the "convergent parallel" approach, where "the researcher uses concurrent timing to implement the quantitative and qualitative strands during the same phase of the research process, prioritizes the methods equally, and keeps the strands independent during analysis and then mixes the results during the overall interpretation." That sounds *almost* right, but it doesn't adequately represent the tacking-back-and-forth nature of the use of both "strands" of information during catalysis. The two strands are most definitely not kept "independent during analysis," but neither are they entirely intermingled either.

Another intriguing possibility is the "embedded" research design, in which one strand dominates the research, obviously in this case the qualitative strand, being the stories themselves. You could argue that the stories in any PNI project dominate questions asked about them and patterns in the answers to those questions.

However, the "transformative" design is also appealing: there the way in which qualitative and quantitative data come together are not determined by a simple rule of mixing but by the role of a "theoretical perspective" that "shapes" the approach. I take this statement to mean that the researcher combines the two strands in whatever way best fits the goals and principles of the research. So a transformative design may be the best categorization of narrative catalysis. It blends qualitative and quantitative data in a way that best supports the creation of thought-provoking materials to support sensemaking.

That's a pigeonhole I can live in; but if you want to explore this topic, why not read the book and see what sort of mixing *you* want to include in your projects?

An example quote:

> One might argue that quantitative research is weak in understanding the context or setting in which people talk. Also, the voices of participants are not directly heard in quantitative research. Further, quantitative researchers are in the background, and their own personal biases and interpretation are seldom discussed. Qualitative research makes up for these weaknesses. On the other hand, qualitative research is seen as deficient because of the personal interpretations made by the researcher, the ensuing bias created by this, and the difficulty in generalizing findings to a large group because of the limited number of persons studied. Quantitative research, it is argued, does not have these weaknesses. Thus, the combination of strengths of one approach makes up for the weaknesses of the other approach.

The Applied Theatre Reader

Prentki, T. and Preston, S. (Eds.). 2008. *The Applied Theatre Reader*. London: Routledge.

Editors: Tim Prentki and Sheila Preston, experts in "theatre for development." Authors: artists, dramatists, teachers, activists, and researchers. Audience: primarily practitioners of applied theatre in community settings. Style: varied, from theoretical to practical to personal. Length: 400 pages. Price: $40 new, half that used.

Why you might want to read it: Books that call themselves "readers" are supposed to bring together everything the editors think people need to read on a topic. This book does the job well. It includes portions of must-read works such as those by Augusto Boal (from "Theatre of the Oppressed") and Paulo Friere (from "Pedagogy of the Oppressed"). It provides a broad overview of the theory and practice of applied theatre today, covering examples of projects in locations from health clinics to prisons to war zones. And the book addresses some of the thorniest issues in applied theatre, those of power and voice. For example, a chapter by Ananda Breed declares, "Participation may be used for liberation, but can also become a tool for imprisonment and persecution." Food for thought!

You may or may not be interested in pursuing theatrical means in your story work to the extent that some of the authors in this book have. I can imagine that some of my readers might consider this book a little too far "out there" for their own story practice, especially if they come from a more scientific field such as qualitative research or narrative inquiry. But don't let the puppets and masks put you off! All participatory work must address the same issues, whether the work entails high drama or quiet conversation. You will find much to support your story work here.

An example quote (from Adrian Jacksons's chapter "Provoking intervention"):

> The theatre must provoke, if the target is truly to move people beyond the normative conventions which keep the spectator passive, the citizen obedient. Of course if you simply provoke, you run the risk of meaningless outrage—the ques-

tion is what you do with that provocation and the resulting release of energy. You also have to seduce, by the power of the narrative and the quality of the theatrical experience. Seduction and provocation in equal measure.

An example quote (from bell hooks' chapter "Choosing the margin as a space of radical openness"):

Often this speech about the "Other" annihilates, erases: "No need to hear your voice when I can talk about you better than you can speak about yourself. No need to hear your voice. Only tell me about your pain. I want to know your story. And then I will tell it back to you in a new way. Tell it back to you in such a way that it has become mine, my own. Re-writing you, I write myself anew. I am still author, authority."

An example quote (from Sarah Thornton's chapter "The complexity and challenge of participation"):

In terms of local participation, the first, key challenge was overcoming the barriers of scepticism and entrenched suspicion. Having lived through a myriad of unsuccessful short-term interventions, having explained their stories to a host of professional consultants and been offered empty promises, having built relationships with agency representatives only to have staff change and find themselves back at square one, local people were unsurprisingly wary of taking the time and trouble to expose themselves again. ... In the face of justifiable scepticism there was little to do but accept it, respect it, and maintain contact with those who articulated these feelings in the hope that over time (but probably not during the lifetime of this project) [we] could earn people's trust.

Do It Yourself Social Research

Wadsworth, Y. 2011. *Do It Yourself Social Research (Third Edition)*. Sydney, Australia: Allen & Unwin.

Author: Yoland Wadsworth, action researcher and consultant. Audience: pretty much everybody. Style: *extremely* accessible and clear. Length: 224 pages. Price: $25 new, $20 or less used.

Why you might want to read it: If you have never done a "research project" in your life, Wadsworth's book will ease your path. Every step of a participatory action research project is laid out with perfect clarity, using everyday words, concrete examples, and witty cartoons. If most of the other books in this list have left you feeling overwhelmed, this book will not. If *my* book overwhelms you, take *Do It Yourself Social Research* with you into a quiet corner, then come back and see if what I have written makes more sense to you.

If you have much experience conducting research, maybe *too* much, this book will serve not as a guide but as a reminder: of what participation means; of what people need to know about research so they can participate as co-researchers; of what you may not be telling people that they need to know; of the kinds of jargon and assumptions you might be using (perhaps without knowing it) that create barriers to participation; of how to demolish those barriers so everyone in your project can work together. If you feel you don't need to be told how to do research "yourself," read this book anyway. It will help you share "your" research with everyone involved and avoid hoarding knowledge or plans or goals.

An example quote:

Most often the researchers or commissioners of research tend to 'study down' (the anthropologist Laura Nader's term, 1972)—that is, more powerful people or researchers on behalf of more powerful people go and study less powerful people (typically the recipients of professional human services). In most cases the effect (even if unintended) is to suppress or distort the voices of the less empowered and results in decisions being made for and about those people on imperfect input. ... For these purposes you will need to attend carefully to how to convert 'studying down' to self-study, or studying 'across' and even 'up'. You may even need a research design which carefully gives a separate voice to parties with different values, interests, degrees of power so they can be heard and responded to, and so on.

Participatory Workshops: A Sourcebook of 21 Sets of Ideas & Activities

Chambers, R. 2002. *Participatory Workshops: A Sourcebook of 21 Sets of Ideas & Activities.* London: Earthscan.

Author: Robert Chambers, development practitioner and scholar. Audience: anyone who wants to work with people in participatory groups. Style: disarming; funny; spare; enticing. Length: 224 pages. Price: $18 new, $15 used.

Why you might want to read it: In terms of experience helping people in groups do things together, Robert Chambers is a giant. His book doesn't try to tell you everything he knows about facilitating participatory groups, which is even better proof that he knows what he is doing. Instead, *Participatory Workshops* pokes and prods you into thinking for yourself with twenty-one lists of twenty-one items: questions, ideas, activities, mistakes. The tone throughout the book is provocative, witty, insightful, and motivating. But don't let the jokes fool you: there is much anyone can learn from this book. It is not the kind of book you sit down and read once; it is the kind you keep coming back to over and over, because each time you come back (after more experience working with groups) it will teach you new things. Like a multifaceted jewel, it reflects the light differently each time you look at it.

An example quote:

> In the workshop process itself, sometimes things being wrong or going wrong makes the best things happen. You are forced to improvise. Instead of showing slides, you demonstrate on the floor. Instead of making a presentation, you facilitate something more participatory. Disasters and difficulties are anyway for enjoying. The scope they offer for learning is generous. Treasure them. The worse they are, the better stories they will be for later.

GROUNDING YOUR UNDERSTANDINGS IN STORIES

To complete your PNI bookshelf, I suggest you add two more books: one of folk tales from a culture you know well, and one of folk tales from a culture you do *not* know well. By "from a culture you know well" I mean that includes at least a few stories you already knew from childhood. Avoid collections created around a theme, and try to find collections gathered from real people. Looking at my own bookshelf, some examples of "other culture" collections I have read are Russian, Slovak, Dutch, Irish, Indian, Pakistani, Arab, Egyptian, West African, Yoruba, Japanese, Chinese, Tibetan, Hmong, Australian, Italian, Israeli, Jewish, Greek, Native North American, Native Latin American, Chilean. Books I consider to be "from my own culture" are "American" (Johnny Appleseed, Davy Crockett, Brer Rabbit, and the like), and European (Grimm and Andersen). I'm not saying you should read *this* many books of folk tales, but the more you read the better you will understand stories. You can read all you like about theory, but folk tales are the horse's mouth.

If you were to buy all sixteen of the books I recommend here (choosing at random two books of folk tales), the total cost (at the time of writing) would come to about $480 if you select only new titles, or about $260 if you are willing to buy used books. I think, if you go the used-book route, this is a pretty reasonable budget to set yourself up with the materials you need to learn more about working with stories. And of course library books are free if you have access to them. The most valuable materials can't be found in books—they are your time and the help of others—but still, I hope this book list will be of use to you.

If you want to go even further than these sixteen books, take a look at the Bibliography appendix. If I found a book useful enough to reference it or quote from it, I must think it's worth reading. So you can consider the bibliography an expanded list for further reading.

Appendix C

Bibliography

Adams, K. 2007. *How to Improvise a Full-Length Play: The Art of Spontaneous Theater.* Allworth Press.

Alexander, C. 1977. *A Pattern Language: Towns, Buildings, Construction.* Oxford: Oxford University Press.

Amabile, T. 2011. *The Progress Principle: Using Small Wins to Ignite Joy, Engagement, and Creativity at Work.* Boston, Massachusetts: Harvard Business Review Press.

Anonymous. University of Minnesota discovery gives insight into brain 'replay' process. *EurekAlert!* March 11, 2010. Accessed online February 2014 at eurekalert.org/pub_releases/2010-03/uom-udg031110.php. (Refers to original article: Anoopum S. Gupta, Matthijs A.A. van der Meer, David S. Touretzky, A. David Redish. Hippocampal Replay Is Not a Simple Function of Experience. Neuron, 2010; 65 (5): 695.)

Bakhtin, M. M. 1981. *The Dialogic Imagination: Four Essays.* Ed. Michael Holquist. Trans. Caryl Emerson and Michael Holquist. Austin and London: University of Texas Press. (Originally written, in Russian, in the 1930s.)

Bal, M. 1992. *Narratology: Introduction to the Theory of Narrative.* Toronto: University of Toronto Press.

Baldwin, C. 2005. *Storycatcher: Making Sense of Our Lives through the Power and Practice of Story.* Novato, California: New World Library.

Baldwin, C. and Linnea, A. 2010. *The Circle Way: A Leader in Every Chair.* San Francisco: Berrett-Koehler Publishers, Inc.

Barger, J. 1993. *Was: Barger@ILS (memoirs of an a.i. hacker).* Essay originally posted to comp.ai newsgroup in January 1993; accessed February 2014 at archive.is/svrn. (If that link is not available, try searching on the essay's title; the essay is on the web in other places.)

Bartle, R. 1996. *Hearts, Clubs, Diamonds, Spades: Players who Suit MUDs.* Online essay, accessed February 2014 at mud.co.uk/richard/hcds.htm.

Bauman, R. 1986. *Story, Performance and Event.* Cambridge: Cambridge University Press.

Bear, S. and Wind, W. 1992. *The Medicine Wheel: Earth Astrology* (25th Anniversary Edition). New York: Fireside.

Bear, S., Wind, W. Mulligan, C. 1991. *Dancing with the Wheel: The Medicine Wheel Workbook.* New York: Fireside.

Belbin, M. 1993. *Team Roles at Work* (Second edition). Oxford: Elsevier.

Bennett, L. 1997. Storytelling in Criminal Trials. In *Memory, Identity, Community: The Idea of Narrative in the Human Sciences*, eds. L.P Hinchman and S.K. Hinchman. Albany, New York: State University of New York Press.

Boal, A. 1979. *Theatre of the Oppressed.* New York: Theatre Communications Group. (English translation; originally published in Spanish as *Teatro de Oprimido* in 1974.)

Boal, A. 2002. *Games for Actors and Non-Actors* (Second edition, Jackson, A. translator). London: Routledge.

Boal, A. 2006. *The Aesthetics of the Oppressed.* (Translation by Adrian Jackson.) London: Routledge.

Boje, D.M. 1991. The Storytelling Organization: A Study of Story Performance in an Office-Supply Firm. *Administrative Science Quarterly* 36: 106-126.

Boisot, M. H. 1999. *Knowledge Assets: Securing Competitive Advantage in the Information Economy.* Oxford: Oxford University Press.

Boyce, M. 1995a. Collective centering and collective sense-making in the stories and storytelling of one organization. *Organization Studies* 16(1): 107–137.

Boyd, B. 2009. *On the Origin of Stories: Evolution, Cognition, and Fiction.* Cambridge, Massachusetts: Belknap Press of Harvard University Press.

Brice Heath, S. 1983. *Ways With Words: Language, Life, and Work in Communities and Classrooms.* Cambridge: Cambridge University Press.

Brice Heath, S. 2012. *Words at Work and Play: Three Decades in Family and Community Life*. Cambridge: Cambridge University Press.

Budrys, A. 2010. *Writing to the Point: A Complete Guide to Selling Fiction*. Action Publishing LLC.

Caddell, J. 2013. *The Mistake Bank: How To Succeed By Forgiving Your Mistakes And Embracing Your Failures*. Caddell Insight Group.

Caddell, J. 2014. Forget Big Data. Use Little Data for Incremental Improvement. 99U, online journal. Accessed March 2014 at 99u.com/articles/23147/a-fitbit-for-work-using-little-data-to-make-yourself-better.

Campbell, J. 2008. *The Hero with a Thousand Faces* (Third Edition). Novato, California: New World Library.

Carse, J.P. 1997. *Finite and Infinite Games*. New York: Ballantine Books.

Chambers, R. 2002. *Participatory Workshops: A Sourcebook of 21 Sets of Ideas and Activities*. New York: Earthscan.

Cialdini, R. B. 1984. *Influence: The Psychology of Persuasion*. New York: William Morrow and Company.

Cohen, C. 2004. *The Seuss, The Whole Seuss and Nothing But the Seuss: A Visual Biography of Theodor Seuss Geisel*. New York: Random House.

Crites, S. 1997. The Narrative Quality of Experience. In *Memory, Identity, Community: The Idea of Narrative in the Human Sciences*, eds. L.P Hinchman and S.K. Hinchman. Albany, New York: State University of New York Press.

Cross, N. and Barker, R. 1998. The Sahel Oral History Project. In *The Oral History Reader*. Perks, R. and Thomson, A., eds. pp. 246–257. New York: Routledge.

Deitz, K. and Silverman, L.L. 2013. *Business Storytelling for Dummies*. Hoboken, New Jersey: John Wiley and Sons.

Denton, A. 2008. *Enough Rope* (Television show with Australia's ABC1 network). Accessed February 2014 at abc.net.au/tv/enoughrope/transcripts/s2338596.htm.

Dervin, B. et. al. (Eds.) 2003. *Sense-Making Methodology Reader: Selected Writings of Brenda Dervin*. Hampton Press.

Field, S. 2005. *Screenplay: The Foundations of Screenwriting* (Revised edition). Delta.

Fisher, W. R. 1989. *Human Communication as Narration: Toward a Philosophy of Reason, Value, and Action*. Columbia: University of South Carolina Press.

Freire, P. 2000. *Pedagogy of the Oppressed* (30th Anniversary edition, translated by M.B. Ramos). London: Bloomsbury Academic.

Freytag, G. 1895. *Freytag's Technique of the Drama: An Exposition of Dramatic Composition and Art*. Authorized translation from the sixth German edition by MacEwan, E. J. Chicago: S. C. Griggs and Company.

Gabriel, Y. 1995. The Unmanaged Organization: Stories, Fantasies, and Subjectivity. *Organization Studies* 16(3): 477-501.

Gabriel, Y. 2000. *Storytelling in Organizations: Facts, Fictions and Fantasies*. Oxford: Oxford University Press.

Gargiulo, T. L. 2005. *The Strategic Use of Stories in Organizational Communication and Learning*. Armonk, New York: M. E. Sharpe.

Graves, T. 2012. *SCAN: A Framework for Sensemaking and Decision-Making*. Published online through Leanpub; accessed Feburary 2014 at leanpub.com/tp-scan

Greenspun, P. 2007. Interview with Peter Menzel and Faith D'Aluisio. Photo.net, April 2007. Accessed February 2014 at photo.net/photographer-interviews/peter-menzel.

Inayatullah, S. (Ed.) 2004. *The Causal Layered Analysis (CLA) Reader: Theory and Case Studies of an Integrative and Transformative Methodology*. Tamkang University Press, Taipei. Available at metafuture.org.

Keidel, R.W. 1995. *Seeing Organizational Patterns*. San Francisco: Berrett-Koehler Publishers.

Klein, G. 1999. *Sources of Power: How People Make Decisions*. Cambridge, Massachusetts: MIT Press.

Kovacs, M. and Ellenbecker, T. 2011. An 8-Stage Model for Evaluating the Tennis Serve. *Sports Health* 3(6): 504–513.

Kurtz, C.F. 2009. *The Wisdom of Clouds*. Self-published white paper, accessed online February 2014 at cfkurtz.com/Kurtz%202009b%20Wisdom%20of%20Clouds.pdf.

Labov, W and Waletzky, J. Narrative Analysis: Oral Versons of Experience. 1967. In *Essays on the Verbal and Visual Arts: Proceedings of the 1966*

Annual Spring Meeting of the American Ethnological Society. June Helm, ed. pp. 12–44. Seattle: University ofWashington Press.

Lear, G. 2009. *Leadership Lessons From The Medicine Wheel: The Seven Elements of High Performance*. Advantage Media Group.

MacIntyre, A. 1984. *After Virtue: A Study in Moral Theory (Second Edition)*. Notre Dame, Indiana: University of Notre Dame Press.

MacIntyre, A. 1997. The Virtues, The Unity of a Human Life, and the Concept of a Tradition. In *Memory, Identity, Community: The Idea of Narrative in the Human Sciences*, eds. L.P Hinchman and S.K. Hinchman. Albany, New York: State University of New York Press.

Mandler, I. M. and Johnson, N. S. 1977. Remembrance of things parsed: story structure and recall. *Cognitive Psychology* 9:111–51.

Mandler, J. and Goodman, M. 1982. On the psychological validity of story structure. *Journal of Verbal Learning and Verbal Behavior*. 21: 507–523.

Martin, J., Feldman, M.S., Hatch, M.J., and Sitkin, S.B. 1983. The Uniqueness Paradox in Organizational Stories. *Administrative Science Quarterly* 28: 438-453.

Martin, J. and Powers, M. 1983. Truth or corporate propaganda: The value of a good war story. In Pondy, L., Frost, P., Morgan, G. and Dandridge, T. (Eds.) *Organizational Symbolism*. Greenwich, Connecticut: JAI Press.

Masinter, L. and Ostrom, E. 1993. Collaborative Information Retrieval: Gopher from MOO. *Proc. INET'93*. Accessed February 2014 at larry.masinter.net/MOOGopher.pdf.

McKee, R. 1997. *Story: Substance, Structure, Style, and the Principles of Screenwriting*. New York: HarperCollins.

Menzel, P. 1994. *Material World: A Global Family Portrait*. San Francisco: Sierra Club.

Monk, G. et al. 1997. (Eds.) *Narrative Therapy in Practice*. San Francisco: Jossey-Bass.

Moore, J. 2008. Sierra Leone's 'family talk' heals scars of war. *Christian Science Monitor*, July 7.

Morrissey, C.T. 1998. On Oral History Interviewing. In *The Oral History Reader*. Perks, R. and Thomson, A., eds. pp. 246–257. New York: Routledge.

Norrick, N. 2000. *Conversational Narrative: Storytelling in everyday talk*. Amsterdam/Philadelphia: John Benjamins Publishing Company.

Novitz, D. 1997. "Art, Narrative, and Human Nature." In *Memory, Identity, Community: The Idea of Narrative in the Human Sciences*, eds. L.P Hinchman and S.K. Hinchman. Albany, New York: State University of New York Press.

Okada, A., Buckingham Shum, S., and Sherborne, T. 2008. *Knowledge Cartography: Software Tools and Mapping Techniques*. London: Springer.

Olson, D. H. and Gorall, D. M. 2003. Circumplex model of marital and family systems. Pp. 514–547 in F. Walsh (Ed.), *Normal Family Processes* (3rd Ed). New York: Guilford.

Patow, C. A. 2005. Advancing Medical Education and Patient Safety through Simulation Learning. *Simulation Learning* March/April 2005. Accessed February 2014 at: psqh.com/marapr05/simulation.html.

Patterson, K., et al. 2008. *Influencer: The Power to Change Anything*. New York: McGraw-Hill.

Pogue, D. 2012. Behind the Dancing Matt Videos. *New York Times*, July 12, 2012.

Prentki, T. and Preston, S. (Eds.). 2008. *The Applied Theatre Reader*. London: Routledge.

Quinn, R.E. & Rohrbaugh, J. 1983. A spatial model of effectiveness criteria: Towards a competing values approach to organizational analysis. *Management Science* 29: 363–377.

Rokeach, M. 1973. *The Nature of Human Values*. New York: The Free Press.

Rosenberg, D. and Grafton, A. 2010. *Cartographies of Time: A History of the Timeline*. Princeton, New Jersey: Princeton University Press.

Schank, R. 1990. *Tell Me a Story: Narrative and Intelligence*. Evanston, Illinois: Northwestern University Press.

Shneiderman, B. 1996. "The Eyes Have It: A Task by Data Type Taxonomy for Information Visualizations." In *Proceedings of the IEEE Symposium on Visual Languages*, Sept 1996, pp. 336–343.

Silverman, L. 2006. *Wake Me Up When The Data Is Over: How Organizations Use Stories To Drive Results*. New York: Jossey-Bass.

Slim, H., et al. 1998. Ways of listening. In *The Oral History Reader*. Perks, R. and Thomson, A., eds. pp. 114–125. New York: Routledge.

Smith, K. A. 2012. Where the Hell is Matt? Everywhere. Smithsonian.com. Accessed February 2014 at smithsonianmag.com/travel/Where-the-Hell-Is-Matt-Everywhere--166023206.html.

Spolin, V. 1986. *Theater Games for the Classroom.* Evanston, Illinois: Northwestern University Press.

Stein, N. and Glenn, C. 1979. An analysis of story comprehension in elementary school children. In R. D. Freedle (Ed.), *Advances in discourse processes: Vol. 2. New directions in discourse processing* (pp. 53–119). Norwood, NJ: Albex.

Stern, J. 2003. *Terror in the Name of God: Why Religious Militants Kill.* New York: HarperCollins.

Sween, E. 1998. The one-minute question: What is narrative therapy? Some working answers. *Gecko: A journal of deconstruction and narrative ideas in therapeutic practice* 2: 3–6.

Symington, R. 2011. *Thomas Mann's The Magic Mountain: A Reader's Guide.* Newcastle upon Tyne: Cambridge Scholars Publishing.

Todorov, T. 1969. Structural Analysis of Narrative. *Novel: A Forum on Fiction* Fall 3(1): 70–76.

Tom, M. 2012. Q&A: Matt Harding on his unlikely career as a YouTube star. GeekWire. Accessed February 2014 at geekwire.com/2012/qa-matt-harding-adventures-traveling-youtube-sensation.

Underwood, P. 1993. *The Walking People.* California: The Tribe of Two Press.

Wadsworth, Y. 1984. *Do It Yourself Social Research.* Victorian Council of Social Service and the Melbourne Family Care Organization.

Waxler, J. 2007. *Learn to Write Your Memoir in 4 Weeks.* Neuralcoach Press.

Weick, K. E., Sutcliffe, K. M. and Obstfeld, D. 2005. Organizing and the Process of Sensemaking. *Organization Science* 16(4): 409–421.

White, M. 2007. *Maps of Narrative Practice.* New York: W. W. Norton & Company.

Wiggins, J. S. 2003. *Paradigms of Personality Assessment.* New York: Guilford Press.

Wilkins, A. L. 1983. Organizational stories as symbols that control the organization. Pp. 81–92 in Pondy, L., et al. (Eds.) *Organizational Symbolism.* Greenwich, Connecticut: JAI Press.

Appendix D

Acknowledgements and Biography

Ideas are like giant but kind whales that let us swim along with them, if we behave ourselves. This book is a portrait of an idea I have come to know and love. I have had the good luck to swim alongside "my" idea—I call it "my" idea not as a possession but as a relationship—in the company of many other people. I would like to thank them here.

Since what I've done is mixed in with how other people have helped me and my work grow, I might as well blend biography and acknowledgement together. That is the most honest way to tell the story.

I grew up loving animals and visual form, so I started my education determined to become an artist, a biologist, or both. I took biology in college with an art minor, but dropped out of art in the mistaken idea that I had no natural talent for it. (That was my mind at twenty; I know now that a taste for hard work is the only natural talent worth having.)

After college I spent five years in an ecology and evolution Ph.D. program studying ethology, or more specifically the evolution of social behavior in animals. My driving passion was to become a field biologist and spend my life wrapped up in nature.

After trying several ideas, I settled on a research project studying harbor seals, to investigate their poorly understood social dynamics and to help reduce the impact of fishing on seal populations. In the cold of winter I walked to my research site, a little wooden blind perched on a hill above a beach where a group of seals hauled out.

I planned to do this for years, but one day I slipped on a patch of ice and fell while carrying some heavy equipment, hurting my back badly enough to remove the possibility of strenuous physical work for years to come. It sounds strange to say it now, but at the time I felt like the ocean brushed me off like a gnat.

Over the next year I spent a lot of time lying in bed, staring at the ceiling, and sampling the modern pharmacopeia of painkillers in various states of confusion. It was then that I discovered chaos and complexity theory. I remember staying up all night two nights in a row reading James Gleick's *Chaos*, to which the drugs in my system added a wonderfully fractal quality. It was 1988 and as far as I knew, nobody had yet applied these ideas to the study of animal behavior. New research ideas jumped out of every chapter.

In the few hours I could work each day, I restarted my work using simulation. I wrote what I hoped would be the first simulation of many, was surprised by it, surprised my advisor by it, and attended a conference in Paris to present my ideas. I hoped for a new beginning. But the academic department I was in was not the right place at the right time to marry complexity with ethology, at least not on a computer. They rejected my plan, considering only field work or laboratory experimentation worthy of a degree. Field work was out of the question; for years I couldn't even pick up a glass of water with one hand. And I hated lab experimentation. I had already killed too many small animals in my first projects, before the seals, to ever want to do that again. So I quit school and took the consolation prize of a M.A. degree.

I remember the day I made the decision to leave science. I was sitting in Notre Dame cathedral in Paris watching a mass, having hobbled there like some old woman from my hotel. I wrote in my journal, "Aujourd'hui je suis un ecrivain." Which is probably awful French, but it was *meant* to mean: Today I am a writer.

I now think this was a horrible mistake. I should have done anything they asked to get that little slip of paper, because its absence has haunted me ever since. But it was *my* mistake; and I guard it fiercely.

We now find our heroine jettisoned from science yet unable to pick up a bag of groceries. Luckily I had caught the programming bug way back in high school (on punched cards no less) so I had a sideline going. I took a job working for a professor in my former department and helped him build software for environmental decision support.

Then I met my husband and married him. That part's none of your business. Anyway, he had this crazy idea to build and sell environmental simulation software that would help regular people learn more about nature. I said, why not? I'm footloose and fancy free, and it's a fitting revenge to tear down the walls of academic science. Let's help the world learn.

So we spent the next several years doing that. As it happened, Paul was a far better programmer than I was, so I apprenticed with him and earned my stars as a software designer. In 1998 we released three software packages: a garden simulator, a plant growth simulator, and an interactive story creator. (That last was his idea and creation; I only wrote him some stories to start it off. My discovery of the world of story work was yet to come.)

Our work on environmental education software was a great success in terms of helping people; I think at least a million copies of our garden simulator have made it onto computers worldwide. We have been proud of our contribution to international science literacy. We also discovered that we make an excellent work team, with such perfect complements in skill and natural talent that we seem made for each other intellectually and professionally as well as in life. We have since collaborated on several software projects, done for love or money or both, and have never been disappointed in our ability to do far more together than we can alone.

But financially, our grand project was a disaster. When we started the work, educational software was selling for about $60; at the end it was $20 if you could get that. We set the software free to roam the internet and turned to the world of big business to work off our debts.

At first I worked on Wall Street doing technical writing. The work was challenging, but the commute was endless, so I looked around for something better. My husband had found work as a contractor at IBM Research, and he showed me an advertisement for a technical writing job in a group doing something called organizational storytelling. I had never heard of such a thing. But the commute was easy, so I applied for the job.

The group was called the Knowledge Socialization group, and my boss was John C. Thomas. John is fairly well known in the world of what used to be called human factors and is now called user experience (UX). John had gotten excited about stories, and he had gotten some internal sponsors at IBM excited about stories, and he pulled together some funding to build a research group. I was its second member. On paper I was a type of temporary worker called a "technical supplemental." I had this image of a giant IBM reaching down and swallowing me like a tiny vitamin pill.

I thank John to this day for his exceptional ability to realize that I was not really a technical writer; I was a researcher in disguise. I did do some writing for John, but he let me expand the definition of "writing" far beyond what my official position said I should do. So I spent my first year at IBM describing wide circles through the realms of possibility where stories, organizations, communities, and computers (it was IBM after all) meet.

I remember the moment when I realized that organizational narrative meshed with ethology. It was like coming home to find an old friend unchanged and waiting to meet me. I plunged into the subject with the energy of a convert.

It was during this year that I first had the idea to ask questions about stories and discovered the dimensions of story form, function, and phenomenon. John added a few other people to the group, including Annita Alting and Andrew Gordon, and we participated in a hearty exchange of ideas.

About six months into 1999, I went to the second IBM-wide "story meeting" of everyone in IBM interested in story work. This meeting brought together people who designed software, marketed products, thought about the future, supported services, everything. There I met Dave Snowden, Sharon Darwent, and Rob Peagler. Dave and Sharon worked in Global Services, IBM's huge consulting arm, and they and we were the two groups working most strongly on stories. We exchanged some ideas, but our work was for the most part separate. As I recall it, I didn't exactly agree with everything they were doing, and I suspect they thought our group's work was boring in a computer nerd sort of way. Rob was in a marketing group, and he and I bounced ideas off each other starting then (and still do).

I remember helpful discussions at that time with Tom Erickson, Irene Greif, Daniel Gruen, Wendy Kellogg, Debbie Lawrence, Peter Malkin, Michael Muller, Peter Orton, Matthew Simpson, Carl Tait, Ted Taptiklis, and Jaya Vaidyanthan. I'm sure there are others I've forgotten from that time and for that I beg their forgiveness.

IBM had a rule about tiny vitamins; they could only stay in the body of the beast for one year. However, over the course of my year there I had made some friends. One of these was Neal Keller, who worked in … I don't remember the official name, but his group helped everybody at IBM Research who was *doing* research do it better. They helped people use the software they got on their laptops, fixed problems, held training courses, and made the research facility more efficient as a whole (a daunting task and well done). Neal found out about our work on stories and wanted to use it in his work, so we started talking. Our group had a general mandate to help *anybody* in IBM who wanted to think about how to use stories in their work, and I remember quite a few meetings with people in software, training, internet, and lots of other divisions, dispensing my newly acquired knowledge.

Near the end of my first year Neal discovered an internal call for proposals to the E-Business Technology Institute. Together we put in a proposal for a one-year project to fund work on stories in e-learning. We succeeded in getting the funding and in getting special permission for me to remain on as a temporary employee for another year. I got right back to work.

It was in my second year at IBM Research, working with Neal, that I really began to learn about people and stories. The most significant moment in my entire career, in fact, took place partway through that year's project. It was when I discovered *that raw stories of personal experience* were more useful than any fictional story could be. (I describe that moment in the "Incorporating narrative into e-learning" project story in *More Work with Stories*.) I also spent many hours watching people tell stories in workshop and interview settings, and many more hours carefully listening to and transcribing tapes of conversations.

It was also during this time that I first "sat with" several collections of stories and learned how answers to questions about them could form patterns that revealed insights impossible to see from simply reading the stories or thinking about the topic. My many discussions with Neal and John had a positive impact on all of this work. What Neal brought was an amazing ability to cut through the intellectual crap and make things happen with people. He knew people better than I did, and you can thank him for some of the insights that ended up in this book.

As my second year at IBM ended, Dave Snowden convinced the IBM's Institute for Knowledge Management (IKM) to hire me as an independent contractor. I started work for the IKM in 2001. This new start had a slightly different mandate than the previous one. Because the IKM (and all the corporate world) was in the midst of discovering complexity theory, I was asked specifically to consider how organizational narrative could work with ideas from complexity. Another old friend met, unchanged and ready for a new embrace.

It turned out, again to my surprise and excitement, that narrative and complexity had met before and were old friends from tens of thousands of years back. You see, stories form complex, emergent patterns; and all complex patterns have stories.

Thus I began a close collaboration with Dave Snowden and Sharon Darwent that lasted several years, off and on. There were several other people in "the group" that was first at the IKM, then IBM's Cynefin Centre. Some were more and some less involved, but I can't recall the details now. Let me see, I can think of Rich Az-zarello, Steve Bealing, Shawn Callahan, Steve Barth, Rob Peagler, Friso Gosliga, Fiona Incle-don, Tony Mobbs, Peter Stanbridge, and War-wick Holder, but I am sure there other people whose names I have forgotten (or can only re-member parts of: was there another Steve?) and for this I apologize.

My collaboration with Sharon was always and unequivocally excellent. We enjoyed a perfect synergism of ideas, and many of the practical insights described in this book came in part from her capable mind. Sadly for me, she be-came a rising star at British Telecom and con-centrates her attention there these days. My collaboration with Dave was a paradox: the best and worst of times. Some of our work to-gether was the finest I've ever done (with any-one other than my husband; he gets first place of course), and some of the disappointments were my worst as well.

In any case, my work with Dave and Sharon had a huge impact on the development of par-ticipatory narrative inquiry. Some of the ideas came from only myself, Dave, or Sharon, and were later refined and improved by the other two (and by others named or unnamed). Some ideas were joint affairs from the start and can-not be easily teased apart. Some came from my work before we joined up, and some came from theirs before we joined up, but all of the ideas changed and improved as we worked together. If you have learned anything useful from this book, Sharon and Dave deserve your thanks.

Besides supporting quite a few consulting projects in various parts of IBM, Sharon and Dave and I put a lot of work into the Genoa program, which was supported by the Defense Advanced Research Projects Administration (DARPA) of the U.S. government. I remember attending a "dog and pony show" that preceded this program (meaning, we line up and show you what we can do) at the end of 2000. I was just coming out of IBM Research and looking for work. A copy of my never-published form-function-phenomenon paper had made its way into the hands of Admiral John Poindexter and (I was told) was among the influences that got him interested in the idea of using stories to make sense of threats and opportunities in na-tional defense and other future-looking spheres of government. After the meeting the Admiral asked me to join the project and asked whether I wanted to work independently or through IBM. I chose IBM for safety, though I later re-gretted the loss of freedom (isn't that always the choice). Dave also impressed and was asked to work with me (or me with him, if he would prefer it that way).

We did quite a lot of work over the next few years for the Genoa program, whose primary goal was to augment human capacities to make sense of complex situations (and which con-tained many other projects along those lines). Many of the experiences that formed the nar-rative sensemaking methods described in this book were based on experimentation in the workshops we held as part of the Genoa pro-gram. That work gave us the essential resource of having some top-notch thinkers to work with—analysts, historians, policy makers, engi-neers, cognitive scientists. They helped us im-measurably in developing and testing methods to help people work with stories to discover new insights about difficult problems.

I would like to thank all of the workshop partic-ipants and collaborators in that work. Among them were Tom Boyce and John Lowrance at the Stanford Research Institute, Mark Lazaroff and Steven Sickels, then at General Dynam-ics, and Dennis Gormley, then an intellectual at large. All of these people (and some whose names I have forgotten) were important to the work and helped inform and improve the ideas developed as a result.

The other major outcome of the Genoa project with respect to this book was a research project I carried out to discover and prototype ideas for visualizing large quantities of stories and an-swers to questions about them. I had built the first "narrative database" of stories in 2001 for an IBM consulting client, marrying my ques-tions about stories with Dave's and Sharon's archetypes (which I now call story elements and use more broadly than the original form of archetypes). I slowly improved the prototype software for use in various projects, but when we left IBM for good it was time to start over.

As part of Genoa's mission to augment human sensemaking with computer tools, I was asked to consider and compare all plausible ways to look at stories (and answers to questions about them) that might help people discover useful insights. I built what I then called the "Mass Narrative Representation" prototypes. I think there were five or six of them, each based on applying published research in visualization to the problem of looking at stories and answers to questions. I later combined the prototypes into what Dave's new company (Cognitive Edge) called SenseMaker Explorer. Some of what I learned about asking questions and considering answers came from work on Explorer and use of it in client projects (of which more later). For some years I kept updating and improving Explorer, and my husband built and maintained Sensemaker Collector.

Another important source of ideas was Singapore's RAHS (Risk Assessment and Horizon Scanning) system. As the Genoa program wound down, Dave was frequently asked by the government of Singapore to visit there, and eventually he convinced the powers-that-be of the utility of narrative work. Unlike the DARPA work, I had nothing to do with getting that project started, other than spending two weeks in Singapore sick with bronchitis, which I doubt helped much. (I don't mind saying that I am not much of a go-getter; I relied on, and admire, Dave's obvious talents in that area.) The RAHS project had similar goals to Genoa and, like Genoa, it lasted for three years. I conducted about ten research projects as contributions to RAHS. Some resulted in software, and some resulted in papers I later published (or self-published).

All of the work I did on RAHS had an impact on the methods and ideas described in this book. I had more opportunities to work with people telling and working with stories in workshops; I sat with more story collections; I read related scientific literature; I built prototype software; and Dave and I conducted more explorations and experiments on group sensemaking methods. Some of the RAHS work benefited from collaborations with Alicia Juarrerro (specifically the work on narrative landscapes), Steve Bealing, and Warwick Holder.

Alongside all this research was ongoing project work for a variety of clients, of IBM, then Cognitive Edge, then myself personally. I wish I had kept a better count of the projects! My best guess is that I have done about thirty research projects and more than fifty story collection projects, though I suspect there may be another ten or twenty early collection projects I lost track of. In most of the fifty-plus collection projects, I "sat with" the stories, dozens or hundreds or thousands of them, and saw what patterns they made.

I am not sure when I first began supporting projects with catalysis work, that is, helping people see what patterns can be found in stories and answers. It may have been sometime around 2004. It was not my original intention to do this. Clients were supposed to use the software to find patterns themselves. But people wanted help making sense of stories and answers to questions, and since I wrote the software, I knew how to use it well. People wanted somebody to use the software for them and with them, to help them find things to ponder.

So I started building reports that helped people think. I learned from my mistakes, some of which were shall-we-say quite educational, and improved my techniques as a result. I hope I have sufficiently described the methods of catalytic work I have developed so that you can do this as well as I can (with practice).

On some of the later client projects with Cognitive Edge, I collaborated strongly with Michael Cheveldave. This was another excellent and wholly positive meeting of minds, and some of Michael's good ideas can also be found in this book. For example, he was the one who came up with the "is this a common story" question, which has proved exceptionally useful in practice.

When I started working on my own, one of the first things I wanted to do was to write down what I knew so other people could do what I did. In the "Why I wrote this book" section of the introduction to this book (page 6) you will find my account of what led me to want to do this. Writing the book, then improving the book through its second and third editions, has been a driving force since I started work on the book in 2008.

I have not yet mentioned a change that had a big impact on my work. For the first several years of my work in this area, I traveled frequently, sometimes as often as monthly, to meet with clients and to facilitate group sessions. After my son was born in 2003, I stopped traveling almost entirely. As a result, at the time of this writing, it has been several years since I have physically stood in a room facilitating a group session. I have not stopped *thinking* about facilitation—I have helped people plan and prepare to facilitate sessions, and I have reviewed videos and transcripts and notes of sessions—but I haven't been *physically* present in a facilitated session for quite a while.

In recent years I have done more work on project planning and catalysis. To some extent this could be seen as a weakness of the book, that its writing on facilitation is based in part on dated experiences. But on the other hand, if I *had* kept traveling frequently, I would not have been able to develop the methods of narrative catalysis I use and describe in the book. I'm not even sure I would have been able to write the book at all if I had kept traveling frequently. I hope the book will meet your needs regardless of where and how I worked on its subject matter.

In the past several years, alongside work on the book, I have continued to do projects for clients around the world. I have developed NarraCat, my own set of open source tools for narrative catalysis, which I use and invite you to use. And I wrote Rakontu, open source software for helping groups share and work with their stories. I hope to continue all of this work in the future.

In recent years I have made many new friends with whom I have shared ideas, and their influence is also felt in this book.

John Caddell was the very first person who wrote me a thank-you note for writing the first edition of the book in 2008. His project story ("Helping a community market listen to its customers," in *More Work with Stories*) was a featured element of edition two, and his unflagging support has helped me to keep writing when the task I had set myself seemed impossible to achieve. (John has written his own story-related book, *The Mistake Bank*, which I strongly recommend.)

I talked with Stephen Shimshock about his Ph.D. research on participatory evaluation methods, and his thoughtful questions and feedback on the book's second edition spurred me to fill many of the gaps in what I had written before. I enjoyed our collaboration so much that I asked Stephen to write the foreword for this edition of the book as well as a project story ("Evaluating effectiveness helping youth in foster care," in *More Work with Stories*). Stephen is a perfect example of someone who saw the benefit of PNI and lost no time applying it with original flair to a goal worth pursuing. His ideas have informed many parts of the book.

Thaler Pekar stands out as the correspondent who has provoked the most exploratory thought in recent years, with her excellent questions and relevant discussions. I also thank her for contributing her insightful interview to the book, and for allowing me to include her essay, "Everyone Wants to Be a Hero."

Thanks to Shawn Callahan and Karen Dietz for adding their excellent interviews to the book, as well as for their steady encouragement.

Jonathan Carter added a valuable story of hard-won project experience ("Collecting stories in a poor urban community," in *More Work with Stories*) and some more great ideas to the mix.

Stéphane Dangel has been a model of patient encouragement in his ideas for translating the book to French, a prospect I view with great excitement (though after all this time I do not hold him to any promises!). He has also contributed his own ideas in a project story about a method of his own design ("Using a specific narrative process to face conflictual situations," in *More Work with Stories*).

Tom Graves encouraged me to keep writing, and graciously allowed me to include a figure from his SCAN model.

Carol Mase, Tom Roy, and Cynthia Weeks improved the book tremendously by listening to me chatter on for hours about projects I had worked on. The transcripts of those discussions turned into most of the project stories in *More Work with Stories*, and they also helped me think of stories to include in this book. Carol, Tom, and Cynthia told me that they learned a lot from the experience, but I think I learned more, and I could not have written about (or thought about) my experiences in such depth without their encouraging presence and thoughtful questions.

I asked Niels Schuddeboom, Stephen Shimshock, and Jim Webber to read the sensemaking chapters early, because I was unsure if my explanations were sufficiently comprehensible. Their thoughtful suggestions helped me improve the clarity of my explanations.

Keith Fortowsky, Niels Schuddeboom, and Harold van Garderen provided careful, detailed, and thoughtful feedback on the whole book, helping me to find and fix many mistakes I failed to notice. Harold in particular helped out with advice on many little decisions that plagued me as I prepared the manuscript for publication.

I have been fortunate to have the expert help of Ellen Kaplan-Maxfield, who hand-crafted a high-quality, professional index for the book. I hope you noticed her index. I don't know about you, but I find that reading through Ellen's index makes this book seem like a whole new book; and that's exciting, because it gives you more ways to make use of it. Ellen also read the book very carefully and found many small mistakes and grammatical faux-pas I had not seen.

The book has also benefited from a wondrous variety of useful discussions with Ajit Alwe, Mark Anderson, Katrina Andrews, Steve Barth, Hannah Beardon, Madelyn Blair, Sonja Blignaut, Tom Cagley, Zarrin Caldwell, Khoon Min Chin, Lilia Efimova, Lang Elliott, Peter Goldsbury, Katharine Hansen, Yvette Hyater-Adams, David Hutchens, Mireille Jansma, Tony Joyce, Tom Kadel, Mary Klinger, Marco Koning, John McGarr, Terry Miller, Steve Newton, Rob Peagler, Marc Maxson, Limor Shiponi, David Vanadia, Jerry Waxler, Graham Williams, and Frank Wood. If this list leaves anyone out, please forgive my oversight.

Finally, I must thank my husband and son, who have patiently endured years of endless discussion about "the book I could write," which transitioned through "the book I'm writing" all the way up to "this damn book!" Thanks to both of them for their faithful encouragement and emotional support through my endless preoccupations with this monster of a project.

I cannot close this autobiography of gratitude without giving my son Elliot special mention. Over the years I have shared many of my goals and dilemmas in this work with him. After I finished writing each book section, I read it out loud to him. As I read, I frequently stopped and asked him to explain, in his own words, what I had just read. If he couldn't explain what he had heard, or if his attention drifted while I read, I knew I had some clarification work to do. Putting the book through its paces in this way helped me improve its accessibility.

Even more importantly, I have had the privilege of watching and helping my son tell and listen to stories, not just a few but thousands upon thousands. We have spent years spinning the finest of yarns from the fibers of daily life, creating worlds within worlds while tackling every hope and fear known to humanity. Watching his mind grow and change has had as important an impact on the ideas in this book as my interactions with any other collaborator in story work, expert as many may be. Because my work is in stories and everyone tells stories, a child is as much an expert as any other human can be, and maybe more of an expert than any adult can hope to be. Everything I have done since he was born has benefited from his ever-present contribution. The ideas I have now are not the ideas I had then; they are deeper and richer, and for that I have my favorite storyteller in the world to thank.

Cynthia F. Kurtz

cfkurtz@cfkurtz.com

Glossary

abstract The beginning of a conversational story, in which storyteller and audience negotiate over exactly what story will be told, by whom, and how.

backflow story A story that starts out with one explanation of events, then changes in such a way that a second story forms with a different explanation of the same events.

catalysis Using mixed-methods analysis to discover patterns in collected stories and other data, then generating multiple competing interpretations of the patterns, all to prepare material that enhances sensemaking.

catalytic material A series of patterns, observations, interpretations, and ideas, generated during narrative catalysis, based on collected stories and other data, and used to deepen and enhance sensemaking.

change In the context of sensemaking, differences in perspective and understanding that come about as a result of contact, churning, and convergence.

churning In the context of sensemaking, people, project, and stories coming into repeated, varied contact.

clustering Placing things together, like with like, so that they form associated groups.

coda The end of a conversational story, in which storyteller and audience negotiate the return to a normal conversational rhythm.

cognitive budget How much time, attention, interest, and ability to concentrate people have to bring to a task.

commitment situation A story collection situation in which partipants feel that the project connects to an essential part of their identity; thus they can be relied on participate (to a reasonable extent) in the project.

complexity theory A research field that studies self-organization, or the formation of emergent patterns in situations where elements interact repeatedly without central coordination.

complication The part of a story after the introduction of setting and characters, when tensions rise and characters react.

composite story A story built from stories.

contact In the context of sensemaking, people, project, and stories coming into proximity and becoming exposed to each other.

convergence In the context of sensemaking, the creation of coherent, resonant meaning through the repeated, varied contact of people, project, and stories.

conversational storytelling The way people tell and listen to stories in everyday conversation, with its rhythms and negotiations.

counter-story A story told in contrast to another story.

decision support A research field that studies how people make decisions and considers how they can be helped to make better decisions.

discovery story A story that stands out in a story collection because it helps people understand something important about the topic of the story collection.

dominant story A story that appears to be uniquely important to a community, organization, or society, but whose importance is an illusion based on superficial qualities.

dramatic action An action, whether large or small, that has an impact on the drama, or story, of a community or organization.

evaluation A statement within a conversational story whose purpose is to support claims to tellability, veracity, and utility of the story as it is being told.

exemplar story A story chosen to illustrate the meaning of a story element.

gleaned story A story drawn from a record in which people exchanged stories outside of the context of a purposeful story collection.

group interview A method of collecting stories in which an interviewer collects stories from multiple interviewees at the same time.

group story session A story collection method in which a facilitator gives participants tasks that involve exchanging stories.

half-story An utterance that is nearly a story but not quite, because it describes only a situation (no resolution), only a scenario (nothing specific), or only a reference to a story (not the story itself).

idea In the context of narrative catalysis, an action that could be taken based on an interpretation.

interpretation In the context of narrative catalysis, a statement about what an observed pattern might mean; must be paired with at least one competing interpretation of the same pattern.

journaling A method of story collection in which participants are asked to tell stories by filling out forms on a periodic or episodic basis.

kiosk situation In the context of story collection, a situation in which participation is minimal, contingent, and fleeting.

landscape In the context of story collection and sensemaking, an exercise in which participants fill a two-dimensional space with stories and/or other elements in order to facilitate recall and discover insights.

mixed-methods research A form of research analysis in which qualitative (quality-based) and quantitative (quantity-based) analysis strands are intermingled.

narrated event An event that takes place inside a story; that is, an event that happens to characters in a story.

narrative completeness How whole or entire a story appears to be, how free of omissions or gaps.

narrative compression The representation of a complete story by a compressed copy of itself, such that the compressed story can stand in for the expanded story, with the missing details filled in by shared understanding.

narrative consistency How well a story works as a coherent communication through conforming to cultural standards of story form.

narrative cycle The cycle of telling, hearing, remembering, and recalling in which stories spread through human society.

narrative displacement The withdrawal from direct attribution of feelings, beliefs, and opinions when expressed in indirect, oblique story form.

narrative distance Emotional, cultural, temporal, and experiential differences between storyteller and listener which make stories more difficult to understand.

narrative diversity Variation in told and retold stories that matches variation in personalities, viewpoints, and experiences within a community, organization, or society.

narrative event The telling of a story, or an event that takes place during the telling of a story (not within the story itself).

narrative flow The extent to which people in a community or organization share stories as a comfortable and familiar daily habit.

narrative freedom The extent to which people in a community or organization feel free to tell stories, to challenge told stories, and to negotiate during storytelling events.

narrative health The strength and vitality of story sharing within a community or organization.

narrative incident report A method of story collection in which participants are asked to observe events and record stories of the events and their reactions.

narrative inquiry A form of qualitative research in which the primary texts of study are stories.

narrative knowledge The extent to which people in a community or organization collectively understand how the social processes of story sharing (negotiation, co-telling, accountability) work in groups.

narrative ombudsman A person (or office) who helps people overcome difficult situations, in part by listening to their stories.

narrative presentation The telling of a story or stories for the purpose of education or persuasion.

narrative pulse The momentary urge to tell and reflect on a story when an event has occurred, or when a person has heard or recalled a story.

narrative richness The degree to which a story collection addresses the goals of the project that collected it; can be achieved through volume, depth, connection, or a combination of these.

narrative sensemaking The place where making sense of situations and sharing stories about situations come together.

narrative simulation A narrative presentation set up as an interactive game in which the audience chooses from options (and sees how their choices affect the story) in order to learn more about a topic.

narrative suggestion box A way for people to make suggestions by recounting events.

narrative therapy A form of therapy that helps people work with the stories in and of their lives to solve problems and improve well-being.

narrative unity The extent to which people in a community or organization share the same stories.

narrative veracity How well a story connects to other stories that corroborate (and do not contradict) its claims.

narrative wave The collective urge, within a community, organization, or society, to tell and reflect on a particular story, or type of story, usually when associated trends are taking place.

naturally occurring story A story told in everyday conversation that has no purpose beyond the daily task of making sense of events as they happen.

non-story A direct statement of fact or opinion, one in which no events or experiences are recounted.

observation In the context of narrative catalysis, a factual statement about an observed pattern.

official story An officially sanctioned, purposeful story, told through the official channels of a community, organization, or society.

one-on-one interview A story collection method in which one interviewer collects stories from one interviewee.

oral history The practice of collecting and studying historical information about people, communities, and organizations, primarily through spoken words.

orientation The first part of a story, in which the setting and characters are introduced.

participatory action research A research practice that blends inquiry with participation and action; also called action research.

participatory theatre A form of theatre in which distinctions between performers and audiences are blurred and sometimes removed entirely.

pattern In the context of narrative catalysis, a graphical visualization of collected data, or the result of a statistical test.

peer interview A story collection method in which participants interview each other.

pivot story A story that stands out in a story collection because it sits at the intersection of important aspects of the collection.

purposeful story A story told not simply because it happened but because the storyteller has some goal to which the story has been applied.

qualitative analysis A form of research analysis in which the primary materials of study are qualities of texts (statements, opinions, stories).

quantitative analysis A form of research analysis in which the primary materials of study are quantities (counts, ratings, rankings).

raw story A story that has not been altered or improved during its collection and distribution.

reframing When people pause and restate some portion of a story using different words; shows negotiation over the form a spoken story will take.

resolution The part of a story when tensions are resolved and the story reaches an end.

sacred story A story that is uniquely important to the community, organization, or society in which it is found, and whose importance may not be obvious to outsiders.

sensemaking Making sense of things in ways that are pertinent to decision making, of practical utility, and experimentally playful.

sensemaking pyramid A practice in which people help other people learn how to support sensemaking, and those people help other people, and so on.

spect-actor In Theatre of the Oppressed terms, an audience member who stops passively watching a drama and begins to actively participate in it.

steganography Hiding a signal in noise.

sticky note A piece of paper that can be attached, removed, and re-attached to a surface due to reusable, partially adhering glue on its back.

story Most broadly, a communicative device with elements of structural form, cognitive function, and social phenomenon. For the purposes of this book, a recounting of events based on emotional experiences from a perspective.

story card A piece of paper, usually small, on which a collected story is written or printed, usually with answers to questions about the story, so the story can be arranged with other such stories in group sensemaking.

story element A representation of meaning in a body of stories, linked to a canonical element of story form (e.g., situation, character, theme), created during sensemaking around a topic of concern, and useful for building new stories to explore the same topic.

story form The internal structure of a story: its setting, plot, characters, and communicative nuances.

story function The cognitive utility of a story: its impact on memory, thinking, and planning.

story phenomenon The social life of a story: its origin, transmission, and variation.

story reference A story whose meaning is compressed so much that it means little or nothing to people who don't know the full story to which it refers.

story sharing The spontaneous, casual exchange of stories, as opposed to the purposeful performance of storytelling.

story work Making sense of events and possibilities by telling, listening to, and thinking about stories.

storytelling The telling of a story as a purposeful performance, as opposed to the spontaneous, casual exchange of story sharing.

survey A story collection method in which participants are asked to tell stories by filling out forms.

timeline In the context of story collection and sensemaking, an exercise in which participants build a graphical representation of events or elements along a line representing time.

trickster A mythological character who disobeys conventional behavior, sometimes maliciously, sometimes helpfully, and sometimes in both ways at once.

turning point In a timeline exercise, an event or story marked as representing a significant change in the overall timeline being built or considered.

voice story A story that stands out in a story collection because it brings to light a perspective or experience that is relatively unknown.

volunteer situation A story collection situation in which participants feel a social obligation to participate, and will participate as long as the boundaries of that obligation are not exceeded.

zooming Looking at things in detail, then from afar, then in detail again; and so on.

Index

Italicized page numbers refer to figures. Page numbers in bold refer to glossary pages. Figures are not noted on page ranges. The current title is abbreviated as *WWS* (Kurtz).

Printed in Great Britain
by Amazon